Introduction to

CRIMINAL JUSTICE

sixth edition

Lawrence F. Travis III
University of Cincinnati

 LexisNexis®

 anderson publishing
A member of the LexisNexis Group

Introduction to Criminal Justice, Sixth Edition

Copyright © 1990, 1995, 1998, 2001, 2005, 2008
Matthew Bender & Company, Inc., a member of the LexisNexis Group
Newark, NJ

ISBN-10: 1-59345-505-4
ISBN-13: 978-1-59345-505-7

Phone   877-374-2919
Web Site   www.lexisnexis.com/anderson/criminaljustice

LexisNexis and the Knowledge Burst logo are trademarks of Reed Elsevier Properties, Inc.
Anderson Publishing is a registered trademark of Anderson Publishing, a member of the LexisNexis Group

Library of Congress Cataloging-in-Publication Data

Travis, Lawrence F.
    Introduction to criminal justice / Lawrence F. Travis III.--6th ed.
        p. cm.
    Includes bibliographical references and indexes.
    ISBN-13: 978-1-59345-505-7 (softbound)
    ISBN-10: 1-59345-505-4 (softbound)
    1. Criminal justice, Administration of--United States. I. Title.
HV9950.T7 2008
364.973--dc22   2008000910

Cover design by Tin Box Studio, Inc./Cincinnati, Ohio

EDITOR   Ellen S. Boyne
ACQUISITIONS EDITOR   Michael C. Braswell

Preface

Writing the sixth edition of *Introduction to Criminal Justice* was a humbling experience. This revision to the fifth edition, and by extension, to the first edition was both frustrating and rewarding in the extreme. The basic system of criminal justice is unchanged and the critical, central issues of criminal justice do not vary over the years. To be sure, there are new concerns, such as homeland security and computer crime, but these issues are framed in familiar contexts such as due process versus crime control and system effectiveness.

This edition maintains the same approach to criminal justice that characterized the first edition. The central purpose of the text is to provide students with a relatively brief, affordable, and comprehensive introduction to and overview of the field of criminal justice. This edition continues to rely on three basic themes: the system-like nature of criminal justice, the core conflict between due process and crime control, and the importance of discretion.

The structure of the text also remains the same. The first part sets the context for the study of criminal justice. The second part is comprised of 10 chapters that address the justice process (including the juvenile justice system), and the final chapter looks to the future. As in earlier editions, the style and vocabulary are set at the reading level of the typical college freshman. Important terms are presented at the start of each chapter and are highlighted within the chapter. Review questions for each chapter and the glossary have been repeated to help students/teachers master the language and concepts of criminal justice.

New in the Sixth Edition

As with previous editions, the most important and widespread changes in this edition of the text involve updating the references and statistical reports. It is disappointing how many facets of criminal justice operations lack up-to-date descriptions, but wherever possible, the data have been revised with the most recent information available. Similarly, the text discussion includes reference to contemporary thinking and research to ensure up-to-date coverage of these important topics.

While the core of criminal justice does not seem to change substantially, the level and breadth of scholarship and research in the field grows at a geometric rate. Whenever possible, detailed tables are replaced with graphs and figures to enhance both readability and student comprehension. Photographs have been updated, and the number of photographs has been increased to add to the "visual" appeal of the book. I still believe criminal justice is a "fun" topic, and I hope that reading the book is exciting and entertaining for students as well.

There is increased discussion throughout the book of important topics like the impact of current federal attention to terrorism and homeland security and the growing emphasis on crime prevention and community quality of life that characterizes all parts of the justice system. In the process, the continuing expansion of federal influence in local criminal justice is explored throughout the book. Similarly, there is continuing coverage of the role of the victim, or the privatization of criminal justice throughout our examination of the components of the criminal justice process.

The expanded coverage given to these topics is purposely less noticeable than the new figures and photos. One goal in writing this book is to give students a view of the forest rather than the trees. I hope to provide students with a broad grounding in criminal justice in preparation for further study. With a focus on the entire system, specific topics are not centers of attention but examples of basic principles and issues. The reader's attention is drawn not to analyzing the growth of federal influence in local justice operations, but rather to how that federal role compares to other factors that influence practice, and how the justice system responds. After all, we want to understand the criminal justice process, not federal politics. Politics are an important influence on criminal justice operations, but only one of many. I expect that this edition, like its predecessors, will encourage readers to raise questions and help them begin to find answers. I hope it also will pass the ultimate test of student use.

Acknowledgments

Writing this edition, like the earlier five, was a group project even if the book has only one author listed. Each edition adds to the number of people to whom I owe a debt of gratitude. It is not possible to list all of those who have influenced my thinking about criminal justice or whose comments and suggestions have found their way into the pages of this book. All of those who are cited in the references have contributed to my understanding of criminal justice and my "take" on the topic. Still, there are some people whom I must single out for special recognition.

From LexisNexis (and the former Anderson Publishing), Bill Simon, Mickey and Susan Braswell, and Kelly Grondin were (and are) always supportive of this effort. I have had the extreme good fortune to work with Ellen Boyne as my editor. As with the previous editions, this one is a better book because of her efforts, and I am a better writer. Her dedication, competence, insight, hard work, and her patience with the author are unsurpassed. That she can work with (or in spite of?) someone as stubborn as I is simply incredible.

My colleagues at the University of Cincinnati also deserve special recognition. It is a pleasure to cite their work, and it is relatively easy to keep abreast of a rapidly developing field when surrounded by scholars of their caliber. We have grown into a large faculty over the past few years, so I will not list everyone. Mitch Chamlin, Frank Cullen, John Eck, Robin Engel, Jim Frank, Ed Latessa, Pat VanVoorhis, Pam Wilcox, John Wooldredge, and John Wright have each given me pause to think and reconsider issues and topics in criminal justice. Their influence finds its way into how I approach the topic of criminal justice, and therefore, what I write.

I have also relied on the able assistance of my professional colleagues. Steve Lab and John Whitehead wrote Chapter 14 on juvenile justice. Harry Allen, Todd Clear, Bob Langworthy, Gerry Vito, George Wilson, and others have made a lasting impression. My own professors, including the late Donald Newman, Rita Warren, Hans Toch, Leslie Wilkins, and Vincent O'Leary, have left an indelible mark. My students, undergraduate and graduate, have influenced me as well. I feel proud (and old) to cite their works in the book.

My greatest thanks go to my family. My sons Larry IV, Chris, and Greg have always kept me from becoming a hermit and encouraged me in their own ways. Larry actually used the book when a student at Bowling Green State University and pronounced it "pretty interesting." I felt that was high praise indeed. My wife, Pat, did much of the editorial work. It is only with her help that I am able to work. Thank you, Pat; I love you.

As always, while I have written the book and must take ultimate responsibility for any errors it contains, I deny that responsibility. Any mistakes are clearly the product of my trusting nature and the failures of those named above.

Lawrence F. Travis III
Monroe, Ohio

Contents

Chapter 1

Criminal Justice Perspectives

Imagine that you are standing on a busy street corner. You look at the people around you. What do you see?

A woman drops a postcard in a mailbox.

Across the street, a man carrying a small suitcase steps off a bus.

Several feet away from you, a couple is arguing about something.

A police car slowly passes through the intersection.

Less than a half a block away, someone is "jaywalking" while a small child nearby is reading a street sign.

A man deposits money in a nearby parking meter.

A stranger approaches and asks that you sign a petition in support of banning cell phone use by drivers.

What you probably do not see is that the mix of pedestrian and vehicular traffic is orderly. You do not notice that almost everyone watches the police car, at least briefly. You do not realize that all of these strangers at the intersection are going about their own business, apparently unaware of each other. Yet, in a well-rehearsed routine, they stop and go on cue from the traffic light. You probably do not see a crime (with the possible exception of the jaywalker).

Without realizing it, you have observed the criminal justice system in action. What you did not know is that the postcard was a monthly report the woman was sending to her probation officer. Nor was it clear that the man with the suitcase just left the state penitentiary on parole. The arguing couple may be tonight's domestic disturbance (or last night's). The slow-moving police car is searching for the small child, who is reading the street signs because he is lost. The jaywalker crossed the street to avoid walking past a group of teens gathered on the sidewalk. The man at the parking meter wants to avoid a citation. The person with the petition hopes to ensure that motorists wear their seat belts by making it criminal not to do so.

The entire street corner scene just described, and all of the individuals in it, are affected by the workings of the criminal justice system. Interestingly, the individuals also directly affect the workings of that system. Should the argumentative couple become too boisterous, the shopper fail to deposit the correct coins in the parking meter, the woman not mail the postcard, and so on, you would expect some sort of official response from the justice system. Criminal justice is an integral part of our society and social living.

Sociologists often speak of the purposes of social institutions as "functions" (Parsons, 1966). Functions are the goals served by a social institution. For instance, schools serve the function of education. Institutional functions can be classified as either manifest or latent. Manifest functions are the stated purposes of the institution, while latent functions are the unstated or hidden goals. Schools serve the manifest function of education through teaching students various academic subjects. They also meet the latent functions of providing child care and controlling the workforce by otherwise occupying millions of young people.

Social Control

Albert Cohen (1966:3) observed that "if human beings are to do business with one another, there must be rules, and people must be able to assume that, by and large, these rules will be observed." The making and enforcement of rules is a requirement for organized social living. Social control is the label given to the processes and structures that seek to limit rule-breaking behavior, or deviance.

There are a number of instruments of social control in any society, of which the law and criminal justice process are only one. Most discussions of social control attempt to classify the different means by which conformity is achieved (Black, 1976; Ross, 1926; Travis & Langworthy, 2008). These classifications focus on the procedures and processes that support conformity. The social control mechanisms in a society or community can influence individual behavior by assigning "blame" and sanctions, or by prevention and education.

Types of Social Control

One of the most common ways of classifying social control processes is to distinguish between "formal" and "informal" social controls. Formal social control includes those sanctions that are applied by some authorized body after a public finding of fault. Informal social control, in contrast, refers to those mechanisms that influence behavior without the need for a public finding of fault or the use of group-"authorized" sanctions. A student who is disruptive in class can be formally sanctioned by expulsion. In this case the instructor, acting in his or her "official" (formal) capacity, or the educational institution itself, can apply the sanction of "banishment" on the offender. Alternatively, other members of the class can "hush" the offender by showing their disapproval without going through any formal process and punishment.

In the ideal, of course, the disruption would not happen because the student would view the behavior as wrong or inappropriate. However we achieve control over the behavior—formal sanctions, informal influence, or self-control—the disruption is stopped or prevented. The social business of the class can continue with relative order and predictability. The means of control vary, but the goal of social control remains the maintenance of order in social relations. Because the goal is uniform regardless of the means, the distinction among types of social control is often artificial. Rather than being completely distinct types of control, informal and formal mechanisms lie along a continuum of controls ranging from those that are internal to the individual to those that are imposed on the individual.

Suppose the student wishes to be disruptive, but refrains from doing so because of a fear of expulsion. The student has demonstrated self-control, but the impetus for control is the threat of a formal sanction. Has social control in this case been established by informal or formal methods? Generally speaking, if the use or threat of a formal sanction is the mechanism by which social order is maintained, we call the process "formal social control." If a formal sanction is not necessary (even if such a sanction exists), then we call it "informal social control."

Criminal Justice as Social Control

The primary function of criminal justice is social control. The components of the justice process are police, courts, and corrections. These components have the manifest function of controlling different kinds of deviance that are defined as crime. "Crime" is only a small part of the total activities and behaviors that are the targets of social control. Most social control works through "informal" mechanisms, such as shunning or ostracizing the person who is rude, insensitive, or bothersome. Other forms of deviance are defined as mental illness and are handled through the mental health system. In 1929, Roscoe Pound (1929:4) remarked, "Law does but a part of this whole task of social control; and the criminal law does but a part of that portion which belongs to the law."

Criminal justice is the formal social institution designed to respond to deviance defined as crime. Crime control is the primary purpose of the criminal justice system, but it also serves other latent functions. Police, courts, and corrections do much more than merely fight crime. Still, our examination of the criminal justice process cannot progress until we understand this central purpose. Whatever other functions it may serve, and whatever methods it may employ, the justice system can be measured (or judged) as an institution of formal social control.

Focusing upon the social control function of criminal justice (specifically, the control of crime) makes it easier to study and understand criminal justice practices and policies. We assess the value of a policy and procedure, or proposed changes in them, by how well they meet the objective of crime control. Theoretically, it seems easy enough to maintain an "objectives" perspective, but it is often very difficult to do so in practice. Frederic Kellogg (1976:50) has observed that this perspective:

> has never made much of an impact on the administration of criminal justice, most likely because there is so little agreement as to the "objectives" of criminal justice, the purposes of punishment, and the most appropriate strategy to reduce crime.

The disagreement to which Kellogg refers concerns the means by which the justice system is expected to achieve crime control. It is not enough that criminal justice efforts control crime, those efforts must protect individual rights and otherwise be acceptable to our society. While it is true that criminal justice practices may be controversial in particular instances, the overriding interest in controlling crime is a constant goal. Although we may disagree over the use of the death penalty, wiretaps, plea bargaining, or probation, we can agree that what we want to do is reduce the incidence of crime. Unfortunately, criminal justice practices too often become focal points for debates that are stated in terms of the purposes of the justice system. The President's Commission on Law Enforcement and Administration of Justice aptly illustrated this confusion in its report (1967:70):

> Any criminal justice system is an apparatus society uses to enforce the standards of conduct necessary to protect individuals and the community. It operates by apprehending, prosecuting, convicting, and sentencing those members of the community who violate the basic rules of group existence. The action taken against lawbreakers is designed to serve three purposes beyond the immediately punitive one. It removes dangerous people from the community; it deters others from criminal behavior; and it gives society an opportunity to attempt to transform lawbreakers into law-abiding citizens.

A debate may arise over whether deterring others from criminal behavior or transforming violators into law-abiding citizens is the best means of achieving the objective of social control, but the objective itself is not questioned. This confusion of means and ends is not limited to disagreements over specific practices such as capital punishment, but also includes ideological conflicts. People not only disagree over the appropriate forms of capital punishment (e.g., beheading, burning at the stake, electrocution, poison gas, lethal injection), but also over the appropriateness of capital punishment in general (e.g., the sanctity of life versus "an eye for an eye"). Yet, what would happen to these debates if the justice system could eliminate murder?

To further complicate an already complicated picture, the justice system is not the only social control institution in operation. The mental health system deals with many of the "rule violators" deemed inappropriate subjects for the justice system. Families, churches, schools, social organizations, and the media all serve social control purposes by informing us of what is and what is not acceptable behavior. The usefulness of the justice system must be understood within the total context of social control institutions. These other social control devices are often very effective (perhaps more effective than the criminal law), as is illustrated in Box 1.1. Fred Markowitz reported that when we lower capacity of mental hospitals, the criminal justice system workload increases, writing (2006:63), "In sum, public psychiatric hospital capacity is an important source of control of those whose behavior or public presence may at times threaten the social order."

Box 1.1   Social Institutions in America

Social control is achieved in many ways: through lessons learned by the individual about what is appropriate or inappropriate behavior, through structured opportunity that does not allow the individual the chance to deviate, through the exercise of coercive force to limit behavior. Nearly all social life affects social control, but the principal institutions in our society achieve social control in the following ways:

LESSONS	serve to teach us what behaviors are acceptable.
STRUCTURES	limit our opportunities for misbehavior.
COERCION	forces us to behave correctly, or prevents us from misbehaving.

LESSONS

The Family	Children learn to respect others' property and opinions, how to resolve conflict peacefully.
Schools	Students learn appropriate behavior, work habits, and respect for others.
Churches	Members learn rules for behavior (e.g., the Ten Commandments).
Social Groups	Members learn tolerance and rules for personal relations and behavior (e.g., majority rule).
Recreation	Players learn rules and discipline, ways of behaving (e.g., fair play).
Employment	Workers learn discipline, work habits, "chain of command."
Mental Health	Patients learn coping skills and ways of behaving (e.g., through token economies).
Law	Defendants and observers learn rules of behavior (laws) through their application.

STRUCTURES

The Family	Children are supervised, must abide by constraints on behavior (e.g., curfews).
Schools	Students follow fairly regimented academic schedules, are supervised by teachers.
Churches	Members participate in legitimate activities (e.g., weekly services, "Sunday School," service projects).

Box 1.1 *(continued)*

Social Groups	Members engage in activities (e.g., formal meetings).
Recreation	Players participate in organized activities and competitions.
Employment	Workers engage in defined activities and meet performance standards (e.g., production quotas).
Mental Health	Patients participate in organized activities (e.g., group meetings).
Law	Statutes require certain behaviors (e.g., providing care to children, maintenance of rental property).

COERCION

The Family	Children are punished for wrongdoing (e.g., "grounding," spanking).
Schools	Students who misbehave are punished (e.g., detention, suspension from school, written assignments).
Churches	Offending members are penalized (e.g., excommunication, threat of eternal damnation).
Social Groups	Offending members are sanctioned (e.g., ridicule, expulsion from the group, ostracism).
Recreation	Wrongdoers are punished (e.g., game forfeiture, penalties, loss of eligibility).
Employment	Misbehavior is penalized (e.g., loss of pay, dismissal, demotion).
Mental Health	Behavioral problems are controlled (e.g., passive restraint, sedation, forcible restraint).
Law	Offenders are sanctioned (e.g., fines, incarceration, execution, assessment of damages).

That most of the pedestrians and vehicles in the illustration that opens this chapter obey the traffic lights and signs is evidence of social control. How are these individuals controlled? Some may be controlled by fear of a citation (justice system); others may react as a result of learning traffic safety at home, in school, or from the media. All of these sources of social control converge at this intersection to produce an orderly and predictable flow of traffic. How much credit for this level of conformity should go to the justice system?

In general, the criminal justice process is a formal social control mechanism. The basic social control tool available to agents of the criminal justice process is group-authorized punishment. The threat of coercive force is the ultimate sanction available for social control. The criminal justice process can be seen as the social control institution of last resort. Returning to our earlier idea of a continuum of social control, we can think of the criminal justice process as occupying the extreme end of the "formal" side of the continuum. Ideally the individual will personally see some behavior (say, theft) as wrong, and avoid engaging in theft. If not, then the disapproval of others (family, friends, even strangers) may stop the individual from stealing. If not, then perhaps some more formal mechanism such as mental health counseling may prevent the theft. When all else fails, we can call upon the criminal justice process to try to force the individual to stop stealing.

One need only consider two examples of traffic behavior to realize the complex interaction of the many sources of social control. First, compare the orderliness of most street traffic to the relative "free-for-all" chaos characteristic of most shopping mall parking lots. Second, think of the number of times you (as driver or passenger) have waited at a stoplight on a deserted street. It is clear that the presence or absence of others does not completely explain the differences in behavior. Rather, it may be the public nature of the road as opposed to the private nature of the parking lot. The criminal justice system is addressed to the issue of public social behavior, but it is not the only working mechanism of social control in those cases.

People's behavior is influenced by a number of factors, including personality, motivations, beliefs, peer pressure, and opportunities. Why people do or do not engage in crime is a complex question. Some of the explanation may be that the criminal justice process exists to punish criminal behavior, but that is not the complete answer. Gertz and Gould (1995) reported a survey of college students that revealed that the chances of a student committing criminal acts were influenced more by the student's own personal beliefs that the acts were wrong than by their perceptions of being caught and punished. Similarly, Burton et al. (1995) found that parental discipline was an important factor in explaining why some juveniles committed delinquent acts while others did not. DeLisi and Berg (2006) suggest that people having low self-control share other personality characteristics (short-tempered and generally unlikeable) that might explain why they are more likely to be caught up in the criminal justice process. These studies and others indicate that social control is the product of both formal and informal processes, and they are interrelated. The existence of formal controls, such as the criminal law and criminal justice process, serves to "educate" people about what is right and wrong. In this way the law supports informal social control mechanisms, even while the law itself is a formal social control mechanism (Bianchi, 1994).

Over the past quarter century, the criminal justice process in the United States has undergone substantial change. Increasingly, the function of the justice process is being defined more broadly than crime control. David Karp and Todd Clear (2000:324) describe this change, "Among justice professionals there is growing interest in a new concept of justice more often referred to as 'community justice.'" Community justice, as an approach to social control, sees the criminal process as an integral part of other community institutions. Crime is seen as a symptom of problems in communities, and criminal justice agents and organizations work with offenders, victims, community groups, and other governmental agencies to solve those problems. As Karp and Clear (2000:324) see it, ". . . these disparate approaches share a common core, in that they address community-level outcomes by focusing on short- and long-term problem solving . . . priority is given to the community, enhancing its responsibility for social control while building its capacity to achieve this and other outcomes relevant to the quality of community life."

In short, community justice entails recognizing that social control is an important requirement of community life, and that traditional criminal justice activities have often been ineffective at social control. As the social control institution of last resort, we have historically used the criminal process when all else had failed, and after crime had occurred. How much better would it be to prevent crimes from occurring in the first place? To prevent crime, the agents of the criminal process should work to strengthen and facilitate informal social control institutions.

Evidence of this shift in thinking abounds. Recent programs exemplify this new emphasis on proactive, preventive efforts that involve the criminal process with other services and institutions. "Operation Weed and Seed" was launched by the U.S. Department of Justice in 1991 in three pilot sites and supports local community efforts to arrest and remove drug and violent offenders. The traditional policing action (arrest) represents the "weeding out" of criminals from high crime areas. The program includes a second component where ". . . community-focused human services programs and neighborhood improvement initiatives" are linked with the police action (Dunworth & Mills, 1999). The program seeks to rebuild communities and informal social control by removing law-breakers and improving community services, organization, and institutions at the same time. The efforts to improve the community constitute the "seeding" with the capacity to maintain law-abiding behavior. Today, there are more than 250 high-crime neighborhoods participating in Operation Weed and Seed (U.S. Department of Justice, 2004).

Another initiative, "The Comprehensive Communities Program," was started in 1994. This initiative has goals very similar to those of Operation Weed and Seed. The comprehensive communities program is based on the principles that communities must take a leadership role in combating crime and violence, and that state and local jurisdictions must establish coordinated, multidisciplinary approaches to deal effectively with the issues of crime and violence (Kelling et al., 1998:2). Preliminary evaluation findings indicate that cities involved in the comprehensive communities program have developed broad-based partnerships between police, courts, citizens, governmental agencies, and a variety of community agencies. The structure of service delivery among government and private agencies has also changed.

Anyone studying criminal justice today will recognize the widespread use of words such as "community" and "partnership." After decades of evolution in which criminal justice professionals were increasingly isolated from the people they served, and where the "job" of criminal justice was defined narrowly as responding to crime, contemporary thinking holds that the best criminal justice is preventive, and that crime prevention is best accomplished by informal social control. As Charles Friel (2000:15) explains, past efforts to improve public safety and reduce crime by professionalizing the criminal justice system had a downside.

"The downside, however, has been growth in government bureaucracy, coupled with a tangle of laws, regulations, and red tape, which, although intended to restore the "community," instead has removed the government from that community." Building closer links between the criminal justice process and the broader community has complicated the criminal justice picture in America.

Supancic and Willis (1998) studied what they called "extralegal justice" and its relationship to the formal criminal justice process. They distinguish between the two, writing (1998:193), "Legal justice includes all formal responses to crime by the police, the court system, and the corrections system. On the other hand, extralegal justice is that form of informal collective action directed against deviant and criminal conduct which is administered outside the formalized legal authority and not legally sanctioned by such authority." Extralegal justice is, they contend, an important part of a total system of social control and justice. It is directly related to the quality and quantity of legal justice. They suggest that an understanding of criminal justice (legal justice) cannot exist without also paying attention to informal social control in the community (extralegal justice). Barbara Warner (2006) studied the use of formal and informal social control in neighborhoods, and her findings support this observation. Warner (2006:124) concludes that relying too much on the justice system may ultimately weaken informal social control but that using informal controls without support from the justice system can lead to vigilantism or some other abuse of power.

Criminal justice, as a topic of study, involves a high level of complexity. First, the study of the justice process involves the examination of social control, which itself is a complex topic. Further, the justice process serves a number of conflicting—and often contradictory—purposes while achieving social control, and is characterized by a wide and expanding variety of agents, agencies, and structures. The immediate task is to develop a perspective that allows us to integrate these many components into a cohesive framework.

Perspectives on Criminal Justice

As an academic field, criminal justice has frequently been accused of being "atheoretical," or lacking a unifying perspective or set of perspectives in which the operations of criminal justice agents and agencies can be understood (Hagan, 1989). As Marenin and Worrall (1998:465) note, "Criminal justice, however, has not yet achieved theoretical integrity and coherence. There is little agreement on what criminal justice theory is or should be about, beyond the acknowledgment that criminal justice concepts and theories are to be drawn from a variety of established disciplines." They argue that criminal justice still has a ways to go before it can claim independence as an academic discipline. Todd Clear (2001:711) argues that although still underdeveloped, criminal justice has come of age as an academic field.

Criminal Justice Theory

Theory is a logical explanation of something. A theory is a statement about how things work to produce outcomes. As we are interested in criminal justice, we might want to know why some places have lots of criminal justice, and others have little. Why do some cities experience high crime rates; employ many police, prosecutors, judges, and correctional personnel; and have high criminal justice caseloads? A theory of criminal justice would give us guidance in trying to understand differences in the size, structure, and operations of criminal justice processes in different places. Critics of criminal justice point to the lack of commonly held explanations and conclude that there is no theory in the field of criminal justice (Kraska, 2004).

Nonetheless, there are a number of theoretical works that are aimed specifically at understanding the development and operation of the criminal justice process. Gorecki (1979) and Duffee (1980) have proposed broad theories of criminal justice aimed at explaining the process as a whole. Others have written more narrow explanations or provided organizing perspectives designed to guide an understanding of criminal justice decisions and practices (Allen, 1964; Beccaria, 1764; Black, 1976; Chambliss & Seidman, 1971; Foucault, 1979; Kolonski & Mendelsohn, 1970; Packer, 1969). In reality, there are many theories of criminal justice. What is missing is a way of classifying and comparing those theories (Bernard & Engel, 2001; Kraska, 2004).

Unlike other areas of study, criminal justice researchers do not often test their theories. Rather, they examine topics and apply theories to explain their findings (Bernard & Engel, 2001). Physicists, for example, might test the theory of gravity, the theory of relativity, or chaos theory by studying the movement of planets or subatomic particles. Criminal justice scholars are more likely to study official decisions to arrest, levy charges, or impose sentences, and then apply a theory to explain what they have found (Zalman, 2007). Criminal justice has a large body of research on all sorts of topics, but lacks a structure in which to organize these findings (Kraska, 2006). Because of this, the study of criminal justice tends to be somewhat fragmented. Still, it is a mistake to conclude that there is no theory in criminal justice. Peter Kraska (2004:9-10) argues about criminal justice that, "It is impossible to conduct theory-less research. Theory influences the questions asked, the selection of the phenomenon under study, the way in which data are collected, the interpretation of those data, and the type of policies recommended." Kraska is saying that everything we do in relation to criminal justice is shaped by our "theory" (understandings and expectations). While not formally stated as a theory, if someone believes hiring different people will change the way criminal justice is done, that person has a "theory" that criminal justice is a product of the officials making decisions.

Part of the problem with finding or identifying criminal justice theory is the complexity of the subject (Kraska, 2006). Not only do we have to explain the actions of individual criminal justice officials, we also have to explain differences in the size and operations of entire organizations and the relationships between organizations like police departments and criminal courts. Added to this is the fact that criminal justice, by definition, contains two related, but distinct topics—crime and justice. Castellano and Schafer (2005) reported that criminal justice educational programs exhibit different characteristics that reflect different understandings of criminal justice.

First, they say (2005:76) that criminal justice programs focus on either a vocational/managerial model aimed at preparing students for work in the justice system, or a model focused on science and critical questioning of criminal justice practice. Next, within the more scientific and critical approach, programs focus either on scientific values or ethical values. The theoretical and scientific study of criminal justice comes in two modes. One way to study criminal justice is to assess the impact of the justice process and changes in justice operations on crime. Castellano and Schafer call this a "problem-solving" focus. What can we do to the justice process, its agencies, or officials that will result in changes in the level and types of crime? The second approach focuses on "justice" or more ethical concerns. Are people treated fairly in the justice system?

As we try to study criminal justice then, we are faced with a complicated process that can be understood or tested in different ways. The study of criminal justice is like moving a 50-pound watermelon; you are sure you could lift the melon, if only you could get a firm grasp on it. Our "grasp" on the study of the justice process comes from an analytic perspective. Several different approaches have been used to study criminal justice. We will examine five of these perspectives: (1) disciplinary, (2) comparison, (3) process, (4) thematic, and (5) systems analyses of criminal justice.

Disciplinary Analyses

Different aspects of the criminal justice process have been the topic of study in a variety of social science disciplines. Each discipline contains at least an implicit theory of what "causes" or explains criminal justice. How one views any particular decision in the process depends partly upon whether the analyst is trained as a sociologist, psychologist, lawyer, political scientist, economist, or something else.

An arrest may be seen as an interpersonal interaction, the product of the police officer's perceptions, an exercise of legal authority, a power relation, a rational decision, or something different. In fact, most arrests probably result from a combination of these factors. The study of criminal justice operations in the United States is perhaps best described as multidisciplinary or interdisciplinary (Marenin & Worrall, 1998).

A discipline is a branch of study or learning. Thus, sociology or political science are branches of a more generic area of learning that could be called the study of "human behavior." In earlier years, the fact that programs in criminal justice at colleges and universities tended to include courses in psychology, sociology, law, political science, social work, and other disciplines illustrated the multidisciplinary nature of criminal justice study. More recently, Southerland reports that criminal justice programs now rarely require supporting courses in sociology, psychology, political science, and law (Southerland, 2002). Still, justice issues have been approached from a number of specialties. Box 1.2 briefly describes the approaches that analysts trained in different social science disciplines might prefer in studying justice topics.

Box 1.2 Disciplinary Approaches to Criminal Justice

Criminal justice professors (and researchers) come from a variety of disciplinary backgrounds. These backgrounds prepare them to approach justice topics and issues from different perspectives:

Sociologists look to the social organization of groups and interactions among people to explain how things occur.

Historians look to larger social and intellectual movements over time to explain how things occur.

Psychologists look to individual motivations and perceptions to explain how things occur.

Political scientists look to the processes of influence and the distribution of power to explain how things occur.

Lawyers look to established legal principles, statutes, and rules to explain how things occur.

Economists look to costs and benefits as an explanation of how things occur.

A full understanding of arrests, criminal penalties, or other parts of criminal justice is achieved through the application of several disciplinary approaches. Thus, in studying the arrest decision, the analyst should be aware of the legal, political, rational, perceptual, organizational, and personal factors in operation.

Observers have commented upon both the multidisciplinary and interdisciplinary nature of criminal justice (Toder, 1987). Orsagh (1983) suggested that economics has much to offer the study of crime and crime control. In discussing the combination of economics and what he termed "traditional criminology," he stated: "Taken together, they significantly broaden and enrich the study of crime and criminal justice" (1983:395). The link between economic "rational choice" theories of behavior and traditional criminology has more recently been explicitly recognized in a number of theoretical approaches to the explanation of crime (Cohen & Felson, 1979; Cornish & Clarke, 1986; Miethe & Meier, 1994). Others have noted that an effect of interdisciplinary approaches would appear to be a lack of theory (Williams, 1984; Willis, 1983). These scholars argue that the use of many disciplines yields descriptive data without a clear theoretical, interpretative scheme.

Multidisciplinary approaches remind one of the old story about the blind men meeting an elephant. Each man feels a different part of the beast and concludes that it is something different. The man touching the trunk believes it is a snake; the one with the tail believes it is a horse; the one at the leg believes he faces a tree; and so on. The result is that there are several interpretations of the same phenomenon, each shaped by the unique perspective of the observer. Critics of the interdisciplinary approach believe that the sighted observer would describe the elephant as a large gray or brown beast with a snake-like frontal appendage, a tail, and four large legs. In other words, he would be able to describe the elephant, but not know what it is.

Disciplinary approaches to the study of criminal justice provide important interpretations of criminal justice, but interpretations that are necessarily limited. Multidisciplinary approaches often yield conflicting information, while interdisciplinary approaches may provide accurate descriptions yet lack true understanding or valid interpretations. Thus, while useful and necessary, studies of criminal justice based on disciplinary perspectives may be unduly restricted.

Comparison Analyses

As the title suggests, comparison strategies for the study of criminal justice establish standards to which actual practices of justice agencies or an entire justice system are compared. Perhaps the best known example of this approach was suggested by Herbert Packer (1969) through the application of "ideal types" of justice systems (either due process or crime control). In this approach, the analyst first constructs a model or ideal justice system to which the actual justice system will be compared.

As illustrated in Box 1.3, Packer suggested that two conflicting goals characterize the United States' criminal justice process. On the one hand, we seek to control crime so that we can expect the justice system to respond quickly to criminal acts. On the other hand, we seek to preserve liberty so that we can expect the justice system to be highly constrained in interfering with individual rights.

The first step in this type of analysis is to envision the "perfect" justice system if only one of these goals is dominant. For example, the **crime control model** would support efficiency with an emphasis on speedy case processing. We would expect an enhancement of police powers to search and arrest, and a relaxation in the rules of evidence to allow relevant information to be presented in court. The emphasis on speed would support plea bargaining, prosecutorial discretion, and mandatory sentences as methods for hastening the disposition of cases. While consistent with the basic tenets of a democratic society (e.g., no coerced confessions), the crime control system would operate on a presumption of guilt. In contrast, the **due process model** would vigorously protect individual rights. It would put restrictions on searches and arrests without warrants, require full trials with strict rules of evidence, and support separate sentencing hearings to protect the interests of the individual offender.

Having created these models, the analyst would next observe a justice system in operation, carefully noting case processing, and compare the reality to the ideals. Then, the analyst would be able to classify the justice process as more or less "due process" or "crime control."

Box 1.3 Two Models of the Criminal Justice Process

	Crime Control	Due Process
	"assembly line"	"obstacle course"
Goal:	repression of crime	fairness and propriety
Objectives:	speed finality	deliberateness review
Procedures:	informal uniform	formal individualistic
Outcome:	efficiency	accuracy

Source: Adapted from H.L. Packer (1968), *The Limits of the Criminal Sanction* (Stanford, CA: Stanford University Press).

Other observers have used similar methods to classify and compare law enforcement agencies (Wilson, 1968), officers (Muir, 1977), sentencing judges (Levin, 1972), and correctional agencies (O'Leary & Duffee, 1971). Other strategies rely on a comparison of media portrayals with actual practice (Durham, Elrod & Kinkade, 1995). All of these approaches employ a comparison of observed criminal justice practices with some standard. This standard may be an artificial ideal or a standard presented by the operations of other justice agencies. The task then becomes one of explaining or understanding the differences and similarities.

Process Analyses

Another perspective on the justice system can be found in analyses that focus on case processing. These approaches focus less on the outcome of the system and more on how the system "runs." Rather than viewing concepts such as due process or crime control as guides for the entire system, this perspective traces the flow of cases from detection of crime through ultimate disposition. It focuses on the decisionmaking of actors in the justice process. Plea bargaining, from this perspective, does not represent a commitment to "crime control" as much as it does a concession to heavy caseloads (Gomme & Hall, 1995). Researchers try to discover how criminal justice actors make decisions about people and cases across the justice process from arrest (Engel, Sobol & Worden, 2000), through the courts (Sorenson & Wallace, 1999), sentencing (Pratt, 1998), and corrections (Turpin-Petrosino, 1999).

The American Bar Foundation provided perhaps the best illustration of this approach (Walker, 1992). Beginning in the 1950s, the Foundation undertook massive case studies of the justice process in three states. The results of these studies were published in five volumes, describing investigation (Tiffany, McIntyre & Rotenberg, 1967), arrest (LaFave, 1965), prosecution (Miller, 1970), conviction (Newman, 1966), and sentencing (Dawson, 1969).

As indicated by the topics covered, the focus of this analysis was on the decisions of justice system actors at major stages of the justice process. The studies investigated how the system "processed" cases in order to determine what factors influenced decisions to pass a case further along the system or to divert a case from further processing. This perspective describes the ways police, courts, and corrections handle different cases. The task is one of explaining or understanding deviations from the "normal" processing routine.

Thematic Analyses

Still others studying the justice process examine one or more issues as they apply across the entire system. For example, Remington et al. (1969) suggested such an approach using the themes of evidence sufficiency, consent, fairness and propriety, effectiveness, and discretion. Newman (1978) applied functions such as the punitive, deterrent, community protection, corrective, and due process functions of criminal justice.

This thematic approach compares different points or aspects of the justice process with each other in regard to the theme. Thus, arrest and sentencing might be compared in terms of how much evidence is required to justify each type of decision (evidence sufficiency). Similarly, the granting of bail, probation, or parole release may be compared and contrasted with reference to how well each serves the corrective function, the deterrent function, or both.

As are process approaches, this technique is based on the various decisions that comprise the justice system. Here, however, the focus is on the characteristics of the decision (e.g., level of evidence required, degree of consent involved) or the effects of the decisions (e.g., deterrent effect, punitive effect, etc.). This approach results in descriptions of common themes or purposes of criminal justice decisions rather than of the nature of the decisions themselves.

Comparing process and thematic approaches as applied to the decision to buy a new car, one finds that process analysts focus on the decision to buy or not, while thematic analysts look at why people come to their decisions. Thus, the process analyst might determine that 50 percent of shoppers actually purchase a new automobile. The thematic analyst, looking at new car buyers, might determine that a rebate program increases car sales by 10 percent. The process analyst might next look at the decision to buy a new refrigerator, while the thematic analyst will study the effect of rebate programs on refrigerator sales.

Systems Analyses

The final perspective that we will examine is the systems approach. This perspective views the criminal justice process as a whole comprised of the separate, but interrelated, parts of law enforcement, courts, and corrections. These parts work together to achieve the goal of crime control in our society.

Although the roots of what is called general systems theory can be traced back hundreds of years (Van Gigch, 1974:49-52), it was best espoused by Ludwig von Bertalanffy in 1950 and later expanded by him in 1968. The heart of systems theory is an emphasis on context. Whatever they study, systems analysts strive to see the "big picture." They are concerned with how their units of study fit into a larger environment.

A **system** is a set or collection of interrelated parts working together to achieve a common goal. Systems seek balance and operate in equilibrium. As a result, a system will react and adapt to pressures in ways that maintain or restore equilibrium. The disruption of a system's balance affects each of its component parts and alters its total operation. Therefore, systems are generally resistant to change.

The systems analyst attempts to understand both how and why decisions are made, and looks for reasons or explanations that are internal to the justice process, or that arise from the larger environment. The systems approach compels the analyst to assess the big picture and to determine whether the parts are interconnected. This perspective also sensitizes the analyst to the complexity of the criminal justice system. For example, the analyst not only attempts to understand how police decide to arrest offenders, but also seeks to learn how this arrest decision affects prosecutors, judges, and correctional authorities.

Choosing a Perspective

This book relies on the systems approach because of its flexibility. The major shortcoming of the other approaches is that they can be too restrictive. Analysts employing one of the other perspectives often hold a "systems" view of the justice process. To explain different levels of discretion, evidence sufficiency, deterrent value, or community protection, they seek reasons outside the narrow realm of their approach.

The process approach yields excellent descriptions of how cases move along the justice system, but often fails to provide adequate explanations for deviations from normal operation. To explain why a particular case or set of cases receives special treatment, these analysts frequently refer to external (environmental) factors. Those using a comparative approach also refer to environmental factors to explain observed deviations from the ideal or to explain differences between models. The systems approach is multidisciplinary and grounded in the context or environment of the justice system. It includes not only the capacity to seek external causes for practices of the justice process, but also requires the analyst to search for those causes.

The systems approach is broad enough to allow the analyst to employ any (or all) of the other perspectives within it, and flexible enough to include many different disciplinary backgrounds and approaches to the study of the justice process. An analyst might concentrate on the psychological motivations of prosecutors in plea bargaining, but do so with reference to the organizational needs of the courts, police, and prosecutors, as well as sensitivity to the evidentiary standards of arrest, charging, and conviction.

The systems approach forces the analyst to remember that many factors influence each decision and decisionmaker in the justice process. The analyst is able to consider not only how a change in the criminal law might affect police enforcement, but also how prosecutors, judges, and correctional officials may react to those changes.

The systems approach provides a "picture window" through which to view criminal justice, as compared to the "portholes" available with other perspectives. For this reason, we take a systems perspective on criminal justice for the remainder of this book. We hope to see the big picture, as well as its component parts.

Systems Theory and the Systems Approach

The properties of systems are easily understood within the common-sense meaning and use of the term "system." We all know, for example, that one cannot "beat the system" (because it resists change). Many people have a "system" for filing, doing the laundry, or even betting on horse races. How many times have we learned that our application, payment, or request for information cannot be processed because "the system is down"? These phrases illustrate the characteristics of a system: the interrelatedness of parts, common purpose, and resistance to change.

The system cannot be beaten because it reacts and adapts to maintain normal functioning. In some way, over the long run, things will even out. A system for filing papers or doing the laundry is a process composed of interrelated steps that, when taken in proper sequence, yield the desired result (e.g., being able to find papers quickly or to produce laundry with "white whites and bright colors"). Any breakdown in the system leads to undesired results such as lost papers or discolored laundry.

The System of Criminal Justice

Systems theory is sensitive to the interdependency of the parts of the entire process. As Sutherland (1975:3) observed, systems theory requires the adoption of the "systems approach." The approach to study and problem-solving that comes from systems theory is very appropriate to the study of criminal justice. It compels the analyst to consider the interconnectedness of parts. It also sensitizes the analyst to the complexities inherent in the criminal justice system. In the next chapter, we will apply this perspective to the justice process and see how well suited it is to the study of crime control, but for now it is important to understand the development of the systems perspective in criminal justice.

Samuel Walker (1992) observed that the systems perspective is the dominant scientific paradigm of criminal justice. That is, most people studying criminal justice use a systems model to understand the process. Walker suggests that this model came to dominate thinking about criminal justice because of the American Bar Foundation survey of criminal justice in the 1950s. Those who worked on that research project assumed leadership roles in the President's Commission on Law Enforcement and Administration of Justice in the mid-1960s. As a result of the intensive study of criminal justice operations, these researchers developed a paradigm (explanatory model) for understanding criminal justice. This paradigm was based on five general observations (Walker, 1992:66-70):

1. Criminal justice is complex, involving much more than law enforcement.

2. The role of the police, as a result, is also very complex, involving more than crime control.

3. The administration of justice is largely discretionary.

4. Discretionary decisions are not well controlled by law or formal rules.

5. The agencies of criminal justice are interrelated and form a system.

These observations have directed the development of criminal justice as a field of inquiry. The focus of criminal justice study became the decision-making processes of agents and agencies of the justice process. Rather than a simple question of law enforcement or the application of rules, each decision in the process was affected, or could be affected, by a variety of forces. Further, the decisions made at one point in the process (e.g., arrest) were recognized to have implications for later decisions.

What emerged from this orientation was a definition of criminal justice as a complex process of social control in which decisions reflected conflicting goals and expectations. The decisions themselves were variable. Contrary to expectations, an arrest was not solely or even primarily dependent on the existence of sufficient evidence of criminality. In addition, the separate decisions of criminal justice agents and agencies were linked in a sequential fashion, so that the choices of police officers constrained prosecutors, whose choices constrained judges, and so on. The goal of reforming criminal justice processing hinged on the ability to understand and thereby control the decision-making process. Understanding this process seemed to require viewing criminal justice as a system (Conley, 1994).

Types of Systems

There are a number of ways in which systems can be identified and classified (Sutherland, 1975). For our purposes, we need only differentiate between "closed" and "open" systems. These terms refer to the sensitivity of a system to its environment. Those systems that are relatively impervious and insensitive to the environment are closed, while those that more freely interact with their environments are open.

A closed system is often self-contained. One simplistic example of a closed system is an astronaut in a space suit. Whether standing on earth, conducting a spacewalk, or exploring another planet, the astronaut is insulated from the environment. To the degree that it functions regardless of surroundings, the life-support system of a space suit is a closed system.

An open system is sensitive to its environment, like a business. Among other things, changes in tax laws, wage rates, markets, environmental protection regulations, shipping rates, or costs of raw materials will affect profits. To remain profitable, a business must constantly adapt not only to internal pressures, but also to external or environmental changes. Most organizations are best understood as open systems.

It is most accurate and useful to classify the justice system as an open system. Clearly, the justice process in American society must react to changes in the economy, population, and political components of its environment. Perhaps less clearly, it must also adapt to changes in social values, ideology, and information. We shall see in later chapters how influential the environment of the justice system is in explaining the operations of the justice process. Finally, we must recognize that the criminal justice system influences the broader society.

Before concluding this brief overview of systems theory, it is necessary to address one more aspect of this approach to the study of criminal justice. The systems analyst is faced with the task of defining system boundaries. In studying criminal justice, for example, must we include the economic system, the educational system, and the state of mass transportation? Sutherland (1975:22-24) referred to this concept as the level of abstraction.

Level of abstraction refers to the degree of complexity of the system selected for study. General systems theory includes concepts of the whole system, of the total system, and of subsystems, as described in Box 1.4. The whole system is comprised of everything. It would include the criminal justice system, the American social system, and several larger sets of systems. In short, the whole system is the entire universe of systems. At this level, the analyst is dealing with issues far too complex to understand or explain fully.

Each system in turn is composed of various components. Depending upon the scope of the system in question, these components may themselves be full systems. A full system that is a component of a larger system is known as a subsystem. Thus, criminal justice is a subsystem of the American social system; it is itself comprised of the subsystems of law enforcement, courts, and corrections. These subsystems, in turn, are also comprised of subsystems. The delineation of components is nearly endless, so it is important for the analyst to define the level of abstraction (complexity) of the system to be analyzed. Sutherland (1975:23) stated: "The problem however, is in determining (for any given phenomenon or class of phenomena) just what the appropriate level of abstraction might be."

Box 1.4 Criminal Justice in the Whole System

Three system levels: The Subsystems (Agencies), the Total System (Criminal Justice System), and the Whole System.

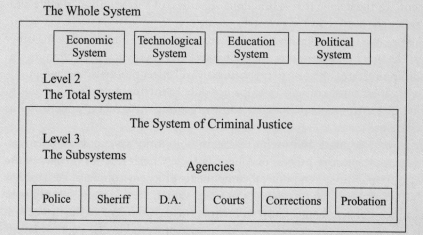

Source: J.P. Van Gigch (1974), *Applied General Systems Theory* (New York: Harper & Row):25.

The systems approach serves to sensitize the analyst to the various degrees of complexity without requiring the selection of any particular level of abstraction. The analyst may decide to study the law enforcement subsystem of the justice process, examining decisions to investigate crime and arrest suspects. Yet, understanding different outcomes of decisions may require reference to community characteristics (e.g., small towns versus large cities) or prosecutorial policies (e.g., willingness to prosecute "victimless" crimes).

The analyst has the flexibility to expand or increase the level of abstraction as needed in order to understand some aspect of the particular system being studied. This feature of the systems perspective is what makes it most appropriate to the study of criminal justice.

The Nonsystem of Criminal Justice

While the justice process would seem to have the properties of a system, and the systems approach appears to be well suited to the study of criminal justice, there are those who argue that such an approach is inappropriate. The Omnibus Crime Control and Safe Streets Act of 1968 provided the impetus for the development of a systems perspective on criminal justice planning. This law established that states wishing to receive federal funds for crime control efforts would be required to create State Planning Agencies (SPAs). These SPAs were charged with administering federal funds and with the development of comprehensive, long-range plans for improvement of the total criminal justice system. It was not long before criticisms of the systems approach to criminal justice were raised.

In 1973, the National Advisory Commission (NAC) on Criminal Justice Standards and Goals reported that "[f]ragmented," "divided," "splintered," and "decentralized" are the adjectives most commonly used to describe the American system of criminal justice (1973:59)." Early attempts to apply systems analysis to criminal justice planning ran afoul of the nature of the justice process. Criminal justice, in practice, does not seem to be the holistic entity envisioned in the systems approach (see Box 1.5).

Box 1.5 The Nonsystem of Criminal Justice

The effectiveness of the system or the mission and priorities of the system are going to be viewed differently by the policeman, the trial judge, the prosecutor, the defense attorney, the corrections administrator, the appellate tribunal, the slum dweller and the residents of the suburbs. Isolated and antagonistic within their traditional responsibilities, each component analyzes its problems from its own point of view and each vies with the others for public funds. Each is jealous of its authority and each proceeds according to a different set of priorities. This attitude reflects a lack of guidance oriented toward a single criminal justice system.

—Richter Moore (1976:6)

Source: R.H. Moore (1976), "The Criminal Justice Nonsystem." In R.H. Moore, T.C. Marks & R.V. Barrow, *Readings in Criminal Justice* (Indianapolis: Bobbs-Merrill):5.

Robin (1984:52-53) classified criticisms of the systems approach to criminal justice into four categories, according to what aspects of the justice system the critic examined to make the case. These categories include: (1) jurisdictional problems, (2) differences in roles and goals, (3) differences in personnel, and (4) substantive issues. The federal government, the District of Columbia, and the 50 states each have a subsystem of justice. Indeed, it can be argued that every municipality represents a system of justice. It is axiomatic that police, prosecutors, judges, and correctional personnel differ among themselves about what strategies best control crime, and each group seeks to protect and enhance its position. Finally, the inefficiency of the system has been presented as evidence that it is, in reality, a nonsystem.

While these arguments are persuasive, they do not refute the systemic nature of the criminal justice process. It cannot be denied that criminal justice is complex, contradictory, inefficient, and decentralized; criminal justice is not a "model" system. Yet, crime control is a manifest function or goal of each agency. Moreover, the interrelatedness of the components of the justice process and the resistance of criminal justice to change also cannot be easily refuted (Walker, 1993). Whether we can establish that criminal justice in the United States is a true system is less important than recognizing that the operation of criminal justice in American society exhibits the characteristics of a system. For this reason, the systems approach still appears to be well suited to the study of criminal justice.

Reliance upon the systems approach (which will characterize our treatment of criminal justice) is founded on its usefulness in understanding the operations of justice agencies. This perspective enables us to study decisions in areas such as arrest or sentencing within a broad context. It highlights the inconsistencies that exist in the justice system and directs our attention to explaining them. The systems approach provides us with a framework for the evaluation and comparison of various subsystems. It requires us to be open to viewing any number of factors as contributing to our understanding of the justice process. This openness in analysis is often lacking in other approaches (Van Gigch, 1974:21-31).

The Environment of Criminal Justice

Having defined the criminal justice process as an open system, we must briefly examine the environmental factors that affect its operations. These factors have direct impact on all aspects of criminal justice. The environment of criminal justice is both material and ideological. The material environment includes concrete resources such as money, personnel, equipment, and the like. The ideological environment is comprised chiefly of values and beliefs about how the justice process should operate. Box 1.6 illustrates the placement of criminal justice within this environment.

Box 1.6 The Environment of Criminal Justice

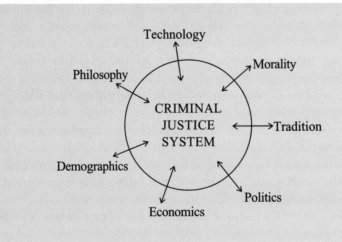

The Material Environment of Criminal Justice

In simple terms, each system has three stages: (1) input, (2) throughput, and (3) output. In manufacturing, for example, input is the reception of raw materials, throughput is the production process, and output is the final product. For the criminal justice system, criminal offenses are the input, the transformation of crime suspects into convicts is the throughput, and ex-convicts are the output.

As with manufacturing, the input stage of the criminal justice system involves labor, machinery, and capital. Law enforcement officers, prosecutors, judges, defense attorneys, correctional staff, police cars, courthouses, jails, and even paper clips for reports are parts of the justice system input. In addition, the output of the justice system is not limited to "ex-convicts." Some nonguilty suspects are released at various stages in the process, as are some persons who are guilty yet not convicted of a crime. Many ex-convicts do not retain that label long before they again are arrested for a new crime. This illustration serves the purpose of identifying the principal material factors in the criminal justice system's environment: raw materials and the means of production.

Raw Materials

The raw material of the criminal justice system consists of criminal offenses. Thus, the system is affected by changes in the nature and distribution of crime. Suppose our "petition-pusher" from the opening part of this chapter is successful and has a law passed prohibiting all drivers from using cell phones while driving. Use of cell phones while driving becomes a new source of "raw material" for the criminal justice system. On the other hand, if all criminal laws were repealed, there would be no raw materials for criminal justice.

Unlike the manufacturing firm, the justice system has little control over the volume of raw material it receives. Imagine the effects on a manufacturing plant of deliveries of materials that far exceed the plant's capacity to produce. For example, imagine the delivery of one million barrels of crude oil each day to a refinery that can process only 100,000 barrels every 24 hours. Similar situations have occurred in the justice process.

In cases of large crowds or demonstrations, police officers are often instructed to overlook minor violations and concentrate on the maintenance of order. In large measure, this is because large crowds are potentially dangerous, but it is also because there may be no capacity to handle mass arrests. In one massive demonstration in Washington, DC, resulting in thousands of arrests, suspects were held in RFK Stadium until they could be processed. While this example is perhaps the exception, there is a long-recognized problem of an abundance of raw material for the justice system. Increasing demands on the justice system may result in lower levels of output. Decker, Varano, and Greene (2007) report that when faced with the demands of providing additional security and dealing with an influx of some

In cases of large crowds or demonstrations, police officers are often instructed to overlook minor violations and concentrate on the maintenance of order. *Photo credit: Mark C. Ide.*

two million visitors during the 2002 Winter Olympics, routine police enforcement activity by the Salt Lake City Police Department decreased significantly. After the Olympics had ended, police enforcement activity returned to its previous levels. It is still not clear what will be the impact of contemporary concerns about the terrorist threat. Unless we expand the size of police agencies, adding counter-terrorism responsibility is most likely to detract from other aspects of police work.

One response to the heavy caseloads of criminal justice agencies seeks to alter this aspect of the environment. Proponents of decriminalization would remove certain categories of criminal behavior from the justice system. They suggest that the justice system devotes too many resources to the control of essentially harmless or victimless crimes such as vagrancy, public intoxication, and disorderly conduct (see Luna, 2003).

Means of Production

The means of production for the criminal justice system are the personnel, facilities, and equipment of the various justice agencies. Changes in the capacity to process criminal cases will have an effect on the entire justice system. Increases or decreases in the numbers of police, prosecutors, judges, prisons, or other components of the justice system will result in changes in the number of cases processed, or in the manner in which cases are handled (Brandl, Chamlin & Frank, 1995). Zhao, Scheider, and Thurman (2003) found that the increased number of police officers and improved police technology provided by the federal Office of Community Policing Services grants to local police agencies resulted in increased numbers of arrests over the years.

Returning to our example of the manufacturing firm, a dramatic increase in the sales force, or a vast improvement in efficiency in the sales force, will result in a tremendous increase in orders. The manufacturing plant will be required to expand production to keep pace with demand. So too, dramatic increases in the number of police officers or in the level of police efficiency can require enhanced capability in the courts and correctional aspects of the justice process. Those increased arrests mean increased caseloads for the courts. Several observers have argued that increasing the capacity of parts of the justice process will have the effect of increasing their use. For example, Nagel (1973) suggested that any prison cells that are created are likely to be filled, and that building more prisons will result in the imprisonment of more offenders. In contrast, the recent problem of prison and jail crowding has meant that many offenders who would otherwise have been imprisoned have been released early or placed on probation instead of being sent to prison or jail.

The actual outcome of changes in the means of production of the criminal justice system are not as important as the fact that the alterations will lead to adaptations in the system. Thus, a person considering reform in one part of the justice system (more or better police, prosecutors, judges, prisons, or what have you) must be sensitive to the fact that such changes will have a "ripple effect" on the remainder of the justice process. Indeed, systems theory suggests that fluctuations in the environment will be met with changes in the system to limit the disruption of equilibrium. One of the most salient characteristics of the criminal justice system (and one strongly supporting the use of a systems perspective) is that it is resistant to change (Travis, 1982).

The Ideological Environment of Criminal Justice

As a social institution, and particularly one of social control, perhaps the most important aspect of the environment in which the criminal justice system operates is ideological rather than material. The criminal justice system is rife with value conflicts, political and social controversy, and inefficient organization. These attributes of criminal justice reflect our deep ambivalence about social control.

Value Conflicts

Perhaps the most fundamental value conflict characteristic of criminal justice in the United States is that between individual freedom and social regularity. In his discussion of policing, Richard Lundman (1980) determined that this conflict was one between liberty (freedom) and civility (order). Packer's two justice system models of due process and crime control reflect the same controversy. As Culbertson has observed (1984:vii):

> We demand that our police apprehend suspects, that our courts convict the accused, and that our correctional system, in some way, punish the convicted. We demand order. The tasks involved in insuring order would be relatively straightforward were it not for our simultaneous demand that the police, courts and correctional agencies operate within the constraints placed upon them by the law.

With some degree of irony, it could be stated that America is constitutionally unsuited for criminal justice. Our emphasis on individual liberty and constrained governmental authority requires that a certain level of inefficiency in criminal justice be tolerated. We generally do not allow potentially effective crime control practices such as random wiretaps, warrantless searches, censorship of mail, or the use of "truth serum" during interrogation. We do provide defense counsel, pretrial release, and appellate review of trials and sentences in most cases. In an effort to preserve individual liberty, we not only constrain justice agencies from engaging in many activities, but we also actively impose barriers to the agencies' swift and simple operation. Dean Spader (1987) remarked that criminal justice practice represents a "golden zigzag" between social protection and individual rights.

A statue of George Washington on the steps of Federal Hall looms over protesters holding up a signs critical of the USA PATRIOT Act during a demonstration near the New York Stock Exchange. The protesters, numbering several hundred, gathered within distant earshot of Attorney General John Ashcroft as he delivered a speech defending the Act as a vital safeguard of American lives. The controversy over the PATRIOT Act highlights the competing values of social protection and individual rights. Photo credit: AP Photo/Scout Tufankjian.

The criminal justice system is designed for crime control, but the control of crime must be consistent with our social and political heritage. The justice system must achieve a balance between competing values of federalism and uniformity, vengeance and assistance, and differing political persuasions, as well as between individual actors and social regularity. It is the balance of these opposing forces that renders the justice system so complex.

The tension between our concerns for crime control (order or safety) and due process (limited governmental power or individual liberty) is clearly visible as we struggle to respond to the threat of terrorist attacks. As Timothy Lynch (2002:2) puts it, "If one examines the history of the federal government's responses to terrorism, a disturbing pattern emerges. The federal government responds to terrorist attacks on U.S. soil—such as the Oklahoma City bombing in 1995—by rushing to restrict civil liberties." From expanded wiretap authority to increased surveillance of citizens, efforts to prevent terrorism often require (or produce) increases in governmental authority and limits on individual liberty.

Federalism and Uniformity. One of the major criticisms of the systems approach to criminal justice is based on the fact that the justice process is decentralized, disorganized, and lacks consistency. Yet, these limitations of the criminal justice system are congruent with two of our social and political values: federalism and the separation of powers.

The basic principle of governmental organization in the United States is that of federalism. Our nation is the result of a federation of sovereign states. The

United States Constitution enumerates the rights and obligations of the federal government, and the Tenth Amendment includes the "reservation clause." The amendment reads:

> The powers not delegated to the United States by the Constitution, nor prohibited by it to the states, are reserved to the states respectively, or to the people.

This amendment enables states to pass and enforce criminal laws, and to create the offices and agencies necessary to perform these tasks. Thus, a federal justice system is created to deal with federal offenses (e.g., counterfeiting), and separate justice systems are created to enable each state to deal with state crimes (e.g., theft).

States, in turn, have constitutions under which they charter municipalities. These counties, cities, towns, and villages are allowed (or required) to provide for their own criminal offenses, and to create and maintain offices and agencies to enforce local and state laws. This organizational structure of government ensures local autonomy, so that the citizens of each state and community have a fairly large degree of freedom from central control.

For the justice system, the result is thousands of police agencies at federal, state, and municipal levels; thousands of jails, courts, probation agencies, prosecutors, and defense offices; and scores of prison and parole agencies. It also results in differences in the definitions of crimes and the levels of punishments applicable to criminal behavior. Variety is central to criminal justice in the United States.

The Constitution of the United States also creates and maintains a separation of powers between the executive, judicial, and legislative branches of government. In simplistic terms, the legislature makes the law, the judiciary interprets the law, and the executive enforces the law. Each branch of government is checked and balanced by the other two branches. This tripartite governmental structure is found at the federal, state, and municipal levels of government.

This complex organization of the crime control function in America causes inefficiency. Yet, to preserve our interests in local autonomy and constrained governmental power, we must tolerate the inefficient organization of governmental service (Forst, 1977). Barbara Stolz (2002:52) observes:

> In the United States, governmental authority is constitutionally distributed among three levels of government—the federal, fifty state, and thousands of local governments . . . Moreover, at each level of government, policy making authority is shared among three branches—the executive, legislative, and judicial . . . These are the formal institutions of government and within these institutions the formal processes of government are carried out. In the criminal justice area, most policy making occurs at the local or state level but, particularly since the 1960s, the role of the federal government has expanded.

In short, a centralized, uniform system of criminal justice would be unconstitutional. Any efforts to understand the justice system and to promote consistency and simplicity in organization and in the processing of criminal cases must be sensitive to the values our society places on federalism. Effectiveness and efficiency of operation in the criminal justice system are not the only goals to be considered when analyzing its structure and operation.

Vengeance and Assistance. The age-old dilemma of what to do for, with, and about criminal offenders plagues the justice system. The system is required to penalize and stigmatize offenders, while at the same time under an obligation to return law-abiding citizens to the streets. The United States is essentially a utilitarian society. We generally are not content with punishment for punishment's sake (Finckenauer, 1988). Rather, we expect some ultimate "good" to arise from governmental action.

In this vein, John Griffiths (1970) suggested a third model of the justice system in opposition to those described by Packer. This third type is the family model. This approach assumes that the interests of society and those of the offender are the same. The net effect of criminal justice processing of an offender should be beneficial to both the offender and the society.

The term "family model" is an apt description of the conflict between vengeance and assistance. While a parent may want or need to punish a child's misbehavior, the purpose of the punishment is to correct the child's error and to restore harmony in the family. Thus, actions taken by agents of the justice system are continually compared against two standards:

> Has punishment been administered?
>
> Has the offender been "helped"?

Jay Albanese (1996) captured the essence of this conflict in his presidential address to the Academy of Criminal Justice Sciences. As have others before him, Albanese called for a merging of the choices between punishment and rehabilitation into a choice of punishment and rehabilitation. Still, despite decades of observations that we can both punish and help at the same time, current thinking is still dominated by a conception that the two are distinct and opposite.

Depending upon the political persuasion of criminal justice policymakers (i.e., liberal or conservative), radically different strategies may be adopted to control crime (Reckless & Allen, 1979). The attitudes, perceptions, and tendencies of criminal justice agents and offenders are important factors in understanding the operations of the criminal justice system. The ability of individual actors to affect criminal justice decisions and processing is known as "discretion."

Individual Actors. In 1928, Sheldon Glueck observed that the criminal justice system was a "clumsy admixture of the oil of discretion and the water of rule" (1928:480). By this he meant that the rule or "law" serves to place constraints on the actions of agents of the criminal justice system, but the system relies upon discretion to process cases smoothly. Regardless of the specificity of applicable law, there is always room for "judgment calls."

Kenneth Davis (1969) studied the pervasiveness of discretion in the justice process. He observed police, prosecutors, parole authorities, and judges, and noted their wide-ranging discretionary powers. In any specific instance, a decision to arrest, charge a suspect, impose a sentence, or grant release from prison is a judgment call. For example, the discretionary power of police officers is illustrated by our hope for a mere warning when we are caught exceeding the speed limit.

The fact of discretion in criminal justice decisionmaking renders the explanation of specific case decisions very complex. However, an understanding of the forces at work in any given decision sheds light on the process. This chapter has attempted to illustrate these forces.

It is important to realize that discretion is not totally unfettered. Every discretionary decision is made within a context of forces operating at all levels of the justice system previously described. Therefore, the day-to-day workings of the justice system are structured by these larger and more distant factors, which must be kept in balance.

A police officer detains a man matching the description of a suspect in a drive-by shooting. Police have wide discretionary power, evident in the decision whether to arrest a person. *Photo credit: Mark C. Ide.*

Examining Criminal Justice

So far this chapter has served as a basic introduction to the study of criminal justice in the United States. The remainder of this book will explore criminal justice practices, agents, and agencies, building on what has been described here. Three themes emerging from this introduction will guide our examination of the United States' system of criminal justice. The first is the notion of a systems approach to understanding the operations of the justice process. Criminal justice is part of the system of social control in American society, as well as part of the larger society. Changes in the environment (materials, ideas, values, etc.) will influence the justice process. A second theme is that there is a fundamental conflict between individual liberty and collective needs for predictability. The criminal justice system, each of its decision points, and all of the decisionmakers involved in the system must strike a balance between the interests of the individual citizen and the interests of the community. Finally, the existence of discretion in the justice system is the third theme in our approach to studying criminal justice. In most cases, criminal justice agents (police, prosecutors, judges, corrections officials, and others) have some latitude in deciding what to do about offenses and offenders. Much of our attention will be devoted to identifying what sorts of factors help us to understand the kinds of decisions that are made.

As we progress in our examination of criminal justice in the United States, we will describe the justice system and its structure, organizations, and agents. We will investigate the range of decisions that are made in cases at each stage of the justice process, and explore the factors that are associated with different decisions. Finally, we will try to place things into the larger context of seeking a balance between due process and crime control.

See Box 1.7 for a chart that seeks to present a simple yet comprehensive view of the movement of cases through the criminal justice system.

Preview of Forthcoming Chapters

In the chapters to follow, we will examine the criminal justice system. The first four chapters set the stage for analyzing criminal justice operations. Chapter 1 has provided a foundation of criminal justice perspectives. Chapter 2 presents an overview of the operations and structure of the criminal justice system of the United States. Chapter 3 includes a discussion of law and a description of some recent changes in criminal justice, and illustrates how the system reflects changes in our thinking about crime and criminals. In Chapter 4, sources of data on the nature and extent of crime are reviewed, and an overview of the way in which cases are "selected" for justice processing is provided. The next 10 chapters address the subsystems of the criminal justice system, from the detection of crime through investigation and arrest; to initial appearance in court; through formal charging, trial, and conviction; and finally to sentencing and the goals of criminal penalties. Incarceration and community-centered punishments are described and discussed, and the juvenile justice system is evaluated in a separate chapter. The last chapter is devoted to a discussion of system-wide developments and issues, and to the future of criminal justice in the United States.

Box 1.7   The Criminal Justice System

Procedures in individual jurisdictions may vary from the pattern shown here. The differing weights of the lines indicate the relative volumes of cases disposed of at various points in the system. This information, however, is only suggestive because no nationwide data of this sort exist.

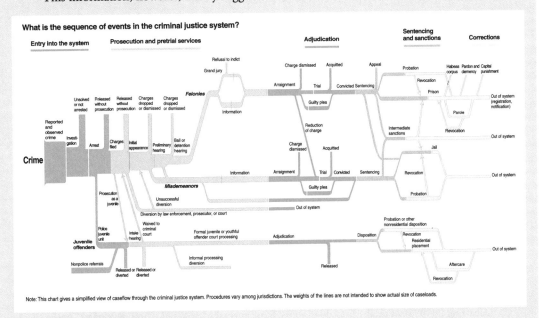

What is the sequence of events in the criminal justice system?

Note: This chart gives a simplified view of caseflow through the criminal justice system. Procedures vary among jurisdictions. The weights of the lines are not intended to show actual size of caseloads.

1. May continue until trial.

2. Administrative record of arrest. First step at which temporary release on bail may be available.

3. Before magistrate, commissioner, or justice of peace. Formal notice of charge, advice of rights. Bail set. Summary trials for petty offenses usually conducted here without further processing.

4. Preliminary testing of evidence against defendant. Charge may be reduced. No separate preliminary hearing for misdemeanors in some systems.

5. Charge filed by prosecutor on basis of information submitted by police or citizens. Alternative to grand jury indictment; often used in felonies, almost always in misdemeanors.

6. Reviews whether government evidence sufficient to justify trial. Some states have no grand jury system; others seldom use it.

7. Appearance for plea; defendant elects trial by judge or jury (if available); counsel for indigent usually appointed here in felonies. Often not at all in other cases.

8. Charge may be reduced at any time prior to trial in return for plea of gulity or for other reasons.

9. Challenge on constitutional grounds to legality of detention. May be sought at any point in the process.

10. Police often hold informal hearings, dismiss or adjust many cases without further processing.

11. Probation officer decides desirability of further court action.

12. Welfare agency, social services, counseling, medical care, etc., for cases where adjudicatory handling not needed.

Source: President's Commission on Law Enforcement and Administration of Justice (1967), *The Challenge of Crime in a Free Society* (Washington, DC: U.S. Government Printing Office).

Review Questions

1. What is the purpose of the criminal justice system?

2. What is a system?

3. Distinguish between "open" and "closed" systems.

4. How has criminal justice been characterized as a nonsystem?

5. In addition to a systems approach, what are three other common approaches to the study of criminal justice?

6. What components comprise the material and ideological environments of the criminal justice system?

7. What is the relationship between support for crime control and support for due process?

References

Albanese, J. (1996). "Presidential Address: Five Fundamental Mistakes of Criminal Justice." *Justice Quarterly* 13(4):549-565.

Allen, F. (1964). *The Borderland of Criminal Justice.* Chicago: University of Chicago Press.

Beccaria, C. (1764). *On Crimes and Punishments and Other Writings.* R. Bellamy (ed.), R. Davies (translator) & V. Cox (1995). Cambridge: Cambridge University Press.

Bernard, T.J. & R.S. Engel (2001). "Conceptualizing Criminal Justice Theory." *Justice Quarterly* 18(1):1-30.

Bianchi, H. (1994). *Justice as Sanctuary: Toward a New System of Crime Control.* Bloomington, IN: Indiana University Press.

Black, D. (1976). *The Behavior of Law.* New York: Academic Press.

Brandl, S., M. Chamlin & J. Frank (1995). "Aggregation Bias and the Capacity for Formal Crime Control: The Determinants of Total and Disaggregated Police Force Size in Milwaukee, 1934-1987." *Justice Quarterly* 12(3):543-562.

Burton, V., F. Cullen, T. Evans, R. Dunaway, S. Kethineni & G. Payne (1995). "The Impact of Parental Controls on Delinquency." *Journal of Criminal Justice* 23(2):111-126.

Castellano, T. & J. Schafer (2005). "Continuity and Discontinuity in Competing Models of Criminal Justice Education: Evidence from Illinois." *Journal of Criminal Justice Education* 16(1):60-78.

Chambliss, W. & R. Seidman (1971). *Law, Order, and Power.* Reading, MA: Addison-Wesley.

Clear, T.R. (2001). "Presidential Address: Has Academic Criminal Justice Come of Age?" *Justice Quarterly* 18(4):709-726.

Cohen, A. (1966). *Deviance and Control.* Englewood Cliffs, NJ: Prentice Hall.

Cohen, L. & M. Felson (1979). "Social Change and Crime Rate Trends." *American Sociological Review* 44:555-608.

Conley, J. (ed.) (1994). *The 1967 President's Crime Commission Report: Its Impact 25 Years Later.* Cincinnati: Anderson.

Cornish, D. & R. Clarke (1986). *The Reasoning Criminal.* New York: Springer-Verlag.

Culbertson, R.G. (ed.) (1984). "Order Under Law." In *Readings in Criminal Justice,* 2nd ed. Prospect Heights, IL: Waveland.

Davis, K.C. (1969). *Discretionary Justice.* Baton Rouge: Louisiana State University Press.

Dawson, R.O. (1969). *Sentencing.* Boston: Little, Brown.

Decker, S., S. Varano & J. Greene (2007). "Routine Crime in Exceptional Times: The Impact of the 2002 Winter Olympics on Citizen Demand for Police Services." *Journal of Criminal Justice* 35(1):89-101.

DeLisi, M. & M. Berg (2006). "Exploring Theoretical Linkages between Self-control Theory and Criminal Justice System Processing." *Journal of Criminal Justice* 34(2):153-163.

Duffee, D. (1980). *Explaining Criminal Justice: Community Theory and Criminal Justice Reform.* Prospect Heights, IL: Waveland Press.

Dunworth, T. & G. Mills (1999). *National Evaluation of Weed and Seed.* Washington, DC: National Institute of Justice.

Durham, A., H. Elrod & P. Kinkade (1995). "Images of Crime and Justice: Murder and the 'True Crime' Genre." *Journal of Criminal Justice* 23(2):143-152.

Engel, R.S., J.J. Sobol & R.E. Worden (2000). "Further Exploration of the Demeanor Hypothesis: The Interaction Effects of Suspects' Characteristics and Demeanor on Police Behavior." *Justice Quarterly* 17(2):235-258.

Finckenauer, J.O. (1988). "Public Support for the Death Penalty: Retribution as Just Deserts or Retribution as Revenge." *Justice Quarterly* 5(1):81-100.

Forst, M.L. (1977). "To What Extent Should the Criminal Justice System Be a System?" *Crime & Delinquency* 23(4):403.

Foucault, M. (1979). *Discipline and Punish: The Birth of the Prison.* New York: Vintage Books.

Friel, C. (2000). "A Century of Changing Boundaries." In C. Friel (ed.), *Boundary Changes in Criminal Justice Organizations.* Washington, DC: National Institute of Justice, Criminal Justice 2000, Volume 2:1-17.

Gertz, M. & L. Gould (1995). "Fear of Punishment and the Willingness to Engage in Criminal Behavior: A Research Note." *Journal of Criminal Justice* 23(4):377-384.

Glueck, S. (1928). "Principles of a Rational Penal Code." *Harvard University Law Review* 41:453.

Gomme, I. & M. Hall (1995). "Prosecutors at Work: Role Overload and Strain." *Journal of Criminal Justice* 23(2):191-200.

Gorecki, J. (1979). *A Theory of Criminal Justice.* New York: Columbia University Press.

Griffiths, J. (1970). "Ideology in Criminal Procedure or a Third 'Model' of the Criminal Process." *Yale Law Journal* 79:359.

Hagan, J. (1989). "Why Is There So Little Criminal Justice Theory? Neglected Macro- and Micro-Level Links Between Organization and Power." *Journal of Research in Crime and Delinquency* 26(1):116-135.

Karp, D.R. & T.R. Clear (2000). "Community Justice: A Conceptual Framework." In C. Friel (ed.), *Boundary Changes in Criminal Justice*. Washington, DC: National Institute of Justice, Criminal Justice 2000, Volume 2:323-368.

Kelling, G., M.R. Hochberg, S.L. Kaminska, A.M. Rocheleau, D.P. Rosenbaum, J.A. Roth & W.G. Skogan (1998). *The Bureau of Justice Assistance Comprehensive Communities Program: A Preliminary Report*. Washington, DC: National Institute of Justice.

Kellogg, F.R. (1976). "Organizing the Criminal Justice System: A Look at Operative Objectives." *Federal Probation* 40(2):9.

Kolonski, J. & R. Mendelsohn (1970). *The Politics of Local Justice*. Boston: Little, Brown.

Kraska, P.B. (2006). "Criminal Justice Theory: Toward Legitimacy and an Infrastructure." *Justice Quarterly* 23(2):167-185.

Kraska, P.B. (2004). *Theorizing Criminal Justice: Eight Essential Orientations*. Long Grove, IL: Waveland Press.

LaFave, W.R. (1965). *Arrest*. Boston: Little, Brown.

Levin, M.A. (1972). "Urban Politics and Policy Outcomes: The Criminal Courts." In G.F. Cole (ed.), *Criminal Justice: Law and Politics*, 4th ed. Belmont, CA: Brooks/Cole, 1984:289.

Luna, E. (2003). "Overextending the Criminal Law." *Cato Policy Report* 25(6):1, 15-16.

Lundman, R.A. (1980). *Police and Policing: An Introduction*. New York: Holt, Rinehart & Winston.

Lynch, T. (2002). "Breaking the Vicious Cycle: Preserving our Liberties while Fighting Terrorism: Executive Summary." *Policy Analysis* (June)443. Washington, DC: CATO Institute.

Marenin, D. & J. Worrall (1998). "Criminal Justice: Portrait of a Discipline in Process." *Journal of Criminal Justice* 26(6):465-480.

Markowitz, F. (2006). "Psychiatric Hospital Capacity, Homelessness, and Crime and Arrest Rates." *Criminology* 44(1):45-72.

Miethe, T. & R. Meier (1994). *Crime and Its Social Context*. Albany, NY: SUNY Press.

Miller, F.W. (1970). *Prosecution*. Boston: Little, Brown.

Moore, R.H., Jr. (1976). "The Criminal Justice Nonsystem." In R.H. Moore, T.C. Marks & R.V. Barrow (eds.), *Readings in Criminal Justice*. Indianapolis: Bobbs-Merrill, 5.

Muir, W. (1977). *Police: Streetcorner Politicians*. Chicago: University of Chicago Press.

Nagel, W.G. (1973). *The New Red Barn: A Critical Look at the Modern American Prison*. New York: Walker & Co.

National Advisory Commission on Criminal Justice Standards and Goals (1973). *A National Strategy to Reduce Crime*. New York: Avon.

Newman, D.J. (1966). *Conviction*. Boston: Little, Brown.

Newman, D.J. (1978). *Introduction to Criminal Justice*. Philadelphia: J.B. Lippincott.

O'Leary, V.I. & D. Duffee (1971). "Correctional Policy: A Classification of Goals Designed for Change." *Crime & Delinquency* 18(3):379.

Orsagh, T. (1983). "Is There a Place for Economics in Criminology and Criminal Justice?" *Journal of Criminal Justice* 11(5):391-402.

Packer, H.L. (1969). *The Limits of the Criminal Sanction.* Stanford, CA: Stanford University Press.

Parsons, T. (1966). *Societies: Evolutionary and Comparative Perspectives.* Englewood Cliffs, NJ: Prentice Hall.

Pound, R. (1929). *Criminal Justice in America.* New York: Henry Holt.

Pratt, T. (1998). "Race and Sentencing: A Meta-Analysis of Conflicting Empirical Research Results." *Journal of Criminal Justice* 26(6):513-523.

President's Commission on Law Enforcement and Administration of Justice (1967). *The Challenge of Crime in a Free Society.* New York: Avon.

Reckless, W.C. & H.E. Allen (1979). "Developing a National Crime Policy: The Impact of Politics on Crime in America." In E. Sagarin (ed.), *Criminology: New Concerns.* Beverly Hills, CA: Sage.

Remington, F.J., D.J. Newman, E.L. Kimball, M. Melli & H. Goldstein (1969). *Criminal Justice Administration: Cases and Materials.* Indianapolis: Bobbs-Merrill.

Robin, G.D. (1984). *Introduction to the Criminal Justice System,* 2nd ed. New York: Harper & Row.

Ross, E.A. (1926). *Social Control: A Survey of the Foundations of Order.* New York: Macmillan.

Sorenson, J. & D.H. Wallace (1999). "Prosecutorial Discretion in Seeking Death: An Analysis of Racial Disparity in the Pretrial Stages of Case Processing in a Midwestern City." *Justice Quarterly* 16(3):559-578.

Southerland, M. (2002). "Presidential Address: Criminal Justice Curricula in the United States: A Decade of Change." Justice Quarterly 19(4):589-601.

Spader, D.J. (1987). "Individual Rights vs. Social Utility: The Search for the Golden Zigzag between Conflicting Fundamental Values." *Journal of Criminal Justice* 15(2):121-136.

Stolz, B.A. (2002). "The Roles of Interest Groups in U.S. Criminal Justice Policy Making: Who, When, and How?" *Criminal Justice* 2(1):69.

Supancic, M. & C.L. Willis (1998). "Extralegal Justice and Crime Control." *Journal of Crime and Justice* 21(2):191-215.

Sutherland, J.W. (1975). *Systems: Analysis, Administration and Architecture.* New York: Van Nostrand Reinhold.

Tiffany, L.P., D.M. McIntyre & D. Rotenberg (1967). *Detection.* Boston: Little, Brown.

Toder, H.A. (1987). "The Necessity of Taking an Interdisciplinary Perspective in Criminal Justice Education." *The Justice Professional* 2(2):92-99.

Travis, L. & R. Langworthy (2008). *Policing in America: A Balance of Forces,* 4th ed. Upper Saddle River, NJ: Prentice-Hall.

Travis, L.F., III (1982). "The Politics of Sentencing Reform." In M.L. Forst (ed.), *Sentencing Reform.* Beverly Hills, CA: Sage, 59.

Turpin-Petrosino, C. (1999). "Are Limiting Enactments Effective? An Experimental Test of Decision Making in a Presumptive Parole State." *Journal of Criminal Justice* 27(4):321-332.

United States Department of Justice (2004). *The Weed and Seed Strategy.* Washington, DC: Community Capacity Development Office.

Van Gigch, J.P. (1974). *Applied General Systems Theory.* New York: Harper & Row.

Von Bertalanffy, L. (1950). "The Theory of Open Systems in Physics and Biology." *Science* 3:23.

Von Bertalanffy, L. (1968). *General Systems Theory.* New York: Braziller.

Walker, S. (1992). "Origins of the Contemporary Criminal Justice Paradigm: The American Bar Foundation Survey, 1953-1969." *Justice Quarterly* 9(1):47-76.

Walker, S. (1993). *Taming the System: The Control of Discretion in Criminal Justice 1950-1990.* New York: Oxford University Press.

Warner, B. (2006). "Directly Intervene or Call the Authorities? A Study of Forms of Neighborhood Social Control within a Social Disorganization Framework." *Criminology* 45(1):99-130.

Williams, F. (1984). "The Demise of the Criminological Imagination: A Critique of Recent Criminology." *Justice Quarterly* 1(1):91-106.

Willis, C.L. (1983). "Criminal Justice Theory: A Case of Trained Incapacity." *Journal of Criminal Justice* 11(5):447-458.

Wilson, J.Q. (1968). *Varieties of Police Behavior.* Cambridge, MA: Harvard University Press.

Zalman, M. (2007). "The Search for Criminal Justice Theory: Reflections on Kraska's Theorizing Criminal Justice." *Journal of Criminal Justice Education* 18(1):161-181.

Zhao, J., M. Scheider & Q. Thurman (2003). "A National Evaluation of the Effect of COPS Grants on Police Productivity (Arrests) 1995-1999." *Police Quarterly* 6(4):387-409.

Chapter 2

The Justice Process

Important Terms

arraignment

arrest

circuits

conditional release

discharge

drug courts

initial appearance

investigation

preliminary hearing

private court

revocation

sentencing

trial

undetected crime

unfounded

unreported crime

unsolved

voir dire

Cases move through the justice system from the first stage of detection by law enforcement through subsequent stages to final discharge from the system. While there are some feedback mechanisms by which a case can move back to an earlier decision point, on the whole, cases flow in one direction through the system. This processing of cases represents the "total system" of criminal justice. It includes the subsystems of law enforcement, the courts, and corrections.

In this chapter we will trace the criminal justice system of the United States. In doing so, we will skip many of the details and nuances of criminal justice processing in the interests of developing an understanding of the total justice system. In other words, to some extent we will ignore the "trees" in order to get a better look at the "forest." Later chapters will examine the subsystems of criminal justice in more detail.

Perhaps the greatest constant of criminal justice is variety. Even things as simple as titles differ among jurisdictions. For example, prosecutors are variously known as state's attorneys, district attorneys, U.S. attorneys, prosecutors, and other titles. In most states, the highest court is called the state supreme court; in New York, the supreme court is a trial court, and the highest court is the New York Court of Appeals. With an appreciation that what follows here is a sketch of the justice system, we are ready to proceed.

The Decision Points
of the Criminal Justice System

The President's Commission on Law Enforcement and Administration of Justice (1967a) created the flow chart of the justice system presented as Box 1.7 in the previous chapter. While we follow the general model of the President's Commission, we use slightly different terminology. The criminal justice system begins with the detection of crime, proceeds through investigation, arrest, initial appearance before the court, preliminary hearing, charging (arraignment), trial, sentencing, and possible revocation, and ends with discharge. We will examine these decision points.

Detection

As the formal social institution charged with the control of deviance that is identified as crime, the justice system does not start until a criminal offense is detected. Crime that goes undetected does not influence the justice process directly. It is only when the justice system (usually through the police) notices a possible criminal offense that the process begins.

Perhaps more than half of all crime is never discovered by the justice system (Rand, Lynch & Cantor, 1997). Many crimes remain undetected because no one realizes that a crime was committed. Many others are detected but are not reported to the police, so that the justice system is not aware that criminal offenses have occurred.

Have you ever reached into your pocket or wallet for money you knew you had, only to discover that it was missing? Most of us at some time have experienced missing money. We cannot be certain that we did not spend it or lose it, but we also cannot remember when it was spent. Have we been the victims of theft? Do we report the money as stolen?

If we assume that we spent or lost the money and do not believe it was stolen, a theft may go undetected. Similarly, if we are convinced the money was stolen, we may still not report it because the sum is so small and the chance of recovery so slim. In the latter case, a crime has gone unreported. Undetected crime is crime that is not known to the criminal justice system or the victim—crimes that are not recognized as crimes. An unreported crime is one that victims recognize as law-breaking behavior but is not brought to the attention of authorities.

If a person has a fight with a friend or relative and assumes it is "personal," an assault may go undetected or at least unreported. The first decision to influence the criminal justice process is determining whether a crime may have occurred. This decision is made most frequently by a civilian rather than a justice system official. A second decision is reporting a crime; again, this decision is made most often by someone other than a justice system official (Avakame, Fyfe & McCoy, 1999). Surveys of crime victims indicate that most crimes are not reported to the police, and that the rates of reporting crime have been relatively stable over the past several years (Catalano, 2006; Hart & Rennison, 2003; Rand, 1998). Over the past few decades, while the number of crimes reported to the police decreased slightly, the number of crimes recorded by the police increased dramatically (Rand, Lynch & Cantor, 1997). In recent years, the rate at which crimes have been reported to the police has increased, especially the rate of reporting for violent crimes (Rennison & Rand, 2003).

Violent crimes have traditionally been reported at higher rates than property crimes, with the exception of sexual assault and rape. Still, nearly half of violent crimes are not reported to police. In a study of reasons for reporting or not reporting domestic violence, Felson, Messner, Hoskin, and Deane (2002) found that victims don't report crime for reasons of privacy, protecting the offender, or fear of reprisal. They note that researchers have focused on reasons for not reporting, but have ignored reasons to report victimization. Felson and his colleagues found that victims of domestic violence were encouraged to report the crime for self-protection, because they viewed the offense as serious, and because they felt the police would take the offense seriously. Goudriaan, Lynch, and Nieuwbeerta (2004) studied crime reporting across several nations and found that social and individual characteristics of the victims influence the likelihood of crime reporting.

Nonreporting of crime limits the ability of criminal justice agents and agencies to respond to crime. Box 2.1 presents the frequency with which different types of crimes are reported to the police, and Box 2.2 describes reasons typically given by people for not reporting violent crimes.

Box 2.1   Percent of Crimes Reported to Police by Type of Crime, 2005

Type of Crime	Percent of Responses
Violent Crimes:	47.4
Rape/Sexual Assault	38.3
Robbery	52.4
Aggravated Assault	624
Simple Assault	42.3
Personal Theft	35.2
Property Crimes:	39.6
Burglary	56.3
Motor Vehicle Theft	83.2
Theft	32.3

Source: S. Catalano (2006). *Criminal Victimization, 2005*. Washington, DC: Bureau of Justice Statistics:10.

Box 2.2	Reasons Given for Not Reporting Violent Crimes, 1992-2000

Reason	Percent of Cases
Private/Personal Matter	20
Not Important Enough	17
Reported to Other Official	14
Not Important to Police	6
Fear of Reprisal	5
Not Clear a Crime Occurred	4
Lack of Proof	4
Protect Offender	3
Inconvenient	3
Other	25

Source: T. Hart & C. Rennison (2003). *Reporting Crime to the Police, 1992-2000.* Washington, DC: Bureau of Justice Statistics: 7.

When a crime or suspected crime is reported to the police, the justice system is mobilized. If agents of the justice system decide that crime has occurred, they have made the detection decision. The police respond to the report of a crime. It is then that case decisionmaking rests with official agents of the justice process. Once the police come to believe that a crime may have been committed, it is their decision whether and how to proceed. We can say that the criminal justice system starts when justice system officials (usually the police) believe a crime has occurred. At that point, the agents of the justice system take control over the official societal response to the crime.

Investigation

Upon deciding that a crime may have been committed, the next decision is whether to investigate, and if so, how thoroughly to investigate. Investigation is the search for evidence that links a specific person to a specific crime. It is a process in which the results of initial inquiries often determine the intensity of the investigation. If, for example, someone reports a prowler, the responding officers may make a visual check of doors and windows, find nothing suspicious, and leave. Alternatively, they may note footprints near a window or find scratch marks on a door or window frame, and then intensify their investigation.

At the conclusion of the investigation, three outcomes are possible. First, no evidence of criminal activity may be found and, thus, the possible crime is classified as unfounded, or not real. Second, evidence of possible criminal activity may support the finding that a crime was committed or attempted, but there is not sufficient evidence for an arrest. In this case, the crime will be left unsolved (i.e., no offender is known), and the investigation, at least theoretically, will continue. Finally, the investigation may yield evidence of both a crime and a probable guilty party. In the last outcome, the next decision stage is reached: arrest.

Arrest

Despite expectations, media portrayals, or legal mandates, police officers do not have to arrest every violator of the criminal law. The police officer makes a decision whether to arrest a suspected offender. Many factors affect the arrest decision.

Perhaps the two most important factors that determine whether an arrest— i.e., taking a person into custody—will be made are (1) the seriousness of the suspected offense, and (2) the quality of the evidence against the suspect. The officer can exercise tremendous discretion in this decision, especially for less serious offenses. For example, if a traffic officer stops you for speeding, a citation is not the only possible outcome, even if you actually were speeding. How often does a person give the officer excuses for his or her violation of the traffic laws? How does a person feel about the officer who issues a citation when he or she knows that the officer could have given a warning?

Discretionary decisions not to arrest are often the result of an officer's attempts to achieve "street justice." Street justice is a term used to describe attempts by police to deal with problems without formal processing. For example, an officer may counsel or warn loitering juveniles, rather than arresting them. In these cases, the officer tries to solve the problem in a way that avoids the negative consequences of formal processing. As we shall see in our discussion of the police, much police work is problem solving, and arrest is only one tool used for that purpose. Many times, however, police officers do decide to arrest a suspect. If an arrest is made, the next decision stage is reached: initial appearance.

Initial Appearance

Persons arrested for crimes are entitled to a hearing in court to determine whether they will be released pending further action. This initial appearance or hearing occurs relatively quickly after arrest, usually within a matter of hours. The hearing does not involve a determination of guilt, but rather an assessment of the defendant's likelihood of appearing at later proceedings. Arrested suspects are usually entitled to release before trial. With the exception of some serious crimes (murder, terrorism, kidnapping, etc.) specified in some statutes, arrested persons may be released while awaiting trial. Traditionally, this release has been accomplished by the posting of bail.

The primary purpose of bail is to ensure that the suspect will return to court for later hearings. The theory of bail is that a person will return to court if it would cost too much not to return. Thus, traditional bail involves the defendant "posting bond," or leaving money on deposit at the court. If the defendant returns, the bond is refunded. If the defendant does not return for the next hearing, the court keeps the bail money and issues a warrant for his or her arrest.

Since the 1970s, criminal justice reforms have witnessed the rebirth of "release on recognizance" systems whereby suspects obtain pretrial release without posting bond as long as they have a job, house, family, and other ties to the community. If a person is expected to appear in court to avoid losing a few thousand dollars, it seems reasonable that he or she would also appear to keep a home, job, or family ties.

In some jurisdictions, it is possible for the prosecutor to ask for "preventive detention." In these cases, the prosecutor believes that, if released on bail, the defendant will present a danger of continued crime in the community. Upon a hearing that establishes that the defendant is indeed dangerous, the magistrate is authorized to deny pretrial release.

In many courts, bail schedules have been developed by which different levels of bail amounts are tied to different types of crime. For instance, the rate for burglary might be $5,000, but for robbery, $10,000. The bail decision, however, is not automatic. If the magistrate believes that the suspect will flee or fail to appear for later hearings, a higher bail may be set. In other cases, a lower bail than usual may be set to allow the defendant to keep his or her job or to maintain family contacts. In either case, after the initial appearance, the next decision relates to the justification for governmental (i.e., justice system) intervention in the life of the citizen.

Charging

Between the time of arrest and arraignment, the prosecutor reviews the evidence in the case and determines a formal criminal charge. The offense for which a person is arrested is not necessarily the one with which he or she will be charged. For example, the police may arrest someone for armed robbery, but be unable to prove that a weapon was used in the crime. The prosecutor may then formally charge the offender with traditional (unarmed) robbery.

Charges are brought in two principal ways: indictment by grand jury or by information. With the indictment, the prosecutor presents the case in secret to a grand jury, which decides whether the evidence is strong enough to warrant the issuance of an indictment. With the information, the prosecutor presents the case in open court before a magistrate, who determines if the evidence is sufficient to warrant a formal charge.

In the information process, a judge reviews the strength of the evidence against a suspect and decides if it is sufficient to have the defendant "bound over" to the felony court. While not a determination of guilt or innocence, the preliminary hearing involves a judge ruling on the strength of the case against the defendant. While the defendant ultimately may be found not guilty, if the available evidence supports probable cause to believe the defendant may be found guilty, the judge will typically order the case bound over to trial, allowing the state to continue.

About a quarter felony arrests in large counties are dismissed before trial (Rainville & Reaves, 2003). The number of cases resulting in dismissal has been dropping over the past decade. Earlier studies of criminal prosecution (Boland, Mahanna & Sones, 1992) reported that nationally, 45 percent of felony arrests were dismissed before trial. Nearly one-half of these are dismissed by the judge. The rates of dismissal of charges at preliminary hearings vary based on the procedures used to bring cases to court. In places where the prosecutor reviews evidence before appearing in court, the weakest cases are rejected before a preliminary hearing is held, and the number of cases

A courtroom artist rendering of Atlanta Falcons quarterback Michael Vick appearing at his arraignment hearing at the federal courthouse in Richmond, Virginia. Vick pleaded not guilty on July 26, 2007, to federal dogfighting charges. Vick was eventually sentenced to 23 months in prison for promoting and funding the dogfighting operation. *Photo credit:* AP Photo/Dana Verkouteren.

dismissed by the judge is low. Where no such review occurs, the rate of dismissal at the preliminary hearing may exceed 40 percent.

Arraignment

At the **arraignment**, the defendant is notified of the formal criminal charges against him or her and is asked to plead to the charges. The arraignment is not a hearing on the facts of the case. The defendant may plead not guilty, guilty, or *nolo contendere* (no contest), or may stand silent. When the defendant pleads guilty or *nolo contendere*, a finding of guilt is entered. If the defendant remains silent, a plea of not guilty will be entered on his or her behalf and a trial date will be set. Most criminal defendants plead guilty at arraignment, often as part of an agreement negotiated with the prosecutor (McDonald, 1979; Newman, 1966; Rosett & Cressey, 1976). In the typical plea bargain, the prosecutor drops charges or otherwise changes the seriousness of the formal charge in exchange for certain conviction without trial arising from a guilty plea from the defendant.

Trial

While most cases result in a guilty plea, those that receive the most media attention and publicity are those that involve a trial at which the defense and prosecution contest the facts and law before a neutral decisionmaker. Most cases that go to trial are what Samuel Walker (2001:29) terms "celebrated cases." In these cases, defendants receive full-blown trials, very often jury trials. Because these are the cases that receive the most publicity, much of the public believes that the jury trial is the normal operating procedure of the justice system.

At trial, the state (prosecutor) must prove, beyond a reasonable doubt, that the defendant committed the criminal offense for which he or she has been charged. The defense attorney seeks to discredit the state's case and, at a minimum, establish that there is some doubt as to whether the defendant committed the offense. Depending upon the nature of the case, one of two types of trials will be requested by the defense: a jury trial or a bench trial.

The jury trial is the ideal of the justice system. A panel of the defendant's peers hears all of the evidence and decides whether the defendant is guilty or not guilty. The bench trial is held before a judge alone, who hears all of the evidence and then decides whether the defendant is guilty or not guilty. If the verdict is "not guilty," the justice process ends with the acquittal of the defendant. On the other hand, if the verdict is "guilty" (or if the defendant pleads guilty), the defendant stands convicted of the crime and the next decision point in the justice system is reached: sentencing.

Sentencing

The sentencing decision has been described as bifurcated (i.e., having two parts). First, the judge decides the type of sentence. This can range from a fine to incarceration and covers a wide variety of alternatives, including probation, confinement in jail or prison, and combinations such as probation with a fine. In capital cases, such as murder, the type of sentence may be death. The second part of the decision involves the conditions of sentence. These include the conditions of supervised release (probation), such as curfew, employment, and so on, as well as the length of prison term for those incarcerated. In states where offenders are convicted of capital crimes, this part of the decision may involve the method of execution (see Box 2.3).

Sentencing power is shared among the three branches of the government. The legislative branch sets limits on penalties by establishing minimum and maximum prison terms and fine amounts, by declaring some offenses ineligible for probation, and by other similar actions. The judicial branch is where the sentencing judge selects the actual type and conditions of sentence from alternatives allowed by the legislature. The executive branch has the power to pardon, to offer clemency, and, often, to authorize parole. This shared power is indicated in Box 2.4.

Most convicted offenders are sentenced to probation or a fine and are not incarcerated. Fewer than half of those convicted of felonies in 2000 were sentenced to prison (Rainville & Reaves, 2003). Those who are incarcerated most frequently gain release from prison through parole or mandatory release, and are required to live in the community under supervision and to obey conditions of release similar to those placed on probationers (Travis & Latessa, 1984). Failure to obey these conditions can lead to the next possible decision point in the justice process: revocation.

Revocation

The overwhelming majority of criminal offenders who are sentenced to correctional custody serve some portion of their sentence under community supervi-

Box 2.3   Method of Execution

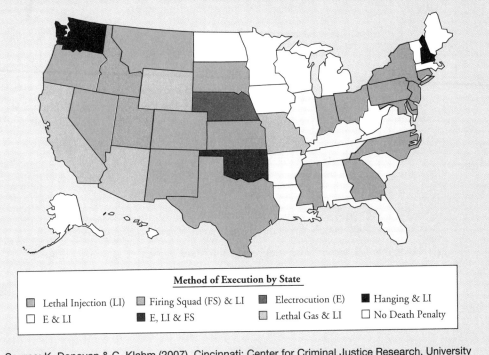

Method of Execution by State

- Lethal Injection (LI)
- Firing Squad (FS) & LI
- Electrocution (E)
- Hanging & LI
- E & LI
- E, LI & FS
- Lethal Gas & LI
- No Death Penalty

Source: K. Donovan & C. Klahm (2007). Cincinnati: Center for Criminal Justice Research, University of Cincinnati.

sion on either probation or parole. Both of these sentences are a form of **conditional release**, whereby the offender is allowed to remain in the community if he or she abides by certain conditions, such as reporting regularly to a supervising officer, observing a curfew, or refraining from further criminal activity. Violation of the conditions of release constitutes grounds for the **revocation** of liberty. For instance, a probationer who is ordered not to consume alcohol can lose his or her liberty if caught drinking. The revocation process is a miniature justice system in which the probation or parole officer detects and investigates violations of conditions, and arrests and prosecutes violators who are tried by the sentencing judge (if on probation) or parole authority (if on parole). Upon "conviction" of violating the conditions of release, the violator may be sentenced to incarceration or continued supervision.

When the author of this book was employed by the Oregon State Board of Parole, nearly half of all inmates admitted to that state's prisons each year were admitted as probation or parole violators. Between 1990 and 2000, the percent of prison admissions in the United States accounted for by parole violators rose from 29 to 35 percent (Hughes, Wilson & Beck, 2001:13), and parole violators still comprised one-third of prison admissions in 2002 (Harrison & Beck, 2005:6).

Box 2.4 Distribution of Sentencing Power Among Branches of Government

States vary in the degree of judicial and parole board discretion in sentencing and release decisions provided by law. Today, the range of state sentencing systems involves the following:

Indeterminate sentencing. The judge has primary control over the type of sentence given (such as prison, probation or fine, and the upper and lower bounds of the length of prison sentences within statutory limits), but the actual time served is determined by the parole board.

Determinate sentencing. The judge sets the type of sentence and the length of prison sentences within statutory limits, but the parole board may not release prisoners before their sentences have expired, minus time off for good behavior, or "good time."

Mandatory prison terms. Legislation requires imposition of a prison sentence, often of specified length, for certain crimes and/or categories of offenders.

Presumptive sentencing. The judge is required to impose a sentence whose length is set by law for each offense or class of offense. When there are mitigating or aggravating circumstances, however, the judge is allowed to shorten or lengthen the sentence within specified boundaries.

Some states have other practices that affect sentencing and the actual time served:

Sentencing guidelines. The courts set sentences by using procedures designed to structure sentencing decisions, usually based on offense severity and criminal history.

Parole guidelines. Parole boards use procedures designed to structure release decisions based on measurable offender criteria.

Good-time policies. In nearly all states, legislation allows for reduction of a prison term based on the offender's behavior in prison.

Emergency crowding provisions. These are policies that relieve prison crowding by systematically making certain inmates eligible for early release.

In recent years many states have been moving away from sentencing systems that allow judges and parole boards wide discretion in sentences and time served. They are moving toward more certain and fixed punishments for crimes through mandatory sentences, sentences of fixed length (determinate sentencing), and the abolition of parole boards.

Source: Bureau of Justice Statistics (1989), *BJS Data Report, 1988* (Washington, DC: U.S. Department of Justice):20-21.

With the exception of the death penalty, incarceration in prison is this country's most severe penalty. Convicted offenders receive this sentence either directly from the court or, more circuitously, through the revocation of conditional liberty.

In comparison to the total number of convicted offenders, less than 1 percent is sentenced to death or life imprisonment (Rainville & Reaves, 2003). Thus, for most offenders, a day comes when they are no longer under the control of the justice system. The last point in the justice process is discharge.

Discharge

Most criminal offenders will eventually be discharged from their sentences. **Discharge** is final release from criminal justice control or supervision. For some, this discharge will occur at the expiration of their term. For someone sentenced to a 10-year prison term, discharge will take place 10 years after the date of sentencing, whether the person was incarcerated for the full 10 years or was granted an earlier release by parole or reduction in term for good behavior.

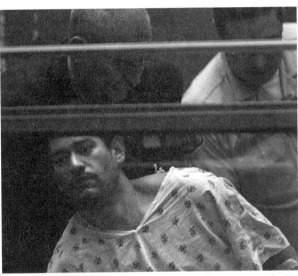

Many states, however, have adopted procedures for "early" discharge. An offender serving a 10-year term may be paroled after serving three years, and then, after successfully completing three years (for example) under parole supervision, may receive an early discharge; thus, the offender may be released from sentence after serving only six years. Other jurisdictions in which no formal early discharge procedure exists may place similar offenders on "unsupervised parole status" after some time. In this case, the offender technically is still under sentence but is not being supervised in the community, and, for all practical purposes, has been discharged.

Juan Manuel Alvarez appears in a Los Angeles courtroom for his arraignment on murder charges, January 28, 2005, in Los Angeles. Alvarez, who faced murder charges for allegedly triggering the deadly collision of two commuter trains during an aborted suicide attempt, was granted a delay of his arraignment for further medical evaluation. *Photo credit: AP Photo/Nick Ut, Pool.*

Upon discharge from sentence, the convicted offender becomes a member of the free society again. In most cases, the record of conviction and collateral effects of conviction (limits on civil rights, employability, and the like) will haunt the ex-convict. Conviction of a crime, especially a felony, often disqualifies the offender from certain types of occupations, such as those requiring licensure or certification (teaching school, practicing law or medicine, and the like). In some cases, felony conviction leads to "civil death," that is, the offender has no rights to enter contracts (including marriage), borrow money, vote, or hold public office (Buckler & Travis, 2003; Burton, Cullen & Travis, 1987).

Box 2.5 Method of Execution

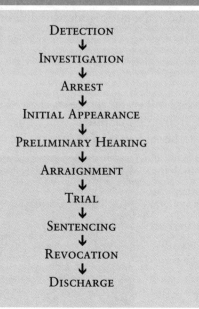

DETECTION
↓
INVESTIGATION
↓
ARREST
↓
INITIAL APPEARANCE
↓
PRELIMINARY HEARING
↓
ARRAIGNMENT
↓
TRIAL
↓
SENTENCING
↓
REVOCATION
↓
DISCHARGE

Box 2.5 graphically portrays the decision points of the criminal justice system.

The Total Criminal Justice System

As our brief description of the justice system illustrates, cases move through the various decision points on a contingency basis. If a crime is detected, an investigation may begin. If the investigation yields sufficient evidence, an arrest may be made. If an arrest is made, formal charges may be brought. The operative word is "if." Approaching this issue from the other direction, the sentence depends upon the conviction, which depends upon the charge, which depends upon the investigation, which depends upon the detection of crime. To paraphrase an old song about how bones are connected, we might say detection is connected to investigation; investigation is connected to arrest; arrest is connected to charging; charging is connected to arraignment; arraignment is connected to sentencing; sentencing is connected to correction; and correction is connected to discharge.

Each decision in the justice process is in large part determined by previous decisions. To a certain degree, earlier decisions depend upon past practices in later points of the justice process. For example, if a county prosecutor routinely dismisses cases involving possession of minor amounts of marijuana, law enforcement officers are more inclined to stop arresting persons for possession of small amounts of that drug.

As the concept of a system implies, the various components of the justice process (the decisions) are interdependent. As a result, the practices of all the justice agencies affect those of every other agency to some extent. Similarly, environmental pressures will affect the operations of each justice agency to some degree. Some examples illustrate the manner in which environmental pressures and agency changes have system-wide effects: the effort to control drunk driving, the "war" on drugs, and the redefinition of domestic violence arrest policies.

Controlling the Drunk Driver

Drunk driving, while a serious safety problem on the nation's highways, was not viewed as a particularly serious offense historically. In the 1980s, however, drunk driving came to be seen as a serious crime. It was no longer fashionable to drink and drive, and sketches and jokes about drunk drivers in the entertainment media were replaced with dramas depicting the devastating effects of drunk driving. "In short, attitudes have changed. Today's drunk driver is a pariah. It is no longer socially acceptable to stagger out from a pub and sit behind the wheel" (Balko, 2003:9). Applegate et al. (1996) noted that surveys generally reveal that the public takes a punitive stance toward drunk driving. However, the punitiveness of the public is related to how much harm is caused by the drunk driving, with drunk drivers who injure or kill others most likely to be seen as deserving harsh penalties. Over the past quarter century all states have taken steps to control drunk driving, most often by redefining the offense as a more serious misdemeanor or felony, and by requiring mandatory incarceration of those convicted of drunk driving, regardless of harm. Every state now has defined a blood alcohol content (BAC) of .08 as a presumptive standard of intoxication. That is, if the BAC measures .08 or higher, the driver is assumed to be impaired. Box 2.6 describes statutory provisions affect-

Box 2.6	Statutory Provisions Concerning Driving Under the Influence	

Statutory Provision	Jurisdictions With Provision	Jurisdictions Without Provision
Felony D.U.I.	46	5
Mandatory Jail for 2nd Offense	47	4
Zero Tolerance	51	0
Penalty for Test Refusal Greater than for Test Failure	34	17
Vehicle Confiscation	30	21
.08 BAC Per Se Intoxicated	51	0

Source: Mothers Against Drunk Driving. Found at: http://www.madd.org (accessed July 7, 2007).

ing driving under the influence. Persons convicted of driving while intoxicated accounted for nearly 6 percent of the jail population nationally and around 10 percent of convicted offenders serving sentences in jails (see Box 2.7).

Box 2.7 Impact of DUI Enforcement on Jail Populations

Percent of persons in jail by sex, race, and conviction status with most serious offense being DUI.

Offender Characteristic	Percent
Sex:	
Male	6.6
Female	4.9
Race/Ethnicity:	
White	10.9
Black	1.1
Hispanic	7.7
Status:	
Convicted	8.9
Unconvicted	2.3

Source: D. James (2004), *Profile of Jail Inmates, 2002* (Washington, DC: Bureau of Justice Statistics):3, 4.

This shift in public attitude regarding drunk drivers—and the associated legislative changes—placed considerable strains on the criminal justice system. More persons were arrested for driving under the influence of alcohol; more of those arrested refused to plead guilty; and many more of those found guilty were incarcerated in jails. Further, many of those sent to jail were first offenders with no prior record, and were not typical jail inmates. In many ways, these offenders required a different institutional setting than the jail, which is generally used for other types of criminal offenders.

With drunk driving defined and viewed as a more serious offense, police officers are more likely to investigate erratic drivers, to charge the offender with driving under the influence (DUI) rather than with reckless operation, to arrest rather than warn, and, generally, to "process" offenders. Robyn Cohen (1992) reported that between 1980 and 1989 the number of arrests for drunk driving rose by 22 percent, while the number of licensed drivers increased by only 14 percent. In addition, prosecutors are more likely to charge drunk drivers. Moreover, with higher stakes (e.g., loss of driving privileges, stiff fines, mandatory incarceration), defendants are less likely to plead guilty (Meyer & Gray, 1997). As a result, the courts must hold more trials, and mandatory sentences create overcrowding in the jails. All three components of the justice process had to adapt to this new emphasis on DUI enforcement, as is seen in Box 2.8.

Box 2.8   Effects of Mandatory Jail Terms for Drunk Driving

To gauge the impact of tougher sanctions on the criminal justice system, National Institute of Justice researchers examined the effects of mandatory confinement for drunk driving in jurisdictions in Washington, Tennessee, Ohio, and Minnesota. The findings revealed:

- When mandatory confinement is introduced and well publicized, drunk driver arrests usually increase.

- The introduction of mandatory confinement imposes new and heavy demands on courts, incarceration facilities and probation services.

- The adoption of mandatory confinement is frequently accompanied by increased public concern about drunk driving and is associated with a decline in traffic fatalities.

- Mandatory confinement can be imposed either through legislation or through judicial policy.

- The implementation of mandatory confinement often requires additional resources for the criminal justice system.

- Appropriate systemwide planning can minimize dysfunction and substantially reduce the impact of mandatory confinement on criminal justice operation.

Source: National Institute of Justice (1985), "Jailing Drunk Drivers: Impact on the Criminal Justice System." *NIJ Reports* (July):2.

The effort to control drinking and driving has continued and gotten more intense. Balko (2003) reports more than 100 new pieces of drinking-and-driving legislation were considered in 31 states between 2002 and 2003. In 2000, the U.S. Congress passed a law creating a federal presumptive intoxication standard at a blood alcohol level of .08. This legislation tied federal highway money to adoption of the new standard. States that did not adopt the lower standard would not receive federal highway funds. Some states estimated that the increased costs of criminal justice processing of drivers found to have blood alcohol levels between .10 and .08 would exceed the amount of highway funds they received from the federal government. Those states initially chose not to adopt the new standard (Vartebedian, 2002), but all states now have this standard.

Interestingly, an early evaluation of changes in drunk driving enforcement (1985) revealed how justice agency policies can affect the total system as well. In Memphis, Tennessee, with little publicity about drunk driving, law enforcement attitudes did not change, and thus arrest rates, court loads, and jail populations of drunk drivers also did not change. In Minnesota, however, although no legislation was enacted, judges adopted a policy of mandatory incarceration; successfully anticipated problems for police, courts, and corrections; and took steps to minimize the problems.

Other analyses of drunk driving laws and enforcement practices show that organizational patterns of police agencies affect arrest decisions (Mastrofski, Ritti &

Hoffmaster, 1987). Individual officer characteristics also were found to be related to arrest decisions in drunk driving cases (Meyers et al., 1987). These studies indicate that an understanding of the effect of justice reform is difficult. Knowledge of the changes in the law is only part of the answer. Organizational and individual characteristics of justice agencies and agents affect how a reform is implemented. Finally, research on the effects of stiff punishments for drunk driving reveals that the deterrent effect of these laws is limited. Yu, Evans, and Clark (2006) reported that persons having an alcohol addiction or serious drinking problem were not likely to be deterred by DUI penalties.

The War on Drugs

In 1973, the state of New York adopted legislation hailed as "the nation's toughest drug law" (U.S. Department of Justice, 1978). This law was intended to "crack down" on those who sold heroin and other dangerous drugs. It had provisions for very stiff sentences and placed controls on plea bargaining. Further, to cope with the anticipated increase in drug offense cases, it provided for the creation of 49 new judgeships. The intent of the legislation was clear: to apprehend, convict, and punish those who sold heroin.

The effect of the law, however, is less clear. The officers and agencies of the justice system appear to have adapted to the changes in order to reduce the potentially disruptive effects on normal court operations that would result from the new law. While there were no dramatic increases in arrests for sale of heroin, fewer of those arrested were indicted, fewer of those indicted pleaded guilty, and fewer were convicted. For those convicted, both the rate of incarceration and the length of prison terms increased after the law took effect. However, in the final analysis, three years after the law was passed, the percentage of those arrested for heroin sale or possession who went to prison remained stable at 11 percent, a figure identical to that occurring before the law was passed in 1973.

There are several possible explanations. First, a probable reason why the number of arrests did not increase was because the sale and possession of large quantities of heroin were already considered serious offenses (even before the new law was enacted). Neither law enforcement nor public attitudes were changed by the new legislation. The fact that fewer defendants pleaded guilty meant that prosecutors needed to be more certain of getting a guilty verdict before taking a case to trial. Thus, indictments decreased as marginal cases were dismissed or downplayed. The increased number of trials created a backlog for the courts so that fewer cases were processed, and further, acquittals were handed down in some cases in which previously a plea of guilty had ensured conviction.

The mandatory sentencing provisions of the legislation may account for the higher incarceration rate and more severe prison terms imposed after the legislation was enacted. This suggests that there was no conscious effort to undermine the intent of the tough anti-drug law, but rather, the court component of the justice process adapted to new pressures reflexively. As part of a system, the courts sought to maintain equilibrium and adapted to stresses and strains so as to minimize their impact.

In this example, the effect of the legislation was initially and most specifically directed at the criminal courts, and an effort was made to alleviate the strains through the creation of new courts. Had these new courts not been provided, it is likely that even more cases would have been dismissed and/or the backlog of cases would have been even greater. The law did not directly affect law enforcement. The effect of changes in prison sentences on corrections was not dramatic for two reasons. First, because heroin dealers are only a very small proportion of all those sentenced to prison, even large increases in their terms or rate of incarceration would not dramatically affect prisons. Second, the percentage of those arrested who were actually sentenced to prison did not change, and the effects of longer terms would not be felt until several years after those who received longer sentences had been imprisoned.

The war on drugs, having raged now for more than a two decades in its most recent form, has produced changes in the characteristics of prison populations, with convictions for drug law violations being the most common crimes for which persons are sentenced to prison (Durose & Langan, 2003; White & Gorman, 2000). Most offenders serving prison terms at any time were convicted of violent crimes, but drug offenders account for the largest part of total prison population growth (Harrison & Beck, 2003). This has contributed to the continued problem of prison and jail crowding and prompted the development of intermediate sanctions, specialized drug courts, and other adaptations in the criminal justice system. It has also had a disproportionately harsh impact on the poor, women, and members of minority groups (Welch, Wolff & Bryan, 1998).

Domestic Violence Arrest Policies

The redefinition of domestic violence also illustrates the interdependency of the criminal justice system. The movement toward policies calling for mandatory arrests in cases of domestic violence has been complicated (Sherman, 1992). Some evaluators have noted that despite clear policy statements requiring arrest, police officers arrest domestic violence offenders in less than half of all cases (Belknap & McCall, 1994). This may be a result of the fact that the offender is not present when the police arrive (Feder, 1996), as well as because prosecutors and courts often still do not treat the offense as a serious matter (Kane, 1999). Whatever else has happened, there is some evidence that victims are increasingly likely to complain to the police, and that the police are increasingly likely to write formal reports, even if no arrests are made (Lanza-Kaduce, Greenleaf & Donahue, 1995).

Johnson and Sigler (2000) compared public opinion about violence against women over a 10-year period and reported that public tolerance for violence has decreased as criminalization of such behavior has become more common. A more recent study indicates that the public is still intolerant of domestic violence, whether in the form of physical or verbal abuse (Boatwright-Horowitz, Olick & Amaral, 2004). It is not possible to tell if opinion changes cause legal changes, or if the reverse is true. Still, domestic violence policy and law demonstrate the link between public opinion and criminal justice practice. Jones and Belknap (1999), studying the practices of the Boulder, Colorado, police, report that the police response to domestic violence appears more formal and serious currently than it has in the past. Again, public perceptions of offense seriousness and the severity of justice system response are related.

One of the most important policy changes in the response to domestic violence has been a proliferation of preferred or mandatory arrest policies and laws. These reforms require the police to arrest offenders involved in domestic assaults. The impact of such policies is unclear. It appears that arrest generally reduces later instances of domestic violence, but the impact of arrest is different for white offenders and for black offenders, and may be different for people of different economic levels (Maxwell, Garner & Fagan, 2002). There is also evidence that mandatory arrest policies

Actress Carmen Electra is escorted by police to the Miami-Dade County jail after she and then-husband, former basketball star Dennis Rodman, were arrested at a hotel on charges of domestic violence. Mandatory and preferred arrest policies have increased the numbers and rates of arrest for both male and female parties to domestic violence incidents. *Photo credit: AP Photo/Wilfredo Lee.*

have increased the arrests of domestic violence victims (Chesney-Lind, 2002). In most jurisdictions adopting these policies, the numbers and rates of arrests for both male and female parties to the incidents have increased dramatically. The unintended consequences of these policies, such as deterring victims from reporting offenses, increasing the number of victims subjected to arrest, and long-term effects on relationships and families, are still unknown (Humphries, 2002). Efforts to make prosecution of domestic violence easier may result in less effort by police to obtain victim cooperation, and ultimately in weaker cases and fewer convictions (Davis, Smith & Taylor, 2003). What is clear is that the adoption and implementation of policy reforms in this area has been neither easy nor trouble-free (Ostrom, 2003; Whitcomb, 2002).

All of these issues have proven to be difficult for criminal justice policymakers and reformers to manage. Experience with these efforts to change criminal justice practices in dealing with drunk drivers, drug offenses, and domestic violence illustrates how the justice system interacts with its environment. In some cases, changes occur in all aspects of the justice process, such as drug enforcement, resulting in more arrests, convictions, and changes in the correctional population. In other cases, the system is sometimes able to adapt so as to minimize the impact of a reform by increasing rates of case dismissal or plea bargaining, or reducing the severity of sentences. All of these examples show that the criminal justice process operates as a system, adapting to change and pressure. They also indicate the complexity of evaluating the operations of the criminal justice process. This complexity becomes clearer when one examines the structure and organization of the agencies that comprise system of criminal justice in the United States.

The Components of Criminal Justice

As was done in Chapter 1, it is common to divide the criminal justice system into three parts: law enforcement, courts, and corrections. Each of these three parts of the justice system is itself comprised of a multitude of separate agencies and actors. The organizations that make up the total criminal justice system are differently structured and funded, and draw from different personnel pools.

One of the most important distinctions among similar agencies is jurisdiction. Police departments, courts, and correctional agencies may be municipal (village, township, city, or county), state, or federal in nature. They may be specialized, like the United States postal inspectors, or they may have general duties, as does a typical police department. They may be public or private (such as security guards, many halfway houses, and other entities that provide crime control services). In this section, we will examine the nature of criminal justice agencies in law enforcement, courts, and corrections.

Law Enforcement

There are so many agencies with law enforcement mandates that it is not possible to state their true number with confidence. In 1967, the President's Commission on Law Enforcement and Administration of Justice (1967b) estimated (in its task force report on police) that more than 40,000 police agencies were in existence. Later, the U.S. Department of Justice reported that there were close to 20,000 state and local law enforcement agencies. This report, however, did not include townships with populations of less than 1,000 (1980:24), nor did it include federal law enforcement agencies. Most recently, the Bureau of Justice Statistics (Reaves, 2007) identified about 18,000 state and local police agencies.

Federal Law Enforcement

A number of federal law enforcement agencies exist. These agencies tend to be small with specific mandates, yet in total, federal law enforcement is very complex. We are all aware of the Federal Bureau of Investigation (FBI), and most of us have heard of the U.S. Marshals; the Postal Inspectors; the Drug Enforcement Administration (DEA); the Bureau of Alcohol, Tobacco, Firearms, and Explosives (ATF); the Immigration and Naturalization Service; Customs; the Internal Revenue Service (IRS); and the Secret Service. Yet, many are unaware of the law enforcement duties of the National Park Service, the United States Supreme Court Police Department, the National Gallery of Art Protection Staff, and other federal "police" agencies. We seldom consider the military police, the tribal police departments on Native American reservations, or the investigative duties of auditors and staff of such organizations as the Federal Trade Commission (FTC) (Travis & Langworthy, 2008). Reaves and Bauer (2003) reported that in mid-2002, the federal government employed about 93,000 full-time officers with arrest powers who were authorized to carry firearms. The bulk of these employees worked for the Immigration and Naturalization Service, and they included 14,000 employees of the Federal Bureau of Prisons. At least 16 other federal agencies employed 500 or more such officers and agents. These numbers excluded law enforcement personnel in the military and those working overseas, but did include some 1,300 federal officers in U.S. Territories. These federal employees do not include the officers of the Transportation Security Administration, created in the wake of the September 11, 2001, terrorist attacks.

Creation of the Department of Homeland Security resulted in organizational changes in federal law enforcement. The Department of Homeland Security is now the single largest employer of federal law enforcement officers, administering the U.S. Coast Guard, Secret Service, Federal Protective Service, and U.S. Customs Service (except for some revenue functions), and has taken over the responsibilities of the Immigration and Naturalization Service, which was abolished. With these changes, the Department of Homeland Security employs 38 percent of federal officers, and the Department of Justice employs 37 percent (Reaves & Bauer, 2003:5).

Because they serve the entire nation, these agencies recruit nationally and tend to have more stringent entry requirements than do most police departments. The FBI, for example, requires a bachelor's degree in combination with investigatory experience or postgraduate training. Because federal law enforcement is funded at the federal level, salary and benefits for federal law enforcement officers are often higher than those paid to municipal police.

State Law Enforcement

The most common form of state police agency is the highway patrol. The highway patrol is charged with enforcing traffic laws on state and federal highways. Many states, however, also charge their state police with general law enforcement duties (International Association of Chiefs of Police, 1975). The New York State Police, for example, not only serve as traffic officers on that state's highways, but also have as a primary duty the provision of general law enforcement service to residents in rural and unincorporated areas. In addition, several states have specialized state units to combat drug offenses, organized crime, liquor and cigarette tax violations, and the like. Finally, many states also charge their park services with law enforcement obligations. Reaves and Hickman (2002) reported that 49 primary state police agencies employed more than 87,000 officers.

Like federal agencies, state agencies recruit from a pool of candidates that is considerably larger than that tapped by most local police departments. Moreover, in many states, the salary and benefits paid to state police officers are higher than those paid in most local departments (Bureau of Justice Statistics, 1989).

Municipal Law Enforcement

The bulk of law enforcement services are provided through municipal or local police departments, as shown in Box 2.9. These include the traditional city or township police department, as well as the county sheriff. The majority of police departments in the United States are local ones, and most police agencies are small, employing fewer than 25 officers (Reaves, 2007:4). Most police officers, however, work for large departments, because the relatively few large departments employ a great many officers.

Box 2.9	Distribution of Police Personnel and Costs by Level of Government	
Level of Government	% Police Personnel	% Police Costs
Federal	14.0	16.7
State	9.5	9.6
Local	76.5	73.6

Source: A. Pastore & K. Maguire (eds.) (2007). *Sourcebook of Criminal Justice Statistics* [online]. Found at: http://www.albany.edu/sourcebook/ (accessed August 1, 2007).

Municipal police departments rarely conduct national searches or recruitment drives, with the exception of a few (usually larger) police departments. Most local police departments recruit locally and employ civil service testing to enlist new officers (Sanders, Hughes & Langworthy, 1995). Sheriffs generally are elected, but many sheriff's deputies are recruited through civil service. It is common for police protection to comprise a major portion of a municipality's budget. In more than 40 states, law enforcement officers must first pass a required training curriculum before being sworn in, and new recruits must complete at least 800 hours of academy and field training. Recruits in the largest agencies must complete about twice as many hours of training (nearly 1,600) than those employed in smaller ones (Hickman & Reaves, 2003:5).

On average, there are about 1.5 local police officers for every 1,000 residents. In 2000, local police agencies costs were approximately $179 per resident per year. The average starting salary for a full-time local police officer was $31,700 per year. As might be expected, departments serving smaller communities generally pay lower salaries than those serving larger communities (Hickman & Reaves, 2003:6-7). By 2004, local police departments employed more than 446,000 full-time sworn officers (Reaves, 2007). The more than 3,000 sheriff's offices employed another 175,000 sworn officers, bringing the total number of sworn officers in general-purpose local police and sheriff agencies to more than 600,000 full-time sworn officers (Reaves, 2007:5).

Private and Other Public Law Enforcement

In addition to the agencies described above, there are hundreds of special-purpose law enforcement agencies in cities and counties, ranging from parkway and transit authority police to housing authority police. Reaves (2007) identified nearly 1,500 public, special purpose police agencies including housing authority, school, airport, university, and park police. Further, there are thousands of private and semi-public law enforcement agencies in the United States. For example, most factories, amusement parks, and hospitals have security staff, as do most retail chain stores. Many residential buildings and developments also have private security. Private police and private security personnel outnumber the public police by a ratio of at least three to one (Maahs & Hemmens, 1998). Additionally, the coroner or medical examiner is often considered to be a law enforcement official because of the investigative duties of that position.

As we have seen, it may not be possible to speak accurately of law enforcement—or even of the police—in the United States. The diversity of agencies, standards, and duties is nearly mind-boggling. Because law enforcement is the largest (numerically) component of the justice process, a review of justice agencies in courts and corrections is less complicated, but only marginally so.

Courts

In 1977, the U.S. Department of Justice reported that there were more than 3,600 courts of general or appellate jurisdiction in the United States, exclusive of tribal courts and the federal judiciary. In 1994, the Bureau of Justice Statistics surveyed a sample of more than 3,000 state felony courts of general jurisdiction (Langan & Brown, 1997). There are thousands of courts of limited jurisdiction also in operation. Ostrom, Kauder, and LaFountain reported that there are more than 15,550 state courts alone. Like law enforcement, the court system is fragmented and complicated (National Survey of Court Organization, 1977). There are federal, state, and municipal courts. These courts are divided further in terms of the types of cases they may hear and the types of decisions they may reach.

There are more than 300 justices of the Supreme Court and other courts of last resort in the 50 states, District of Columbia, and federal systems. More than 1,100 additional justices serve in intermediate courts of appeal, with more than

9,000 judges serving in general trial courts (Rottman et al., 2000). State supreme court justices are paid an average of $107,905 per year, with intermediate and trial court judges earning average salaries of $106,395 and $96,475, respectively (Maguire & Pastore, 1999:68).

Federal Courts

In 1996, there were more than 1,850 federal justices, judges, and magistrates, with a total judiciary staff exceeding 24,000 (Administrative Office of the U.S. Courts, 1996; Maguire & Pastore, 1996). Federal judges and justices of the U.S. Supreme Court are nominated by the President and appointed with the advice and consent of the United States Senate. These judges have lifetime tenure. Federal magistrates are appointed to eight-year terms by federal district judges.

The federal courts are organized by circuits, with 11 circuits covering the entire nation. Within these circuits, 89 district courts are trial courts. In addition, more than 400 federal magistrates within these districts may hear minor offenses and conduct the early stages of felony trials and more serious civil trials. Compensation for federal judicial officers ranges from more than $142,000 per year for magistrates to more than $198,000 per year for the Chief Justice of the U.S. Supreme Court (Maguire & Pastore, 2003:75).

Federal courts decide cases of federal interest: for example, charges of federal law violation. Federal appeals courts also decide federal constitutional issues, even if such issues were raised during state trials or proceedings.

State Courts

State judicial systems are similar to the federal judiciary in structure. They are generally comprised of trial courts, intermediate appellate courts, and a state supreme court. State judges and justices are either appointed (as is the federal judiciary) or elected. Members of most state judiciaries are in office for specified terms of office (unlike federal judges, who have lifetime tenure). Rhode Island's judges have lifetime tenure, and judges in Massachusetts and New Hampshire serve terms that do not expire until the judge reaches age 70 (Ostrom, Kauder & LaFountain, 2003).

While federal judges are recruited nationally (although district court judges and circuit court judges are generally selected from among candidates residing in the particular district or circuit), state court judges are elected statewide (or appointed) for statewide posts (e.g., the office of justice of the state supreme court), or from the jurisdiction of the lower court (e.g., the county of a specific county court). While there may be no constitutional provision (Maine and Massachusetts do not require a law degree), as with United States judges, or statutory requirement that judges be members of the bar, most judges are attorneys. By late 2002, the average salaries for judicial officials in state courts were $123,525 for justices of the highest court, $121,086 for intermediate appellate court justices, and $111,222 for general trial court judges (Maguire & Pastore, 2003:81).

Local Courts

There are a plethora of local courts in the United States. These are courts of limited jurisdiction because they are not allowed to decide felony cases, serious misdemeanors, or civil suits seeking damages above fairly low dollar amounts. Often these are known as "justice of the peace" courts. In many places, these limited-jurisdiction courts are known as police courts or mayor's courts. They usually decide traffic offense cases, hear violations of local ordinances and petty offenses, and make bail determinations.

Some of these judgeships are "ex officio." For example, upon being elected mayor in Ohio, the new mayor becomes the "judge" of mayor's court. In states that still retain the office of justice of the peace, frequently there is no formal legal training required for this position. These limited-jurisdiction courts are not authorized to conduct jury trials, and their decisions may be appealed to courts of general jurisdiction, which are also known as "trial courts."

Salaries for these local courts are usually not commensurate with what an attorney could earn in the private practice of law. However, many of these courts operate on a part-time basis, and members of the bar may serve as justices of the peace.

Other Courts

Every court system has a number of special-jurisdiction courts. For example, the federal judiciary has a tax court, and states usually have a court of domestic relations and/or a juvenile court. Several jurisdictions also have bankruptcy courts and other special jurisdiction courts. A relatively recent innovation is what may be called a private court. In some places, offices or commissions for dispute resolution have been developed to divert cases away from the formal courts (Aaronson et al., 1977). Here, the parties to a dispute sit with a lay negotiator (or team of negotiators) and attempt to resolve their problem without resorting to the courts. Most of these private courts are staffed by volunteers or by paid staff whose salaries are lower than that of a judge. An example of this type of private court was seen on television as "The People's Court." Court specialization within the criminal justice system has also increased with the development and spread of special drug courts dedicated to the processing and supervision of drug cases, as illustrated in Box 2.10. Other special courts are increasingly common. Rottman and Casey (1999) describe these as "problem-solving courts" where courts (judges, prosecutors, and the defense bar) work with offenders, victims, service providers, and the broader community to develop long-term solutions to the problems that bring cases to court.

Box 2.10	Special Jurisdiction/Problem Solving Courts in the United States, 2004

Court Specialty	Number of Courts
Drug Court	1,315
Family Court	202
Domestic Violence	123
Mental Health	115
Community	25
Re-entry	14
Other	214

Source: D. Rottman & S. Strickland (2006), *State Court Organization 2004* (Washington, DC: Bureau of Justice Statistics):185-186.

Prosecution

At all levels of courts, from local to federal, the interests of the state (not the victim) are represented by the prosecutor. In the federal system, the prosecutor is the U.S. Attorney or the Deputy U.S. Attorney. These are lawyers appointed by the nomination of the President with the consent of the Senate. Local prosecutors are common in most states; for the most part, they are lawyers elected at the county level. Prosecutors have many titles, including district attorney, state's attorney, county attorney, circuit attorney, commonwealth's attorney, solicitor, and others (DeFrances, 2002:11). The Bureau of Justice Statistics reported the existence of more than 2,300 prosecutor's offices responsible for felony cases in state criminal courts in 2001 (DeFrances, 2002). These offices employed more than 79,000 people, including more than 31,000 attorneys (DeFrances, 2002:3).

The salary of a prosecutor generally is not very high in comparison to potential private practice earnings or judicial salaries. The median salary for chief prosecutors in all jurisdictions was $85,000. In large jurisdictions in 2001 the median salary was $136,700 per year (DeFrances, 2002:2). Many assistant prosecutors (also known as assistant district attorneys) seek these positions at the start of their careers in order to gain trial experience prior to starting their own practices (Rubin, 1984).

Defense

There are three basic structures for the provision of defense counsel: private retention, public defenders, and assigned counsel. Private retention refers to the possibility of the defendant retaining his or her own attorney. Private retention is unusual because most criminal defendants cannot afford attorney fees. However, in cases involving wealthy or notorious defendants, celebrated defense attorneys are often retained. Fewer than one-fifth of felony defendants in the largest counties and less than one-third of defendants in federal courts used privately retained counsel (Harlow, 2000:1). Public defenders are organized like prosecutors; that is, they usually work with an appointed director or administrator who hires a sufficient staff of attorneys to represent indigent clients in court (*Guide to Establishing a Defender System*, 1978). The most common form of criminal defense system is the public defender, but most criminal courts use two or more methods of providing defense counsel, including assigned counsel and contract systems. In the provision of assigned counsel, judges are presented either with a list of all attorneys practicing in their jurisdiction, or with a list of those attorneys willing to take on criminal defense cases. The judge then appoints an attorney for each indigent defendant from this list; he or she usually moves down the list from the first name to the last. The attorneys selected and assigned are then paid a set fee, which is usually on an hourly rate not to exceed some upper limit per case. In contract systems, the court enters an agreement with a law firm, bar association, or private attorney for indigent defense services for a specified period of time at a specified rate (Harlow, 2000).

Like prosecutors, defense attorneys employed in public defender offices (and most assigned counsel schemes) are not paid as well as judges, nor are they paid as much as they could earn in private practice as retained defense attorneys. Again, like prosecutors, young attorneys often seek this kind of work to gain trial experience.

In the cases of both prosecutors and defense attorneys, staff are recruited from local bar associations. While the local nature of the recruitment is comparable to recruiting for most police officers and judges, the requirement of membership in the bar limits the pool of possible applicants.

Witnesses and Jurors

Many other persons are involved in the court process in addition to prosecutors, defense counsel, and judges. There are court support staff members, such as court clerks, stenographers, bailiffs, and administrators; however, we will focus here on witnesses and jurors.

A variety of persons may serve as witnesses in a criminal case (Victim/Witness Legislation, 1984). Generally the arresting officers and any investigators are called as witnesses in a criminal case. If any passersby saw the offense, they too may be called to testify. Sometimes the defendant (or a codefendant) is called to testify in criminal cases (but the defendant cannot be required to be a witness). Depending on the nature of the case, or of the defense, expert witnesses may be called. These individuals are first established as having special knowledge not commonly available to the average citizen. Experts in areas such as ballistics, forensic medicine, and psychology or psychiatry (for instance, when an insanity defense is raised) are asked to bring special knowledge to bear on issues at trial. The victim of a crime is "useful" only as a witness. Crimes are public wrongs; individual suffering is not at issue in criminal trials. In recent years, however, there has been an increased emphasis on using the criminal process to redress the harms suffered by individual victims. Balancing the interests of the victim with those of the defendant is a complicated task (Office for Victims of Crime, 2002).

Citizens participate directly and most strongly in the criminal justice process in the courts. Citizens make up the two types of juries used in the courts. Grand juries of citizens sit and listen to the prosecutor's case before deciding whether an indictment should be issued. Trial juries sit and listen to the criminal trial before deciding if the defendant should be convicted. In several states, and in death penalty cases, the jury also recommends a sentence to the judge after deciding to convict the defendant. Box 2.11 describes the use of jurors in the federal courts.

Box 2.11   Juror Usage in the Federal Courts, 2005

Grand Juries:

Total number of:	
Sessions	9,854
Jurors in Session	196,197
Hours in Session	48,582
Average number of:	
Jurors per Session	19.9
Hours per Session	4.9
Petit Juries	
Jury Trial Days	30,775
Total Jurors Selected	612,032

Source: A. Pastore & K. Maguire (eds.) (2007). *Sourcebook of Criminal Justice Statistics* [online]. Found at: http://www.albany.edu/sourcebook/ (accessed August 1, 2007).

Jurors are selected from lists of residents in the court's jurisdiction. Often these lists are voter registration rolls, telephone books, or the billing records of utility companies. Trial jurors are then subjected to voir dire, a process by which the prosecutor and defense attorney seek to discover whether the jurors have any prejudices that could affect their decision in the trial. A juror suspected of being unable to make an objective decision may be challenged by the attorneys and dismissed by the judge.

Corrections

Corrections can be divided into the general categories of incarceration and community supervision. This general classification, however, grossly oversimplifies this complex component of the justice system. In the area of incarceration are found both prisons and jails, while both probation and parole comprise the nonincarceration sectors of corrections. With this dichotomy, it is not clear where such sanctions as halfway houses or "split sentences" fall.

Incarceration

The most frequent place of incarceration for criminal offenders and those suspected of criminal acts is the jail. There are more than 3,300 jails in the United States (Perkins, Stephan & Beck, 1995), most of which are municipal—either city or (more frequently) county jails. Most jails do not have treatment staffs of counselors, psychologists, and therapists. The major occupational group in jails is correctional officers. Most jail correctional officers are poorly trained and low-paid. Often, jail officers are members of the police department or the sheriff's department that is responsible for jail operation. Starting salaries for jail officers in 1982 were reported to be at an average of less than $11,000 per year (Kerle & Ford, 1982), which was $1,700 per year lower than the average starting salary of a patrol officer in the same jurisdiction. In 1996, the average starting salary for a jail officer was about $22,600 (Camp & Camp, 1996). Jail officers often are recruited in the same way as police officers, which is through local searches and civil service testing.

The nation's jails supervise some 690,000 inmates on any given day, but because of the relatively short time most persons stay in jail, 10 million or more people may "do time" in jail each year. The U.S. Department of Justice reported more than 13 million admissions to jails in 1993 (Perkins, Stephan & Beck, 1995). More than half of those held in jail are not yet convicted and are awaiting trial (Harlow, 1998). It is not possible to determine how many jail admissions are repeat offenders.

The nation's more than 1,600 prisons and state and federal correctional facilities house more inmates than do jails on any given day (more than 1.2 million), but because of the longer terms, fewer people serve prison time each year than jail time. While jails usually are municipal, prisons are operated by the state or federal governments. Prisons are more apt than jails to have counselors, therapists, industries, and educational programs, partly because prisons are larger and hold inmates longer, and partly because they have a larger resource base (state taxes) than do city and county jails. Still, the most common occupational category in prisons is that of correctional officers (Stephan & Karberg, 2003). Like jail officers, correctional officers in prisons are typically selected through civil service and are not particularly well paid (Camp & Camp, 1984). State and federal correctional facilities employed almost 350,000 personnel in 1995, with about two-thirds of these designated as custody or security staff (Maguire & Pastore, 1999:81).

Nonincarceration

The most common form of nonincarcerative sanction (after fines, perhaps) is probation. On any day there are more than 3.9 million persons under probation supervision (Glaze, 2003:1). Probation officers supervise these persons in the community and are also responsible for writing presentence investigation reports and other programs, depending upon the jurisdiction.

Probation officers are typically assigned to courts, although more than one-half of the probation departments in the country are run by states. Unlike police or correctional officers, it is common for a probation officer to be required to have a college degree. Recruitment of probation officers tends to be local, on the basis of the court's jurisdiction. In 1996, Camp and Camp (1996) reported that there were more than 29,500 probation and parole officers (not counting supervisory staff). The average salary for entry-level probation officers reported by Camp and Camp (1996:135) was $25,126 per year.

Parole is similar to probation, except that parole is handled by a state agency; parole officers are, therefore, state employees. At any given time, more than 750,000 persons are under parole supervision. These persons have been granted an early release from incarceration (mostly from prison) and are supervised by parole officers. Thirty-eight states have parole boards in the executive branch of government that are responsible for deciding which inmates to whom early release will be granted, as well as what should be the proper conduct of the prisoners' parole periods.

A parole officer is often required to have a college education and to perform duties similar to those of a probation officer, except that a parole officer typically has a smaller caseload comprised of ex-inmates. Parole officers, on the average, receive slightly higher wages than do probation officers, and are selected from statewide pools through civil service procedures. Camp and Camp (1996) reported that the average annual salary for an entry-level parole officer was $26,829.

Private-Sector Corrections

As with law enforcement and the courts, there is also private involvement in corrections as well. Traditionally, many correctional practices were the province of voluntary or private initiatives. Throughout the 1980s until the present, there has been a growing movement to "privatize" corrections, with private companies constructing and operating prisons and jails in addition to providing other services on a contract basis (Travis, Latessa & Vito, 1985). Box 2.12 gives an indication of the growth of private involvement in corrections.

In addition to these for-profit private correctional enterprises, volunteer service is relatively common in corrections. Volunteers write to and visit prison inmates, provide services to probation and parole offices and clients, and serve on

Box 2.12 — Growth of Private Correctional Facilities, 1995-2000

	Number	
Facility Characteristics	1995	2000
Confinement Facility	29	101
Community-Based	81	163
Total Personnel	5,248	24,357
Custody/Security Personnel	3,197	14,589
Size:		
Fewer than 250 Beds	93	175
250 to 1,499 Beds	17	79
1500 Beds and Larger	0	10
Rated Capacity	19,294	105,133
Percent Occupied	86%	89%

Source: A. Pastore & K. Maguires (eds.) (2007). *Sourcebook of Criminal Justice Statistics* [online]. Found at: http://www.albany.edu/sourcebook/ (accessed August 1, 2007).

a variety of boards and commissions. The boards and commissions range from those that govern halfway houses to citizen court-watching groups. "Neighborhood Watch" programs and other citizen crime-prevention projects have also increased the citizens' role in law enforcement. One of the most important trends in criminal justice over the past decade has been the resurgence of private initiative in the criminal justice system. Corrections is being affected by this development.

Systems and Criminal Justice Structure

What this chapter has demonstrated is that the criminal justice system in the United States is extremely complex. The various agencies that comprise the system are organized at different levels of government, utilize different resource bases, and select differentially qualified personnel in different ways. In short, although the justice system appears too diverse to be a system, the interdependence of its parts and its sensitivity to environmental changes support a systems approach.

There are at least 52 criminal justice systems in the United States: one for each state, the federal government, and the District of Columbia. This may, in fact, be an underestimate of their numbers. For example, if city police can arrest someone for violating a city ordinance, and that person can be convicted and fined in mayor's court, do we have a city justice system? While it may be argued that there are many criminal justice systems in the United States, we will continue to examine and discuss the criminal justice system as a whole.

This systems approach to the study of criminal justice seems especially appropriate. Without a prevailing approach, we might be forced to throw up our hands in despair, unable to make sense of the confusion. Why do we have so many agencies? Why do these different agencies have conflicting and sometimes competing jurisdictions and goals? The answer is because they are part of an open system. The large number of agencies and the various levels and branches of government involved can be understood as a manifestation of the environmental impact on American criminal justice. Given our political and cultural values of federalism, local autonomy, and the separation of powers, we should not be surprised at the confusion in the justice system; it would be more surprising if there was no confusion. A single, well organized, monolithic criminal justice system for the entire nation may well be "un-American."

Review Questions

1. Identify the 10 decision points of the criminal justice process discussed in this chapter.

2. How does the justice process work as a directional flow of cases in the total system?

3. Give two examples of how the environment of the justice process affects the operations of all justice agencies.

4. What are the basic components of the justice process?

5. Describe the different types, levels, and staffing patterns of the components of the justice process.

6. Why is the "systems" approach especially appropriate to the study of American criminal justice?

References

Aaronson, D.E., N.N. Kittrie, D.J. Saari & C.S. Cooper (1977). *Alternatives to Conventional Criminal Adjudication.* Washington, DC: U.S. Government Printing Office.

Administrative Office of the U.S. Courts (1996). *Annual Report of the Director, 1995.* Washington, DC: Administrative Office of the U.S. Courts.

Applegate, B., F. Cullen, B. Link, P. Richards & L. Lanza-Kaduce (1996). "Determinants of Public Punitiveness Toward Drunk Driving: A Factorial Survey Approach." *Justice Quarterly* 13(1):57-80.

Avakame, E.F., J.J. Fyfe & C. McCoy (1999). "'Did You Call the Police? What Did They Do?' An Empirical Assessment of Black's Theory of the Mobilization of Law." *Justice Quarterly* 16(4):765-792.

Balko, R. (2003). "Back Door to Prohibition: The New War on Social Drinking." *CATO Policy Analysis* 501.

Belknap, J. & K. McCall (1994). "Woman Battering and Police Referrals." *Journal of Criminal Justice* 22(2):223-236.

Boatwright-Horowitz, S., K. Olick & R. Amaral (2004). "Calling 911 During Episodes of Domestic Abuse: What Justifies a Call for Help?" *Journal of Criminal Justice* 32(1):89-92.

Boland, B., P. Mahanna & R. Sones (1992). *The Prosecution of Felony Arrests, 1988.* Washington, DC: Bureau of Justice Statistics.

Buckler, K. G. & L.F. Travis (2003). "Reanalyzing the Prevalence and Social Context of Collateral Consequence Statutes." *Journal of Criminal Justice* 31(5):435-53.

Bureau of Justice Statistics (1989). *Profile of State and Local Law Enforcement Agencies, 1987.* Washington, DC: U.S. Department of Justice.

Bureau of Justice Statistics (1991). *Census of Local Jails 1988.* Washington, DC: U.S. Department of Justice.

Bureau of Justice Statistics (1996). *Correctional Populations in the United States, 1994.* Washington, DC: U.S. Department of Justice.

Burton, V.S., F.T. Cullen & L.F. Travis III (1987). "The Collateral Consequences of a Felony Conviction: A National Study of State Statutes." *Federal Probation* 51(3):52-60.

Camp, G.M. & C.C. Camp (1984). *The Corrections Yearbook.* South Salem, NY: Criminal Justice Institute.

Camp, G.M. & C.C. Camp (1996). *The Corrections Yearbook.* South Salem, NY: Criminal Justice Institute.

Chesney-Lind, M. (2002). "Criminalizing Victimization: The Unintended Consequences of Pro-Arrest Policies for Girls and Women." *Criminology and Public Policy* (2)1:81-90.

Cohen, R. (1992). *Drunk Driving.* Washington, DC: Bureau of Justice Statistics.

Davis, R., B. Smith & B. Taylor (2003). "Increasing the Proportion of Domestic Violence Arrests that are Prosecuted: A Natural Experiment in Milwaukee." *Criminology and Public Policy* 2(2):263-282.

DeFrances, C.J. (2002). *Prosecutors in State Courts, 2001.* Washington, DC: Bureau of Justice Statistics.

Durose, M. & P. Langan (2003). *Felony Sentences in State Courts, 2000.* Washington, DC: Bureau of Justice Statistics.

Feder, L. (1996). "Police Handling of Domestic Calls: The Importance of Offender's Presence in the Arrest Decision." *Journal of Criminal Justice* 24(6):481-490.

Felson, R., S. Messner, A. Hoskin & G. Deane (2002). "Reasons for Reporting and Not Reporting Domestic Violence to the Police." *Criminology* 40(3):617-648.

Glaze, L. (2003). *Probation and Parole in the United States, 2002*. Washington, DC: Bureau of Justice Statistics.

Goudriaan, H., J. Lynch, & P. Nieuwbeerta (2004). "Reporting to the Police in Western Nations: A Theoretical Analysis of the Effects of Social Context." *Justice Quarterly* 21(4):933-969.

Guide to Establishing a Defender System (1978). Washington, DC: U.S. Government Printing Office.

Harlow, C. (1998). *Profile of Jail Inmates 1996*. Washington, DC: Bureau of Justice Statistics.

Harlow, C. (2000). *Defense Counsel in Criminal Cases*. Washington, DC: Bureau of Justice Statistics.

Harrison, P.M. & A.J. Beck (2003). *Prisoners in 2002*. Washington, DC: Bureau of Justice Statistics.

Harrison, P.M. & A.J. Beck (2005). *Prisoner and Jail Inmates at Midyear 2004*. Washington, DC: Bureau of Justice Statistics.

Hart, T.C. & B.A. Reaves (1999). *Felony Defendants in Large Urban Counties, 1996*. Washington, DC: Bureau of Justice Statistics.

Hart, T.C. & C. Rennison (2003). *Reporting Crimes to the Police, 1992-2000*. Washington, DC: Bureau of Justice Statistics.

Hickman, M.J. & B.A. Reaves (2003). *Local Police Departments, 2000*. Washington, DC: Bureau of Justice Statistics.

Hughes, T. A., D.J. Wilson & A.J. Beck (2001). *Trends in State Parole, 1990-2000*. Washington, DC: Bureau of Justice Statistics.

Humprhies, D. (2002). "No Easy Answers: Public Policy, Criminal Justice, and Domestic Violence." *Criminology and Public Policy* (2)1:91-96.

International Association of Chiefs of Police, Division of State and Provincial Police (1975). *Comparative Data Report*. Gaithersburg, MD: IACP.

Jailing Drunk Drivers (1985). Washington, DC: U.S. Department of Justice.

Johnson, I. & R. Sigler (2000). "Public Perceptions: The Stability of the Public's Endorsements of the Definition and Criminalization of the Abuse of Women." *Journal of Criminal Justice* 28(3):165-179.

Jones, D. & J. Belknap (1999). "Police Responses to Battering in a Progressive Pro-Arrest Jurisdiction." *Justice Quarterly* 16(2):249-273.

Kane, R. (1999). "Patterns of Arrest in Domestic Violence Encounters: Identifying a Police Decision-Making Model." *Journal of Criminal Justice* 27(1):65-79.

Kerle, K.E. & F.R. Ford (1982). *The State of Our Nation's Jails, 1982*. Washington, DC: National Sheriffs' Association.

Langan, P. & J. Brown (1997). *Felony Sentences in State Courts, 1994*. Washington, DC: Bureau of Justice Statistics.

Lanza-Kaduce, L., R. Greenleaf & M. Donahue (1995). "Trickle-up Report Writing: The Impact of a Proarrest Policy for Domestic Disturbances." *Justice Quarterly* 12(3):525-542.

Maahs, J. & C. Hemmens (1998). "Guarding the Public: A Statutory Analysis of State Regulation of Security Guards." *Journal of Crime and Justice* 21(1):119-134.

Maguire, K. & A. Pastore (1996). *Sourcebook of Criminal Justice Statistics—1995*. Washington, DC: U.S. Government Printing Office.

Maguire, K. & A. Pastore (1999). *Sourcebook of Criminal Justice Statistics—1998*. Washington, DC: U.S. Government Printing Office.

Maguire, K. & A. Pastore (2003). *Sourcebook of Criminal Justice Statistics—2002*. Washington, DC: U.S. Government Printing Office.

Maguire, K., A. Pastore & T. Flanagan (1993). *Sourcebook of Criminal Justice Statistics—1992*. Washington, DC: U.S. Government Printing Office), 90.

Mastrofski, S.D., R.R. Ritti & D. Hoffmaster (1987). "Organizational Determinants of Police Discretion: The Case of Drinking-Driving." *Journal of Criminal Justice* 15(5):387-402.

Maxwell, C. D., J.H. Garner & J.A. Fagan (2002). "The Preventive Effects of Arrest on Intimate Partner Violence: Research, Policy and Theory." *Criminology and Public Policy* 2(1):51-80.

McDonald, W. (ed.) (1979). *The Prosecutor*. Beverly Hills, CA: Sage.

Meyer, J. & T. Gray (1997). "Drunk Drivers in the Courts: Legal and Extra-Legal Factors Affecting Pleas and Sentences." *Journal of Crime and Justice* 25(2):155-163.

Meyers, A., T. Heeren, R. Hingson & D. Kovenock (1987). "Cops and Drivers: Police Discretion and the Enforcement of Maine's 1981 DUI Law." *Journal of Criminal Justice* 15(5):361-368.

National Survey of Court Organization (1977). Washington, DC: U.S. Department of Justice

Newman, D.J. (1966). *Conviction: The Determination of Guilt or Innocence without Trial*. Boston: Little, Brown.

Office for Victims of Crime (2002). "The Crime Victim's Right to Be Present." *Legal Series Bulletin #3* (January). Washington, DC: Office for Victims of Crime.

Ostrom, B., N. Kauder & R. LaFountain (2003). *Examining the Work of State Courts 2002: A National Perspective from the Court Statistics Project*. Washington, DC: National Center for State Courts.

Ostrom, B. (2003). "Domestic Violence: Editorial Introduction." *Criminology and Public Policy* 2(2):259-262.

Perkins, C., J. Stephan & A. Beck (1995). *Jails and Jail Inmates, 1993-94*. Washington, DC: U.S. Department of Justice.

President's Commission on Law Enforcement and Administration of Justice (1967a). *The Challenge of Crime in a Free Society*. Washington, DC: U.S. Government Printing Office.

President's Commission on Law Enforcement and Administration of Justice (1967b). *Task Force Report: The Police*. Washington, DC: U.S. Government Printing Office.

Rainville, G. & B. Reaves (2003). *Felony Defendants in Large Urban Counties, 2000*. Washington, DC: Bureau of Justice Statistics.

Rand, M. (1998). *Criminal Victimization 1997: Changes 1996-97 with Trends 1993-1997*. Washington, DC: Bureau of Justice Statistics.

Rand, M., J. Lynch & D. Cantor (1997). *Criminal Victimization, 1973-95*. Washington, DC: Bureau of Justice Statistics.

Reaves, B. (2007). *Census of State and Local Law Enforcement Agencies, 2004*. Washington, DC: Bureau of Justice Statistics.

Reaves, B. & M. Hickman (2002). *Census of State and Local Law Enforcement Agencies, 2000*. Washington, DC: Bureau of Justice Statistics.

Reaves, B.A. & L.M. Bauer (2003). *Federal Law Enforcement Officers, 2002.* Washington, DC: Bureau of Justice Statistics.

Rennison, C. & M.R. Rand (2003). *Criminal Victimization, 2002.* Washington, DC: Bureau of Justice Statistics.

Rosett, A. & D. Cressey (1976). *Justice by Consent.* Philadelphia: J.B. Lippincott.

Rottman, D. & P. Casey (1999). "Therapeutic Jurisprudence and the Emergence of Problem-Solving Courts." *National Institute of Justice Journal* (July):12-19.

Rottman, D., C. Flango, M. Cantrell, R. Hansen & N. LaFountain (2000). *State Court Organization, 1998.* Washington, DC: Bureau of Justice Statistics.

Rubin, H.T. (1984). *The Courts: Fulcrum of the Justice System,* 2nd ed. New York: Random House.

Sanders, B., T. Hughes & R. Langworthy (1995). "Police Officer Recruitment and Selection: A Survey of Major Police Departments in the U.S." *Police Forum* 5(4):1-4.

Sherman, L. (1992). *Policing Domestic Violence: Experiments and Dilemmas.* New York: Free Press.

Smith, S. & C. DeFrances (1996). *Indigent Defense.* Washington, DC: Bureau of Justice Statistics.

Stephan, J. & J. Karberg (2003). *Census of State and Federal Correctional Facilities, 2000.* Washington, DC: Bureau of Justice Statistics.

Travis, L.F. & R.H. Langworthy (2008). *Policing in America: A Balance of Forces,* 4th ed. Englewood Cliffs, NJ: Prentice Hall.

Travis, L.F. & E.J. Latessa (1984). "A Summary of Parole Rules Thirteen Years Later: Revisited Thirteen Years Later." *Journal of Criminal Justice* 12(6):591-600.

Travis, L.F., E.J. Latessa & G.F. Vito (1985). "Private Enterprise in Institutional Corrections: A Call for Caution." *Federal Probation* 49(4):11-16.

U.S. Department of Justice (1978). *The Nation's Toughest Drug Law.* Washington, DC: U.S. Government Printing Office.

U.S. Department of Justice (1980). *Justice Agencies in the United States.* Washington, DC: U.S. Government Printing Office.

Vartebedian, R. (2002). "A Spirited Debate Over DUI Laws." *Los Angeles Times* (December 30, 2002):A1.

Victim/Witness Legislation: An Overview (1984). Washington, DC: U.S. Department of Justice.

Walker, S. (2001). *Sense and Nonsense about Crime and Drugs: A Police Guide,* 5th ed. Belmont, CA: Wadsworth.

Welch, M., R. Wolff & N. Bryan (1998). "Decontextualizing the War on Drugs: A Content Analysis of NIJ Publications and their Neglect of Race and Class." *Justice Quarterly* 15(4):719-742.

Whitcomb, D. (2002). "Prosecutors, Kids, and Domestic Violence Cases." *National Institute of Justice Journal* (March):2-9.

White, H.R. & D.M. Gorman (2000). "Dynamics of the Drug-Crime Relationship." In G. LaFree (ed.), *The Nature of Crime: Continuity and Change.* Washington, DC: National Institute of Justice, Criminal Justice 2000, Volume 1.

Yu, J., P. Evans & L. Clark (2006). "Alcohol Addiction and Perceived Sanction Risks: Deterring Drunk Drivers." *Journal of Criminal Justice* 34(2):165-174.

Chapter 3

Crime and Crime Control

Important Terms

The business of the American criminal justice process is "crime"; yet, this does not explain much. One obstacle to the study of the system of criminal justice is our lack of precision in discussing the issue of crime. In short, what is crime?

Although it is relatively easy to provide examples of crime, it is not so easy to define it. There is a tendency to assume a common meaning for the word "crime." The variety of actions and nuances of behavior that constitute crime is nearly infinite. If asked to name a crime, how many of us would say shoplifting, drunken driving, price fixing, or failure to register for the selective service? We are far more likely to mention murder, bank robbery, rape, or burglary. In that sense, we have a fairly clear common definition of crime, but one that is inadequate for the study of criminal justice.

These mental images of crime reflect those offenses that cause the most concern. Of the many different types of behaviors that we have defined as criminal, some types are more commonly agreed upon to be criminal than others. There tends to be consensus among us about the criminality of the more serious offenses that involve actual physical harm or direct economic harm to individuals (Cullen, Link & Polanzi, 1982). There is considerably less agreement about those offenses that do not cause such direct and potentially personal harm (Miethe, 1982; Newman & Trilling, 1975).

Similarly, we carry mental images of criminals about which there is general agreement. The average criminal probably appears as a relatively young, mean, menacing male. Most people seem to believe that the criminal knows—but does not care—that his or her behavior is wrong and harmful. The criminal is simply bad or lazy, preferring crime to some other more appropriate mode of earning a living or settling arguments. Yet, as with crimes, there is a wide variety of criminals. The hulking street offender, bullying rapist, calculating white-collar offender, college student selling drugs, and political terrorist are all criminals.

Brenda Vogel (1998) reported on a study of perceptions of crime seriousness among African Americans. In this study, respondents were given descriptions of six crimes that involved information about the actual behavior as well as the context of the offense. The context information included the motive of the offender, the amount of harm caused, and the actions of the victim. She found that there was little consensus about crime seriousness. While there may be widespread agreement about what behaviors are the most serious crimes in some abstract way, knowing the details about specific criminal behaviors produces less agreement among observers.

Faced with the wide array of crimes and criminals, we need to organize our understanding of each in order to appreciate the demands placed upon the justice system. Both crimes and criminals have been sorted into classes for ease of understanding. Before turning to these, however, we should try to answer the question: what is crime?

Defining Crime

"Crime" refers in part to a set of behaviors that society deems to be wrong and in need of control. Most often, classifying a behavior as a crime includes a reference to the "intent" of the actor. The specification and definition of crimes is a legislative function in our society. It is the legislature that declares certain behaviors to be "criminal" and describes the conditions under which a person may be said to have committed a crime. (Box 3.1 provides an example of a criminal statute.) Therefore, from a legalistic perspective, we can conclude the "cause" of crime in America is the legislature. Without legislative action, there would be no conduct designated as "crime." Crime is an act or omission in violation of a law that is punished by the state. In the United States, the requirement that the behavior violate the law means that legislative action is needed.

Of course, without the designation of certain conduct as "crime," we would still have troublesome behavior, such as the taking of property or the infliction of injury. These actions would not be crimes, however, unless they were first so defined by the legislature. A crime is "an act or omission in violation of the law and punishable by the state."

While most of us do not think of legislative action as a necessary "cause" of crime, we understand the legislative role. If asked what is the cause of crime, most people will contend that bad companions, ignorance, poverty, psychological

Box 3.1	Sec: 2911.12 Ohio Revised Code (1995) Burglary

(A) No person, by force, stealth, or deception, shall do any of the following:

(1) Trespass in an occupied structure or in a separately secured or separately occupied portion of an occupied structure, when another person is present, with purpose to commit therein any criminal offense;

(2) Trespass in an occupied structure or in a separately secured or separately occupied portion of an occupied structure that is a permanent or temporary habitation of any person when any person is present or likely to be present, with purpose to commit in the habitation any criminal offense;

(3) Trespass in an occupied structure or in a separately secured or separately occupied portion of an occupied structure, with purpose to commit in the structure or separately occupied portion any criminal offense;

(4) Trespass in a permanent or temporary habitation of any person when any person is present or likely to be present . . .

(C) Whoever violates this section is guilty of burglary. A violation of division (A)(1) or (2) of this section is a felony of the second degree. A violation of division (A)(3) of this section is a felony of the third degree. A violation of division (A)(4) of this section is a felony of the fourth degree.

disturbance, or some other factor is what makes people break the law. Yet, when we see someone doing something that we believe is wrong, we are also apt to say, "There ought to be a law." This statement reflects an understanding of the role of the legislature. No matter how wrong is the behavior in question, we cannot do anything about it unless there is a law against it.

This is an important concept for understanding the criminal justice system. The justice system is constrained by the law. We generally cannot use the justice process to control behavior that is unpleasant but not criminal. There are limits, then, to what level of control can be asserted by agents of the criminal process. Of course, the power of the justice system to control behavior often leads people to pass laws. Luna (2003:15) has described the expansion of criminal law in the United States, noting that there are more than 3,000 offenses punishable as federal crimes.

Criminologists have debated the definition of crime for many years (Schwendinger & Schwendinger, 1975). Some argue that only those behaviors identified in criminal laws are crimes. Others seek a broader definition that includes actions that are socially harmful or immoral. The issue of defining crime is somewhat different for these criminologists than it is for our purposes because they are trying to explain deviance, of which crime is one type. If the focus is on deviant behavior, there is no need to consider legal status. Deviance is behavior that violates socially accepted standards of proper conduct.

The approach we are using in this book requires a definition of crime that identifies those behaviors on which the criminal justice system focuses. Criminologists, on the other hand, are seeking to identify a set of behaviors that can be explained by theories of criminal behavior (Tittle, 2000). Criminologists usually seek to explain the behavior of individuals (Willis, Evans & LaGrange, 1999), while we wish to understand the criminal justice system and its parts as a social institution.

The definitions of most crimes contain two components. First, there is an action (or lack of action) known as *actus reus*. Second, there is the intent or mental condition of the offender, known as the *mens rea*. To be considered a criminal, it is usually not enough to do something illegal; one must also intend to do what is illegal to be convicted of a crime.

Most jurisdictions define the crime of burglary as the unlawful entry of a place for the purpose of committing a crime therein. To be convicted of burglary, one must unlawfully enter a place (a home, business, storage building, etc.). Simply entering, however, does not make one a burglar. The entry is the *actus reus*. To be a burglar, it is also necessary that one enter with the intent to commit a crime while inside. This intent to commit a crime is the mental state of the offender, the *mens rea*.

Neither of the two hypothetical persons below is a burglar.

> P. was invited to a party at a neighbor's home. P. did not care much for these neighbors, but cared greatly for several of their possessions. P. accepted the invitation and attended the party for the express purpose of obtaining the property of the neighbors. P. is not a burglar, for the entry was achieved lawfully. In this case, P. is a thief.

> Q. was walking home from a party at which large quantities of alcoholic refreshments were consumed (the largest quantity by Q). Passing a furrier, Q. blacks out from the combined effects of too many beverages and a long, tedious conversation with someone named P., a neighbor of the host. Q. falls over and crashes through the display window of the furrier's shop, landing in a huge pile of fur coats, on which Q. falls fast asleep. The police arrive within minutes, responding to the alarm at the furrier's, to discover the quietly resting Q. Q. is not a burglar, for there was no intent to commit a crime in the furrier shop. (Indeed, there was not even intent to enter.)

In order to obtain a criminal conviction, the state must prove all elements (both *actus reus* and *mens rea*) of an offense beyond a reasonable doubt. Television murder-mystery plots often include a missing victim when there is reason to believe that someone has been murdered but the body cannot be found. The characters remark that it will be difficult to bring charges without the *corpus delicti*. Because of the plot, and the similarity between the words "corpus" and "corpse," audiences sometimes think that *corpus delicti* refers to the dead body. In fact, it refers to the body of the crime. The lack of a motive (also a frequent plot line) also hinders the filing of charges because, without a motive, it is difficult to establish intent, another part of the *corpus delicti*.

For some crimes, the job of the state in proving the guilt of an offender is somewhat easier. Some crimes, known as **strict liability** offenses, presume *mens rea* (Lilly & Ball, 1982). In these cases, if it can be proved that the defendant engaged in the prohibited behavior, a conviction will occur. Regardless of the intent of the offender, she or he is strictly liable for the consequences of the behavior.

Strict liability often applies to white-collar crimes. For example, the law may presume the head of a company is responsible for the wrongdoing of his or her employees, even if the company head is unaware of the activity. Especially with strict liability offenses, the old adage "Ignorance of the law is no excuse" is true.

This brief explanation of the definition of crimes and of the elements of an offense is needed to understand the nature of crime. However, this explanation alone does not help us to obtain a perspective on crime that will be useful to our examination of the criminal justice process. The legislatures in the various United States criminal jurisdictions have managed to define a large number of widely divergent behaviors and mental states as crimes. The justice system must respond to all of them with limited resources and ability. To better organize and deploy the limited resources for the control of crime, this plethora of offenses must be sorted and ranked.

Classification of Crimes and Criminals

One simple classification of crimes has already been mentioned as the difference between "serious" and "less serious" offenses. This same simplistic distinction is frequently drawn between "dangerous" and "normal" crimes. Those offenses that are most threatening to individuals are usually defined as serious (or dangerous), while those that are less directly threatening are classed as less serious (or normal).

Sometimes this distinction between dangerous and normal crimes is explained as the difference between offenses that are wrong in themselves (*mala in se*) and those that are wrong because they are prohibited (*mala prohibita*). That is, certain crimes appear to be obviously criminal, while others are apparently criminal only because we say they are wrong.

Mala in se offenses encompass traditional or street crimes that seem wrong regardless of their legality. Purposely or carelessly causing physical harm or suffering to someone, or taking the property of others, are acts that most people believe to be simply wrong. One does not need a criminal law to realize that killing a person without cause (and often with cause) is "wrong." These are the very offenses about which we have the most agreement and around which most of our mental images of crime focus. As Luna (2003:1) puts it, ". . . every U.S. jurisdiction has on its books a set of crimes and punishments that are incontrovertible, involving acts and attendant mental states that must be proscribed in order to constitute a just society—murder, rape, robbery, arson and the like."

Mala prohibita offenses, on the other hand, are those acts that are wrong because they are defined as wrong. The use of narcotics by adults within the confines of their own homes and the refusal to pay income taxes (especially if the money might be better spent on something else) are not behaviors that are necessarily wrong (at least in a secular perspective). What makes these behaviors criminal, and therefore wrong, is that we have prohibited them and defined them as crimes. These are the offenses about which we have the least agreement and that raise the most serious issues of individual liberty and the needs of the state. Luna (2003:15) writes, "These offenses are marked by the absence of violence or coercion, with parties engaged in voluntary transactions for desired goods or services."

A second major way in which criminal offenses have been classified is into categories of felony, misdemeanor, or violation. These three levels of crime reflect the different seriousness of behaviors, in large part on the basis of the extent of punishment authorized. Before explaining this difference, it is important to remember that there are exceptions to every rule. The following are merely rules of thumb.

A felony is the most serious level of offense and generally is punishable by a term of more than one year in a state prison. A misdemeanor is a less serious offense, generally punishable by a term of no more than one year in a local jail. A violation is the least serious offense and typically does not carry an incarceration penalty; the penalty is limited to a fine or loss of privilege. For example, in most states, theft of $1,000 or more is a felony and can be punished by imprisonment for a number of years, while theft of $50 is a misdemeanor and can be punished by a jail term of up to several months. Exceeding the speed limit is a violation and is punished by a fine of less than $100 (except for repeated offenses). As these examples illustrate, the classes of crimes reflect the amount of harm caused by the criminal behavior.

Still another distinction drawn between crimes is to label them as being either ordinary (normal) or aggravated (dangerous) (Newman, 1987:28-30). It is possible to rate crimes as being "better" or "worse" than each other, within the same crime type. A burglar may not do any more damage to a home than that required for entry and theft; this is an ordinary burglary. On the other hand, the burglar may vandalize the home in addition to breaking in and stealing; this might be an aggravated burglary. (We will return to this type of classification system later when sentencing is discussed.)

The ordinary-versus-aggravated distinction is generally used within some less precise classification (such as "robbery") in order to differentiate between the seriousness of several instances of the "same" behavior. As with the other classifications of crimes, the purpose of this distinction is to clarify the response that should be taken by the justice system. Typically, the agents and agencies of the justice system are more willing to expend resources in response to aggravated felonies than in response to ordinary violations. Indeed, many people express this rational choice upon being stopped for a traffic violation by wondering why the officer is not out "fighting crime" rather than focusing on trivial matters.

There is ample evidence to suggest that the type of crime is an important consideration in criminal justice decisions. More serious crimes are more likely to be reported by victims and witnesses, and are more likely to be investigated and processed by the police (Wilson & Ruback, 2003). Criminal justice officials at all points of the system devote more attention and resources to aggravated, *mala in se* felonies than to other, less serious crimes. When trying to understand criminal justice processing then, offense seriousness is an important consideration.

Michael Gottfredson and Donald Gottfredson reviewed the research on criminal justice processing. Across all types of criminal justice decisions from detection through parole, and even the crime victim's decision to report the offense to the police, three factors were most important predictors of decisions. Gottfredson and Gottfredson wrote (1988:257-258), "...from the host of offender, offense, victim, decision-maker, and situational factors that potentially influence individual decisionmaking, three appear to play a persistent and major role throughout the system: the seriousness of the offense, the prior criminal record of the offender, and the personal relationship between the victim of the crime and the offender." Crime seriousness or the type of crime is an important influence on criminal justice processing.

When crimes are defined as felonies, they are more likely to be investigated than misdemeanors. Felonies result in incarceration sentences more often, and for longer periods of time, than less serious offenses. Jogerst, Daly, Brinig, and Bibas (2005) studied the relationship between crime seriousness and the reporting and investigation of those crimes. They found that in cases of elder abuse, the crime was more likely to be reported and more likely to be investigated in states that defined elder abuse as a more serious offense (criminal rather than civil; felony rather than misdemeanor).

Defining Criminals

Like crimes themselves, the people who commit them are of an infinite variety. Assuming that there is a preventive component to the justice system's overall mission to control crime, knowledge of the type of offender is as important as knowledge about the type of crime (Holmes, 1989). Certain types of offenders have been identified as deserving specific types of justice system responses. A Bureau of Justice Statistics Report stated (1985:1):

> Programs aimed at the serious, recidivistic offender require the capability to identify dangerous offenders at key decision points in the criminal justice system, such as pre-trial release and sentencing . . .

> These programs are designed primarily to increase the effectiveness of criminal justice by targeting resources on offenders considered most likely to recidivate and on offenders whose detention is most likely to have an incapacitative or deterrent effect.

One common method of classifying offenders is by the crime they committed—someone guilty of murder is a murderer, someone guilty of robbery is a robber, someone guilty of burglary is a burglar, and so on. This is often how the media and correctional authorities identify offenders. Police frequently improve on this simple scheme by adding details of crimes, such as the time of the crime, type of weapon used, and characteristics of the victim. These added details comprise a *modus operandi* (M.O.) file. This type of classification is limited because it does not tell much about the offender. A study conducted by the RAND Corporation (Chaiken & Chaiken, 1982) showed that offenders often engage in a variety of criminal behavior. Today's robber may have been yesterday's thief and may be tomorrow's burglar. More recent research suggests that offenders may specialize at least in terms of types of crime. Deane, Armstrong, and Felson (2005) report that some offenders are likely to commit crimes of violence while others are unlikely to be violent. Offenders may not specialize along the lines of specific crimes as much as within violent or nonviolent crimes. Similarly, there are certain crime types that seem to "go together" and might represent something of a criminal lifestyle. Deane and his colleagues reported a link between armed robbery, other armed violence, selling drugs, and serious property crime. Criminals who engage in one of these crimes are more likely to also be involved in the others. Osgood and Schreck (2007) also reported finding evidence of a specialization in violence among a sample of juvenile offenders. These studies suggest that while it may not be accurate to speak of "burglars" or "robbers," it may be true that offenders can be classified by crime type in terms of property offenders, violent offenders, or other types of offense such as drug offenders.

Another typical classification of offenders is similar to the ordinary/aggravated distinction applied to crimes. Here, offenders are identified as either "first-time" (ordinary) or "repeat" (more dangerous) offenders. Many jurisdictions have special procedures for the handling of repeat offenders, known as career criminals. The distinction drawn is one between periodic (or occasional) criminality and a criminal lifestyle. Those who lead a criminal life—that is, who routinely engage in criminal behavior—are responsible for a disproportionate share of crime committed (Greenwood, 1982).

Criminal Careers versus Career Criminals

Criminologists have studied criminal behavior through examination of the "criminal careers" of offenders (Gibbons, 1973; Nettler, 1982). These researchers seek to identify the paths followed by offenders throughout their lives that lead them into and out of crime. They recognize that criminality is not always central to the personality of an offender. The average person probably has committed (or will someday commit) a crime. Yet, few of us are (or will be) "criminals." In contemporary parlance, this approach to the study of criminals is known as the study of **lifecourse criminality**—how people engage in or refrain from crime over the course of their lives (Farrington, 2003).

The career criminal is someone for whom crime is a normal activity and for whom being a criminal is part of self-identification. This person is often called a "hardened criminal" or persistent offender. It has been suggested that these persistent offenders commit the majority of crimes. By attempting to focus attention on these individuals, justice officials hope to have the greatest impact on the crime rate.

For decades, some criminologists argued that the most useful classification of offenders would be one based on behavioral characteristics. They advanced several means of distinguishing among criminals based on the psychological or sociological traits of the offender. These have been used for prison classification (Bonta & Motiuk, 1992; Fox, 1983:59-62), probation and parole classification (Bonta, 1996; Clear & Gallagher, 1985; Warren, 1973), and prevention programs. Perhaps the most wide-ranging classification system that retained links to type of crime was suggested by Clinard, Quinney, and Wildeman (1994).

The principal goal of these criminologists is the explanation of criminal conduct, that is, to understand why persons commit crimes or why certain persons commit certain crimes (Cullen, 1983). For criminal justice agencies, this knowledge is useful only insofar as it can guide reactions to crime and criminals (Vito & Holmes, 1994). Clinard, Quinney, and Wildeman classified offenders by the major forms of crime committed. They identified nine categories, ranging from violent personal criminal behavior through professional criminal behavior (see Box 3.2). Agents of the criminal justice system appear to use a similar classification scheme in their handling of offenders.

Typologies of crimes and criminals are used to plan and evaluate the uses to which criminal justice resources are put. Without such "shorthand" categorization of its basic types of business, the justice system would be overwhelmed by idiosyncrasies. While by no means perfect, these classification schemes allow an organization of the justice system that is necessary to making the system's operation more efficient.

For example, police officers may distinguish burglars as either juvenile burglars, average burglars, or "cat burglars." The juvenile burglar, as the name implies, is a youth who commits an opportunistic burglary with little forethought and perhaps less care in the commission of the offense. The average burglar plans his or her crime and is careful to avoid detection. The cat burglar is someone who burglarizes a dwelling while the occupants are on the premises (Gibbons, 1973:14).

While all of these are correctly labeled or categorized as "burglars," it is clear that they pose different levels of risk to citizens and that they require different responses by the police. The juvenile burglar is likely to grab whatever valuables can be quickly obtained and easily carried. The average burglar is unlikely to be discovered during the crime and generally will take more property. The cat burglar, while also unlikely to be detected, usually restricts his or her thefts to cash, jewels, or specific high-value items.

Agents and agencies of the justice system have organized to better combat the more serious offenses and offenders. The career criminal became the target of special crime control efforts and programs in the 1980s. "The concept of the career criminal has led to police and prosecutor programs that target resources on those offenders identified as the most persistent and frequent in their com-

Box 3.2   Criminal Behavior Systems

	Violent Personal Criminal Behavior	Occasional Property Criminal Behavior	Public Order Criminal Behavior
Legal Aspects of Selected Offenses	The criminal laws of homicide, assault and forcible rape are of ancient origin. Yet the legal categories are qualified and interpreted in their respective social and historical contexts. Likewise, the ruling class is able to exclude the forms of violence that enhance its own position.	Criminal laws protect the material interests of the propertied classes. Specific laws prohibit forgery, shoplifting, vandalism and auto theft.	Specific criminal laws embody the moral sense of particular segments of the community. Such offenses as prostitution, homosexuality, drunkenness and drug use are disturbing to some community members. Many of the crimes are "victimless" in that only willing participants are involved. Yet it is easier for the power elite to outlaw these behaviors than to either accept them or to change the social arrangements that produced the behaviors.
Criminal Career of the Offender	Crime is not part of the offender's career. He or she usually does not conceive of self as criminal.	Little or no criminal self-conception. The offender does not identify with crime. He or she is able to rationalize his or her behavior.	Most offenders do not regard their behavior as criminal. They do not have a clearly defined criminal career. Ambiguity in self-concept produced in continued contact with legal agents.
Group Support of Criminal Behavior	Little or no group support. Offenses committed for personal reasons. Some support in subcultural norms.	Little group support. Generally individual offenses. Associations tend to be recreational.	Offenses such as prostitution, homosexual behavior and drug use grow out of, and are supported by, rather clearly defined subcultures. Considerable association with other offenders.
Correspondence between Criminal and Legitimate Behavior	Violations of values on life and personal safety.	Violation of value on private property. Offenders tend to be committed to the general goals of the society.	Some of the offenses are required by legitimate society. Much of the behavior is consistent with legitimate behavior patterns.
Societal Reaction and Legal Processing	Strong social reaction. Harsh punishments. Long imprisonment.	Social reaction is not severe when the offender does not have a previous record. Leniency in legal processing. Probation.	Strong reaction by some segments of society, weak reaction by others. Only a small portion of the offenses result in arrest. Sentences are strong for some offenses, such as the possession of narcotic drugs.

Box 3.2 *(continued)*

Conventional Criminal Behavior	Political Criminal Behavior	Occupational Criminal Behavior
The laws that protect private property include such crimes as larceny, burglary and robbery. Since the primary interest is in protecting property, general laws regarding property do not need to distinguish the career nature of many property offenders.	Criminal laws are created by governments to protect their own existence. Specific criminal laws, such as conspiracy laws, as well as traditional laws, are made to control and punish those who threaten the state. Yet the government and its officials often violate criminal laws. Political criminal behavior thus includes crimes *against* government and crimes *by* government.	Legal regulation of occupations has served to protect the interests of occupational groups, and in some cases to regulate harmful occupational activities. The legal codes that control occupations and professions tend to be made by the occupations and the professions themselves, representing their material interests.
Offenders begin their careers early in life, often in gang associations. Crimes committed for economic gain. Vacillation in self-conception. Partial commitment to a criminal subculture.	Political offenders do not usually conceive of themselves as criminals and do not identify with crime. They are defined as criminal because they are perceived as threatening to the status quo (as in crime against government) or they are criminal when they violate the laws that regulate the government itself (crime by government).	Little or no self-conception. Occasional violation of the law, accompanied by appropriate rationalizations. Violation tends to be a part of one's work. Offenders accept the conventional values in the society.
Behavior supported by group norms. Early association with other offenders in slum areas. Status achieved in groups. Some persons continue primary association with other offenders, while others pursue different careers.	Support is received by particular groups or by segments of society. They identify or associate with persons who share similar values. Behavior is reinforced by specific norms.	Some occupations (or groups within occupations), tolerate or even support offenses. The offender is integrated into social groups and societal norms.
Consistent with goals of economic success, but inconsistent with sanctity of private property. Gang delinquency violates norms of proper adolescent behavior.	Crimes against government usually correspond to basic human rights. The actions and beliefs, however, are opposed by those who are threatened by these freedoms. Crimes by government correspond to contrary behavior patterns that promote the sovereignty of government rulers.	Behavior corresponds to the pursual of business activity. "Sharp" practices and "buyer beware" philosophy have guided work and consumption patterns.
A series of arrests and convictions. Institutionalization and rehabilitation of the offender. Agency programs that preserve the status quo without changing social conditions.	Official reactions tend to be severe in the case of crimes against government. Considerable harassment may be experienced and heavy sentences may be imposed. Public acceptance of political offenses depends on the extent to which the policies and actions of the government are accepted. Reactions to governmental crime depend on the consciousness of the public regarding the activities of the government.	Reactions have traditionally been mild and indifferent. Official penalties have been lenient, often restricted to the sanctions administered by professional associations. Public reaction is becoming less tolerant.

Box 3.2 *(continued)*

	Corporate Criminal Behavior	Organized Criminal Behavior	Professional Criminal Behavior
Legal Aspects of Selected Offenses	With the growth of corporations, criminal laws have been created to regulate such activities as restraint of trade, false advertising, fraudulent sales, misuse of trademarks and manufacture of unsafe foods and drugs. Criminal laws—especially administrative regulations—have been established by the corporations themselves to secure a capitalist economy.	Many traditional laws have been used in the attempt to control organized crime, especially those regarding gambling, prostitution and drug trafficking. The government has more recently enacted special criminal laws in order to infiltrate organized criminal activity in legitimate business and racketeering. But since organized crime is closely tied to the general business economy, these laws tend to invade the privacy of all citizens rather than control organized crime.	Professional crimes are distinguished by the nature of the criminal behavior rather than by specific criminal laws. Such professional activities as confidence games, pickpocketing, shoplifting, forgery and counterfeiting are regulated by the traditional laws that protect private property.
Criminal Career of the Offender	The violating corporate official and the corporation have high social status in society. Offenses are an integral part of corporate business operations. Violations are rationalized as being basic to business enterprise.	Crime is pursued as a livelihood. There is a progression in crime and an increasing isolation from the larger society. A criminal self-conception develops.	A highly developed criminal career. Professional offenders engage in specialized offenses, all of which are directed toward economic gain. They enjoy high status in the world of crime. They are committed to other professional criminals.
Group Support of Criminal Behavior	Crime by corporations and corporate officials receives support from similar (even competing) businesses and officials. Lawbreaking is a normative pattern within many corporations. Corporate crime involves a great amount of organization among the participants.	Support for organized criminal behavior is achieved through an organizational structure, a code of conduct, prescribed methods of operation and a system of protection. The offender is integrated into organized crime.	Professional offenders associate primarily with other offenders. Behavior is prescribed by the norms of professional criminals. The extent of organization among professional criminals varies with the kind of offense.
Correspondence between Criminal and Legitimate Behavior	Corporate crime is consistent with the prevailing ideology that encourages unlimited production and consumption. Only recently has an alternative ethic developed that questions practices that support corporate crime.	While organized crime may be generally condemned, characteristics of American society give support to organized crime. The values underlying organized crime are consistent with those valued in the free enterprise system.	Professional criminal activity corresponds to societal values that stress skill and employment. Some of the offenses depend upon the cooperation of accomplices. The operations of professional crime change with alterations in the larger society.
Societal Reaction and Legal Processing	Strong legal actions have not usually been taken against corporations or their officials. Legal actions often have been in the form of warnings and injunctions, rather than in terms of criminal penalties. Public reactions and legal actions, however, are increasing in respect to corporate crime.	Considerable public toleration of organized crime. Offenses are not usually visible to the public. Immunity of offenders, as provided by effective organization, prevents detection and arrest. Convictions are usually for minor offenses.	Considerable public toleration because of the low visibility of professional crime. Offenders are able to escape conviction by "fixing" cases.

Source: M.B. Clinard, R. Quinney & J. Wildeman (1994), *Criminal Behavior Systems: A Typology*, 3rd ed. (Cincinnati: Anderson).

mission of serious crimes" (National Institute of Justice, 1986). Many police departments and prosecutor's offices have special repeat offender or career criminal bureaus. Some states have initiatives that support (or require) local justice agencies to focus attention on career criminals. The State of California supports a Career Criminal Prosecution Program with special state funding. In Virginia, the state supports the Serious or Habitual Offender Comprehensive Action Program (SHOCAP).

Criminologists have begun to focus (in some cases, refocus) on different dimensions of criminality. There has been a resurgence of "rational choice" theory, which treats criminals as economic decisionmakers who calculate the costs and benefits of crime before deciding to commit an offense (Tittle, 2000:62-67). Daniel Nagin (2007) has argued that a focus on how offenders make choices about whether and which crimes to commit would expand our understanding of crime and our ability to control and prevent crime. He warns that rational choice approaches must be sensitive to the fact that decisions involve not only reason, but also emotion. It may well be that certain decisions appear rational to us under some emotional circumstances such as when we are angry, afraid, or excited.

We hear less about "career criminals" today, and more about crime in the "life course" (Laub & Sampson, 1993; Thornberry, 1997). One of the best known theories of crime over the course of offenders' lives was suggested by Terrie Moffitt. She suggests that some individuals engage in crime over their entire lives, while others experience certain periods (usually adolescence) when they have a greater risk of criminality. Lifecourse criminology is a subset of criminological theory that seeks to understand how people start, continue, and stop engaging in crime over the span of their lives.

Another theme relates to place, or environmental criminology. Cohen and Felson (1978) described a "routine activities" theory of crime. They suggested that crime occurs when a motivated offender and a suitable target (victim or property) come together in time and space in the absence of an effective guardian. That is, there are criminals and victims in society. At some times, and in certain locations, they come into contact. Unless someone is there to prevent it (the guardian), a crime will occur. Crime, then, depends on the interaction of offenders, targets, and guardians. This theory suggests a structural approach to crime. By increasing guardianship, for example, crime can be reduced. More recently, criminologists have focused attention on repeat victims—those people who are frequently the victims of crime (Pease & Laycock, 1996).

Controlling Crime and Criminals

Francis A. Allen, Professor of Law and Dean of the University of Michigan Law School, was one of the first observers of American criminal justice to identify the increasing burden placed on the justice system by expansions of the criminal sanction. Allen studied the tremendous growth of criminal laws and increasing use of the justice system to deal with social problems ranging from substance abuse to health care. He considered the most important task to be the definition of what could reasonably be expected from the criminal justice system. In 1964, he wrote:

> The time has long been ripe for some sober questions to be asked. More and more it seems that the central issue may be this: What may we properly demand of a system of criminal justice? What functions may it properly serve? There is a related question: What are the obstacles and problems that must be confronted and overcome if a system of criminal justice is to be permitted to serve its own proper ends? These are broad and difficult questions, and the way in which they are answered will affect much that is important to the community at large (Allen, 1964:4).

At base, Allen was attempting to set priorities for the use of the criminal law. His position was that the criminal law was increasingly being applied to social welfare problems (such as public intoxication) and regulatory needs. He decried the growing reliance on the criminal law to solve social problems. He urged that we decide upon those behaviors that would best be the objects of criminal law, and that we limit the activities of the justice system to the control of these particular behaviors.

Other observers of American criminal justice shared this sentiment (American Friends Service Committee, 1971; National Advisory Commission, 1973). During the 1970s, a growing number of scholars and practitioners came to agree that the most sensible approach to crime control required the identification of "serious" crimes and the focusing of enforcement resources on those crimes. As the National Advisory Commission on Criminal Justice Standards and Goals (1973:84) explained, "The empire of crime is too large and diverse to be attacked on all fronts simultaneously."

Observers and agents of the justice system have long recognized the fundamental truth of this comment. Traditionally, police officers, prosecutors, judges, correctional personnel, and parole boards have adopted ad hoc strategies to maximize the effectiveness of criminal justice processing in controlling crime. In this vein, Kenneth C. Davis (1975:1) noted:

> The police make policy about what law to enforce, how much to enforce it, against whom, and on what occasions. Some law is always or almost always enforced, some is never or almost never enforced, and some is sometimes enforced and sometimes not.

With a large number of criminal laws applied to a broad variety of behavior, agents of the justice system often must choose which laws to enforce and when to enforce them. Moreover, with the wide variety of offenders, it is similarly common for laws to be enforced differently against different types of individuals. The dangerous, repeat offender is not likely to be ignored, regardless of the violation. In a sense, this approach to the "rationing" of justice resources seeks to maximize effectiveness. Officials use the criminal law to control the most serious offenses and offenders.

Criminal justice officials historically have devoted most of their resources to the control of more dangerous crimes and criminals. For example, police investigate suspected felonies more thoroughly than misdemeanors, and prosecutors are less willing to negotiate for guilty pleas from repeat felons. For the most part, this focus of attention on serious crimes (such as felonies and violent acts) had not been a conscious policy decision.

In the recent past, this unconscious rationing of resources (by justice officials choosing cases on which to concentrate) was exposed and adopted as

Citizens sit outside their home watching members from License and Inspection board up and condemn their neighbor's home in a troubled area of North Philadelphia's Kensington section. "Operation Sunrise," a landmark offensive aimed at the most crime-ridden square mile of the city, brought a brigade of police officers, street crews, and inspection workers to the area to make arrests and board up drug houses. *Photo credit: AP photo/Dan Loh.*

formal policy in many jurisdictions. Twenty years ago, Walker (1985:117) observed, "Career-criminal programs are the hottest fad in criminal justice these days." A brief review of the programs that flowed from these policies serves to illustrate the point and identify priorities in the justice system. Policies and programs directed at the control of serious offenses and offenders exist in law enforcement, courts, and corrections.

Law Enforcement Programs

There are several types of police activities aimed at the control of serious crime and criminals. In one, the police focus attention on identified serious offenders and carefully watch them for evidence of criminal conduct. In another, the police identify high-risk areas where serious crimes appear likely to occur, and devote increased patrol to those areas. In yet another, the police identify likely victims and intervene to reduce the chances of crime by changing victim behavior or characteristics. In each case, a decision is made that the best investment of police resources involves targeting specific individuals or locations. Often police departments have responded to "crime waves" by increasing police presence in a given area (Sherman, 1990).

Several police departments started programs that identified specific individuals as "repeat offenders." In California, scores of police agencies developed "repeat offender programs." Kansas City, Missouri, experimented with what was called "perpetrator-oriented patrol." Minneapolis, Minnesota, instituted a "Target 8" program in which eight suspects were identified as career criminals and all officers were expected to be alert for these suspects. (Walker, 1985). The police in Washington, DC, perhaps attracted the most attention with a program called the "Repeat Offender Project" (ROP, pronounced "rope"), described in Box 3.3. This program assigned a special unit of more than 60 officers to focus attention on persons thought to be committing at least five major offenses each week. A team of officers was given 48 hours to make an arrest. If, after that time, there was no arrest, the team was reassigned to another suspected repeat offender (Walker, 1985). More recently, "Operation Cease Fire" in Boston sought to reduce youth violence by targeting gang leaders for special enforcement (Kennedy, 1998). A search of the Internet for mentions of "repeat offender," "career criminal," or "habitual offender" will turn up scores of law enforcement agency web sites describing police units and programs aimed at dangerous offenders.

Box 3.3   Career Criminals and the Police

The jury is still out on the effectiveness of the Washington, DC. Repeat Offenders Project (ROP). But the new program has attracted the attention of other metropolitan police departments who eagerly await the results of a study on the program by the Police Foundation, under a $100,000 grant from the U.S. Justice Department's National Institute of Justice.

It was the boss' idea. Captain Edward J. (Caesar) Spurlock, 49, blond-haired and thick-necked with a deep, toothy laugh, remembers that during his years in uniform, "I knew the names of a small number of crooks who were all the time hittin' us, constantly committin' crimes, constantly comin' in to my station. It became obvious to me that if you could knock out those guys, you could make an impact on crime and make maximum use of your resources."

. . . Often the ROP officers arrest felons on relatively minor charges, a practice that cops in other parts of the city and prosecutors in the U.S. attorney's office say isn't cost-effective.

The ROP officers vehemently disagree. To them, if a few days of waiting and watching for a bigger crime doesn't materialize, it's better to take the smaller offense and move on to another target. If that results in a light sentence, as often happens, that's not the end of it.

"We're not too concerned with what they do in court . . . All we know is that if they let him out again, we'll target him again."

Source: A. Epstein (1983), "On the Hunt for Career Criminals," *National Centurion Magazine* 1(6):23-24, 26.

In each of these programs, police administrators decided to devote resources to the control of specific crimes and criminals—or to the control of crime in areas where there was reason to believe that serious crime was most likely to occur. At the same time, regular police patrol and response to calls for service in the jurisdiction continued. In the departments mentioned, and in others with similar programs, police administrators have at least tacitly decided that some crimes or criminals are more deserving of police attention than others.

Court Programs

The repeat or career criminal is the subject of special treatment in at least two points of the court process: prosecution and sentencing. The goal of these special procedures is to ensure the conviction and punishment of offenders posing the greatest threat of future criminality.

Today, many trial jurisdictions have "career-criminal programs." In these programs, the prosecutor's office develops criteria to select cases involving repeat or career criminals. These cases become a priority in the system. Officials try to secure convictions in these cases even when, under normal circumstances, the case might have been dropped. Brosi (1979) explained the justification for these programs:

> Given the disproportionately large share of crime committed by repeat offenders, prosecutors seem justified in structuring their discretion so that an appropriate percentage of time and staff is focused on recidivists, even though this might mean that other cases with as much or more evidence and involving less frequent offenders would have to be rejected or pursued with less than normal intensity.

The organization of career criminal prosecution programs differs by jurisdiction. The theory behind the use of these programs is the same as that underlying the law enforcement programs described earlier. If identifiable individuals exist who will be continuing targets of prosecution, it is a wise investment of resources to devote attention to them in the present (INSLAW, 1977:8). That is, it makes sense to devote crime control resources to those cases in which the greatest payoff in crime control can be expected. Several jurisdictions in Florida have developed "repeat offender courts" in which the focus on repeat offenders means the court has a smaller caseload and is better able to ensure tough punishment (Florida Corrections Commission, 2007).

Brosi (1979) described career criminal prosecution programs operating in the United States 30 years ago. In large, busy jurisdictions it is common for prosecutors to be assigned to specific decision points such as initial appearance, preliminary hearing, arraignment, and so on. For career criminal prosecution programs, all but the District of Columbia used a procedure called **vertical prosecution** that assigned a single prosecutor to each career criminal case. That prosecutor stayed with the case from arrest through final disposition. The District of Columbia program used one prosecutor to stay with the case from arrest through indictment, and then the case became the responsibility of another prosecutor in the trial division. The idea is that the prosecutor will be more familiar with the case and the offender and less likely to accept a plea of guilty to a lesser charge or otherwise treat the offender leniently.

Each program established criteria for selecting cases for treatment in the career criminal program. In the District of Columbia, the program, which was known as "Operation Doorstop," took cases involving those arrested for a crime of violence or a felony while on probation or parole. Those arrested for a crime of violence

Box 3.4	Scoring Criteria for Selection of Career Criminals for Special Attention by Federal Prosecutor

Variable	Points	
Heavy use of alcohol	+ 5	
Heroin use	+10	
Age at time of instant arrest		
Less than 22	+21	
23 - 27	+14	
28 - 32	+ 7	
33 - 37	0	
38 - 42	- 7	
43+	-14	
Length of criminal career		
0-5 years	0	
6-10	1	
11-15	2	
16-20	3	
21+	4	
Arrests during last 5 years		
Crimes of violence	4	per arrest
Crimes against property	3	per arrest
Sale of drugs	4	per arrest
Other offenses	2	per arrest
Longest time served, single term		
1-5 months	4	
6-12	9	
13-24	18	
25-36	27	
37-48	36	
49+	45	
Number probation sentences	1.5	per sentence
Instant offense was crime of violence*	7	
Instant offense was crime labeled "other"**	-18	

Critical Value to Label of Offender
As a Career Criminal:
47 points

*Violent crimes consist mostly of bank robberies, but also include homicide, assault, sexual assault, and kidnapping.

**Other crimes include military violations, probation, parole, weapons and all others except arson, burglary, larceny, auto theft, fraud, forgery, drug sale or possession, and violent crimes.

Source: B. Forst, W. Rhodes, J. Dimm, A. Gelman & B. Mullin (1983), "Targeting Federal Resources on Recidivists: An Empirical View," *Federal Probation* 46(2):18.

who were possibly subject to pretrial detention also received special attention. The Prosecutor's Repeat Offender Bureau (PROB) in Detroit selected cases involving arrests for burglary or violent felonies by those having three prior felony convictions, and arrests of those having a combination of three prior convictions or pending charges. Other jurisdictions developed different methods of choosing cases.

Career criminal prosecution programs in other jurisdictions have used a "point" system for selecting cases. Box 3.4 gives an example of one such scoring system. The Indianapolis program assigned points for previous violent and burglary convictions, any felony convictions or arrests, and pending cases. Milwaukee County employed a similar point system, assigning points for prior convictions, current status on bail, probation or parole, and current charges involving injury or weapons. Other jurisdictions target specific crimes, such as burglary or robbery.

In general, these career criminal prosecution programs have the effect of flagging specified cases for special treatment (Chaiken & Chaiken, 1991). This results in slightly higher rates of conviction and greatly increased rates of incarceration for those identified as career criminals. In most programs, career criminal cases also are disposed of more quickly than cases in the regular caseload. Again, prosecutors decide which cases deserve increased attention and investment of limited prosecutorial resources (Chaiken & Chaiken, 1991).

Increasingly prosecutors' offices have established specialized units devoted to particular crimes as well. It is not uncommon for a prosecutor's office to have a domestic violence unit or a drug unit. Here again, criminal justice agents have decided to focus effort and resources on particular types of crime or criminals. At the national level, the U.S. Department of Justice has implemented Project Safe Neighborhoods, which focuses criminal justice attention on firearms offenders. The program is administered by the U.S. Attorney (federal prosecutor) in each of the 94 U.S. District Courts. The project involves the creation of local task forces comprised of the U.S. Attorney and representatives from federal, state, and local law enforcement; prosecutors; other justice agencies; and other local leaders. The task forces identify gun crime problems and develop strategies to reduce gun crime, often involving federal prosecution of gun law violators (Bureau of Justice Assistance, 2004).

Differential handling of career criminals at sentencing has long been a tradition in America. Most states have had habitual offender or recidivist sentencing statutes for decades. These statutes essentially make it criminal and thereby separately punishable for someone to have prior felony convictions. In many states, upon conviction of a third felony offense, one can be tried as a "habitual offender" and receive an extended prison term, even life imprisonment (Sigler & Culliver, 1990).

Other sentencing programs have been receiving increasing attention and support: selective incapacitation, mandatory sentencing, and "three-strikes" laws. In each, the goal is to control the incidence of either specific crimes, or to lessen (through incarcerating offenders) the opportunity of specific criminals to commit crime in the future.

Selective incapacitation seeks to identify those offenders who are most likely to commit future crimes. This program reserves incarceration for these habitual offenders (Greenwood, 1982). Research showing that the majority of crimes are committed by a minority of offenders supports the idea that imprisoning those few would result in less crime. Selective incapacitation argues that because prison space is a scarce resource, reserving space for the most prolific offenders is a wise investment.

Mandatory sentencing is another strategy to control crime. In practice, mandatory sentencing really means mandatory incarceration. This approach relies on deterrence and does not target specific criminals, focusing instead on specific crimes. The examples discussed earlier dealing with drunk driving and the New York state drug law illustrate the strategy of mandatory sentencing. By "ensuring" that those convicted of specific crimes we believe to be dangerous will be imprisoned, the hope is that the program will deter those who might consider committing the offense.

Finally, following in this tradition, with the passage of the Violent Crime Control and Law Enforcement Act of 1994, offenders convicted of specific felonies for the third time were expected to be imprisoned for life (Saint-Germain & Calamia, 1996). This repeat offender sentencing provision came to be known as "three strikes and you're out." An earlier three-strikes law, with similar goals, was passed in California (Turner et al., 1995). These laws seek to identify serious, repeat criminal offenders and ensure that they are sentenced to long terms of imprisonment. More recently, with federal incentives, states have moved to ensure the imprisonment of those convicted of violent crimes under what is known as "Violent Offender Incarceration/Truth in Sentencing" programs (Ditton & Wilson, 1999).

As with law enforcement and criminal prosecution programs, sentencing programs either target criminals (selective incapacitation) or crimes (mandatory sentencing). In both cases, a decision has been made that resources (e.g., prison) should be targeted to specific cases of criminality.

Corrections Programs

Efforts to identify and provide special services and controls for repeat offenders in correctional settings are traditional. Correctional officials have given increased attention to classification of offenders, and have developed special "intensive supervision" programs for probationers and parolees. These efforts try to focus correctional resources on those offenders most in need of such attention.

Van Voorhis (1986) indicated the importance of classification for the organization and delivery of correctional services. She suggested that the greatest return on the correctional investment would be obtained through matching the available services and programs with the needs of individual offenders. The implications of classification decisions for the effectiveness of correctional treatments is only one incentive for the increasing emphasis on this process (Bonta, 1996; Bonta & Motiuk, 1992).

In an age of prison crowding, classification became important as a check on the efficient use of correctional resources. Clear and Cole (1986:320) noted:

The prison crowding crisis and litigation challenging existing procedures have forced many correctional systems to reexamine their classification procedures. As space becomes a scarcer and more valuable resource, administrators feel pressured to ensure that it is used as efficiently as possible: that levels of custody are appropriate and that inmates are not held in "oversecure" facilities.

The other side of this, of course, is that certain dangerous prisoners should not be held in "undersecure" facilities. Among other things (such as amenability to certain types of treatment or aptitude for certain job assignments), classification also reflects risk of future criminality. A large part of the classification decision in prisons, or within probation or parole caseloads, reflects a desire to identify and control the repeat offender.

A related development in corrections involves the use of "intensive supervision" with probationers and parolees. In these programs, offenders under community supervision are classified by risk and need. Those posing the greatest risk of future crime and those presenting the greatest needs for service are assigned to special "intensive supervision" caseloads. These caseloads are smaller than the average probation or parole caseload, and the supervising officer is expected to make more contacts with his or her clients each month. Thus, the title "intensive supervision" reflects a greater concentration of traditional probation and parole resources on offenders who are selected because this greater investment is expected to produce higher returns in the control of future criminality (Latessa, 1985; Travis, 1984).

With many of the policies and programs being at least 20 years old, all of this discussion of career criminals and the justice system response to them may seem dated, until we realize these programs and others like them continue today. They

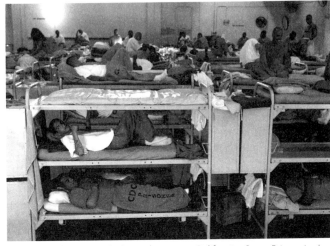

Inmates endure crowded conditions at California State Prison in Los Angeles. In an age of prison crowding, classification has become an important check on the efficient use of prison resources. *Photo credit: AP Photo/California Department of Corrections.*

illustrate how criminal justice resources are devoted to those crimes and criminals defined as most serious, dangerous, or threatening. In the past 20 years, however, the percentage of released prisoners who return to crime has remained relatively unchanged (Langan & Levin, 2002). About one-half of those released from prison in 15 states in 1994 were returned within three years (see Box 3.5). What has changed is the rate and number of persons sentenced to prison. Over the past 20 to 30 years we have increasingly sentenced offenders to prison, leading to what some observers have called a policy of "mass incarceration" (Crutchfield, 2004). This suggests that the ability of the traditional criminal justice system to control or prevent crime is limited.

| **Box 3.5** | New Arrest, Conviction, Return to Prison, and New Prison Sentences of Prisoners Released |

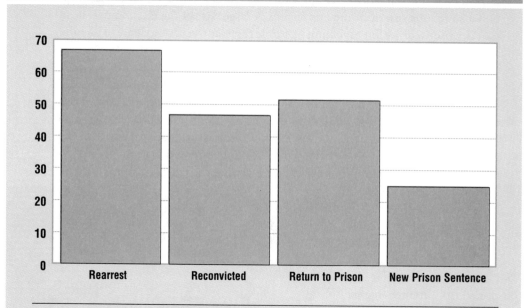

Source: P. Langan & D. Levin (2002), *Recidivism of Prisoners Released in 1994* (Washington, DC: Bureau of Justice Statistics):7.

A New Direction for Crime Control

Research into the causes of crime and the effectiveness of crime prevention practices over the past 30 years has produced some changes in how criminal justice system officials seek to control crime. David Weisburd (1997) has suggested that crime control policy should shift from a focus on the causes of crime to a consideration of the context in which crime occurs. He wrote (1997:1), "This approach, which is often associated with situational crime prevention, looks to develop greater understanding of crime and more effective crime prevention strategies through concern with the physical, organizational, and social environments that make crime possible." That is, crime is more likely under some circumstances than others. Rather than viewing crime as a product of individual offenders and seeking crime prevention through control of those offenders, we should see crime as product of a social context and seek to control crime by changing those contexts.

We have known for decades that crime is more likely to occur in some places than in others, and that some particular crimes are more likely to occur in certain places than in others. What Weisburd and others are suggesting is that we seek to understand the set of factors, or context, in which crimes are likely to occur and move to change the context in order to reduce the incidence of crime. Changes can take many forms. In some cases, changing the physical environment by better lighting, altering traffic patterns, installing locks and bars, removing shrubbery, and the like may reduce the chances of crime. In other cases, increased police patrol or organizing Neighborhood Watch groups can reduce the chances of crime. In still other instances, it may be that we need to identify and control specific high-rate offenders.

A new focus on the context of crime does not ignore offenders, but treats the criminal as only one of several factors that account for crime. The core logic of this argument is that offenders are only part of the crime problem, and focusing crime control efforts on offenders will then control only some of all crime. If the factors that account for crime vary, our crime control efforts should target various factors (Sherman et al., 1997).

There is a noticeable movement today in the direction of addressing the context of crime. Over the past decade there has been increasing emphasis on the role of the community in crime control (Ward, 1997). Returning to our earlier discussion of social control, current strategies of crime control seek to strengthen informal social control by removing obstacles to informal control and strengthening mechanisms of control other than the criminal justice process. Changing traffic patterns by blocking streets, for example, reduces the number of strangers in a neighborhood, thereby making it easier for residents to recognize those who belong in the neighborhood and those who do not belong. Using civil laws to close bars, evict tenants who sell drugs, and similar efforts reduce the chances that crimes will occur. The use of curfews to remove juveniles from the streets in the late night hours also works to reduce the likelihood of crime and misbehavior. Rather than waiting for a fight or robbery to occur and then calling the police, these strategies work to prevent the fight or robbery in the first place.

In support of this more preventive approach to dealing with problems of crime, police and other criminal justice agencies have begun to use sophisticated geographic analyses to identify and respond to specific types of crimes (Harries, 1999; LaVigne & Wartell, 2000). Plotting the location of reported crimes and calls for police service on maps, and combining these with the locations of targets, offenders, and measures of guardianship, police agencies have begun to analyze patterns in crime and identify strategies for preventing future problems.

Scores of programs across the nation have been implemented and assessed. Box 3.6 highlights efforts to deal with the problem of youth violence in Boston (Office of Juvenile Justice and Delinquency Prevention, 1999). This effort involved a wide range of criminal justice and community agencies, evolved over several years, and has been recognized nationally as an exemplary project. Recognizing that homicide was an especially pressing problem among youths, the Boston Police Department organized a Youth Violence Strike Force. Working with the federal Bureau of Alcohol, Tobacco, Firearms, and Explosives, as well as the prosecutor's office (both local and federal) and the probation department, strategies for reducing homicides

Box 3.6 A Coordinated Approach to Youth Violence Boston, MA

Beginning in 1994, the Boston Police Department identified serious violence among youths as a major problem. Over the next several years, a coordinated city-wide strategy emerged that involved a combination of law enforcement and crime prevention programs. Criminal justice, local government, and private social service and commercial organizations combined their efforts to address the problem. Among others, the strategy involved:

Operation Cease Fire—A collaboration between the ATF (the U.S. Bureau of Alcohol, Tobacco, and Firearms), the Boston Police Department, the U.S. Attorney, the local prosecutor, the state probation department, the State Department of Youth Services, clergy, schools, and social service agencies to identify gang members and to warn them that violence would be met with severe sanctions.

Boston Gun Project—A collaboration between the Boston Police, the ATF, the U.S. Attorney, and the local prosecutor to reduce the number of guns available to youths, and to disrupt the illegal gun market.

Operation Night Light—A collaboration between the Boston Police and the probation department to increase surveillance and supervision of youthful offenders on probation through increased unannounced visits to probationers in their homes, schools, and workplaces during nontraditional hours (7 P.M. to midnight).

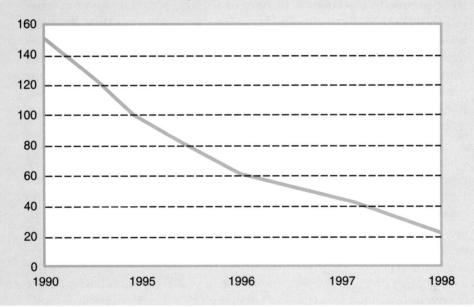

were implemented. The "targets" of these efforts were gun traffickers (including licensed gun dealers) and gang members. Enforcement strategies involved inspections of gun dealers and targeted investigations of gun traffickers. Police officers tried to obtain gun market information from offenders charged with serious non-gun charges. Gang members were identified and warned that violence (especially gun violence) would no longer be tolerated. In cooperation with prosecutors and probation personnel, the police met with gang members and warned that any violence would receive swift, severe consequences. In the end, these efforts seem to have reduced the incidence of homicide, and gang-related homicide in particular. The combined, coordinated efforts of police, courts, and corrections, at local, state, and federal levels, in conjunction with community service agencies, were brought to bear on the problem of juvenile homicides. One of the most remarkable things about the Boston project is not its results, but rather, the coordination of so many different agents and agencies to focus on one specific problem.

Lorraine Mazerolle and Janet Ransley (2005) have described this development in regard to policing. They write about a phenomenon they call "third-party policing" in which the role of the police is increasingly that of convincing or forcing others to exercise social control. Mazerolle and Ransley describe what they call "nodes of regulation" or sources of crime prevention and control that lay outside the justice system, such as landlords, business owners, other governmental agencies, neighbors, and others. In third-party policing the public police work with these outside parties to exert control over offenders or criminal contexts. For example, the police might pressure a landlord to evict a tenant who is selling drugs from his apartment. Alternatively, the police may work with a local merchant to improve lighting and security in the parking lot. Rather than directly intervening, the police mobilize third parties to exert a crime control influence.

A situational or contextual approach to crime prevention holds great promise of reducing the incidence of crime, but it is not without its limits. Recall our discussion of the central conflict between due process and crime control (see Box 3.7). A juvenile curfew may prevent much crime, but it is unlikely that the juveniles af-

Box 3.7 Due Process vs. Crime Control: A Delicate Balance

Individual Liberty vs. Social Order
Costs vs. Benefits
Rights vs. Obligations

fected by the curfew appreciate the limits placed on their freedom. Blocking streets to reduce through traffic may prevent some offenders from entering a neighborhood, but it also inconveniences residents who live in the area (Lasley, 1998). The current effort to go beyond traditional criminal justice practices to achieve greater crime control poses the threat of expanding crime control at the cost to individual liberty or due process.

A final product of this broader view of crime control is the integration of criminal justice and community services. It is now common for inter-agency task forces to work toward the solution of crime problems. The Boston gun project is only one example. Across the country police, court, and correctional agencies are joining together in efforts to address crime and criminal justice problems (Sigmon et al., 1999). Similar efforts include partnerships between criminal justice agencies and other governmental and community offices and groups not directly parts of the criminal justice system.

Crime Control in General

This chapter began with a definition of crime and an explanation of the elements of criminal offenses. It then moved to a discussion of criminals and criminal types. Throughout these topics, it was suggested that the variety of behaviors and individuals included in the concepts of "crime" and "criminal," respectively, are exceedingly diverse. The justice system must respond to a large number of widely divergent instances and individuals.

To organize our perspective of this otherwise cumbersome task, the use of classes of crime or classes of offenders to allocate justice system resources was discussed. Descriptions of current efforts of police, court, and correctional agencies to focus attention and resources on the most serious crimes and criminals were provided. Given the broad crime-control mandate of the criminal justice system, priorities must be established.

In practice, agents and agencies of criminal justice will respond to more serious crimes and more dangerous offenders before the less serious incidents. For the most part, felonies and repeat offenders are more likely to attract the attention of the justice system and to receive full-scale justice processing than are misdemeanants and first offenders.

A redefinition of crime control that encompasses a broader range of social issues covering the context of crime promises to improve crime prevention, but raises concerns about individual liberty. The task of the criminal justice system and criminal justice policymakers is to achieve a balance between crime control needs and due process requirements. Dean Spader (1994) has suggested that this balance involves weighing costs and benefits and competing values. The central questions that emerge in the conflict between due process and crime control in the American criminal justice system reflect these issues. Under what circumstances does the value of social control outweigh the value of individual liberty? How preventive should the agents and agencies of criminal justice be in their approach to crime control? How should we decide (and who should decide) which crimes and criminals deserve criminal justice attention? How much of our limited criminal justice resources should be devoted to "noncriminal" prevention activities versus detecting and apprehending criminals? We will return to these topics in later chapters.

Review Questions

1. Define "crime."

2. What are the elements of a criminal offense?

3. Identify at least two ways in which crimes can be classified according to the level of their seriousness.

4. Define what is meant by the term "career criminal."

5. Give an example of career criminal programs in each segment of the criminal justice system (law enforcement, courts, and corrections).

6. What is the situational approach to crime control/prevention, and how does it differ from traditional approaches?

7. What key issues emerge when agents of the justice system choose crimes and criminals on which to focus attention?

References

Allen, F.A. (1964). *The Borderland of Criminal Justice*. Chicago: University of Chicago Press.

American Friends Service Committee (1971). *Struggle for Justice*. New York: Hill & Wang.

Bonta, J. (1996). "Risk-Needs Assessment and Treatment." In A. Harland (ed.), *Choosing Correctional Options That Work*. Thousand Oaks, CA: Sage, 18-32.

Bonta, J. & L. Motiuk (1992). "Inmate Classification." *Journal of Criminal Justice* 20(4):343-352.

Brosi, K.B. (1979). *A Cross-City Comparison of Felony Case Processing*. Washington, DC: Institute for Law and Social Research.

Bureau of Justice Assistance (2004). *Program Brief: Project Safe Neighborhoods: America's Network Against Gun Violence*. Washington, DC: Bureau of Justice Assistance.

Bureau of Justice Statistics (1985). *Special Report: Crime Control and Criminal Records*. Washington, DC: U.S. Department of Justice.

Chaiken, J.M. & M.R. Chaiken (1982). *Varieties of Criminal Behavior*. Santa Monica, CA: RAND.

Chaiken, M.R. & J.M. Chaiken (1991). *Priority Prosecution of High Rate Dangerous Offenders.* Washington, DC: National Institute of Justice.

Clear, T.R. & G.F. Cole (1986). *American Corrections.* Monterey, CA: Brooks/Cole.

Clear, T.R. & K. Gallagher (1985). "Probation and Parole Supervision: A Review of Current Classification Practices." *Crime & Delinquency* 31(3):423-443.

Clinard, M.B., R. Quinney & J. Wildeman (1994). *Criminal Behavior Systems: A Typology,* 3rd ed. Cincinnati: Anderson.

Cohen, L. & M. Felson (1979). "Social Change and Crime Rate Trends: A Routine Activities Approach." *American Sociological Review* 44(August):588-608.

Crutchfield, R. (2004). "Commentary: Mass Incarceration, Editorial Introduction." *Criminology and Public Policy* 3(2):265-266.

Cullen, F.T. (1983). *Rethinking Crime and Deviance Theory: The Emergence of a Structuring Tradition.* Totowa, NJ: Rowman & Allenheld.

Cullen, F.T., B.G. Link & C.W. Polanzi (1982). "The Seriousness of Crime Revisited." *Criminology* 20(1):83-102.

Davis, K.C. (1975). *Police Discretion.* St. Paul, MN: West.

Deane, G., D. Armstrong, & R. Felson (2005). "An Examination of Offense Specialization Using Marginal Logit Models." *Criminology* 43(4):955-988.

Ditton, P. & J. Wilson (1999). *Truth in Sentencing in State Prisons.* Washington, DC: Bureau of Justice Statistics.

Farrington, D. (2003). "Developmental and Life-Course Criminology: Key Theoretical and Empirical Issues—The 2002 Sutherland Award Address." *Criminology* 41(2):221-256.

Felson, M. (1998). *Crime and Everyday Life,* 2nd ed. Thousand Oaks, CA: Pine Forge Press.

Florida Corrections Commission (2007). Found at: http://www.fcc.state.fl.us/fcc/reports/courts/ctrec.html, accessed July 12, 2007.

Forst, B., W. Rhodes, J. Dimm, A. Gelman & B. Mullin (1983). "Targeting Federal Resources on Recidivists: An Empirical View." *Federal Probation* 46(2):18.

Fox, V. (1983). *Correctional Institutions.* Englewood Cliffs, NJ: Prentice Hall.

Gibbons, D.C. (1973). *Society, Crime, and Criminal Careers,* 2nd ed. New York: Prentice Hall.

Gottfredson, M. & D. Gottfredson (1988). *Decision Making in Criminal Justice: Toward the Rational Exercise of Discretion,* 2nd ed. New York: Plenum.

Greenwood, P.W. (1982). *Selective Incapacitation.* Santa Monica, CA: RAND.

Harries, K. (1999). *Crime Mapping: Principle and Practice.* Washington, DC: National Institute of Justice, Crime Mapping Research Center.

Holmes, R. (1989). *Profiling Violent Crimes: An Investigative Tool.* Beverly Hills, CA: Sage.

INSLAW (1977). *Curbing the Repeat Offender: A Strategy for Prosecutors.* Washington, DC: U.S. Department of Justice.

Jogerst, G., J. Daly, M. Brinig & S. Bibas (2005). "The Association Between Statutory Penalties and Domestic Elder Abuse Investigations." *Journal of Crime & Justice* 28(2):51-69.

Kennedy, D. (1998). "Pulling Levers: Getting Deterrence Right." *NIJ Journal* (July):2-13.

Langan, P. & D. Levin (2002). *Recidivism of Prisoners Released in 1994.* Washington, DC: Bureau of Justice Statistics.

Lasley, J. (1998). *"Designing Out" Gang Homicides and Street Assaults.* Washington, DC: National Institute of Justice.

Latessa, E.J. (1985). "Community Supervision: Research, Trends, and Innovations." In L.F. Travis III, M.D. Schwartz & T.R. Clear (eds.), *Corrections: An Issues Approach,* 2nd ed. Cincinnati: Anderson, 159-167.

Laub, J. & R. Sampson (1993). "Turning Points in the Lifecourse: Why Change Matters in the Study of Crime." *Criminology* 31(3):301-326.

LaVigne, N. & J. Wartell (2000). *Crime Mapping: Case Studies,* Volume 2. Washington, DC: The Police Foundation.

Lilly, J.R. & R.A. Ball (1982). "A Critical Analysis of the Changing Concept of Criminal Responsibility." *Criminology* 20(2):169-184.

Luna, E. (2003). "Overextending the Criminal Law." *CATO Police Report* 25(6):1;15-16.

Mazerolle, L. & J. Ransley (2005). *Third Party Policing.* Cambridge, UK: Cambridge University Press.

Miethe, T.D. (1982). "Public Consensus on Crime Seriousness." *Criminology* 20(3-4):515-526.

Moffitt, T. (1997). "Adolescence-limited and Life-course Persistent Offending: A Complementary Pair of Developmental Theories." In T. Thornberry (ed.), *Developmental Theories of Crime and Delinquency.* New Brunswick, NJ: Transaction.

Nagin, D. (2007). "Moving Choice to Center State in Criminological Research and Theory." *Criminology* 45(2):259-272.

National Advisory Commission on Criminal Justice Standards and Goals (1973). *A National Strategy to Reduce Crime.* Washington, DC: U.S. Government Printing Office.

National Institute of Justice (1986). *Research Program Plan: Fiscal Year 1987.* Washington, DC: U.S. Department of Justice.

Nettler, G. (1982). *Explaining Criminals.* Cincinnati: Anderson.

Newman, D.J. (1987). *Introduction to Criminal Justice,* 3rd ed. New York: Random House.

Newman, G.R. & C. Trilling (1975). "Public Perceptions of Criminal Behavior." *Criminal Justice & Behavior* 2(2):217.

Office of Juvenile Justice and Delinquency Prevention (1999). *Promising Strategies to Reduce Gun Violence.* Washington, DC: OJJDP.

Osgood, D. & C. Schreck (2007). "A New Method For Studying the Extent, Stability, and Predictors of Individual Specialization in Violence." *Criminology* 45(2):273-312.

Pease, K. & G. Laycock (1996). *Revictimization: Reducing the Heat on Hot Victims.* Washington, DC: National Institute of Justice.

Saint-Germain, M. & R. Calamia (1996). "Three Strikes and You're In: A Streams and Windows Model of Incremental Policy Change." *Journal of Criminal Justice* 24(1):57-70.

Schwendinger, H. & J. Schwendinger (1975). "Defenders of Order or Guardians of Human Rights?" In I. Taylor, P. Walton & J. Young (eds.), *Critical Criminology.* London: Routledge & Kegan Paul, 113-146.

Sherman, L. (1990). *Police Crackdowns.* Washington, DC: National Institute of Justice.

Sherman, L., D. Gottfredson, D. MacKenzie, J. Eck, P. Reuter & S. Bushway (1997). *Preventing Crime: What Works, What Doesn't, What's Promising?* Washington, DC: National Institute of Justice.

Sigler, R. & C. Culliver (1990). "Effectiveness of the Habitual Offender Act: An Assessment of Criminal Histories." *American Journal of Criminal Justice* 15(1):105-121.

Sigmon, J., M. Nugent, J. Goerdt & S. Wallace (1999). *Key Elements of Successful Adjudication Partnerships.* Washington, DC: National Institute of Justice.

Spader, D. (1994). "Teaching Due Process: A Workable Method of Teaching the Ethical and Legal Aspects." *Journal of Criminal Justice Education* 5(1):81-106.

Thornberry, T. (1997). *Developmental Theories of Crime and Delinquency.* New Brunswick: Transaction.

Tittle, C. (2000). "Theoretical Developments in Criminology." In G. LaFree (ed.), *The Nature of Crime: Continuity and Change.* Washington, DC: National Institute of Justice, Criminology 2000, Volume 1:51-101.

Travis, L.F., III (1984). "Intensive Supervision in Probation and Parole." *Corrections Today* 46(4):36-38.

Turner, M., J. Sundt, B. Applegate & F. Cullen (1995). "'Three Strikes and You're Out' Legislation: A National Assessment." *Federal Probation* 59(3):16-35.

Van Voorhis, P. (1986). "The Promise of Confronting Important Gaps between Knowledge and Applications." Paper presented at The First International Conference on Reaffirming Rehabilitation, Alexandria, VA, June, 1986.

Vito, G. & R. Holmes (1994). *Criminology: Theory, Research and Policy.* Belmont, CA: Wadsworth.

Vogel, B. (1998). "Perceptions of Crime Seriousness in the African American Community: Exploring the Presence of Consensus." *Journal of Criminal Justice* 26(3):227-236.

Walker, S. (1985). *Sense and Nonsense About Crime: A Policy Guide.* Monterey, CA: Brooks/Cole.

Ward, C. (1997). "Community Crime Prevention: Addressing Background and Foreground Causes of Criminal Behavior." *Journal of Criminal Justice* 25(1):1-18.

Warren, M.Q. (1973). "All Things Being Equal . . ." *Criminal Law Bulletin* 9:482.

Weisburd, D. (1997). *Reorienting Crime Prevention Research and Policy: From the Causes of Criminality to the Context of Crime.* Washington, DC: U.S. Department of Justice.

Willis, C., T. Evans & R. LaGrange (1999). "'Down Home' Criminology: The Place of Indigenous Theories of Crime." *Journal of Criminal Justice* 27(3):239-247.

Wilson, M. & R. Ruback (2003). "Hate Crimes in Pennsylvania, 1984-99: Case Characteristics and Police Responses." *Justice Quarterly* 20(2):373-398.

Chapter 4

Counting Crimes and Criminals

Important Terms

cohort studies

Crime Index

crime rate

"dark figure" of crime

defounding

forgetting

"funnel effect"

"hot spots" of crime

National Crime
    Victimization
    Survey (NCVS)

observations

official statistics

self-report studies

telescoping

unfounding

Uniform Crime Reports
    (UCR)

unofficial statistics

victimization data

If the criminal justice system can be likened to a business, it is a business run by individuals who have no clear understanding of the market, the production and distribution process, or customer satisfaction. Not many commercial enterprises could succeed in such a state of ignorance. Yet, the criminal justice system does operate in ignorance.

Lack of knowledge about the types of crimes and criminals is not the only form of ignorance that hinders the criminal justice system in the United States. Not only do we not know very much about the nature of crimes and offenders, we also have difficulty in determining their numbers. For decades, critics have written about the "dark figure" of crime; that is, the unknown amount of crime that occurs.

The "dark figure" represents the portion of crime of which we are ignorant. Like a half-moon where part of the moon is in shadow and we can see only one-half of the lunar surface, current official crime statistics may reveal only one-half (more or less) of the actual amount of crime; the remainder is hidden in the "shadows." It is this crime in the shadows that is the "dark figure."

The Need for Numbers

At first we may be tempted to ask, so what? How important can it be that we do not know how much crime there really is? Even when we cannot see the full moon, we know that it is there. Paradoxically, the problem is that without knowing what is in the shadows, we cannot know the importance of the crimes of which we are ignorant. Old sayings such as "Ignorance is bliss" and "What you don't know can't hurt you" do not always apply. This problem becomes clearer when we examine the uses to which we put criminal statistics.

Nettler (1984) listed four reasons for counting crime:

1. description

2. risk assessment

3. program evaluation

4. explanation

Description is exactly what the term implies: painting an accurate picture of the number and distribution of criminal offenses. Such information is useful for the allocation of resources (Rich, 1995). It is used to determine where to concentrate police patrol and to estimate the number of prosecutors or judges needed. Descriptive measures of crime allow planners to detect changes in crime patterns over time and to adjust criminal justice operations accordingly.

Risk assessment was discussed earlier when we examined the differences between ordinary and dangerous criminals. Accurate data about crime allow us to make estimates about the risks of people becoming offenders, and of people becoming victims of crime. Not knowing how much crime actually occurs makes it impossible to predict how much crime is likely to occur. To the degree that the justice process attempts to reduce criminality, lack of knowledge about the actual level of crime hinders our ability to affect future levels. Knowing what kinds of crimes occur, and where and when they occur, enables criminal justice agents to allocate resources more efficiently (Rich, 1996).

In 1989, Sherman, Gartin, and Buerger coined the term "hot spots" of crime to refer to locations where much more crime can be found than at other places. The notion of a crime hot spot is useful to decisions about where to assign police patrol. Several researchers have reported that focusing police efforts in places that have lots of crime is the most effective use of patrol in terms of crime prevention and control (Weisburd & Eck, 2004). Similarly, if we know a certain location has more crime than others, we can try to avoid that place and reduce our chances of becoming a crime victim. Naturally, the effectiveness of these "strategies" depends on the accuracy of our identification of the "hot spots."

Program evaluation is an effort that often relies on estimates of a program's effect on crime. In the previous chapter, we discussed several programs aimed at controlling career criminals. Evaluations of these programs attempted to compare the program's effects on the criminality of offenders with the effects of "normal" criminal justice processing. Should we continue or expand these programs? We do not know. Assuming a dark figure of crime, there is no way to tell what effect these programs have had on that figure.

Explanation is the most troublesome of all the reasons we need accurate numbers about crime and criminals. Why do some people break the law? Being unaware of many criminal offenses, we can offer only partial explanations. Many people believe that poverty causes crime, and most persons whom we know to have committed crimes can be classified as "poor." However, a problem arises in that we do not know whether those who commit the dark figure of crime offenses are poor or wealthy. If these unknown offenders are not poor, then poverty only offers an explanation for the criminality of those whom we can identify.

The Impact of Ignorance

One result of our ignorance about the nature and extent of crime is an inability to assess or predict the effects of policy changes on levels of crime. Changing our emphasis on enforcing laws against certain crimes also may have unintended and unpredictable effects. The "war on drugs" indicates the problem that the dark figure of crime poses for evaluations of criminal justice policy (see Box 4.1).

Box 4.1 The Dark Figure of Crime

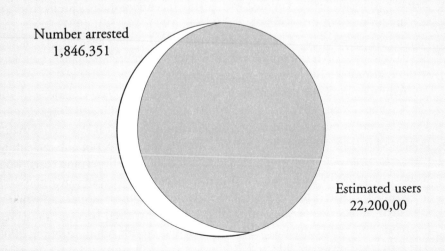

Number arrested
1,846,351

Estimated users
22,200,00

Source: Federal Bureau of Investigation (2006), *Crime in the United States, 2005*; and Substance Abuse and Mental Health Administration (2006). Results of the *2005 National Survey on Drug Use and Health* (see http://www.oas.samhsa.gov/p0000016.htm#2k5).

During the 1980s, beginning with the Reagan administration, the United States declared (or more accurately, redeclared) a war on drugs, and a national antidrug campaign developed (Albanese & Pursley, 1993:265-270). Law enforcement agencies, prosecutors, and criminal courts increased their efforts to catch, convict, and punish drug law violators. Since that time, the number of drug cases and drug offenders has grown as a proportion of the criminal justice system's "business" far more rapidly than other types of offenses and offenders. Arrests, convictions, and prison sentences for drug offenders have increased dramatically, yet we do not appear any closer to winning the "war" than we were almost two decades ago.

One reason we may not be able to see any progress in terms of reducing the number of drug offenses and offenders is that for years many of these crimes have been a part of the dark figure. With increased emphasis on drug crimes, agents and agencies of the justice system have uncovered offenses that have been present for years. Because drug offenses have gone unreported in the past, Zeisel (1982) noted that they present an almost limitless supply of business for the police. Changing public perceptions of the seriousness of drug offenses has supported increased drug enforcement efforts. Given large numbers of casual or "small-time" drug users who had been ignored in the past, vast increases in arrests, convictions, and imprisonment may signal small increases in the proportion of drug offenders caught and processed.

Kraska (1992:524) observed that with drug offenders, police "can seek actively to detect drug crimes, as opposed to violent and property crimes, for which they have little choice but to react to complaints." Thus, the volume of drug offenders entering the justice system is more a product of police activity than is that of violent or property offenders. Political pressure to treat drug offenses more seriously (Hagan, 1989), coupled with giving incentives such as profit from seizing the property of drug offenders (Holden, 1993; Worrall, 2001), spurs more aggressive police action. When applied to offenses that have been largely underenforced, these activities can produce dramatic increases in criminal justice caseloads without affecting basic levels of offense behavior.

Assuming available data are accurate, arrests for drug law violations in 2005 affected about 8 percent of the population reporting use of illegal drugs that year. Doubling the number of arrests for drug violations would still leave more than 80 percent of users untouched. In terms of assessing the impact of doubling enforcement efforts, an evaluator would conclude that doubling efforts (and costs) would reduce the problem by less than 10 percent. Indeed, between 2002 and 2005, the number of arrests for drug offenses increased by almost 17 percent while the estimated number of persons using illegal drugs increased between those years by about 9 percent (Substance Abuse and Mental Health Administration, 2006). The difference between 2002 and 2005 was that of all estimated drug users (persons eligible for arrest), only about 1.5 percent more were arrested (8.3%) in 2005 than in 1994 (6.9%). The number of arrests for drug offenses increased by more than one-quarter million, while the percentage of those arrested among persons estimated to have used drugs during the year increased by only 20 percent. Even doubling the number of drug arrests results in only about 16 percent of those who used drugs being arrested. By 2005, the number of arrests for drug offenses had increased, but changes in arrests do not make much change in the number of persons using drugs (see Box 4.2). For comparison, consider the case of gambling. If we were to declare a war on gambling, how could we know what effect criminal justice efforts were having on the scope of the problem? What commitment of resources would it take to stamp out gambling?

We have long recognized the inadequacies of our data about crimes and criminals. Yet, with repeated calls for improvement in the collection and use of statistics on crime, how is it that we have made so little progress? The answer lies within the complex nature of criminal justice in the United States.

Information is gathered by thousands of agencies in thousands of separate jurisdictions. These agencies often use their own definitions of crimes and criminals, and report their data to national centers on a voluntary basis. To further complicate matters, each agency needs different types of information for its own planning and operation. It is very difficult to follow cases through the justice process, as the police, prosecutor, criminal court, and correctional agencies use their

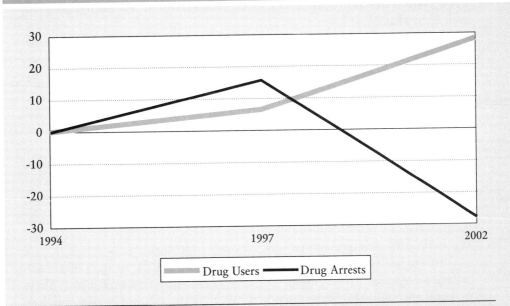

Box 4.2   Percent Changes in Estimated Number of Persons Using Illegal Drugs and Being Arrested for Drug Offenses, 1994-2002

Source: Figure constructed from Federal Bureau of Investigation (2003), *Crime in the United States, 2002* (Washington, DC: U.S. Government Printing Office), and U.S. Department of Health and Human Services (2003), *National Household Survey on Drug Abuse* (Washington, DC: U.S. Department of Health and Human Services).

own forms to collect the information that is useful to them, with little regard to a system-wide need for information.

Much data are available concerning the number of crimes and criminals, justice agencies, and operations of the justice system. However, we do not know exactly how much crime exists and where it occurs. The crime problem is one without clearly marked boundaries. The sources of information about crime and criminal justice are of two basic types: official statistics and unofficial statistics.

Official Statistics

Official statistics are statistics that are provided by criminal justice agencies as official records of their activities. The most familiar of all official crime statistics is the Uniform Crime Reports (UCR), published annually by the Federal Bureau of Investigation (FBI) from reports received by the nation's police departments. These data describe the volume of business handled by the law enforcement agencies of the country. The basic statistic of the UCR is "crimes known to the police."

Only those offenses detected by the police are crimes known to the police. Should someone steal your wallet and you do not report the theft to the police, the crime is not known to the police and is not counted in the UCR. If you report the theft, or a police officer witnesses the crime, then the offense will be "known to the police." In addition, the police officer decides whether a crime has occurred and, if so, what crime it was.

In the example above, suppose you report the theft to a police officer, but the officer decides that you are not telling the truth. The process of unfounding occurs if the officer decides that your criminal complaint is "unfounded"; that is, the officer believes that the crime you reported is not supported by available evidence and, therefore, has reason to believe that no crime occurred. In this instance, the theft will remain "unknown" to the police because the officer considers your report untrustworthy.

A similar decision is defounding a crime for which a police officer decides that an offense was less serious than reported. If the criminal stole your wallet by threatening to harm you with a knife, an armed robbery occurred. If the police officer does not believe that you were actually threatened, he or she may simply record a theft of your wallet. In this instance, a crime is known to the police, but it is a crime less serious than that which actually happened.

An English economist, Sir Josiah Stamp, warned of the dangers of official statistics. He stated: "[t]he government are very keen on amassing statistics. They collect them, raise them to the nth power, take the cube root and prepare wonderful diagrams. But you must never forget that every one of these figures comes in the first instance from the village watchman, who just puts down what he damn pleases" (Platt, 1989).

The Uniform Crime Reports (UCR)

The Uniform Crime Reports covers 29 different crimes, including eight crimes known as the **Crime Index**. The total number of these eight crimes (known to the police) represent the "Index of Crime." This total is used to compare levels of crime over time. The eight Index offenses are: homicide, forcible rape, robbery, aggravated assault, burglary, larceny-theft, auto theft, and arson. Box 4.3 illustrates the Crime Index for 2005.

Participating police agencies voluntarily report data to the FBI. Most (but not all) police departments report to the FBI. The UCR has been published since 1930 (U.S. Department of Justice, 2004), and thus has provided information on the rate and level of crime in the United States for more than 70 years. Nonetheless, criminologists question the value of the UCR on several grounds (Kleinman & Lukoff, 1981; Menard, 1987, 1991).

Many criminologists warn that UCR data must be used cautiously (Maltz, 1999). The data are voluntarily reported and may reflect different definitions of offenses employed by the multitude of police departments participating. Moreover, the UCR excludes many types of crimes (such as white-collar crime) and is open to police manipulation. The data also mask the actual numbers of offenses and offenders through reporting procedures. For example, if a number of crimes are committed during a single criminal episode (say a bank robber kills a teller, kidnaps a hostage, steals a car for the escape, and flees across state lines), only the most serious offense is counted (in this case, the homicide). Gilbert Geis (1986) noted that changes in UCR data may reflect police efficiency more than changes in crime.

Other criticisms have been leveled about the reporting of crimes as the **crime rate** in which the amount of crime is "adjusted" for population size. Using the "crime rate" formula, the number of crimes is reported as a function of population such that:

$$\frac{Crime \times 100,000}{Total\ Population} = Crime\ Rate$$

In this way, the Crime Index treats crimes such as homicide and theft as equal. In addition, until recently, the FBI used the decennial (10-year) census for the population total. As a result, the UCR based the 1969 crime rate on the same population as it did the 1960 rate. This caused an artificial inflation of the crime rate because the actual increase in the population was not reflected in the formula (Eck & Riccio, 1979).

The purpose of the crime rate is to make fairer comparisons between jurisdictions. If we have a city of 100,000 people where 20 murders occurred last year, and a town of 5,000 people where one murder occurred last year, which is safest? The raw numbers indicate that murder is 20 times as likely to occur in the city as in the town. In fact, however, if you reside in either community, your chances of

Box 4.3   Estimated Number and Rate (per 100,000) of Crimes Known to the Police, 2006

By offense and extent of urbanization, 2006

Area	Population[a]	Violent crime					Property crime			
		Total	Murder and non-negligent manslaughter	Forcible rape	Robbery	Aggravated assault	Total	Burglary	Larceny Theft	Motor Vehicle theft
United States, total	299,398,485	1,417,745	17,034	92,455	447,403	860,853	9,983,568	2,183,746	6,607,013	1,192,809
Rate per 100,000 inhabitants	X	473.5	5.7	30.9	149.4	287.5	3,334.5	729.4	2,206.8	398.4
Metropolitan Statistical Area	248,798,842									
Area actually reporting[b]	95.6%	1,202,186	14,572	72,878	403,380	711,356	8,226,522	1,766,498	5,392,106	1,067,918
Estimated totals	100.0%	1,280,264	15,429	77,384	430,003	757,448	8,707,148	1,862,416	5,730,014	1,114,718
Rate per 100,000 inhabitants	X	514.6	6.2	31.1	172.8	304.4	3,499.7	748.6	2,303.1	448.0
Cities outside metropolitan areas	20,027,212									
Area actually reporting[b]	86.3%	67,421	561	6,665	10,770	49,425	669,526	139,065	497,254	33,207
Estimated totals	100.0%	76,594	653	7,720	12,470	55,751	770,898	159,800	573,692	37,406
Rate per 100,000 inhabitants	X	382.4	3.3	38.5	62.3	278.4	3,849.3	797.9	2,864.6	186.8
Nonmetropolitan counties	30,572,430									
Area actually reporting[b]	88.1%	55,924	850	6,483	4,446	44,145	456,828	145,329	274,342	37,157
Estimated totals	100.0%	60,887	952	7,351	4,930	47,654	505,522	161,530	303,307	40,685
Rate per 100,000 inhabitants	X	199.2	3.1	24.0	16.1	155.9	1,653.5	528.4	992.1	133.1

Note: See Note, table 3.106.2006. These figures are aggregated from individual State statistics presented in table 3.108.2006. These data include estimated offense totals for agencies submitting less than 12 months of offense reports (Source, Table 2). Complete data for 2006 were not available for Illinois; crime counts for Illinois were estimated by the Source. For definitions of offenses and areas, see Appendix 3.

a Populations are U.S. Census Bureau provisional estimates as of July 1, 2006, and are subject to change.
b The percentage representing "area actually reporting" is based on the population covered by law enforcement agencies providing 3 or more months of crime reports to the FBI.

Source: A. Pastore & K. Maguire (eds.) (2008), *Sourcebook of Criminal Justice Statistics* [online]. Found at: http://www.albany.edu/sourcebook/pdf/t31072006.pdf (accessed February 8, 2008).

being a homicide victim are equal. The city has a homicide rate of 20 per 100,000 population. The town has a homicide rate of 1 per 5,000 (or 20 per 100,000), which is equal to the homicide rate in the city, because the city is 20 times larger than the town in population. James Nolan (2004) has shown that the level of crime increases with city size so that larger cities have higher crime rates than smaller cities. This means using the crime rate to make comparisons between different-sized cities more fair is only partly successful.

Despite the problems with UCR data, the UCR is still considered an important indicator of the nature and extent of crime in the nation (Hindelang, 1974; Lab & Allen, 1984). Rosenfeld and Decker (1999) tested the accuracy of official arrest reports as a measure of substance abuse. In comparison to public health and drug test data, they found that the arrest data were quite similar to other measures for drugs like heroin and cocaine, but that the various measures differed for marijuana. The UCR also includes data on the characteristics of persons arrested for crimes and on the numbers of police officers killed and assaulted in the line of duty. As long as the user is aware of the limitations of the UCR and is cautious in its interpretation, it is an important source of information. In some ways, the UCR represents the internal marketing data of the criminal justice system. A company that keeps track of its customers may be unable to describe the entire potential market, but it can describe its clients.

Improving the UCR

In late 1982, a task force composed of representatives of the U.S. Bureau of Justice Statistics and the Federal Bureau of Investigation began to study ways of improving the Uniform Crime Reports (Bureau of Justice Statistics & Federal Bureau of Investigation, 1985). While this revision of the crime reporting program has had broad support, the task is not yet completed. The new reporting system is called the National Incident Based Reporting System (NIBRS). In comparison to the traditional UCR, the NIBRS will gather much more detailed information about crimes known to the police.

The NIBRS format asks police to record information for each incident of crime, as opposed to recording information about only the most serious crime. Instead of eight Index offenses, the NIBRS has 22 Group A offense categories and 11 Group B offenses. Some crime definitions have also been changed. For example, the UCR defines rape as a crime by a male against a female, while NIBRS uses a sexually neutral definition. Finally, for each incident included in NIBRS, information is recorded in six segments representing data about the case (administrative), crime (offense), property, victim, offender, and arrestee. The result is a much richer and more detailed set of information about crimes known to the police.

This information enables analysts to study relationships among offenders and victims, characteristics of places and times when offenses occur, and other topics (Reaves, 1993). The new reporting format, however, results in higher

Police officers are required to complete reports whenever they make an arrest. This information is funneled into UCR and NIBRS reporting systems, upon which much criminal justice research is based. *Photo credit: Mark C. Ide.*

numbers of crimes reported as known to police. Not all law enforcement agencies participating in the Uniform Crime Reports are using the NIBRS reporting format yet. It is likely to be some time before the new reporting format will achieve widespread use. After more than 10 years, many law enforcement agencies still do not report with the NIBRS format. In the long run, the changes brought by NIBRS will go a long way toward fixing most of the problems identified with the UCR.

Other Official Statistics

Other criminal justice and governmental agencies also collect and publish data that are relevant to measuring crime and criminals in the United States. Increasingly over the past three decades, the U.S. Bureau of Justice Statistics has gathered and published information about the operations of criminal justice agencies by surveying law enforcement, court, and correctional organizations. Periodic censuses of the nation's jails also are conducted and reported, as are data on case filings in the courts of the United States. Still more official data are available regarding the numbers and distribution of juvenile offenders, operations of pretrial release programs, and other aspects of justice processing. Some of the more common and more important sources of official information about criminal justice operations in the United States include the Law Enforcement Management and Administrative Statistics, National Pretrial Reporting, National Judicial Reporting, and National Corrections Reporting programs. These programs are administered by the Bureau of Justice Statistics (http://www.ojp.usdoj.gov/bjs).

Unofficial Statistics

Recognizing that official statistics tell only part of the story of crime in the United States, criminologists have developed other ways of estimating how much crime occurs and who commits criminal offenses. Unofficial statistics are those measures of the rate and nature of crime that do not rely upon the reporting of official agencies and agents of criminal justice. Two basic sources of crime data (collected without relying upon the official reports of justice agencies) are victim surveys and self-reports. These data reveal that official statistics cover only about half of all crime. They also show that persons arrested for criminal offenses are not representative of all those who commit crimes. To avoid the problems and limitations of official statistics, particularly the UCR, researchers developed these other methods of counting crimes and criminals (Salas & Surette, 1984). Each gives a slightly different view of the overall crime picture and thus serves as an aid to understanding the true nature and extent of crime in the United States.

Victim Surveys

In 1965, the National Opinion Research Center (NORC) of the University of Chicago conducted the first survey of crime victims. The researchers used the results to estimate the nature and extent of crime. The President's Commission on Law Enforcement and Administration of Justice instructed the NORC to conduct a survey of 10,000 households (President's Commission, 1967:96). The survey results indicated that crimes known to the police were only a fraction of all crimes committed.

The NORC survey contacted a spokesperson for each household surveyed and asked if that person, or anyone else residing in the household, had been the victim of certain crimes in the past year. Respondents were also asked whether the crime had been reported to the police and, if not, why it had not been reported. Since the original 1965 survey, similar data have been collected annually by the U.S. Bureau of the Census through the National Crime Victimization Survey (NCVS).

Results of the survey over the years continue to indicate that the UCR data are incomplete. Respondents to victim surveys report that many crimes, especially less serious property crimes and violent crimes among friends and acquaintances, remain unreported to the police. Box 4.4 compares the victim surveys of the NCVS with the UCR. Victimization data provide information about the nature and extent of crime as it is perceived by those reporting that they have been crime victims.

The National Crime Victimization Survey asks about the number of times that members of the responding household have been the victims of assault, personal larceny, robbery, and forcible rape. It also counts automobile theft, burglary, and household larceny as crimes against households. The data are not directly comparable to the UCR. Nonetheless, the wide gap between the number of victimizations reported in the surveys and the number of crimes reported in the UCR indicates that much more crime occurs than is brought to the attention of the justice system. However, victim survey reports reveal that the types of crimes and their relative numbers are accurately portrayed in the UCR (Booth, Johnson & Choldin, 1977; Cohen & Lichbach, 1982; Hindelang, 1978; O'Brien, 1990). Box 4.5 shows a sample NCVS Incident Report.

While victim surveys and the UCR differ over the absolute number of crimes committed, their respective findings are similar in other regards. Both show similar relative proportions of crime that consist of burglaries or robberies, and both have sim-

Box 4.4 Comparison of the NCVS and the UCR

The National Crime Victimization Survey (NCVS)

Using stable data collection methods since 1973, the NCVS has the following strengths:

- It measures both reported and unreported crimes.

- It is not affected by changes in the extent to which people report crime to police or improvements in police record-keeping technology.

- It collects information that is not available when the initial police report is made including contacts the victim has with criminal justice system after the crime, extent and costs of medical treatment, and recovery of property.

- It collects detailed information about victims and characteristics of the victimization including who the victims are, what their relationship is to the offender, whether the crime was a part of a series of crimes occurring over a 6-month period, what self-protective measures were used and how the victims assess their effectiveness, and what the victim was doing when victimized.

- On occasion, it includes special supplements about particular topics such as school crime and the severity of crime.

The Uniform Crime Reports (UCR)

The UCR program measures police workload and activity. Local police departments voluntarily report information to the Federal Bureau of Investigation (FBI) including the numbers of crimes reported to police, arrests made by police and other administrative information. The UCR program has the following strengths:

- It can provide local data about states, counties, cities and towns.

- It measures crimes affecting children under age 12, a segment of the population that experts agree cannot be reliably interviewed by the NCVS.

- It includes crimes against commercial establishments.

- It collects information about the number of arrests and who was arrested.

- It counts the number of homicides (murders and nonnegligent manslaughters), crimes that cannot be counted in a survey that interviews victims. UCR also collects detailed information about the circumstances surrounding homicides and the characteristics of homicide victims.

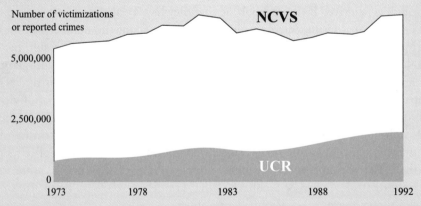

Violent Crimes measured by NCVS and UCR*

*Includes NCVS violent crimes of rape, robbery, aggravated assault, and simple assault; and UCR violent crimes of murder and nonnegligent manslaughter, forcible rape, robbery, and aggravated assault.

Source: Bureau of Justice Statistics (1994), *Criminal Victimization in the United States, 1992* (Washington, DC: U.S. Department of Justice):9.

Box 4.5 Sample NCVS Incident Report

NOTICE — Your report to the Census Bureau is **confidential** by law (U.S. Code 42, Sections 3789g and 3735). All identifiable information will be used only by persons engaged in and for the purposes of the survey, and may not be disclosed or released to others for any purpose.

Sample	Control number				HH No.
J ____	PSU	Segment	CK	Serial	

FORM **NCVS-2(X)**
(10-13-92)

U.S. DEPARTMENT OF COMMERCE
BUREAU OF THE CENSUS

ACTING AS COLLECTING AGENT FOR THE
BUREAU OF JUSTICE STATISTICS
U.S. DEPARTMENT OF JUSTICE

CRIME INCIDENT REPORT
REDESIGN PHASE III
NATIONAL CRIME VICTIMIZATION SURVEY

Notes

PGM 6

1a. LINE NUMBER OF RESPONDENT ⟶ | 601 | _____ Line number

1b. SCREEN QUESTION NUMBER ⟶ | 602 | _____ Screen question number

1c. INCIDENT NUMBER ⟶ | 603 | _____ Incident number

CHECK ITEM A   See item 33a on the NCVS-1(X). Has the respondent lived at this address for more than 6 months? *(If not sure, ask.)*

☐ Yes (more than 6 months) – **SKIP** to 3
☐ No (6 months or less) – *Ask 2*

---

2. **You said that during the last 6 months —**
(Refer to appropriate screen question for description of crime.) **Did (this/the first) incident happen while you were living here or before you moved to this address?**

| 605 | 1 ☐ While living at this address
2 ☐ Before moving to this address

---

3. **(You said that during the last 6 months —**
Refer to appropriate screen question for description of crime.) **In what month did (this/the first) incident happen?** *(Show calendar if necessary. Encourage respondent to give exact month.)*

| 606 | ☐☐ ☐☐
Month   Year

---

4. *If known, mark without asking. If not sure, ASK —*
Altogether, how many times did this type of incident happen during the last 6 months?

| 607 | _____ Number of Incidents

CHECK ITEM B   Refer to 4.
How many incidents?

| 608 | 1 ☐ 1–5 incidents (not a "series") — **SKIP** to 5b
2 ☐ 6 or more incidents — *Fill Check Item C*

Box 4.5 *(continued)*

CHECK ITEM C	Are these incidents similar to each other in detail, or are they for different types of crimes? *(If not sure, ask.)*	609	1 ☐ Similar — *Fill Check Item D* 2 ☐ Different (not a "series") — **SKIP** *to 5b*
CHECK ITEM D	Can you (respondent) recall enough details of each incident to distinguish them from each other? *(If not sure, ask.)*	610	1 ☐ Yes (not a "series") — **SKIP** *to 5b* 2 ☐ No (is a "series") — *Reduce entry in screen question if necessary — Ask 5a*

5a. The following questions refer only to the most recent incident.

5b. Was it daylight or dark outside when (this/the most recent) incident happened?

| 611 | 1 ☐ Light — *Ask 6*
2 ☐ Dark — *Ask 6*
3 ☐ Dawn, almost light, dusk, twilight — *Ask 6*
4 ☐ Don't know — **SKIP** *to 7* |

6. About what time did (this/the most recent) incident happen?

During day

| 612 | 1 ☐ After 6 a.m. — 12 noon
2 ☐ After 12 noon — 6 p.m.
3 ☐ Don't know what time of day |

At night

4 ☐ After 6 p.m. — 12 midnight
5 ☐ After 12 midnight — 6 a.m.
6 ☐ Don't know what time of night

Or

7 ☐ Don't know whether day or night

ilar findings as to the location of crimes (urban areas, lower classes, etc.). Thus, UCR data may underestimate the amount of crime, but may accurately reflect the types of crimes committed, and where and when criminal offenses are likely to occur.

In addition to the National Crime Victimization Survey, researchers have adopted the victim survey to measure the level and extent of crime for other purposes. While the NCVS allows us to compare national victim survey results with the UCR, the technique of surveying crime victims is useful for any measure of changes in crime. In addition to official police reports, researchers have conducted victim surveys in evaluations of several programs. The victim survey has become an important tool in studying crime (Cantor & Lynch, 2000).

Victim surveys also have their limitations (O'Brien, 1986). It has been suggested that the victim survey's major problems may revolve around the phenomena known as "telescoping" and "forgetting." The interviewer asks the respondent if anyone in the household has been the victim of a particular crime in the past six months. In telescoping, the respondent errs by including an offense that may have occurred seven months earlier, thereby "telescoping" it into the covered time period. Forgetting occurs when the respondent forgets about a crime that did occur in the period under study (Schneider & Sumi, 1981). Moreover, it is always possible when interviewing a person that (for whatever reason) the person is not telling the truth in answering the questions.

Another limitation on victim surveys is that many crimes may have gone unnoticed by—or unreported to—the respondent. The NCVS interviewer relies on one individual to have knowledge of the criminal victimizations experienced by the entire household. Finally, certain offenses are not covered in the victim surveys (Cantor & Lynch, 2000). For example, the National Crime Victimization Survey asks about only a small number of offenses, and it is not possible to gather data about homicide, for example, from the victims of the crime. In recent years the increasing cost of collecting data has meant that the size of the victimization sample has been reduced. The combination of a smaller sample size and crime rates at their lowest levels in decades during the recent past means that it is difficult to detect significant changes in rates of victimization from year to year (Catalano, 2006).

Improving the National Crime Victimization Survey

In 1992, responding to many of the problems identified with the National Crime Victimization Survey, the Bureau of Justice Statistics changed the interview used to gather victimization information. Among other changes, the survey now interviews all persons age 12 or older residing in households included in the sample. Some offense classifications have been changed so that thefts, for example, are now all classified as household victimizations. Interviewers now specifically ask respondents about their experiences as victims of rape or sexual assault, and the interview gathers more detailed information about victimization and some offenses such as assault (Bureau of Justice Statistics, 1996). The changes in the interview were phased into use over several years, with the final form of the new survey implemented between 1992 and 1993. The results of the changes in interview format and content included finding much higher rates of victimization. The greatest changes occurred in estimates of rape and assault (Rand, Lynch & Cantor, 1997). In 2003, changes in federal regulations allowed survey participants to choose more than one racial category, making it difficult to compare recent victims with past victims in terms of race.

Self-Reports

Both the UCR and victim surveys attempt to describe criminal offenders. The FBI reports the characteristics of persons arrested for crimes, and thereby provides descriptions of those persons who have been officially recognized as probably having committed crimes. The respondents to victim surveys are asked to describe the offenders involved, if possible. These data provide a description of criminal offenders as seen by the victims of crime. Both efforts at describing criminal offenders are severely limited. Moreover, although there is a fair degree of agreement between victim surveys and UCR data, it is possible that neither measure accurately reflects all crime. Thus, a third method of counting crimes has been employed: surveys of criminal offenders.

Self-report studies attempt to measure the amount of crime committed and describe the characteristics of criminal offenders by asking people if they have committed offenses. In these studies, researchers ask a sample of the public if they have committed any crimes (Thornberry & Krohn, 2000). This crime measure yields information on the types of persons likely to commit crimes as well as another estimate of the amount of crime that is committed each year.

Traditionally, self-report studies have been conducted with juvenile populations. As such, the studies frequently include questions about behaviors that would not necessarily be crimes if committed by adults. For example, disobeying teachers or parents and skipping classes are "delinquent" acts for those with the status of juvenile, but such acts are not crimes for adults. Such "status offenses" included in self-report surveys cloud the issue of how much crime is committed and by whom (Hood & Sparks, 1970).

These studies also have other limitations. They share the problems of telescoping and forgetting that afflict victim surveys, and it is difficult to determine whether respondents are telling the truth. There is reason to believe that some may exaggerate to make themselves appear to be notorious and that some will be reticent, fearing that disclosure of their criminality will lead to punishment. When researchers have compared reported crimes and arrests with official records, however, respondents were generally found to be telling the truth (Cantner, 1982; Lab & Allen, 1984; but also see Nettler, 1984).

In a test of the validity of self-reported drug use, McElrath, Dunham, and Cromwell (1995) found that most of the arrestees they interviewed truthfully reported their drug abuse behavior. However, they also reported that rates of truthful responses varied across jurisdictions and types of people interviewed. African-American arrestees were less truthful in reporting cocaine use than were whites, while no differences were found between rates of valid reports among opiate abusers. Truthful reporting was higher in some places than others; it depended on the characteristics of the interviewer and was related to the type of charge for which the offender had been arrested. McElrath, Dunham, and Cromwell (1995:538) concluded, "The major finding of this study is that many factors affect reporting and that these factors differ by site."

Nonetheless, self-report studies indicate that almost everyone will admit to having violated some criminal law. The most important finding of self-report studies is not who does or does not break the law, but rather how often crimes are committed and how serious are those violations. Institutionalized populations of delinquents or adult criminals report more frequent and more serious law violations than do "free citizens." Males report more criminal activity than females; African Americans report more frequent and more serious offenses than whites. In general, with the exception that self-reports indicate that everyone probably breaks some law, the findings of these studies echo those of victim surveys and official reports.

Other Measures of Crime and Criminal Justice

Researchers have used several other methods to measure crime and study the criminal justice process. Information gathered from cohort studies and observations helps to better describe and explain the operations of the criminal justice process and the nature and extent of crime.

Cohort studies begin with an identifiable group (or "cohort") and trace the group's interaction with the justice system over a period of time. The individuals studied in such research are members of a cohort. The cohort is a collection of all persons sharing a common selection characteristic. Thus, a cohort might include all entering freshmen at a university or all persons married in a given year. For criminal justice research, the selection criterion normally relates to a justice system decision (such as all those arrested in a given time period) or to an age limit (such as all those born in a specified year).

The most famous cohort study selected cases by specifying all males born in Philadelphia in the year 1948. *Delinquency in a Birth Cohort* (Wolfgang, Figlio & Sellin, 1978) was the report of a study designed to examine the criminal careers of youths. All males born in 1948 were tracked for a 20-year period to determine which of them were arrested, tried, and sentenced for delinquent behavior. Additionally, the distribution of delinquent offenses among the cohort was studied, as were characteristics of individuals most often involved in delinquent behavior.

This study allowed the researchers to estimate the proportion of youths that would become entangled in the juvenile justice process, how serious the youths' misbehavior would be, and who among them were most likely to be delinquent. Marvin Wolfgang has been involved in at least three cohort studies of delinquency (Navares, Wolfgang, & Tracy, 1990; Tracy, Wolfgang, & Figlio, 1990). Similar cohort analyses of persons arrested for crime could be used to estimate how the justice system processes cases from arrest to final disposition. Such data would be invaluable to an understanding of the justice process. The problem with cohort studies is one of expense. By definition, most cohort studies must be extensive; that is, they involve large numbers of cases followed over a period of several years.

For *Delinquency in a Birth Cohort*, the researchers actually identified their cohort in 1976, and backtracked through official records to estimate the subjects' involvement in juvenile delinquency. A similar study of those born this year could not be completed for 20 years. Despite this limitation, cohort studies allow us to examine the operations of criminal justice agencies in a broader context than is normally possible. Cohort studies provide an estimate of the distribution of crime across an entire population over time.

Observations, as the term implies, involve researchers watching the behavior of criminals, agents of the justice system, or other samples of people. The American Bar Foundation series, mentioned in Chapter 1, which reported observations of police, prosecutors, judges, and correctional personnel at the investigation, arrest, conviction, and sentencing decisions, is one example of an observation study. Other observation studies have been conducted that seek to determine when people break the law, when they report lawbreaking, what factors justice system agents consider in their decisionmaking, and how cases move from one stage of the justice process to the next.

Like cohort studies, observational methods are fairly expensive to use and, thus, often result in limited data confined to one location, or in a few decisions rather than national, system-wide descriptions. As mentioned earlier, there has been increased interest in and use of geographic data in the analysis of crime (Anselin et al., 2000). These data provide a different perspective from which to view crime and criminal justice, giving us a better feel for the reasons behind decisions and behaviors.

Summary of Crime Statistics

While each of these methods of counting crimes and criminals uses different means of gathering data and collects information from different sources, in total, the "picture" each gives us of crime is generally consistent (Nettler, 1984:98-156). Absolute numbers may vary (for instance, victim surveys may show much more crime than police reports), but the relative frequency of crimes (e.g., more thefts than robberies, more robberies than assaults, more assaults than rapes) reported by all three procedures is similar.

Where these three research methods differ is in the picture they paint of offenders. In a comparison of self-report, victim survey, and arrest data, Hindelang (1978) noted that self-report studies show little difference between race and offense behavior, while the other two measures are in general agreement that African Americans are more likely to be offenders. Self-report studies also show little difference between social classes in the likelihood of engaging in crime. Both upper- and lower-class respondents admit to committing criminal offenses. However, lower-class youths are more likely to commit crimes more frequently, and to commit more serious crimes than middle- or upper-class youths (Williams & Gold, 1972).

One point that is apparent (assuming that victim and self-report measures are accurate) is that persons arrested, and therefore subjected to justice system processing, are not representative of the general population (O'Brien, 1985). Poor, urban dwellers and minority group members are far more likely to be arrested and processed than their numbers in the population suggest. In addition, females are less likely to become involved in the justice process than their numbers in the population would indicate (Wolfe, Cullen & Cullen, 1984). One exception here is the juvenile justice system, where girls are often subjected to more justice processing than boys (Kempf-Leonard & Sample, 2000).

One of the questions raised in response to these findings concerns the fairness of the justice process. If nearly everyone admits to committing some crimes, why is it that minorities and the poor are most often arrested, convicted, and incarcerated? Why are women less likely to be arrested and convicted for crimes than are men? Is the justice system racist, sexist, and prejudiced against the poor? In short, the evidence of differential treatment of certain classes of the population has led some observers to suggest that the justice system is discriminatory.

Discrimination in the Justice System

The data suggest that the justice process appears to identify and select certain offenders for processing in a manner that reflects their relative involvement in crime. Yet some have argued that the justice process is discriminatory and repressive because it differentially selects and processes members of disadvantaged groups, such as youth, minorities, the poor, and urban residents (Petersilia, 1983). Others suggest that the justice system is sexist because it does not subject females to equal treatment as offenders (Visher, 1983). On the basis of the data presented in Box 4.6, these criticisms seem well-founded. Yet, there are some other possible explanations.

Box 4.6   Characteristics of Persons Processed in the Criminal Justice System

	Violent Crime Arrest	Property Crime Arrest	Conviction	Percent of Prison Population
Sex:				
Male	82.1%	68.0%	83.0%	90.1%
Female	17.9%	32.0%	17.0%	9.9%
Race:				
White	59.0%	68.8%	60.0%	36.1%
Black	38.8%	28.6%	37.0%	44.7%*
Other	2.2%	2.6%	3.0%	19.2%
Age:				
<18	15.8%	26.0%	7.0%	0.2%
18+	84.2%	74.0%	93.0%	99.8%

*Race/Ethnicity of prison population classifies black and white Hispanics as one category. All Hispanics are included in the "other" category here.

Source: A. Pastore & K. Maguire (2007), *Sourcebook of Criminal Justice Statistics* [online]. Found at: http://www.albany.edu/sourcebook/ (accessed August 8, 2007).

Recall that the justice system exists in an ideological environment that contains our society's values and biases. Differences are more understandable between victim and self-report surveys' conclusions as to who are criminals and who actually is apprehended and processed through the justice system. Females are less likely to engage in most crimes than are males, partly because of socially defined opportunities for women (both criminal and noncriminal). Additionally, the types of offenses for which women are most often apprehended, and in which most women offenders appear to engage, are less serious and less threatening than crimes dominated by males. We are far more likely to fully process robbers, rapists, and assaulters than we are prostitutes, thieves, and drug offenders. Even if they are aware of the relatively large number of female offenders, agents of the justice system are likely to concentrate their resources on the more serious offenses. Until there are greater numbers of female offenders engaged in homicide, rape, and robbery, it is not possible to assess accurately the extent of the sexism and paternalism operating in the justice system. Some observers think that these changes are afoot and that females are becoming more involved in traditional crimes, and taking a more active role in the crimes they commit (Decker et al., 1993; Fagan & Chin, 1991; Maher & Curtis, 1992). In a study of incarcerated female offenders, however, Alarid et al. (1996) reported that fewer than one-half of these women said they were leaders or even equal partners in their crimes. Thus, in this study at least, even among women subjected to full justice system processing, the majority reported that the crime, and their role in it, was not their idea. There is some evidence too, that not only are the crimes committed by females less likely to be reported, those committed by black offenders are more likely to be reported (Mastrofski, Reisig & McCluskey, 2002). If the behaviors of males and minorities are socially defined as more serious, the justice system will be activated more frequently to deal with those offenders.

As for the disparities among those arrested for crime and those who report having committed crimes (or whom victims report having seen commit crimes), the explanation is equally plausible. Research has documented that minority group members are likely to engage in more serious crimes over a longer period of time than are white offenders. Thus, the arrest statistics will reflect the increased probability of being caught, which is a result of the greater frequency of criminal conduct. The concentration of justice system resources on the more serious offenses also produces disproportionate numbers of arrests of minority group members as compared to the numbers of whites arrested. Still, data from observational studies and reviews of arrests, as well as the outcomes of arrest (charges dropped/trial/conviction), indicate that, as Weitzer (1996:312) notes, "... police are involved in at least some discrimination against members of racial and ethnic minorities..." Research into the effect of a driver's race on police decisions to stop motorists indicates that minority drivers are more likely to be stopped than white motorists when police are engaged in law enforcement and order maintenance activities than when the police are focused on traffic enforcement (Warren et al., 2006). There is additional evidence to suggest that cultural differences between white and minority citizens are related to police officer development of suspicion. Johnson (2006) reports that African-American and Hispanic citizens are less likely to maintain eye contact with police officers and were also likely to speak and smile differently than white citizens. These differences in behavior while dealing with police tended to make the officers more suspicious of African-American and Hispanic citizens.

The greater number of youths in arrest statistics reflects the fact that crime tends to be a young person's game. The idleness, good physical condition, and lack of responsibilities that many youths enjoy may create special opportunities for them to commit crime. As one who engages in crime grows older, she or he generally risks longer prison terms as a habitual offender. Giving longer terms to older offenders means they are less likely to have the opportunities to commit the crimes that are available to the young. Finally, in a "Catch-22" fashion, the police actually are more likely to look for crimes among the young precisely because so many of the young have been found to be engaged in crime.

Similar reasoning applies to members of minority groups. Idleness (even if forced by unemployment) allows more time for crime and subjects people to greater police scrutiny. However, the greatest factor appears to be urbanism. Most arrests are of young, urban offenders. Minority groups tend to be concentrated most greatly in the cities of the United States. Simply put, both the police and young, minority males are overrepresented in the cities (Akins, 2003; Swanson, 1981). The justice system statistics reflect the organization, both social and geographical, of our society. Nelson (1992) observed that discriminatory handling of minorities may not be recognizable in statewide statistics, but is visible in county-level analyses. Thus, when minority populations are concentrated in a few urban counties, checks of statewide conviction or incarceration data will not reveal discriminatory patterns. Neighborhood disadvantage, living in poverty in places with few social services, and the presence of little informal social control all lead to greater levels of crime and greater reliance on the justice system. In the United States, African Americans are disproportionately found in the most disadvantaged neighborhoods

A police officer arrests a man for disorderly conduct at a night club. The majority of arrests are of young, urban offenders. *Photo credit: Mark C. Ide.*

(McNulty, 2001; Schaefer, Huebner & Bynum, 2003; Velez, 2001). Pauline Brennan (2006) found that sentences imposed on female misdemeanants in New York City reflected social class and not race. However, because African-American and other minority women were more likely to be from the lower class, they were more likely to receive jail sentences than were white women.

In rural and suburban areas, the population is more dispersed, and there are fewer police officers. It is more difficult for police to observe crimes and respond quickly to reports of crime. In addition, in smaller communities, more informal mechanisms of social control are available. People are less frequently strangers to one another and can, therefore, resolve differences more easily without involving the police. It is more likely that disputes will be defined as "personal" and not demanding of police intervention. In the future, however, differences between rural and urban areas in terms of crime are likely to diminish. As urban sprawl continues, and with the increasing importance of a global economy and improved communications, many of the problems of cities are likely to also affect rural areas (Weisheit & Wells, 1999).

We will return to the question of discrimination in the justice system a little later. For now, it is enough to say that the presence or absence of discrimination in criminal justice processing, the degree to which discrimination exists, and the effects of possible discrimination in the justice system are complex questions. In a review of the discrimination literature, Weitzer (1996) concluded that discrimination appears to exist in the justice system, but not to the degree we might expect.

Understanding the Justice System

Counting the number of crimes and criminals yields an estimate of the volume of "business" conducted by the criminal justice system. Other data are available that lend insight into the complex operations of criminal justice in the United States. The workings of the system are described by statistics that detail the numbers of persons arrested, prosecuted, tried, convicted, sentenced, incarcerated, or placed under community supervision, released, and discharged.

Ideally, data obtained from all of the methods discussed above would be available for answering whatever questions we might have about crime and criminal justice. Unfortunately, such data (at least on a national level) are not always available, and the student of criminal justice is forced to rely upon limited information, or to make inferences from what information can be obtained. Yet another problem is that the periodic revisions of how we collect information, like the development of the NIBRS and revised NCVS, often mean that it is not possible to make direct comparisons of data collected before the changes with data collected after changes.

One fact readily apparent in an overview of these data is that the criminal justice system operates like a giant sieve. It continuously filters the huge volume of crimes and criminals to the relatively small number of offenders who are incarcerated in the nation's prisons. By beginning with crimes known to the police and then using different data sources to track arrests, prosecutions, convictions, and sentences, it is possible (as is illustrated in Box 4.7) to observe this "funnel effect."

The flowchart of the justice system presented in Chapter 1 (Box 1.7) is drawn in scale to the volume of cases involved. It is clear that the starting point, "Crime & Law," is much wider (containing many more cases) than any of the later points. As one reads along the diagram from crime, through police, courts, and correctional processing, to discharge, the volume of cases becomes progressively smaller.

At each successive stage, the less serious offenses and less dangerous offenders are diverted from the justice system. "Weak cases"—those in which the evidence against the offender is less complete or less compelling—are also dropped. Some

Box 4.7 "Funnel Effect" of the Criminal Justice System

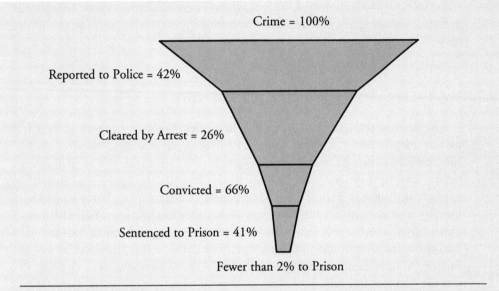

Crime = 100%

Reported to Police = 42%

Cleared by Arrest = 26%

Convicted = 66%

Sentenced to Prison = 41%

Fewer than 2% to Prison

Source: Figure compiled from *Crime in the United States 2005*; *Criminal Victimization 2005*; *Felony Defendants in Large Urban Counties, 2002*; and *Felony Sentences in State Courts, 2002*.

accused offenders who are innocent are removed from the process. In the end, it is a very select group that is subjected to the full force of the criminal law.

From this perspective, it is clear that crime does indeed pay, at least in the case of an individual offense. Wilson and Abrahamse (1992:375) note, "To someone contemplating the commission of any given crime, the answer is that it pays reasonably well." They go on, however, to observe that a career in crime does not pay. Of course, this conclusion about a criminal career's costs and benefits was based on a study of unsuccessful criminals: inmates in three state prisons. The chances of going to prison for a criminal act are slim (except regarding certain criminal acts, such as homicide, which have higher risks of imprisonment). It may be that we have too many criminals for the justice system to accommodate and that this selection process is required so that the entire justice system does not collapse under the number of cases. This is the argument most commonly raised in support of such practices as plea bargaining: that the courts could not handle the volume of criminal trials if bargaining were abolished. It is in the close observation of the filtering process that we begin to understand our society's crime control priorities. It is here, too, that we most clearly see the systemic nature of the criminal justice process. Our task is to develop an understanding of how it is that the criminal justice system in the United States works in the ways it does.

Recalling our earlier discussion of systems theory, the total system of criminal justice exists within the whole "system" of American society. As an open system, criminal justice is sensitive to a variety of social values and social forces. That is, criminal justice processing cannot be fully understood in isolation from its place within American society. While a comprehensive study of society is beyond our scope (and may be impossible), certain aspects of American society are relevant to our understanding of criminal justice operations. One of the most important of these is the emphasis we place on democratic values.

Criminal Justice in a Democracy

At its base, the criminal justice system is a legal system, or more accurately, part of a legal system. Donald Black (1980) observed that legal systems can be characterized as being more or less democratic. Further, the degree of democracy shown in a legal system has implications for how the law develops, how it is applied, and what it accomplishes (Meehan & Ponder, 2003). Black concluded that more democracy in a legal system means that the law is mobilized (or applied) by the citizens more so than by governmental agents. Thus, "crimes" are brought to the attention of authorities more by citizen complaints than by police investigation. In democratic societies, the law is reactive-responsive to citizens. As a result, the law will reflect existing patterns of social stratification, and will be more responsive to changes in social morals and social structure. Thus, one effect of the high value Americans place on democracy is the creation of a legal system (criminal justice system) that reflects society in the United States.

Democracy also leads to the development of constraints on the powers of government and the ability of the criminal justice system to affect crime. Packer (1960) identified "due process" and "crime control" models of criminal justice. In the first, concerns about individual rights and liberty dominate a justice system's actions. In the latter, concerns for crime control and social order dominate. Similarly, Lundman (1980) noted that the police in American society reflect a "dynamic tension" between liberty (individual freedom) and civility (social order). Similarly, O'Leary and Duffee (1971) characterized correctional policies as variously emphasizing concern for the individual or concern for the community.

Each of these views suggests that the criminal justice system must achieve a balance between the rights of the individual and society's need for order. This balance may change over time, but the essential conflict between individual interests and social interests is central to criminal justice in the United States. How this conflict is resolved is the product of the thousands of individual decisions made in the criminal justice system each day. These decisions, in turn, reflect how that balance exists throughout American society.

With regard to the question of discrimination in the criminal justice system, the effect of democracy on the workings of the criminal justice process is evident. William Wilbanks (1987) and Coramae Richey Mann (1987) debated the existence of racial discrimination in United States criminal justice processing. Relying on empirical studies of official decisionmaking, Wilbanks concluded that differential treatment of minority group members at arrest, bail, trial, and sentencing does not represent discrimination based on race. Rather, he concluded that minority group members commit more serious offenses, and thus it is their behavior, not their ethnicity, that explains justice decisions. Mann argued, to the contrary, that data (especially the greater prior arrest/conviction records of minorities) represent racial discrimination. Moreover, she suggested that some of the strongest evidence of discrimination is not "quantified," like arrest statistics, but exists in the qualitative experiences of minority group members.

Who is correct? It is entirely likely that both Wilbanks and Mann are correct in their assertions about the existence of discrimination in criminal justice processing. Wilbanks is essentially saying that the data do not indicate, for example, that criminal justice officials consciously apply more severe treatment to minority group members. Thus, it would appear that most police, prosecutors, judges, juries, and correctional officials are not racist in their individual decisions. Mann is suggesting that minority group members are more often the targets of justice system processing because of their minority status. The aggregate data clearly indicate that this is the case. Zatz (1987), for instance, suggests that relatively high rates of case dismissal for racial minorities may be evidence of discrimination in arrest. That is, minorities are arrested on the basis of less evidence than whites (Barnes & Kingsnorth, 1996). Others suggest that different outcomes of criminal justice processing may be the product of different choices made by members of minority groups. For example, Meyer and Gray (1997) reported that minority defendants charged with driving under the influence were more likely to plead guilty to the charge than were white defendants.

An alternative resolution of the question might be that while agents of the justice system are generally "color-blind" in their decisionmaking, society in the United States is structured so that minority group members are more likely to come under justice system control. Society may grant minority group members less access to adequate education, resulting in less employment and fewer resources. These citizens then may be less able to defend themselves from criminal charges (unable to afford bail, private defense counsel, fines, etc.) and may be less suitable for leniency in treatment (e.g., probation sentences) because of a lack of community resources such as stable residence, job, family ties, and so on. As Black's thesis would suggest, if the society in which a legal system exists is discriminatory, a democratic legal system will also discriminate. Avakame, Fyfe, and McCoy (1999) studied the characteristics of who calls the police, as well as what the police do when called. Among other things, they observed that minorities and the poor are more likely to call the police to deal with problems. Perhaps because they lack access to other resources, poor people and members of minority groups are likely to have greater exposure to the police, and thus a greater chance of being involved in the criminal justice process (Mastrofski, Reisig & McCluskey, 2002).

The enforcement of drug laws provides an example of institutional or systemic discrimination. Carole Barnes and Rodney Kingsnorth (1996) examined sentences imposed on persons convicted of drug law violations in a California court. Among other things, their findings suggested that possession of drugs favored by minority ethnic groups (crack cocaine and heroin) was defined in the law as a more serious offense (a felony) than possession of drugs favored by whites (marijuana and methamphetamines), which was more likely to be defined as a misdemeanor offense. Thus, defining some drugs as more dangerous than others has been coupled with the tendency of the police to focus on street drug markets, which tend to be located in minority neighborhoods. A combination of forces—including ethnic differences in drugs of choice and "drug marketing," police availability and strategies, and court decisions based on statutory definitions—together produce disproportionate rates of arrest, conviction, and incarceration for minority group members.

Beckett, Nyrop, and Pfingst (2006) studied drug enforcement in Seattle, Washington, and found that the drug crimes of minority group members and poor people were more likely to be the targets of police enforcement efforts than were the crimes of whites. For example, the police were more likely to investigate and arrest crack cocaine offenses than those involving powder cocaine, and to focus on crime in the downtown area than in suburban or other neighborhoods. In these cases, African Americans and other minorities were more at risk for being arrested than whites. In terms of sentencing, the combined impact of mandatory minimum sentencing for certain types of offenses and the influence of guidelines may produce differential rates of incarceration for whites and minority groups (Kautt & Spohn, 2002). It also seems that sentences imposed on minorities are more severe (Steffensmeier & Demuth, 2001).

This is not to say that discrimination is acceptable or inevitable. However, this observation has important implications for those who would seek to change the system. If the discrimination that exists in the justice process is rooted in the social system, changes in the justice process alone will have limited impact on levels of discrimination (Meehan & Ponder, 2002). Gilbert Geis (1990) suggested that if the roots of crime are found in the society, the ability of the justice system to control crime is limited. Changes in the social system would be required to achieve either a reduction in discrimination or a reduction in crime. In a democratic society, the criminal justice system is a part of—and a reflection of—the society in which it exists.

On a more positive note, some research has failed to discover evidence of racial discrimination. Kingsnorth and his colleagues (1998) investigated race effects on prosecutions of sexual assault cases. They found no combination of offender and victim race was any more important in understanding charging or plea bargaining. Similarly, Delisi and Regoli (1999) tested five hypotheses based on an assumption of racial discrimination in criminal justice decisionmaking. Based on their research, Delisi and Regoli concluded that the available evidence does not support the notion that overt racial discrimination explains criminal justice operations. This does not mean that discrimination does not exist in the system, but rather that discrimination, where it exists, is only one of many factors that explain criminal justice operations.

The next chapters of this book are dedicated to an in-depth examination of the practices and decisions of the agents and agencies of the criminal justice system. In this examination, we will identify the factors that seem to be most important in determining which cases will be retained in the system and which ones will be diverted. Our focus will be on the decisions made in the criminal justice system and on the identification of explanations for those decisions.

Review Questions

1. What is meant by the "dark figure" of crime?

2. Give four reasons for counting crime.

3. What are "official statistics"? Give an example.

4. Define the terms "unfounding" and "defounding."

5. Explain how to calculate a "crime rate." What does the term mean?

6. Describe two types of "unofficial" crime statistics.

7. What do the data reveal about discrimination in the criminal justice system?

8. Describe "cohort" and "observation" studies of crime and criminal justice.

9. Explain how it can be said that the criminal justice system operates like a funnel.

10. What is the effect of democratic values on the criminal justice system?

References

Akins, S. (2003). "Racial Segregation and Property Crime: Examining the Mediating Effect of Police Strength." *Justice Quarterly* 20(4):675-695.

Alarid, L., J. Marquart, V. Burton, F. Cullen & S. Cuvelier (1996). "Women's Roles in Serious Offenses: A Study of Adult Felons." *Justice Quarterly* 13(3):431-454.

Albanese, J. & R. Pursley (1993). *Crime in America: Some Existing and Emerging Issues.* Englewood Cliffs, NJ: Prentice Hall.

Anselin, L., J. Cohen, D. Cook, W. Gore & G. Tita (2000). "Spatial Analysis of Crime." In D. Duffee (ed.), *Measurement and Analysis of Crime and Justice.* Washington, DC: National Institute of Justice, Criminal Justice 2000, Volume 4:85-138.

Avakame, E., J. Fyfe & C. McCoy (1999). "Did You Call the Police? What Did They Do? An Empirical Assessment of Black's Theory of Mobilization of Law." *Justice Quarterly* 16(4):765-792.

Barnes, C. & R. Kingsnorth (1996). "Race, Drug, and Criminal Sentencing: Hidden Effects of the Criminal Law." *Journal of Criminal Justice* 24(1):39-56.

Beckett, K., K. Nyrop & L. Pfingst (2006). "Race, Drugs, and Policing: Understanding Disparities in Drug Delivery Arrests," *Criminology* 44(1):105-137.

Black, D. (1980). *The Manners and Customs of the Police.* New York: Academic Press.

Booth, A., D.R. Johnson & H.M. Choldin (1977). "Correlates of City Crime Rates: Victimization Surveys versus Official Statistics." *Social Problems* 25:187-197.

Brennan, P. (2006). "Sentencing Female Misdemeanants: An Examination of the Direct and Indirect Effects of Race/Ethnicity." *Justice Quarterly* 23(1):60-95.

Bureau of Justice Statistics (1996). *Criminal Victimization in the United States, 1994.* Washington, DC: U.S. Department of Justice.

Bureau of Justice Statistics/Federal Bureau of Investigation (1985). *Blueprint for the Future of the Uniform Crime Reporting Program.* Washington, DC: U.S. Department of Justice.

Cantor, D. & J. Lynch (2000). "Self-Report Surveys as Measures of Crime and Criminal Victimization." In D. Duffee (ed.), *Measurement and Analysis of Crime and Justice.* Washington, DC: National Institute of Justice, Criminal Justice 2000, Volume 4:85-138.

Cantner, R.J. (1982). "Sex Differences in Self-Report Delinquency." *Criminology* 20(3-4):373-393.

Catalano, S. (2006). *Criminal Victimization, 2005.* Washington, DC: Bureau of Justice Statistics.

Cohen, L.J. & M. Lichbach (1982). "Alternative Measures of Crime: A Statistical Evaluation." *Sociological Quarterly* 23:253-266.

Decker, S., R. Wright, A. Redfern & D. Smith (1993). "A Woman's Place is in the Home: Females and Residential Burglary." *Justice Quarterly* 10(1):143-162.

Delisi, M. & R. Regoli (1999). "Race, Conventional Crime, and Criminal Justice: The Declining Importance of Skin Color." *Journal of Criminal Justice* 27(6):549-557.

Eck, J.E. & L.J. Riccio (1979). "Relationship Between Reported Crime Rates and Victimization Survey Results: An Empirical and Analytical Study." *Journal of Criminal Justice* 7(4):293-308.

Federal Bureau of Investigation (2006). *Crime in the United States, 2005.* Washington, DC: Federal Bureau of Investigation.

Fagan, J. & K. Chin (1991). "Social Processes of Initiation into Crack." *Journal of Drug Issues* 21(2):313-343.

Geis, G. (1986)."On the Declining Crime Rate: An Exegetic Conference Report." *Criminal Justice Policy Review* 1(1):16-36.

Geis, G. (1990). "Crime and Criminal Justice: Where Have We Been, Where Are We Going?" *Journal of Contemporary Criminal Justice* (December):254-263.

Hagan, J. (1989). "Why is There So Little Criminal Justice Theory? Neglected Macro- and Micro-level Links between Organization and Power." *Journal of Research in Crime and Delinquency* 26(2):116-135.

Hindelang, M.J. (1974). "The Uniform Crime Reports Revisited." *Journal of Criminal Justice* 2(1):1-17.

Hindelang, M.J. (1978). "Race and Involvement in Crimes." *American Sociological Review* 43(1):93-109.

Holden, R. (1993). "Police and the Profit-Motive: A New Look at Asset Forfeiture." *ACJS Today* 12(2):1, 3, 24-25.

Hood, R. & R. Sparks (1970). *Key Issues in Criminology.* London: World University Library.

Johnson, R. (2006). "Confounding Influences on Police Detection of Suspiciousness." *Journal of Criminal Justice* 34(4):435-442.

Kautt, P. & C. Spohn (2002). "Crack-ing Down on Black Drug Offenders? Testing for Interactions among Offenders' Race, Drug Type, and Sentencing Strategy in Federal Drug Sentences." *Justice Quarterly* 19(1):1-35.

Kempf-Leonard, K. & L. Sample (2000). "Disparity Based on Sex: The Interaction of Formal and Informal Social Controls." *Justice Quarterly* 17(1):89-128.

Kingsnorth, R., J. Lopez, J. Wentworth & D. Cummings (1998). "Adult Sexual Assault: The Role of Racial/Ethnic Composition on Prosecution and Sentencing." *Journal of Criminal Justice* 26(5):359-371.

Kleinman, P.H. & I.F. Lukoff (1981). "Official Crime Data: Lag in Recording Time as a Threat to Validity." *Criminology* 20(2):169-184.

Kraska, P. (1992). "The Processing of Drug Arrestees: Questioning the Assumption of an Ambivalent Reaction." *Journal of Criminal Justice* 20(6):517-525.

Lab, S.P. & R.B. Allen (1984). "Self Report and Official Measures: A Further Examination of the Validity Issue." *Journal of Criminal Justice* 12(5):445-456.

Lundman, R. (1980). *Police and Policing: An Introduction.* New York: Holt, Rinehart & Winston.

Maher, L. & R. Curtis (1992). "Women on the Edge of Crime: Crack Cocaine and the Changing Contexts of Street-Level Sex Work in New York City." *Crime, Law, and Social Change* 18(2):221-258.

Maltz, M. (1999). *Bridging Gaps in Police Crime Data.* Washington, DC: Bureau of Justice Statistics.

Mann, C.R. (1987). "Racism in the Criminal Justice System: Two Sides of a Controversy." *Criminal Justice Research Bulletin* 3(5):1-5.

Mastrofski, S., M. Reisig & J. McCluskey (2002). "Police Disrespect Toward the Public: An Encounter-Based Analysis." *Criminology* 40(3):519-552.

McElrath, K., R. Dunham & P. Cromwell (1995). "Validity of Self-Reported Cocaine and Opiate Use Among Arrestees in Five Cities." *Journal of Criminal Justice* 23(6):531-540.

McNulty, T. (2001). "Assessing the Race-Violence Relationship at the Macro Level: The Assumption of Racial Invariance and the Problem of Restricted Distributions." *Criminology* 39(2):467-490.

Meehan, A. & M. Ponder (2002). "Race and Place: The Ecology of Racial Profiling African American Motorists." *Justice Quarterly* 19(3):399-430.

Menard, S. (1987). "Short-term Trends in Crime and Delinquency: A Comparison of UCR, NCVS and Self-Report Data." *Justice Quarterly* 4(3):455-474.

Menard, S. (1991). "Encouraging News for Criminologists (In the Year 2050)? A Comment on O'Brien (1990)." *Journal of Criminal Justice* 19(6):563-567.

Meyer, J. & T. Gray (1997). "Drunk Drivers in the Courts: Legal and Extra-Legal Factors Affecting Pleas and Sentences." *Journal of Criminal Justice* 25(2):155-164.

Navares, D., M. Wolfgang & P. Tracy (1990). *Delinquency in Puerto Rico: The 1970 Birth Cohort Study*. New York: Greenwood Press.

Nelson, J. (1992). "Hidden Disparities in Case Processing: New York State, 1985-1986." *Journal of Criminal Justice* 20(3):181-200.

Nettler, G. (1984). *Explaining Crime*, 3rd ed. New York: McGraw-Hill.

O'Brien, R. (1985). *Crime and Victimization Data*. Beverly Hills, CA: Sage.

O'Brien, R. (1986). "Rare Events, Sample Size, and Statistical Problems in the Analysis of NCS City Surveys." *Journal of Criminal Justice* 14(5):441-448.

O'Brien, R. (1990). "Comparing Detrended UCR and NCS Crime Rates Over Time: 1973-1986." *Journal of Criminal Justice* 18(3):229-238.

O'Leary, V. & D. Duffee (1971). "Correctional Policy: A Classification of Goals Designed for Change." *Crime & Delinquency* 18(3):379.

Packer, H. (1960). *The Limits of the Criminal Sanction*. Englewood Cliffs, NJ: Prentice Hall.

Petersilia, J. (1983). *Racial Disparities in the Criminal Justice System*. Santa Monica, CA: RAND.

Platt, S. (ed.) (1999). *Respectfully Quoted: A Dictionary of Quotations*. Requested from the Congressional Research Service. Found at: http://www.Bartleby.com/73/; accessed January 26, 2005.

President's Commission on Law Enforcement and Administration of Justice (1967). *The Challenge of Crime in a Free Society*. Washington, DC: U.S. Government Printing Office.

Rand, M., J. Lynch & D. Cantor (1997). *Criminal Victimization, 1973-95*. Washington, DC: Bureau of Justice Statistics.

Reaves, B. (1993). Using NIBRS Data to Analyze Violent Crime. Washington, DC: Bureau of Justice Statistics.

Rich, T. (1995). *The Use of Computerized Mapping in Crime Control and Prevention Programs*. Washington, DC: National Institute of Justice.

Rich, T. (1996). *The Chicago Police Department's Information Collection for Automated Mapping (ICAM) Program*. Washington, DC: National Institute of Justice.

Rosenfeld, R. & S. Decker (1999). "Are Arrest Statistics a Valid Measure of Illicit Drug Use? The Relationship Between Criminal Justice, and Public Health Indicators of Cocaine, Heroin, and Marijuana Use." *Justice Quarterly* 16(3):685-699.

Salas, L. & R. Surette (1984). "The Historical Roots and Development of Criminological Statistics." *Journal of Criminal Justice* 12(5):457-466.

Substance Abuse and Mental Health Administration (SAMHA) (2006). *Results of the 2005 National Survey on Drug Use and Health: National Findings*. Rockville, MD: Office of Applied Studies, SAMHA.

Schaefer, J., B. Huebner & T. Bynum (2003). "Citizen Perceptions of Police Services: Race, Neighborhood Context, and Community Policing." *Police Quarterly* 6(4):440-468.

Schneider, A.L. & D. Sumi (1981). "Patterns of Forgetting and Telescoping: An Analysis of LEAA Survey Victimization Data." *Criminology* 23(1):41-50.

Sherman, L., P. Gartin & M. Buerger (1989). "Hot Spots of Predatory Crime: Routine Activities and the Criminology of Place." *Criminology* 27(1):27-55.

Steffensmeier, D. & S. Demuth (2001). "Ethnicity and Judges' Sentencing Decisions: Hispanic-Black-White Comparisons." *Criminology* 39(1):145-178.

Swanson, C.R. (1981). "Rural and Agricultural Crime." *Journal of Criminal Justice* 9(1):19-28.

Tracy, P., M. Wolfgang & R. Figlio (1990). *Delinquency Careers in Two Birth Cohorts.* New York: Plenum Press.

Thornberry, T. & M. Krohn (2000). "The Self-Report Method for Measuring Delinquency and Crime." In D. Duffee (ed.), *Measurement and Analysis of Crime and Justice.* Washington, DC: National Institute of Justice, Criminal Justice 2000, Volume 4:33-84.

U.S. Department of Justice (2004). *The Nation's Two Crime Measures.* Washington, DC: U.S. Department of Justice.

Velez, M. (2001). "The Role of Public Social Control in Urban Neighborhoods: A Mutilevel Analysis of Victimization Risk." *Criminology* 39(4):837-864.

Visher, C.A. (1983). "Gender, Police Arrest Decisions and Notions of Chivalry." *Criminology* 21(1):5-28.

Warren, P., D. Tomaskovic-Devey, W. Smith, M. Zingraff & M. Mason (2006). "Driving While Black: Bias Processes and Racial Disparity in Police Stops." *Criminology* 44(3):709-738.

Weisburd, D. & J. Eck (2004). "What Can Police Do to Reduce Crime and Fear?" *Annals of the American Academy of Political and Social Science* 593:42-65.

Weisheit, R. & L. Wells (1999). "The Future of Crime in Rural America." *Journal of Crime and Justice* 22 (1):1-26.

Weitzer, R. (1996). "Racial Discrimination in the Criminal Justice System: Findings and Problems in the Literature." *Journal of Criminal Justice* 24(4):309-322.

Wilbanks, W. (1987). "Racism in the Criminal Justice System: Two Sides of a Controversy." *Criminal Justice Research Bulletin* 3(5):1-5.

Williams, J. & M. Gold (1972). "From Delinquent Behavior to Official Delinquency." *Social Problems* 20:209-228.

Wilson, J. & A. Abrahamse (1992). "Does Crime Pay?" *Justice Quarterly* 9(3):359-377.

Wolfe, N.T., F.T. Cullen & J.B. Cullen (1984). "Describing the Female Offender: A Note on the Demographics of Arrest." *Journal of Criminal Justice* 12(5):483-492.

Wolfgang, M.E., R.M. Figlio & T. Sellin (1978). *Delinquency in a Birth Cohort.* Chicago: University of Chicago Press.

Worrall, J. (2001). "Addicted to the Drug War: The Role of Civil Asset Forfeiture as a Budgetary Necessity in Contemporary Law Enforcement." *Journal of Criminal Justice* 29(3):171-187.

Zatz, M. (1987). "The Changing Forms of Racial/Ethnic Biases in Sentencing." *Journal of Research in Crime and Delinquency* 24(1):69-92.

Zeisel, H. (1982). *The Limits of Law Enforcement.* Chicago: University of Chicago Press.

Chapter 5

Police and Policing

Important Terms

community-oriented
  policing

constable

cynicism

legalistic style

order maintenance

paramilitary structure

proactive

quality-of-life policing

reactive

service style

shire reeve

watchman style

No simple count of the number of police agencies or police officers in the United States exists. Available data suggest that there are more than 20,000 police agencies in the United States, but even this number is not certain. A variety of federal, state, municipal, special jurisdiction (housing authority, transit authority, etc.), and private agencies provide law enforcement services. The Bureau of Justice Statistics (Reaves, 2007) identified 12,766 local agencies alone, and another 3,067 sheriff's departments. More than two-thirds of municipal police employees are sworn police officers. The 2004 census identified local police departments and sheriff's agencies, with another 1,481 special jurisdiction police and 513 Texas constables.

More than 90 percent of municipalities with a population of 2,500 or more operate their own police agency (Reaves, 1996), so the majority of local police organizations are relatively small (see Box 5.1). The largest police agencies, however, employ the most officers, meaning that although the typical police organization is small, the typical police officer works in a large agency. Regardless of agency size, most sworn police personnel are assigned to patrol and similar field operations duties. Patrol officers do the bulk of police work in the United States, and the work of patrol officers is varied.

Box 5.1 Distribution of Police Officers and Agencies, 2004

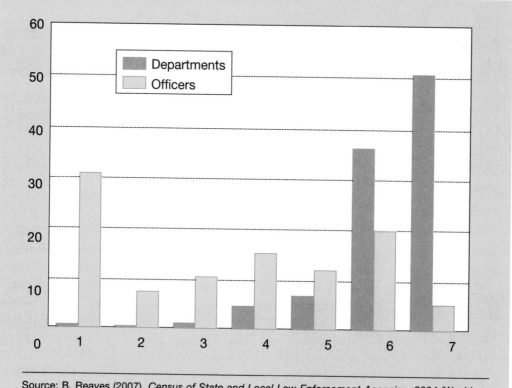

Source: B. Reaves (2007), *Census of State and Local Law Enforcement Agencies, 2004* (Washington, DC: Bureau of Justice Statistics):2.

Police agencies provide a variety of services to the communities they serve, ranging from travelers' aid through ambulance service. Yet, we continue to think of them as "law enforcement." Indeed, enforcing criminal laws is, at most, a part-time activity for most police departments and police officers. The police are what James Q. Wilson (1968) called the "agency of last resort." While we must focus upon the law enforcing duties of police agencies because of our interest in criminal justice, it is also important to remember other demands placed on police.

Because police are available 24 hours each day, are mobile, and carry authority, we call upon them to resolve many issues and problems (Goldstein, 1990). Most of these problems are not, strictly speaking, law enforcement–oriented in nature (Kennedy, 1983). The principal task of a police agency is best described as "order maintenance." The peacekeeping function of police is far more important than the law enforcement function. Law enforcement is a small part of order maintenance (Eck & Spelman, 1987).

The criminal law is only one of many tools available to police officers and police agencies in their efforts to keep peace in our communities. The police are responsible for dealing with stray children and dogs, lost travelers, injured persons, stranded motorists, traffic accidents, parades, domestic disputes, and crime. It seems that almost any disruptive event can be resolved by "calling the cops" (Bittner, 1970). In many cases, people have reported fires to the police first, rather than to the fire department. The police are often called to deal with abandoned cars, but the reason they are called is not because the car may have been involved in a crime. People call the police because the police are the first agency that comes to mind.

People also call the police because they have come to know that the police can (and probably will) do something about the problem. Egon Bittner (1970) observed that the police have a monopoly on the legitimate use of coercive force. The ability to use force and to make people behave in certain ways defines the police role in society. The police are called to deal with a variety of problems that may require

Mounted police keep watch over Boston's Quincy Market during the 2004 Democratic National Convention. The peacekeeping function of police is considered by many to be far more important than the law enforcement function. *Photo credit: E.S. Boyne.*

force (Klockars, 1985). For example, the police may be called to intervene with a mentally disturbed person because, if all else fails, they can arrest and remove the individual (Lurigio & Swartz, 2000). This action may not cure the mental disorder, but it will solve the immediate problem.

Given the scope of police responsibilities (some assigned, some assumed, and some simply evolved), it is clear that law enforcement is only a small part of police duties. Studies of police tasks have revealed that actual crimes consume a small portion of police resources and comprise a small percentage of police tasks (Liederbach & Frank, 2006; Webster, 1970; Wilson, 1968). Depending upon the definitions used by the researchers, the majority of police time is devoted to general patrol, service calls, and paperwork (Mastrofski et al., 1999a, 1999b; Parks et al., 1999). Nonetheless, the public, the media, and the police themselves continue to define policing as principally crime-fighting (Manning, 1978). This conception of the police as "crime fighters" developed historically as a response to difficulties encountered in the police role.

The Development of American Policing

The idea of police controlling the behavior of individuals is a relatively recent addition to society. The American colonists did not employ police, and no police forces were created in the United States until the 1840s. In colonial times, law enforcement was the duty of every citizen, and no specialized occupational group was given a mandate to ensure public order. As with so much of our justice system, the origins of public police can be traced to our English tradition.

Law Enforcement in England

Most of England had no specialized police force or public office charged with maintaining public order until after the Norman Conquest in 1066 (Critchley, 1972; Stewart-Brown, 1936). At that time, the Normans, having gained control over England and occupying a hostile population, created a centralized governmental structure based on feudalism. High-ranking officers and nobles of William the Conqueror's army were given control of large parcels of England. These nobles were expected to provide a percentage of the production from these lands to the king as taxes, and to supply soldiers in time of war. They also were required to obey the commands of the king and to ensure the "king's peace" in their lands.

To accomplish this administrative task, these nobles further subdivided their lands to lesser officers and nobles, and required them to remit a portion of their profits and to supply a number of soldiers when necessary. The subdivision continued, with each successive rank being required to pay a larger portion of taxes but supply a smaller number of soldiers. The increased taxes represented the need to meet the demands of the king and the higher nobility for income. The lower number of soldiers reflected the increased number of "officers" who were granted lands. If a duke promised to provide 10,000 soldiers and 5 percent of profits to the king, this could be accomplished by dividing the land among 10 barons. Each baron might be required to provide 1,000 soldiers (10,000 total) and 8 percent of profits (5% for the king; 3% for the duke). Feudalism provided a structure for government in medieval times.

Essentially rural and agrarian, England was divided into 10 family units called "tythings." Each tything was responsible for its own tax collection and order maintenance. With the advent of Norman control, new units of 100 families, called "shires," were created. Being an occupied country, maintenance of the Norman king's law was problematic, and tax collection was difficult. The office of "shire reeve" was created.

The shire reeve was responsible for the collection of taxes and the maintenance of the king's peace within the shire, which was usually an area similar to a county or parish in the United States today. The reeve was elected from a list of candidates approved by the lord of the manor. Over time, the shire reeve became known as the "sheriff." The resistance of the English to this new structure can be seen in the tales of Robin Hood, whose nemesis was the Sheriff of Nottingham.

Each manor also operated a manorial court. To assist in the day-to-day operation of the court functions, the office of constable was created. The lord of the manor selected the **constable** from among qualified property holders. The constable performed the clerical duties of the court and housed prisoners awaiting trial. Over time, these functions were expanded to include general "peacekeeping."

As villages and towns developed, this rural order-maintenance apparatus proved to be inadequate to the task of law enforcement in congested areas. Traditionally, every citizen was responsible for order maintenance. Drawing on this tradition, town constables were empowered to draft citizens for a "watch" system. In this system, citizens were required to provide unpaid watch service (typically at night) to patrol for fires and breaches of the peace. As towns grew larger and cities developed, it became increasingly difficult to find either adequate "watchmen" or persons willing to take the role of constable.

By the early 1800s, English towns and cities were crowded and unruly. The nobility and wealthy citizens traveled with hired guards (footmen) and avoided the more dangerous sections of town. Several experiments with paid watches, "private" law enforcement, and rejuvenated constabulary offices had all failed to provide adequately for order maintenance. One of the most famous of these experiments was the organization of the Bow Street Runners by Henry Fielding. Also known as "thief-takers," this group of men was organized to provide police protection in the Bow Street area of London. There was clearly a need to create a specialized body charged with maintaining the peace.

During the 1820s, Sir Robert Peel, British Home Secretary, proposed the creation of a police force for England. This force would be comprised of paid, uniformed, armed, and disciplined officers whose job would be the enforcement of the law, the maintenance of order, and the prevention of crime. Crime prevention was expected to result from the presence of police on the streets. Patrolling police officers would act to deter criminal offenders. Parliament, fearing the effects of such an armed force on the "rights of Englishmen," resisted Peel's idea. In democratic societies, and especially in the Anglo-American tradition, there has always been a tension or conflict between liberty and civility (Lundman, 1980). Our need for order (civility) is in direct conflict with our desire for personal freedom (liberty). The English Parliament had to be convinced that the new police would not unduly threaten English liberty. Peel revised his proposal and, in 1829, Parliament agreed to "experiment" with a Metropolitan Police Force in London. This force would not be armed, but in every other respect, it would mirror Peel's original plan. If it worked in London, the idea might be expanded. The Metropolitan Police Force of London, created in 1829, was the first modern police force.

The Colonial and Early American Experience

Like many other areas of social life, the American colonists relied upon their traditions and experiences from England in developing a social control system. Colonial villages and towns normally had the offices of constable and/or sheriff. The

A member of the professional police force organized by Sir Robert Peel. Initially referred to as "Peelers," they later came to be known as "Bobbies." *Photo credit: Metropolitan Police, New Scotland Yard, London.*

duties of each were similar to those of its English counterpart (Johnson & Wolfe, 2001). As towns and cities grew, the Americans experimented with watch systems. In time, it became clear that these less formal systems for order maintenance were inadequate.

Unlike England, however, there was no strong central government in America, and weapons and violence were more commonplace in the New World. While the same general pattern of development was followed in America, these differences would result in a modification of the English police structure. If anything, American concerns with liberty were even more strongly felt than those of the English, and distrust of centralized governmental power meant that any police would be limited.

By the 1840s, waves of immigrants began arriving on the shores of America, and industrialization was beginning. The population of American cities swelled, and the cities became unruly and dangerous places. The urban poor, especially immigrants, came to be defined as prerevolutionary by the upper and middle classes. It became common to speak of the immigrant poor in America's congested cities as the "dangerous classes."

To control these "dangerous" people, and to bring order and stability to the cities, Americans began to consider the creation of police forces. On many occasions, the militia or the army was used to quell riots or to break strikes (and would still be used for these purposes in the future), but these were extraordinary circumstances. Many people believed a more permanent solution to the problems of day-to-day disorder was required. The importance of ethnic and cultural conflict to the emergence and development of policing in America cannot be overstated (Barlow & Barlow, 2000).

Knowing about the English experiments and developments, many reformers began to advocate the creation of police forces for the cities. In 1844, New York City created a police force modeled after the Metropolitan Police Force of London, but with several significant differences (Johnson & Wolfe, 2001:217-219). The New York City Police were appointed by the mayor from among candidates recommended by political ward leaders. The police force was to be administered by a Board of Police Commissioners. Each officer was to be a resident of the ward in which he would work; these officers objected to wearing uniforms and being unarmed.

The New York City Police were created and funded locally. This new American police department was characterized by a weak central administration, municipal organization, and direct political involvement. Over the years, the issues of uniforms and arms were resolved, so that municipal police were both armed and uniformed. Each city created its own police force and organizational structure. In the next 10 years, the New York City Police were followed by the creation of police in most major American cities (see Box 5.2). Eric Monkonnen (1981) notes that local police in America were first modeled on the police of London, but that American police agencies quickly grew independent of this original model. It is important to note that the police in America were developed in specific cities and towns, with no effort to create a national police force. This ensured that the American police would be under local control and direction.

Box 5.2   Milestones in American Law Enforcement

1748	Bow Street Runners organized by Henry Fielding.
1829	Metropolitan Police Force created in London, England.
1838	Boston Police created with nine officers.
1844	New York City Police created with 800 officers.
1852	Cincinnati and New Orleans Police created.
1854	Philadelphia and Boston Police establish formal patrol.
1855	Chicago Police created.
1857	Baltimore Police created.
1893	Organization of the Police Chief's Union in Chicago.
1905	August Vollmer elected Marshal of Berkeley, CA.
1908	Bureau of Investigation (later FBI) created. Berkeley Police School started.
1924	J. Edgar Hoover named Director of FBI.
1930	Uniform Crime Reports first published.
1931	Police Science Program started at San Jose State University.
1935	FBI National Police Academy opened.
1960	O.W. Wilson named Chicago Police Commissioner.
1974	Kansas City Preventive Patrol Experiment initiated.
1982	"Broken Windows" thesis appears.
1994	Passage of Violent Crime Control and Law Enforcement Act (creation of The Office of Community Policing Services).

The American Police

Like New York's, most early police departments in America were not centrally organized and did not have strong leadership. This was in response to a fear of the effect of police on the exercise of rights by individuals (similar to the English Parliament's fears regarding the Metropolitan Police). It was common to employ a "police commission" to govern the department so that no single individual would gain too much power. With the growth of political machines in the cities, however, this weak administrative structure left city police forces open to manipulation and corruption.

Initially, the principal duty of the police was to maintain order. The success of a police officer was most easily established by the absence of disorder on the patrol beat. The fact that officers were recruited from the neighborhoods they were to patrol and were sometimes unwilling to arrest their friends and acquaintances meant that officers tolerated much "deviance," which the upper and middle classes found frightening. Drinking of alcohol, for example, was viewed with suspicion by many city leaders, yet tolerated (even shared) by many officers. The failure of the police to remain free of political influence and corruption, coupled with neighborhood enforcement styles, led to an early call to reform the police.

In the latter part of the nineteenth century, a reform effort was mounted to enhance police accountability and to professionalize the police (Fogelson, 1977; Travis & Langworthy, 2008; Walker, 1977). August Vollmer, perhaps the foremost proponent of police professionalism, led the reform. Vollmer sought higher personnel standards and stronger police leadership. The push for police professionalism continued well into the twentieth century and is still felt (Vogel & Adams, 1983). The police were given strong central administration and a clear "crime control" mandate. The focus on law enforcement was supposed to circumvent the difficulties that accompanied the more general role of maintaining order (Johnson, 1981). According to many policing historians, the movement to professionalize the police was an effort by middle-class, native-born citizens to gain control over the police and to restrain the growing immigrant population (Toch, 1997).

With the crime control mandate came an equally important definition of the police as serving a crime-prevention function. The police were not only expected to detect and apprehend offenders, but police presence on the streets of a city was expected to deter others from committing crimes. From this came the tradition of preventive patrol. The uniformed officer on patrol would not only be better able to detect crime, but the patrol presence would prevent crime as well. While the technology may have changed from foot patrol to motorized patrol (and perhaps back again), the idea is essentially the same.

The tradition of police as peacekeepers (order maintenance), however, has also remained (Kappeler, 1996). While the definition of the police became (and remains) one of a crime control force, the functions of a modern police department are far broader. The police are the most visible representatives of government in a community, and they represent the legitimate authority of the law. As they are always (theoretically) present and available, the police have become ombudsmen for all social and legal problems.

The Functions of Police

The role of the police has been broadly classified into three categories. Wilson (1968) suggested that the police are responsible for law enforcement, order maintenance, and service. Further, he argued that, of the three, order maintenance is at once both the most important and the most troublesome. Order maintenance is the main purpose of police. If they do nothing else, the police must ensure that the citizens can go about their daily business safely and efficiently.

Order maintenance activities include settling disputes, dispersing crowds, keeping sidewalks and streets clear and traffic flowing smoothly, and other important activities. These are troublesome responsibilities because the officer often must operate in the "gray areas" of the law and must choose whether to intervene and, if so, how and with whom (Eck & Spelman, 1987).

The service functions of police have evolved over time out of necessity. Police are called upon to provide a variety of services, from giving directions to travelers to finding missing children. Partly because of a potential link to criminal behavior, police also investigate traffic accidents, provide first aid to victims, and, often, transport the injured to medical facilities. Whatever the reasons, modern police provide a wide variety of services to the community that do not strictly conform to the role of crime control (Bittner, 1970; Das, 1987; Trojanowicz et al., 1998).

Law enforcement activities are those that relate directly to the detection and apprehension of criminal offenders. Responding to alarms and citizen complaints of crime, investigating suspicious persons and circumstances, and arresting suspected offenders are all law enforcement activities. Although crime control does not comprise the bulk of police tasks, it is this function of the police that will be our focus. Before turning our attention to the crime control activities of the police, however, we must more fully explore the diverse obligations of contemporary police.

The Police as a Human Services Agency

To understand the role of the police, it is helpful to describe what it is that the police do. Ideally, perhaps, it would be possible to determine what it is that police are supposed to do and, from that, develop a definition of the police role. The problem is that it is not clear what it is that we want the police to do. Historically, the police acquired responsibilities because no other agency existed to perform particular tasks. Today, the police role is shaped by a variety of social, political, legal, and administrative factors.

Whatever it is that the police do, research shows that most of what they do is not criminal law enforcement. Box 5.3 displays the results of several analyses of police work. While the exact percentages for each category differ, in all cases, the majority of police resources were not spent on enforcing the criminal laws. Rather, administrative tasks and service provision appear to be important components of the police task, and thus, the police role. Based on observations of police officers in Indianapolis, Indiana, Stephen Mastrofski and his colleagues (1999a) concluded that police spent about one-quarter of their time interacting with citizens, and only one-half of that (less than 13% of total time) involved with potentially criminal matters. Christine Famega (2004) reviewed studies of police officer activity and concluded that in general, only about one-quarter of a patrol officer's time is spent responding to calls for service or dispatches.

Box 5.3 Workload Analysis of Police Patrol Officers' Time

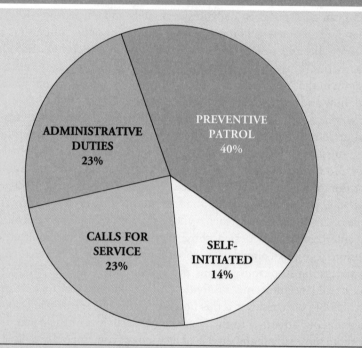

Source: W. Gay, T. Schell & S. Schack (1977), *Improving Patrol Productivity, Volume 1: Routine Patrol* (Washington DC: U.S. Department of Justice):3.

Many of the services provided to citizens by police departments have already been identified. If you think of your own interactions with the police over the course of your lifetime, how often have you dealt with police officers in non–law enforcement situations? The investigation of traffic accidents and crowd control at parades, demonstrations, sporting events, and the like, are important, non–law enforcement services provided by the police. Box 5.4 shows that many local police departments have primary responsibility for safety functions such as search and rescue, animal control, and civil defense. Other police departments that do not have primary responsibility for these functions still must often respond to calls about such safety problems.

Despite the fact that most police activities do not involve enforcing criminal laws, the view of the police as crime fighters persists. This definition of the police role is reinforced by the entertainment media, politicians, and the police themselves (Goldstein, 1978; Graber, 1979; Van Maanen, 1978). One reason for the continuation of such a narrow and distorted image of the police is the historical rationale behind giving priority to the crime control mandate. There is general societal agreement that the police ought to enforce the criminal laws. In comparison to all other police tasks, crime control is the least controversial. Order

Box 5.4	Public Safety Functions of Local Police: Percent of Departments

Search & Rescue	21%
Emergency Medical	26%
Civil Defense	19%
Animal Control	65%
Fire Services	10%
Underwater Recovery	4%
Bomb Disposal	3%

Source: M. Hickman & B. Reaves (2006), *Local Police Departments, 2003* (Washington, DC: Bureau of Justice Statistics):18.

maintenance and service activities present the greatest role definition problems for police in the United States.

David Kennedy (1983) argued that the police qualify as a human services agency. After reviewing the literature on human services, Kennedy concluded that five characteristics identify human services agencies: (1) systemic integration of services, (2) comprehensiveness and accessibility, (3) client troubles defined as problems in living, (4) generic helping activities, and (5) service provider accountability. In an overview of police activities, Kennedy established that each of these factors applies to contemporary police work, although the public (and often the police themselves) object to the "human services" definition.

The police serve as a referral center for people in trouble, linking victims, the ill, and others in need of service with available community resources (e.g., hospitals, mental health clinics, travellers' aid societies, etc.). The police are available all day and every day throughout their jurisdiction. Whether crime, injury, illness, or disputes cause the police to intervene, police problems generally can be reduced to problems in living. The sheer scope and variety of situations in which the police are called to intervene are evidence of their generic helping activities. Finally, the police, like all governmental agencies, are ultimately responsible to the public (their clients) and the courts.

Historically, as a human services agency, the most important role of the police was that of "first aid." Whether, the problem is a lost child, domestic disturbance, landlord/tenant dispute, public intoxication, or traffic accident, the police are normally first on the scene. In this role, the police provide first aid by taking charge of the situation, providing immediate help and counseling, and giving referrals for further care (Fritsch et al., 2004). It is common, especially in larger police departments, to give officers a directory of social service agencies to which the officers can refer citizens. The fact that the police do not always provide complete human services to resolve the living problems of those with whom they come into contact does not negate the important role of the police in the first stages of human service (Das, 1987). More recently, the police role has been redefined as prevention, as we shall see.

The Police as a Crime Control Agency

The police control crime in one of two basic ways: reactively or proactively (Black, 1972). These types of policing represent ideal types. A reactive police department would only respond (or react) to crime. A proactive police department would use its own initiative in aggressively seeking out crimes and criminals. The most strict type of reactive police department would remain at the police station, watching television, cleaning cruisers, and the like, until a complaint of a crime was received or an alarm sounded, when the officers would rush to their cruisers and speed to the scene of the crime. Having investigated or made an arrest, the officers then would return to the station to await their next call.

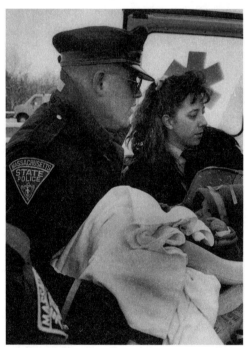

Service functions are an important, but often over-looked, aspect of policing. Here a police officer assists medical technicians at the scene of an accident. The infant's mother was injured in the accident. *Photo credit: Mark C. Ide.*

In contrast, a fully proactive police department would resemble the vice squad. All officers would be in the field seeking out crime. Much of the work of the police would be accomplished by undercover officers, because marked cars and uniforms would forewarn offenders. Traffic officers would establish "speed traps" rather than patrol stretches of highway. Decoy teams and "sting operations" would be prevalent.

In reality, of course, one does not find either ideal type. Rather, it is possible to classify police departments as being more or less proactive or reactive. As a result of the democratic nature of our society, and of the municipal organization of the majority of our police forces, police in the United States are more reactive than proactive (Travis & Langworthy, 2008). As a society, we prefer to set policing priorities through our complaints and calls. The alternative is for the police to set priorities through deciding how and when to combat crime. Proactive police seeking to prevent crime are required to act on their own initiative to avoid citizen com-plaints about crime. In a study of proactive police efforts in two cities, Sun (2003) concluded that officers in the study were less proactive than had been expected, engaging in relatively few problem-focused or aggressive preventive patrol activities.

The Police as a Peacekeeping Agency

In television and motion picture westerns, the marshal is charged with "keeping the peace." At base, peacekeeping means the maintenance of order. The police control disruptions such as fights and riots. They maintain traffic flow and ensure a general level of satisfaction with living in the community. Police protect and enhance orderly social interactions. James Q. Wilson (1968:16) argued that order maintenance is at the core of the police task. He wrote:

> The patrolman's role is defined more by his responsibility for maintaining order than by his responsibility for enforcing the law. By "order" is meant the absence of disorder, and by disorder is meant behavior that either disturbs or threatens to disturb the public peace or that involves face-to-face conflict among two or more persons. Disorder, in short, involves a dispute over what is "right" or "seemly" conduct or over who is to blame for conduct that is agreed to be wrong or unseemly.

As Wilson's explanation implies, disorder is often noncriminal. Order-maintenance problems usually involve questions of propriety rather than questions of legality. Youths loitering on a street corner, a neighbor who plays her stereo too loudly, homeless persons congregating in a park, and other noncriminal events are frequently the basis for order-maintenance calls to the police. In these situations, the responding officer is expected to resolve the conflict and thereby restore order.

Most order-maintenance problems fall into a gray area of the law where frequently the officer is not authorized to act. As a matter of practicality, the officer is compelled to do something. Order maintenance is the most common activity of police officers. These tasks often expose officers to physical danger and involve the exercise of discretion by the officer. Order maintenance is the least "consensual" part of the police task (Wilson, 1968). For these reasons, order maintenance is perhaps the most difficult aspect of policing. Allen Jiao (1998) suggests that different communities hold different expectations of their police. He urges police to develop policies and practices based, in large part, on the expectations of the community. Other research has indicated that community characteristics tend to be correlated with some police decisions. Arrick Jackson and John Wade (2005) observed that the police are more proactive in their enforcement efforts in neighborhoods characterized by high rates of crime than in low-crime areas. It seems the likelihood of criminal activity influences the decisions of officers to intervene with citizens.

While there may be a consensus that robbery will not be tolerated, that police should arrest robbers, that accident victims should be helped, and that the police should help them, there often is no such consensus for order-maintenance questions. In the case of the neighbor with the loud stereo, it is clear that dissension or disagreement exists; one party feels that the stereo is too loud and the other feels that it is set at an acceptable level. Into this conflict steps the officer. Regardless of the outcome, at least one (if not all) of the parties will be dissatisfied.

Difficult as it is, order maintenance is a critical component of policing. Left unattended, minor disputes can escalate into criminal acts (such as assault or vandalism if the complaining neighbor takes the matter of the loud stereo into his or her own hands). Further, the police and the entire justice system must serve the major function of social control. We should be able to go about our daily lives in a relatively smooth and predictable fashion. It is order maintenance, more than any other police function, that ensures the routine functioning of society.

A police help and information center in a midwestern shopping mall. Community-friendly programs such as this are a component of the trend toward community policing. *Photo credit: E.S. Boyne.*

Despite all this, Moore, Trojanowicz, and Kelling (1988:1) observed that crime control is the core mission of the police in the United States. The police can work to control crime by enforcement of laws and by prevention. Police efforts to maintain order and provide services often have the effect of preventing crime. There is growing evidence that citizens appreciate and support police efforts at crime control, even when those efforts involve tactics such as aggressive traffic enforcement (Chermak, McGarrell & Weiss, 2001; Hawdon, Ryan & Griffin, 2003). In contrast, efforts to engage citizens in community development and order maintenance activities are not associated with improved citizen perceptions of the police. Further, as we will discuss in more detail later, the police can (and do) use the criminal law to achieve order maintenance and service functions.

Community Policing: A Revised Role for the Police

Throughout the past 20 to 30 years, the role of the police has been redefined as that of crime control through order maintenance. In 1982, James Wilson and George Kelling published an article in which they argued that signs of neighborhood decay and disorder led to increased crime. Coined the "broken windows" theory, Wilson and Kelling's contention was that signs of disorder, including broken windows, graffiti, and litter, indicate that no one is in charge of a neighborhood. In these "chaotic" neighborhoods, criminals feel safe from apprehension because no one appears to be responsible for maintaining order. Thus, crime is higher in disorganized neighborhoods.

The logic of the argument supports the idea that if we are to prevent and control crime, we must strengthen and improve neighborhoods. Because disorder is linked to crime, preventing disorder through strengthening neighborhoods will ultimately prevent crime. With other developments, including the suggestion by Herman Goldstein (1990) that police should view crime as a symptom of larger problems that they should seek to solve, the broken windows theory led to a revised view of the police role. John Worrall (2006) reports enforcement against minor offenses does seem to be associated with reductions in more serious crimes. The focus on minor crimes as a means of preventing serious crime is sometimes referred to as quality-of-life policing because police efforts are focused on day-to-day issues like loitering, littering, loud noises and the like. Improving the "quality of life" in the neighborhood leads to effective informal social control and, ultimately, less serious crime.

Community-oriented policing is the title given to this conception of what the police should do. Community-oriented policing can be considered an approach to policing that relies on community definitions of police functions and a partnership between the police and the community in the production of public safety. Community-oriented policing, however, is still elusive of definition. Many agencies report that they practice community-oriented policing, but each agency seems to describe something different with this title. Still, community-oriented policing involves an expansion of the police role from reactive crime fighters to proactive problem solvers. In partnership with the community, the police identify community problems that contribute to crime and seek solutions designed to alleviate those problems. Box 5.5 describes the variety of police practices that have fallen under the general title of community-oriented policing.

Box 5.5   Community-Oriented Policing

Programmatic Elements:

- Foot Patrol
- Bicycle Patrol
- Mounted (Horse) Patrol
- Neighborhood Mini-Stations
- Citizen Police Academies
- Neighborhood Watch
- School Resource Officers
- D.A.R.E. Programs
- Citizen Ride-Along Programs
- Neighborhood Police Officers
- Prioritizing Calls for Service
- Geographic Mapping

While community-oriented policing is often discussed as a fundamental philosophical shift in the way police agencies do business, departments reporting the existence of community policing initiatives often point to the implementation of special programs such as these as evidence that they are "doing community policing."

Community policing initiatives have swept the police departments of the country, with the majority of police agencies reporting that they have implemented some type of community policing program (see Box 5.6). The rapid acceptance of this new role definition of policing has led some commentators to suggest that community-oriented policing is the new "orthodoxy," or commonly accepted purpose for the police. The police, under community-oriented philosophies, are supposed to be more closely tied to the communities they police, more accessible to the public, and less bureaucratic. The range of issues that are now defined as legitimate police problems is enormous, including street lighting, sanitation removal, recreational and health programming, housing, and almost every other public problem.

Box 5.6	Percent of Local Police Departments Engaging in Community Policing Activities, 2003
C.O.P. Officers	58%
Partnerships	60%
Citizen Feedback	37%
Trained Citizens	18%
Citizen Police Academy	17%
Formal Agency Plan	14%

Source: M. Hickman & B. Reaves (2006), *Local Police Departments, 2003* (Washington, DC: Bureau of Justice Statistics):19, 21.

In practice, community-oriented policing has supported decentralized organization in police agencies, alternative patrol strategies and resource allocation, and increased police involvement in civic issues. In theory, the police should be involved in this wide range of problems because they are broadly responsible for public order, and because they are perhaps best organized (jurisdiction-wide, 24-hour availability) to learn about problems, develop solutions, and monitor outcomes. In most places where formal community-oriented policing programs have been instituted, each neighborhood is assigned at least one "neighborhood officer." Permanent assignment to a specific beat is expected to help the officers develop a better understanding of the area and its residents, and to take greater responsibility for public safety and problem-solving in the beat.

Robert Kane (2000) examined the effect of permanent assignments on how officers worked in their beats. He concluded that within a few weeks, officers permanently assigned to an area "took ownership" of the beat and began to engage in more proactive, problem-solving efforts. Residents quickly come to appreciate having their own officer, and unserved neighborhoods call for their own officers as well. Early evidence suggests that community-oriented policing improves citizens' satisfaction with local government and reduces fear of crime.

The central question for community policing remains unanswered (Duffee, Fluellen & Renauer, 1999). If successful, community policing will support the development of non-police social controls in communities so that crime and disorder are prevented (Buerger & Mazerolle, 1998) and communities are strengthened. Evaluations to date have identified a number of successes (Plummer, 1999; Rojek, 2003), but the long-term impact of community policing remains to be seen (Carter, 1999). At the same time, there is evidence to suggest that American policing has not changed all that much as a result of the emergence of community policing. Jihong Zhao and his colleagues have been tracking changes in American police agencies since the emergence of community policing, and they conclude that there is little evidence that the basic structure or core functions of American police have changed substantially (Zhao, He & Lovrich, 2003; Zhao, Lovrich & Robinson, 2001).

The Structure of American Policing

The structure and organization of law enforcement agencies in the United States reflect the influences of historical development and the conflicting tasks expected of them. Unlike the police agencies of other countries, most American police agencies exist at a local level. This fragmentation of police service supports the value we place on federalism and local autonomy. Americans do not want national police, and we insist on maintaining a civilian police force that is distinct from the military (Kraska, 1994; Moore, 1987).

Geoffrey Alpert and Roger Dunham (1988) stated that police organization and administration focus on standardizing the use of civil force. The police must weigh the mandate to control behavior against the requirement that they respect individual rights. This double responsibility places a premium on controlling and directing the actions of individual police officers.

Organizational options were limited when police departments came into being in the mid-1800s. The only organizational model available that allowed control of large groups of personnel was the military model. For this reason above any other, the police often adopted a **paramilitary structure**. This structure included ranks and a chain of command. The trappings of a military organization are still a part of American policing in most places (King, 2003).

In the military model, information flows up the chain of command from the street officers to the police administrator. Orders and commands flow down the chain to the street officers. In this fashion, the police administrator controls the actions of the officers on the street. Organizationally, this structure enables the police to meet their conflicting functions in a routine manner.

In practice, the structure of policing is different from the military model. James Q. Wilson (1968) noted that, unlike other organizations, street officers have more discretion than police administrators. The reality of police work is that officers on the street must react to a variety of situations. It is not practical for police officers to report every call and await instructions from above.

The fear of a strong, centralized police force was one cause of decentralization. The variety of calls for service received by the police further supported allowing individual initiative among officers. Most police departments did not closely supervise street officers (Kelling, 1988). Rather, patrol officers were generalists who were expected to deal appropriately with the majority of calls for assistance without guidance from higher ranks.

As policing entered the twentieth century, the advent of the automobile as well as changes in American cities affected the structure of police departments. While the paramilitary model was retained, policing became increasingly bureaucratic. The radio and the telephone allowed more communication between officers and supervisors. In addition, the new communication tools increased demand for police service because a citizen only had to pick up a telephone to request help. However, these changes also served to alienate the officer from the community (Sherman, 1988).

The separation of the police from the community led to increased concern about controlling police behavior. The bureaucratic response to this concern was the creation of rules and procedures for officers to follow. These departmental policies, or "standard operating procedures" (SOPs), became a factor determining the actions of individual officers. While they are not perfect, the rules affect how officers decide to handle cases (Fyfe, 1979; Mastrofski, Ritti & Hoffmaster, 1987). Like other organizations, police agencies change slowly in response to external pressures (King, 1999).

Early police officers were sworn into office, issued uniforms and weapons, and sent to the streets. Most states now require training and certification of recruits prior to the assignment to patrol. Beginning in 1972, many police agencies developed field training programs to evaluate how well new officers apply laws and departmental policies to field situations (McCampbell, 1986). These programs help ensure that police officers know and follow the rules of the police bureaucracy.

Another development in policing during the twentieth century was specialization. Large police departments, especially those in our biggest cities, use task specialization to assign officers. These departments divide tasks into special units or divisions. While departments differ among themselves in how tasks are divided and named, Alpert and Dunham (1988:59) identified four basic elements: (1) administration, (2) communication, (3) patrol, and (4) internal review. They observed that many police agencies use more precise divisions. Patrol and investigation are two units that include the crime control function of the police. A traffic division and community relations unit may combine with the patrol unit to provide service and order maintenance. Administrative services and internal affairs units assist police administrators in running and controlling the department.

A typical large police department may have several divisions. The investigation unit, for example, may be further divided into homicide, robbery, fraud, vice, and other squads. Similarly, the patrol unit may be organized by geography into precincts or districts. Regardless of the complexity of the police bureaucracy, the military ranks and chain of command are retained. Box 5.7 presents a model organizational chart for a specialized police department. This chart shows an

Box 5.7   Organizational Chart for a Police Department

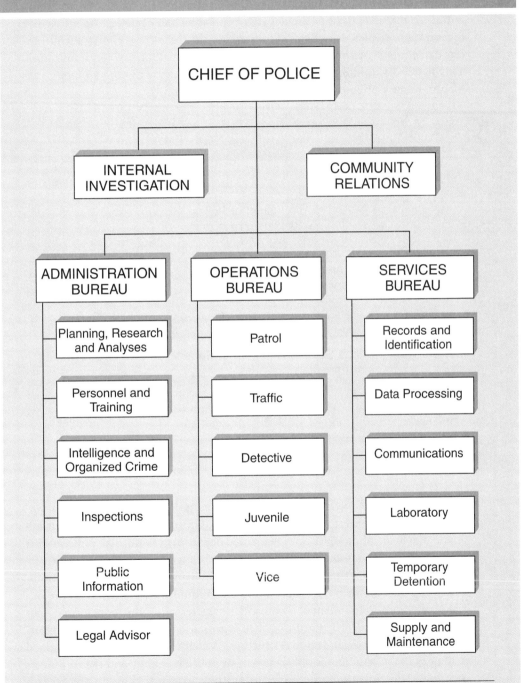

Source: President's Commission on Law Enforcement and Administration of Justice (1967), *Task Force Report: Police* (Washington, DC: U.S. Government Printing Office):47.

organization that has a well-defined hierarchy—there are many steps between the individual patrol officer and the chief of police. Most police departments, however, are small and do not have such a detailed and specialized organization. Still, even the smallest of police departments has a chief of police. An alternative organization, depicted in Box 5.8, "flattens" this hierarchy, giving patrol officers easier input into policy development and shortened lines of communication. This flatter organizational structure is more consistent with contemporary calls for community-oriented policing (Maguire et al., 2003).

Box 5.8 A Flattened Organizational Structure

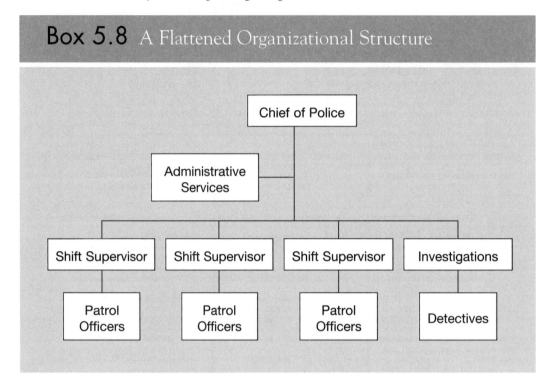

The movement toward community-oriented policing promised to "flatten" the organizational hierarchy of police agencies (Greene, 2000). If a community-oriented policing philosophy is implemented department-wide, each police officer is expected to have responsibility for his or her beat area. The officers are usually expected to work with residents to identify problems and implement solutions. This direct link between the officer and the community naturally lessens the bureaucratic control and "chain of command" characteristic of the more formal, specialized police agency. So far, must police organizations have not shown substantial change in their organizational structure. William King (2005) has suggested that a rigid rank structure is only one part of police hierarchy and that if officers are allowed discretion to make decisions, the police organization can operate in a decentralized fashion while keeping the traditional rank structure.

We must remember that even in the most specialized city police department, patrol officers are generalists. Patrol has been called the "backbone of policing."

The majority of police services are still performed by patrol officers. It is unlikely that the decentralized performance of police service by patrol officers will change in the future. What may change is the amount of direction and supervision these generalist patrol officers receive from the central administration.

The degree of specialization in any police department is at least partly the result of the size of the department (Langworthy, 1985). Larger departments are more likely to be specialized than are smaller ones. Additionally, the police in larger departments are less likely to reflect neighborhood values in police activities (Alpert & Dunham, 1988). This is a result of specialization and bureaucracy. The varying sizes of American police departments influence how the tasks of police are accomplished and how the public perceives the police.

Recall that the majority of police officers work in the large, bureaucratic departments, but that most departments are small. This fact of police organization means duplication and inefficiency are part of American policing. Our police serve communities as much as (or more than) than they serve in the enforcement of the criminal law. The price we pay for local control of police is inefficiency. To ensure that we have police who are responsive to local needs, we must be willing to tolerate multiple jurisdictions and thousands of separate police agencies. However, the existence of many police agencies in a relatively small area does not necessarily translate into a large amount of overlap and wasted effort. Ostrom, Parks, and Whitaker (1978) noted that in metropolitan areas the norm is cooperation among police agencies, not conflict and duplication in service delivery.

Understanding Police

Because we are examining the criminal justice system, we will proceed to discuss policing almost exclusively in terms of law enforcement. In doing so, it is easy to forget the other complex demands placed on the police. The purpose of the previous discussion was to recognize and highlight the fact that enforcing the criminal law is only one part of the police function. In dealing with many social problems, the police must develop workable, immediate responses. King and Dunn (2004) report on police "dumping"—the practice of transporting mentally-ill, substance-impaired, or other troublesome people out of the local jurisdictions. This may not solve the long-term problem of mental illness, homelessness, or substance abuse, but it does solve the immediate problem of what to do with a disorderly person.

Requiring our police to provide services, to maintain order, and to serve crime control ends means that police resources cannot be totally devoted to law enforcement. It also means that law enforcement is not entirely comprised of detecting and apprehending serious criminal offenders. On occasion, the criminal law is used by police officers to achieve order-maintenance or service ends. It is not uncommon, for example, for the police in some large cities to employ "mercy bookings" to provide shelter and medical care for the poor (Finn & Sullivan,

1988; *Newsweek*, 1987:48). Robert Panzarella and Justin Alicea (1997) reported a survey of officers assigned to a special unit having responsibility for dealing with emotionally disturbed persons. These officers noted that they were unlikely to arrest such persons, but often took them into custody and delivered them to medical or psychiatric services. Bittner (1990) noted that police officers seek to control disturbances on the street, and will use arrest as a means to achieve order even when the circumstances of the event would not otherwise justify arresting the citizen. Teplin (2000) suggests that officers may arrest mentally ill persons when the lack of mental health resources leaves them with no other alternative. In contrast, Engel and Silver (2001) observed that officers often resort to informal dispositions because they lack access to mental health treatment yet the criminal law is inappropriate. Cooper, McLearen, and Zapf (2004) reported that police officers recognize a responsibility to deal with the mentally ill, but often complain that there are inadequate community resources available for these people. These examples illustrate how the multiple goals of policing complicate an analysis of the crime control actions of police departments. Nonetheless, we shall endeavor to focus on the role of the police in the criminal justice system—and that role includes crime control. Several factors influence the practice of policing, but two of the most important are the characteristics of the police organization and the characteristics of the police officer.

Police Organizations

Beyond recognizing the multiple functions served by police, we must also remain aware of the structure and organization of policing. The actions of police officers and police departments reflect different patterns of organization (Holmes, 1997). Departmental policies and procedures, as well as recruit training, serve as boundaries on police behavior. The diversity of organizational sizes, structures, and policies ensures variety in the practice of policing.

Finally, we must be sensitive to the local nature of law enforcement in the United States. The police serve their various communities. As James Wilson (1968) reported, there are varieties of police behavior. It is our goal to understand and explain police behavior as it relates to crime control. We cannot accomplish that goal if we ignore the contributions of community and department size and structure in the decisions of police officers.

Wilson (1968) distinguished police department styles on the basis of the frequency and formality with which officers intervened in the lives of citizens. Formality was defined as the use of the criminal law, while frequency referred to the rate at which police interacted with citizens. He identified three basic styles of policing: (1) legalistic, (2) service, and (3) watchman. The legalistic style involved relatively frequent and formal interventions. In the service style, police intervened frequently, but informally (there was little law enforcement). In contrast, in the watchman style, police intervened infrequently. For example, in the case of a curfew violation, legalistic policing would involve the police stopping and issuing a citation (formal intervention); the service style would involve a stop followed by a warning (informal intervention); and the watchman style would predict that the officers were likely to ignore the violation (no intervention).

Because these are ideal types, we can expect variety in practice. Sometimes officers in a legalistic-style department will ignore the violation, those in a service-style department will issue a citation, and those in a watchman-style department will stop the citizen. However, the police department as a whole develops a style of policing that is generally maintained. Wilson suggests that these different styles reflect differences in the communities served by the police. Thus, police departments develop policing styles that are appropriate to the desires and needs of the communities in which they work.

Police Officers

The police officer is a very important component of the justice process. In some ways, he or she is the most important component: police officers decide who will be subjected to justice processing, what crimes will be investigated, and how vigorously laws will be enforced. In addition, as the most numerous and most visible agents of criminal justice, police officers are disproportionately responsible for citizens' opinions about the entire justice system. Finally, police officers are ordinary people entrusted with extraordinary powers, and they are charged with what some have called "an impossible mandate" (Manning, 1978).

Many observers have identified what they have termed "the police personality" (Evans, Coman & Stanley, 1992; Niederhoffer, 1967; Skolnick, 1966).

New York City Police Academy graduates stand at attention during the presentation of colors at Madison Square Garden in New York. More than 1,500 men and women graduated after seven months of training. The 2005 class claimed to be the most diverse class to have ever graduated. *Photo credit: AP Photo/Julie Jacobson.*

Some have suggested that policing as a career attracts persons who are more cynical, authoritarian, suspicious, brutal, and so on. Others argue that the nature of the job changes an average person into the police personality. Whatever causes the police officer to have this unique personality, it is important to understand the complex set of forces that affects the policing activities of the individual officer.

Studies of the police show that officers frequently act as if they are cynical (Regoli et al., 1987). **Cynicism** entails distrust or suspicion. In terms of police, the term refers to a perception or belief that citizens, department leaders, politicians, and other criminal justice officials are not truthful and honest in their dealings with officers. Some observers say that this apparent cynicism does not mean that police officers do not trust citizens or that the police do not hope to improve conditions (Langworthy, 1987a, 1987b). Part of the explanation for police cynicism may be the stress of the job (Terry, 1985; Travis & Vukovich, 1990).

The existence and nature of police officer stress has been an important but elusive topic of research for several decades. The evidence about the level of stress experienced by police officers in comparison to those in other occupations is unclear. Policing, as an occupation, contains some unique stressors, such as the chance of killing someone, the threat of attack, and the need to deal with human misery and crime. Police officers also face many of the same stressors faced by other workers, such as rotating shifts, organizational insensitivity, red tape, and the like (Vila & Kenney, 2002). Recent investigations of police stress indicate that what causes stress and how much stress is felt may differ between officers (Violanti & Aron, 1995). Contemporary reforms aimed at implementing community-oriented policing appear to be stressful for some officers, especially for police supervisors (Lord, 1996). Because different officers may respond differently to potential stressors, it may be, as Storch and Panzarella (1996:106) conclude, that ". . . police officers seem to experience about the same level of stress as other people." Research (Haar & Morash, 1999; Morash, Kwak & Haar, 2006) reveals that officers experience stress differently, and develop different coping patterns based on their gender, race, and length of service. While police may experience stress as do other people, not all police experience it to the same degree, nor cope with it as well. Some officers respond to stress by leaving the profession (Wood, 2001, 2002). Burnout and turnover represent costly problems for police organizations, as replacing officers requires extensive and expensive selection and training processes.

The police officer is a member of an organization and, as such, must be careful to serve the ends of the organization. She or he is also a bureaucrat, and must abide by the rules and regulations of the bureaucracy. Finally, the officer is a member of an occupational group that is larger than his or her individual department. Thus, in any given situation, the behavior of the officer reflects the limits imposed by (1) the department, (2) the goals of the organization, and (3) the prestige of the occupational group. The officer is (at least subliminally) aware that his or her actions will be judged against all of these criteria. Indeed, Bazemore and Senjo reported that officers assigned as neighborhood police interacted with juveniles differently than officers with traditional assignments. They note that the neighborhood officers engaged in more preventive and coalition-building activities, and displayed a more positive attitude toward youths (1997:77).

To this mix of standards must be added the social context of the situation in which the officer is operating (Worden, 1989). The victim/witness has a set of expectations about how the officer will behave. The officer has expectations about himself or herself and about the victim/witness. Finally, onlookers also have their expectations. The officer is aware of many of these expectations, and they affect his or her behavior. Thus, while every call to which the police respond is not dangerous or difficult, there are no simple calls. As we discovered when we examined the arrest decision, the law is only one influence on police officer decisions. Other "contextual" factors that may influence the decisions of officers include characteristics of the citizens (Chermak, 1998; Mastrofski, Parks & Worden, 1998). The presence of witnesses and bystanders can also influence the officer's decisions (Connolly, Huzurbazar & Routh-McGee, 2000).

The discretionary nature of the decisions officers make concerning the criminal justice system means that the forces that influence their decisions also influence the workings of the justice system (Brooks, 1989). If a police officer is prejudiced, the system will be prejudiced to some extent. Thus, the characteristics of officers, as well as their relationship to the organization and the citizenry, are important influences on criminal justice system operations. The characteristics of individual officers, including demographic factors (age, gender, ethnicity) and experience (rank, years on the job, etc.) have been linked to officer decisions (Bayley & Garafalo, 1989; Fridell & Binder, 1992; Hale & Wyland, 1993; Riksheim & Chermak, 1993; Worden & Brandl, 1990).

Just as Wilson (1968) suggested that there are types of police organizations, others have suggested that there are types of police officers. William Muir (1977), for example, argues that officers differ in terms of their willingness to use coercive force and their ability to empathize with or understand citizens. These differences result in four distinct types of officers differing in the ways they do policing. Muir used the term "enforcers" to describe those officers who are willing to use force but unable to empathize with citizens. Those comfortable with force and able to empathize were called "professionals." Officers who were unwilling to use force were either "reciprocators," who could empathize with citizens, or "avoiders," who did not understand citizens. While there are many anecdotal and qualitative data to support the notion that police officer types exist, these types have not been identified in attitudinal surveys of officers (Hochstedler, 1981). Nonetheless, it is reasonable to conclude that police officers probably differ among themselves, and that these differences are relevant to an understanding of their criminal justice decisions (Travis & Langworthy, 2008).

Because we believe that individual officer characteristics influence police decisions, the selection and training of police officers is an important topic. Police selection typically involves a number of steps that are designed to produce the best qualified police officers. Research into the police selection process, however, indicates that it is not always effective. Metchik (1999) suggests that our reliance on a "screening out" model aimed at dismissing unsuitable candidates is not as effective as one that seeks to identify and retain good candidates. Similarly, Gaines and Falkenberg (1998) argue that current written examinations may not adequately identify the best candidates, and may have the negative effect of excluding female and minority candidates. Zhao and Lovrich (1998) suggest that the presence of a formal affirmative action policy does not automatically increase the number of female and minority officers hired in a jurisdiction.

Beyond selecting police officers, training and experience also produce differences among officers, and training is frequently used as a vehicle to change officer attitudes and practices (Buerger, 1998). Hoath, Schneider, and Starr (1998) and Travis and Winston (1998) have suggested that officer attitudes are related to job satisfaction.

Russell and MacLachlan (1999) found that while officers in their sample felt that community policing resulted in their having more input into decisions, they also felt that it was less likely that they could accomplish goals. In short, part of the task in police officer selection and training is to develop a good match between the skills and orientations of officers and the tasks and goals of the police organization.

The characteristics of the officers involved in a situation also help determine actions (Terrill & Mastrofski, 2002). One of the recent changes in American policing has been the hiring of women and minority group members. Some observers feared that women would be unable to endure the danger and rigors of police work (Hale & Wyland, 1993; Potts, 1983). Others felt that the inclusion of women and minorities would improve community relations. Analyses of the effects and effectiveness of these new police officers are incomplete. Thus far, however, the data show that female and minority group members make good police officers (Burke, Richardsen & Martinussen, 2006; Grennan, 1987). Box 5.9 shows, however, that by 2000, only about 10 percent of sworn officers were female, and almost 23 percent were members of ethnic minority groups. Robin Haar (1997) studied the integration of female and minority police officers into one police department. She noted that minority and female officers faced several problems in their interpersonal interactions with white, male officers. In part, this is because efforts by the organization to assist integration, such as vigorous support of affirmative action, served to drive a wedge between the patrol officers, dividing them by race and sex. More recent challenges to affirmative action policies are threatening to limit diversity among police personnel. Eric Moore (2001) contends that the solution to challenges to affirmative action policies in police agencies involves careful planning and research to determine and justify the goals of the policy. At the same time, there is evidence that traditional officer selection practices such as physical ability testing still work to exclude qualified female and minority candidates (Lonsway, 2003).

Box 5.9	Distribution of Full-Time Police Officers by Race and Sex, 2003

Sex:	
Male	88.7%
Female	11.3%
Race:	
White	76.4%
Black	11.7%
Hispanic	9.1%
Other	2.8%

Source: M. Hickman & B. Reaves (2006), *Local Police Departments, 2003* (Washington, DC: Bureau of Justice Statistics):7.

The complexity of the job facing the individual officer is multiplied several times when we analyze the complexity of policing in society on an organizational level. The department has expectations and goals; the community has expectations and goals; and the prosecutor's office, the courts, and the local government also have expectations and goals for the department. Many times the goals or expectations of the audiences of a police department conflict with each other and with those of the department.

Policing in the Whole System

Returning to our discussion of the location of the criminal justice system within the whole system of American society, Wilson's observations about the police indicate the influence of environmental factors. He saw police agency styles as being related to community characteristics. The size, structure, and composition of the community, Wilson (1968) argued, create a "political culture" in which the police exist. Part of this culture defines the limits of police actions that are acceptable in the community. Service-style agencies were found in suburban, middle-class communities. Watchman-style and legalistic agencies were found in more heterogeneous (mixed population in terms of social class and ethnicity) cities. The distinction between whether the police would demonstrate a watchman or legalistic style seemed to be related to the type of government in the cities. Those with "professional" governments (city managers) were legalistic; those in "political" governments (strong mayor) were watchman-style.

Wilson did not contend that city governments directly influenced policing practices, but that differences in communities created different environments and police styles reflected those environments. Thus, the job the police do and the way in which they do it reflect the values and structure of the community in which they exist (Travis & Langworthy, 2008). As a subsystem of the criminal justice and social systems, the police department adapts to its environment so as to support the existing equilibrium. For example, consider the likely public reaction to a watchman style of policing in a homogeneous, middle-class, suburban community. It is likely that citizens would complain about the failure of the police to enforce the laws, and would demand police reform. On the other hand, a legalistic style would also generate complaints about overzealous enforcement. The service style is most likely to fit the desires and expectations of the citizens in such a community.

Finally, given the essentially democratic nature of government (and policing in particular) in the United States, it is logical that the police reflect the desires of the citizens. After all, if it is the citizens who define the police job through their calls for service, it is the citizens who, at some level, direct the police. The spread of community-oriented policing promises to increase variety in policing. Each large police department can potentially become comprised of a large number of distinct "neighborhood" or "community" police. The types of issues that attract police attention, and the ways in which police react to problems, may begin to vary not just between departments but within departments between neighborhoods.

The next chapter examines the law enforcement role in the criminal justice system. It continues with a brief discussion of the forces that affect discretionary decisions by police officers. The final part of the chapter examines some contemporary issues in law enforcement. Each of these topics must be understood within the context of police history, functions, and organization.

Review Questions

1. What is meant by calling the police the "agency of last resort"?

2. Briefly trace the development of policing in the United States.

3. Describe how the police can be considered to be a human services agency.

4. How can community policing be considered a revised role for the police?

5. Differentiate between reactive and proactive policing.

6. How do the multiple tasks expected of the police affect them as part of the justice system?

7. What factors influence the decisions and behavior of police officers?

References

Alpert, G. & R. Dunham (1988). *Policing Urban America*. Prospect Heights, IL: Waveland.

Barlow, D. & M. Barlow (2000). *Police in a Multicultural Society: An American Story*. Prospect Heights, IL: Waveland.

Bayley, D. & J. Garafalo (1989). "The Management of Violence by Police Patrol Officers." *Criminology* 27(1):1-25.

Bazemore, G. & S. Senjo (1997). "Police Encounters with Juveniles Revisited: An Exploratory Study of Themes and Styles in Community Policing." *Policing* 20(1):60-82.

Bittner, E. (1970). *The Functions of Police in Modern Society*. Rockville, MD: National Institute of Mental Health.

Bittner, E. (1990). *Aspects of Police Work*. Boston: Northeastern University Press.

Black, D.J. (1972). "The Mobilization of Law." *Journal of Legal Studies* 2(1):125-149.

Brooks, L. (1989). "Police Discretionary Behavior: A Study of Style." In R. Dunham & G. Alpert (eds.), *Critical Issues in Policing: Contemporary Readings*. Prospect Heights, IL: Waveland, 121-145.

Buerger, M. (1998). "Police Training as Pentecost: Using Tools Singularly Ill-Suited to the Purpose of Reform." *Police Quarterly* 1(1):27-64.

Buerger, M. & L. Mazerolle (1998). "Third-Party Policing: A Theoretical Analysis of an Emerging Trend." *Justice Quarterly* 15(2):301-327.

Burke, R., A. Richardsen & M. Martinussen (2006). "Gender Differences in Policing: Reasons for Optimism?" *Policing: An International Journal of Police Strategies and Management* 29(3):513-523.

Carter, D. (1999). "A Response to 'Community Policing: Thriving Because It Works.'" *Police Quarterly* 2(1):103-109.

Chermak, S. (1998). "Predicting Crime Story Salience: The Effects of Crime, Victim, and Defendant Characteristics." *Journal of Criminal Justice* 26(1):61-70.

Chermak, S., E. McGarrell & A. Weiss (2001). "Citizens' Perceptions of Aggressive Traffic Enforcement Strategies." *Justice Quarterly* 18(2):365-391.

Connolly, C., S. Huzurbazar & T. Routh-McGee (2000). "Multiple Parties in Domestic Violence Situations and Arrest." *Journal of Criminal Justice* 28(3):181-188.

Cooper, V., A. McLearen & P. Zapf (2004). "Dispositional Decisions With Mentally Ill: Police Perceptions and Characteristics." *Police Quarterly* 7(3):295-310.

Critchley, T. (1972). *A History of Police in England and Wales,* 2nd ed. Montclair, NJ: Patterson Smith.

Das, D. (1987). *Understanding Police Human Relations.* Metuchen, NJ: Scarecrow Press.

Duffee, D., R. Fluellen & B. Renauer (1999). "Community Variables in Community Policing." *Police Quarterly* 2(1):5-35.

Eck, J. & W. Spelman (1987). "Who You Gonna Call? The Police as Problem Busters." *Crime & Delinquency* 33(1):31-52.

Engel, R. & E. Silver (2001). "Policing Mentally Disordered Suspects: A Reexamination of the Criminalization Hypothesis." *Criminology* 39(2):225-252.

Evans, B., G. Coman & R. Stanley (1992). "The Police Personality: Type A Behavior and Trait Anxiety." *Journal of Criminal Justice* 20(5):429-442.

Famega, C. (2004). "Variation in Officer Downtime: A Review of the Research." *Policing: An International Journal of Police Strategies and Management* (28(3):388-414.

Finn, P.E. & M. Sullivan (1988). "Police Respond to Special Populations." *NIJ Reports* (May/June):2-8.

Fogelson, R. (1977). *Big-City Police.* Cambridge, MA: Harvard University Press.

Fridell, L. & A. Binder (1992). "Police Officer Decisionmaking in Potentially Violent Confrontations." *Journal of Criminal Justice* 20(5):385-399.

Fritsch, E., T. Caeti, P. Tobolowsky & R. Taylor (2004). "Police Referrals of Crime Victims to Compensation Sources: An Empirical Analysis of Attitudinal and Structural Impediments." *Police Quarterly* 7(3):372-393.

Fyfe, J.J. (1979). "Administrative Intervention on Police Shooting Discretion: An Empirical Examination." *Journal of Criminal Justice* 7(4):309-324.

Gaines, L. & S. Falkenberg (1998). "An Evaluation of the Written Selection Test: Effectiveness and Alternatives." *Journal of Criminal Justice* 26(2):175-183.

Goldstein, H. (1978). *Policing a Free Society.* Cambridge, MA: Ballinger.

Goldstein, H. (1990). *Problem-Oriented Policing.* New York: McGraw-Hill.

Graber, D. (1979). "Evaluating Crime-Fighting Policies: Media Images and Public Perspective." In R. Baker & F. Meyer, Jr. (eds.), *Evaluating Alternative Law-Enforcement Polices.* Lexington, MA: Lexington Books, 179-199.

Greene, J. (2000). "Community Policing in America: Changing the Nature, Structure, and Function of the Police." In J. Horney (ed.), *Policies, Procedures, and Decisions of the Criminal Justice System.* Washington, DC: National Institute of Justice, Criminal Justice 2000, Volume 3:299-370.

Grennan, S. (1987). "Findings on the Role of Officer Gender in Violent Encounters with Citizens." *Journal of Police Science and Administration* 15(1):78-85.

Haar, R. (1997). "Patterns of Interaction in a Police Patrol Bureau: Race and Gender Barriers to Integration." *Justice Quarterly* 14(1):53-85.

Haar, R. & M. Morash (1999). "Gender, Race and Strategies of Coping with Occupational Stress in Policing." *Justice Quarterly* 16(2):303-336.

Hale, D. & S. Wyland (1993). "Dragons and Dinosaurs: The Plight of Patrol Women." *Police Forum* 3(2):1-6.

Hawdon, J., J. Ryan & S. Griffin (2003). "Policing Tactics and Perceptions of Police Legitimacy." *Police Quarterly* 6(4):469-491.

Hoath, D., F. Schneider & M. Starr (1998). "Police Job Satisfaction as a Function of Career Orientation and Position Tenure: Implications for Selection and Community Policing." *Journal of Criminal Justice* 26(4):337-348.

Hochstedler, E. (1981). "Testing Types: A Review and Test of Police Types." *Journal of Criminal Justice* 9(6):451-466.

Holmes, S. (1997). "The Occupational Definition of Police Use of Excessive Force." Unpublished doctoral dissertation. Cincinnati: University of Cincinnati, Division of Criminal Justice.

Jackson, A. & J. Wade (2005). "Police Perceptions of Social Capital and Responsibility: An Explanation of Proactive Policing." *Policing: An International Journal of Police Strategies and Management* 28(1):49-68.

Jiao, A. (1998). "Community-Oriented Policing and Policing-Oriented Community." *Journal of Crime and Justice* 20(1):135-158.

Johnson, D.R. (1981). *American Law Enforcement: A History.* St. Louis: Forum Press.

Johnson, H.A. & N.T. Wolfe (2001). *History of Criminal Justice,* 3rd ed. Cincinnati: Anderson.

Kane, R. (2000). "Permanent Beat Assignments in Association with Community Policing: Assessing the Impact on Police Officers' Field Activity." *Justice Quarterly* 17(2):259-280.

Kappeler, V. (1996). "Making Police History in Light of Modernity: A Sign of the Times?" *Police Forum* 6(3):1-6.

Kelling, G. (1988). *Foot Patrol. Crime File Study Guide.* Washington, DC: National Institute of Justice.

Kennedy, D.B. (1983). "Toward a Clarification of the Police Role as a Human Services Agency." *Criminal Justice Review* 8(2):41-45.

King, W. (1999). "Time, Constancy, and Change in American Municipal Police Organizations." *Police Quarterly* 2(3):338-364.

King, W. (2003). "Bending Granite Revisited: The Command Rank Structure of American Police Organizations." *Policing: An International Journal of Police Strategies and Management* 26(2):208-230.

King, W. (2005). "Toward a Better Understanding of the Hierarchical Nature of Police Organizations: Conception and Measurement." *Journal of Criminal Justice* 33(1):97-109.

King, W. & T. Dunn (2004). "Dumping: Police Initiated Transjurisdictional Transport of Troublesome Persons." *Police Quarterly* 7(3):339-358.

Klockars, C. (1985). *The Idea of Police.* Beverly Hills, CA: Sage.

Kraska, P. (1994). "The Police and the Military in the Post -Cold War Era: Streamlining the State's Use of Force Entities in the Drug War." *Police Forum* 4(1):1-8.

Langworthy, R.H. (1985). "Police Department Size and Agency Structure." *Journal of Criminal Justice* 13(1):15-28.

Langworthy, R.H. (1987a). "Police Cynicism: What We Know from the Niederhoffer Scale." *Journal of Criminal Justice* 15(1):17-36.

Langworthy, R.H. (1987b). "Comment: Have We Measured the Concept(s) of Police Cynicism Using Niederhoffer's Cynicism Index?" *Justice Quarterly* 4(2):277-280.

Liederbach, J. & J. Frank (2006). "Policing the Big Beat: An Observational Study of County Level Patrol and Comparisons to Local Small Town and Rural Officers." *Journal of Crime and Justice* 29(1):21-44.

Lonsway, K. (2003). "Tearing Down the Wall: Problems with Consistency, Validity, and Adverse Impact of Physical Agility Testing in Police Selection." *Police Quarterly* 6(3):237-277.

Lord, V. (1996). "An Impact of Community Policing: Reported Stressors, Social Support, and Strain Among Police Officers in a Changing Police Department." *Journal of Criminal Justice* 24(6):503-522.

Lundman, R. (1980). *Police and Policing: An Introduction.* New York: Holt, Rinehart & Winston.

Lurigio, A. & J. Swartz (2000). "Changing the Contours of the Criminal Justice System to Meet the Needs of Persons with Serious Mental Illness." In J. Horney (ed.), *Policies, Processes, and Decisions of the Criminal Justice System.* Washington, DC: National Institute of Justice, Criminal Justice 2000, Volume 3:45-108.

Maguire, E., Y. Shin, J. Zhao & K. Hassell (2003). "Structural Change in Large Police Agencies During the 1990s." *Policing: An International Journal of Police Strategies and Management* 26(2):251-275.

Manning, P.K. (1978). "The Police: Mandate, Strategies and Appearances." In P.K. Manning & J. Van Maanen (eds.), *Policing: A View from the Street.* Santa Monica, CA: Goodyear, 7-31.

Mastrofski, S., R. Parks & R. Worden (1998). *Community Policing in Action: Lessons from an Observational Study.* Washington, DC: National Institute of Justice.

Mastrofski, S., R. Parks, A. Reiss & R. Worden (1999a). *Policing Neighborhoods: A Report from Indianapolis.* Washington, DC: National Institute of Justice.

Mastrofski, S., R. Parks, A. Reiss & R. Worden (1999b). *Policing Neighborhoods: A Report from St. Petersburg.* Washington, DC: National Institute of Justice.

Mastrofski, S.D., R.R. Ritti & D. Hoffmaster (1987). "Organizational Determinants of Police Discretion: The Case of Drinking-Driving." *Journal of Criminal Justice* 15(5):387-402.

McCampbell, M.S. (1986). *Field Training for Police: State of the Art.* Washington, DC: National Institute of Justice.

Metchik, E. (1999). "An Analysis of the 'Screening Out' Model of Police Officer Selection." *Police Quarterly* 2(1)79-95.

Monkonnen, E. (1981). *Police in Urban America: 1860-1920.* Cambridge, UK: Cambridge University Press.

Moore, E. (2001). "Emerging Legal Constraints on Affirmative Action in Police Agencies and How to Adapt to Them." *Journal of Criminal Justice* 29(1):11-19.

Moore, M., R. Trojanowicz & G. Kelling (1988). *Crime and Policing.* Washington, DC: U.S. Department of Justice.

Moore, R. (1987). "Posse Comitatus Revisited: The Use of the Military in Civil Law Enforcement." *Journal of Criminal Justice* 15(5):375-386.

Morash, M., D. Kwak & R. Haar (2006). "Gender Differences in the Predictors of Police Stress." *Policing: An International Journal of Police Strategies and Management* 29(3):541-563.

Muir, W. (1977). *Police: Streetcorner Politicians.* Chicago: University of Chicago Press.

Niederhoffer, A. (1967). *Behind the Shield: The Police in Urban Society.* Garden City, NJ: Anchor Books.

Newsweek (1987). "Forcing the Mentally Ill to Get Help." (November 9, 1987):47-48.

Ostrom, E., R. Parks & G. Whitaker (1978). *Patterns of Metropolitan Policing.* Cambridge, MA: Ballinger.

Panzarella, R. & J. Alicea (1997). "Police Tactics in Incidents with Mentally Disturbed Persons." *Policing: An International Journal of Police Strategies and Management* 20(2):326-338.

Parks, R., S. Mastrofski, C. DeJone & M. Gray (1999). "How Officers Spend Their Time With the Community." *Justice Quarterly* 16(3):483-518.

Plummer, L. (1999). "Community Policing: Thriving Because It Works." *Police Quarterly* 2(1):96-102.

Potts, L. (1983). "Equal Employment Opportunity and Female Employment in Police Agencies." *Journal of Criminal Justice* 11(6):505-524.

Reaves, B. (2007). *Census of State and Local Law Enforcement Agencies, 2004.* Washington, DC: Bureau of Justice Statistics.

Reaves, B. (1996). *Local Police Departments, 1993.* Washington, DC: Bureau of Justice Statistics.

Reaves. B. & A. Goldberg (2000). *Local Police Departments 1997.* Washington, DC: Bureau of Justice Statistics.

Regoli, R.M., J.P. Crouch, R.G. Culbertson & E.D. Poole (1987). "Police Professionalism and Cynicism Reconsidered: An Assessment of Measurement Issues." *Justice Quarterly* 4(2):257-275.

Riksheim, E. & S. Chermak (1993). "Causes of Police Behavior Revisited." *Journal of Criminal Justice* 21(4):353-382.

Rojek, J. (2003). "A Decade of Excellence in Problem-Oriented Policing: Characteristics of the Goldstein Award Winners." *Police Quarterly* 6(4):492-515.

Russell, G. & S. MacLachlan (1999). "Community Policing, Decentralized Decision Making, and Employee Satisfaction." *Journal of Crime and Justice* 22(2):33-54.

Sherman, L. (1988). *Neighborhood Safety. Crime File Study Guide.* Washington, DC: National Institute of Justice.

Skolnick, J. (1966). *Justice without Trial.* New York: John Wiley.

Stewart-Brown, R. (1936). *The Serjeants of the Peace in Medieval England and Wales.* Manchester, UK: Manchester University Press.

Storch, J. & R. Panzarella (1996). "Police Stress: State-Trait Anxiety in Relation to Occupational and Personal Stressors." *Journal of Criminal Justice* 24(2):99-108.

Sun, I. (2003). "Officer Proactivity: A Comparison Between Police Field Training Officers and Non-Field Training Officers." *Journal of Criminal Justice* 31(3):265-277.

Teplin, L. (2000). "Police Discretion and Mentally Ill Persons." *NIJ Journal* (July):8-15.

Terrill, W. & S. Mastrofski (2002). "Situational and Officer-Based Determinants of Police Coercion." *Justice Quarterly* 19(2):215-248.

Terry, W.C. (1985). "Police Stress as a Professional Self-Image." *Journal of Criminal Justice* 13(6):501-512.

Toch, H. (1997). "The Democratization of Policing in the United States: 1895-1973." *Police Forum* 7(2):1-8.

Travis, L. & R. Langworthy (2008). *Policing in America: A Balance of Forces,* 4th ed. Englewood Cliffs, NJ: Prentice Hall.

Travis, L.F. III & C. Winston (1998). "Dissension in the Ranks: Officer Resistance to Community Policing, Cynicism, and Support for the Organization." *Journal of Crime and Justice* 21(2):139-156.

Travis, L.F., III & R. Vukovich (1990). "Cynicism and Job Satisfaction in Policing: Muddying the Waters." *American Journal of Criminal Justice* 15(1):90-104.

Trojanowicz, R. & B. Bucqueroux (1990). *Community Policing: A Contemporary Perspective.* Cincinnati: Anderson.

Trojanowicz, R., V. Kappeler, L. Gaines & B. Bucqueroux (1998). *Community Policing: A Contemporary Perspective,* 2nd ed. Cincinnati: Anderson.

Van Maanen, J. (1978). "Observations on the Making of Policemen." In P.K. Manning & J. Van Maanen (eds.), *Policing: A View from the Street.* Santa Monica, CA: Goodyear, 292-308.

Vila, B. & D. Kenney (2002). "Tired Cops: The Prevalence and Potential Consequences of Police Fatigue." *NIJ Journal* (248):16-221.

Violanti, J. & F. Aron (1995). "Police Stressors: Variations in Perception Among Police Personnel." *Journal of Criminal Justice* 23(3):287-294.

Vogel, R. & R. Adams (1983). "Police Professionalism: A Longitudinal Cohort Study." *Journal of Police Science and Administration* 11(4):474-484.

Walker, S. (1977). *A Critical History of Police Reform: The Emergence of Professionalism.* Lexington, MA: Lexington Books.

Webster, J.A. (1970). "Police Task and Time Study." *Journal of Criminal Law, Criminology and Police Science* 60(1):94-100.

Wilson, J.Q. (1968). *Varieties of Police Behavior.* Cambridge, MA: Harvard University Press.

Wilson, J. & G. Kelling (1982). "Broken Windows: Police and Neighborhood Safety." *Atlantic Monthly* 249(March):29-38.

Wood, D. (2001). "Rural Alaskan Police Face High Turnover." *NIJ Journal* (January):16-23.

Wood, D. (2002). "Explanations of Employment Turnover Among Alaska Village Public Safety Officers." *Journal of Criminal Justice* 30(3):197-216.

Worden, R. (1989). "Situational and Attitudinal Explanations of Police Behavior: A Theoretical Reappraisal and Empirical Assessment." *Law & Society Review* 23(4):667-711.

Worden, R. & S. Brandl (1990). "Protocol Analysis of Police Decision-making: Toward a Theory of Police Behavior." *American Journal of Criminal Justice* 14(2):297-318.

Worrall, J. (2006). "Does Targeting Minor Offenses Reduce Serious Crime? A Provisional, Affirmative Answer Based on an Analysis of County-Level Data." *Police Quarterly* 9(1):47-72.

Zhao, J., N. He & N. Lovrich (2003). "Community Policing: Did It Change the Basic Functions of Policing in the 1990s? A National Follow-Up Study." *Justice Quarterly* 20(4):697-724.

Zhao, J. & N. Lovrich (1998). "Determinants of Minority Employment in American Municipal Police Agencies: The Representation of African American Officers." *Journal of Criminal Justice* 26(4):266-277.

Zhao, J., N. Lovrich & T. Robinson (2001). "Community Policing: Is It Changing the Basic Functions of Policing? Findings from a Longitudinal Study of 200+ Municipal Police Agencies." *Journal of Criminal Justice* 29(5):365-377.

Chapter 6

Law Enforcement in the Criminal Justice System

Important Terms

arrest

booking

cold case squads

crackdown

decoy operation

detection

entrapment

exclusionary rule

frisk

good faith exception

"hot pursuit"

interrogation

inventory search

lineups

low visibility

Miranda warnings

plain view doctrine

probable cause

search

sting operation

street sense

throw-downs

Three principal decision points of the criminal justice system occur in the law enforcement segment of the process: (1) detection of crime, (2) investigation, and (3) arrest. As decisions, the police have choices about what, when, how, and whom to detect, investigate, or arrest. The existence of choices means that the police have discretion in these decisions. These activities comprise the scope of police crime control, with the exception of preventive practices such as uniformed patrol, and proactive problem-solving efforts. It is these three decision points to which we will devote most of our attention in this chapter.

Detection

Detection is the discovery of crime or probable crime by the police. Once the police come to believe that a crime has been committed, the justice process begins. Detection hinges on many factors, ranging from the seriousness of the alleged crime and the observation powers of the officer, to the credibility of the complainant or witness. As indicated by our earlier discussion of "unfounding," sometimes the officer decides that a reported crime did not, in fact, occur. In this case, she or he would label the complaint "unfounded," and would proceed as if nothing out of the ordinary had happened (Sudnow, 1964).

Detection of crime by police takes place in the two major ways described in the previous chapter: reactively or proactively. The most common way in which police come to learn about crime is reactively, through the receipt of citizen complaints. Most crimes are brought to the attention of the police rather than discovered by them (Tiffany, McIntyre & Rotenberg, 1967). Some, however, are detected proactively, through undercover operations or through the observations of officers on patrol. Still other crimes are discovered through the actions of related agents, such as investigative grand juries, legislative committees, and the like. These latter means of detection can best be categorized under the heading of reactive detection, because in these cases police gain knowledge of the existence of crimes from complaints.

We refer to detection as a decision process because often what appears to be a decision made on the spur of the moment is actually the culmination of months or years of training or effort. This is particularly true of many of those crimes that are discovered by the police. What seems to be a nearly arbitrary decision to stop and question someone, or to check the license of a particular automobile, is in fact the result of a long process of learning and intelligence gathering. What the officer does is decide that further investigation is warranted.

Smith, Makarios, and Alpert (2006) reported a study of police officer decisionmaking in Miami. The results suggest that police officers form suspicion based on prior experience. For instance, if the officer has primarily encountered crime among males, the officer will be more suspicious of men. In the end, this means officers will be more observant of males, more likely to search and question males, and more likely to arrest males. The researchers note that in the long run, this may lead to a sort of "self-fulfilling prophecy" because police will look for crime where they expect to find it—among males, for example. In turn, they will find more crime among males because that is where they look, and that will encourage them to continue to be more suspicious of men than of women. Of course, other data (self-report and victimization) suggest that men are more likely to be criminal, so increased police suspicion of males may simply be reasonable.

Harvey Sacks (1978) described **street sense**, which he called an "incongruity procedure." Street sense is the ability of experienced police officers to "know" who is likely to be a criminal or to be dangerous. Sacks's term is appropriate because what the police officer relies upon is that something about the individual or circumstances is incongruous or "not right"; that is, something does not fit. What appears normal to the average citizen may appear strange to the experienced officer. Police officers are taught to look for certain clues, such as overcoats being worn on warm days, mud splatters on rear license plates, and the like. The average citizen either does not notice such things or does not interpret them as possibly being crime-related. After several years of experience, most officers become quite adept at the use of the incongruity procedure. The detection of crime then often rests on the police officer's perception or interpretation of the incongruous circumstances.

Officer perceptions have traditionally been attributed to training and experience. That is, over time, and with training, police officers are sensitized to crime and potentially criminal circumstances. Police officers see (and seek) evidence of potential crime in circumstances that the typical citizen would not view as suspicious. In recent years, efforts have been made to improve officer accuracy in identifying criminal situations. One of the most controversial of these has been the use of "profiles" in the enforcement of drug laws. Based on data taken from arrests, some jurisdictions have developed "profiles" of people who are likely to be engaged in certain types of crimes. For example, young, male, minority group members driving late-model automobiles might be targeted for traffic stops and preliminary investigations as potential drug couriers. These profiles understandably antagonize law-abiding citizens who are so targeted and contribute to poor public relations with the police (Reitzel & Piquero, 2006).

Investigation

Investigation is a process that continues throughout the law enforcement segment of the criminal justice system, and that often continues into the court segment as well. The decision involved in investigation is split into two parts: (1) whether to investigate a suspected crime, and (2) how best to proceed with the investigation if one is initiated. Box 6.1 presents a model of police activity in responding to crime.

Box 6.1 The Criminal Apprehension Process

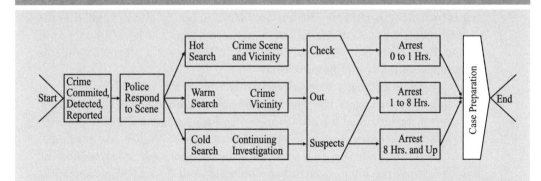

Source: P. Weston & K. Wells (1986), *Criminal Investigation: Basic Perspectives*, 4th ed. (Englewood Cliffs, NJ: Prentice Hall):3. Reprinted by permission of Prentice Hall, Inc., Upper Saddle River, NJ.

An investigation is the accumulation of information and evidence that links a particular person or group of persons to a particular crime or set of crimes. It is the process by which formal criminal charges can be brought against identified individuals. As an evidence-gathering activity, the principal tools of investigation are search and interrogation. Other tools and skills are employed, depending on the nature of the offense and the resources that are available to the police, for example, forensic analyses, lineups, and surveillance (Palmiotto, 1984).

Search

Search involves the seeking out of evidence of a crime or the location of a suspect. It entails the physical inspection of papers, premises, and possessions by the police. The U.S. Constitution provides that searches can be conducted only upon the issuance of a warrant based upon probable cause. In practice, however, the warrant requirement has proven impractical and problematic. The U.S. Supreme Court has recognized a number of exceptions to the warrant requirement. Most of these are based on a determination of reasonable behavior by the police under the circumstances. If the police have behaved reasonably, the search will be construed to be valid.

Police can obtain a search warrant from a judge or magistrate if they provide the court with information that establishes the existence of probable cause (evidence that leads a reasonable person to conclude that a crime has occurred and evidence of the crime may be found) to support the search. In this case, the court has the chance to review the police decision and protect the right of the suspect to be free from unreasonable intervention by the police.

To control unreasonable or improper police behavior in regard to searches, the Supreme Court has adopted the exclusionary rule. This rule states that illegally or improperly obtained evidence cannot be used in a trial. The logic of the rule is that the police conduct a search in order to obtain evidence of criminal behavior, and excluding this evidence from trial defeats the purpose of the search. Thus, theoretically, if the police cannot conduct a legal search, they will not conduct any search.

The Supreme Court developed and imposed an exclusionary rule on federal law enforcement in 1914, in *Weeks v. United States*, but refused to apply it to the states, hoping instead that the various state systems would arrive at a better solution to the problem of illegal searches. Finally, in 1961, the Court applied the rule to the states in the case of *Mapp v. Ohio*.

Acting on a tip that a suspect (wanted in connection with a bombing) and gambling equipment would be found at the home of Dolree Mapp, Cleveland police went there and asked for admission, which Mapp refused. Three hours later, more officers arrived and again the police asked to enter. When Mapp refused, one of the officers displayed papers that he claimed to be a search warrant and the officers entered the home, searched the premises, and discovered pornographic materials in a trunk in the basement of the house. Mapp was arrested and charged with possession of obscene materials.

The Supreme Court ruled that the police behavior in this case was unacceptable and that the evidence (the obscene materials) must be excluded from any future trial of Mapp. Weighing heavily in the Court's decision were the facts that the police had time to secure a warrant but did not do so, that the officers claimed to have had a warrant (but never introduced one in Mapp's trial), and that Mapp was apparently not guilty of the crimes of which she was suspected. In the end, the Court held that the exclusionary rule used to support the Fourth Amendment of the U.S. Constitution was applicable to state cases through the due process clause of the Fourteenth Amendment.

The *Mapp* case and the *Miranda* decision (discussed below) led to charges that the Supreme Court was "handcuffing" the police. Critics of the Court launched virulent attacks on this interpretation of the Constitution. They believed that an "overly liberal" stance characterized these and similar decisions of the Court. Nonetheless, the Supreme Court had interpreted the Constitution, and the exclusionary rule became the law of the land (Wilson, 1988).

Given that the Court would distinguish between the types of searches that would yield admissible evidence and those that would not, it was possible to determine exceptions to the warrant requirement by learning the circumstances under which warrantless searches had been held admissible by the Court. Generally, the Court has identified the following circumstances to be exempt from the warrant requirement:

- limited protective searches (frisks)

- searches incident to lawful arrest

- searches conducted by police in emergency situations or "hot pursuit" of a suspect

- border searches, upon consent of the person being subjected to the search

- searches of automobiles

- inventory searches

- seizure of evidence "in plain view" of the officer.

The **frisk** is a traditional police practice that has been upheld by the Supreme Court when conducted under specific circumstances. The Court outlined the requirements for a valid frisk in 1968 when it decided the case of *Terry v. Ohio*. In this case, an experienced Cleveland police officer conducted a limited "pat down" of the outer garments of suspected robbers to ensure his own safety as well as that of innocent bystanders.

In the *Terry* case, a 39-year veteran officer observed two suspects repeatedly walk past and look into a store. The officer came to the conclusion that the men were "casing" the store for a robbery, and he approached them to investigate. When the two stopped to confer with another man, the offi-

Fresno (California) police search the trunk of a car before letting it leave the area. Police were searching for bank robbery suspects who shot at police while trying to flee. In *Warden v. Hayden* (1967), the Supreme Court determined that officers may follow and search for a suspect when in "hot pursuit." *Photo credit: AP Photo/The Fresno Bee, Craig Kohlruss.*

cer approached and asked for their names. When they mumbled in response, he turned one of them around and patted him down, finding a revolver. He frisked the other men, found another gun, and placed the men under arrest.

The Supreme Court ruled that the officer had acted reasonably under the circumstances and that the evidence (guns) was taken in a reasonable search. Therefore, the evidence could be used at trial. If an officer has a reasonable suspicion that criminal activity is occurring, the officer has the authority to stop persons and to request identification and information. Moreover, if the officer has a reasonable belief that these individuals may be armed, and if nothing in the initial investigation dispels this reasonable fear, an officer may conduct a "frisk" to protect self and others.

The frisk is a protective search limited in scope to only that which is required to assure that the person with whom the officer is dealing is not capable of injuring the officer. Upon a lawful arrest, however, the officer's authority to search is broader. Whereas frisking is limited to a "pat down" of the outer garments to discover weapons, a full search by the officer is permissible in the case of an arrested person. Searches incident to lawful arrest are allowed in order to protect officers through discovery of any weapons, and to secure any evidence of the crime that the offender might otherwise be able to destroy. This type of search is limited to the area within the immediate control of the offender (*Chimel v. California*, 1969).

A "hot pursuit" exception to the warrant requirement was recognized by the Court in the case of *Warden v. Hayden* (1967). While the Court generally would prefer that police officers obtain warrants before conducting a search, it recognizes that there are times when this is impractical. In the *Hayden* case, the police were informed of the crime (a robbery) by a cab driver who followed the suspect to a building. The police arrived at the scene within minutes after the suspect entered the building and were informed by the cab driver that the suspect had gone inside. The police entered the building and searched the premises for evidence of the robbery and for the suspect described to them by the cab driver. The Court decided that, under the circumstances, while the police could have cordoned off the building and awaited a warrant, the time lag involved might have allowed the suspect to destroy the evidence of the crime, or to escape. Thus, when in "hot pursuit," officers may follow and search for the suspect.

The law regarding search at international borders is different from the law of searching residences, according to the Court. As a result of the volume of traffic that crosses our borders and faces the U.S. Customs Service, as well as the potential for smuggling, the Court allows searches of persons and possessions at the nation's borders without the requirement of warrants. Indeed, the U.S. Customs Service periodically conducts random searches at border points.

It is possible for a competent adult to voluntarily waive his or her right to be protected from unreasonable searches. In a consent search the suspect consents or agrees to the search so any evidence found will be admissible. In the *Mapp* case, for example, if Mapp had voluntarily allowed the police to enter her home and search for the bombing suspect, she would not have been successful in her efforts to have the evidence excluded from trial. Anyone with a right to grant consent may do so. In *United States v. Matlock* (1974), the Court ruled that a co-occupant of an apartment could grant consent to a search. In a later case, *Georgia v. Randolph* (2006), the court ruled that police must observe the objections of an occupant even if a co-occupant has given consent for the search.

As a result of the mobility of automobiles, the Court treats automobile searches differently from searches of houses or buildings. In *United States v. Ross* (1982), the Court ruled that police officers could conduct a full search of an automobile that the officers had legitimately stopped, as long as they had probable cause to believe that the automobile contained contraband. The Court has applied the warrant standard of probable cause to the search of automobiles. Thus, as long as the police have probable cause to believe that an automobile contains contraband or evidence, they may search the vehicle and any containers in it.

A related issue surrounding automobiles in particular is the inventory search. If the police seize an automobile or other item, they generally search it to determine the contents for the purpose of inventory. They do not want the owner to claim that valuable property is missing after retrieving the car. In *Chambers v. Maroney* (1970), the Court ruled that a search of an automobile shortly after it was seized was permissible. In *Coolidge v. New Hampshire* (1981), however, the Court held that a search of an automobile required that the officers first obtain a warrant. The fact that the police had held the car for a long period before the search negated the possibility that the *Coolidge* case involved an inventory search. Because the car was in police custody and could not be moved, the probable cause standard of *Ross* was inapplicable because the officers could have obtained a warrant.

Not only may officers search an automobile they have legitimately stopped, they can also order the driver and passengers from the car and "frisk" those individuals (*Maryland v. Wilson*, 1997). Beyond this, in the event the police legitimately arrest the driver, they are authorized to search the passenger compartment of the automobile (*Thornton v. United States*, 2004).

The plain view doctrine does not pertain to a type of search. What it means is that if an officer sees criminal evidence in plain view (i.e., the evidence did not have to be searched for), the officer may seize that evidence. Thus, if you approach an officer for directions, and you are openly carrying a controlled substance, the officer may seize the substance with no other justification than that it was in plain view. In *New York v. Class* (1986), an officer trying to read the VIN (vehicle identification numbers) through the windshield of a stopped automobile reached into the car to clear material from the number. While doing so, the officer saw a gun under the seat. The Court ruled that the officer had a right to check the VIN and thus the discovery of the gun "in plain view" was not violation of the warrant requirement. A related issue is that of "open fields": the issue of whether or when police can search for evidence of crime in fields that are fenced but visible. The Supreme Court has ruled that police may make special arrangements to fly over these areas to look for evidence and as long as the police view the evidence from publicly accessible areas, the search and seizure is acceptable (*Florida v. Riley*, 1989).

The purpose of the exclusionary rule and the general requirement of a warrant is to protect the liberty of the individual citizen. The fact that there are exceptions indicates a consideration for order and crime control. The police must walk a fine line between what is necessary for the protection of the public and the control of crime, and what is demanded for the protection of individual liberties. The warrant process, whereby a magistrate reviews the evidence and either confirms the judgment of the police (issues a warrant) or rejects it, and court rulings as to the admissibility of evidence, are examples of how the justice system attempts to check the discretionary powers of the police.

Decisions whether to search, how to search, and what to search are governed by evidentiary standards such as "reasonable suspicion" or "probable cause," but in practice are discretionary in nature. The officer on the street must decide whether to take investigatory steps. Although this decision is ruled by the evidentiary standards of the courts, many other factors come into play when the decision is made.

Rubinstein (1973) wrote that the decision to pursue an investigation hinges on the seriousness of the crime reported, the credibility of the witness/complainant, and the circumstances of the event. The less serious the crime, the less likely the police are to invest scarce investigation resources in solving it. Jogerst, Daly, Brinig, and Bibas (2005) report that the police are more likely to devote resources to investigating allegations of elder abuse when the offense is defined as more serious (e.g., a felony rather than a misdemeanor). The less believable or sympathetic the witness/complainant, the less likely the police are to investigate. Finally, the busier the police are, the less likely they are to take the time to investigate a given complaint. Brandl (1993) reports that evidence sufficiency has perhaps the greatest influence on investigation decisions. If there is enough evidence to suggest that the case can be solved, detectives are likely to devote time to its investigation. Given equal probabilities of solving cases, however, other concerns exert an effect, including the seriousness of the crime. As with other criminal justice decisions, police exert more effort responding to cases that are seen as more serious (involving physical harm, threats, or substantial property loss). Wilson and Ruback (2003) found that in "hate crime" cases, police responses were determined in large part by the seriousness of the offense—how much harm was done.

Other factors also can affect the decisions of police officers when a crime is detected. A rash of crimes, negative press pressure, the importance or status of the victim, political interference, and similar factors all can play roles in the decision to investigate. Increasingly police agencies are instituting what are known as **"cold case squads."** These are teams of detectives dedicated to pursuing cases (usually homicide cases) that have not been solved and lack significant leads. Turner and Kosa (2003) described such squads and note that they can effectively reduce the backlog of unsolved cases. As cold case squads proliferate, the traditional wisdom that police devote attention to new cases with the greatest chance for successful resolution may have to change.

Interrogation

Interrogation of suspects and witnesses has long been a mainstay of criminal investigation. We are all familiar with entertainment-media portrayals of police investigations in which detectives "grill" the suspect or continually return to the witness to extract details of the crime. Most often, it is the interrogation that leads the officers to the needed evidence and ultimately seals the case. Interrogation is a "search" for evidence through seeking testimony or responses to questions put to the suspect.

Just as the Fourth Amendment to the U.S. Constitution protects the homes, papers, and possessions of the citizenry from unreasonable searches, the Fifth Amendment protects citizens from overzealous interrogation by the police. The Fifth Amendment states that no one can be compelled to give testimony against oneself. *Miranda v. Arizona* (1966), perhaps the most famous of the Court's exclusionary rule cases, involved the Fifth Amendment.

In the *Miranda* case, as in many other cases preceding it, the police arrested the suspect and held him in custody for several hours while questioning him about the crime. At the conclusion of the interrogation, the suspect had confessed to the crime. Miranda's attorneys appealed the conviction on the grounds that Miranda was not aware that he did not have to speak during the interrogation and that he had a right to an attorney during questioning. Thus, the attorneys contended that the confession was obtained improperly and should not have been allowed as evidence at the trial. The Supreme Court agreed, ruling that when police have a suspect in custody, they must advise the suspect that he or she may remain silent, that what is said may be used against the suspect in court, and that the suspect has the right to either a retained (hired) or appointed attorney during questioning (see Box 6.2).

Box 6.2 Miranda Warnings

You have the right to remain silent. Anything you say can and will be used against you in a court of law.

You have the right to an attorney during questioning. If you cannot afford an attorney, one will be appointed for you by the court.

Do you understand these rights?

The *Miranda* decision revolutionized police interrogation practices. One of the reasons the case is so well known is that the Court required that police provide suspects with warnings as to their rights at interrogation, and these required warnings became known as the *Miranda* warnings. Traditional practices of "incommunicado" (not permitting the suspect to see or speak with anyone except the investigating officers), as well as the psychological advantage held by the police in such interrogations, were abolished.

Within two years of the decision, the United States Congress included language in the Omnibus Crime Control Act of 1968 that redefined the conditions under which a confession was considered voluntary. The U.S. Department of Justice, however, never sought to implement that statute (*Dickerson v. United States*, 2000). As long as the confession was voluntary, the statute did not require that the *Miranda* warning be given to the suspect. In 2000, the U.S. Supreme Court reviewed this issue and held that the requirements of the *Miranda* ruling still apply. Essentially, the Court ruled that absent the warnings it would not be possible to conclude that a suspect voluntarily confessed, because the warnings ensure that the suspect knows his or her rights and that he or she need not cooperate with the police.

The *Miranda* decision, most of all, led some commentators to charge that the Supreme Court was "handcuffing the police." These critics expressed fears that, as a result of this decision, the police would be unable to obtain confessions, and thereby far fewer offenders would be convicted and far less stolen property would be recovered by the police (Inbau, 1966). However, evaluations of the effects of the *Miranda* warnings on conviction rates and the recovery of stolen property have failed to support these earlier criticisms (Witt, 1977). Box 6.3 shows that, for California cases, evidence problems (including possible exclusionary rule violations) are most common in drug cases. These data do not support critics of the exclusionary rule, who argued that the rule would result in robbers, burglars, and other street criminals being released from custody. More recent research indicates that police officers do not believe that *Miranda* rulings prevent them from successfully identifying criminals. Indeed, many police chiefs report that one outcome of the *Miranda* ruling has been a proliferation of more professional and effective police officers (Time & Payne, 2002). In part, the critics were wrong in their contention

Box 6.3 — Felony Cases Rejected for Prosecution in California (1976-79) for Search and Seizure Problems, by Most Serious Charge

Most Serious Charge	Number of Cases	Percent
Total Cases	4,130	100.0
Drug	2,953	71.5
Other Felonies*	641	15.5
Burglary	217	5.3
Robbery	134	3.2
Assault	88	2.1
Grand Theft Auto	48	1.2
Grand Theft	33	.8
Rape	12	.3
Murder	4	.1

*Includes weapons and other felonies not listed separately

Source: National Institute of Justice (1982), *The Effects of the Exclusionary Rule: A Study in California* (Washington, DC: U.S. Department of Justice):12.

because they probably did not consider the system qualities of the justice process and the ability of systems to resist change and to maintain equilibrium. Several practices developed that may have served to blunt the effect of *Miranda*.

Lewis and Allen (1977) described a post-*Miranda* interrogation style that, they argued, allowed the police to overcome the limits placed upon them by the Supreme Court. According to Lewis and Allen, the interrogating officers would give the suspect his or her warnings, but would do so over the course of the interrogation; that is, the warnings were part of the questioning. After several hours, the interrogation would be over, and the warnings would have been given. As an example, this type of interrogation might proceed as follows:

> Officer: You have the right to remain silent, but if you have nothing to hide, we just want to ask a few questions about what you were doing last night. The sooner we can get on with this, the sooner we can all go home. So, tell me, where were you about 10 P.M. last night?
>
> Suspect: (Speaks for a while, answers a few questions.)
>
> Later . . .
>
> Officer: Anything you tell us could be used against you in a court of law, although frankly, I don't think you've done anything. When you were telling us about the car, you mentioned . . .
>
> Suspect: (Continues speaking and answering questions)
>
> Later . . .
>
> Officer: You have the right to an attorney, but it's late and it would be hard to get an attorney to come down here now. Besides, I don't see any reason why an innocent person would waste money on an attorney . . .

Over the span of several hours, the entire *Miranda* warning would be given. If the officers obtained a confession, they would have it typed up for the suspect's signature, along with the waiver of Fifth Amendment rights. Should the suspect complain, the officers need only ask whether the suspect told them what was in the statement, and whether the officers gave the suspect the *Miranda* warnings. The answers to both questions would be yes, although the warnings were not given in the way the Court envisioned.

A second practice that enabled police to get around the *Miranda* requirement was "psychological warfare." One effect of the *Miranda* decision may have been to increase the skill of police interrogators. In *Brewer v. Williams* (1977), a suspect in the murder of a little girl finally led police to the body after listening to officers talk about how tragic it was for the girl's parents to not be able to provide a proper burial for their daughter. Similar practices were revealed in other cases in which police officers preyed upon the guilt of the suspect by speculating about what could happen if neighborhood children found guns that were used in crimes. A guilt-ridden offender often would lead the officers to the guns, thereby providing the police with sufficient evidence to obtain a conviction.

The "Good Faith" Exception

Generally, the Supreme Court has determined the admissibility of evidence obtained in these cases on the basis of the intent of the police officers involved. If it deems the officers were consciously trying to provoke the suspect and to obtain evidence, the court usually rules that the interrogation was improper. On the other hand, if the Court believes the police were merely speaking among themselves, and the suspect (upon overhearing a conversation that was not directed at him or her) merely volunteered information, it is treated as a valid confession.

In 1967, the U.S. Supreme Court decided the case of *Katz v. United States*. In this case, federal investigators who suspected Katz of involvement in gambling placed an electronic eavesdropping device on the exterior of a telephone booth they believed Katz used to transmit betting information. Katz was convicted of transmitting betting information by telephone in violation of a federal law. He appealed, stating that the federal agents had violated the Fourth Amendment by not securing a warrant for the eavesdropping. Prior to this case, the general rule of thumb was that the Fourth Amendment was designed to protect places. By locating the device on the exterior of a public telephone booth, the agents believed they had not violated Katz's rights. The Supreme Court, however, reversed the conviction, ruling that the Fourth Amendment protected people, not places. The decision turned on Katz's expectation of privacy. In this case, although law enforcement officials took pains to comply with the Constitution and believed they were behaving appropriately, a guilty defendant was nonetheless set free.

The *Katz* case illustrates one problem with the exclusionary rule. The rule is designed to deter police officials from violating citizens' rights. What happens when the police believe they are obeying the law? If the police make an "honest" mistake, their behavior cannot be deterred. What was needed, many observers believed, was a "good faith" exception to the exclusionary rule. If the police work in good faith in the belief that they are not violating the Constitution, then any evidence they obtain should be admissible.

In 1984, the Court established such a good faith exception in the case of *United States v. Leon*. In this case, officers relied on information from a confidential informant to obtain a search warrant. At trial, Leon's attorneys argued that the information on which the warrant was based was insufficient to establish probable cause, and thus the evidence from the search should be suppressed (excluded). The judge agreed. Here, officers sought and obtained a warrant, executed the search, found large quantities of drugs, and yet the evidence was still suppressed because of an error by the magistrate issuing the warrant. The Supreme Court ruled that because the exclusionary rule is designed to deter police misconduct rather than punish errors of judges or magistrates, the evidence could be used. If the police conduct a search believing in good faith that the search is permissible, then the evidence can be used at trial, making a **good faith exception**.

Since then, the Court has expanded on the good faith exception. In *Arizona v. Evans* (1995), the Court ruled that a police search of Evans based on a mistaken belief that he was a fugitive was legal. Evans was stopped for a traffic violation, and the subsequent computer check revealed an outstanding arrest warrant. The officer arrested Evans based on the warrant, and then searched the car, finding marijuana. The arrest warrant, however, had been removed two weeks earlier. There was no warrant for Evans's arrest at the time of the search. Still, the officer believed, in good faith, that Evans was wanted and that the arrest and subsequent search were constitutional. The Supreme Court ruled that the exclusionary rule is not designed to prevent clerical errors (the computer record of the warrant had not been updated), and thus the officer was acting reasonably and the evidence was admissible. In 1995, the U.S. Congress considered legislative action to curtail the exclusionary rule. In separate bills, both the House of Representatives and the Senate considered legislation that would have statutorily instituted and defined a good faith exception to the exclusionary rule (Davis, 1997). Neither house's version of exclusionary rule reform was passed, but the exclusionary rule remains a topic of intense debate in criminal justice.

The USA PATRIOT Act (Uniting and Strengthening America by Providing Appropriate Tools Required to Intercept and Obstruct Terrorism Act of 2001) has raised concerns about potential governmental intrusion on individual rights. Among other things, the act authorizes investigators to execute search warrants without notifying the owner or occupant of the location, and has eased restrictions on the use of wiretaps and other electronic surveillance. While aimed at counterterrorism and national security, the powers given law enforcement officers to detect and prevent terrorism can and will also be used to detect and apprehend more traditional criminal offenders.

Other Investigatory Practices

In addition to search and interrogation, police obtain evidence in a number of ways. The offender's age, race, sex, and size can be determined from hairs found at the scene of the crime. The clothes worn by the offender can be identified from fibers collected at the crime scene. The weapon used in the crime can be ascertained from ballistics examinations. All of these techniques are staples of a forensic scientist's investigation. While rarely employed because of costs and a lack of necessity, the techniques of a forensic scientist sometimes provide the answers to investigators (Peterson, 1987). Forensic science is becoming increasingly important in criminal investigations, as can be seen in the increased attention paid to DNA typing. The Office of Law Enforcement Standards recently identified the growing need for training, equipment, and improvements in forensic sciences. Television dramas based on crime scene investigators have popularized forensic science and crime scene analysts. While still relatively rarely used, investigation technology has experienced amazing advances in the past several years (National Institute of Justice, 2003).

Identification Techniques: Throw-downs and Lineups

More common is the identification of offenders through throw-downs and lineups, whereby the police seek the identity of the suspect from a pool of possibilities by having witnesses examine photographs (throw-downs) or observe possible offenders (lineups). The major concern of the courts in regard to these practices is that the police not be too suggestive in their behavior. For example, the identification of a white male suspect from a lineup comprised of the man and six black females would be too suggestive. To protect against the possibility that the police would encourage a false identification, the Supreme Court has held that suspects in custody have the right to have an attorney present during lineups (*United States v. Wade*, 1967). Unless the offender is known to the victim or witness, it is unlikely that these procedures by themselves will yield the offender. More often, such procedures are employed after the police already have enough evidence to conclude that the suspect is probably guilty of the offense. Thus, these identifications tend to constitute supporting evidence and are not the heart of the case.

Surveillance

Still another investigation tool is surveillance. Both physical and electronic surveillance techniques are used to gather evidence of criminal activity. Wire taps, hidden microphones, cameras, and other forms of surreptitious surveillance generally require warrants and are therefore used infrequently. The point of most surveillance is to gather evidence on persons suspected of crimes, but against whom insufficient evidence exists to obtain a search warrant. Usually, surveillance does not involve tapping telephone lines or watching individual residences. The bulk of surveillance conducted by police agencies is physical surveillance, by which officers watch a certain location or follow a suspect to gather evidence (Nunn et al., 2006). One exception is the use of video surveillance of public areas. The British have been using video surveillance of public areas for years, and the practice is becoming more common in the United States (see Box 6.4). British research suggests that the use of surveillance cameras has a modest effect in reducing crime (Welsh & Farrington, 2002). Surette (2006) reported the results of video surveillance in an American city. He concluded that the evidence suggests that cameras produce a deterrent effect on crime.

Box 6.4	Percent of U.S. Local Police Departments Regularly Using Video Surveillance in 2003
Any Use	60%
In Patrol Cars	55%
Fixed Site	14%
Traffic Enforcement	11%
Mobile Surveillance	8%

Source: M. Hickman & B. Reaves (2006), *Local Police Departments, 2003* (Washington, DC: Bureau of Justice Statistics):28.

Surveillance techniques yield evidence of specific criminality and information (or "intelligence") on suspicious persons and places. In the former case, officers generally have reason to believe that a particular person is engaged in criminal activity, or that crimes are occurring at a particular place, and the surveillance is designed to provide evidence about those specific offenses. In intelligence-gathering, police suspect an individual or location and conduct a surveillance in hopes of obtaining further evidence or information to confirm or reject their suspicions.

Informers

Informers are another investigation tool used by the police. To some, the use of informers seems inappropriate because it frequently requires the police to join forces with criminals in order to enforce the law. Nonetheless, informants are extremely useful to police in intelligence-gathering. The informer is usually not respected by either the criminals or the police, in keeping with a norm that one should not be a "rat." However, informers are often able to learn and observe things that an undercover officer would find difficult to discover even after months of work—and that a uniformed officer would find impossible to obtain. Police can use information from informants, even anonymous tips, but they must be able to convince the magistrate that the informant's information is credible. In *Illinois v. Gates* (1983), the Supreme Court allowed police to rely on an anonymous tip about the Gateses' involvement in drug trafficking as long as the police had taken reasonable steps to verify the accuracy of the tip.

Informers do not make particularly good witnesses. Typically, their credibility is questioned either because of their own criminal pasts, or because their information is provided with the expectation of a reward and not as a matter of civic responsibility. Add to this the fact that many informers are not willing to testify in open court, and this valuable source of information for police becomes less than ideal for solving crimes. To combat these weaknesses, many police departments employ undercover police officers. These officers are assigned to work in "plain clothes" and are directed to mix with the general public so that their identities as police officers will not be readily apparent.

Crackdowns

Yet another police response to crime that combines investigation with detection and arrest is the crackdown (Sherman, 1990a). In crackdowns, the police devote increased attention and resources to either specific types of crime (drug sales, prostitution, street robberies, etc.) or to crime in particular places (downtown areas, parking lots, schools, etc.). Crackdowns are temporary in nature and often involve practices of saturation patrol, in which a large number of uniformed officers are used to flood a locale with police, or policy directives, in which officers are directed to arrest in certain crime situations whenever possible. Crackdowns allow the police to show that they are "doing something" about crime, and tend, at least in the short run, to depress levels of criminal activity in the affected areas. During the past decade, crackdowns have been used by the police to affect general levels of disorder, drug trafficking, serious crime, prostitution, and drunk driving (Mazerolle, Soole & Rombouts, 2007; Sherman, 1990b).

In more sophisticated applications, the notion of a crackdown has evolved into a specific policing strategy for preventing crime in areas known as "hot spots" of crime. Sherman, Gartin, and Buerger (1989) reported that some places have much higher rates of crime (or citizen complaints of crime) than do others. They labeled these high-rate locations as "hot spots" of crime. Once hot spots are located, the police must determine how to respond. A typical response is to increase police presence in these areas, or crack down on the hot spot. A number of studies have shown that such efforts have at least short-term effects of reducing crime and disorder (Green, 1995; Koper, 1995; Sherman & Weisburd, 1995; Weisburd & Green, 1995). Lawton, Taylor, and Luongo (2005:449) had this to say about a crackdown effort in Philadelphia, "Crackdowns respond to current crises. Because they are 'out of the ordinary,' they cost a lot, they attract attention, and as we show here, they get results. But they are rarely sustainable because of high costs."

Undercover Operations

Certain types of crimes, such as the "victimless" offenses associated with vice enforcement, are not likely to yield complainants. The customer who solicits a prostitute or purchases drugs is unlikely to complain to the police. In so doing, of course, the complainant would implicate himself or herself in criminal behavior. Thus, the police must aggressively (proactively) seek evidence of these crimes. Almost every major police department has a vice unit comprised of officers who attempt to uncover instances of victimless crimes. These officers pose as either potential consumers or potential providers of the illicit goods and services, and then wait to be approached by would-be offenders.

There are other crimes that are approached in a proactive manner in some places. Robberies, especially street robberies, have been detected through the use of plainclothes "decoys." Areas of high incidence of specific crimes are determined through reviews of police reports, and police use a decoy operation using officers disguised as potential victims in those areas, with other officers serving as "back-ups" (Halpher & Ku, 1976). When the criminal strikes, the backup officers close in and an arrest is made. These types of undercover operations have proven to be very successful with specific types of crimes.

The "sting" is an additional form of undercover operation that has been employed to detect and arrest burglars and other forms of criminal offenders. The sting operation gets its name from the slang of confidence artists. These "con artists" gain the trust of their victims and then take the victim's money. The actual taking of the money is called the "sting." Because the police pretend to be criminals to gain the trust of offenders until they have sufficient evidence to make an arrest, these undercover operations also are called stings. One of the most famous sting operations was the Federal Bureau of Investigation's ABSCAM operation, in which FBI agents posed as wealthy foreign representatives and attempted to uncover bribery activity among members of Congress and other governmental officials (Coleman, 1985:104-106; *Time*, 1980).

The most common sting operation involves the establishment of a "fencing" operation; that is, police officers pose as dealers of stolen goods. Burglars and thieves then are photographed when they come to sell ("fence") goods they have stolen. Later, these offenders are arrested and charged on the basis of the evidence obtained in the fake fence operation.

There are two commonly raised criticisms of undercover operations. First, there are those who argue that these operations, especially sting operations, create crime because they provide an easily identifiable outlet for stolen property, which encourages people to steal (Langworthy, 1989; Langworthy & LeBeau, 1992, 1993). Second, and perhaps more important, there are those who suggest that such operations ensnare the innocent through entrapment.

The **entrapment** defense to criminal charges is applicable when the entrapped offender did not have the inclination to commit a crime absent police enticement. If the police entice an otherwise innocent individual to commit a crime, that individual may have a defense of entrapment (Park, 1976). Assuming that you would not generally think of committing a crime, how would you respond if I offered you $1 million to transport some drugs across town for me?

For many people, this offer is too good to refuse. If you were to say yes to my offer and I then wished to arrest you for transporting drugs, you could say you were entrapped. You only committed the crime because I came to you with the idea and offered you an inducement too great to refuse. The same logic applies if an officer suggests a price and activity to a suspected prostitute. This is true regardless of the price offered; the law does not question judgment and worth as much as it does motive.

It is important to distinguish between entrapment and encouragement. Unlike entrapment, it is permissible for the police to "encourage" someone to complete a crime the person is already contemplating. An officer who approaches a prostitute and offers to pay for a service may be placing the idea in the mind of the prostitute. Someone contemplating an act of prostitution, however, already has the criminal idea. The fact that an officer allows a person to make a proposition is not entrapment; it is encouragement.

The investigation of crimes, through whatever means the police employ, provides a basis for the next decision of importance in the law enforcement segment of the justice process: arrest. When police have probable cause to believe that an individual has committed a crime, they are expected to place that person under arrest. Yet, as with investigation and detection, arrest is a decision process that depends upon a number of factors.

Arrest

Arrest is taking a person into custody. Once arrested, a person is no longer free to leave. The authority to arrest offenders is but one of a number of tools available to the police officer in his or her efforts to maintain order. There are times when this authority is the best or most appropriate tool, and other times when it is inappropriate. The decision regarding the appropriateness of arrest is often a discretionary one for the officer.

Teenage students register for the Connecticut Coalition to Stop Underage Drinking conference in North Haven, Connecticut, to participate in sting operations targeting illegal sales of liquor to minors. *Photo credit: AP Photo/Douglas Healey.*

Joseph Goldstein (1960) discussed police discretion in deciding whether to employ the criminal law. He identified the decision not to arrest as "noninvocation discretion" (decision not to invoke the law). He termed the process "low-visibility decisionmaking." If an officer decides not to make an arrest when an arrest is justified, who has knowledge about the decision? Generally, only the officer and the offender are aware of the failure to arrest. Thus, this decision has low visibility, meaning that most people (including the police administration) do not see it. If an officer decides not to issue a traffic citation to you, no one will know unless the officer or you report this decision. How many times have you reported to the police station that an officer should have issued you a citation but did not?

The other face of noninvocation discretion is, logically, "invocation discretion" (the decision to invoke the law). This decision is more visible, as the officer must report the arrest, the suspect will most likely have legal counsel, and eventually the case may get into the courts. Yet, the decision to arrest someone is often as discretionary as the decision not to arrest. There are rules of thumb that officers or departments follow in deciding to invoke the criminal law. Occasionally, an officer will opt to enforce the law when the rule of thumb would suggest noninvocation. Exemplifying this are "tolerance limits" regarding excessive speed. Most departments attempt to avoid bad public relations (and close court decisions) in traffic cases by suggesting that offenders not be cited if they are traveling at a rate within a specified difference from the speed limit. Thus, if the speed limit is 55 mph, traffic officers might be expected to cite only those motorists traveling in excess of 60 mph. However, a motorist stopped for traveling 58 mph could be cited instead of warned (regardless of the tolerance limit) if the motorist's behavior is deemed inappropriate by the officer. Schafer and Mastrofski (2005) describe traffic enforcement in one community in which the policy of the department supported leniency by officers, but also noted that citizen behavior was associated with the use of more formal and more severe sanctions.

Similarly, a responding officer might decide that arrest is necessary to separate combatants in a dispute, or that such an arrest might prove more harmful than beneficial in a given situation. An officer might arrest an ill child to secure needed medical treatment in the absence of parents, or might fail to arrest a known offender in return for information about other offenses or offenders. In all of these situations, it is apparent that arrest is a tool for the officers involved, or a means to an end. To understand the exercise of the arrest power in a particular instance, one must understand the intent of the officer involved.

A number of researchers have investigated the arrest decision by police officers. With regard to domestic violence cases in which agencies have mandatory or preferred arrest policies, police still often fail to make arrests (Jones & Belknap, 1999). Robert Kane (1999) found that police officers' decisions to arrest in domestic violence situations became less predictable as the seriousness of the offense decreased. As have other researchers (Berk, Fenstermaker & Newton, 1988; Buzawa & Austin, 1993), he noted that officers take more factors into account in deciding about arrest when the legal requirements for arrest are less clear. So too, Richard Lundman (1998) contends that despite the increased attention paid to drunk drivers in the last 20 years, police today are likely to avoid arrests in many drunk driving cases. Robin Engel and her colleagues (2000) reported that police decisions to use coercive tactics, including arrest, are influenced by the demeanor of citizens. That is, citizens who are disrespectful to the police, or who challenge police authority, face a greater likelihood of being arrested or subjected to police force. Clearly, the available research indicates that police officers decide between arrest and nonarrest in many cases.

When an arrest is made, the justice process becomes fully involved. The arresting officer must file reports, and the offender/suspect must be transported to a detention facility and booked (whereby the arrest is entered on official records). Shortly after the arrest, the suspect must be given the opportunity to contact an attorney. The suspect has the right to be considered for pretrial release. These procedures quickly move the case from the law enforcement segment of the justice system into the courts.

As is evident in the *Miranda* ruling, the behavior of police officers is much more tightly controlled after arrest than before it. Once the suspect is in custody, the procedures designed to protect the liberty of individuals are initiated. Police officers often complain that suspects are returned to freedom on the streets through bail before the officers have completed their paperwork. Typically these officers are expressing frustration with the justice system because it seems to be "stacked" in favor of the suspect.

Booking, the official public recording of an arrest, is designed to prevent the police from holding an offender/suspect incommunicado; anyone can check the booking records to determine whether a person is in police custody. Bail or pretrial release is a provision of the Eighth Amendment of the U.S. Constitution, which is designed to prevent a suspect from unnecessary confinement prior to conviction and to allow the defendant to be free to cooperate in his or her own defense. A third stage, the preliminary hearing (which will be discussed in the next chapter), is a review of the evidence and the arrest decision by a magistrate or judge. The hearing is held to determine whether the police had sufficient grounds for placing a person in custody. All of these procedures illustrate the care with which the rights of the individual are guarded in conformity with the presumption of innocence. Frustration arises because, while police and other actors in the justice system are expected (at least theoretically) to presume that the suspect is innocent, in order to do their jobs, they often have to believe in the probable guilt of suspects.

Due Process, Crime Control, and the Police

Even if the core mission of the police is crime control, crime control is not the only criterion on which the police and police actions are assessed. The police must not only strive to reduce, prevent, and respond to crime, they must do so in a constrained fashion. We require the police not only to enforce the law and protect the public, but to observe and protect individual rights in the process (Bayley, 2002). Our discussion of entrapment illustrates the tension that exists between due process and crime control in policing. It is not enough for the police to establish that someone broke the law; they must do so without unduly influencing the person to engage in crime. The requirements of due process support a reactive style of policing by restricting what police can do to detect and arrest potential criminals.

The exclusionary rule also illustrates the tension between due process and crime control. The exclusionary rule applies to only those cases in which the police find evidence that crime has occurred. If the police search a home without a warrant and find no criminal evidence, there is no evidence to exclude. It is only when there is evidence that someone is guilty of a crime that the exclusionary rule applies. Thus, the exclusionary rule works to release the guilty. In doing so, the rule implies that due process concerns outweigh crime control concerns. The courts would rather let a criminal go free than allow the police to violate constitutional rights.

The Supreme Court has wrestled with this question of balance. In 1984, the Court decided the case of *United States v. Leon*, in which it defined a good faith exception to the exclusionary rule. In *Leon* (and later cases), the police took all reasonable steps to protect the rights of the accused, but still made a technical error. The Court noted that the police believed the warrant they had obtained was valid, and conducted a search based on that warrant. It later turned out that the warrant was issued erroneously. The Supreme Court ruled that if police obtain evidence of crime based on what they, in good faith, believe to be a valid warrant, the evidence need not be excluded even if the warrant is invalid.

Rather than view the exclusionary rule as universal, the Court recognized a circumstantial test of police behavior. The purpose of the exclusionary rule is to deter or prevent police misconduct. The Court suggested that in cases in which the police believe they are obeying procedural law, there is no police behavior to deter. Thus, if the exclusionary rule would not be working to protect individual rights (due process), the social cost of letting the guilty go free is unjustified. Crime control proponents applaud this decision because it allows the police and justice system to avoid ignoring crime based on legal technicalities. Due process proponents worry that the *Leon* decision signals a shift in the balance between due process and crime control away from an emphasis on individual liberty.

The good faith exception to the exclusionary rule represents the balancing act that characterizes all of the American system of criminal justice. It seeks to define when, and under what conditions, our interests in individual liberty outweigh our interests in crime control. When do we trust the police to act in our best interests, and when are we suspicious of police powers?

This balancing act can also be seen in the recent movement toward community-oriented or problem-oriented policing. As the police become more proactive in seeking to prevent and control crime, the ability of citizens to control police behavior through calls for service is reduced. When the police are encouraged to identify and select problems that seem to produce crime, and when they are urged to focus on disorder at least as much as crime, the role of the police expands. Rather than responding to citizen calls for service, the police themselves determine when and how they will intervene.

This discretion can cause problems between the police and the community. If there is disagreement among members of the community about what is acceptable behavior, the police end up taking sides when they decide whether to act to control such behavior (Kelling, 1999). As important, when the behavior in question relates to order more than crime, the authority of the police to act is unclear. If citizens believe that they are not violating any laws, they may be resistant to police efforts to control them. Facing resistance, the officers often must rely on force, or the threat of force, to make citizens obey. This, in turn, leads to citizen views of the police as brutal and authoritarian. Many researchers have studied citizen attitudes toward the police (e.g., Cao, Stack & Sun, 1998; Cheurprakobkit & Bartsch, 1999; Frank, Smith & Novak, 2005). In general, citizens who have had negative experiences with the police, or who have friends, family, and acquaintances who report negative experiences with the police, are less likely to report positive feelings toward the police themselves. When, and for what types of disorder, should the police direct citizen behavior? If behavior is not criminal in itself, should the police be able to intervene to prevent future crime?

These issues have become even more important as local law enforcement has been called to take a more active role in homeland security. Recent federal legislation and growing public concern about the threat of terrorist attacks have resulted in increased demands that police take steps to prevent terrorist activity (DeLone, 2007). Preventive actions, of course, are in some sense less democratic, as the police work under their own initiative. Critics of our reaction to the terrorist threat point out that efforts to prevent future terrorist acts that negate our freedoms are, in the end, proof that the terrorist attacks have been successful (Lynch, 2002).

To the extent that concerns about the harm of terrorist attacks outweigh our concerns about individual liberty, we can expect a shift in police practice toward a greater emphasis on crime control and a reduced concern with due process.

See Box 6.5 for a brief summary of some important cases in law enforcement.

Box 6.5 Selected Court Cases in Law Enforcement

Weeks v. United States 232 U.S. 383 (1914)	Evidence illegally obtained by law enforcement officers is not admissible in federal criminal prosecutions. This is referred to as the "exclusionary rule."
Mapp v. Ohio 367 U.S. 643 (1961)	The exclusionary rule, which prohibits the use of evidence obtained as the result of unreasonable searches and seizures, is applicable in state criminal proceedings. (See *Weeks v. United States* for the exclusionary rule.)
Miranda v. Arizona 384 U.S. 436 (1966)	Police must advise a suspect in custody of his or her right to remain silent, the fact that what is said may be used against him or her in court, and of the right to the counsel of a hired or appointed attorney during questioning.
United States v. Wade 388 U.S. 218 (1967)	A suspect in custody has the right to an attorney during post-indictment lineups.
Warden v. Hayden 387 U.S. 294 (1967)	A warrantless search may be valid under circumstances of "hot pursuit."
Terry v. Ohio 392 U.S. 1 (1968)	Stop and frisk is valid on "reasonable suspicion" in order to ensure the safety of police and bystanders.
Chimel v. California 395 U.S. 752 (1969)	When making a valid arrest, police may search the area of the arrestee's "immediate control," whether the arrest is with or without a warrant.
Chambers v. Maroney 453 U.S. 42 (1970)	Police may perform a warrantless search of automobile shortly after it is seized.
Brewer v. Williams 430 U.S. 387 (1977)	Conversations with or appeals to a suspect that may induce a confession constitute an interrogation that requires both *Miranda* warnings and the right to counsel.
Coolidge v. New Hampshire 403 U.S. 443 (1981)	A search is valid only if the warrant is issued by a neutral and detached magistrate. Search of a car after it is in police possession for a period of time does not constitute a valid inventory search.

Box 6.5 *(continued)*

United States v. Ross 456 U.S. 798 (1982)	Police can conduct a full search of an automobile as long as they have probable cause to believe that the automobile contains contraband.
Illinois v. Gates 462 U.S. 213 (1983)	The two-pronged test established under *Aguilar* and *Spinelli* is abandoned in favor of a "totality of circumstances" approach. The task of an issuing magistrate is to make a practical decision whether, given all the circumstances, there is a fair probability that the evidence of a crime will be found in a particular place.
United States v. Leon 484 U.S. 897 (1984)	Even if the warrant relied upon is eventually found invalid, the exclusionary rule allows the use of evidence obtained by officers acting in reasonable reliance on the validity of the warrant.
Dickerson v. United States 530 U.S. 428 (2000)	*Miranda* waivers are still required when police officers are interrogating suspects who are in custody. This supersedes the provision of the Omnibus Crime Control Act of 1968, which provides that a defendant's statement is admissible in federal court if given voluntarily, regardless of whether *Miranda* rights have been waived.

Source: Portions of this table were adapted from R.V. del Carmen & J.T. Walker (2006), *Briefs of Leading Cases in Law Enforcement*, 6th ed. (Newark, NJ: LexisNexis Matthew Bender).

Issues in Law Enforcement

It is difficult to identify a limited set of important issues in contemporary policing. Almost everything about the police is problematic, and given the dilemma inherent in policing a free society, all of these problems are important. For instance, the increasing tendency of civilians to sue the police is evidence of a conflict between police practice and citizen expectancies (Kappeler, Kappeler & del Carmen, 1993). For our purposes, however, it is necessary to narrow the field and examine only a few of the problems. Corruption, for example, is a traditional problem in policing, with the police almost always suspected of being corrupt. Additionally, the use of force, especially deadly force, has been an issue in policing since the first use of force by police. The relationship between the police and the community also has traditionally been a source of conflict. Finally, the role of the police in controlling crime remains unclear.

Corruption

In terms of corruption, police in the United States have a flawed tradition. From the beginning, when police were loosely controlled, political patronage and the influence of politicians and criminals on police operations contributed to a perception among the general public of the police as corruptible at least, if not corrupt (Sherman, 1974). The public, aware of past practices, tends to believe that police will treat their friends and political leaders differently than they do the average citizen (Dowler & Zawilski, 2007). This perception of favoritism supports a view of the police as corrupt.

Legendary police corruption whistleblower Frank Serpico testifies in 1997 at a City Council hearing in New York. Serpico, who testified as a police officer before the Knapp Commission hearings on police corruption in 1971, here endorsed an independent monitoring board to investigate complaints made by cops about corruption and brutality in the department. *Photo credit: AP Photo/Kathy Willens.*

Periodic scandals exposing police acceptance of bribes further reinforce this perception. Corruption is an issue not simply because it means the police are criminal, but because it raises the question of who controls the police. Public fears of police corruption are based more on the fact that a corrupt police department is out of control than on the belief that graft is, in itself, morally wrong. In recent years, concern about police corruption has again risen to prominence. Renewed interest in police corruption is partly a product of the recent war on drugs. Revelations of widespread and serious police misconduct in New York, Miami, Los Angeles, and other cities have attracted attention.

The police have broad powers, and yet they operate with decentralized patrols. The discretionary authority of police officers is generally well-known (that is, we all hope for a "break," even if we do not get it). This combination of power and lack of accountability is what makes corruption possible. In fact, given the nature of American policing, it might be more surprising that there is so little widespread corruption than that there is so much of it. In the end, police corruption is difficult to define. Withrow and Dailey (2004) suggest that corruption lies on a continuum that includes lawful and proper activity. Police behavior is corrupt, they suggest, when the police officer comes to expect or demand special treatment or reward.

David Carter (1990a, 1990b) has classified police officer corruption associated with drug enforcement. He characterizes the opportunities for corruption as being of two basic types: (1) for personal benefit, and (2) for organizational gain. Personal benefit corruption exists when police officers take bribes, convert seized evidence (drugs) and property to personal use, or similarly use their position to advance their individual well-being. Organizational gain characterizes police corruption that involves lying or perjury to secure convictions of drug offenders, undercover officers engaging in criminality to gain access to higher levels of drug organizations, and similar practices designed, not for personal benefit, but to achieve the goals of the organization in drug enforcement. To further complicate matters, Holden (1993) suggests that statutes allowing police seizure of the property of drug offenders may work to corrupt the police agency by instilling a profit motive into law enforcement, and by reducing the ability of the government to control police through the budgetary process. What makes corruption such an important issue is this concern about the negative effects of police that are beyond citizen control.

Police corruption is a term that almost everyone understands, but that has a variety of meanings to different people. Clearly, taking bribes not to enforce the law, stealing from crime scenes, and similar acts of crime are felt to be corrupt by most people. Other actions in which police officers may engage, however, find less agreement. Police officers who conduct background checks on persons for their friends, or who use their access to criminal and driving records for personal information, may be corrupt. Often, what is called corruption by a police officer is something that is "not right," but is not a violation of the law. Some police "corruption" consists of violations of departmental regulations and can be sanctioned, whereas other improper police behavior is not covered by any rules. In an exploratory study of police officer sexual violence, Kraska and Kappeler (1995) developed a continuum of police misbehavior with regard to sexual behavior. This continuum ranged from unobtrusive acts such as viewing photographs of victims and other forms of invasion of privacy, through criminal behavior that included sexual assault and rape. The continuum illustrates one problem with police corruption: some misbehavior is clearly illegal (rape), while other behavior is inappropriate but not yet defined as a punishable wrong.

Police misconduct is an especially vexing problem. It raises the question: who polices the police? Perceived police misconduct is often at the root of tension between the police and citizens, especially minority citizens (Jesilow & Mayer, 2001; Lersch, 1998; Weitzer, 2002). Walker and Graham (1998) studied citizen perceptions of police misconduct. They found that most incidents that generate complaints involve relatively minor forms of misconduct and perceptions that the police failed to provide service. They also found that, faced with perceived police misconduct, the majority of citizens did not report the incident. Box 6.6 presents the reasons citizens gave for not reporting police misconduct. Nonetheless, concern about excessive force, brutality, and bullying are considered to be core to public perceptions of police misconduct. It is to this topic that we turn next.

Use of Force

Similar fears surround the issue of justified use of force by the police. Among all police powers, the ability to employ physical force legitimately in order to secure compliance with police orders, or with the law, is one of the most problem-

Box 6.6 Reasons for Not Reporting Police Misconduct

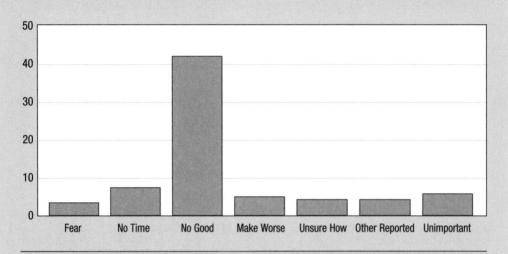

Source: S. Walker & N. Graham (1998), "Citizen Complaints in Response to Police Misconduct: The Results of a Victimization Survey," *Police Quarterly* 1(1):78.

atic issues in law enforcement (Bittner, 1970). Police officers resent having their decisions to employ force "second guessed" by civilians or by the internal affairs unit of the department. Citizens fear the unbridled use of force by the police. The issue revolves around the definition of excessive force, that is, force that is greater than what would be required to achieve the lawful aims of the officer.

Fears of excessive police force are particularly clear in cases of the use of deadly force. Few people seriously question an officer's ability and duty to use deadly force to protect self or others from death or serious harm. Most observers (e.g., Bazley, Lersch & Mieczkowski, 2007; Brandl & Stroshine, 2003) report that assaults on police officers are, statistically speaking, relatively rare events and most police use of force is of a minor nature. Still, Box 6.7 illustrates that the need for self-defense by police officers is real. It should be remembered, however, that officers are also at great risk of injury through accident (Brandl, 1996). Many believe that police officers should be allowed to use deadly force to prevent the escape of dangerous offenders who are likely to injure people again. Questions arise, however, when a police officer strikes an offender "too many times" or when an officer shoots and kills an innocent or unarmed person.

The Bureau of Justice Statistics (Hickman, 2006) reports citizen complaints about excessive force by police officers are quite common in large local law enforcement agencies employing 100 or more officers. For those agencies there were 6.6 complaints for every 100 full-time sworn officers. The complaint rate was higher in the largest departments. Fewer than 10 percent of these citizen complaints were sustained on review. However, in agencies that allowed citizens to

Box 6.7 Law Enforcement Officers Assaulted, by Circumstances at Scene of Incident and Type of Weapons, United States, 2005

Circumstances at scene of incident	Total	Type of Weapon			
		Firearm	Knife/Cutting instrument	Other weapon	Personal weapon
Total	57,546	2,145	1,059	8,314	46,028
Percent of total	100%	3.7	1.8	14.4	80.0
Disturbance calls (family quarrels, bar fights, etc.)	17,534	755	543	1,643	14,593
Percent	100%	4.3	3.1	9.4	83.2
Robbery/burglary	1,333	158	28	263	884
Percent	50%	5.9	1.1	9.9	33.1
Attempt other arrest	9,602	240	98	1,173	8,091
Percent	100%	2.5	1.0	12.2	84.3
Handling/transporting prisoners	7,356	30	34	541	6.751
Percent	100%	0.4	0.5	7.4	91.8
Traffic pursuits/stops	6,360	259	46	2,346	3,709
Percent	100%	4.1	0.7	36.9	58.3
Investigating suspicious persons	5,520	255	103	808	4,354
Percent	100%	4.6	1.9	14.6	78.9
Dealing with mentally ill	1,110	73	71	107	859
Percent	100%	6.6	6.4	9.6	77.4
Civil disorder	727	13	12	106	596
Percent	100%	1.8	1.7	14.6	82.0
Ambush situations	181	32	8	37	104
Percent	100%	17.7	4.4	20.4	57.5
All others	7,823	330	116	1,290	6,087
Percent	100%	4.2	1.5	16.5	77.8

Source: Table constructed from Federal Bureau of Investigation (2006), *Law Enforcement Officers Killed and Assaulted, 2005* [online]; Table 71. Found at: http://www.fbi.gov/ucr

appeal decisions about use-of-force complaints, the percentage of complaints sustained was more than twice as great as in those not allowing appeals.

Illustrating this concern are cases like that of Rodney King in Los Angeles, as well as more recent instances of police excessive force against citizens in New York City and similar cases involving allegations of excessive force in many other cities. Police officers in some cases were convicted of criminal charges, ranging from denial of civil rights to homicide, for the beatings and killings of African-American citizens. In many cases, the defense offered by the officers was that their use of force was justified by the citizen's resistance or refusal to obey lawful police commands. African Americans are not the only targets of police use of force, of course, but they are disproportionately subjected to police assaults. Because of the discretionary nature of decisions to employ force, citizens are suspicious of officer motives in these cases. Many people believe that King would not have been beaten, or beaten so severely, had he been white. While there is no way to know the real impact of race in this case, knowledge that the use of force is discretionary to some degree makes racial prejudice a viable explanation. In a review of the processing of excessive force complaints against the Chicago Police, Kerstetter, Rasinski, and Heiert (1996) found that complaints by citizens that were of a different race than the officer accused of excessive force were generally taken seriously by the investigators. So too, Son, Davis, and Rome (1998) found that police officers did not consider the race of the citizen involved when they were asked to assess the seriousness of police misconduct by other officers. On the other hand, Barkan and Cohn (1998) reported that whites who displayed racially prejudiced attitudes were more likely to support police use of force against citizens than nonprejudiced persons.

The actual use of substantial force by police officers against citizens is a relatively rare event (Adams, 1999). However, given the weapons and uniforms of police and the need for police to take charge of situations, the use of force, at least in terms of threats, is pervasive but low-level (Terrill, 2003). Further, it appears that the police are more likely to threaten force or be disrespectful to certain citizens, including minorities and youths (Mastrofski, Reisig & McCluskey, 2002). The appearance of officers, complete with baton, firearm, and uniform, coupled with officers' issuance of commands, creates a perception of the police as threatening in the minds of many citizens. Added to this is the fact that police officers and citizens may hold different views toward those incidences in which force is used. Box 6.8 compares the perceptions of force used by police and by criminal suspects in Phoenix, Arizona.

Joel Garner and his colleagues (1996) asked officers and suspects to report what kinds of force were used. In a later report, Garner and colleagues conclude that police use of force is dependent upon suspect/citizen resistance. Suspects tended to report more instances of officers using force at low levels (hitting or pushing) than

Box 6.8	Police Officer and Suspect Reports of Police Use of Force	

Type of Force Used	Police Report	Suspect Report
No Force	82.2%	79.5%
Hit or Push	2.2%	5.4%
Other Weaponless	9.7%	9.7%
Use/Threaten Weapon	5.9%	5.4%

Source: J. Garner, J. Buchanan, T. Schade & J. Hepburn (1996), *Understanding the Use of Force by and Against the Police* (Washington, DC: National Institute of Justice):7.

did officers, but less instances of force at the highest level (threat or use of a weapon). Perceptions of excessive force by police translate into lower citizen satisfaction with the police and a greater reluctance to cooperate with the police (Browning et al., 1994; Son et al., 1997). MacDonald, Alpert, and Tennebaum (1999) note that police use of deadly force is linked to the level of violent crime that exists in a community. That is, the police are most likely to use force in places and at times when violent crime is also most likely to occur. They suggest that knowledge of the risk of violence influences officers decisions to use deadly force.

The core of the problem is that we have granted our police the power to inflict death and injury without a clear understanding of the fact that the officer must decide when to use this power. We are troubled by the decisional aspect of police use of force more so than by the use of force itself (Terrill, 2005). When the evidence reveals that force is not applied randomly and that certain people are more likely to be victims than others, we fear discrimination based on factors other than the threat posed to the officer or to the law. If we could control the decisions of officers to employ force, we would be less troubled by the issue. David Griswold investigated complaints against police in one sheriff's office. He found that one-fifth of complaints involved allegations of excessive force, consistent with earlier studies (1994:218). Further, he found that complaints of excessive force were least likely to be upheld by the complaint review board. Griswold speculated that the low rate of sustained complaints may be explained by several facts. Use of force complaints are serious, and consequences for accused officers are also serious. It might be that the evidentiary standard used by the review board for such serious complaints is higher than that applied to less serious complaints. It may be that persons accusing officers of excessive force are not credible witnesses because they tend to have been subjects of arrest. It also may be that the combination of higher evidentiary standards and less credible complainants combines to produce a low rate of sustained complaints. Whatever the reason, the fact that it is difficult to lodge a complaint of excessive use of force successfully contributes to citizen suspicion of police use of force.

Most police agencies attempt to constrain the use of force by officers through training and policy (Morrison, 2006; Alpert & Smith, 1994). McEwen (1997) reported wide variation in the comprehensiveness and thoroughness of use-of-force policies. While most agencies had policies that specified the purpose of using force, implemented training and reporting requirements, and identified authorized weapons, none of these components was found in the policies of every agency. Further, less than one-half of the policies reviewed defined less-than-lethal force, listed unauthorized weapons, or gave instructions to officers concerning seeking medical aid for suspects. A little more than 50 percent of the agencies had policies that specifically directed officers to avoid excessive force. Increasingly police agencies are turning to technological solutions such as less lethal weapons as a means to overcome concerns about the use of force. While there is still some concern about the safety of electronic control devices (e.g., "stun guns" like the TASER), many police departments are issuing less lethal weapons to their officers (White & Ready, 2007).

Community Relations

"Community relations" is a police issue of relatively recent designation; it became an important topic as a result of the civil protests and riots of the late 1960s. However, the problem of police and community relations has always plagued the police departments of the United States. To what extent should the community determine policing policy and priorities? In the early days of American policing, police officers were appointed to serve in their own neighborhoods, and the officers very clearly reflected community standards and norms in the enforcement of the laws. Later, policing became more centralized and more impersonal. Communities now desire closer control of their police departments and more input in the setting of police policy. The problem arises when the police are defined as experts about policing matters but oppose what they term "political interference."

It is estimated that less than one-fifth of U.S. residents age 16 or older had a face-to-face contact with the police in 2005 (Durose, Smith & Langan, 2007). Police and citizen contact is most common among younger, white, male citizens and most typically occurs during traffic stops. This limited amount of citizen contact with the police contributes to strained relations between the police and the community. Not only is there little interaction, most of it takes place in stressful circumstances. Police officers typically assume a professional, detached role in dealing with citizens, suggesting that the police are separate from the communities they serve.

In reality, the police are dependent upon, and responsible to, the community. At the same time, the community has charged the police with controlling the behaviors of community members while complaining about the fact that the police control behavior. The dilemma is that the community has hired the police to do many things, and some of these are things that the community does not really want to see done. Community relations problems center on those issues in which it is not clear who (the police or the community) should directly define the police role (Radelet & Carter, 1994).

The current movement to community-oriented policing seeks to increase the role of the citizenry in setting police policy. The police work with the community to identify problems and select solutions. The community is expected to define problems, suggest and/or approve solutions, and cooperate in police efforts to improve the quality of life in the community. One problem that arises is when the community and the police disagree about which police actions are appropriate. Webb and Katz (1997) report that citizens do not believe that the preventive activities of police officers are as legitimate and important as more traditional enforcement activities. Further, satisfaction with the police and support for police appear to be linked to feelings of personal safety. Those who feel safest in their communities are most likely to be supportive of the police and of community policing initiatives (Dietz, 1997). Interestingly, it seems that those persons least in need of police assistance are most happy with police service. The very people the police most need to engage— those living in high-crime neighborhoods—are the ones least likely to trust the police or be satisfied with police service. In addition, when the police seek to prevent disorder in these neighborhoods as a route to improving community conditions and preventing more serious crime, the targets of disorder control are often the community members the police are seeking to assist. When the police crack down on loitering, for example, the persons confronted by the police tend to be those who live in the neighborhood. The attempt to improve community conditions has the effect of undermining police and community relations (Reibstein, 1997).

A final issue for our consideration is the role of the police in the control of crime. The police do not define what behaviors are criminal, do not control their own budget, and do not control the social and psychological forces that lead individuals to commit crimes, yet they are responsible for the control and prevention of crime. In large part, this is what is meant by the "impossible mandate" of the police (Manning, 1978). The police are responsible for the control of something over which they have no control.

To control crime, police have adopted a number of strategies throughout the years that theoretically appear to serve the function of crime control. Many of these, however, have been discovered to be of questionable utility. Rapid response and preventive patrol are but two of these strategies.

For decades, the typical police force has been distributed over the entire jurisdiction for which it is responsible. This distribution has been based in part on the belief that officers would be able to respond more quickly to calls for aid, and that quicker responses would prove more successful in apprehending offenders. More recent research indicates that this is not true, at least insofar as complainants often do not notify the police soon enough that an offense has occurred. By the time the police are notified, responding within a minute of the call normally is not important (Cordner, Greene & Bynum, 1983).

Another reason for placing officers out in the community is to provide a "police presence" in order to deter potential violators and reassure law-abiding citizens. Further, when they are not responding to calls for help, the police are expected to patrol and to prevent crime. Recent research has brought into question the assumption that patroling prevents crime. There is little reason to believe that preventive patrol is the crime-reduction strategy that it has traditionally been thought to be (Kelling et al., 1974; Sherman, 1997). While the effectiveness of preventive patrol requires further study, the general effectiveness of the police in controlling crime has come into question.

The primary issue involved in the question of police effectiveness appears to be one of preventing crime. While there is interest in how to improve police efficiency in apprehending and processing offenders, and there is hope of success in this area, the greatest questions revolve around the ability of the police to prevent crimes. Recent suggestions range from increased technological adaptations to community crime watch to environmental design (Fleissner & Heinzelmann, 1996; Lab, 1990). In each of these prevention strategies, the role of the police in actual crime prevention is minimal. Perhaps we must reconsider the long-held view that police can prevent most crime if they are given sufficient resources (Kelling & Coles, 1996). The question to be decided is whether the police role should continue to cover the dual mandates of crime control and crime prevention.

As an outgrowth of the recognition that police efforts to control crime are limited and that police relationships with citizens are strained, there has been a call to reform policing in the United States. Many police experts, administrators, and observers support the movement toward crime prevention as the major purpose of policing. Indeed, the shift to a greater cooperation between the police and the community has been termed a "quiet revolution" (Kelling, 1988). The revolution involved is a restructuring of the relationship between the police and the community, and a redefinition of the police task. The central idea is that if the police, working with the community, can minimize disorder, more serious crime will also decline.

There is the emerging notion that while the police cannot do much to control actual levels of crime, police can have an effect on levels of disorder and the fear of crime (Wilson & Kelling, 1982). To be successful in this effort, the police must take direction from the community in order to determine what are the most important community problems relating to crime and fear of crime. The police then should work with community leaders to develop necessary resources to solve those problems from within both the private and public sectors. To do this, the police must decentralize decisionmaking to the level of the patrol officer as well as take policy direction from the community. These changes reflect very different arrangements than were evident in the policing of the recent past (Skolnick & Bayley, 1986).

Police bike patrols are often developed as a facet of a department's proactive approach to law enforcement and community service. They are designed to be both an aid to positive community relations as well as a sensible approach to policing neighborhoods. Supporters believe that police interaction with the community will result in stronger communities with more effective informal social controls. *Photo credit: E.S. Boyne.*

Community policing, in theory at least, suggests a model in which the police can organize a reactive form of crime prevention (Travis & Langworthy, 2008). Thus, the police are still reactive (democratic), while crime control becomes proactive through community organizations. While supporters of community policing believe this will result in stronger communities with more effective informal social controls, there are those who are skeptical (Sampson, 2002).

Skeptics believe that this task will prove to be impossible for a variety of reasons. Some suggest that early police were organized in this fashion, that is, closely tied to the community, and point out that this close link led to corruption (Strecher, 1991; Travis, 1992). They fear that a return to decentralized policing may produce increased amounts of ethnic discrimination and disparity in law enforcement. Others (Williams & Wagoner, 1992) argue that the reality of police crime prevention efforts is that they must be antidemocratic in the sense that the police will not be able to simply enact the wishes of the community. Still others argue that as the police emphasize order maintenance in an attempt to prevent serious crime, they will lose legitimacy in the eyes of the public. This loss of legitimacy will be manifest in increased resentment and resistance by citizens (Piquero & Bouffard, 2003; Taylor et al., 2001). In response to this resistance, the police will increasingly rely on force, leading to further resistance and poisoning the relationship between the police and the public.

The increasing emphasis on proactive, problem-solving approaches to crime raise questions about citizen support for the police (Davis, Mateu-Gelabert & Miller, 2005). Overly zealous enforcement efforts may cause citizens to question whether or not the police are concerned about helping citizens. If people feel they are simply the targets of police enforcement and that police are not concerned about their welfare, they may begin to question the legitimacy of the police, and of the law more generally. In the end, public perceptions of unjust and uncaring enforcement can lead to "rebellion," with higher rates of crime and less citizen cooperation with police. The control and prevention of crime by the police requires a balance between the needs for crime control and requirements of due process.

Review Questions

1. Identify and explain the three principal justice system decision points contained in the law enforcement component of the system.

2. Under what circumstances has the U.S. Supreme Court ruled that police need not obtain a warrant prior to conducting a search?

3. What is meant by the "exclusionary rule," and how does it reflect the conflict between due process and crime control?

4. What is the significance of the *Miranda* ruling, and what does it require of the police?

5. What is the good faith exception to the exclusionary rule?

6. Define what is meant by the term "entrapment."

7. What pressures influence the decisions and behavior of police officers?

8. Identify three contemporary issues in American law enforcement.

References

Adams, K. (1999). "What We Know About Police Use of Force." In National Institute of Justice, *Use of Force by Police: Overview of National and Local Data*. Washington, DC: National Institute of Justice:1-14.

Alpert, G. & W. Smith (1994). "How Reasonable is the Reasonable Man?: Police and Excessive Force." *Journal of Criminal Law and Criminology* 85(2):481-501.

Barkan, S. & S. Cohn (1998). "Racial Prejudice and Support by Whites for Police Use of Force: A Research Note." *Justice Quarterly* 15(4):743-753.

Bayley, D. (2002). "Law Enforcement and The Rule of Law: Is There a Tradeoff?" *Criminology & Public Policy* 2(1):133-154.

Bazley, T., K. Lersch & T. Mieczkowski (2007). "Officer Force Versus Suspect Resistance: A Gendered Analysis of Patrol Officers in an Urban Police Department." *Journal of Criminal Justice* 35(2):183-192.

Berk, R., S. Fenstermaker & P. Newton (1988). "An Empirical Analysis of Police Responses to Incidents of Wife Battering." In G. Hotaling, D. Finkelhor, J. Kirkpatrick & M. Straus (eds.), *Coping with Family Violence: Research and Policy Perspectives*. Newbury Park, CA: Sage.

Bittner, E. (1970). *The Functions of Police in Modern Society*. Rockville, MD: National Institute of Mental Health.

Brandl, S. (1993). "The Impact of Case Characteristics on Detectives' Decision Making." *Justice Quarterly* 10(3):395-415.

Brandl, S. (1996). "In the Line of Duty: A Descriptive Analysis of Police Assaults and Accidents." *Journal of Criminal Justice* 24(3):255-264.

Brandl, S. & M. Stroshine (2003). "Toward an Understanding of the Physical Hazards of Police Work." *Police Quarterly* 6(2):172-191.

Browning, S., F.T. Cullen, L. Cao, R. Kopache & T.J. Stevenson (1994). "Race and Getting Hassled by the Police: A Research Note." *Police Studies* 17(1):1-10.

Buchanan, G. (1993). "Managing Police Use of Force." *The Police Chief* 60(August):20-24.

Buzawa, E. & T. Austin (1993). "Determining Police Response to Domestic Violence Victims." *American Behavioral Scientist* 36(5):610-623.

Cao, L. & B. Huang (2000). "Determinants of Citizen Complaints Against Police Abuse of Power." *Journal of Criminal Justice* 28(3):215-226.

Cao, L., S. Stack & Y. Sun (1998). "Public Attitudes Toward the Police: A Comparative Study Between Japan and America." *Journal of Criminal Justice* 26(4):279-289.

Carter, D. (1990a). "Drug-Related Corruption of Police Officers: A Contemporary Typology." *Journal of Criminal Justice* 18(2):85-98.

Carter, D. (1990b). "An Overview of Drug-Related Misconduct of Police Officers: Drug Abuse and Narcotic Corruption." In R. Weisheit (ed.), *Drugs and the Criminal Justice System*. Cincinnati: Anderson, 79-109.

Cheurprakobkit, S. & R. Bartsch (1999). "Police Work and the Police Profession: Assessing Attitudes of City Officials, Spanish-Speaking Hispanics, and Their English-Speaking Counterparts." *Journal of Criminal Justice* 27(2):87-100).

Coleman, J.W. (1985). *The Criminal Elite*. New York: St. Martin's.

Cordner, G.W., J.R. Greene & T.S. Bynum (1983). "The Sooner the Better: Some Effects of Police Response Time." In R.R. Bennett (ed.), *Police at Work: Policy Issues and Analysis*. Beverly Hills, CA: Sage, 145-164.

Davis, R. (1997). "What Fourth Amendment? HR666 and the Satanic Expansion of the Good Faith Exception." *Policing* 20(1):101-112.

Davis, R., P. Mateu-Gelabert & J. Miller (2005). "Can Effective Policing Also be Respectful? Two Examples in the South Bronx." *Police Quarterly* 8(2):229-247.

DeLone, G. (2007). "Law Enforcement Mission Statements Post-September 11th." *Police Quarterly* 10(2):218-235.

Dietz, A. (1997). "Evaluating Community Policing: Quality Police Service and Fear of Crime." *Policing* 20(1):83-100.

Dowler, K. & V. Zawilski (2007). "Public Perceptions of Police Misconduct and Discrimination: Examining the Impact of Media Consumption." *Journal of Criminal Justice* 35(2):193-203.

Durose, M., E. Smith & P. Langan (2007). *Contacts Between Police and the Public, 2005*. Washington, DC: Bureau of Justice Statistics.

Engel, R., J. Sobol & R. Worden (2000). "Further Exploration of the Demeanor Hypothesis: The Interaction Effects of Suspects' Characteristics and Demeanor on Police Behavior." *Justice Quarterly* 17(2):235-258.

Fleissner, D. & F. Heinzelmann (1996). *Crime Prevention Through Environmental Design and Community Policing*. Washington, DC: National Institute of Justice.

Frank, J., B. Smith & K. Novak (2005). "Exploring the Basis of Citizens' Attitudes Toward the Police." *Police Quarterly* 8(2):206-228.

Garner, J., C. Maxwell & C. Heraux (2002). "Characteristics Associated with the Prevalence and Severity of Force Used by the Police." *Justice Quarterly* 19(4):705-746.

Garner, J., J. Buchanan, T. Schade & J. Hepburn (1996). *Understanding the Use of Force by and Against the Police*. Washington, DC: National Institute of Justice.

Goldstein, J. (1960). "Police Discretion Not to Invoke the Criminal Process: Low Visibility Decisions in the Administration of Justice." *Yale Law Journal* 69(March):543-594.

Green, L. (1995). "Cleaning up Drug Hot Spots in Oakland, California: The Displacement and Diffusion Effects." *Justice Quarterly* 12(4):737-754.

Griswold, D. (1994). "Complaints Against the Police: Predicting Dispositions." *Journal of Criminal Justice* 22(3):215-222.

Halpher, A. & R. Ku (1976). *An Exemplary Project: New York Police Department Street Crime Unit*. Washington, DC: U.S. Government Printing Office.

Hickman, M. (2006). *Citizen Complaints About Police Use of Force*. Washington, DC: Bureau of Justice Statistics.

Holden, R.N. (1993). "Police and the Profit Motive: A New Look at Asset Forfeiture." *ACJS Today* 12(2):1.

Hurst, Y. & J. Frank (2000). "How Kids View Cops: The Nature of Juvenile Attitudes Toward the Police." *Journal of Criminal Justice* 28(3):189-202.

Inbau, F.E. (1966). "Playing God: Five to Four." *Journal of Criminal Law, Criminology and Police Science* 57:377.

Jesilow, P. & J. Mayer (2001). "The Effects of Police Misconduct on Public Attitudes." *Journal of Crime & Justice* 24(1):109-121.

Jogerst, G., J. Daly, M. Brinig & S. Bibas (2005). "The Association Between Statutory Penalties and Domestic Elder Abuse Investigations." *Journal of Crime and Justice* 28(2):51-69.

Jones, D. & J. Belknap (1999). "Police Responses to Battering in a Progressive Pro-Arrest Jurisdiction." *Justice Quarterly* 16(2):249-273.

Kane, R. (1999). "Patterns of Arrest in Domestic Violence Encounters: Identifying a Police Decision-Making Model." *Journal of Criminal Justice* 27(1):65-79.

Kappeler, V.E., S.F. Kappeler & R.V. del Carmen (1993). "A Content Analysis of Police Civil Liability Cases: Decisions of the Federal District Courts, 1978-1990." *Journal of Criminal Justice* 21(4):339-352.

Kelling, G. (1999). *"Broken Windows" and Police Discretion.* Washington, DC: National Institute of Justice.

Kelling, G. (1988). *Police and Communities: The Quiet Revolution.* Washington, DC: U.S. Department of Justice.

Kelling, G. & C. Coles (1996). *Fixing Broken Windows.* New York: Free Press.

Kelling, G., T. Pate, D. Dieckman & C.E. Brown (1974). *The Kansas City Preventive Patrol Experiment: A Summary Report.* Washington, DC: The Police Foundation.

Kerstetter, W., K. Rasinski & C. Heiert (1996). "The Impact of Race on the Investigation of Excessive Force Allegations Against Police." *Journal of Criminal Justice* 24(1):1-15.

Koper, C. (1995). "Just Enough Police Presence: Reducing Crime and Disorderly Behavior by Optimizing Patrol Time in Crime Hot Spots." *Justice Quarterly* 12(4):649-672.

Kraska, P. & V. Kappeler (1995). "To Serve and Pursue: Exploring Police Sexual Violence Against Women." *Justice Quarterly* 12(1):85-111.

Lab, S. (1990). "Citizen Crime Prevention: Domains and Participation." *Justice Quarterly* 7(3):467-492.

Langworthy, R.H. (1989). "Do Stings Control Crime? An Evaluation of a Police Fencing Operation." *Justice Quarterly* 6(1):27-45.

Langworthy, R.H. & J. LeBeau (1992). "The Spatial Distribution of Sting Targets." *Journal of Criminal Justice* 20(6):541-551.

Langworthy, R.H. & J. LeBeau (1993). "Spatial Evolution of a Sting Clientele." *Journal of Criminal Justice* 20(2):135-146.

Langworthy, R.H. & L.F. Travis III (2003). *Policing in America: A Balance of Forces,* 3rd ed. Englewood Cliffs, NJ: Prentice Hall.

Lawton, B., R. Taylor & A. Luongo (2005). "Police Officers on Drug Corners in Philadelphia, Drug Crime, and Violent Crime: Intended, Diffusion, and Displacement Impacts." *Justice Quarterly* 22(4):427-451.

Lersch, K. (1998). "Predicting Citizen Race in Allegations of Misconduct Against the Police." *Journal of Criminal Justice* 26(2):87-97.

Lewis, P.W. & H.E. Allen (1977). "Participating Miranda: An Attempt to Subvert Certain Constitutional Safeguards." *Crime & Delinquency* 23(1):75.

Lundman, R. (1998). "City Police and Drunk Driving: Baseline Data." *Justice Quarterly* 15(3):527-546.

Lynch, T. (2002). *Policy Analysis: Breaking the Vicious Cycle: Preserving Our Liberties While Fighting Terrorism.* Washington, DC: CATO Institute.

MacDonald, J. G. Alpert & A. Tennenbaum (1999). "Justifiable Homicide by Police and Criminal Homicide: A Research Note." *Journal of Crime and Justice* 22(1):153-166.

Manning, P.K. (1978). "The Police: Mandate, Strategies and Appearances." In P.K. Manning & J. Van Maanen (eds.), *Policing: A View from the Street.* Santa Monica, CA: Goodyear, 7-31.

Mastrofski, S., M. Reisig & J. McCluskey (2002). "Police Disrespect Toward the Public: An Encounter-Based Analysis." *Criminology* 40(3):519-552.

Mazerolle, L., D. Soole & S. Rombouts (2007). "Drug Law Enforcement: A Review of the Evaluation Literature." *Police Quarterly* 10(2):115-153.

McEwen, T. (1997). "Policies on Less-Than-Lethal Force in Law Enforcement Agencies." *Policing* 20(1):39-59.

Morrison, G. (2006). "Deadly Force Programs Among Larger U.S. Police Departments." *Police Quarterly* 9(3):331-360.

National Institute of Justice (2003). "Without a Trace? Advances in Detecting Trace Evidence." *NIJ Journal* (July):2-9.

Nunn, S., K. Quinet, K. Rowe & D. Christ (2006). "Interdiction Day: Cover Surveillance Operations, Drugs, and Serious Crime in an Inner-City Neighborhood." *Police Quarterly* 9(1):73-99.

Office of Law Enforcement Standards (1999). *Forensic Sciences: Review of Status and Needs.* Gaithersburg, MD: National Institute of Standards and Technology.

Palmiotto, M. (ed.) (1984). *Critical Issues in Criminal Investigation.* Cincinnati: Anderson.

Park, R. (1976). "The Entrapment Controversy." *Minnesota Law Review* 60:163-274.

Peterson, J.L. (1987). *Use of Forensic Evidence by the Police and Courts.* Washington, DC: National Institute of Justice.

Piquero, N. & L. Bouffard (2003). "A Preliminary and Partial Test of Specific Defiance." *Journal of Crime and Justice* 26(1):1-22.

Priest, T. & D. Carter (1999). "Evaluations of Police Performance in an African American Sample." *Journal of Criminal Justice* 27(5):457-463.

Radelet, L. & D. Carter (1994). *The Police and the Community,* 5th ed. New York: Macmillan.

Reibstein, L. (1997). "NYPD Black and Blue." *Newsweek* (June 2):66.

Reitzel, J. & A. Piquero (2006). "Does It Exist? Studying Citizens' Attitudes of Racial Profiling." *Police Quarterly* 9(3):161-183.

Rubinstein, J. (1973). *City Police.* New York: Farrar, Straus & Giroux.

Sacks, H. (1978). "Notes on Police Assessment of Moral Character." In P.K. Manning & J. Van Maanen (eds.), *Policing: A View from the Street.* Santa Monica, CA: Goodyear, 187-202.

Sampson, R. (2002). "Transcending Tradition: New Directions in Community Research, Chicago Style—The American Society of Criminology 2001 Sutherland Address." *Criminology* 40(2):213-230.

Schafer, J. & S. Mastrofski (2005). "Police Leniency in Traffic Enforcement Encounters: Exploratory Findings From Observations and Interviews." *Journal of Criminal Justice* 33(3):225-238.

Sherman, L., P. Gartin & M. Buerger (1989). "Hot Spots of Predatory Crime: Routine Activities and the Criminology of Place." *Criminology* 27(1):27-55.

Sherman, L. & D. Weisburd (1995). "General Deterrent Effects of Police Patrol in Crime 'Hot Spots': A Randomized, Controlled Trial." *Justice Quarterly* 12(4):625-648.

Sherman, L.W. (ed.) (1974). *Police Corruption: A Sociological Perspective.* Garden City, NJ: Anchor Books.

Sherman, L.W. (1990a). "Police Crackdowns." In C. Klockars & S. Mastrofski (eds.), *Thinking about Police: Contemporary Readings.* New York: McGraw-Hill, 188-211.

Sherman, L.W. (1990b). "Police Crackdowns." *NIJ Reports* (March/April)219:2-6.

Sherman, L. (1997). "Policing for Crime Prevention." In L. Sherman, D. Gottfredson, D. MacKenzie, J. Eck, P. Reuter & S. Bushway (eds.), *Preventing Crime: What Works, What Doesn't, What's Promising?* Washington, DC: National Institute of Justice.

Skolnick, J. & D. Bayley (1986). *The New Blue Line: Police Innovation in Six American Cities.* New York: Free Press.

Smith, M., M. Makarios & G. Alpert (2006). "Differential Suspicion: Theory Specification and Gender Effects in the Traffic Stop Context." *Justice Quarterly* 23(2):271-295.

Son, I., M. Davis & D. Rome (1998). "Race and Its Effect on Police Officers' Perceptions of Misconduct." *Journal of Criminal Justice* 26(1):21-28.

Son, I., Tsang, C., D. Rome & M. Davis (1997). "Citizen's Observations of Police Use of Excessive Force and Their Evaluation of Police Performance." *Policing* 20(1):149-159.

Strecher, V. (1991). "Histories and Futures of Policing: Readings and Misreadings of a Pivotal Present." *Police Forum* 1(1):1-9.

Sudnow, D. (1964). "Normal Crimes: Sociological Features of the Penal Code in the Public Defender's Office." *Social Problems* 12:81.

Surette, R. (2006). "CCTV and Citizen Guardianship Suppression: A Questionable Proposition." *Police Quarterly* 9(1):100-125.

Taylor, T., K. Turner, F. Esbensen & L. Winfree (2001). "Coppin' An Attitude: Attitudinal Differences Among Juveniles Toward the Police." *Journal of Criminal Justice* 29(4):295-306.

Terrill, W. (2005). "Police Use of Force: A Transactional Approach." *Justice Quarterly* 22(1):107-138.

Terrill, W. (2003). "Police Use of Force and Suspect Resistance: The Micro Process of the Police-Suspect Encounter." *Police Quarterly* 6(1):51-83.

Tiffany, L.P., D.M. McIntyre & D.J. Rotenberg (1967). *Detection of Crime: Stopping and Questioning, Search and Seizure, Encouragement and Entrapment.* Boston: Little, Brown.

Time, V. & B. Payne (2002). "Police Chiefs' Perceptions about Miranda: An Analysis of Survey Data." *Journal of Criminal Justice* 30(1):77-86.

Time (1980). "The F.B.I. Stings Congress." *Time* (February 18, 1980):10-14; 18-21.

Travis, L.F., III (1992). "Making History: Explaining the Development of the Police." *Police Forum* 2(2):6-10.

Travis, L.F. & R. H. Langworthy (2008). *Policing in America: A Balance of Forces,* 4th ed. Upper Saddle River, NJ: Prentice Hall.

Trojanowicz, R. & B. Bucqueroux (1990). *Community Policing: A Contemporary Perspective.* Cincinnati: Anderson.

Turner, R. & R. Kosa (2003). "Cold Case Squads: Leaving No Stone Unturned." *BJA Bulletin* (July). Washington, DC: Bureau of Justice Assistance.

Walker, S. & N. Graham (1998). "Citizen Complaints in Response to Police Misconduct: The Results of a Victimization Survey." *Police Quarterly* 1(1):65-89.

Webb, V. & C. Katz (1997). "Citizen Ratings of the Importance of Community Policing Activities." *Policing* 20(1):7-23.

Weisburd, D. & L. Green (1995). "Policing Drug Hot Spots: The Jersey City Drug Market Analysis Experiment." *Justice Quarterly* 12(4):711-735.

Weitzer, R. (2002). "Incidents of Police Misconduct and Public Opinion." *Journal of Criminal Justice* 30(5):397-408.

Welsh, B. & D. Farrington (2002). *Crime Prevention Effects of Closed-Circuit Television: A Systematic Review.* London: Home Office Research, Development, and Statistics Directorate.

White, M. & J. Ready (2007). "The TASER as a Less Lethal Force Alternative: Findings on Use and Effectiveness in a Large Metropolitan Police Agency." *Police Quarterly* 10(2):170-191.

Williams, R. & C. Wagoner (1992). "Making the Police Proactive: An Impossible Task for Improbable Reasons." *Police Forum* 2(2):1-15.

Wilson, J.Q. (1988). *The Exclusionary Rule: Crime File Study Guide.* Washington, DC: U.S. Department of Justice.

Wilson, J.Q. & G. Kelling (1982). "Broken Windows: Police and Neighborhood Safety." *Atlantic Monthly* 249 (March):29-38.

Wilson, M. and R. Ruback (2003). "Hate Crimes in Pennsylvania, 1984-99: Case Characteristics and Police Responses." *Justice Quarterly* 20(2):373-398.

Withrow, B. & J. Dailey (2004). "A Model of Circumstantial Corruptability." *Police Quarterly* 7(2):159-178.

Witt, W. (1977). "Non-Coercive Interrogation and the Administration of Criminal Justice: The Impact of Miranda on Police Effectuality." *Journal of Criminal Law, Criminology and Police Science* 64:320-332.

Worden, R. (1989). "Situational and Attitudinal Explanations of Police Behavior: A Theoretical Reappraisal and Empirical Assessment." *Law & Society Review* 23(4):667-711.

Important Cases

Arizona v. Evans, 115 S. Ct. 1185 (1995).

Brewer v. Williams, 430 U.S. 387 (1977).

Chambers v. Maroney, 453 U.S. 42 (1970).

Chimel v. California, 395 U.S. 752 (1969).

Coolidge v. New Hampshire, 403 U.S. 443 (1981).

Dickerson v. United States, 530 U.S. 428 (2000).

Florida v. Riley, 488 U.S. 455 (1989).

Georgia v. Randolph, 547 U.S. __ (2006).

Illinois v. Gates, 462 U.S. 213 (1983).

Katz v. United States, 389 U.S. 347 (1967).

Mapp v. Ohio, 367 U.S. 643 (1961).

Maryland v. Wilson, 519 U.S. 408 (1997).

Miranda v. Arizona, 384 U.S. 436 (1966).

New York v. Class, 475 U.S. 106 (1986).

Terry v. Ohio, 392 U.S. 1 (1968).

Thornton v. United States, 541 U.S. 615 (2004).

United States v. Class, 475 U.S. 106 (1986).

United States v. Leon, 484 U.S. 897 (1984).

United State v. Matlock, 415 U.S. 164 (1974)

United States v. Ross, 456 U.S. 798 (1982).

United States v. Wade, 388 U.S. 218 (1967).

Warden v. Hayden, 387 U.S. 294 (1967).

Weeks v. United States, 232 U.S. 383 (1914).

Chapter 7

The Criminal Courts

Important Terms

There are more than 16,000 courts in operation in the United States (Rottman & Strickland, 2006). Most of these are at the local level in cities and counties across the country and employ more than 30,000 justices, judges, magistrates, or other judicial officers (Schauffler et al., 2006). As we saw with police agencies, the large number of individual courts in the United States is a reflection of our belief in local autonomy. Almost 21 million criminal cases (excluding traffic cases) were filed in American state courts in 2005 (Schauffler et al., 2006). There were also nearly 55 million cases filed for traffic offenses. In addition, more civil cases than nontraffic criminal cases are filed. About 2 percent of all cases filed involved felony offenses, which number 2 to 2.5 million cases each year.

Every county is served by a felony court (sometimes a court serves more than one county), but most cases arise in the few populous counties. The 42 largest jurisdictions (in terms of population) accounted for more than one-quarter of criminal cases closed in 2005 (Perry, 2006). In 2001, slightly less than 5 percent of prosecutor's offices serving jurisdictions having 500,000 or more persons represented 45 percent of the nation's population and accounted for nearly one-half of all felony case closures (DeFrances, 2001). In terms of crime control, then, American courts mirror the police. Crime control activities are a relatively small part of the total workload of the courts, and criminal cases are concentrated in a few, populous areas.

A **crime** is a public wrong. Crime cases comprise the criminal justice component of United States courts. Thus, crime is a part-time function for our courts. Box 7.1 describes the workload of America's courts. The basic purpose of the courts is to resolve disputes (Neely, 1983; Stumpf, 1988). As our society becomes increasingly complex, we not only encounter more disputes, but informal mechanisms of dispute resolution become less effective. Added to this is the fact that the large and increasing number of attorneys in our society makes it easier for people to obtain legal counsel and to use the courts. Thus, more people are bringing their disputes to the courts each year. Each of these individuals is seeking justice. In discussing the purpose of the courts, Rubin (1984:4) noted:

> If we try to describe the purpose of the courts, someone will usually first suggest that their purpose is to "do justice," to provide individualized justice in individual cases. This is true, but whether justice is done depends typically upon the interests or viewpoints of the affected or interested parties. We are confident that some guilty people have been found innocent in our courts, and that innocent persons have been found guilty. These trials may have been conducted fairly, but was justice done?

Box 7.1 Types of Cases Filed in State Trial Courts, 2005 (in millions)

Case Type	Total Number	General	Jurisdiction Limited	Unified
Traffic	54.7	1.6	40.8	12.3
Civil	16.9	4.5	9.3	3.0
Criminal	20.7	3.1	14.2	3.3
Domestic	5.7	3.1	1.6	1.0
Juvenile	2.1	1.0	.8	.4
Total	100.0	13.3	66.7	20.0

Source: R. Schauffler, R. LaFountain, S. Strickland & W. Raftery (2006), *Examining the Work of State Courts, 2005* (Washington, DC: National Center for State Courts):13.

The point here is that justice is elusive of definition. Indeed, the courts are perhaps better understood as jugglers attempting to keep many divergent interests in motion without dropping anything. The courts must strike a balance between the rights of disputing parties. In the criminal courts, the principal balance to be maintained is between the rights of an individual (and by extension, all individuals) and the rights of the state. The resolution of criminal cases more often entails compromise than competition. Perhaps the best example of this "juggling act" quality of the criminal courts is seen in the practice of plea bargaining.

In plea bargaining, the state and the individual defendant compromise, with neither side getting all that it would hope to achieve. The judge serves as the juggler, balancing the interests of the state (in securing a conviction and punishing a criminal) against the interests of the individual (in protecting his or her liberty and constitutional rights). The alternative to plea bargaining is trial. Trial is the epitome of competition. It is filled with costs and uncertainties for both parties involved in the dispute. Either side may "win" the trial, but both sides will have to expend time and money, experience aggravation, and risk losing to the competition. In plea bargaining, the accused is convicted, but avoids the full measure of punishment for the offense of which he or she is accused. Neither side is completely satisfied with the outcome, but both can accept it.

These compromises, which characterize the workings of the criminal courts, must be understood within the organizational context of the courts. They involve not only a defendant and a prosecutor as two competing parties, but also a defense attorney (or defender's office), a prosecutor's office, a judge, witnesses, other court staff, the police, possibly jurors, and others. Each actor or set of actors in every criminal case affects the final outcome (Panzarella & Shapiro, 1988). However complex the issues involved in any case, the complexity of the issues is matched or exceeded by the complexity of the court process (Mays & Taggart, 1986).

The Organization of American Courts

The term "courts" covers a wide range of decision-making bodies, ranging from part-time justice of the peace (or mayor's) courts, in which the "judge" often is not trained in the law, to the nine-member U.S. Supreme Court. There are many different types of courts. They are organized on two basic levels: federal courts and state courts. The existence of two sets of courts in the United States, one federal and the other state, has led observers to speak of a dual system of courts. Box 7.2 provides a diagram of the American court process.

Court systems contain two basic types of courts: trial courts and appellate courts. Trial courts are fact-finding bodies whose job it is to determine the facts of a case (i.e., did the defendant commit the crime?). Appellate courts are law-interpreting bodies whose job it is to determine if the laws were correctly applied and followed (i.e., should the defendant have been provided defense counsel at trial?). Within trial courts, distinctions are made based on jurisdiction, which is the definition of a court's authority. Determination of a court's jurisdiction typically involves both geography (a county court hears cases arising in its county) and type of case. A court of general jurisdiction can hear civil and criminal cases of all sorts. A court of limited jurisdiction typically is constrained to hearing only minor cases, or conducting the early parts of more serious cases. There are also special jurisdiction courts that are created to deal with specific types of cases, such as family matters (court of domestic relations) or wills and estates (probate court).

Box 7.2   The Structure of American Courts

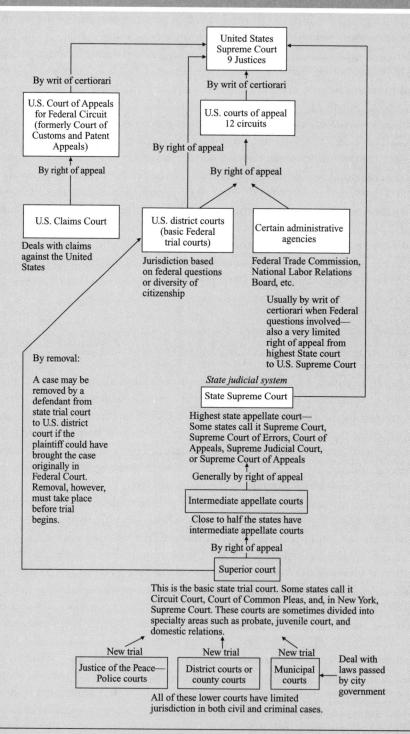

Source: Bureau of Justice Statistics (1988), *Report to the Nation on Crime and Justice*, 2nd ed. (Washington, DC: U.S. Department of Justice).

Federal Courts

The federal judicial system is comprised of the U.S. Supreme Court, 12 U.S. Courts of Appeals, 94 district courts, more than 400 magistrates assigned to the district courts, and a number of special courts for tax, patent, customs, and contract cases. In comparison to most state court systems, the federal courts are relatively simply organized. United States magistrates are appointed by district court judges and are empowered to issue warrants, hear petty cases, and conduct the preliminary stages of more serious criminal cases.

District courts exist in each of the 50 states, the District of Columbia, and the federal territories. District courts are trial courts of the federal system and, combined with magistrates, they comprise the lower courts in the federal system. They hear both civil and criminal cases involving the federal government or violations of federal laws.

U.S. Courts of Appeals represent the 50 states, the District of Columbia, and the federal territories. Eleven of these courts are identified by number; the twelfth is the Court of Appeals for the District of Columbia. These courts receive appeals from the decisions of the district courts and also decide appeals from the decisions of many federal administrative agencies. Their decisions become binding on all federal district courts under their jurisdiction.

The U.S. Supreme Court is the nation's highest court. Its nine justices hear appeals from the U.S. Courts of Appeals as well as those from state courts of last resort (usually state supreme courts) that involve questions of federal law or the U.S. Constitution. In most cases, the Supreme Court is not obligated to decide a case and only selects to do so by granting a writ of certiorari. This writ is an order to the lower court to send its records of the case so that the Supreme Court can determine whether the law has been applied properly. The Court grants certiorari in less than 5 percent of the cases brought before it (Schmalleger, 1993:276).

State Courts

In terms of general organization, state court systems mirror the federal courts. They are divided into triers of limited or special jurisdiction, general jurisdiction courts, and a court of last resort. Boxes 7.3 and 7.4 illustrate two state court systems that differ in terms of their complexity. From state to state, the courts vary greatly in name, number, administration, and power. In 2005, the court systems of the 50 states, Puerto Rico, and the District of Columbia reported general-jurisdiction trial courts as using the following names: "circuit," "district," "superior," "chancery," "common pleas," "supreme," "county," or simply "trial" courts. Several court systems had multiple court names, such as circuit courts and district courts. Courts at this level employed nearly 10,000 judges, ranging from 16 in Maine to more than 2,000 in Texas (Rottman & Strickland, 2006).

State court systems take one of two basic organizational structures. A traditional court structure involves separate general-jurisdiction and limited-jurisdic-

Box 7.3 Texas Court Structure, 2004

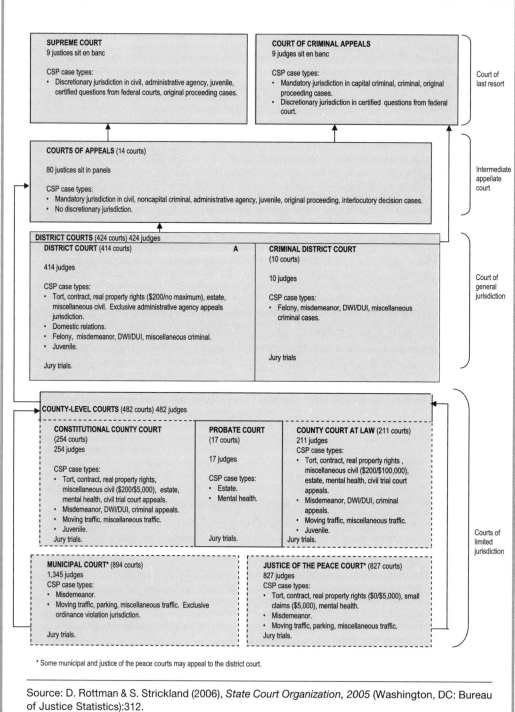

SUPREME COURT
9 justices sit en banc

CSP case types:
• Discretionary jurisdiction in civil, administrative agency, juvenile, certified questions from federal courts, original proceeding cases.

COURT OF CRIMINAL APPEALS
9 judges sit en banc

CSP case types:
• Mandatory jurisdiction in capital criminal, criminal, original proceeding cases.
• Discretionary jurisdiction in certified questions from federal court.

Court of last resort

COURTS OF APPEALS (14 courts)

80 justices sit in panels

CSP case types:
• Mandatory jurisdiction in civil, noncapital criminal, administrative agency, juvenile, original proceeding, interlocutory decision cases.
• No discretionary jurisdiction.

Intermediate appellate court

DISTRICT COURTS (424 courts) 424 judges

DISTRICT COURT (414 courts)   A

414 judges

CSP case types:
• Tort, contract, real property rights ($200/no maximum), estate, miscellaneous civil. Exclusive administrative agency appeals jurisdiction.
• Domestic relations.
• Felony, misdemeanor, DWI/DUI, miscellaneous criminal.
• Juvenile.

Jury trials.

CRIMINAL DISTRICT COURT
(10 courts)

10 judges

CSP case types:
• Felony, misdemeanor, DWI/DUI, miscellaneous criminal cases.

Jury trials

Court of general jurisdiction

COUNTY-LEVEL COURTS (482 courts) 482 judges

CONSTITUTIONAL COUNTY COURT
(254 courts)
254 judges

CSP case types:
• Tort, contract, real property rights, miscellaneous civil ($200/$5,000), estate, mental health, civil trial court appeals.
• Misdemeanor, DWI/DUI, criminal appeals.
• Moving traffic, miscellaneous traffic.
• Juvenile.
Jury trials.

PROBATE COURT
(17 courts)

17 judges

CSP case types:
• Estate.
• Mental health.

Jury trials.

COUNTY COURT AT LAW (211 courts)
211 judges
CSP case types:
• Tort, contract, real property rights , miscellaneous civil ($200/$100,000), estate, mental health, civil trial court appeals.
• Misdemeanor, DWI/DUI, criminal appeals.
• Moving traffic, miscellaneous traffic.
• Juvenile.
Jury trials.

Courts of limited jurisdiction

MUNICIPAL COURT* (894 courts)
1,345 judges
CSP case types:
• Misdemeanor.
• Moving traffic, parking, miscellaneous traffic. Exclusive ordinance violation jurisdiction.

Jury trials.

JUSTICE OF THE PEACE COURT* (827 courts)
827 judges
CSP case types:
• Tort, contract, real property rights ($0/$5,000), small claims ($5,000), mental health.
• Misdemeanor.
• Moving traffic, parking, miscellaneous traffic.
Jury trials.

* Some municipal and justice of the peace courts may appeal to the district court.

Source: D. Rottman & S. Strickland (2006), *State Court Organization, 2005* (Washington, DC: Bureau of Justice Statistics):312.

Box 7.4   Indiana Court Structure, 2004

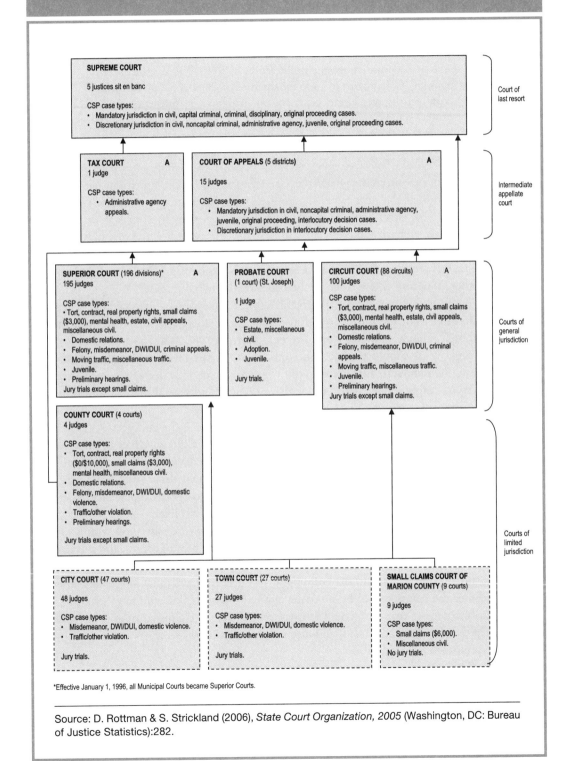

SUPREME COURT

5 justices sit en banc

CSP case types:
- Mandatory jurisdiction in civil, capital criminal, criminal, disciplinary, original proceeding cases.
- Discretionary jurisdiction in civil, noncapital criminal, administrative agency, juvenile, original proceeding cases.

Court of last resort

TAX COURT   A
1 judge

CSP case types:
- Administrative agency appeals.

COURT OF APPEALS (5 districts)   A

15 judges

CSP case types:
- Mandatory jurisdiction in civil, noncapital criminal, administrative agency, juvenile, original proceeding, interlocutory decision cases.
- Discretionary jurisdiction in interlocutory decision cases.

Intermediate appellate court

SUPERIOR COURT (196 divisions)*   A
195 judges

CSP case types:
- Tort, contract, real property rights, small claims ($3,000), mental health, estate, civil appeals, miscellaneous civil.
- Domestic relations.
- Felony, misdemeanor, DWI/DUI, criminal appeals.
- Moving traffic, miscellaneous traffic.
- Juvenile.
- Preliminary hearings.
Jury trials except small claims.

PROBATE COURT
(1 court) (St. Joseph)

1 judge

CSP case types:
- Estate, miscellaneous civil.
- Adoption.
- Juvenile.

Jury trials.

CIRCUIT COURT (88 circuits)   A
100 judges

CSP case types:
- Tort, contract, real property rights, small claims ($3,000), mental health, estate, civil appeals, miscellaneous civil.
- Domestic relations.
- Felony, misdemeanor, DWI/DUI, criminal appeals.
- Moving traffic, miscellaneous traffic.
- Juvenile.
- Preliminary hearings.
Jury trials except small claims.

Courts of general jurisdiction

COUNTY COURT (4 courts)
4 judges

CSP case types:
- Tort, contract, real property rights ($0/$10,000), small claims ($3,000), mental health, miscellaneous civil.
- Domestic relations.
- Felony, misdemeanor, DWI/DUI, domestic violence.
- Traffic/other violation.
- Preliminary hearings.

Jury trials except small claims.

Courts of limited jurisdiction

CITY COURT (47 courts)

48 judges

CSP case types:
- Misdemeanor, DWI/DUI, domestic violence.
- Traffic/other violation.

Jury trials.

TOWN COURT (27 courts)

27 judges

CSP case types:
- Misdemeanor, DWI/DUI, domestic violence.
- Traffic/other violation.

Jury trials.

SMALL CLAIMS COURT OF MARION COUNTY (9 courts)

9 judges

CSP case types:
- Small claims ($6,000).
- Miscellaneous civil.
No jury trials.

*Effective January 1, 1996, all Municipal Courts became Superior Courts.

Source: D. Rottman & S. Strickland (2006), *State Court Organization, 2005* (Washington, DC: Bureau of Justice Statistics):282.

tion courts. A **unified court system** combines the two types of courts into one. The numbers and names of state courts and their organization are diverse. Rubin (1984:11) observed:

> At the state level, courts are created by state constitutions and legislative enactments, and by municipal and county-level legislation. In too many jurisdictions the proliferation of courts has left the citizen unsure of what court to go to for a particular cause of action (divorce, contract dispute, crime, etc.), and for that matter attorneys are not always sure of where to file a particular suit. Some actions can be filed in two or three different courts, and appeals can be taken to several forums.

Indeed, very often the greatest service an attorney can provide his or her client is to ensure that the proper papers are filed with the appropriate court. Donald Jackson (1974) described the current structure of American courts as one that would "make a chart-maker collapse in despair." He described the organizational chart of courts in the United States as "a bewildering maze of parallel, perpendicular, crisscrossing, and overlapping lines." It is frequently difficult to determine whether, how, and where to enter the courts with any given case.

Suppose that you have a disagreement with a neighbor about parking spaces on the street. For the moment (because your car is already parked in front of the neighbor's house), you have won. The next morning, you awaken to discover four flat tires. What should you do? The options are many. First, you may "grin and bear it." Not knowing for sure who did you wrong, you may opt to repair the tires and try to forget the incident (although you may spend several nights monitoring your car, or you may be more selective in deciding where you park). Second, you may confront your neighbor because you surmise that he is the guilty party. (If relations between you and your neighbor were better, you would have had an informal mechanism to avoid this incident in the first place.) Third, you may seek revenge by slashing your neighbor's tires that evening. Fourth, you may decide to call the police and report the vandalism. Calling the police could lead to a court appearance. There may be other options, but these four appear to be the most likely.

If the first three options are unacceptable, in all probability you would call the police. This allows you to collect insurance payment for damages, and it transfers the decision of what to do to the responding officer. The dispute then may reach the courts as a criminal complaint, but deciding whether, where, and how to enter the courts would be someone else's problem. Unless you have extraordinarily expensive tires, you could take your case to small claims court and sue your neighbor for damages. You could also secure counsel by hiring an attorney or by contacting a legal aid office.

This hypothetical case resulted from a dispute among neighbors about parking privileges. It could go to a number of different courts as a tort (a dispute between private parties over a wrongful injury suffered; that is, damaged tires), a crime (willful destruction of property by your neighbor), or both. How is the average citizen to know how and where to file a court case?

The general structure of state courts includes courts of limited jurisdiction (more than 12,000 of them) that are empowered to hear petty cases such as traffic violations, and to conduct the preliminary stages of more serious cases (much like federal magistrates). At a second level of courts are those of general jurisdiction, in which trials for civil and criminal cases are conducted. Most states also have a juvenile or family court. This court is a special-jurisdiction trial court empowered to hear juvenile delinquency cases, but is not otherwise involved with criminal matters. Such courts also hear divorce, child custody, and related domestic relations cases. Finally, there are frequently other special-purpose courts, such as probate and surrogate's courts.

Specialized criminal courts, such as drug courts, are also on the rise (Rottman & Strickland, 2006). Another trend is imposing specialized caseloads so that one judge hears most or all of certain types of offenses, such as domestic violence, gun crimes, or violent crimes. By 2003, there were more than 1,000 drug courts in the United States (Casey & Rottman, 2003:6). Drug courts focus on delivering drug treatment services to substance-abusing offenders, using the criminal process to ensure that needed treatment is available (Wenzel et al., 2001). Other specialized courts include teen courts (Butts & Buck, 2000) and dispute resolution programs. All of these types of courts are referred to as the "lower courts" because they are the first courts in the hierarchy of tribunals to receive cases. Lower courts decide issues of fact. They conduct trials, receive evidence, and establish guilt or innocence. Lower-court judges preside over trials and impose criminal sentences upon convicted offenders.

In most states, a third level of appellate courts exists, at which the courts operate like the U.S. Courts of Appeals (that is, they hear appeals from the lower courts). Some states have more than one intermediate appeal level, so that a case may go through two or more appeals before reaching the third level of courts. Each state has a court of last resort or a supreme court, which receives appeals from all lower courts in the state and from the intermediate appellate courts. The decisions of these courts are binding on all other courts in the state.

Appellate courts do not decide issues of fact; rather, appellate courts serve to interpret the law. Appellate courts accept the findings of fact from the lower courts, and then decide whether the lower-court judges interpreted and applied the law correctly. They resolve questions of law raised by those who lost in the lower courts. Decisions of higher courts on the interpretation and application of the law are binding on all the courts beneath them. Thus, when the U.S. Supreme Court decides upon an interpretation of the U.S. Constitution, that interpretation is binding on all other courts in the nation.

Problem-Solving Courts

As indicated, in the past two decades there has been a growing emphasis on specialized courts aimed at solving specific problems. These courts range from drug courts that deal exclusively with offenders who have substance abuse problems to domestic violence courts and re-entry courts that specialize in returning prisoners to productive lives in the community. As is occurring in policing, there is a growing movement to develop and implement community courts in the United States. Some community courts are actually diversion programs or mediation centers that focus on less serious disputes. In some places, however, actual community courts have been created. They tend to practice restorative justice—the **community courts** attempt to resolve problems and disputes that addresses all concerned, including the community at large (Quinn, 1998). The courts are also linked to community resources and seek to solve problems rather than simply find facts. Thus, the court tries not only to resolve a conflict but to understand its underlying causes and secure necessary community services to prevent the conflict from happening again (Rottman & Casey, 1999).

The movement to community courts was described by David Rottman (1996). His description of the development and spread of community courts mirrors similar accounts of the development of community policing. Initially, courts represented the community and served as forums for dispute resolution in which the resolution process was attuned to community life. As the courts became more professional and centralized, courts became divorced from the communities they served, in part to reduce the impact of "politics" on court processing.

Box 7.5	Community Courts: Types of Community Involvement by Purpose

PURPOSE	TYPE
Better Court Practices	Citizen's Advisory Committee
	Futures Commissions
	Public Opinion & Exit Surveys
	Community Volunteer Programs
	Court-Watching Programs
	Teen Courts
	Judicial Evaluation Programs
	Citizen Sentencing Panels
Better Public Access	Telephone Hotlines
	Divorce Workshops
	Day-care Facilities
	Information Kiosks
Increase Public Knowledge	Courthouse Tours
	Citizen Guides
	"Meet Your Judge" Programs
	School Outreach
	Media Outreach
	Public Service Announcements

Source: D. Rottman (1996), "Community Courts: Prospects and Limits," *NIJ Journal* (August):47.

The community court movement seeks to reestablish the link between courts and communities (see Box 7.5). The community court, it is hoped, will uphold the values of the community and work for the good of all parties. A key component of community courts is citizen involvement (Terry, 2000). A part of this general movement involves **community prosecution**, in which the prosecutor is assigned to the case from initial appearance through disposition and works with the police, community, and other agencies not just to secure conviction, but to solve the problems that led to the criminal behavior (Jansen & Dague, 2006).

While not yet well-evaluated, community courts hold promise for improving justice for less serious disputes and crimes that often find their way into the lower courts of the criminal justice system. Casey and Rottman (2003) report that the limited evaluations to date indicate that community courts rely on community service sentencing, are viewed favorably by the public, and conclude cases more quickly than traditional criminal courts. On the other hand, these courts tend to be more expensive and may result in more severe sentences for offenders who fail to comply with community court orders and are sent to criminal courts. Community courts tend to focus on low-level offenses and devote considerable attention and resources to these less serious crimes.

Community courts are seen as problem-solving courts designed to address not just specific instances of criminal behavior, but community problems that lead to crime (Casey & Rottman, 2003). As with community and problem-solving policing, the emergence of problem-solving courts raises a number of important questions. It remains to be seen how a proliferation of community and other problem-solving courts will affect case processing and outcomes across communities. It is not clear what will happen if one party to a dispute is not a member of the community. The questions revolve around the issue of how community courts will affect the balance between individual liberty and community interests.

The Development of American Courts

During the colonial period, most political power was placed in the hands of the colonial governor (Neubauer, 1984:36). The colonists generally adopted the existing English system of courts and government, but modified the system to fit the less complicated nature of colonial life. The many specialized courts that had evolved in Britain were not fully transplanted to the colonies. Rather, the county court was created as the basic tool of adjudication. Appeals from rulings of the county court were taken directly to the governor. While it was possible to appeal a gubernatorial decision to the English courts, it was seldom done (Glick, 1983:35).

As the colonies grew and commerce developed, the county courts became increasingly less able to handle the number and intricacy of cases that were filed. Each colony created special courts to expedite the handling of cases. New courts of general jurisdiction also were created to reduce the need for litigants to travel great distances to have their cases heard in county courts. The addition and cre-

The District of Columbia Court of Appeals is the equivalent of a state supreme court. As the highest court for the District of Columbia, the Court of Appeals is authorized to review all final orders, judgments, and specified interlocutory orders of the Superior Court of the District of Columbia. *Photo credit: L.F. Travis III.*

ation of new courts took place on a haphazard basis. New courts were created to resolve specific problems, not with any grand scheme of court structure in mind. Further, court development occurred independently in each colony (Stumpf, 1988:70-73). One result of this method of development is that courts performing the same functions often have different names.

After the American Revolution, the greatest issues facing the courts were those surrounding the balance between federal and state powers. The nature of the U.S. Constitution, with its limitations on federal powers and reservation of certain governmental powers to the states, ensured the continuation of state judicial systems. The Federal Judiciary Act of 1789, designed to create a court system for the resolution of cases arising from federal laws, was a compromise between the federalists (who favored a strong central government) and the antifederalists (who championed states' rights and feared the results of a strong central government). The compromise was that federal courts would be created, but that these courts would not cross state lines. To this day, no United States district court has more than one state within its jurisdiction.

State judges were required to swear an oath of allegiance to the U.S. Constitution. The Judiciary Act of 1789 gave the Supreme Court of the United States authority to review state decisions involving questions of a constitutional or federal nature. Although this fact gave the appearance that state courts were subservient to the federal courts (Jacob, 1984:162), state courts retained tremendous powers. The federal courts did not gain significantly in authority until social changes in the United States caused state courts to become ineffective.

Throughout the nineteenth century, the development of industry, the completion of the transcontinental railroad, and the growth in interstate commerce combined to create conditions in which state courts were not capable of resolving a large number of cases. In time, federal courts were increasingly called upon to resolve disputes. As Jacob (1984:163) noted:

> Just as state governments in general became less important to national policymaking, so state courts, to a somewhat lesser degree, lost their pre-eminent position in the judicial system and increasingly concentrated on private law cases, which enforce existing norms and affect only the immediate parties to a case.

The Functions of Courts

In describing the role of the courts, one of the first goals of the process is likely to be "justice" (Rubin, 1984). That is, the purpose of the courts is to do justice. However, we are not able to agree upon exactly what is "just." Alan Dershowitz (1982:xvi) suggested that, in fact, "nobody wants justice." Rather, parties to a suit are only interested in winning.

It is not possible to understand the operations of the criminal courts without having an appreciation for the complexity of the job performed by the courts. Addressing this issue, Neely (1983:16) noted:

> As long as we are talking only about criminal courts, the questions are relatively simple. As soon, however, as civil courts enter the picture, all bets are off. For while improved funding of the criminal courts would return economic dividends to the public, improved funding of the civil courts has mixed income effects.

Neely cited the example of New York City, where increased funds were given to courts of general jurisdiction to help alleviate caseload backlogs. The creation of more courts and the appointment of more judges opened more opportunities for people to press civil lawsuits. In many of these accelerated cases, the defendant in the civil suits was the City of New York. In effect, the citizens of New York City had paid more money to create more courts that could then be used by plaintiffs to sue the city for still more money in damages.

Because most courts empowered to hear criminal cases are also authorized to hear civil cases (as is true in New York City), it is not possible to enhance court capacities selectively. Creating new judgeships and courts for the purpose of speeding criminal trials, for example, will necessarily also serve to speed civil trials. In fact, the civil docket may be so crowded that increasing the number of courts or judges will not substantially affect the outcome of criminal cases. While our focus is on the criminal courts for the remainder of this chapter and the next, we must remember that the civil caseload lurks in the background and represents the largest portion of court workload (with the exception of traffic cases).

The functions of the criminal courts are twofold: the repression of crime and the protection of the rights of individuals accused of crimes. These goals are served within an environmental context that includes many factors. These factors include the characteristics of the various actors (defendants, witnesses, juries, judges, prosecutors, defense attorneys, etc.), the organizational goals of involved agencies, the political climate, present social forces, and the like. The law is only one of several factors that impinge on judicial outcomes. As Glick (1983:18) stated, "Most cases also are settled through informal negotiation, not trials. Personal decisionmaking and compromise are the keys to understanding how disputes are settled."

The Criminal Court Process

The basic dispute addressed in criminal courts is that between the need to control criminal behavior and the desire to protect individual rights and liberties. This dispute is at the core of each decision in the court segment of the justice system. After arrest, the suspect is processed into the court stage of the criminal justice process and moves along a series of hearings and decisions that result in either conviction and punishment, or release from custody. The principal decision points in the courts are initial appearance (bail determination), formal charging, preliminary hearing, arraignment on charges, and trial. Sentencing, or punishment, is the subject of Chapter 9.

Initial Appearance

Shortly after arrest, the suspect is taken before a magistrate for the setting of bail. **Bail** is a security posted by the defendant to ensure appearance at later court proceedings. The Eighth Amendment to the U.S. Constitution provides that "excessive bail shall not be required." There is some controversy as to whether this provision creates a right to bail for criminal defendants, or whether it merely protects them from facing an excessive bail. The leading U.S. Supreme Court decision on bail was rendered in the case of *Stack v. Boyle* (1951). Under federal law, defendants in noncapital cases are entitled to bail. The issue in this case was whether bail set at $50,000 was excessive, given the defendant's inability to post that amount. The Court decided that the purpose of bail is to ensure appearance at later proceedings and, absent evidence to support an exception, bail that is not reasonably calculated—or that is higher than that normally fixed for a similar offense—is excessive.

Neubauer (1984:213) reported that federal law and the constitutions of most states expressly provide a right to bail in most cases. In the latter part of the 1960s and in the early 1970s, bail was the subject of great scrutiny and debate (Wice, 1974). The Vera Institute of New York City conducted an experiment on the effects of bail on criminal defendants that demonstrated that many of those accused of crimes were unable to meet even relatively low bail amounts, and that those who were unable to make bail suffered with higher rates of conviction and incarceration (Ares, Rankin & Sturz, 1963). As a result of this report, and of the general interest in bail reform in the United States, a number of bail projects were created and implemented across the country. The ways in which a defendant could "make bail" were expanded. In addition to monetary bail, in which the defendant posts cash in the amount specified by the court, a number of alternatives were developed. These were created largely in response to perceived problems with the role of the bail bond agents.

Bail bond agents are often small business owners who provide bail for criminal defendants for a fee. Usually, the bond agent charges 10 percent of the bail amount, which is not refundable. Thus, if you face a bail of $2,500, the bond agent will charge you $250 and post the full bond to secure your release. If you appear at the later stages of your trial, the bond agent is refunded the full $2,500, but you are out the $250. Should you fail to appear at later hearings, the bond agent will seek you out and return you to court in order to protect his or her investment (Burns, Kinkade & Leone, 2005). Some observers of the bail process were uncomfortable with several factors: profit as the motive behind pretrial release; the errors made by bond agents in apprehending those who "skipped" bail; and irregularities in the posting of bond (using the same assets to secure release for several defendants) (Goldfarb, 1965; Goldkamp, 1980).

A 2002 Bureau of Justice Statistics study of felony case processing in large urban counties (Cohen & Reaves, 2006) supports the initial Vera Institute results. More than two-thirds of felons with bail amounts set at less than $10,000 secured release, while only about one-third of those with amounts more than $10,000 were released (see Box 7.6). More than 80 percent of defendants who did not secure release were convicted, compared to only 60 percent of defendants who were released. A 1992 study of similar cases showed that released defendants were more likely than detained defendants to avoid incarceration as a sentence (Reaves & Perez, 1994). Box 7.7 displays these findings.

Box 7.6 Percent of Defendants Securing Release by Bail Amount, 2002

Bail Amount	Percent Released
Under $5000	74%
$5,000 – $9,999	67%
$10,000 – $24,999	56%
$25,000 – $49,999	38%
$50,000 +	16%

Source: T. Cohen & B. Reaves (2006), *Felony Defendants in Large Urban Counties, 2002* (Washington, DC: Bureau of Justice Statistics):19.

Box 7.7 Pretrial Release Status of Felony Defendants and Percent Convicted, 2002

Case Characteristic	Released	Not Released
Total of All Cases	60%	81%
Violent Offense Charged	46%	76%
Property Offense Charged	64%	83%
Drug Offense Charged	61%	82%
Public Order Offense Charged	69%	82%

Source: T. Cohen & B. Reaves (2006), *Felony Defendants in Large Urban Counties, 2002* (Washington, DC: Bureau of Justice Statistics):24.

In reaction to its findings, the Vera Institute and other programs initiated **release on recognizance (ROR)**, whereby a defendant with ties to the community (a job, family, stable residence, etc.) would be released on his or her own recognizance without posting bail, as there was reason to believe that he or she would not flee the jurisdiction (Maxwell, 1999). In other places, courts allowed

defendants to post only 10 percent of the full amount (because 10 percent was the percentage risked by a defendant whose bail was paid by a bond agent) or to post surety (such as property deeds or automobile titles) rather than cash. Another innovation was the use of issuing citations in lieu of arrest (Kalmanoff, 1976). Here, defendants are issued a summons to appear in court (much like a traffic citation), rather than being arrested.

A bail bond office near a midwestern city's jail and courthouse. Bail bond agents often seek to attract clients by conspicuously locating their offices close to county and municipal jails. *Photo credit: E.S. Boyne.*

Hirschel and Dean (1995) investigated the effects of citation release versus arrest in Charlotte, North Carolina. They found that persons issued citations were significantly more likely to miss later court appearances, but that citation releases, on average, cost $100 less than arrests. Box 7.8 summarizes the major forms of pretrial release that are available to defendants.

A central question in bail determinations is to what extent the setting of a bail amount should reflect concern for protecting public safety. While the only constitutionally recognized purpose of bail is to ensure appearance by the defendant at later court proceedings, a common concern of police, prosecutors, and magistrates (not to mention the general public) is to keep suspected offenders off the streets until they can be convicted and punished. To accomplish this goal, some persons advocate preventive detention, in which defendants suspected to be dangerous are denied bail until their cases are tried (Sorin, 1988).

The federal Bail Reform Act of 1984 authorizes pretrial detention for certain categories of offense or offenders. In 1987, the United States Supreme Court ruled that pretrial detention of defendants was permissible under the Eighth Amendment. In *United States v. Salerno* (1987), the court held that when adversarial procedures are used in open court to determine that a defendant poses a risk of pretrial crime, it is permissible to deny pretrial release. Reaves (1994) reported that federal defendants who had a record of failing to appear in court or who were charged with serious crimes were likely to be denied bail. Similarly, those who had lengthy criminal records or who were under criminal justice custody at the time

Box 7.8   Pretrial Release Procedure

Both financial bonds and alternative release options are used today

Financial bond

Fully secured bail—The defendant posts the full amount of bail with the court.

Privately secured bail—A bondsman signs a promissory note to the court for the bail amount and charges the defendant a fee for the service (usually 10% of the bail amount). If the defendant fails to appear, the bondsman must pay the court the full amount. Frequently, the bondsman requires the defendant to post collateral in addition to the fee.

Deposit bail—The courts allow the defendant to deposit a percentage (usually 10%) of the full bail with the court. The full amount of the bail is required if the defendant fails to appear. The percentage bail is returned after disposition of the case, but the court often retains 1% for administrative costs.

Unsecured bail—The defendant pays no money to the court but is liable for the full amount of bail should he or she fail to appear.

Alternative release options

Release on recognizance (ROR)—The court releases the defendant on the promise that he or she will appear in court as required.

Conditional release—The court releases the defendant subject to his or her following specific conditions set by the court, such as attendance at drug treatment therapy or staying away from the complaining witness.

Third-party custody—The defendant is released into the custody of an individual or agency that promises to assure his or her appearance in court. No monetary transactions are involved in this type of release.

Citation release—Arrestees are released pending their first court appearance on a written order issued by law enforcement personnel.

The traditional objective of bail or other pretrial release options is to assure appearance at trial

In medieval times, the accused was bailed to a third party who would be tried in place of the accused if the accused failed to appear. As the system evolved, the guarantee became the posting of a money bond that was forfeited if the accused failed to appear. In the United States, the Eighth Amendment states that bail shall not be excessive, but it does not grant the right to bail in all cases. The right to bail for many offenses was established by Federal and State laws early in our history.

Source: Bureau of Justice Statistics (1988), *Report to the Nation on Crime and Justice,* 2nd ed. (Washington, DC: U.S. Department of Justice):76; Bureau of Justice Statistics (1983), *Report to the Nation on Crime and Justice: The Data* (Washington, DC: U.S. Department of Justice):59.

of their new crime were also likely to be denied bail. Cohen and Reaves (2006) reported that fewer than half of felony defendants in large jurisdictions who had a prior criminal record were able to secure pretrial release.

There have been many cases in which persons released on bail committed several crimes while on pretrial release—crimes that could have been avoided if the defendant were not released (Ervin, 1971). Cohen and Reaves (2006) reported

Box 7.9   Provisions for Pretrial and Preventive Detention of Defendants in American Courts

About three-fifths of the states have one or more provisions to ensure community safety in pretrial release

Type of provision	States that have enacted the provision
Exclusion of certain crimes from automatic bail eligibility	Colorado, District of Columbia, Florida, Georgia, Michigan, Nebraska, Wisconsin
Definition of the purpose of bail to ensure appearance and safety	Alaska, Arizona, California, Delaware, District of Columbia, Florida, Hawaii, Minnesota, South Carolina, South Dakota, Vermont, Virginia, Wisconsin
Inclusion of crime control factors in the release decision	Alabama, California, Florida, Georgia, Minnesota, South Dakota, Wisconsin
Inclusion of release conditions related to crime control	Alaska, Arkansas, Colorado, Delaware, District of Columbia, Florida, Hawaii, Illinois, Iowa, Minnesota, New Mexico, North Carolina, South Carolina, South Dakota, Vermont, Virginia, Washington, Wisconsin
Limitations on the right to bail for those previously convicted	Colorado, District of Columbia, Florida, Georgia, Hawaii, Indiana, Michigan, New Mexico, Texas, Utah, Wisconsin
Revocation of pretrial release when there is evidence that the accused committed a new crime	Arizona, Arkansas, Colorado, District of Columbia, Georgia, Hawaii, Illinois, Indiana, Maryland, Massachusetts, Michigan, Nevada, New Mexico, New York, Rhode Island, Texas, Utah, Vermont, Wisconsin
Limitations on the right to bail for crimes alleged to have been committed while on release	Arizona, Arkansas, Colorado, District of Columbia, Florida, Georgia, Illinois, Indiana, Maryland, Massachusetts, Michigan, Minnesota, Nevada, New Mexico, New York, Rhode Island, Tennessee, Texas, Utah, Vermont, Wisconsin
Provisions for pretrial detention to ensure safety	Arizona, Arkansas, California, Colorado, District of Columbia, Florida, Georgia, Hawaii, Illinois, Indiana, Maryland, Massachusetts, Michigan, Nebraska, Nevada, New Mexico, New York, Rhode Island, South Dakota, Texas, Utah, Vermont, Virginia, Washington, Wisconsin

Source: Bureau of Justice Statistics (1988), *Report to the Nation on Crime and Justice*, 2nd ed. (Washington, DC: U.S. Department of Justice):77.

that about 18 percent of released defendants in 75 large urban counties were arrested for new offenses, and fully one-third engaged in some sort of misconduct with fewer than 80 percent making all scheduled court appearances. Only 6 percent of all felony defendants in these large jurisdictions were denied bail.

In practice, this dilemma is resolved through the establishment of bail schedules and the criteria employed to determine whether a defendant is suitable for ROR. Those with prior criminal records, who have no visible means of support, who are accused of serious offenses, or are otherwise thought to be dangerous usually do not qualify for ROR or low-amount bail. As shown in Box 7.9, most jurisdictions have enacted preventive detention statutes that establish the criteria and procedures that will be followed in establishing the dangerousness of a defendant and deciding whether to deny pretrial release (Kennedy, 1980). Nonetheless, problems remain with the bail decision. Sheila Maxwell (1999:129) observed, "Criteria used in making pretrial release decisions in many jurisdictions, are often arbitrary and laws guiding pretrial release are vague with no clear policies for judges to follow, nor are judges required to note reasons for their decisions to release, set bail, or detain a defendant prior to trial."

With the exception of preventive detention hearings, the bail decision is usually not concerned with assessing evidence. For defendants arrested without a warrant, the U.S. Supreme Court has held that there must be a "prompt" judicial determination of probable cause. In those cases, the magistrate or judge must assess the adequacy of the evidence on which the arrest was based. This assessment occurs at the initial appearance for defendants arrested without warrants. In *County of Riverside v. McLaughlin* (1991), the Supreme Court ruled that such a review must occur within 48 hours of the arrest.

Preliminary Hearing

Whether or not bail or other pretrial release is granted, the next decision point in the court process is the preliminary hearing. At this stage, the case against the accused is reviewed by a neutral magistrate to determine whether the evidence is sufficient to justify binding the defendant over for trial (Chen, 1991). The preliminary hearing is not a full trial of the case but is an open court process in which the strength of the state's case against the defendant is tested. The prosecution must establish that there is sufficient evidence to show probable cause that the defendant committed a crime. The defense may cross-examine witnesses, testify, and call witnesses on his or her behalf.

If the magistrate decides that there is sufficient evidence to justify further action, the defendant may be bound over for trial. In many states, this action means that the case will go to the grand jury for a decision about formal criminal charges. In other states, the preliminary hearing serves as a charging process. The purpose of the hearing, however, is to ensure that the state is justified in continuing to proceed against the defendant.

Formal Charging

At some point in the pretrial segment of the court process the state must file formal charges against a defendant. These charges are allegations of the specific crimes for which the defendant will stand trial. They are termed "formal charges" to distinguish them from the arrest charge, which may not actually reflect the offense for which the accused will be tried. In charging, the prosecutor (or state's attorney or district attorney) applies the criminal law to the facts of the case and identifies which provisions of the criminal code have been violated.

For example, the police may arrest someone who is holding a screwdriver while standing on the porch of a home and charge him or her (in the arrest report) with attempted burglary. Upon reviewing the case and the law, the prosecutor may decide that the evidence will not support so serious a charge and opt instead to charge criminal trespassing and possession of burglar's tools. Similarly, the police may arrest for first-degree murder, but use the formal charge of manslaughter.

The evidentiary standard for charging is the same as that for arrest: probable cause. However, there is a subtle difference in interpretation of probable cause among police and prosecutors. Police tend to be "backward-looking" in attempting to justify an arrest, while the prosecutor is "forward-looking" in attempting to predict the likelihood of successful prosecution (Newman, 1978). That is, the police require probable cause to believe the suspect has committed a crime, while the prosecutor requires probable cause to believe the suspect (now defendant) can be convicted of the crime (Adams, 1983; Boland & Forst, 1985).

There are two methods by which formal charges can be leveled against a defendant. One is by the information process through the preliminary hearing. The second is indictment by the grand jury. In about one-half of the states and in the federal jurisdiction, the grand jury indictment is the normal method of charging. In the remaining states, the information process is the routine manner in which formal charges are brought (Senna & Siegel, 1984:265). Grand jury charging for felony offenses is required in only 12 states, the District of Columbia, and the federal system. An additional four states require grand jury indictments in capital (death penalty) cases. In most instances the defendant can waive the right to a grand jury indictment (Rottman et al., 2000:215-217).

The grand jury is a part of the court processes of all but one American criminal jurisdiction. Pennsylvania abolished the indicting grand jury, and no grand jury has been convened in Wisconsin in decades, though the state still has a grand jury statute on the books. The grand jury is a panel of citizens (often sitting for a month or longer) that reviews evidence in criminal cases to determine whether sufficient evidence exists to justify trial of an individual (Acker & Brody, 2004). Grand juries are usually larger than trial juries (sizes range from a minimum of five jurors in Virginia, to 23 jurors in the federal, District of Columbia, and 11 state jurisdictions). In addition to this charging function, grand juries also have investigation powers and occasionally are used to investigate suspected criminality and to issue formal charges based on the results of that investigation (Alpert & Petersen, 1985; Rottman et al., 2000).

In *United States v. R. Enterprises* (1991:292, 299), the Supreme Court had this to say about the grand jury: "A grand jury may compel the production of evidence or the testimony of witnesses as it considers appropriate, and its operation is unrestrained by the technical procedural and evidentiary rules governing the conduct of criminal trials." This virtually unrestrained investigatory power can be abused both by the grand jury itself and by the prosecutor. Some critics of the grand jury argue that the investigation powers of the grand jury are wrongly used by police and prosecutors to obtain evidence by subpoena that they could not secure by search warrant (Dillard, Johnson & Lynch, 2003).

The grand jury sometimes has been criticized as being a "rubber stamp" of the prosecutor. Cases are presented to the grand jury by the prosecutor in secret proceedings without a magistrate or judge to instruct the jury. Dillard, Johnson, and Lynch (2003:3) state, "As a practical matter, the prosecutor calls the shots and dominates the entire grand jury process." In about 95 percent of cases the grand jury issues a "true bill" or indictment. This is a formal document that lists the specific violation of the criminal code of which the defendant is accused. In cases in which the defendant is accused of more than one crime, each violation of the law identified in the indictment is called a count. In only about 5 percent of cases does the grand jury go against the wishes of the prosecutor and issue a "no bill," or fail to indict. Thus, it appears that the grand jury does not perform its function of checking the discretion of the prosecutor. The problem with this type of analysis, however, is that the assumption is made that the prosecutor indeed wants an indictment in every case presented to the grand jury, and that a 5 percent rejection rate is evidence of inefficiency. Critics suggest that prosecutors probably have insufficient evidence for charging in more than the 5 percent of cases that grand juries reject.

In contrast, the information process occurs in open court and the defendant and his or her attorney are present and allowed to examine witnesses. The proceedings of the preliminary hearing become part of an official record, and the hearing takes place before a magistrate or judge who ensures that rules of evidence are followed. The result of both processes is the same: either the defendant is bound over for trial on formal charges or the evidence is found to be insufficient to support the charges and the case is dismissed. The choice of charging process often depends on jurisdictional tradition and laws and is at the discretion of the prosecutor. In some places, it is the prosecutor's choice regarding which process to follow.

The grand jury is more under the control of the prosecutor, but it does not allow a test of evidence sufficiency at trial (i.e., how well witnesses will "hold up" under cross-examination), and it yields no evidence that can be entered into the trial record directly. The U.S. Supreme Court has consistently held that the grand jury process is not subject to the same due process requirements as other decision points. In *United States v. Williams* (1992), the court held that the prosecutor is not required to disclose exculpatory evidence to the grand jury. Exculpatory evidence is evidence that tends to establish the innocence of the accused or defendant. Normally at trial, prosecutors are bound to disclose such evidence to the defense. The Supreme Court reasoned that such issues are dealt with at trial, and requiring strict due process protections at the grand jury stage would only delay proceedings and not add to trial fairness.

The grand jury also has the advantage of not disclosing the nature of the case or evidence to the defense attorney. The preliminary hearing, on the other hand, allows the state to test the strength of its case and, because the defendant is allowed to face his or her accusers and to cross-examine witnesses, testimony presented at this hearing can be used at trial if necessary. The disadvantage to the prosecution is that rules of evidence must be more strictly followed and, therefore, the defense is given a good indication of the nature and strength of the case against the defendant. For the defendant, the information process is preferred because of the stricter rules of evidence and the chance to preview the prosecution's case.

Traditionally, the prosecutor has had broad, almost uncontrolled discretion in charging decisions. Prosecutors have the ability to "nol pros" cases, meaning they can decide not to press formal charges regardless of the available evidence. The term comes from the Latin, *nolle prosequi,* which means "I do not prosecute." Many observers—especially proponents of more serious criminal treatment of domestic violence —have criticized the broad charging discretion of prosecutors. In response, some prosecutor's offices have adopted "mandatory filing" policies by which the prosecutor files charges in every case in which a suspect has been arrested for domestic violence. In an evaluation of this policy, Peterson and Dixon (2005) found that the mandatory filing jurisdiction had a final conviction rate of only half that of the nonmandatory filing jurisdiction. Among other things, it appears that prosecutors exercise their charging discretion so as to reduce the number of charges filed in cases that are unlikely to result in conviction.

Regardless of which method of filing formal charges is employed, once the defendant is bound over for trial on the charges, the next decision point is conviction. The popular media generally depict this decision as being the result of a jury trial characterized by calculated strategy and dignified, formal courtroom demeanor and drama. In reality, most criminal cases are decided at the next stage of the court process, the arraignment. This is the point at which the defendant is asked to plead to the charges.

Arraignment

After being formally charged with a crime, the defendant is called into court to be notified of the charges against him or her, and is asked to plead to the charges. In most criminal cases, the defendant will enter a plea of guilty at this point, and avoid a trial of the case on the facts. This high percentage of guilty pleas clearly illustrates the "compromise" nature of the court process. It is most often the result of what is known as plea bargaining.

At arraignment, the formal charges are read and the defendant is asked, "How do you plead?" The defendant (usually it is the defense attorney who speaks at this point) can answer in one of five ways: (1) not guilty, (2) not guilty by reason of some defense (that is, a special, affirmative defense such as insanity or self-defense), (3) guilty, (4) *nolo contendere,* or (5) the defendant can stand silent. If the defendant is silent, the judge will enter a plea of "not guilty" for the defendant.

The only plea a judge must accept at this point is "not guilty." The plea of *nolo contendere* means that the defendant, by not contesting the charge, will be convicted of the offense. The difference is that the conviction cannot be used against the defendant in other proceedings, especially civil actions. This can be very important, depending upon the nature of the offense. It is a relatively common plea in "white-collar" offenses.

Suppose you drank too much at a party, and while driving home, struck and injured a pedestrian. The responding officer who investigates the accident will probably discover that you are drunk, and charge you with driving under the influence. At arraignment, you plead *nolo contendere* and stand convicted, with all that the conviction entails (such as loss of driving privileges, mandatory jail term, a fine, and the like). The pedestrian you injured files a tort suit against you for pain and suffering, alleging negligence on your part. Conviction of drunken driving would establish your blame for the civil case in itself. By pleading *nolo contendere*, the pedestrian is now required to establish your negligence at the civil trial, without reference to the outcome of your criminal trial.

Certain affirmative defenses involve special pleadings in which the defense states the reason for asserting innocence (e.g., "not guilty by reason of insanity"). In these cases, the defense generally is not contesting the facts of the case in regard to the criminal act (*actus reus*), but rather is asserting that the requisite mental state (*mens rea*, or intention to commit a crime) does not exist for the act to be a crime. This special plea gives notice to the state that an affirmative defense will be raised, and shifts the burden of proof from the state to the defense. As we will see, the state generally is required to prove all elements of a criminal offense beyond a reasonable doubt. Failure to do so results in an acquittal. With affirmative defenses, the defense is required to raise a question about the case; for example, the defense may give evidence that the defendant might have been legally "insane" at the time of the crime (Klofas & Weisheit, 1987). Box 7.10 summarizes the requirements and burdens of proof for insanity pleas.

Conceivably, the defense could remain silent throughout an entire trial and, when all the state's evidence has been entered, move for a directed verdict (dismissal) because the state failed to meet the burden of proof beyond a reasonable doubt. If the state's case is indeed not strong enough, the defendant will be acquitted. With most affirmative defenses, the defendant admits the act but denies some element crucial to the mental aspect of the crime, such as intent. The burden then falls upon the defense to raise a reasonable doubt about that element, which the state must then prove (beyond a reasonable doubt) actually existed at the time of the offense.

The "not guilty" plea results in the establishment of a trial date and subsequent moving for trial. This stage includes jury selection and the filing of pretrial motions for disclosure of evidence, suppression of evidence, and the like, in preparation for the trial itself. While this is a typical outcome of arraignment on television and in the movies, it is very rare in the actual operations of the criminal courts. Brown, Langan, and Levin (1999:8) reported that 91 percent of felons convicted in state courts were convicted on the basis of a guilty plea. Only 9 percent of cases went to trial. Ostrom, Kauder, and LaFountain (2004:61) report that in 2001, only about 3 percent of all criminal cases (including misdemeanors and DWI offenses) were resolved by trial.

Box 7.10   Evidentiary Standards and Burdens of Proof for Insanity Pleas

Test	Legal Standard Because of Mental Illness	Final Burden of Proof	Who Bears Burden of Proof
M'Naghten	"didn't know what he was doing or didn't know it was wrong"	Varies from proof by a balance of probabilities on the defense to proof beyond a reasonable doubt on the prosecutor	
Irresistible Impulse	"could not control his conduct"		
Durham	"the criminal act was caused by his mental illness"	Beyond reasonable doubt	Prosecutor
Brawner-A.L.I.	"lacks substantial capacity to appreciate the wrongfulness of his conduct or to control it"	Beyond reasonable doubt	Prosecutor
Present Federal Law	"lacks capacity to appreciate the wrongfulness of his conduct"	Clear and convincing evidence	Defense

Source: N. Morris (1988), *Insanity Defense: Crime File Study Guide* (Washington, DC: National Institute of Justice):3.

The "guilty" plea is an admission of the offense and obviates the need for a trial. It is left to the judge's discretion whether to accept a plea of guilty, for it entails a waiver of the right to trial. In many states, it is also a waiver of the right to appeal rulings on the admissibility of the evidence and other controversies. The Federal Rules of Criminal Procedure (see Box 7.11) instruct the judge to investigate the factual nature of the plea, the voluntariness of the plea, and the defendant's awareness of the effects of the plea before a guilty plea can be accepted.

If the defendant does not plead guilty, the next stage of the court process is trial. This is the point at which the decision is made about conviction. Here the state presents the case against the defendant, and the defense attempts to discredit or otherwise cast doubt on the case presented by the prosecutor. The act of pleading guilty means that the state's case will go uncontested. While contested trials are the exception in criminal law (if not all law), it is at trial that the full strength of the value placed on individual liberty is evident.

Box 7.11   Federal Rules of Criminal Procedure, Rule 11—Pleas

A defendant may plead not guilty, guilty or, with the consent of the court, nolo contendere. The court may refuse to accept a plea of guilty, and shall not accept such plea or a plea of nolo contendere without first addressing the defendant personally and determining that the plea is made voluntarily with understanding of the nature of the charge and the consequences of the plea. If a defendant refuses to plead or fails to appear, the court shall enter a plea of not guilty. The court shall not enter a judgment upon a plea of guilty unless it is satisfied that there is a factual basis for the plea.

Trial

Although not often used, the jury trial is the "balance wheel" (Neubauer, 1984:284) of the court process. It is the possibility of the jury trial that serves to ensure "justice" in the more common event of plea bargaining. As Jacob (1984:207) explained:

> Although critics focus on plea bargains, bench and jury trials continue to constitute an essential part of the criminal justice process. It is true that only a very small proportion of cases go to trial, and an especially small proportion go to trial by jury. But the possibility of going to trial constrains the plea bargaining process. No one has to accept a bargain that is worse than the decision that could be obtained at a jury trial. Doubtful cases can be brought to a jury or bench trial, even when the prosecutor would rather close the case with a lenient bargain.

Only the more "celebrated" cases (Walker, 1994:29-33) tend to receive the full panoply of rights, including jury trial, but the full justice process is available to all. Trials are held in approximately 10 percent of felony cases in the United States. These trials are of two types: bench trials and jury trials.

A common form of criminal trial is the bench trial, which is held before a judge sitting alone, with no jury. These trials are routine for petty offenses for which the maximum penalty does not exceed incarceration for six months. They are commonly accepted by defendants in more serious cases in lieu of the more costly and time-consuming jury trials. The jury trial involves a panel of citizens who have the task of determining the facts of the case. In these trials, the judge rules on questions of law and presides over the trial, but the jury is responsible for questions of fact, how much weight to give the testimony of a witness, and the final decision about guilt or innocence. Criminal trials are about evenly split between jury trials and bench trials. For persons charged with felonies in the largest jurisdictions, only 5 percent of cases went to trial, and of them, 40 percent were jury trials. The more serious the offense charged, the greater the likelihood that the defendant would choose to go to trial (Cohen & Reaves, 2006).

The right to trial by jury is rooted in our legal tradition and firmly established in the U.S. Constitution. In the case of *Baldwin v. New York* (1970), the U.S. Supreme Court ruled that any criminal defendant facing a punishment of incarceration of more than six months had the right to trial by jury. Individual states may grant the right to trial by jury for those facing less serious charges if they desire, but they are not required to do so by the U.S. Constitution.

Most of us envision the jury as a body of 12 members who come to a unanimous decision about whether the defendant is guilty. To some, the phrase "jury of one's peers" connotes that the members of the jury should be representative of the defendant in terms of age, sex, education, place of residence, race, and other factors. "Peers," however, has been determined to refer to fellow citizens, and thus the jury does not need to reflect the characteristics of the defendant. Moreover, the jury does not have to consist of 12 members, and does not have to reach a unanimous verdict in all states. Box 7.12 shows state requirements of jury size for felony and misdemeanor cases.

Box 7.12 State Requirements for Jury Size, Felony and Misdemeanor Trials

All states with capital punishment require a 12-member jury in capital cases. Nine states allow less than 12 members in at least some felony cases.

Less than 12 members

Arizona	Louisiana
Arkansas	Massachusetts
Connecticut	Pennsylvania
Florida	Utah
Indiana	

Thirty-seven states authorize juries of less than 12 members for at least some misdemeanor cases:

Alaska	Iowa	New Mexico
Arizona	Kansas	New York
Arkansas	Kentucky	North Dakota
California	Louisiana	Ohio
Colorado	Massachusetts	Oklahoma
Connecticut	Michigan	Oregon
Florida	Minnesota	Pennsylvania
Georgia	Montana	South Carolina
Hawaii	Nebraska	Texas
Idaho	Nevada	Utah
Illinois	New Hampshire	Virginia
Indiana	New Jersey	West Virginia
		Wyoming

Source: D. Rottman & S. Strickland (2006), *State Court Organization, 2004* (Washington, DC: Bureau of Justice Statistics):233-237.

The U.S. Supreme Court has addressed the unanimity of jury verdicts and the size of the jury. Many related questions still remain, but in the case of *Williams v. Florida* (1970) the Court decided that it was permissible to use a jury of six members in a robbery trial. The Court further decided that nonunanimous verdicts are permissible. It has upheld convictions based on juror votes of 9–3 (*Johnson v. Louisiana,* 1972) and 10–2 (*Apodaca v. Oregon,* 1972). Nonetheless, only two states and Puerto Rico allow nonunanimous verdicts (Rottman et al., 2000). The Court has not ruled on how close a jury vote could be and still be valid, nor has it ruled on the effect of a split vote on a jury of less than 12 members. The Court has found that cases heard by juries of less than six members are unconstitutional (*Ballew v. Georgia,* 1978), and that in serious criminal cases, a jury of six must render a unanimous verdict (*Burch v. Louisiana,* 1979). Because most states and the federal system require unanimous verdicts,

In this artist's rendering, members of the jury in the trial of accused presidential assailant John W. Hinckley Jr. listen to closing arguments in federal court in 1982. While relatively rare, the full jury trial is the centerpiece of the court process. *Photo credit: AP Photo.*

the failure of the jury to reach consensus means no decision is reached. A jury that cannot reach consensus about the verdict is known as a **hung jury**. The actual rate of hung juries is very low (about 6 percent of jury trials), but it varies widely from court to court (Hannaford-Agor et al., 2002).

If a trial is held, the burden of proving guilt rests with the state, and the rights of the offender are strictly protected. In the case of *In re Winship* (1970), the U.S. Supreme Court ruled that the prosecution must prove every element of the offense "beyond a reasonable doubt." In *Gideon v. Wainwright* (1963), the Court held that an accused must be provided with defense counsel at state expense if he or she is unable to provide for his or her own defense. This case involved a convicted felon who had asked for the assistance of a defense attorney at trial and was denied. The Court ruled that the right to counsel at trial applied to felony cases. In a later case, *Argersinger v. Hamlin* (1972), the Court extended this right to any criminal prosecution in which the possible penalty included incarceration. Thus, not only does the defendant have a right to contest the state at trial, but if he or she is unable to retain an attorney, the defendant has a right to counsel provided by the state.

While relatively rare, the full jury trial is the center of the court process. As such, the trial is what we most often think of when we consider the courts. Our adversary system of justice, in which truth is expected to emerge from the arguments of two sides of a question, is epitomized by the jury trial. If acquitted, the defendant is set free and generally cannot be tried again for the offense.

The U.S. Constitution protects criminal defendants from double jeopardy, that is, being subjected to trial or punishment more than once for a single offense. This point is illustrated by the case of Byron de la Beckwith, who was convicted of the murder of civil rights leader Medgar Evers. While some feel that the double jeopardy protection should support a defendant's right to achieve finality—to put the case behind him or her (Hickey, 1995), double jeopardy applies only if the original jeopardy terminates. In the de la Beckwith case, the defendant was tried twice in 1964, with both trials resulting in hung juries. In 1969, the prosecutor entered a *nolle prosequi* order for this case but did not terminate the case. In 1990, de la Beckwith was indicted, and his subsequent trial resulted in a conviction. In reviewing the double jeopardy issues, the Mississippi Supreme Court ruled (*Beckwith v. State*, 1992) that de la Beckwith was not entitled to double jeopardy protection because his jeopardy (risk of conviction) had never been terminated.

If the defendant is convicted, the case proceeds to the next decision point of the justice system: sentencing. Sentencing and punishment are addressed in Chapter 9.

Due Process, Crime Control, and the Courts

If, as we suggest, the primary purpose of the courts is to resolve conflicts, it should not be surprising that the conflict between due process and crime control is brought into high relief in the criminal courts. As the core issue in the criminal justice system, the conflicting interests in liberty and order are a common theme in court procedures. Our entire system of adversary trial illustrates a "combat" between the individual and the society. The difficulty of resolving this conflict is reflected in the procedures and decisions of the courts. Referring to the problems in bail decisions, Sheila Maxwell summarized this conflict between due process and crime control. She wrote (1999:127), "The difficulty arises in balancing the rights of defendants on the one hand, who are presumed innocent before conviction and should not be unnecessarily detained, and ensuring future court appearances and community safety, on the other."

Those who champion individual rights over public safety tend to support practices that increase the numbers of defendants who secure pretrial release through bail or other programs. They endorse practices such as the preliminary hearing and grand jury process, in which a neutral magistrate or panel of citizens reviews the government's justification for proceeding against a citizen. The provision of defense counsel, the requirement of high evidentiary standards for conviction, and the use of juries to decide criminal matters all promise to protect the rights of individuals. On the other hand, those who wish to protect public safety and control crime tend to support preventive detention of dangerous offenders. They encourage speedy resolution of criminal cases through guilty pleas, less-than-unanimous jury verdicts, and a generally streamlined decision process in the courts.

Community courts and other specialized courts (e.g., drug courts) are being developed to improve the workings of the judicial component of the justice system. Dissatisfaction with current procedures underlies these reform movements. In the drug courts, an effort is made to use the justice system and its coercive control to ensure that drug offenders receive the necessary treatment to prevent future crime. In community courts, an effort is made to restore harmony in the community by both resolving minor disputes and attacking the causes of community conflicts. In both these cases, the criminal justice system is being used to solve individual or community problems that manifest themselves in crime, but that are not limited to criminal behavior. It remains to be seen if these efforts represent an expansion of state power over individuals (crime control), or a focusing of state power for the benefit of individuals (due process). At present, the hope is to achieve a balance between the two by which the interests of the individual and of the community are best served.

Box 7.13 Selected Court Cases on Criminal Procedure

Stack v. Boyle 342 U.S. 1 (1951)	The right to bail established in noncapital cases. Noted the purpose of bail is to secure appearance at later court proceedings.
Gideon v. Wainwright 372 U.S. 335 (1963)	An accused must be provided with defense counsel at state expense if he or she is unable to provide for his or her own defense.
Baldwin v. New York 399 U.S. 66 (1970)	Any criminal defendant facing a punishment of more than six months of incarceration has the right to trial by jury.
In re Winship 397 U.S. 358 (1970)	In deciding the burden of proof required for a juvenile adjudication, the Court held that "the Due Process Clause protects the accused against conviction except upon proof beyond a reasonable doubt of every fact necessary to constitute the crime. . ."
Williams v. Florida 399 U.S. 78 (1970)	In a robbery case it is permissible to use a jury of six members.
Apodaca v. Oregon 406 U.S. 404 (1972)	Nonunanimous verdicts are permissible. Court upheld a jury's vote of 10–2.
Argersinger v. Hamlin 407 U.S. 25 (1972)	A defendant has a right to counsel at trial (either hired or appointed) if the possible penalty for the offense includes incarceration.
Johnson v. Louisiana 406 U.S. 356 (1972)	Nonunanimous verdicts are permissible. Court upheld a jury's vote of 9–3.

Each of the criminal justice system decision points discussed in this chapter revolves around the conflict between due process and crime control. Specific practices in pretrial and trial proceedings represent efforts to achieve a balance between concerns for individual liberties and social needs for order. In later stages of the justice process (sentencing and corrections), the guilt of the defendant has been established. While concerns about the rights and interests of offenders continue, the fact of guilt renders crime control interests more salient.

See Box 7.13 for a table of selected court cases on criminal procedure.

Review Questions

1. Briefly describe the organization of United States courts. Explain how this particular court structure developed.

2. Distinguish between lower and higher courts.

3. Identify the principal decision points in the criminal court process.

4. What is bail, and what is its constitutional purpose?

5. What is meant by preventive detention?

6. Describe two ways in which formal criminal charges are brought against defendants.

7. What are community courts?

8. What is meant by "plea bargaining"? Why is it important?

9. Differentiate between a bench trial and a jury trial.

References

Acker, J. & D. Brody (2004). *Criminal Procedure: A Contemporary Perspective*, 2nd ed. Sudbury, MA: Jones & Bartlett.

Adams, K. (1983). "The Effect of Evidentiary Factors on Charge Reduction." *Journal of Criminal Justice* 11(6):525-538.

Alpert, G. & T.K. Petersen (1985). "The Grand Jury Report: A Magic Lantern or an Agent of Social Control?" *Justice Quarterly* 2(1):23-50.

Ares, C.E., A. Rankin & H. Sturz (1963). "The Manhattan Bail Project: An Interim Report on the Use of Pre-Trial Parole." *New York University Law Review* 38(January):71-92.

Boland, B. & B. Forst (1985). "Prosecutors Don't Always Aim to Pleas." *Federal Probation* 54(2):10-15.

Brown, J., P. Langan & D. Levin (1999). *Felony Sentences in State Courts, 1996.* Washington, DC: Bureau of Justice Statistics.

Burns, R., P. Kinkade & M. Leone (2005). "Bounty Hunters: A Look Behind the Hype." *Policing: An International Journal of Police Strategies and Management* 28(1):118-138.

Butts, J. & J. Buck (2000). *Teen Courts: A Focus on Research.* Washington, DC: Office of Juvenile Justice and Delinquency Prevention.

Casey, P. & D. Rottman (2003). *Problem-Solving Courts: Models and Trends.* Washington, DC: National Center for State Courts.

Chen, H. (1991). "Dropping In and Dropping Out: Judicial Decisionmaking in the Disposition of Felony Arrests." *Journal of Criminal Justice* 19(1):1-17.

Cohen, T. & B. Reaves (2006). *Felony Defendants in Large Urban Counties, 2002.* Washington, DC: Bureau of Justice Statistics.

DeFrances, C. (2001). *State Court Prosecutors in Large Districts, 2001.* Washington, DC: Bureau of Justice Statistics.

Dershowitz, A.M. (1982). *The Best Defense.* New York: Vintage Books.

Dillard, W., S. Johnson & T. Lynch (2003). "A Grand Facade: How the Grand Jury was Captured by Government." *Policy Analysis* (May 13). Washington, DC: CATO Institute.

Ervin, S.J. (1971). *Preventive Detention.* Chicago: Urban Research Corp.

Glick, H.R. (1983). *Courts, Politics and Justice.* New York: McGraw-Hill.

Goldfarb, R. (1965). *Ransom: A Critique of the American Bail System.* New York: Harper & Row.

Goldkamp, J. (1980). *Two Classes of Accused.* Lexington, MA: Lexington Books.

Hannaford-Agor, P., V. Hans, N. Mott & G. Munsterman (2002). *Are Hung Juries a Problem? Executive Summary.* Washington, DC: National Center for State Courts.

Hickey, T. (1995). "A Double Jeopardy Analysis of the Medgar Evers Murder Case." *Journal of Criminal Justice* 23(1):41-51.

Hirschel, J. & C. Dean (1995). "The Relative Cost-Effectiveness of Citation and Arrest." *Journal of Criminal Justice* 23(1):1-12.

Jackson, D.D. (1974). *Judges.* New York: Atheneum.

Jacob, H. (1984). *Justice in America.* Boston: Little, Brown.

Jansen, S. & E. Dague (2006). "Working with a Neighborhood Community Prosecutor." *The Police Chief* 73(7). Found at: http://policechiefmagazine.org, accessed July 16, 2007.

Kalmanoff, A. (1976). *Criminal Justice: Enforcement and Administration.* Boston: Little, Brown.

Kennedy, E. (1980). "A New Approach to Bail Release: The Proposed Federal Code and Bail Reform." *Fordham Law Review* 48:6.

Klofas, J. & R. Weisheit (1987). "Guilty but Mentally Ill: Reform of the Insanity Defense in Illinois." *Justice Quarterly* 4(1):39-50.

Maxwell, S. (1999). "Examining the Congruence Between Predictors of ROR and Failures to Appear." *Journal of Criminal Justice* 27(2):127-141.

Mays, G.L. & W.A. Taggart (1986). "Court Clerks, Court Administrators and Judges: Conflict in Managing the Courts." *Journal of Criminal Justice* 14(1):1-8.

Neely, R. (1983). *Why Courts Don't Work.* New York: McGraw-Hill.

Neubauer, D.W. (1984). *America's Courts and the Criminal Justice System.* Monterey, CA: Brooks/Cole.

Newman, D.J. (1978). *Introduction to Criminal Justice,* 2nd ed. Philadelphia: J.B. Lippincott.

Ostrom, B., N. Kauder & N. LaFountain (2004). *Examining the Work of State Courts, 2003.* Williamsburg, VA: National Center for State Courts.

Panzarella, R. & I. Shapiro (1988). "Policy, Job Practices, and Personal Values in Decision Making by Court Officers." *Journal of Criminal Justice* 16(2):111-120.

Perry, S. (2006). *Prosecutors in State Courts, 2005.* Washington, DC: Bureau of Justice Statistics.

Peterson, R. & J. Dixon (2005). "Court Oversight and Conviction Under Mandatory and Nonmandatory Domestic Violence Case Filing Policies." *Criminology & Public Policy* 4(3):535-558.

Quinn, T. (1998). "Restorative Justice: An Interview with Visiting Fellow Thomas Quinn." *NIJ Journal* (March):10-16.

Reaves, B. (1994). *Pretrial Release of Federal Felony Defendants.* Washington, DC: U.S. Department of Justice.

Reaves, B. & J. Perez (1994). *Pretrial Release of Felony Defendants, 1992.* Washington, DC: Bureau of Justice Statistics.

Rottman, D. (1996). "Community Courts: Prospects and Limits." *NIJ Journal* (August):46-51.

Rottman, D. & P. Casey (1999). "A New Role for Courts?" *NIJ Journal* (July):12-19.

Rottman, D., C. Flango, M. Cantrell, R. Hansen & N. LaFountain (2000). *State Court Organization, 1998.* Washington, DC: Bureau of Justice Statistics.

Rottman, D. & S. Strickland (2006). *State Court Organization 2004.* Washington, DC: Bureau of Justice Statistics.

Rubin, H.T. (1984). *The Courts: Fulcrum of the Justice System,* 2nd ed. New York: Random House.

Schauffler, R., R. LaFountain, S. Strickland & W. Raftery (2006). *Examining the Work of State Courts, 2005. A National Perspective From the Court Statistics Project.* Washington, DC: National Center for State Courts.

Schmalleger, F. (1993). *Criminal Justice Today,* 2nd ed. Englewood Cliffs, NJ: Prentice Hall.

Senna, J. & L. Siegel (1984). *Introduction to Criminal Justice,* 3rd ed. St. Paul, MN: West.

Sorin, M.D. (1988). *Out on Bail: Crime File Study Guide.* Washington, DC: National Institute of Justice.

Stumpf, H.P. (1988). *American Judicial Politics.* New York: Harcourt, Brace, Jovanovich.

Terry, W. (2000). *Opening the Courts to the Community: Volunteers in Wisconsin's Courts.* Washington, DC: Bureau of Justice Assistance Bulletin.

Walker, S. (1994). *Sense and Nonsense About Drugs and Crime: A Policy Guide,* 3rd ed. Belmont, CA: Wadsworth.

Wenzel, S., D. Longshore, S. Turner & M. Ridgely (2001). "Drug Courts: A Bridge Between Criminal Justice and Health Services." *Journal of Criminal Justice* 29(3):255-267.

Wice, P.B. (1974). *Freedom for Sale.* Lexington, MA: Lexington Books.

Important Cases

Apodaca v. Oregon, 406 U.S. 404 (1972).

Argersinger v. Hamlin, 407 U.S. 25 (1972).

Baldwin v. New York, 399 U.S. 66 (1970).

Ballew v. Georgia, 435 U.S. 223 (1978)

Beckwith v. State, 615 So. 2d. 1134 (Miss. 1992).

Burch v. Louisiana, 441 U.S. 130 (1979).

County of Riverside v. McLaughlin, 500 U.S. 44 (1991).

Gideon v. Wainwright, 372 U.S. 335 (1963).

In re Winship, 397 U.S. 358 (1970).

Johnson v. Louisiana, 406 U.S. 356 (1972).

Stack v. Boyle, 342 U.S. 1 (1951).

United States v. R. Enterprises, 498 U.S. 292 (1991).

United States v. Salerno, 481 U.S. 739 (1987).

United States v. Williams, 504 U.S. 36 (1992).

Williams v. Florida, 399 U.S. 78 (1970).

Chapter 8

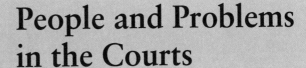

People and Problems in the Courts

Important Terms

assigned counsel

community justice

contract systems

courtroom work group

indigent

innocence projects

jury

jury nullification

Missouri Plan

panel attorneys

peremptory challenges

plea bargaining

priority prosecution

privately retained
   counsel

pro se defense

prosecutorial case
   management

public defender

special prosecutor

venire

vertical prosecution

voir dire

wrongful convicton

Four sets of people play major roles in the court segment of the justice system: (1) defense attorneys, (2) prosecutors, (3) judges, and (4) jurors. These are the people who have a direct effect on decisions in the criminal courts. With the exception of jurors, who are usually typical citizens, all are trained in the law and therefore share a common culture (Glick, 1983:2-3; Holten & Lamar, 1991:115-119). In many ways, prosecutors and defense attorneys are similar, except for the fact that they are adversaries at trial. Very often, judges are recruited from the ranks of prosecutors and (to a lesser extent) defense attorneys. As a result, judges not only share a common training and educational experience, they often share common career paths.

Defense Attorneys

In the field of law, criminal law is not a particularly well-respected specialty (Neubauer, 1984:156). Wice (1978) studied defense attorneys across the country and reported that defense counsel generally were solo practitioners or attorneys working in small offices (with two or three associates). They usually began their private practices late in life, and many obtained their criminal law experience and training in prosecutor's offices. Most were not graduates of the nation's best law schools, and their salaries were generally on the lower end of the earnings scale for the legal profession. As Neubauer

Box 8.1 Characteristics of Public Defender and Assigned Counsel Systems

Summary of public defender system characteristics		Summary of characteristics of assigned counsel systems	
Characteristics	Percent of public defender counties	Characteristics	Percent of assigned counsel counties
Affiliation		Administrative	
County government	38%	Ad hoc (appointments made by individual judges, clerks, public defenders, or others)	75%
State executive agency	25		
Judiciary	23		
Independent nonprofit organization	8	Coordinated	25
Other	6	Lists of available attorneys	
Chief public defenders		• Compiled on basis of:*	
Full-time	78	Lawyers who affirmatively volunteer	43
Part-time	22		
Number of full-time staff attorneys		Inclusion of all lawyers	35
		Volunteers who qualify	27
0	24	Volunteers who participate in continuing legal education	8
1-6	59		
7-20	10		
21-50+	7	• Categorized according to attorneys' specialization in lists	19
Support staffing			
Secretaries	86	• Established procedures for formal removal	15
Investigators	58		
Administrative assistants	18	Caseload	
Law students	16	Cases distributed among most of the attorneys on the list	44
Paralegal employees	10		
Social workers	9		
Fiscal officer	6		
Training director	3	Average of 1 to 10 cases per assigned counsel	75
Salary ranges			
Full-time chief public defenders $6,000-$66,000 (yearly) $20,000-30,000 (modal)		* Total exceeds 100% because multiple methods are used.	

Source: The Spangenberg Group (1986), *National Criminal Defense Systems Study: Final Report* (Washington, DC: U.S. Department of Justice):15, 17.

(1984:157) reported, "Most lawyers view criminal cases as unsavory." Of the hundreds of thousands of attorneys in the United States, fewer than 50,000 will take criminal cases. The number of criminal law specialists is probably in the vicinity of only 5,000 (Bartollas, Miller & Wice, 1983; Glick, 1983; Neubauer, 1984).

Of those attorneys who routinely do take criminal cases, many do so on a part-time basis to supplement their earnings from a general law practice. Criminal defense services typically are provided by young, inexperienced attorneys, or by older, somewhat less successful attorneys. As Holten and Lamar (1991:124) observe, "The field (criminal defense law) does seem to attract more than its share of marginal practitioners." Among several reasons given to explain the attraction of marginal practitioners is that much of criminal defense work is mundane and uncomplicated. One result of the *Gideon* and *Argersinger* decisions (see Chapter 7) has been an increase in criminal defense work for attorneys. By requiring that defense counsel be appointed for indigent (i.e., poor) defendants, these decisions place the burden of paying for defense on the government when the defendant is poor. Nationally the annual cost of providing defense counsel to indigent defendants has been estimated at between 3 and 4 billion dollars.

Traditional defense services were available to a defendant only if he or she could afford to retain the services of an attorney. Privately retained counsel is still an option for criminal defendants today, and involves the defendant hiring his or her own attorney, who for a fee then represents the defendant at trial and in all other stages of the court process. For those unable to pay an attorney, however, the effect of the Supreme Court's decisions on the right to counsel has been the development of alternative systems for the provision of defense services. The most common are the creation of a public defender's office and the use of assigned counsel. Box 8.1 compares these two systems. About half of all criminal jurisdictions use combinations of indigent defense services (see Box 8.2).

Box 8.2   Types of Indigent Defense Systems, Percent of Local Jurisdictions Reporting Each Type

Defense System	Percent
Single Systems:	
Public Defender Only	20.8
Assigned Counsel Only	19.3
Contract Attorney Only	7.1
Combined Systems:	
Public Defender and:	
Assigned Counsel	31.0
Contract Attorney	9.6
Both	6.4
Assigned Counsel and:	
Contract Attorney	5.7

Source: C. Harlow (2000), *Defense Counsel in Criminal Cases* (Washington, DC: Bureau of Justice Statistics):4.

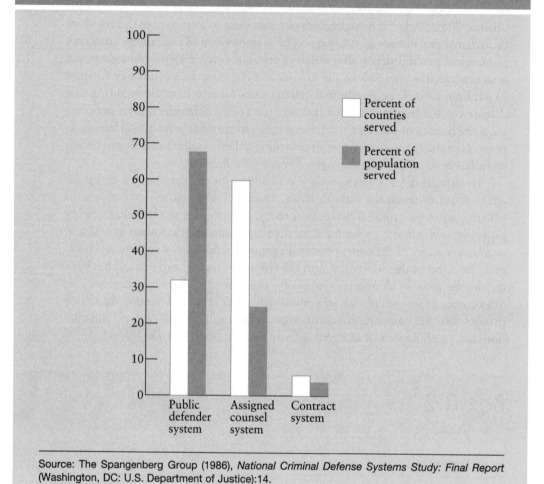

Box 8.3   Distribution of Indigent Syetm Types by Percentage of Counties and Population Served

Source: The Spangenberg Group (1986), *National Criminal Defense Systems Study: Final Report* (Washington, DC: U.S. Department of Justice):14.

Privately retained counsel, public defenders, and assigned counsel comprise the three major methods of securing representation for criminal defendants. A fourth method, **contract systems** (those in which defense services for the poor are secured by contract with a private attorney, the local bar association, or a private law firm), is used in fewer than 10 percent of counties (Harlow, 2000:4). In most states the county is responsible for providing indigent defense services. In the 100 most populous counties, almost 60 percent of indigent defense costs are paid by county governments (DeFrances & Litras, 2000).

In terms of the volume of cases handled, the most common of these forms is the public defender's office (Rubin, 1984:201). Larger jurisdictions (those having the heaviest caseloads) are likely to operate a public defender's office that mirrors the prosecutor's office. In many jurisdictions, the **public defender** is elected and authorized to employ a number of assistant public defenders to serve all indigent defendants. In these systems, the defense attorneys work for the municipality on salary. Young attorneys often seek these positions in order to develop trial experience prior to beginning their own private practices. Some older attorneys, weary of the rigors of private practice, also take positions with the public defender's office. Box 8.3 shows the distribution of criminal defense systems by number of counties and size of the populations served. Box 8.4 shows the major form of defense system used in each state.

The assigned counsel system (often in conjunction with some other form of defense, e.g., a public defender) is used in the majority of criminal jurisdictions, but serves fewer than half of all indigent criminal defendants. In jurisdictions in which criminal caseloads usually are not large enough to justify the expense of developing

Box 8.4   Criminal Defense Systems Most Commonly Used by the States

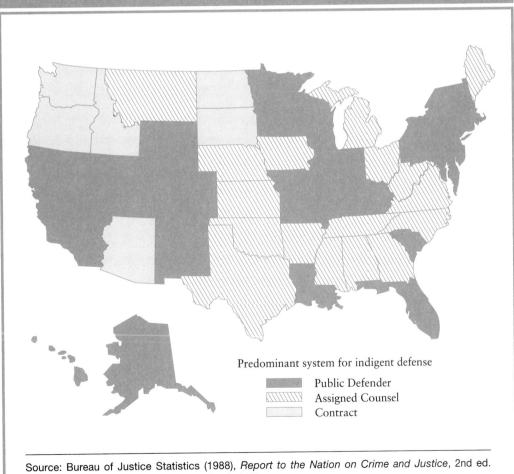

Predominant system for indigent defense

- Public Defender
- Assigned Counsel
- Contract

Source: Bureau of Justice Statistics (1988), *Report to the Nation on Crime and Justice*, 2nd ed. (Washington, DC: U.S. Department of Justice):75.

and operating public defenders' offices, assigned counsel are used. In this system, attorneys voluntarily enter their names to be considered for criminal defense work or, in some places, all members of the local bar are enrolled on the defender's list. As indigents come before the court, the judge appoints an attorney from the list, moving down the list of attorney names as cases are initiated. In this system, the assigned counsel generally is paid a fee based on an hourly rate, but with a maximum. The fee paid generally is less than an attorney would charge a private client (especially when all members of the bar appear on the list). Again, because of the relatively low fees available under this system, only younger, less established attorneys tend to seek out assigned counsel appointments. In the federal system, assigned counsel are referred to as panel attorneys because defense counsel are assigned from a list or panel of approved lawyers. Similarly, the "public defender" system in the federal district courts consists of the federal defender organizations, which include both the federal public defender's office and community defender organizations where applicable.

There is great variation in the cost of publicly provided defense counsel (The Spangenberg Group, 2007). Costs vary from state to state, within states by county or judicial district, and, often, by type of case. In general, death penalty cases are more expensive than noncapital felonies, which are often more expensive than misdemeanor cases. The American Bar Association reported that the hourly compensation for court-appointed counsel in noncapital cases ranged from a low of $35 per hour for work outside of court in Cook County (Chicago) Illinois to more than $120 per hour for some cases in Texas. The federal rate of compensation was $92 per hour. In fiscal year 2002, the state and federal governments spent more than $3 billion for indigent defense.

There has been some debate regarding which of these systems provides the best defense services to the accused. Traditionally, it has been expected that privately retained counsel, as a result of the clear relationship between who is paying for service and who is receiving service, would provide the best defense. However, analyses comparing privately retained counsel with publicly appointed attorneys have not demonstrated any significant differences in the quality of service provided (Wice & Suwak, 1974). There is some research that indicates that defendants with privately retained counsel may fare better in the judicial process than those with public defenders (Champion, 1989).

Harlow (2000) reported that about 80 percent of defendants in the largest counties were represented by public defenders or assigned counsel, and that about 74 percent of prison inmates had been represented by public defenders or assigned counsel, indicating that type of counsel makes no difference in terms of imprisonment. He reported that just over three-quarters of defendants were convicted regardless of form of representation. Defendants represented by publicly paid defense attorneys were more likely to receive a sentence to jail or prison, but for shorter terms than those represented by privately retained counsel. Box 8.5 compares the experiences with defense counsel reported by prison inmates.

A final option for defendants in criminal cases is to defend themselves. Less than 1 percent of felony defendants in the largest counties represented themselves in 1996 (Harlow, 2000:5). Given the adage that "a lawyer who represents himself

Box 8.5   State Prison Inmate Reports of Court Experiences by Type of Defense Counsel

Experience	Type of Counsel	
	Private	Public
Contact with Counsel:		
Within a day of arrest	8.8	26.3%
Within a week of arrest	27.7	33.9
More than a week before trial	32.8	29.6
Within a week of trial	12.6	4.8
At trial	13.6	3.5
None	4.5	1.9
Number of Contacts with Counsel:		
0	4.6%	2.0%
1	24.6	9.6
2-3	44.5	30.6
4-5	13.4	20.7
6 or more	12.9	37.2
Type of Plea:		
Not Guilty	24.3%	31.4%
Guilty	60.6	54.7
No Contest	11.1	10.3
Other	6.7	7.0

Source: C. Harlow (2000), *Defense Counsel in Criminal Cases* (Washington, DC: Bureau of Justice Statistics):8.

has a fool for a client," do defendants have the right to make fools of themselves? The U.S. Supreme Court has decided that they do. In *People v. Faretta* (1975), the defendant, Faretta, sought self-representation, but the trial judge denied his request, insisting that Faretta accept the assistance of appointed defense counsel. Faretta appealed, arguing that it was his right to represent himself at trial. The Supreme Court agreed with Faretta that self-representation (*pro se* defense) is a constitutional right of the defendant. What has not yet been decided, however, is whether a *pro se* defendant who loses in court can appeal the conviction on the basis of incompetent representation.

While relatively rare, *pro se* defenses do occur. Sometimes a defendant feels that no one else can, or will, present the case as well. More often, these defenses occur when the defendant is interested in using the courtroom as a forum for expressing some viewpoint, rather than as a place for settling a criminal case. An article appearing in *Time* (1977) described some of the pitfalls that can upset a *pro se* defense. Among them are cases in which defendants make incriminating statements (e.g., asking a witness how, since the perpetrator was wearing a mask, she could be so sure he was the offender), fail to follow proper procedure, or underestimate the strength of the state's case.

Prosecutors

Unlike defense services, there is no privately retained prosecutor. Rather, prosecutors are usually elected officials whose duty is to provide legal counsel for the state in criminal trials. Only three states (Alaska, Connecticut, and New Jersey) have appointed prosecutors. Depending on the size of the jurisdiction and the size of its criminal caseload, prosecutors may be either full-time or part-time. Nationally, about 75 percent of chief prosecutors are full-time, and 70 percent of prosecutor's offices also employ at least one full-time assistant prosecutor (Perry, 2006:3). Depending on the size of the prosecutor's office, the prosecutor (frequently called the county attorney, state's attorney or district attorney) may actually serve as a manager, rarely engaging in trial preparation or courtroom appearances. Box 8.6 describes the distribution of staff in prosecutor's offices in the United States.

Box 8.6 Personnel Categories in Prosecutor's Offices

Position	Percent of Personnel
Chief Prosecutor	3%
Assistant Prosecutor	31
Support Staff	35
Staff Investigators	9
Managers/Supervisors	6
Civil Attorneys	6
Victim Advocates	6
Other	3
Total	100

Estimated total personnel: 78,000

Source: S. Perry (2006), *Prosecutors in State Courts, 2005* (Washington, DC: Bureau of Justice Statistics):2.

Prosecutors usually are locally elected for a specified term. In 1990, 97 percent of prosecutors were elected, and the average term was about four years (Dawson, 1992:2). In 2001, the average chief prosecutor had been in office for almost seven years. In the largest jurisdictions, prosecutors work full-time and hire assistants who provide the bulk of legal services of the office. These assistants are salaried employees of the municipality. The overwhelming majority of assistant prosecutor positions are full-time appointments. These positions are most attractive to young attorneys seeking trial experience and to older attorneys who do not wish to engage in private practice or who have not been able to secure a position with a larger law firm. In 2001, almost one-third of prosecutor's offices reported having trouble recruiting or retaining assistant prosecutors, most saying the problem was caused by low salaries (DeFrances, 2002:3).

At the federal level, prosecutorial services are provided by United States Attorneys. United States Attorneys are presidential appointees who are empowered to employ assistants to handle federal criminal cases. In addition, the federal government (as well as some state and municipal governments) sometimes creates an Office of the Special Prosecutor, where an attorney is employed to investigate and prosecute cases arising out of some special circumstance, such as the Watergate investigation during the Nixon administration or the Whitewater investigation during the Clinton administration. A **special prosecutor** is employed when there is concern about possible conflicts of interest, or when a case is so complex that the need to perform the ordinary duties of the prosecutor's office would render it impossible for that office to pursue the case adequately. In the Watergate and Whitewater examples, because the United States Attorneys are appointed by the President, it might be difficult for one of them to investigate criminal allegations against the president.

While similar in many respects, one major difference between the prosecutor's office and the public defender's office is that the prosecutor's office traditionally has been a stepping-stone for political careers. Partly as a result of its elective nature, and partly because the prosecutor can garner considerable media coverage by tackling certain cases (pornography, white-collar crime, child abuse, etc.), the office of prosecutor enables incumbents to prepare for political advancement. An attorney who is interested in a political career as a judge or other elected official often begins in the prosecutor's office (Stumpf, 1988:179-181). Unlike the prosecutor, the public defender generally does not gain voter support, mostly because he or she earns a living by defending the accused (who may be pornographers, child molesters, or other unsavory characters).

Judges

In 2005, there were more than 30,000 judgeships, including appellate courts and courts of limited jurisdiction (Rottman & Strickland, 2006). Judgeships are prestigious positions. To many attorneys, becoming a judge represents the pinnacle of a legal career (Neely, 1983). Compared to the general practice of law, being a judge is more prestigious, more secure, and less stressful. The overwhelming majority of the nation's judges achieve their offices through election. Unfortunately, judicial elections—at least as measured by voter turnout—generally do not provoke much citizen interest. Yet, the selection of judges is important because the characteristics of the judge are often what determine the outcome of a case, more so than does the nature of the case itself (Eisenstein & Jacob, 1977; Jackson, 1974; Levin, 1977).

There are two basic methods by which judges are selected in the United States: election and appointment. In the case of elections, states determine whether judicial races are allowed to be partisan or whether they must be nonpartisan in nature. In elections, judges run for office in much the same way as mayors or state legislators. In states having appointment processes, the governor or state legislature is empowered to appoint judges to office. For years there has been debate about how best to ensure that those selected for judicial positions have the requisite qualifications for the job. Generally, the debate has focused on either the election of judges or on the "Missouri Plan."

In the **Missouri Plan** (so named because it originated in the state of Missouri), a judicial nominating commission rates the qualifications of candidates and identifies qualified candidates or recommends appointment to the governor (Reddick, 2002). The governor appoints someone from the list of qualified/recommended candidates. The appointed judge must then periodically face an uncontested "retention election," in which the sole question before the voters is whether the judge should be retained in office. Should the voters decide to oust the judge, the governor appoints another from a list of qualified candidates. The process is then repeated. Supporters of this system of judicial selection argue that it provides the best of all worlds; that is, the system includes direct voter input in the selection of judges through the retention election, yet it ensures that only

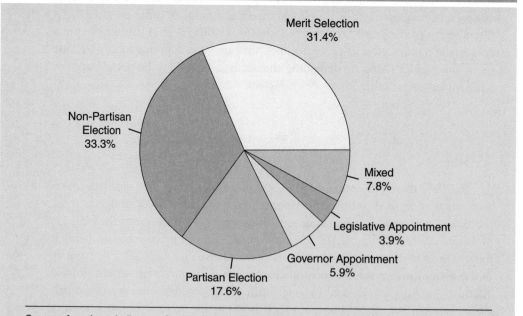

Box 8.7 Methods of Judicial Selection for Judges of State General Jurisdiction Courts

Source: American Judicature Society (2004), *Judicial Selection in the States* (Des Moines: American Judicature Society).

qualified candidates become judges and that those judges are at least somewhat insulated from political pressure and isolated from partisan politics. However, the evidence is not clear that this method of choosing judges is better than direct election (Nagel, 1973). Box 8.7 describes the methods by which judges are selected in the United States.

The federal judicial system operates differently in that federal judges are appointed for life terms by the President of the United States. The President generally accepts nominations from the senators of the state in which the district court judge will serve, but he or she is not required to do so. The candidate is then nominated by the President, whose final appointment of the judge is subject to the advice and consent of the Senate. Controversy about the appointment of Supreme Court justices during the Reagan administration illustrated the hazards of Senate confirmation faced by federal judicial nominees.

In the autumn of 1987, then-President Reagan nominated three candidates before he was able to obtain the consent of the Senate. Seeking conservative justices who would be strict constructionists in their interpretation of constitutional issues, the President nominated Judge Robert Bork, followed by Judge Douglas Ginsburg and Judge Anthony M. Kennedy. An active senatorial committee dominated by Democrats closely investigated all three candidates. Judge Bork was found unacceptable on the basis of his record on equal rights issues. Judge Ginsburg removed his name from consideration after acknowledging that he had experimented with marijuana in his youth (*Criminal Justice Newsletter*, 1987). The third nominee, Judge Kennedy, won Senate approval. The controversy surrounding the confirmation hearings on the appointment of Justice Clarence Thomas (President George H.W. Bush's nominee) also illustrates the confirmation process. Justice Thomas was eventually confirmed, despite great controversy regarding charges of sexual harassment.

The principal difference between the federal and state judiciaries is the tenure of judicial office in each. State judges (except those in Rhode Island), no matter how selected, undergo periodic review and face possible removal without impeachment. Judges in Rhode Island, like federal judges, are granted lifetime tenure upon appointment to the bench. Lifetime tenure insulates the judge from improper political or other influence, but it also means that incompetent or corrupt judges cannot easily be removed from office. The removal of a federal judge, for example, can be accomplished only through impeachment.

Jurors

The last important set of decisionmakers in the criminal courts is the jury. The jury is a panel of citizens, selected through the process of voir dire (literally, to speak the truth), who are charged with hearing cases and determining guilt or innocence. While rarely used, the criminal trial jury is symbolically important as evidence that the citizenry reigns. The right to a jury trial is provided for in the

Constitution of the United States. Regardless of the testimony and other evidence presented at trial, the verdict of the jury is almost totally within its discretion, and it is binding on the court. Only in very rare instances can the defense attorney succeed in convincing the judge to order a directed verdict of acquittal. This occurs when, at the conclusion of presenting its case, the prosecution has failed to provide enough evidence about some important element of the offense. In such cases, the defense counsel requests that charges be dropped because the prosecution has failed to establish its case.

Because of the tremendous discretionary power of the jury, prosecutors and defense attorneys are very careful in the jury selection (*voir dire*) process. Each side is awarded a number of **peremptory challenges**, which allow them to remove otherwise qualified jurors from service. In addition, each side may challenge any number of prospective jurors for cause. Thus, during the selection process, prospective jurors may be asked about how they feel about the defendant, whether they know about the case, and other such questions. Any answer may be cause for a challenge. Peremptory challenges are used by attorneys when they cannot establish a just cause for keeping someone off the jury, yet they believe that the individual will not be receptive to their case.

Both the prosecution and the defense seek to seat jurors whom they believe will support their respective presentations of the case. In many ways, jury selection is the most important part of the trial process (Fried, Kaplan & Klein, 1975). Just as judicial decisions reflect the characteristics of the judge, jury decisions reflect the characteristics of the jury (Kalven & Zeisel, 1966; Simon, 1980). Turner and colleagues (1986) reported that prosecutors and defense attorneys agree, for example, that black jurors are more likely to vote for acquittal, while white jurors are usually in favor of conviction.

Prospective jurors usually are randomly selected from the population within a court's jurisdiction. These prospective jurors form a panel (called the **venire**) from which the attorneys select (through the voir dire process) members who will serve on the jury. Representativeness of the panel of jurors is a thorny issue. In order to ensure that juries reflect the characteristics of the community, courts select prospective juror names from voter registration lists, driver's license records, public utility customer records, city/county directories, tax rolls, and other lists that are likely to include all potential jurors (Rottman & Strickland, 2006). Members of the venire are then randomly sampled from the list. This process, however, frequently fails to produce a representative sample (Fukurai, Butler & Krooth, 1991). Not only do juries frequently lack proportionate representation of minorities, those minorities selected for jury duty tend to come from higher social class standings than might be desired. Thus, jury selection seems to discriminate against minorities in general, and lower-class minorities in particular (Fukurai, 1996). Some persons are exempt from jury duty. The list of exemptions varies from state to state but typically includes certain professions (attorneys, physicians, etc.), public safety and active military members, and those with health problems.

Half the states do not identify any exemptions from jury duty, but the judge can choose to dismiss a prospective juror.

During the voir dire process, both prosecution and defense seek to identify possible biases in the potential jurors through their responses to questions. Seltzer, Venuti, and Lopes (1991) reported that nearly 40 percent of jurors were untruthful during the voir dire. Jurors were most likely to lie about whether they or members of their families had been crime victims and whether they knew police officers. While Seltzer, Venuti, and Lopes conclude that juror dishonesty undermines the prospects for a fair trial, their analysis showed no significant differences in the verdicts rendered by truthful and untruthful jurors.

The selection of jury members is important in part because the jury is empowered to decide the ultimate fate of a case. The tradition of English and American law is that the jury can nullify a law by voting to acquit even if the evidence supports conviction. **Jury nullification** occurs when jurors refuse to convict a guilty defendant because of their belief that the law or the government's use of the law in that case is unjust (Simon, 1992). Reviewing the verdict in the Marion Barry trial, Rita Simon argued that the decision to acquit Barry on the felony perjury charges was an example of jury nullification. She suggests that the six African-American jurors refused to convict the defendant because they saw the case as an example of government injustice in which police entrapped the mayor. Controversy about jury nullification has esca-

O.J. Simpson, center, clenches his fists in victory after the jury finds him not guilty of the murders of his ex-wife Nicole Brown Simpson and her friend Ronald Goldman. Some observers have cited this case as an example of jury nullification, whereby the jury refuses to convict a guilty defendant because of their belief that the government's use of the law is unjust. Later, a jury in a wrongful-death civil trial found Simpson liable in the deaths of Brown Simpson and Goldman. *Photo credit: AP Photo/Myung Chun.*

lated in recent years, especially as crime control policies such as the "war on drugs" are seen to have disproportionate effects on minority group members. The highly publicized murder trial of retired football star O.J. Simpson has been cited by some observers as a case in which the jury ignored the facts and thereby nullified the law (Zatz, 2000). In fact, several jurors believed that the evidence against Simpson had been planted by Los Angeles police. In their view, Simpson had been framed, and the evidence was not believable.

Problems in the Criminal Courts

As with every stage of the justice system, the court process is plagued with problems and issues that defy easy resolution. Some have been touched upon earlier in this chapter, such as the best mechanism for the provision of defense counsel, the effects of judicial selection, and the process of jury selection. Four additional issues have been identified for further consideration in this section: (1) speedy trial, (2) the role of the press in the trial process, (3) the development of "community courts," and (4) plea bargaining. With severe overcrowding in the nation's jails and hundreds of persons accused of terrorist connections or plans, the right to a speedy trial is again an important practical and constitutional issue. Court delay contributes to jail crowding as defendants wait for hearings and trials. There is also a debate about whether suspects arrested after the September 11, 2001, terrorist attacks and as a result of ongoing anti-terror investigations should be tried in criminal or military courts, and how long the government can hold these persons without trial (Lynch, 2002). The role of the press in trials is also still unresolved. This issue, which was particularly important during the political trials of the student anti-war and civil rights activists in the early 1970s, has resurfaced and again gained prominence with the war on terror. Additional issues involve the role of citizens in the courts and the impact of technology on court operations.

Speedy Trial

The issue embodied in the phrase "speedy trial" is most often thought of as court delay. That is, speedy trial is the solution to the problem of what some perceive as unacceptable delays in the processing of criminal cases from arrest to disposition. The concern over court delay is founded on three related, but different, perspectives (Bureau of Justice Statistics, 1986): (1) there are those who advocate speedy trials for the protection of the rights of the defendant; (2) there are those who see speedy trials as the solution to some of the mistreatment of crime victims by the justice system; and (3) there are those who propose speedy trials as a crime-control strategy.

Lengthy delays between arrest and trial (or between charging and trial) can be to the disadvantage of criminal defendants. Especially in those cases in which the defendant is unable to make bail, denial of a speedy trial amounts to incarceration prior to conviction. By virtue of their inability to obtain pretrial release, defendants awaiting trial for long periods of time are likely to suffer further losses, such as loss of income (if not loss of job), possible loss of residence, separation from family and friends, and, upon conviction, higher rates of incarceration. Thus, at least one group proposes speedy trial as a protected right of the defendant (American Bar Association, 1968). Delays in the prosecution of defendants arrested as terror suspects have raised a number of issues about the right to a speedy trial. An example is the case of José Padilla, an American citizen arrested in Chicago and charged with terrorism. Padilla was arrested as an "enemy combatant" and held for more than two years without being formally charged. In 2004 the U.S. Supreme Court avoided ruling in the case when it noted that Padilla's *habeas corpus* appeal against Defense Secretary Donald Rumsfeld was mistaken and should have been filed against the commander of the military prison in which he was housed (*Rumsfeld v. Padilla*, 2004). While the court has allowed continued detention without trial of foreign combatants, as formal hostilities end, the question of speedy trial rights will come to the fore.

Crime victims frequently are ignored by the justice system. Indeed, the role of the victim in the justice process, if anything, is generally that of witness. The justice system is not designed to alleviate the suffering of crime victims. Lengthy court proceedings, especially those in which the victim is involved as a witness, result in lost work days, mental anguish while awaiting resolution of the case, delays in recouping stolen property, and other costs to the victim. While speedy trials act to the advantage of the accused (especially the innocent accused), it has been suggested that the crime victim has a stake in the early resolution of a criminal case (Walker, 1985:141). In the past two decades, concern for the plight of crime victims has led to the development of victim and witness service programs across the country (Smith & Huff, 1992). Today, the federal office for crime victims lists more than 10,000 programs in its online directory (Office for Victims of Crime, 2008).

Yet another reason for speedy trials is the desire to control crime. Pretrial delays are often blamed for high rates of plea bargaining. Plea bargaining, in turn, is blamed for the lack of deterrent effect of the criminal law. A more quantifiable effect of case processing delays on crime, however, may be the amount of crime committed by criminal defendants who are free on bail and at large in the community. Reaves and Perez (1994:11) reported that 14 percent of felons granted pretrial release were rearrested while awaiting trial. The longer a defendant is at liberty on bail, the greater the likelihood that he or she will commit a new crime while awaiting trial. Speedier trials and convictions (especially those resulting in incarceration) would reduce at least this one aspect of crime (Walker, 1985:53). Finally, the longer the period is between when a crime occurs and when the trial is held, the more difficult it is to secure a conviction. Witnesses sometimes move or die, memories fail, outrage at the offense lessens, and general interest in the case wanes. Indeed, defense attorneys often use delay strategies to win cases; that is, they seek repeated continuances in the hope that witnesses eventually will fail to appear. Box 8.8 presents information on case processing time and the right to a speedy trial.

In spite of the relatively widespread support for speedy trials, this is not a reform likely to be easily realized. Speedy trials are not in the best interests of the guilty defendant, nor are they always in the best interests of the prosecutor. Especially when the defendant is incarcerated and awaiting trial, the length of time between arrest and trial serves as an inducement to the defendant to engage in plea bargaining, thereby assuring conviction. Also important is the fact that the general workload of the courts is constantly increasing. A study of American courts revealed that in 2005, fewer than half of all criminal courts were able to close as many cases as were started that year. That means that the caseload of more than half the criminal courts increased by the end of the year (Schauffler et al., 2006).

Box 8.8 Felony Case Processing Times and Speedy Trial

Average elapsed time from arrest to sentencing by type of offense:

Offense Charged	Elapsed Time in days
All Offenses	184
Murder	412
Rape	261
Other Sexual Assault	270
Robbery	222
Aggravated Assault	188
Other Violent	207
Burglary	161
Larceny	168
Motor Vehicle Theft	99
Fraud	194
Drug Possession	175
Drug Trafficking	130
Weapons Offenses	196
Other offenses	184

Right to a Speedy Trial

A criminal defendant's right to a speedy trial is guaranteed by the Sixth Amendment to the U.S. Constitution: "In all criminal prosecutions, the accused shall enjoy the right to a speedy and public trial. . . ." Determining when this right has been violated, however, is rarely a matter of simple objective fact. In *Barker v. Wingo* (407 U.S. 514, 530-533 (1972)) the Supreme Court spelled out four factors for courts to weigh in determining if a defendant's constitutional right to a speedy trial has been denied. The *length of the delay* is the most important consideration, but it must be judged in light of the *reasons for the delay*. Deliberate attempts to delay by the government weigh heavily in favor of the defendant. Certain reasons, such as the absence of a key witness, are considered valid. The court must also determine *if the defendant asserted his rights to a speedy trial* and *if the delay prejudiced the case against the defendant*.

Source: M. Durose & P. Langan (2004), *Felony Sentences in State Courts, 2002* (Washington, DC: Bureau of Justice Statistics).

The most promising development in reducing delay involves changes in **prosecutorial case management** (Jacoby, Ratledge & Gramckow, 1992). Policies and procedures have been developed to expedite case processing, including moves toward early screening of cases to plan for later processing; assignment of cases to tracks that anticipate trial, plea, diversion, and so on; and continuous monitoring of case progress (Cooper, 1994). Jurisdictions implementing such case management systems have experienced dramatic reductions in case processing time. In general, these changes reflect a recognition of "typical" cases so that prosecutors have better guidance concerning how to proceed and what to expect in a given case. Terry Baumer (2007) reported on an evaluation of an expedited case screening process that provided case reviews "24/7" and resulted in significant reductions in detention time and quicker releases of cases that were going to be discharged. Chaiken and Chaiken (1991) described **priority prosecution** programs in operation in the United States. In these programs, certain types of offenders are selected to receive increased attention to ensure conviction. Rather than treating each case as completely unique, screening classifies cases into types that typically receive different treatments (e.g., diversion, plea bargaining, trial). Based on this, prosecutors can know what to expect in each case and better plan and manage the total caseload.

Nearly two-thirds of prosecutor's offices operated diversion programs or deferred prosecution for first offenders. Prosecutors have also adopted what is known as vertical prosecution for specific types of cases. In large prosecutor's offices, the tradition was to assign different assistant prosecutors to different stages of the court process. Thus, one assistant would handle bail hearings, another charging, yet another arraignment, and so forth. No single prosecutor followed a case from the initial appearance up through sentencing. **Vertical prosecution**, on the other hand, refers to the practice of assigning the responsibility of a case to a single prosecutor who then follows that same case throughout the entire court process. DeFrances, Smith, and van der Does (1996:2) report that more than 40 percent of prosecutor's offices use vertical prosecution for all cases. Some offices use this management technique for specific types of crimes such as sexual assault, drug offenses, homicide, and child abuse. One potential benefit of vertical prosecution is that with specialization, prosecutors develop greater consistency in their handling of cases so that defendants and victims are treated more fairly (Kingsnorth, MacIntosh & Wentworth, 1999).

Klemm (1986) reported that case processing time in five cities was more dependent upon the type of plea than on other factors. Thus, defendants who plead not guilty and go to trial experience longer court delays than those who plead guilty. A report from the Bureau of Justice Statistics (1986), based on courts in 12 jurisdictions, echoed Klemm's findings. In addition, Langan and Brown (1997) reported that the time from arrest to sentencing for felony cases differed by type of conviction. While the cases of those convicted at trial took about nine months, cases in which the offender pleaded guilty took only about six months from arrest to sentencing. Moreover, as Feeley (1983) recognized, reforms that aim to promote speedy trials are subject to the desires of the courtroom work group. The judges, prosecutors, and defense attorneys who regularly work in United States courts realize that speedy trials will disrupt their operations and, therefore, generally oppose such reform (even if the opposition is not knowingly and openly voiced). This opposition is usually enough to render the reform ineffective. Case processing delays, in fact, are more likely to be products of this work group and the legal culture of a community than the result of caseload pressures, trial rates, or other factors (Klemm, 1986). In support of this conclusion, a recent comparison of case processing time in nine courts concluded that court "culture" was the most important factor in explaining differences in case processing time (Ostrom & Hanson, 2000). That is, in courts in which judges, prosecutors, and defense counsel understood and shared goals for case-processing time, cases were more quickly resolved. More than types of charges, rates of trial, or other factors, again it was the courtroom workgroup that determined court operations.

The Courtroom Work Group

James Eisenstein and Herbert Jacob (1977) and other observers of the criminal courts have identified what has come to be called the **courtroom work group**. This designation refers to the "regular" players in United Stated criminal courts: judges, prosecutors, and defense attorneys. This group, through close working relationships over time, develops a shared understanding of what are appropriate and inappropriate court procedures and outcomes. The shared norms and definitions among this informal group have real consequences for case outcomes and attempts at court reform. The work group often determines the "going rate" for crimes. For example, what is a suitable penalty for breaking and entering may come to be defined as a six-month jail sentence. Having this shared understanding, all parties are likely to agree to a negotiated plea in which a defendant accused of breaking and entering will be convicted of an offense carrying a six-month jail term (e.g., criminal trespass).

Because all members of the group are responsible for the orderly processing of cases, the development of shared understandings is useful to each of them. Rather than treat every case as unique, it becomes possible to classify cases as typical (i.e., deserving the going rate) or unusual (i.e., requiring alternative processing). Once this informal understanding has been developed, it is exceptionally difficult to change. Myers and Reid (1995) studied efforts to change sentencing outcomes in three Florida county courts. They discovered that sentences imposed on defendants differed across counties, but were quite similar within each county. Thus, they concluded that prosecutors and defense attorneys, as well as judges, were important to efforts to change sentencing. Their research confirms that the courtroom work group is alive and important in those courts.

John Harris and Paul Jesilow (2000) studied the implementation of the three-strikes sentencing law in California. The law was passed as a public initiative, with more than 80 percent of state voters supporting the law. It requires prosecutors to charge defendants who have prior convictions, and it enhances sentences for those who have prior convictions, so that each prior conviction ("strike") results in a longer prison term. It also means that what would be misdemeanor offenses for persons with no prior convictions are sometimes elevated to felonies if the defendant has prior "strikes." In general, Harris and Jesilow found that the effect of the three-strikes law was to destabilize the courtroom work group. The law greatly enhances the importance of the prosecutor's charging decisions (to allege prior strikes), but its popularity with voters prevents prosecutors from avoiding the law in many cases. Harris and Jesilow found some evidence that the work group had already adjusted to reduce the impact of the law, but that new norms for plea negotiations had not yet emerged. They wrote (2000:202): "Despite the obvious need to establish norms within the courtroom workgroup for negotiations concerning strike priors, we find little evidence that such norms will be established in the near future. The situation is clouded further by uncertainty stemming from defendants' willingness to go to trial and by juries' inclination to nullify the law and find defendants not guilty." They suggest that one result of the law is that case outcomes are less predictable, and thus trials are more likely. For this reason, the court process is becoming less efficient, and cases are beginning to backlog. Similar outcomes can be expected whenever efforts are made to treat cases more severely than had been traditional practice.

Free Press and Fair Trial

The circumstance of media coverage compromising the trial process, while relatively rare, is an important concern because it deals with a balance of rights—the right of the defendant to a fair and impartial hearing, and the right of the press to report on operations of the government (or, as might be stated by members of the news media, the public's "right to know"). Press coverage of criminal trials may affect court processes in two significant ways. First, the effects of pretrial publicity may make it difficult, if not impossible, to select a jury that has not been exposed to prejudicial coverage of the case (Brady, 1983). This was the rationale used in the trial of the Los Angeles police officers accused of beating Rodney King. The trial was relocated to a suburban area because the defense argued that the officers could not secure a fair trial in Los Angeles. The change of venue (location of

An artist's drawing shows presiding Judge Steven Taylor urging the jury to steer clear of media accounts of the trial, as courtroom action in the state's murder case against convicted Oklahoma City bombing conspirator Terry Nichols ends for the day on June 8, 2004. Cameras were banned from the Nichols trial. *Photo credit: AP Photo/Pat Lopez.*

trial) for Timothy McVeigh, the individual accused of the bombing of the Oklahoma City Federal Building, was similarly based on a concern that the defendant could not receive a fair trial in the state that was the site of the bombing. Second, in cases in which members of the press are allowed into the courtroom, it is possible that the entire trial will take on a "circus atmosphere." Not only will the behavior of reporters disrupt court proceedings, but the very presence of reporters may alter the behavior of the judge, prosecutor, defendant, jury, and others (Giglio, 1982). Judge Lance Ito was criticized for his failure to control the press in the criminal trial of O.J. Simpson. Despite this concern, there is a cable television network (Court TV) devoted entirely to the legal process, and particularly to the coverage of trials.

Because this issue involves two constitutional guarantees, the right to a fair trial and the right to a free press, the courts generally have adopted a "totality of circumstances" test, wherein they attempt to balance the rights of the media to cover trials against the rights of the state and the accused to proceed in an orderly fashion. The issue becomes important only in those cases that receive the lion's share of media attention—those cases that involve particularly gruesome offenses or are otherwise newsworthy (involving well-known victims or defendants). Ray Surette (1989) concludes that most "media trials" focus on specific types of themes that are typical of entertainment media. These types of trials dominate news coverage of the courts and, Surette argues, distort public understanding and possibly affect future cases. He notes (1989:300): "The significance is that media trials, while publicizing only a single case, probably influence the handling of a large number of defendants, including those who receive no coverage." This influence works in a number of ways, one of which is by sensitizing justice officials to public concern about types of crimes.

It is instructive to compare the American method of handling news media coverage of criminal trials with that of England. In England, the press is strictly forbidden to report on pending criminal cases, under penalty of contempt of court. Once a criminal case has been opened, the British press are banned from commenting on it. Violation of this ban can (and usually does) result in the offending reporter being incarcerated for contempt of court. In the United States, such a ban on reporting would violate the First Amendment's prohibition against "prior restraint" (censoring free speech before it occurs). Rather, United States courts have relied upon posttrial remedies, such as declaring convictions invalid and ordering new trials, as in *Sheppard v. Maxwell* (1966) and *Estes v. Texas* (1965).

The strong American value placed on individual rights, such as free speech, and the nation's commitment to the sovereignty of the citizen prevent us from banning press coverage of trials. The U.S. Supreme Court has ruled that criminal trials must remain public (*Richmond Newspapers, Inc. v. Virginia,* 1980). The other side of the dilemma is the commitment to fairness and a recognition that media coverage of criminal cases can bias juries and result in unfair verdicts. The American solution of posttrial remedies and the British use of prior restraint reflect the different values of the two societies. As Giglio (1982:349) stated, "The British emphasis, therefore, is on justice being done, rather than witnessed." Conversely, the American emphasis is on justice being witnessed, in order to ensure that justice is done.

In practice, much of the problem of balancing the rights to free press and fair trial has been resolved in United States courts through the development of norms of doing business. Occasionally, explicit policies and agreements have been reached among judges, attorneys, and the press. More often, understandings of what constitutes appropriate or inappropriate reporting develop tacitly. The reliance on posttrial remedies for prejudicial media coverage of criminal cases allows the courts and the press to learn from experience and develop policies that will avoid future controversies.

Aside from specific cases, the attention of the media does appear to have effects on the operation of courts. Ray Surette (1999) examined the effect of a well-publicized case on the overall work of courts. Comparing cases processed before and after a highly publicized case of child molestation in a daycare facility, he found that court practices changed in response to the attention. The basic change was that more molestation cases were brought to court. It appeared that one effect of media exposure was to make law enforcement and prosecutors more sensitive to those cases. Prosecutors were less likely to dismiss charges. Of course, this meant that "weaker" cases were brought to trial, and more defendants were acquitted. Other than increasing the number of such cases brought to court, the effects of the publicized case seemed to cancel each other out (more cases, but more acquittals). What is important is that prosecutors (and other justice system actors) do seem to be influenced by the media.

The question of fair trial versus free press is complex because the coverage of criminal cases by the media, although sometimes misleading (for example, by presenting the jury trial as the norm), leads to a better understanding of criminal justice processes for the citizenry. Further, media coverage of criminal cases supports the ultimate accountability of justice system officers to the public. On the other hand, the possible biasing effects of media commentary about criminal cases cannot be denied. In comparing American and British practices, Giglio concluded that one result of freer press coverage of criminal cases in the United States is that American citizens have a better understanding of their system of justice than do citizens of Britain. The inherent difficulty in balancing the good against the bad of media coverage of criminal cases ensures that this issue will remain relevant for some time to come.

The issue of fair trial versus free press has been complicated since the terrorist attacks of September 11, 2001. In response to terrorism, the United States has embarked on a number of practices that raise issues about fair trials. It is not so much media access to trials but rather public access in general. In late 2001, Evan Thomas and Michael Isikoff wrote an article in *Newsweek* entitled "Justice Kept in the Dark." The article examined new policies on the treatment of noncitizen terror suspects, including use of military tribunals for secret trials, holding suspects and witnesses "incognito," and not notifying defendants of the charges against them. While the rights of U.S. citizens are protected, even legal resident aliens could be subjected to secret investigations and trials. The dilemma involves protecting the interests of the defendants in maintaining their freedom while trying to prevent terrorist attacks and not providing terrorists with important information concerning the whereabouts of their personnel.

Community Courts

In Chapter 7 we discussed the development of specialty courts, including such focused tribunals as drug courts, domestic violence courts, and reentry courts. In combination, these have been called "problem-solving courts" (Casey & Rottman, 2003) because the role of the court has been redefined as that of responding to specific problems such as drug abuse or domestic violence. In a broader way, "community courts" have developed and spread. These are designed to deal with a range of community problems through the application of the criminal law (and less formal adjudication options). The proliferation of community courts has occurred in conjunction with the development of "community prosecution" and the expectation that the prosecutor's office will develop working partnerships with a range of community agencies.

As illustrated in Box 8.9, most prosecutor's offices report engaging in at least some community prosecution activities. Community prosecution, according to DeFrances (2002:9), "has been defined by prosecutors as a way to involve the community to solve crime and coordinate their office, law enforcement, local residents, and organizations to improve public safety and quality of life."

Community courts and community prosecution represent an expansion of the role of criminal courts and prosecutors. No longer are prosecutors expected to seek conviction of criminal offenders, or courts expected to simply determine guilt and assign penalties. Rather, prosecutors and judges are to be community advocates and use the resources and power of their offices to solve recurrent

Box 8.9 Community Activities of Prosecutors, 2005

Type of Activity	Percent of Prosecutors Reporting
Define Office as Community Prosecution	39%
Use Tools Other Than Community Prosecution to Solve Problems	66
Involve Community in Problem Definition	51
Assign Prosecutors to Specific Geographic Location	16
Form Relationships with:	
Police	99
Other Government Agencies	88
Community Associations	70
Private Organizations	56
Regularly Meet with:	
Advocacy Groups	62
School Groups	61
Youth Service Organizations	47
Business Groups	45
Neighborhood Associations	30
Religious Groups	24
Tenant Associations	6

Source: S. Perry (2006), *Prosecutors in State Courts, 2005* (Washington, DC: Bureau of Justice Statistics):9.

community problems. It is not enough to process cases. Community courts and community prosecution seek to address the underlying factors that cause criminal cases to develop. Much like community and problem-solving policing, the philosophy of community courts is that justice system agents must become more proactive in preventing crime and should be more responsive to members of the community in selecting cases for prosecution and court attention (Goldkamp, Irons-Guynn & Weiland, 2003).

John Feinblatt and Greg Berman (2001) note that community courts are designed to produce "community justice." They say (2001:1) community justice "takes many forms, but at its core are partnership and problem solving. Community justice is about creating new relationships both within the justice system and with stakeholders in the community, such as residents, merchants, churches, and schools, and testing new and aggressive approaches to public safety rather than merely responding to crime." Among other things, community courts are expected to maintain supervision over offenders and use the criminal sanction to reward treatment progress or punish failure. Court or justice services, such as training and employment assistance, should be made available to all members of the community in order to prevent future problems.

One central question that applies to these efforts (and to problem-solving policing as well) is how a proactive stance toward crime prevention may alter the traditional definition of criminal justice. In the past, a reactive criminal justice process responded to persons who had violated the law, but until there was evidence that someone broke the law, the justice system was not authorized to intervene. More proactive stances by criminal justice officials often call for intervention with citizens based on the likelihood that someone who has not yet broken the law may do so in the future. This too is a dilemma that pits individual interests in being free from government intervention against community interests in solving problems and preventing crime.

Plea Bargaining

As shown in Box 8.10, the overwhelming majority of criminal convictions come as a result of a negotiated plea of guilty. In a study of the processing of felony cases in New York City, the Vera Institute reported that 98 percent of felony arrests resulted in guilty pleas (Vera Institute, 1977). The Bureau of Justice Statistics (Durose & Langan, 2004) reported that 95 percent of felony convictions resulted from guilty pleas. Plea bargaining refers to the process in which the state (through the prosecutor) and the defendant negotiate the terms under which the defendant will enter a plea of guilty. The importance of plea bargaining in the court process cannot be denied. Opinion is divided, however, as to the appropriateness of pleading guilty for considerations (Newman, 1966).

On the one hand, there are those who argue that plea bargaining violates the rights of the accused. Especially in cases in which possible penalties are very severe, or in which the defendant is in jail awaiting trial, the incentives to plead

Box 8.10 Methods of Conviction of Felons, 2003

Conviction Type:	Percent of Cases
Guilty Plea	95%
Bench Trial	3
Jury Trial	2

Source: M. Durose & P. Langan (2004), *Felony Sentences in State Courts, 2003* (Washington, DC: Bureau of Justice Statistics):8.

guilty are thought to be too enticing. In most jurisdictions, by pleading guilty, the defendant has waived his or her right not only to a jury trial but also to appeal questions of evidence admissibility. On the other hand, there are those who suggest that plea negotiations are unfair to the state and the victim. These critics argue that plea bargains serve to let the guilty off without sufficient punishment. They contend that negotiated guilty pleas serve to lessen the deterrent effect of the law because offenders are allowed to avoid their due penalties. Further, the idea that justice is open to negotiation is repugnant to the critics of plea bargaining.

Plea negotiations, however, do have some supporters. It has been suggested that the criminal justice system could not possibly provide the number of trials required if every criminal defendant were to demand one. The justice system would collapse under the burden of so many trials. The plea bargain results in a sure conviction of the offender, whereas a jury trial may not, and the defendant who pleads guilty is entitled to a sentence concession as a result of his or her honesty in admitting guilt, his or her demonstration of remorse in pleading guilty, or his or her cooperation with the state (Champion, 1987). Indeed, in *Santobello v. New York* (1966), the U.S. Supreme Court declared that plea bargaining, when properly carried out, is something to be encouraged.

There are several competing views of the reality and purposes of plea bargaining. Some believe that plea bargaining is the effect of better representation of defendants. Malcolm Feeley (1982) argues that plea bargaining is a product of increased adversariness. Prior to the twentieth century and the court reforms that added protections to defendants, trials were perfunctory. Plea bargaining occurs because the defendant now has an advocate, someone who can negotiate for him or her. Others have noted that one desired outcome of plea bargaining is case dispositions that are seen as just or fair (Douglas, 1988; Garafalo, 1991). That is, when the defense and prosecution engage in bargaining, they settle on a case outcome that seems fair. Plea bargaining can thus allow for the individualization of justice.

In an ideal world, perhaps it would be best if every criminal defendant were given a trial and plea bargaining were not allowed. In reality, however, this is unlikely to occur. The caseload-pressure argument, which explains high levels of plea bargaining on the basis of necessity, has not been supported by empirical study (Klemm, 1986; Parnas, 1980). The abolition of plea bargaining in some jurisdictions (Alaska, for example) has not resulted in a tremendous decrease in the number of cases that are concluded as a result of guilty pleas (Call, England & Talarico, 1983; Rubinstein & White, 1979). Thus, not only does it appear that plea bargaining is not associated with limited ability to provide trials, it further appears that plea bargaining is not a practice that can be easily abolished. Similar results were obtained in an analysis of the abolition of plea bargaining in trials within the U.S. Coast Guard.

Whatever else may be said about plea bargaining, it appears to be a functional practice. Again, the concept of a courtroom work group is important. Whether or not pleas of guilty result from formal negotiations between the prosecution and defense, the negotiations will continue, as will the pleas of guilty. Failure to recognize the informal structure of the courthouse—and the professional relationships that exist among the prosecutors, judges, and defense attorneys—leads reformers to believe that plea negotiations are somehow aberrant. Instead, given that the purpose of the court is to resolve disputes, it is only natural that a certain amount of compromise develops among the set of actors that engage in dispute resolution daily. Indeed, the history of plea bargaining indicates that it is a useful and traditional practice (Sanborn, 1986). Plea bargaining is a good example of the effect of people on the justice system. In assessing the operations of the justice process, it is important to remember that the system is comprised of people and operates through people (Champion, 1989).

Additional Issues in the Courts

Earlier in this chapter we discussed "community courts." These new courts are expected to increase the involvement of citizens in the court process. For at least the past 100 years, the role of average citizens in the court process has been strictly curtailed. Citizen involvement in the courts has been limited to jury service and service as witnesses. Citizens have often tried to avoid jury duty, and the crime victim was considered important as a witness only. In recent decades, however, there has been an effort to expand the role of citizens in the courts and to increase the voice of victims in court proceedings. The reasons for increasing citizen involvement in the courts are both practical and philosophical.

On the practical side, lack of citizen cooperation hinders the orderly process of court cases. When victims and other witnesses refuse to testify, it is impossible for agents of the justice system to gain convictions of guilty offenders. A perception of increased witness and victim intimidation, especially in relation to crimes associated with gang drug activity, spurred efforts to improve witness and juror protection. Healey (1995) reported that more than 50 percent of prosecutors in large jurisdictions identified victim and witness intimidation as a major problem, while more than 80 percent reported intimidation to be at least a moderate problem. To respond to this problem, the courts have developed a number of responses to victim and witness intimidation, including emergency relocation and support, requests for higher bail or denial of release, increased pretrial and courtroom security, protective custody for victims and witnesses, and community outreach programs seeking to better educate the public and gain the cooperation of community service organizations in assisting victims and witnesses.

The voice of the victim has been amplified in criminal court proceedings throughout the past several decades. Prosecutors often consult with crime victims before accepting a negotiated plea (Dawson, Smith & DeFrances, 1993), and most jurisdictions have provisions for victim input into the sentencing decision. Judges, too, will usually thank citizens who serve on juries and recognize their contribution to the workings of the court. One reason for this concern with citizens' experiences in courts, of course, is that most prosecutors and judges are elected officials and thus need to serve the citizenry. A more important reason, however, is the growing recognition that victims, witnesses, and jurors deserve better treatment than they have traditionally received.

In response to this shift in our thinking about what kinds of consideration are owed to victims, witnesses, and jurors, courts have improved jury selection process, streamlined jury service terms, and improved the physical facilities in which

---

Box 8.11 Victim Services Required of Prosecutor's Offices

Type of Service	Percent of Offices
Notification/Alert	
Notify victim	82%
Notify witness	55%
Orientation/Education	
Victim restitution assistance	60%
Victim compensation procedures	58%
Victim impact statement assistance	55%
Orientation to court procedures	41%
Public education	15%
Escort	
Escort victim	23%
Escort witness	17%
Counseling/Assistance	
Property return	38%
Referral	32%
Personal Advocacy	17%
Counseling	10%
Crisis Intervention	10%

Source: C. DeFrances, S. Smith & L. van der Does (1996), *Prosecutors in State Courts, 1994* (Washington, DC: Bureau of Justice Statistics).

jurors convene. Similar changes have improved conditions for witnesses and victims. In the case of victims, legislation in most states requires the courts (generally the prosecutor's office) to provide services to crime victims. These services include notification about case progress; providing help with and information about restitution, compensation, and victim impact statements; and offering an orientation to the court process. In some jurisdictions, prosecutor's offices are required to provide escort services for victims and witnesses and to assist with referral to community services, the provision of counseling, and the return of property held as evidence (see Box 8.11).

A second development affecting the operations of criminal courts consists of the availability of new technologies and the improvement of existing ones. These technological changes include the increasing use of forensic evidence such as DNA testing, videotape evidence, 911 emergency system audiotapes, polygraph evidence, and expert witness testimony. In some cases, courts have used testimony obtained through remote telephone or video links. Increased computerization of prosecutor's offices and courts also has resulted in increased use of criminal history data in decisionmaking. The majority of prosecutor's offices reported using criminal history data in the charging, bail, plea bargaining, trial, and sentencing stages. While these technological developments often improve the efficiency of court functioning, their use requires the development of staff expertise and expands the jobs of court personnel. Beyond that, the spread of computer literacy and use of computers has generated new forms of crime. Box 8.12 reports on the prosecution of "computer crime."

Box 8.12   Computer-Related Crimes Reported by Prosecutor's Offices

Type of Offense	Percent Reporting
State Computer Crime Statute	60%
Credit Card Fraud	80
Bank Card Fraud	71
Identify Theft	69
Transmit Child Pornography	67
Computer Forgery	40
Cyberstalking	36
Unauthorized Access	23
Computer Sabotage	5
Theft of Intellectual Property	5
Unauthorized Copying	4
Other	11

Source: S. Perry (2006), *Prosecutors in State Courts, 2005* (Washington, DC: Bureau of Justice Statistics):5.

These improvements in technology, especially DNA testing and information system technology, have raised new issues about the fairness and accuracy of our courts. Improved evidence and information have increased the recognition of **wrongful conviction**, cases in which innocent persons are convicted of criminal acts. The number of convicted offenders who are later exonerated has increased dramatically in recent years. Samuel Gross and his colleagues (2004) reported that there are more than 40 "innocence projects" in existence in more than 30 states. **Innocence projects** are efforts to investigate claims of innocence maintained by persons convicted of criminal offenses (see http://www.innocenceproject.org). The growth of these projects and the rate of exonerations suggests that many thousands of innocent persons are convicted of crimes each year in the United States (Gross et al., 2004:11). While most of these convictions are for less serious offenses, for which the convicted person serves a relatively short sentence, the likelihood that innocent defendants are convicted of crimes raises questions about the quality of justice. Ron Huff (2002:3) sums up the problem, writing, "Most people can readily understand that convicting an innocent person is unjust, even thought they might express more concern with the guilty who go free. A society that views itself as just and fair simply cannot afford to ignore this problem."

Scandals involving the disclosure of police misconduct that includes fabricating evidence and committing perjury have led to the overturning of convictions of scores of persons in Los Angeles and other cities. Each instance of a wrongful conviction threatens public confidence in fairness and accuracy of the courts. On the other hand, that innocence is ultimately recognized and official misbehavior is eventually punished can be seen as a positive. While not to downplay the seriousness of wrongful conviction, it remains true that exonerations have occurred in only a small percentage of cases. Even counting the thousands of cases in which wrongful convictions might occur, these are in relation to the millions of convictions each year. As perhaps no other issue, the problem of wrongful convictions highlights the tension between due process and crime control. How do we ensure that guilty persons are convicted and punished while preventing the conviction of an innocent person?

Box 8.13 provides a table of selected court cases regarding the judicial process.

Box 8.13 Selected Court Cases on the Judicial Process

Estes v. Texas 381 U.S. 532 (1965)	New trial ordered because of problems with news media coverage of court case.
Santobello v. New York 404 U.S. 257 (1966)	The plea bargaining process, when properly carried out, is to be encouraged.
Sheppard v. Maxwell 384 U.S. 333 (1966)	Verdict declared invalid because of problems with news media coverage of court case.
People v. Faretta 422 U.S. 806 (1975)	Self-representation (pro se defense) is a constitutional right of the defendant.

The Criminal Courts in the Whole System

Like the police, the criminal courts are a subsystem of the criminal justice system, which itself exists within the whole system of American society. This context can be understood clearly when we consider the fact that those courts that hear criminal cases do so on a part-time basis. Most cases are civil in nature, and criminal cases are a part-time responsibility for the courts. Thus, delay in criminal case processing cannot be easily resolved by merely hiring more court personnel and building more courtrooms, because these changes will have the effect of accelerating both civil and criminal cases.

Donald Black's theory of the sociology of law suggests that as a society becomes more diverse and larger, the use of the law will expand. In the criminal courts, we find that the majority of cases and court personnel are found in a few very large jurisdictions. Moreover, the practice of plea bargaining represents, at some level, a less formal means of social control than trial and conviction. While we see proposals to reduce or eliminate plea bargaining and make formal trials more common, we also see a movement to develop less formal, problem-solving courts. We should not be surprised that the majority of cases are disposed of by plea bargaining. Trials seem to be reserved for those cases in which less formal resolutions are unworkable.

As our thinking about the role of citizens in the courts has changed, the courts themselves have become more sensitive to the needs and desires of victims, witnesses, and jurors. With the advent of community-based justice, we see the development of community courts. As communications technology improves, issues emerge surrounding media coverage, especially television coverage, of courts. The courts themselves adopt, and adapt to, new technologies to improve operations.

The courts are affected by changes in the larger society and, in turn, the courts affect the larger society (Calvi & Coleman, 1989). Many of the conflicts and controversies existing in the courts represent efforts to manage the relationship between the courts and social forces. The role of juries and the selection of judges and prosecutors evidence the United States' commitment to a legal system that is sensitive to our perceptions of what is right and what is wrong. As perceptions change (e.g., drug offenses are seen as more serious than in the past), there is pressure for the courts to change. Yet, we want the courts to be predictable and fair as well as free from improper outside influence. Thus, we want to know what the courts are doing, but we do not want court decisions to be biased by preconceived notions. As with achieving a balance between due process and crime control, the courts must seek a balance between responsiveness to social change and the commitment to impartiality.

Review Questions

1. Identify three ways in which defendants in criminal cases may obtain defense counsel.

2. Summarize the case of *Gideon v. Wainwright* and explain how it relates to *Argersinger v. Hamlin*. (Consult Chapters 7 and 8.)

3. Compare criminal defense attorneys with prosecutors. In what ways are their jobs similar?

4. Tell which method of judicial selection you feel is most likely to yield competent judges who are responsive to the public. Explain how the system you select will accomplish this goal.

5. Describe the voir dire process and explain how it allows attorneys to protect the interests of their clients.

6. How can "speedy trial" be expected to reduce strains in other areas of the justice system?

7. The conflict between a free press and a fair trial reflects one of the ideological dilemmas of American criminal justice. Explain this conflict and propose a solution.

8. Take a position on the issue of plea bargaining (i.e., either support or oppose the practice) and give arguments against those who take the opposing position to yours.

9. How do the courts reflect changes in the larger American society?

References

American Bar Association (1968). *Standards Relating to Speedy Trial.* New York: Institute of Judicial Administration.

Bartollas, C., S. Miller & P. Wice (1983). *Participants in American Criminal Justice: The Promise and the Performance.* Englewood Cliffs, NJ: Prentice Hall.

Baumer, T. (2007). "Reducing Lockup Crowding with Expedited Initial Processing of Minor Offenders." *Journal of Criminal Justice* 35(3):273-281.

Brady, J. (1983). "Fair and Impartial Railroad: The Jury, the Media, and Political Trials." *Journal of Criminal Justice* 11(3):241-264.

Bureau of Justice Statistics (1986). *Felony Case-Processing Time.* Washington, DC: U.S. Department of Justice.

Call, J., D. England & S. Talarico (1983). "The Abolition of Plea Bargaining in the Coast Guard." *Journal of Criminal Justice* 11(4):351-358.

Calvi, J. & S. Coleman (1989). *American Law and Legal Systems.* Englewood Cliffs, NJ: Prentice Hall.

Casey, P. &D. Rottman (2003). *Problem-Solving Courts: Models and Trends.* Williamsburg, VA: National Center for State Courts.

Chaiken, M. & J. Chaiken (1991). *Priority Prosecution of High-Rate Dangerous Offenders.* Washington, DC: National Institute of Justice.

Champion, D. (1987). "Felony Offenders, Plea Bargaining, and Probation: A Case of Extra-Legal Exigencies in Sentencing Practices." *Justice Professional* 2(2):1-18.

Champion, D. (1989). "Private Counsels and Public Defenders: A Look at Weak Cases, Prior Records, and Leniency in Plea Bargaining." *Journal of Criminal Justice* 17(4):253-263.

Cooper, C. (1994). *Expedited Drug Case Management.* Washington, DC: Bureau of Justice Assistance.

Criminal Justice Newsletter (1987). "President Cites Crime Issue in Choosing Kennedy for High Court." *Criminal Justice Newsletter* 18(22):4.

Dawson, J. (1992). *Prosecutors in State Courts, 1990.* Washington, DC: U.S. Department of Justice.

Dawson, J., S. Smith & C. DeFrances (1993). *Prosecutors in State Courts, 1992.* Washington, DC: Bureau of Justice Statistics.

DeFrances, C. (2002). *Prosecutors in State Courts, 2001.* Washington, DC: Bureau of Justice Statistics.

DeFrances, C. & M. Litras (2000). *Indigent Defense Services in Large Counties, 1999.* Washington, DC: Bureau of Justice Statistics.

DeFrances, C., S. Smith & L. van der Does (1996). *Prosecutors in State Courts, 1994.* Washington, DC: Bureau of Justice Statistics.

Douglas, R. (1988). "Tolerated Contests? Plea and Sentence in the Victorian Magistrate's Courts." *Journal of Criminal Justice* 16(4):269-290.

Durose, M. & P. Langan (2004). *Felony Sentences in State Courts, 2002.* Washington, DC: Bureau of Justice Statistics.

Eisenstein, J. & H. Jacob (1977). *Felony Justice.* Boston: Little, Brown.

Feeley, M. (1982). "Plea Bargaining and the Structure of the Criminal Process." *Justice System Journal* 7(Winter):338-355.

Feeley, M. (1983). *Court Reform on Trial.* New York: Basic Books.

Feinblatt, J. & G. Berman (2001). *Responding to the Community: Principles for Planning and Creating a Community Court.* Washington, DC: Bureau of Justice Assistance.

Fried, M., K. Kaplan & K. Klein (1975). "Juror Selection: An Analysis of Voir Dire." In R. Simon (ed.), *The Jury System in America.* Beverly Hills, CA: Sage.

Fukurai, H. (1996). "Race, Social Class, and Jury Participation: New Dimensions for Evaluating Discrimination in Jury Service and Jury Selection." *Journal of Criminal Justice* 24(1):71-88.

Fukurai, H., E. Butler & R. Krooth (1991). "Cross-Sectional Jury Representation or Systematic Jury Representation? Simple Random and Cluster Sampling Strategies in Jury Selection." *Journal of Criminal Justice* 19(1):31-48.

Garafalo, J. (1991). "Police, Prosecutors, and Felony Case Attrition." *Journal of Criminal Justice* 19(5):439-449.

Giglio, E. (1982). "Free Press—Fair Trial in Britain and America." *Journal of Criminal Justice* 10(5):341-358.

Glick, H. (1983). *Courts, Politics and Justice.* New York: McGraw-Hill.

Goldkamp, J., C. Irons-Guynn & D. Weiland (2003). *Community Prosecution Strategies.* Washington, DC: National Institute of Justice.

Gross, S., K. Jacoby, D. Matheson, N. Montgomery & S. Patil (2004). *Exonerations in the United States: 1989 through 2003.* Chicago: American Judicature Society.

Harlow, C. (2000). *Defense Counsel in Criminal Cases.* Washington, DC: Bureau of Justice Statistics.

Harris, J. & P. Jesilow (2000). "It's Not the Old Ball Game: Three Strikes and the Courtroom Workgroup." *Justice Quarterly* 17(1):186-203.

Healey, K. (1995). *Victim and Witness Intimidation: New Developments and Emerging Responses.* Washington, DC: National Institute of Justice.

Holten, N.G. & L. Lamar (1991). *The Criminal Courts: Structures, Personnel, and Processes.* New York: McGraw-Hill.

Huff, C.R. (2002). "Wrongful Conviction and Public Policy: The American Society of Criminology Presidential Address." *Criminology* 40(1):1-18.

Jackson, D. (1974). *Judges.* New York: Atheneum.

Jacoby, J., E. Ratledge & H. Gramckow (1992). *Expedited Drug Case Management Programs: Issues for Program Development.* Washington, DC: U.S. Department of Justice.

Kalven, H. & H. Zeisel (1966). *The American Jury.* Boston: Little, Brown.

Klemm, M. (1986). "A Look at Case Processing Time in Five Cities." *Journal of Criminal Justice* 14(1):9-23.

Kingsnorth, R., R. MacIntosh & J. Wentworth (1999). "Sexual Assault: The Role of Prior Relationship and Victim Characteristics in Case Processing." *Justice Quarterly* 16(2):275-302.

Langan, P. & J. Brown (1997). *Felony Sentences in State Courts, 1994.* Washington, DC: Bureau of Justice Statistics.

Levin, M. (1977). *Urban Politics and Criminal Courts.* Chicago: University of Chicago Press.

Lynch, T. (2002). *Breaking the Vicious Cycle: Preserving Our Liberties While Fighting Terrorism.* Washington, DC: CATO Institute.

Myers, L. & S. Reid (1995). "The Importance of County Context in the Measurement of Sentence Disparity: The Search for Routinization." *Journal of Criminal Justice* 23(3):223-241.

Nagel, S. (1973). *Comparing Elected and Appointed Judicial Systems.* Beverly Hills, CA: Sage.

Neely, R. (1983). *Why Courts Don't Work.* New York: McGraw-Hill.

Neubauer, D. (1984). *America's Courts and the Criminal Justice System.* Monterey, CA: Brooks/Cole.

Newman, D. (1966). *Conviction: The Determination of Guilt or Innocence Without Trial.* Boston: Little, Brown.

Office for Victims of Crime (2008). Found at: http://ojp.usdoj.gov/ovc (accessed February 5, 2008).

Ostrom, B. & R. Hanson (2000). *Efficiency, Timeliness, and Quality: A New Perspective From Nine State Criminal Trial Courts.* Washington, DC: National Institute of Justice.

Parnas, R. (1980). "Empirical Data, Tentative Conclusions, and Difficult Questions About Plea Bargaining in Three California Counties." *Federal Probation* 44(2):12.

Perry, S. (2006). *Prosecutors in State Courts, 2005.* Washington, DC: Bureau of Justice Statistics.

Reaves, B. & J. Perez (1994). *Pretrial Release of Felony Defendants, 1992.* Washington, DC: Bureau of Justice Statistics.

Reddick, M. (2002). "Merit Selection: A Review of the Social Scientific Literature." *Dickinson Law Review* 106:729-744.

Rottman, D. & S. Strickland (2006). *State Court Organization 2004.* Washington, DC: Bureau of Justice Statistics.

Rubin, H. (1984). *The Courts: Fulcrum of the Justice System,* 2nd. ed. New York: Random House.

Rubinstein, M.L. & T.J. White (1979). "Plea Bargaining: Can Alaska Live Without It?" *Judicature* 62:266.

Sanborn, J.B. (1986). "A Historical Sketch of Plea Bargaining." *Justice Quarterly* 3(2):111-138.

Seltzer, R., M. Venuti & G. Lopes (1991). "Juror Honesty During the Voir Dire." *Journal of Criminal Justice* 19(5):451-462.

Simon, R. (1980). *The Jury: Its Role in American Society.* Lexington, MA: Lexington Books.

Simon, R. (1992). "Jury Nullification, or Prejudice and Ignorance in the Marion Barry Trial." *Journal of Criminal Justice* 20(3):261-266.

Smith, B. & C.R. Huff (1992). "From Victim to Political Activist: An Empirical Examination of a Statewide Victim's Rights Movement." *Journal of Criminal Justice* 20(3):201-215.

The Spangenberg Group (2003). *State and County Expenditures for Indigent Defense Services in Fiscal Year 2002.* West Newton, MA: The Spangenberg Group, prepared for The American Bar Association Bar Information Program. Found at: http://www.abanet.org/legalservices/sclaid/defender/downloads/2007FelonyCompRatesupdates_nonfelony.pdf, accessed August 12, 2005.

Stumpf, H. (1988). *American Judicial Politics.* New York: Harcourt, Brace, Jovanovich.

Surette, R. (1999). "Media Echoes: Systemic Effects of News Coverage." *Justice Quarterly* 16(3):601-631.

Surette, R. (1989). "Media Trials." *Journal of Criminal Justice* 17(4):293-308.

Thomas, E. & M. Isikoff (2001). "Justice Kept in the Dark." *Newsweek* (Dec. 10, 2001):36-43.

Time (1977). "Fools in Court." (May, 1977):45.

Turner, B., R. Lovell, J. Young & W. Denny (1986). "Race and Peremptory Challenge During Voir Dire: Do Prosecution and Defense Agree?" *Journal of Criminal Justice* 14(1):61-70.

Vera Institute of Justice (1977). *Felony Arrests: Their Prosecution and Disposition in New York City's Courts.* New York: Vera Institute of Justice.

Walker, S. (1985). *Sense and Nonsense About Crime.* Monterey, CA: Brooks/Cole.

Wice, P. (1978). *Criminal Lawyers: An Endangered Species.* Beverly Hills, CA: Sage.

Wice, P. & P. Suwak (1974). "Current Realities of Public Defender Programs." *Criminal Law Bulletin* 10(March):163.

Zatz, M. (2000). "The Convergence of Race, Ethnicity, Gender, and Class on Court Decisionmaking: Looking Toward the 21st Century." In J. Horney (ed.), *Policies, Processes, and Decisions of the Criminal Justice System.* Washington, DC: National Institute of Justice, Criminal Justice 2000, Volume 3:503-552.

Important Cases

Argersinger v. Hamlin, 407 U.S. 25 (1972).

Barker v. Wingo, 407 U.S. 514 (1972).

Estes v. Texas, 381 U.S. 532 (1965).

Gideon v. Wainwright, 372 U.S. 335 (1963).

People v. Faretta, 422 U.S. 806 (1975).

Richmond Newspapers, Inc. v. Virginia, 448 U.S. 555 (1980).

Rumsfeld v. Padilla, 542 U.S. 426 (2004).

Santobello v. New York, 404 U.S. 257 (1966).

Sheppard v. Maxwell, 384 U.S. 333 (1966).

Chapter 9

Sentencing: The Goals and Process of Punishment

Important Terms

After conviction, the next major decision point in the criminal justice system is sentencing, the decision about punishment. In many ways, the sentencing decision represents the crux of the justice system, for it is at this point that we determine what will be done to, for, with, or about the criminal offender.

Criminal sentences may involve the imposition of fines, community supervision, or incarceration. In some cases, a criminal sentence includes a combination of all of these. Excluding fines and short-term incarceration in a local jail, millions of people each year receive criminal sentences of probation or imprisonment. If we include punishments for all sorts of offenses, including traffic citations, sentences are imposed on more than 15 million people each year. In 2004, more than one million people were convicted of felonies in state courts, only 40 percent of whom were sentenced to prison (Durose & Langan, 2007).

In order to understand how the distinction is drawn between who is incarcerated and who is allowed to remain in the community under supervision, we need to understand the purposes of punishment and the motivations of the people who make the punishment decision. This chapter examines these factors.

The Purposes of Punishment

Traditionally, four purposes or justifications for criminal penalties have been advanced: (1) deterrence, (2) incapacitation, (3) treatment (or rehabilitation), and (4) just deserts (or retribution). These theories of punishment answer the question: why punish at all? This is a question the average citizen does not often hear in the context of criminal law. Yet, most of us have heard the expression that "two wrongs do not make a right." Applied to the criminal law, this suggests that imposing a punishment on someone who has broken the law is a "second wrong," which does not make it "right." If I steal your television and am sent to prison for a year because of it, have things turned out right? You are deprived of your television, I am deprived of a year of my life, and all of us pay the costs of trial and imprisonment.

From this point of view, the punishment of crime seems useless, if not wasteful. However, we usually do not think of it this way. Rather, it seems almost automatic that someone who breaks the law will be punished (von Hirsch, 1976). What can justify a system of penalties that can be argued to involve nothing but costs to everyone affected?

Deterrence is a purpose of punishment based on the idea that punishment of the individual offender produces benefits for the future by making the crime less attractive. Deterrence has two parts: specific deterrence, in which the object of the deterrent effect is the specific offender, and general deterrence, in which the object of the deterrent effect is a wider audience (the general public). According to deterrence theory, punishment is an example of what awaits law violators and serves to educate would-be offenders, so that they will weigh the costs of crime against its benefits (Paternoster, 1987).

With specific deterrence, after I am released from prison, I will think twice before I steal another television because I now know that I will face a year in prison if I steal and am caught. With general deterrence, after seeing what happened to me, you will rethink your plan to replace your missing television by stealing your neighbor's set. In both cases, the punishment serves to prevent future crimes. If society does not punish, there may be no reason for us to obey the law.

Deterrence has a certain intuitive appeal. On the surface, it makes sense that deterrence will "work." Unfortunately, the evidence of its effectiveness is not very clear (Newman, 1983:101-105). Few (if any) criminals believe they will be caught and punished (indeed, if they expected to be caught, they most probably would not commit the offense). While we have used the term "educate," deterrence is really based on fear. Would-be offenders must fear the penalty, and thus we are left with a society in which "proper" behavior is based on fear—a basis that most of us do not favor. Finally, when someone has thought about it and decided not to commit a crime, it is unclear whether the person made the decision based on fear of punishment, fear of public ridicule, fear of eternal damnation, or based on some other factor. Deterrence has strong appeal, but it is difficult to prove. Following a long tradition of research into the workings of deterrence, Gertz and Gould (1995) studied a sample of college students and found that the likelihood of students engaging in crime was affected more by their personal perceptions that the behavior was wrong than by fear of arrest and punishment. Others have studied criminal offenders and found that their decisions about engaging in crime are influenced by their perceptions of being caught and the likely penalty they might receive (Shover, 1996; Wright & Decker, 1994). In a study of 15 active residential burglars, Piquero and Rengert (1999) found that while burglars considered the risk of being caught and punished, the potential pay-off of the burglary was a more important factor in their decision to commit a crime. Nagin and Pogarsky (2001) came to similar conclusions in a study of deterrence in which they found that offender preferences for risk-taking influenced the deterrent effects of punishments. These studies and others (Pogarsky, 2002) suggest that different people view the risk of penalty differently so that it may not be possible to deter all potential offenders with a single penalty.

The theory of deterrence assumes that humans are rational beings guided by a pleasure principle. That is, humans do things that please them and avoid things that hurt them. Further, it holds that we are able to assess the likely effects of our behavior and guide ourselves according to these assessments. As rational beings, we will avoid "bad" behaviors, such as committing crimes, when the behaviors will produce unpleasant results (punishments). Rationality, of course, is difficult to establish. Indeed, many crimes, especially violent offenses among friends and family, are more emotional than rational.

In order for a punishment to deter a would-be offender, two conditions must be met. First, the penalty must be severe enough that the pain of the punishment will outweigh the pleasure of the criminal act. Using an economic example, if the penalty for theft were a $100 fine, it may be severe enough to stop one from stealing $50. Given the opportunity to steal $500, however, the rational person may take the money and pay the fine, keeping a $400 profit. Thus, deterrence depends in part on the severity of punishment.

The second condition is whether the punishment is certain to be imposed. Not only must the punishment be severe enough to outweigh the gain realized by crime, but the likelihood of being punished must be high enough that the offender takes the threat seriously. If the punishment for theft were 10 years in prison, but the chance of being caught and punished were only one in a million, the threat of punishment probably would not deter. Deterrence theory suggests the lower the risk of punishment, the higher the likelihood that a crime will be committed.

Research has indicated that, of these two conditions, certainty of punishment is the more important aspect of deterrence. Given a rational offender, uncertainty of punishment makes deterrence even more troublesome. The offender will assess the likelihood of being caught, and then take steps to reduce the chance of detection before committing an offense. Deterrence may best serve to make offenders more cautious rather than less criminal. In a review of the deterrence literature, Paternoster (1987) suggested that neither certainty nor severity appear to affect the behaviors of deterrence research samples. He warned deterrence researchers to prepare for the possibility that people who commit crimes may not be acting rationally. It may well be that people are not motivated by their perceptions of either the certainty or the severity of punishment. In a study of the specific deterrent effects of punishment for DUI offenses, Kingsnorth, Alvis, and Gavia (1993) suggest that offenders have different perceptions of sanction severity. Thus, a sanction or set of sanctions may not be viewed as very severe by some, or may allow others to minimize the severity of the penalty. For white-collar criminals, whose rational crimes seem particularly suited to deterrence, Benson (1990) suggests that punishments induce feelings of anger and resentment rather than remorse and shame. Thus, the penalty may actually have an anti-deterrent effect. Finally, would-be offenders must perceive that the crime is likely to result in arrest and punishment (Schoepfer, Carmichael & Piquero, 2007).

Incapacitation, like deterrence, suggests that punishment serves to prevent future crime, but not by education or fear. An incapacitative punishment prevents future crimes by the specific offender by removing opportunities for crime. One good reason to imprison a criminal is to ensure that he or she does not have the chance to commit a crime in society again. I cannot steal your television if I am in prison. Probably the most effective incapacitative penalty is capital punishment. Not only do the dead tell no tales, but they also commit no crimes.

The major drawbacks to incapacitation as a justification for criminal punishment are the difficulties in predicting who is likely to commit an offense in the future, and the costs of incapacitating offenders. At the current level of sophistication, it is not possible to identify precisely those persons likely to pose a threat of serious crime in the future (Visher, 1987). The prediction problem is simply too complex.

In any attempt to predict "dangerousness" among a population of criminal offenders (not to mention the general population), one runs a risk of making two types of errors: false positives and false negatives. A false positive refers to someone who is predicted to be dangerous (positive on danger), but who turns out not to be a threat (false). A false negative refers to someone who is predicted to be safe (negative on danger), but who turns out to be dangerous (false). False positives are incapacitated as if they were dangerous, and thus prison resources are wasted and individual freedoms are needlessly infringed. False negatives are not incapacitated and thus are free to victimize others. Every crime-prediction scheme available makes both types of errors. Under the best of circumstances, the likelihood is that roughly eight false positives will be incapacitated for each truly dangerous offender imprisoned, and that nearly one-half of the dangerous offenders will be classified as posing little danger and released (Wenk, Robison & Smith, 1972). In addition, most predictive models do not account for the possibility that offenders change over time and that their risk of new crime can increase or decrease based on life experiences after a sentence is imposed (LeClair & Guarino-Ghezzi, 1991). Given these limitations, policymakers must decide how much error they are willing to tolerate (Smith & Smith, 1998), balancing concerns about due process (false positives) with concerns about crime control (false negatives).

Largely as a result of the numerous false positives, incapacitation entails a significant increase in prison space (Greenwood, 1982; Van Dine, Conrad & Dinitz, 1979). If we work with the eight-to-one ratio of false positives to "true positives" (actual dangerous offenders), for us to incapacitate 100 more dangerous offenders each year, we also will need to incarcerate 800 more nondangerous offenders. That is, the prison populations increase nine times as fast as the population of dangerous offenders. In order to provide sufficient prison capacity for these larger populations, it would be necessary to build four to six times as many prisons as are currently in operation. Incapacitation is ultimately rational, but a determination of its effectiveness must await the development of accurate prediction devices. Upon reviewing the available evidence about incapacitation, Visher (1987) concluded, "These findings indicate that 'lock 'em up' strategies . . . are only slightly more effective against crime than current practice."

Treatment (also called rehabilitation) is another rationale based on a reduction of future crime. Unlike deterrence or incapacitation, treatment is concerned with the offender as an individual (Cullen & Gilbert, 1982). Here the punishment imposed is one that fits the individual and is most likely to result in a change in the individual's desire to commit crime. Treatment suggests that individuals commit crimes for a variety of reasons and that the solution to the problem of crime will be achieved through changing individuals so that they will not wish to engage in crime, and by having other options available to them that will allow them to avoid criminality.

As with prediction, the behavioral sciences do not yet have a level of sophistication that allows treatment programs imposed as criminal sentences to be entirely successful. Partly as a result of pragmatic need, the treatment options available for criminal offenders are limited. Generally, offenders receive some type of counseling that is applied to a wide range of offenders. While designed to deal with individuals, the realities of large numbers of offenders and limited treatment resources mean that treatment is applied to groups and tailored (often not very well) to individuals. Adams (1961) reported that such approaches may be very good for some, of no effect for some, and very bad

A Pennsylvania Department of Corrections counselor leads a session called "La Familia Latina En Recuperacion" to treat Spanish-speaking inmates with alcohol and other drug abuse problems at the Camp Hill prison in Camp Hill, Pennsylvania. In 2004, the state legislature passed a law designed to eventually move about 1,500 inmates into treatment. *Photo credit: AP Photo/Carolyn Kaster.*

for others. The net result is that, for the total group, the treatment leads to no marked improvement when those for whom the treatment was harmful cancel out those for whom it was beneficial.

Many studies of the effects of treatment have suggested that treatments for criminal offenders generally are not effective (Bailey, 1966; Martinson, 1974). Reviewing the research on correctional treatment, Doris Mackenzie (1997:9-16) noted, "The important issue is not whether something works but what works for whom." Like incapacitation, treatment is eminently plausible, but must await greater sophistication in the design and delivery of services to offenders, as well as in the investment of sufficient resources, before it meets in practice what is expected in theory (Flores et al., 2005).

Despite discouraging results from many attempts at rehabilitation, efforts to treat criminal offenders continue, and may be increasing (Gendreau & Ross, 1987). Many treatment programs show promise of being effective answers to the criminality of specific populations of offenders. Completing a review of the evidence on rehabilitation effectiveness, Gendreau and Ross (1987) argued that we do have successful programs. What is lacking, they contended, is an ability to translate experimental treatments into routine, effective programs for offenders. In contrast, Logan and Gaes (1993) contend that the research continues to show an inability to treat the causes of criminal behavior effectively. Further, they suggest (1993:261) that treatment is not an appropriate goal of punishment.

What appears from the research on treatment effectiveness is that we have not been very sophisticated in our application of treatments. Van Voorhis (1987) suggests that the evidence available shows that some treatments work for some offenders, and that we need to better match treatments with offenders. Gendreau (1996) maintains that we must focus treatments on high-risk offenders. He suggests that one of the reasons why studies of treatment effectiveness show low impact is because we have "wasted" treatment on those who do not need it. Today treatment as a part of sentencing has experienced a resurgence as we seek to prevent future crime (Harland, 1996). Taxman and Piquero (1998) compared treatment and punishment sentences of drunk drivers in Maryland, concluding that treatment approaches seemed more effective at reducing future instances of drunk driving. The problem-solving courts, like drug courts and domestic violence courts, attempt to use the threat or application of criminal sanctions to support treatment programs and ensure that the offender participates in treatment (Casey & Rottman, 2003).

Just deserts (sometimes called **retribution** or desert) is the only justification for criminal punishment that is not "forward-looking." That is, it does not offer a reduction in future crime as the principal justification for the imposition of a punishment. Rather, just deserts is based on the belief that whoever breaks the law "deserves" to be punished. Breaking the law in itself is justification for punishment, whether that punishment reduces, increases, or has no effect on future levels of crime. Essentially, the criminal law is a promise wherein we (the state) promise to punish anyone who violates the law, and in the desert rationale, the promise must be kept.

As a justification for punishment, just deserts places limits on the degree to which someone may be punished. Punishment is expected to be commensurate with (or proportionate to) the severity of the crime committed. For example, public torture and execution of parking violators would deter most of us from parking illegally (if not from driving altogether), and these methods would be acceptable in a purely deterrent system of punishment. In contrast, these extreme forms of punishment for parking violations would be unthinkable in a desert scheme. Further, while a purely deterrent system of punishment does not require that the person being punished be convicted first, the just deserts rationale holds that only convicted offenders should be punished.

Supporters of deterrence often engage in "penalty escalation" because it is easier to alter the severity of punishment than its certainty (Newman, 1983). In this case, the penalty for a given offense—for example, five years imprisonment for theft—is increased (perhaps to 10 years). It is easier to increase penalty severity than to become more efficient at catching and punishing thieves. Further, deterrence rests on an argument that the good of the penalty (in terms of crimes prevented) must outweigh its harm in terms of injury to the punished. It is possible, then, for a deterrent penalty to be imposed on an innocent person, as long as the social good outweighs the individual harm.

Incapacitative penalties also can be argued to have the effect of punishing the innocent. The determination of how severe a penalty should be for incapacitation does not rest on the seriousness of the crime committed but upon a prediction that the offender will commit another crime. Like the queen in *Alice in Wonderland*, proponents of incapacitation invoke the penalty first, and the crime comes later, after the penalty is served. If there in fact is no crime, so much the better.

Treatment penalties assume an "identity of interest" between the state and the offender. The state wants what is best for the offender, that is, to improve his or her chances in life and to reduce the offender's desire to commit crimes. The offender either wants the same thing, or would want it if he or she were competent. Thus, the imposition of a punishment is for the offender's own good. A sanction that seems disproportionate to the seriousness of the offense is not a problem, as long as it is "good" for the offender.

The just deserts justification for punishment is often stated in biblical terms as "an eye for an eye." It fits rather well with our beliefs that, regardless of the reason, those who break the law should be punished (Johnson & Sigler, 1995). The difficulty with desert is that we cannot yet precisely measure levels of crime severity, or of punishment severity (Durham, 1988). Additionally, we are uncomfortable with the idea that punishment can (or should) be imposed simply for the sake of punishment. Retribution is also difficult to achieve in practice. There tends to be widespread disagreement about how much punishment is deserved by those convicted of different kinds of crimes (Griset, 1995). Further, as Nancy Wonders (1996) observed, sentencing is located in the middle of the criminal justice system. Attempts to make sentencing "fair" must contend with both earlier (investigation, arrest, charging) and later (correctional placements, parole release) decisions. Finally, as Myers and Reid (1995) observed, statewide legislation is implemented in different localities, and each of these has its own courtroom work group and definition of appropriate penalties.

These four rationales for the imposition of criminal punishment—deterrence, incapacitation, treatment, and just deserts—have been presented separately and analyzed as if they were required to stand alone. In practice, however, operating sentencing systems are founded on many purposes. It is not unusual, for example, for the sentencing judge to "throw the book" at a defendant for deterrent purposes, while correctional authorities seek to "treat" the offender's problems and rehabilitate him or her, only to have a paroling authority refuse to release the offender because of a fear that the offender will commit a new crime and, therefore, must be incapacitated.

Not only do most sentencing systems expressly serve all four of these functions, but the decisionmakers in those sentencing systems (judges, parole authority members, correctional workers, and administrators) favor different justifications for punishment. To complicate matters even more, these different actors favor different rationales for punishment of different offenders at different points in time. Further, each criminal jurisdiction has its own structure for the determination and implementation of criminal sentences.

Sentencing Structures in the United States

There are substantial differences among the states with regard to how they go about the sentencing of criminals. As the Bureau of Justice Statistics (1984:1) reported:

> It requires more than 200 pages to describe the basic features of the sentencing laws in each state. In addition to the different laws that govern sentencing, there are differences in how specific offenses are defined and classified by the criminal code in each state.

Criminal sentencing has been the topic of a great deal of interest and debate (Clear, 1994; Tonry, 1996; Travis, 2002; Ulmer, 1997; Zalman, 1987). Since 1975, many states have adopted changes in the structures used for criminal sentencing. The result has been the addition of a number of innovative formats for sentencing. If anything, criminal sentencing in the United States has become even more complicated in the past three decades. Michael Tonry (1999:1) observed, "There are now many approaches to sentencing and corrections in this country. Some States have guidelines with parole release, and some without. Some three-strikes states have adopted truth-in-sentencing; some have not. And so on, through the litany of changes in recent decades." Nonetheless, the traditional distinction made between determinate and indeterminate sentencing is useful.

Determinate sentencing structures are those in which each offender knows the exact length and nature of his or her punishment at the time it is imposed. Indeterminate sentencing structures are those in which the precise length of the penalty is unknown until some time has passed since the imposition of the penalty. Within each of these classes, there are several types of sentencing structures. Each sentencing structure represents a balance of power among the legislative, judicial, and executive branches of government. The structure of sentencing reflects varying degrees of emphasis on each of the goals of criminal sentencing, and it affects how sentencing is conducted.

Box 9.1 depicts sentencing structures found across the United States. The majority of sentencing authority rests with the legislature, which establishes criminal penalties and defines crimes. There traditionally has been a certain level of sentencing power vested in the executive branch in the form of clemency. The governor of a state or President of the United States can grant pardons, commutations, re-

Box 9.1 Basic Sentencing Structures in the United States

The basic difference in sentencing systems is the apportioning of discretion between the judge and parole authorities.

Indeterminate sentencing—the judge specifies minimum and maximum sentence lengths. These set upper and lower bounds on the time to be served. The actual release date (and therefore the time actually served) is determined later by parole authorities within those limits.

Partially indeterminate sentencing—a variation of indeterminate sentencing in which the judge specifies only the maximum sentence length. An associated minimum sentence automatically is implied but is not within the judge's discretion. The implied minimum may be a fixed time (such as 1 year) for all sentences or a fixed proportion of the maximum. In some states the implied minimum is zero; thus, the parole board is empowered to release the prisoner at any time.

Determinate sentencing—the judge specifies a fixed term of incarceration, which must be served in full (less any "good time" earned in prison). There is no discretionary parole release.

Since 1975 many states have adopted determinate sentencing, but most still use indeterminate sentencing.

In 1976 Maine was the first state to adopt determinate sentencing. The sentencing system is entirely or predominantly determinate in these 10 states:

California	Maine
Connecticut	Minnesota
Florida	New Mexico
Illinois	North Carolina
Indiana	Washington

The other states and the District of Columbia use indeterminate sentencing in its various forms. One state, Colorado, after changing to determinate sentencing in 1979 went back to indeterminate sentencing in 1985. The federal justice system had adopted determinate sentencing through a system of sentencing guidelines.

States employ other sentencing features in conjunction with their basic strategies.

Mandatory sentencing—Law requires the judge to impose a sentence of incarceration, often of specified length, for certain crimes or certain categories of offenders. There is no option of probation or a suspended sentence.

Presumptive sentencing—The discretion of a judge who imposes a prison sentence is constrained by a specific sentence length set by law for each offense or class of offense. That sentence must be imposed in all unexceptional cases. In response to mitigating or aggravating circumstances, the judge may shorten or lengthen the sentence within specified boundaries, usually with written justification being required.

Sentencing guidelines—Explicit policies and procedures are specified for deciding on individual sentences. The decision is usually based on the nature of the offense and the offender's criminal record. For example, the prescribed sentence for a certain offense might be probation if the offender has no previous felony convictions, a short term of incarceration if the offender has one prior conviction, and progressively longer prison terms if the offender's criminal history is more extensive.

Sentence enhancements—In nearly all states, the judge may lengthen the prison term for an offender with prior felony convictions. The lengths of such enhancements and the criteria for imposing them vary among the states.

Mandatory sentencing laws are in force in 46 states (all except Maine, Minnesota, Nebraska and Rhode Island) and the District of Columbia. In 25 states, imprisonment is mandatory for certain repeat felony offenders. In 30 states, imprisonment is mandatory if a firearm was involved in the commission of a crime. In 45 states, conviction for certain offenses or classes of offenses leads to mandatory imprisonment, most such offenses are serious, violent crimes, and drug trafficking is included in 18 of the states. Many states have recently made drunk driving an offense for which incarceration is mandated (usually for relatively short periods in a local jail rather than a state prison).

Presumptive sentencing is used, at least to some degree, in about 12 states.

Sentencing guidelines came into use in the late 1970s. They are:
- used in 13 states and the federal criminal justice system
- written into statute in the federal system and in Florida, Louisiana, Maryland, Minnesota, New Jersey, Ohio, Pennsylvania, and Tennessee
- used systemwide, but not mandated by law, in Utah
- applied selectively in Massachusetts, Michigan, Rhode Island and Wisconsin
- being considered for adoption in other states and the District of Columbia

In some states that group felonies according to their seriousness, the repeat offender may be given a sentence ordinarily imposed for a higher seriousness category. Some states prescribe lengthening the sentences of habitual offenders by specified amounts or imposing a mandatory minimum term that must be served before parole can be considered. In other states the guidelines provide for sentences that reflect the offender's criminal history as well as the seriousness of the offense. Many states prescribe conditions under which parole eligibility is limited or eliminated. For example, a person with three or more prior felony convictions, if convicted of a serious violent offense, might be sentenced to life imprisonment without parole.

Sources: Surveys conducted for the Bureau of Justice Statistics by the U.S. Bureau of the Census in 1985 and by the Pennsylvania Commission on Crime and Delinquency in 1986.

Source: Bureau of Justice Statistics (1988), *Report to the Nation on Crime and Justice*, 2nd ed. (Washington, DC: U.S. Department of Justice):91.

prieves, and other forms of mercy. The sentencing power granted to parole authorities and sentencing judges is generally delegated to these offices by the legislature.

In indeterminate sentencing systems, the legislature establishes a range of penalties (minimum to maximum), and the sentencing judge is then authorized to impose a sentence that is not less than the minimum and not more than the maximum. In some cases, the legislature establishes a minimum term and then allows the judge to set a maximum within some absolute outer limit. In other cases, the legislature sets a minimum term that is some fraction of the maximum term decreed by the judge. In any indeterminate sentencing system, a paroling authority is authorized to grant release sometime between the end of the minimum term and the end of the maximum term. Thus, the judge has powers delegated by the legislature, and the paroling authority has power that is limited both by the legislature and by the decision of the judge.

In determinate sentencing systems, the legislature generally reserves most of the sentencing power for itself. In some cases, the legislature actually will determine the sentence to be imposed on persons convicted of a specific offense. Here, the judge and parole authority have no sentencing power. More common is the model in which the legislature describes the expected or normal penalty for an offense, and then allows the sentencing judge to modify it (with reasons given). This is presumptive sentencing; that is, the law establishes what the legislature "presumes" will be the sentence, and then requires the judge to explain any case in which the presumed term length is not imposed. In determinate sentencing systems, the parole authority typically has no sentencing power.

In most cases, the legislature grants the sentencing judge the ability to choose between a sentence of incarceration and one of community supervision. This is considerable sentencing power, even in a system in which the judge's power to determine the length of a prison sentence has been strictly curtailed. The decision as to what decisionmaker receives how much sentencing power reflects a different emphasis on each of the four purposes of criminal sentencing.

Anspach and Monsen (1989) observe that the sentencing process and the achievement of sentencing purposes are complex. In a study of the effects of sentencing reform in Maine, they note that adoption of determinate sentencing alone does not ensure rational sentencing. In abolishing indeterminate sentencing and parole, the legislature in Maine provided sentencing judges with a list of eight purposes of penalties that were themselves contradictory. They conclude that failing to provide a consistent rationale for the imposition of sentences promotes unfair and/or irrational punishments. Thus, while sentencing structures are differently suited to achieving or promoting a specific purpose of punishment, structural reform alone is not enough. The structure of the sentencing process should be coupled with a clear statement about the relative importance of particular sentencing purposes. Similarly, Kramer and Ulmer (1996) found that even within a sentencing structure designed to promote equality in sentencing, judges still imposed different sentences in cases that were similar to each other.

Pamela Griset (2002) examined the development of sentencing policy in Florida over 20 years, as the general sentencing structure in the state moved from essentially indeterminate to determinate sentencing. She observed that sentencing policy is the product of many different decisionmakers, including the legislature, judiciary, and various executive branch officials. With regard to Florida, Griset (2002:299) observed, "Like a dysfunctional family, the three branches of government in different places and at different times, have employed a variety of pathological adaptations in exercising their punishment powers, often resulting in muddled or destructive punishment policy." While one branch might be trying to lengthen terms, another would be seeking to reduce prison terms. One set of decisionmakers might be trying to increase the use of imprisonment while another sought to increase diversion from prison. In short, the shared nature of sentencing power, coupled with the political importance of crime and punishment, often led to inconsistent and contradictory sentencing actions.

Deterrent sentences are best defined and imposed by the legislature, so that it is clear to everyone beforehand that a specific punishment will follow a certain criminal conviction. This is the rationale behind what are known as **mandatory minimum sentences**. In these sentences, the legislature decrees that anyone convicted of a particular offense (say, use of a handgun in the commission of a crime or drunk driving) will be sentenced to a minimum number of days or years of incarceration. The prison sentence is mandatory and is expected to deter offenders. Rottman and Strickland (2006) report that 44 states and the District of Columbia have mandatory minimum prison sentences for offenders convicted of committing at least some felonies while armed with a deadly weapon.

Just deserts, or retributive, sentencing is perhaps best accomplished by granting limited sentencing power to the judge. The legislature sets an expectation or limit on how severe a penalty may be imposed for a particular criminal act, but the judge is expected to "fine tune" the sentence so that the severity of the sentence matches the severity of the offense.

Rehabilitative (treatment) and incapacitative sentences are probably best imposed by granting substantial control in sentencing to the paroling authority. This authority can then determine when the offender is safe for release (that is, cured of criminal tendencies) and can adjust the sentence accordingly. The legislature and sentencing judge are ill-suited to this task because they either do not deal directly with the offender, or their roles occur too early in the process. Both of these rationales require that someone continually monitor the offender for progress.

Alternatively, for the purpose of incapacitation, the legislature can develop **habitual offender statutes** that allow for increased penalties for repeat offenders. One such law is the California "three strikes and you're out" law. This law was enacted as a result of a voter initiative (referendum) and provides for a doubling of the sentence upon a second felony conviction "strike," and a tripling of the sentence (or 25-year term, whichever is longer) on the third "strike" (Harris & Jesilow, 2000). The problem with such laws is that they seek to imprison all offenders meeting the criteria (e.g., a third felony conviction) and thus run the risk of relatively high rates of false positives (Saint-Germain & Calamia, 1996; Turner et al., 1995). Most contemporary **three-strikes laws** increase prison terms for offenders having prior convictions but have been written so that they are applied only to

Children display photos of their father, who is in jail for a term of 25 years to life, during a protest against California's "three strikes" law. California voters and lawmakers approved the three-strikes law amid public furor over the 1993 kidnap and murder of 12-year-old Polly Klaas. Photo credit: AP Photo/Damian Dovarganes.

the most violent repeat offenders, reducing their likely impact on overall prison populations (Clark, Austin & Henry, 1997). Kovandzic and his colleagues (2004) assessed the impact of three-strikes laws in 21 states on crime rates. They concluded that there was little reason to believe that such laws resulted in reduced crime rates through either incapacitation or deterrence. In a separate analysis, however, Kovandzic (2001) reported that the habitual offender sentencing provisions of Florida law appear to result in small reductions of crime through incapacitation. The policy question, of course, is whether the increased costs in terms of incarceration are justified by the modest reductions in future crime. In 2005, all but two states had some provision for the sentencing of habitual felony offenders.

Sentencing in the Justice System

Criminal sentencing is the final decision point in the court segment of the criminal justice system (with the possible exception of probation revocation, which is discussed in Chapter 12). It represents a transitional decision point at which the fate of the offender is determined jointly by correctional and judicial officials. In cases of negotiated pleas of guilty, the prosecutor also plays a large role in determining the sentence (Alschuler, 1978). In noncapital cases in three states (Kentucky, Missouri, and Virginia), the jury sentences those convicted of felonies, and in three more (Arkansas, Indiana, and Texas), the jury recommends a sentence to the judge in felony cases. In these states, however, the judge can alter a jury sentence or recommendation (Rottman & Strickland, 2006).

In capital cases (12 states do not have the death penalty), the jury determines the sentence in 29 states and recommends a sentence to the judge in seven other states. In one state (Nebraska), a panel of judges makes the sentencing decision. In Pennsylvania, the sentence can be decided by either the jury or the judge.

The decision about sentence is bifurcated (Wilkins et al., 1976); that is, it is made in two stages. First, the sentencing judge decides whether to incarcerate the convicted offender. Next, the conditions of sentence are determined. These conditions range from the restrictions and obligations placed upon those who are given probation to the length of term for those incarcerated.

Historically, sentencing judges had a greater voice in setting the conditions of prison confinement for sentenced offenders. The judge used to be able to specify the institution to which an offender would be sent, or to require that the sentence be served "at hard labor." Today, most jurisdictions restrict the judge to setting the term of confinement, and leave to the correctional authorities the discretionary power to establish the place and conditions of confinement.

Especially in indeterminate sentencing systems based on a rehabilitative rationale, the sentencing decision is expected to be based on the results of a **presentence investigation** (PSI) conducted by a probation officer. The PSI report describes the offense and offender, and in many jurisdictions includes a recommendation of sentence from the reporting officer (Czajkoski, 1973). Presentence investigations are common in most felony cases across the nation, thereby involving probation officers in the sentencing decision.

Presentence Investigation

After conviction, the judge generally sets a date for sentencing that is delayed long enough to allow the probation department to conclude a presentence investigation. This investigation includes a detailed assessment of the offense and the offender's criminal and social background. A report on the investigation (the PSI report) is then submitted to the sentencing judge so that it can be relied upon in arriving at an appropriate sentence. In addition to its usefulness at the sentencing stage, the PSI serves many other purposes. It is a basic information source for the correctional programming used in developing probation plans and institutional classification; it provides background data used by parole boards in their decisions; and it serves as a basic resource document for research on correctional authorities, offenders, and corrections (U.S. Division of Probation, 1974).

The typical PSI report includes a face sheet, which contains basic offense and offender demographic information. The textual part of the report generally covers: (1) the offense, that is, it gives the official (police) version and the offender's version of the facts (occasionally the victim's version is also added); (2) the social history of the defendant (describing his or her childhood) and current family, employment, economic, and educational situations; and (3) the prior criminal record of the offender. Much of this information is obtained through interviews with the offender, members of the offender's family, and others who know the offender. The material in the report is not held to the strict evidentiary standards of trial. Michael Weinrath (1999) assessed the accuracy of narrative presentence reports and found that the traditional descriptive report was not an accurate means of predicting whether the offender would successfully complete probation. He urged that we discontinue narrative reports and move to the use of more objective risk assessments for judicial sentencing.

Traditionally, the PSI report did not have to be disclosed to the defendant. In 1949, the U.S. Supreme Court decided the case of *Williams v. New York*, which dealt with the issue of disclosure of the presentence investigation report. Williams had been convicted of capital murder, but the jury had recommended leniency. After reviewing the PSI report, the judge imposed the death penalty. Williams's attorney was not allowed to see the report and verify its accuracy. The Court ruled that there was no constitutional right to review the report. However, in 1977, the Court ruled in *Gardner v. Florida* that when the death penalty is imposed as a result of information contained in a PSI report, the defense has a right to review that report. Therefore, at least in a capital case, the contents of the PSI report must be disclosed to defense counsel.

In jurisdictions where probation officers are allowed to make recommendations to the sentencing judge, sentencing judges have been found to concur with these recommendations in the great majority of cases (Carter & Wilkins, 1967). This is one of the principal reasons why some argue that the defendant should be allowed to review the document. Disclosure of the PSI report, however, is opposed by others, who argue that letting the defendant see the report will cause those interviewed to withhold information, or that disclosure might jeopardize the rehabilitation of the offender, should he or she learn things from the report that would be detrimental to rehabilitative programming.

In many jurisdictions, this issue has been resolved, either through disclosure of the entire report (Dubois, 1981) or, more frequently, through partial disclosure. In **partial disclosure**, the judge either summarizes the facts and the reasons for sentence, allowing the defense to contest any errors, or provides a copy of the body of the report to the defense. In jurisdictions where a copy is provided, there often is a confidential addendum that is not disclosed.

The Sentencing Hearing

There is no constitutional right to a separate hearing for sentencing, but generally a sentencing hearing is held for felony defendants. In most states, there are statutory provisions for sentencing hearings (Rottman et al., 2000). In jurisdictions or cases in which there is no presentence investigation, sentencing typically follows conviction. Although there is not a separate hearing, the defendant is afforded the opportunity to speak on his or her own behalf (usually through counsel), and the state (prosecutor) is asked to comment on sentencing. Sometimes the victim is present and allowed to speak or submit a written statement for consideration at sentencing.

At the point of sentencing, whether or not there is a separate hearing for that purpose, the defendant has the right to counsel. In 1967, in *Mempa v. Rhay*, the U.S. Supreme Court ruled that sentencing was a "critical stage" of the justice system, at which the defendant stands to lose protected rights and interests. The Court held that the offender had the right to be represented at sentencing.

The Parole Hearing

In cases in which the offender is sentenced to incarceration in prison under an indeterminate sentence model, the final sentencing decision is usually rendered by a parole authority. In these cases, the judge imposes a sentence that has a minimum and maximum term, but the actual duration of the penalty is not known. The paroling authority has the power to grant release (that is, limit the duration of confinement) at some point between the end of the minimum term and the end of the maximum term. This decision is usually made by the entire board, or by a panel of board members, after a hearing with the inmate. In Oklahoma, the parole board advises the governor, but it is the governor who holds the authority to grant parole. Only about one-third of the states continue to use parole as the primary means of release for prison inmates. In those states in particular, the parole release decision is an important part of the sentencing process.

Parole eligibility is established by the legislature and defines which types of inmates can be paroled at what points in their sentence. For example, the legislature might require that the offender serve a minimum term before release is authorized. Similarly, the legislature can define certain offenses (or offenders) as ineligible for parole. In cases in which states use the "life without parole" sentence for murder, the legislature has defined murderers as "ineligible" for parole. Given eligibility, the parole authority can grant release to a prison inmate.

At the parole hearing, the paroling authority reviews the criminal and social history of the offender, assesses his or her adjustment to prison, and evaluates the offender's potential for success under parole supervision. The inmate is allowed to speak at this hearing and to present whatever evidence he or she feels is relevant. There is no right to counsel at the parole release hearing. Discretionary release on parole has been criticized for failing to protect the community by releasing dangerous offenders early as well as for violating individual rights through discriminatory decisions. Lawrence Bennett (1995) argues that while these are real problems with traditional parole release systems, the development of guidelines for release decisions and better policies for supervision of parolees can overcome the most serious problems. In contrast, Carolyn Turpin-Petrosino (1999) studied parole in New Jersey and concluded that changes in the law intended to control parole board discretion had no effect on parole decisionmaking. In another study of parole in Nebraska, Jon Proctor (1999) concluded that parole decisions were routine and based primarily on eligibility. He did not find much evidence of discretionary decisionmaking in release determinations. In a study of parole decisions with sex offenders, Huebner and Bynum (2006) report that parole decisions demonstrate effects of both legal and extralegal factors and that protection of public safety is a primary concern.

Conditions of Sentence

Whether the judge chooses probation or incarceration, the second decision in sentencing relates to the conditions of sentence. In cases of probation, the judge retains broad discretionary power to set the conditions of supervision. With incarceration sentences, the power is shared between the legislature and correctional authorities. Box 9.2 describes the basic sentences imposed on those convicted of felonies in 2000.

Box 9.2	Types of Felony Sentences Imposed by State Courts, by Offense, 2003

| Most serious Conviction offense | Percent of Felons Sentenced to Incarceration | | | |
	Total	Prison	Jail	Probation
All offenses	69%	41%	28%	31%
Violent Offenses	77	52	25	23
Murder	95	91	4	5
Sexual Assault	82	59	23	18
Rape	89	67	22	11
Other Sex Assault	78	55	23	22
Robbery	86	71	15	14
Aggravated Assault	71	42	29	29
Other violent	77	42	35	23
Property Offenses	66	38	28	34
Burglary	72	46	26	28
Larceny	67	36	31	33
Motor Vehicle Theft	76	37	39	24
Fraud	59	31	28	41
Drug Offenses	66	39	27	34
Possession	62	34	28	38
Trafficking	68	42	26	32
Weapons Offenses	73	45	28	27
Other Offenses	70	35	35	30

Source: M. Durose & P. Langan (2004), *Felony Sentences in State Courts, 2003* (Washington, DC: Bureau of Justice Statistics):4.

Probation

Probation, as a punishment for criminal behavior, is conditional liberty. The convicted offender is allowed to remain in the community under the supervision of a probation officer, provided that he or she abides by certain conditions of conduct established by the judge. Should the probationer violate the conditions of release, he or she may be taken before the court for a hearing, at which time probation may be revoked and the probationer sentenced to prison.

Probation sentences generally are regarded by offenders and the public as leniency (Gibbs, 1985; Israel & Dawes, 2002; Newman, 1983). Probation may be imposed in a variety of ways. The most common way in which probation is imposed is when a pronounced prison sentence is ordered suspended; that is, when the execution of sentence (the taking of an offender to prison) is suspended. Another very common practice is suspended sentencing, in which the offender is placed on probation before a sentence (prison term) is actually pronounced. A third method entails a direct sentence to probation, in which the sentence is a probation term. However, surprisingly few jurisdictions actually have statutes that specifically recognize and authorize probation as a criminal sentence. Other, less formal mechanisms for probation also may be used, but these more closely mirror "diversion" programs than criminal sentences. That is, there are some jurisdictions in which the conviction will not be entered if the defendant successfully completes the probation term. Spohn, DeLone, and Spears (1998) describe one such practice as a "decision to withhold adjudication" in Miami, Florida.

The offender on probation is supervised by a probation officer who works for the court, but the probationer is responsible to the judge. The judge establishes the conditions of release, including such things as "punish lessons," curfews, partial incarceration, and community service (Parisi, 1980; Umbreit, 1981). Because of the large number of judges, and their individual discretion, probation conditions include a wide variety of restrictions and prescriptions (Jaffe, 1979). These will be discussed more fully in Chapter 12.

Incarceration

While incarceration will be discussed in greater detail in Chapter 10, the conditions of a sentence of incarceration involve two dimensions: the type of facility and the length of term. In any jurisdiction with more than one correctional facility, there will be differences in the experience of being imprisoned depending upon where one is incarcerated. Prisons differ in terms of population (hardened, dangerous criminals, or first offenders), type of programs (educational/vocational or industrial), and level of custody (maximum-, medium-, or minimum-security). As an example of the variance in prison experiences, serving three years by working outside on a prison farm for half of the day and attending school for the other half is qualitatively different from spending the same amount of time locked inside a huge maximum-security prison making automobile tags all day.

The decision as to where an offender will serve his or her sentence is sometimes controlled by statute, so that offenders older than a certain age or those convicted of a specified crime must be incarcerated in a maximum-security prison. What the offender will do while incarcerated, and where he or she will be incarcerated, however, are questions that often are left to the discretion of correctional authorities.

The length of sentence is controlled by statutory provisions that define parole eligibility (minimum term) and by the **good time** (reductions in length of prison sentence for good behavior while incarcerated) policies and laws of the jurisdiction. Most states shorten prison terms for good behavior while incarcerated. Rottman and his colleagues (2000) reported that 30 of the 50 states had provisions for the award of sentence reductions for good behavior. In some states, this good time is credited only against the maximum term, that is, by advancing the date of mandatory release. In others, it is counted against the minimum term, that is, by advancing the date of parole eligibility. In still others, it is credited against both the minimum and maximum terms. Thus, the legislature, judge, and parole board all have some power in regard to sentence length, but correctional administrators who award and revoke good time also share in this decision.

Issues in Sentencing

Like the rest of the justice system, sentencing is fraught with questions and unresolved issues. The sentencing process is constantly emerging and evolving, sometimes returning to earlier practices and procedures that previously had been abandoned as inappropriate. Today sentencing is undergoing considerable scrutiny and reform. In the latter part of the nineteenth century, we began to abandon corporal and capital penalties and long, harsh prison terms in favor of rehabilitative strategies including more flexible prison sentences. In the last quarter of the twentieth century, we abandoned rehabilitative, indeterminate sentences in favor of more retributive fixed terms. Today, we are moving away from retributive sentences toward an unclear future.

Four core issues can be identified that allow us to better understand the complex problems of criminal sentencing. Disparity is a central issue today and is the concern at the base of many of the efforts to change criminal sentencing. Corporal and capital punishment have reemerged (perhaps continued) as issues in sentencing. The calculation of prison time and "truth in sentencing" is still a point of contention and, finally, we continue to grapple with the development of intermediate or alternative sanctions.

Disparity

Disparity refers to the unequal treatment of similar offenders at sentencing (Gottfredson, 1979). Most of us would agree that offenders with similar criminal histories who are convicted of the same offense ought to receive similar penalties. When differences in sentences appear among similar offenders, the differences generally are termed disparity. Yet, disparity actually refers to *unwarranted* differences (Gottfredson et al., 1978).

For example, if a jurisdiction follows an incapacitation sentencing rationale and has two first-offender burglars, it would not be disparity if one offender who was determined to pose a great risk of further crime was imprisoned, while the other, thought to pose little risk, was granted probation. Under the concerns of incapacitation, these offenders are not similar. The current debate over disparity hinges, in large measure, on the definition of "similar" (Vining, 1983).

Since 1976, several states and the federal government have enacted legislation that alters their sentencing structures. In large measure, these changes have been aimed at increasing equity (reducing disparity) in criminal sentences (Anspach & Monsen, 1989; Goodstein & Hepburn, 1983; LaGoy, Hussey & Kramer, 1978; Ulmer, 1997; von Hirsch & Hanrahan, 1979). Several states have implemented presumptive or determinate sentencing to ensure that similarly situated offenders receive similar sanctions. The results of these reforms are now being studied; the evaluation of their success is unclear (Griswold, 1987).

One type of determinate sentencing that states and the federal government have adopted in hopes of controlling disparity and ensuring more certainty in punishment is based on the use of sentencing guidelines. Sentencing guidelines identify the factors that judges should consider in sentencing and give an indication of what would be an acceptable penalty for each of many different types of cases. The federal government adopted a sentencing guideline system in November 1987 (*Criminal Justice Newsletter*, 1987). By 2005, 18 states also had developed sentencing guidelines. As shown in Box 9.3, in five jurisdictions, the guidelines are mandatory; in seven, they are voluntary. In the remaining jurisdictions, the guidelines are advisory, in that the judge may deviate from the guidelines. Most jurisdictions use decision matrices in which offense seriousness and risk or prior criminal record are used to determine appropriate sentences. A few use other types of guidelines in which general principles guide the sentencing judge in selecting an appropriate punishment (Griffin & Katz, 2002).

Box 9.3   Sentencing Guidelines in 2005

Guideline Type:	Number of States	Percent
None	32	64%
Voluntary	7	14
Advisory	6	12
Mandatory	5	10

Source: D. Rottman & S. Strickland (2006), *State Court Organization, 2005* (Washington, DC: Bureau of Justice Statistics):254-259.

The individual whims of justice system officials (judges, parole board members, etc.) that come out in the exercise of discretionary authority have been identified as the culprit for sentencing disparity. This concern is driven in large measure by perceptions that sentencing decisions reflect ethnic and sex discrimination more so than differences in crimes and risk of new crimes (Crew, 1991; Spohn, 2000; Spohn & Cederblom, 1991). To combat the disparity in decisions, reformers have moved to give legislatures tighter control over sentencing power by more closely defining sentences and the factors to be relied upon in determining punishments (Bureau of Justice Assistance, 1996). The effects of reform are unclear, and may involve changes in the rates at which people are incarcerated, the types of crimes for which offenders are imprisoned, and the lengths of terms (Tonry, 1999). Twenty-three states and the District of Columbia have created sentencing commissions, formal bodies assigned to assess and oversee criminal sentencing and recommend reforms.

In the Spring of 2004, the U.S. Supreme Court decided the case of *Blakely v. Washington* (2004). With the sentencing guidelines of the State of Washington, the judge is allowed to increase a prison term if the judge finds that the offense or offender represent an aggravated or more serious case than normal. The Supreme Court ruled that relying only on a judicial determination of facts in this instance violates a Constitutional right to have facts determined by the jury. It is still unclear what might be the full effects of this decision. While some commentators feared the decision spelled the end to sentencing guidelines, a more cautious and restrained assessment of the decision suggests that sentencing guidelines, especially in most state systems, can survive constitutional challenge (Skove, 2004). The next year the Court decided *United States v. Booker* (2005), in which it ruled that while federal judges must consider the federal sentencing guidelines, they are allowed to alter sentences for other factors.

Kathleen Daly and Rebecca Bordt (1995) reviewed available data on sentencing, looking for differences in punishment related to the sex of the defendant. They found that women were generally given less severe sentences than men. Daly and Bordt suggest that these differences are partly explained by differences in the types of offenses and prior records of men and women, but also probably reflect the justice system's recognition of the sex differences that exist in society. Cassia Spohn (1994) has reported similar persistent differences in the sentencing of blacks as compared to whites. Black defendants generally receive more severe sentences than whites, but again the picture is complicated by differences in rates of conviction for certain types of offenses and in prior criminal records of whites and blacks (Pratt, 1998). It may be that these differences in offenses and criminal records explain some of the differences in sentencing, yet it is also likely that criminal sentencing reflects the disadvantaged status of minority group members in American society (Zatz, 2000). Steffensmeier and Demuth (2001) found that sentences in Pennsylvania were harshest for Hispanic defendants and least harsh for white defendants, indicating that minority status, whether racial or ethnic, appears to be associated with sentencing outcomes. Gainey, Steen, and Engen (2005) found that offender characteristics such as sex, race, and the decision to go to trial versus enter a guilty plea explained the use of alternatives to incarceration with drug offenders. Griffin and Wooldredge (2006) reported that the adoption of sentencing guidelines in Ohio had mixed effects on the sentencing of female offenders, but that females might benefit from some "chivalrous" treatment in sentencing. In the end, the research indicates that the problems of sentencing disparity are complex and may not be easily solved.

Corporal and Capital Punishment

In America, from colonial times through the early part of the nineteenth century, most punishments for serious offenses involved physical pain, such as branding, maiming, flogging, and death. In recent history, we have abandoned those forms of punishment in favor of the more humane alternative of incarceration. Yet, more recently, there has been a rebirth of support for physical punishment (Foucault, 1977; Newman, 1978, 1983). The death penalty is back. In 1991, 14 inmates were executed and nearly 2,500 inmates were on death row in the United States. In 2005, 60 inmates were executed, and nearly 3,300 inmates were on death row. Between 1977 and 2001, there were 1,004 executions in 34 states and the federal system (Snell, 2006). The types of offenses for which the death penalty may be imposed are described in Box 9.4, while Box 9.5 describes the offenders who were on death rows around the country in 2005.

Box 9.4 Capital Offenses, by State, 2005

Alabama. Intentional murder with 18 aggravating factors (Ala. Stat. Ann. 13A-5-40(a)(1)-(18)).

Arizona.* First-degree murder accompanied by at least 1 of 14 aggravating factors (A.R.S. § 13-703(F)).

Arkansas.* Capital murder (Ark. Code Ann. 5-10-101) with a finding of at least 1of 10 aggravating circumstances; treason.

California.* First-degree murder with special circumstances; train wrecking; treason; perjury causing execution.

Colorado.* First-degree murder with at least 1 of 17 aggravating factors; treason.

Connecticut.* Capital felony with 8 forms of aggravated homicide (C.G.S. 53a-54b).

Delaware.* First-degree murder with aggravating circumstances.

Florida.* First-degree murder; felony murder; capital drug trafficking; capital sexual battery.

Georgia.* Murder; kidnapping with bodily injury or ransom when the victim dies; aircraft hijacking; treason.

Idaho.* First-degree murder with aggravating factors; aggravated kidnapping; perjury resulting in death.

Illinois.* First-degree murder with 1 of 21 aggravating circumstances.

Indiana.* Murder with 16 aggravating circumstances (IC 35-50-2-9).

Kansas.* Capital murder with 8 aggravating circumstances (KSA 21-3439).

Kentucky.* Murder with aggravating factors; kidnapping with aggravating factors (KRS 32.025).

Louisiana.* First-degree murder; aggravated rape of victim under age 12; treason (La. R.S. 14:30, 14:42, and 14:113).

Maryland.* First-degree murder, either premeditated or during the commission of a felony, provided that certain death eligibility requirements are satisfied.

Mississippi. Capital murder (97-3-19(2) MCA); aircraft piracy (97-25-55(1) MCA).

Missouri.* First-degree murder (565.020 RSMO 2000).

Box 9.4 (continued)

Montana. Capital murder with 1 of 9 aggravating circumstances (46-18-303 MCA); capital sexual assault (45-5-503 MCA).

Nebraska. First-degree murder with a finding of at least 1 statutorily-defined aggravating circumstance.

Nevada. First-degree murder with at least 1of 15 aggravating circumstances (NRS 200.030, 200.033, 200.035).

New Hampshire. Six categories of capital murder (RSA 630:1, RSA 630:5).

New Jersey. Murder by one's own conduct, by solicitation, committed in furtherance of a narcotics conspiracy, or during commission of a crime of terrorism (NJSA 2C:11-3c).

New Mexico. First-degree murder with at least 1 of 7 statutorily-defined aggravating circumstances (Section 30-2-1 A, NMSA).

New York. First-degree murder with 1 of 13 aggravating factors (NY Penal Law §125.27).

North Carolina. First-degree murder (NCGS §14-17).

Ohio. Aggravated murder with at least 1 of 10 aggravating circumstances (O.R.C. secs. 2903.01, 2929.02, and 2929.04).

Oklahoma. First-degree murder in conjunction with a finding of at least 1 of 8 statutorily-defined aggravating circumstances.

Oregon. Aggravated murder (ORS 163.095).

Pennsylvania. First-degree murder with 18 aggravating circumstances.

South Carolina. Murder with 1 of 11 aggravating circumstances (§ 16-3-20(C)(a)).

South Dakota. First-degree murder with 1 of 10 aggravating circumstances; aggravated kidnapping.

Tennessee. First-degree murder with 1 of 15 aggravating circumstances (Tenn. Code Ann. § 39-13-204).

Texas. Criminal homicide with 1 of 9 aggravating circumstances (TX Penal Code 19.03).

Utah. Aggravated murder (76-5-202, Utah Code Annotated).

Virginia. First-degree murder with 1 of 13 aggravating circumstances (VA Code § 18.2-31).

Washington. Aggravated first-degree murder.

Wyoming. First-degree murder.

*As of December 31, 2005, 27 States excluded mentally retarded persons from capital sentencing: Arizona, Arkansas, California, Colorado, Connecticut, Delaware, Florida, Georgia, Idaho, Illinois, Indiana, Kansas, Kentucky, Louisiana, Maryland, Missouri, Nebraska, Nevada, New Mexico, New York, North Carolina, Ohio, South Dakota, Tennessee, Utah, Virginia, and Washington. Mental retardation is a mitigating factor in South Carolina.

Source: T. Snell (2006), *Capital Punishment, 2005* (Washington, DC: Bureau of Justice Statistics):2.

Flogging or whipping as a sanction for offenses was finally abandoned in this country in the 1970s, when the state of Delaware removed the whipping post from its penitentiary. In a review of case law through the year 2000, Maddan and Hallahan (2002) conclude that is possible that corporal punishment, in the form of whipping, could be revived in the United States. The constitutionality of corporal and capital punishment is always subject to question. The U.S. Supreme Court has not ruled the death penalty to be cruel and unusual punishment or to

Box 9.5	Characteristics of the Death Row Population, December 31, 2005

Total Number Under Sentence of Death	3,254
Male	98.4%
Female	1.6
White	55.5%
Black	42.2
Other	2.4
Hispanic	12.7%
Non-Hispanic	87.3
Education:	
Less than 8th Grade	14.3%
9th – 11th Grade	36.9
High School/GED	39.6
Any College	9.2
Median	11th Grade
Married	22.2%
Divorced/Separated	20.5
Widowed	2.9
Never Married	54.4

Source: T. Snell (2006), *Capital Punishment, 2005* (Washington, DC: Bureau of Justice Statistics):6.

be otherwise unconstitutional. Moreover, in the 1976 case of *Gregg v. Georgia*, the Court held that the death penalty, per se, is not unconstitutional. Earlier, in *Furman v. Georgia* (1972), the Court focused on the procedures by which the death penalty was imposed. Having found the existing procedures too vague and unstructured, the Court did not address the issue of the death penalty itself. The *Gregg* decision was the first of several in which revised procedures for imposing the death penalty were reviewed by the Court. Given an acceptable procedure (jury recommendation based on a presentation of aggravating and mitigating factors identified in the statute), the Court also addressed the constitutionality of the death penalty itself.

Some support the death penalty as an incapacitative sanction, saying that murderers pose too great a risk to society. Vito and Wilson (1988) addressed this issue and found that most prisoners in their sample who were sentenced to death were not particularly dangerous. Less than 25 percent of death row inmates who were released committed new crimes, and none committed a new homicide. Others suggest that an alternative to capital punishment is to impose life sentences without possibility of parole (Cheatwood, 1988). The debate over capital punishment continues. The public, it appears, specifically supports capital punishment, and generally is in favor of harsher criminal sanctions (Flanagan, 1987). Public opinion surveys reveal that more than three-quarters of those polled support capital punishment in general. However, general support for the death penalty does not translate into support for capital punishment in specific cases (Vito & Keil, 1998). Durham, Elrod, and Kinkade (1996) presented respondents with examples of specific cases and found that people make distinctions between different kinds of murders and murderers so that the general agreement on support for the death penalty in the abstract translates into different sentencing recommendations in particular cases.

Those supporting corporal punishment argue that physical pain, properly administered, is less destructive, less costly, and more effective than lengthy incarceration (Newman, 1983). Those who are opposed to corporal punishment suggest that such penalties will continue to be considered cruel and unusual and, therefore, unconstitutional. If the issue were raised in the U.S. Supreme Court, it is not clear how the Court would decide the question. A principal rationale in support of corporal punishment is that our current practices are not effective in controlling crime, and that our prisons and jails are too crowded to accommodate many more prisoners. Added to this is the reasoning that as death is allowed as a penalty for crime, penalties less than death should also not be considered too severe.

To date no state has reinstituted corporal punishment, but there are continuing calls for physical punishments, including "chain gang" service. Among intermediate penalties are programs of community service in which convicted offenders are required to perform some labor, often physical, as part of their sentence. It is difficult to predict how the system will respond to suggestions for a return to corporal punishment. On the one hand, it could be seen as a practical alternative to incarceration for those convicted of serious offenses for which probation seems too lenient. On the other hand, it is entirely likely that, if accepted, corporal punishment would be added to current penalties, resulting in sentences to prison with corporal punishment, or bodily punishment as a condition of probation. Whatever the result, the resurgence of this once-discredited response to criminality illustrates the intractable nature of the issues involved in sentencing.

The importance of pain as a component of criminal punishments, however, has regained prominence. Todd Clear (1994) has written about how the imposition of harm (pain) for harm has become a central component of contemporary sentencing and correctional practice. The renewed emphasis on the imposition of physical suffering on criminal offenders is illustrated by the popularity of **boot camp** or "shock incarceration" programs in prisons (Lutze, 1998). By 1996 there were more than 50 boot camp programs operating in 32 states (Bourque, Han & Hill, 1996:7). As seen in Box 9.6, these programs include a heavy emphasis on physical training and manual labor. The programs are expected to be more physically demanding than traditional imprisonment, and are of shorter duration than most prison sentences. In essence, the increase in physical pain involved in the boot camp experience balances a shorter length of confinement. While we may not adopt electric shock or return to flogging offenders, the spread of "boot camps" indicates that we are not opposed to using some forms of corporal sanctions.

Box 9.6	Program Elements of Boot Camp Programs Reported by Correctional Administrators

Program Element	Percentage of Programs
Physical Training	100%
Physical Labor	100%
Drill/Ceremony	100%
Alcohol Treatment	100%
Drug Treatment	100%
Substance Abuse Education	100%
Basic Education	96%
Vocational Education	46%

Source: E. Cowles, T. Castellano & L. Gransky (1995), *"Boot Camp" Drug Treatment and Aftercare Interventions: An Evaluation Review* (Washington, DC: National Institute of Justice):6.

Using Time as a Penalty: Truth in Sentencing

We already have seen how provisions for good time affect sentencing decisions by adding correctional administrators to the list of officials who exercise authority in sentencing decisions. What is not as clear is the complexity of using time as a penalty. Although the death penalty can be used for heinous murders, the basic limitation on criminal penalties in the United States is time. While conditions of confinement vary, for the individual offender the length of term is critical. How long an offender serves is dependent on several factors, each of which has importance for the severity of punishment and the operation of correctional institutions.

Prison time is typically measured in days, although sentences are generally imposed in months and years. Most states with provisions for good-time award reductions of sentence on a "per days served" basis. Good time is expected to be an incentive to encourage inmates to obey prison rules. James Emshoff and William Davidson (1987) recognized that sentence reductions may affect inmate behavior, but contended that other factors are at least as important. A typical model awards one day of good time for every two served, so that after serving 20 days, 10 days are added to complete the month. A six-year sentence is then reduced to four years (one-third reduction). In some states, good time is awarded on a sliding scale so the longer the sentence, or the longer the term served, the more good-time days received. Thus, an inmate could earn 10 days for every 30 for the first three years, and 15 days for every 30 for the next three years, and so on, "sliding" up the scale of good-time award. To this sentence may be added "meritorious" good time, earned by the inmate for special accomplishments such as exceptional industry, donating blood, and the like. Reductions for good behavior, then, can be substantial.

Whatever the reductions for good behavior, there are other time calculations that are questionable. For an offender unable to secure pretrial release on bail, what part of his or her pretrial time counts as time served? The time spent in jail after conviction but before going to prison generally counts toward a prison sentence. The decision whether to count the time spent in jail prior to conviction is generally left to the discretion of the judge or correctional authorities. Thus, an offender who is in jail for six months prior to conviction and three months after conviction, prior to transport to the prison, may be granted nine months off his or her sentence, and generally must be granted three months. A question remains, however, as to whether the offender also should be granted good time for time served before going to prison. Generally, good time is not awarded for time spent in jail.

A final consideration is the ability of the judge to impose terms for multiple convictions to run either consecutively or concurrently. A **consecutive term** is one in which each sentence must be served in order, one following the other. A **concurrent term** is one in which all the sentences run at the same time. Two five-year terms imposed consecutively total 10 years; the same terms imposed concurrently total five years.

The unresolved problem in the calculation of prison time is that the imposed sentence generally is not the same as the actual term served, as can be seen in Box 9.7. Von Hirsch and Hanrahan (1979) suggest that one of the major difficulties faced in sentencing reform is that we do not sentence offenders in "real time." The public sees the sentence imposed as being the maximum term ordered by the judge, without reference to good time or to the fact that concurrent terms are imposed frequently. Thus, if an offender sentenced to three concurrent five-year terms is released in two years, the public may begin to believe that the law does not mean what it says. The Bureau of Justice Statistics (Durose & Langan, 2003) estimates that felons sentenced to prison in state courts in 2000 will serve only 55 percent of their sentences before being released.

Box 9.7	Estimated Percentage of Sentence to be Served in State Prison by Conviction Offense		
Conviction Offense	Mean Sentence	Time to be Served	Percent of Sentence
All Offenses	53 mo.	27 mo.	51%
Violent Offenses	84 mo.	52 mo.	6%
Property Offenses	41 mo.	20 mo.	49%
Drug Offenses	48 mo.	20 mo.	43%
Weapon Offenses	38 mo.	24 mo.	63%
Other Offenses	39 mo.	19 mo.	50%

Source: M. Durose & P. Langan (2004), *Felony Sentences in State Courts, 2003* (Washington, DC: Bureau of Justice Statistics):5.

Concern about the gap between the length of sentence imposed by the court and that actually served by convicted offenders spurred a call for "truth in sentencing." In 1995, Congress passed legislation calling for states to develop **"truth in sentencing"** so that those convicted of violent offenses will serve at least 85 percent of the term they receive. Federal aid is available to states that adopt such truth-in-sentencing laws, and many states have changed or are considering a change in their sentencing laws to achieve more truthful sentences. Thus far, the solutions sought by the states involve reserving prison space for those convicted of violent crimes by reducing the rate of imprisonment and length of terms for nonviolent offenders. Of course, one solution to the problem would be the imposition of prison sentences in "real time." However, most legislators are unwilling to admit to the public that violent offenders, on average, will serve a little more than four years instead of the 10 years to which they are sentenced.

As a result, the impact of truth in sentencing is likely to be the diversion of repeat, nonviolent offenders to community sanctions such as probation, and a substantial lengthening of terms served by violent offenders. The effects of these changes on both community corrections and prison populations are difficult to estimate. It is clear, however, that truth-in-sentencing as currently envisioned will change both prison and community corrections populations. Ditton and Wilson (1999) reviewed the impact of truth-in-sentencing laws through 1998, noting that offenders sentenced under the new laws will not be released for many years and thus it is too early to tell the full effects of the reform. Box 9.8 summarizes their findings. Durose and Langan (2007:3) report that "the average time served in prison for a violent felony remained relatively stable between 1994 and 2004."

Intermediate Sanctions

Throughout the past decade there has been increasing interest in the development and implementation of **intermediate sanctions** for crime or punishments that fall somewhere between imprisonment and traditional probation. Historically, sentencing judges have been given a choice between community supervision and confinement in prison or jail as the primary sanctions for crime. Especially as the numbers of people convicted of crime have increased, and prison and jail populations have exceeded the capacity of institutions, these choices have been seen as inadequate. In 1985, Pierre DuPont called for the development of a meaningful continuum of sanctions ranging from no restriction to maximum-security incarceration. This call has been echoed by others (Klein, 1997; Morris & Tonry, 1990; Petersilia, 1987).

In response to the perceived need for a wider variety of sanctions, a number of innovative practices have emerged. These include various combinations of incarceration and community supervision dispositions. Specific forms of these sanctions will be discussed in more detail in Chapters 12 and 13, but a brief listing is in order. Sanctions combining incarceration with supervision have emerged, including shock probation, shock parole, placement in community residential facilities, home incarceration, and **split sentences** (sentences combining a period

Box 9.8 The "Truth in Sentencing" Reform

Highlights

Three decades of sentencing reform—1970s through 1990s

- *Indeterminate sentencing:* Common in the early 1970s, parole boards have the authority to release offenders from prison.

- *Determinate sentencing:* States introduced fixed prison terms which could be reduced by good-time or earned-time credits.

- *Mandatory minimum sentences:* States added statutes requiring offenders to be sentenced to a specified amount of prison time.

- *Truth in sentencing:* First enacted in 1984, TIS laws require offenders to serve a substantial portion of their prison sentence. Parole eligibility and good-time credits are restricted or eliminated.

- Violent offenders released from prison in 1996 were sentenced to serve an average of 85 months in prison. Prior to release they served about half of their prison sentence or 45 months.

- Under truth-in-sentencing laws requiring 85% of the sentence, violent offenders would serve an average of 88 months in prison based on the average sentence for violent offenders admitted to prison in 1996.

- Nearly 7 in 10 State prison admissions for a violent offense in 1997 were in States requiring offenders to serve at least 85% of their sentence.

- By 1998, States and the District of Columbia met the Federal Truth-in-Sentencing Incentive Grant Program eligibility criteria. Eleven States adopted truth-in-sentencing laws in 1995, 1 year after the 1994 Crime Act.

Discrepancy between sentence and time served

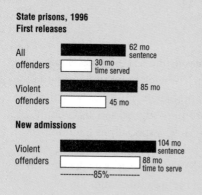

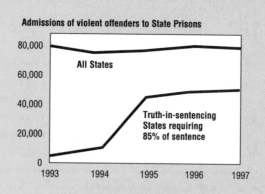

Source: P. Ditton & D. Wilson (1999), *Truth in Sentencing in State Prisons* (Washington, DC: Bureau of Justice Statistics):1.

of incarceration with a period of probation supervision) (Petersilia, Lurigio & Byrne, 1992). So too, penalties have been developed that make the experience of community supervision more severe. These include day reporting, intensive supervision, electronic monitoring, and community service orders.

The growth of these penalties blurs the traditional distinction between incarceration and community supervision. Prison boot camps involve a short, intense incarceration. The offender goes to prison, but for a much shorter period. Observers note that these sanctions allow gradations in punishment along a continuum (Holsinger & Latessa, 1999; McCarthy, 1987; Schwartz & Travis, 1996). Thus, penalties can escalate from traditional probation supervision through intensive supervision to day reporting (offenders report to the probation office daily). If more restrictive punishments are desired, the offender could be placed under house arrest (restricted to his or her home), sent to a residential facility (halfway house), or sent to prison. As Box 9.9 shows, judges often impose multiple penalties on convicted offenders.

Recalling our discussion of sentencing disparity, the development of a range of punishments is potentially troublesome. If sentencing decisions were suspected

Box 9.9	Additional Penalties Imposed on Felons by Conviction Offense, 2003

| | Percent of felons with an additional penalty of: | | | | |
Most serious Conviction offense	Fine	Restitution	Treatment	Community Service	Other
All offenses	25%	12%	3%	4%	7%
Violent Offenses	23%	11%	3%	3%	6%
Murder	17	7	1	1	1
Sexual Assault	22	10	4	2	7
Rape	21	10	4	1	6
Other Sex Assault	23	10	3	2	8
Robbery	13	10	1	2	4
Aggravated Assault	27	11	3	3	7
Other violent	26	12	2	4	9
Property Offenses	24%	21%	2%	4%	6%
Burglary	23	20	2	4	5
Larceny	21	19	1	5	7
Motor Vehicle Theft	22	19	2	3	11
Fraud	28	24	2	5	8
Drug Offenses	27%	6%	6%	4%	7%
Possession	25	3	11	5	11
Trafficking	27	8	2	3	5
Weapons Offenses	18%	4%	2%	4%	6%
Other Offenses	29%	10%	3%	4%	8%

Source: M. Durose & P. Langan (2004), *Felony Sentences in State Courts, 2003* (Washington, DC: Bureau of Justice Statistics):10.

of being based on prejudice when only a few choices were available, the provision of more choices increases the chances of disparate treatment. The more things that can be done to punish an offender, the greater the discretion of sentencing decisionmakers. Conversely, the relative degree of disparity may be reduced. Rather than a simple "either/or" issue of incarceration, disparate sentences may be closer in degree of restrictiveness. The difference between intensive supervision and day reporting is not as great as that between probation and prison.

See Box 9.10 for a table of selected court cases on sentencing.

Box 9.10 Selected Court Cases on Sentencing

Williams v. New York 377 U.S. 241 (1949)	There is no constitutional right to review a presentence investigation (PSI) report. See later controlling case, *Gardner v. Florida* (1977).
Mempa v. Rhay 389 U.S. 128 (1967)	An offender has the right to representation by counsel at the point of sentencing.
Furman v. Georgia 408 U.S. 238 (1972)	Current procedures for imposing the death penalty violate the equal protection clause of the Fourteenth Amendment and the prohibition against cruel and unusual punishment.
Gregg v. Georgia 428 U.S. 153 (1976)	Death penalty statutes that contain sufficient safeguards against arbitrary and capricious imposition are constitutional.
Gardner v. Florida 430 U.S. 349 (1977)	When the death penalty is imposed as a result of information contained in a presentence investigation (PSI) report, the defense has a right to review that report.

Source: Portions of this table were adapted from R.V. del Carmen, S.E. Ritter & B.A. Witt (2005), *Briefs of Leading Cases in Corrections*, 4th ed. (Newark, NJ: LexisNexis Matthew Bender).

Due Process, Crime Control, and Sentencing in the Whole System

The sentencing decision links the court subsystem to the correctional subsystem of the justice process. Sentencing decisions reflect the demands and stresses placed on corrections, and indicate how the justice process reacts to social change. For example, with the emergence of drug abuse as a serious criminal problem, the sentencing of those convicted of drug-related offenses has changed. Many more drug offenders are sentenced to prison than in the past, and their sentences to prison are longer than before. Thus, as society has come to see drug offenders as more serious criminals, the increased seriousness has been reflected in more severe sentences. These sentences have changed the composition of correctional (especially prison) populations (Barnes & Kingsnorth, 1996; Beck, 1997; Kraska, 1992).

Further, as the corrections subsystem has struggled with crowding, the sentencing decisions of criminal courts have changed. The imposition of probation sentences for felons increased (Champion, 1988; Petersilia et al., 1985). Judges are using jail sentences as sanctions for those convicted of felonies (McCarthy, 1989). Moreover, the actual length of sentence served by convicted offenders has frequently been reduced by correctional decisionmakers (Farnsworth, Golden & Tester, 1991). The interplay between corrections and sentencing that is driven by prison and jail crowding illustrates the systemic nature of the justice process.

A Maricopa County female chain gang in traditional black and white striped uniforms is pictured cleaning up trash in Phoenix, Arizona, in April 1997. Convicted criminals laboring by the roadside, linked together with shackles and chains, are no longer ghosts of Southern-style justice, as chain gangs make a comeback across the United States. *Photo credit: AP Photo/Eric Drotter.*

Remember too, that one of the primary motivations for reform of criminal sentencing and the development of alternative sanctions is a desire for fairness. Thus, not only do we seek punitive and incapacitative alternatives to prison for crime control reasons, we seek equitable sanctions for diverse individuals. The sentencing decision is the point at which the full weight of state power can be brought to bear on the individual. The challenge for sentencing is to achieve crime control goals while respecting the rights of the individual offender. Yet, available evidence suggests that criminal sentences reflect differences in sex, race, and age (Spohn, 2000; Steffensmeier, Kramer & Ulmer, 1995). If we seek equal treatment of persons at sentencing, it is likely that we will first have to develop equal treatment of persons in the broader society.

Perhaps the major obstacle to reforming criminal sentencing in the United States lies not in sentencing's considerable complexity of operation and calculation, but more in the lack of effort among our citizens to achieve understanding of the sentencing process. In order to achieve a rational and workable system of sentencing, it may first be necessary to be more open and honest about the meaning of criminal sentences—and more consistent in our purposes served by criminal sanctions.

Review Questions

1. Identify the four traditional purposes of criminal penalties.

2. What types of errors are involved in the prediction of dangerousness at sentencing?

3. Distinguish between determinate and indeterminate criminal sentencing structures.

4. What is the presentence investigation, and what purposes does it serve?

5. What is the sentencing hearing, and what takes place at one?

6. Identify two principal types of sanctions imposed on serious criminal offenders.

7. What is meant by sentencing disparity?

8. Besides sentencing disparity, identify two other current issues in criminal sentencing.

References

Adams, S. (1961). *Effectiveness of Interview Therapy with Older Youth Authority Wards: An Interim Evaluation of the PICO Project.* Sacramento, CA: California Youth Authority.

Alschuler, A.W. (1978). "Sentencing Reform and Prosecutorial Power: A Critique of Recent Proposals for 'Fixed' and 'Presumptive' Sentencing." In *Determinate Sentencing: Reform or Regression?* Washington, DC: U.S. Government Printing Office, 59-88.

Anspach, D. & S. Monsen (1989). "Determinate Sentencing, Formal Rationality, and Khadi Justice in Maine: An Application of Weber's Typology." *Journal of Criminal Justice* 17(6):471-485.

Bailey, W. (1966). "Correctional Outcome: An Evaluation of 100 Reports." *Journal of Criminal Law, Criminology & Police Science* 57:153-160.

Barnes, C. & R. Kingsnorth (1996). "Race, Drug, and Criminal Sentencing: Hidden Effects of the Criminal Law." *Journal of Criminal Justice* 24(1):39-55.

Beck, A. (1997). "Growth, Change, and Stability in the U.S. Prison Population, 1980-1995." *Corrections Management Quarterly* 1(2):1-14.

Bennett, L. (1995). "In Defense of Parole—Is It Worth the Effort?" *Perspectives* 19(3):14-17.

Benson, M. (1990). "Emotions and Adjudication: Status Degradation among White-Collar Criminals." *Justice Quarterly* 7(3):515-528.

Bureau of Justice Statistics (1984). *Sentencing Practices in 13 States.* Washington, DC: U.S. Department of Justice.

Bourque, B., M. Han & S. Hill (1996). *A National Survey of Aftercare Provisions for Boot Camp Graduates.* Washington, DC: National Institute of Justice.

Bureau of Justice Assistance (1996). *National Assessment of Structured Sentencing.* Washington, DC: Bureau of Justice Assistance.

Carter, R.M. & L.T. Wilkins (1967). "Some Factors in Sentencing Policy." *Journal of Criminal Law, Criminology & Police Science* 58:503.

Casey, P. & D. Rottman (2003). *Problem-Solving Courts: Models and Trends.* Williamsburg, VA: National Center for State Courts.

Champion, D. (1988). "Felony Plea Bargaining and Probation: A Growing Judicial and Prosecutorial Dilemma." *Journal of Criminal Justice* 16(4):291-301.

Cheatwood, D. (1988). "The Life-Without-Parole Sanction: Its Current Status and a Research Agenda." *Crime & Delinquency* 34(1):43-59.

Clark, J., J. Austin & D. Henry (1997). *"Three Strikes and You're Out": A Review of State Legislation.* Washington, DC: National Institute of Justice.

Clear, T. (1994). *Harm in American Penology: Offenders, Victims, and Their Communities.* Albany, NY: SUNY Press.

Crew, B. K., (1991). "Sex Differences in Criminal Sentencing: Chivalry or Patriarchy?" *Justice Quarterly* 8(1):59-83.

Criminal Justice Newsletter (1987). "Despite Warnings of 'Chaos,' No Delay on Sentencing Reforms." *Criminal Justice Newsletter* 18(21):1, November 2, 1987.

Cullen, F.T. & K.E. Gilbert (1982). *Reaffirming Rehabilitation.* Cincinnati: Anderson.

Czajkoski, E.H. (1973). "Exposing the Quasi-Judicial Role of the Probation Officer." *Federal Probation* 37:9.

Daly, K. & R. Bordt (1995). "Sex Effects and Sentencing: An Analysis of the Statistical Literature." *Justice Quarterly* 12(1):141-175.

Ditton, P. & D. Wilson (1999). *Truth in Sentencing in State Prisons.* Washington, DC: Bureau of Justice Statistics.

Dubois, P.L. (1981). "Disclosure of Presentence Reports in the United States District Courts." *Federal Probation* 45(1):3-9.

DuPont, P. (1985). *Expanding Sentencing Options: A Governor's Perspective.* Washington, DC: U.S. Department of Justice.

Durose, M. & P. Langan (2007). *Felony Sentences in State Courts, 2004.* Washington, DC: Bureau of Justice Statistics

Durose, M. & P. Langan (2004). *Felony Sentences in State Courts, 2002.* Washington, DC: Bureau of Justice Statistics

Durose, M. & P. Langan (2003). *Felony Sentences in State Courts, 2000.* Washington, DC: Bureau of Justice Statistics.

Durham, A.M. (1988). "Crime Seriousness and Punitive Severity: An Assessment of Social Attitudes." *Justice Quarterly* 5(1):131-153.

Durham, A., H. Elrod & P. Kinkade (1996). "Public Support for the Death Penalty: Beyond Gallup." *Justice Quarterly* 13(4):705-736.

Emshoff, J.G. & W.S. Davidson (1987). "The Effect of 'Good Time' Credit on Inmate Behavior: A Quasi-Experiment." *Criminal Justice and Behavior* 14(3):335-351.

Farnsworth, M., J. Golden & K. Tester (1991). "Felony Court Processing in an Urban County: Coping with a Limited Capacity to Punish." *Journal of Criminal Justice* 19(5):421-438.

Flanagan, T.J. (1987). "Change and Influence in Popular Criminology: Public Attributions of Crime Causation." *Journal of Criminal Justice* 15(3):231-243.

Flores, A., A. Russell, E. Latessa & L. Travis (2005). "Evidence of Professionalism or Quackery: Measuring Practitioner Awareness of Risk/Need Factors and Effective Treatment Strategies." *Federal Probation* 69(2):9-14.

Foucault, M. (1977). *Discipline and Punish.* New York: Pantheon.

Gainey, R., S. Steen & R. Engen (2005). "Exercising Options: An Assessment of the Use of Alternative Sanctions for Drug Offenders." *Justice Quarterly* 22(4):488-520.

Gendreau, P. (1996). "The Principles of Effective Interventions with Offenders." In A. Harland (ed.), *Choosing Correctional Options that Work: Defining the Demand and Evaluating the Supply.* Thousand Oaks, CA: Sage.

Gendreau, P. & R. Ross (1987). "Revivification of Rehabilitation: Evidence from the 1980s." *Justice Quarterly* 4(3):349-407.

Gertz, M. & L. Gould (1995). "Fear of Punishment and the Willingness to Engage in Criminal Behavior: A Research Note." *Journal of Criminal Justice* 23(4):377-384.

Gibbs, J.J. (1985). "Clients' Views of Community Corrections." In L.F. Travis III (ed.), *Probation, Parole, and Community Corrections.* Prospect Heights, IL: Waveland.

Goodstein, L. & J. Hepburn (1983). *Determinate Sentencing and Imprisonment.* Cincinnati: Anderson.

Gottfredson, D.M., C.A. Cosgrove, L.T. Wilkins, J. Wallerstein & C. Rauh (1978). *Classification for Parole Decision Policy.* Washington, DC: U.S. Government Printing Office.

Gottfredson, M.R. (1979). "Parole Guidelines and the Reduction of Sentencing Disparity: A Preliminary Study." *Journal of Research in Crime and Delinquency* 16(2):218-231.

Greenwood, P. (1982). *Selective Incapacitation.* Santa Monica, CA: RAND.

Griffin, B. & L. Katz (2002). "Sentencing Consistency: Basic Principles Instead of Numerical Grids: The Ohio Plan." *Case Western Reserve Law Review* 53(1):1-75.

Griffin, T. & J. Wooldredge (2006). "Sex-Based Disparities in Felony Dispositions Before and After Sentencing Reform in Ohio." *Criminology* 44(4):893-923.

Griset, P. (1995). "Determinate Sentencing and Agenda Building: A Case Study of the Failure of a Reform." *Journal of Criminal Justice* 23(4):349-362.

Griset, P. (2002). "New Sentencing Laws Follow Old Patterns: A Florida Case Study." *Journal of Criminal Justice* 30(4):287-301.

Griswold, D. B. (1987). "Deviation from Sentencing Guidelines: The Issue of Unwarranted Disparity." *Journal of Criminal Justice* 15(4):317-329.

Harland, A. (ed.) (1996). *Choosing Correctional Options That Work: Defining the Demand and Evaluating the Supply.* Thousand Oaks, CA: Sage.

Harris, J. & P. Jesilow (2000). "It's Not the Old Ball Game: Three Strikes and the Courtroom Workgroup." *Justice Quarterly* 17(1):185-203.

Holsinger, A. & E. Latessa (1999). "An Empirical Evaluation of a Sanction Continuum: Pathways Through the Juvenile Justice System." *Journal of Criminal Justice* 27(2):155-172.

Huebner, B. & T. Bynum (2006). "An Analysis of Parole Decision Making Using a Sample of Sex Offender: A Focal Concerns Perspective." *Criminology* 44(4):961-992.

Israel, M. & J. Dawes (2002). "'Something From Nothing': Shifting Credibility in Community Correctional Programmes in Australia." *Criminal Justice* 2(1):5-25.

Jaffe, H.J. (1979). "Probation with a Flair: A Look at Some Out-of-the Ordinary Conditions." *Federal Probation* 43(1):25-36.

Johnson, I. & R. Sigler (1995). "Community Attitudes: A Study of Definitions and Punishment of Spouse Abusers and Child Abusers." *Journal of Criminal Justice* 23(5):477-487.

Kingsnorth, R., L. Alvis & G. Gavia (1993). "Specific Deterrence and the DUI Offender: The Impact of a Decade of Reform." *Justice Quarterly* 10(2):265-288.

Klein, A.R. (1997). *Alternative Sentencing, Intermediate Sanctions and Probation*, 2nd ed. Cincinnati: Anderson.

Kovandzic, T. (2001). "The Impact of Florida's Habitual Offender Law on Crime." *Criminology* 39(1):179-204.

Kovandzic, T., J. Sloan & L. Vieraitis (2004). "'Striking Out' as Crime Reduction Policy: The Impact of 'Three Strikes' Laws on Crime Rates in U.S. Cities." *Justice Quarterly* 21(2):207-239.

Kramer, J. & J. Ulmer (1996). "Sentencing Disparity and Departures from Guidelines." *Justice Quarterly* 13(1):81-106.

Kraska, P. (1992). "The Processing of Drug Arrestees: Questioning the Assumption of an Ambivalent Reaction." *Journal of Criminal Justice* 20(6):517-525.

LaGoy, S.P., F.A. Hussey & J.H. Kramer (1978). "A Comparative Assessment of Determinate Sentencing in the Four Pioneer States." *Crime & Delinquency* 24:385-400.

LeClair, D. & S. Guarino-Ghezzi (1991). "Does Incapacitation Guarantee Public Safety: Lessons from Massachusetts' Furlough and Prerelease Programs." *Justice Quarterly* 8(1):9-36.

Logan, C. & G. Gaes (1993). "Meta-analysis and the Rehabilitation of Punishment." *Justice Quarterly* 10(2):245-263.

Lutze, F. (1998). "Are Shock Incarceration Programs More Rehabilitative Than Traditional Prisons? A Survey of Inmates." *Justice Quarterly* 15(3):547-566.

Mackenzie, D. (1997). "Criminal Justice and Crime Prevention." In L. Sherman, D. Gottfredson, J. Eck, P. Reuter & S. Bushway (eds.), *Preventing Crime: What Works, What Doesn't, What's Promising*. Washington, DC: U.S. Department of Justice, 9-1- 9-76.

Maddan, S. & W. Hallahan (2002). "Corporal Punishment in the 21st Century: An Examination of Supreme Court Decisions in the 1990s to Predict the Reemergence of Flagellance." *Journal of Crime and Justice* 25(2):97-120.

Martinson, R.M. (1974). "What Works?" *The Public Interest* (Spring):22.

McCarthy, B. (1989). "The Use of Jail Confinement in the Disposition of Felony Arrests." *Journal of Criminal Justice* 17(4):241-251.

McCarthy, B. (ed.) (1987). *Intermediate Punishments.* Monsey, NY: Criminal Justice Press.

Morris, N. & M. Tonry (1990). *Between Prison and Probation: Intermediate Punishments in a Rational Sentencing System.* Oxford: Oxford University Press.

Myers, L. & S. Reid (1995). "The Importance of County Context in the Measurement of Sentence Disparity: The Search for Routinization." *Journal of Criminal Justice* 23(3):223-241.

Nagin, D. & G. Pogarsky (2001). "Integrating Celerity, Impulsivity, and Extralegal Sanction Threats Into a Model of General Deterrence: Theory and Evidence." *Criminology* 39(4):865-892.

Newman, G.R. (1978). *The Punishment Response.* Philadelphia: J.B. Lippincott.

Newman, G.R. (1983). *Just and Painful.* New York: Macmillan.

Parisi, N. (1980). "Combining Incarceration and Probation." *Federal Probation* 44(2):3-12.

Paternoster, R. (1987). "The Deterrent Effect of the Perceived Certainty and Severity of Punishment: A Review of the Evidence and Issues." *Justice Quarterly* 4(2):173-217.

Petersilia, J. (1987). *Expanding Options for Criminal Sentencing.* Santa Monica, CA: RAND.

Petersilia, J., A. Lurigio & J. Byrne (1992). "Introduction: The Emergence of Intermediate Sanctions." In J. Byrne, A. Lurigio & J. Petersilia (eds.), *Smart Sentencing: The Emergence of Intermediate Sanctions.* Beverly Hills, CA: Sage, 1992, ix-xv.

Petersilia, J., S. Turner, J. Kahan & J. Peterson (1985). *Granting Felons Probation: Public Risks and Alternatives.* Santa Monica, CA: RAND.

Piquero, A. & G. Rengert (1999). "Studying Deterrence with Active Residential Burglars." *Justice Quarterly* 16(2):451-471.

Pogarsky, G. (2002). "Identifying 'Deterrable' Offenders: Implications for Research on Deterrence." *Justice Quarterly* 19(3):343-369.

Pratt, T. (1998). "Race and Sentencing: A Meta-Analysis of Conflicting Empirical Research Results." *Journal of Criminal Justice* 26(6):513-523.

Proctor, J. (1999). "The 'New Parole': An Analysis of Parole Board Decision Making as a Function of Eligibility." *Journal of Crime and Justice* 22(2):193-217.

Rottman, D. & S. Strickland (2006). *State Court Organization, 2005.* Washington, DC: Bureau of Justice Statistics.

Rottman, D., C. Flango, M. Cantrell, R. Hansen & N. LaFountain (2000). *State Court Organization, 1998.* Washington, DC: Bureau of Justice Statistics.

Saint-Germain, M. & R. Calamia (1996). "Three Strikes and You're In: A Streams and Windows Model of Incremental Policy Change." *Journal of Criminal Justice* 24(1):57-70.

Schoepfer, A., S. Carmichael & N. Piquero (2007). "Do Perceptions of Punishment Vary Between White-Collar and Street Crimes?" *Journal of Criminal Justice* 35(2):151-163.

Schwartz, M. & L. Travis (1996). *Corrections: An Issues Approach,* 4th ed. Cincinnati: Anderson.

Shover, N. (1996). *Great Pretenders: Pursuits and Careers of Persistent Thieves.* Boulder: Westview.

Skove, A. (2004). Blakely v. Washington: *Implications for State Courts.* Williamsburg, VA: National Center for State Courts.

Smith, W. & D. Smith (1998). "The Consequences of Error: Recidivism Prediction and Civil-Libertarian Ratios." *Journal of Criminal Justice* 26(6):481-502.

Snell, T. (2006). *Capital Punishment, 2005.* Washington, DC: Bureau of Justice Statistics.

Spohn, C. (2000). "Thirty Years of Sentencing Reform: The Quest for a Racially Neutral Sentencing Process." In J. Horney (ed.), *Policies, Processes, and Decisions of the Criminal Justice System.* Washington, DC: National Institute of Justice, Criminal Justice 2000, Volume 3:427-501.

Spohn, C. (1994). "Crime and the Social Control of Blacks: Offender/Victim Race and the Sentencing of Violent Offenders." In G. Bridges & M. Myers (eds.), *Inequality, Crime, and Social Policy.* Boulder, CO: Westview.

Spohn, C. & J. Cederblom (1991). "Race and Disparities in Sentencing: A Test of the Liberation Hypothesis." *Justice Quarterly* 8(3):305-327.

Spohn, C., M. DeLone & J. Spears (1998). "Race/Ethnicity, Gender and Sentence Severity in Dade County, Florida: An Examination of the Decision to Withhold Adjudication." *Journal of Crime and Justice* 21(2):111-138.

Steffensmeier, D. & S. Demuth (2001). "Ethnicity and Judges' Sentencing Decisions: Hispanic-Black-White Comparisons." *Criminology* 39(1):145-178.

Steffensmeier, D., J. Kramer & J. Ulmer (1995). "Age Differences in Sentencing." *Justice Quarterly* 12(3):583-601.

Taxman, F. & A. Piquero (1998). "On Preventing Drunk Driving Recidivism: An Examination of Rehabilitation and Punishment Approaches." *Journal of Criminal Justice* 26(2):129-143.

Tonry, M. (1999). "The Fragmentation of Sentencing and Corrections in America." In *Sentencing and Corrections Issues for the 21st Century* (September). Washington, DC: National Institute of Justice.

Tonry, M. (1996). *Sentencing Matters.* New York: Oxford University Press.

Travis, L.F., III (2002). "Criminal Sentencing: Honesty, Prediction, Discrimination, and Ethics." In M. Braswell, B. McCarthy & B. McCarthy (eds.), *Justice, Crime, and Ethics,* 4th ed. Cincinnati: Anderson, 2002:175-187.

Turner, M., J. Sundt, B. Applegate & F. Cullen (1995). "'Three Strikes and You're Out' Legislation: A National Assessment." *Federal Probation* 59(3):16-35.

Turpin-Petrosino, C. (1999). Are Limiting Enactments Effective? An Experimental Test of Decision Making in a Presumptive Parole State." *Journal of Criminal Justice* 27(4):321-332.

Ulmer, J. (1997). *Social Worlds of Sentencing: Court Communities Under Sentencing Guidelines.* Albany, NY: SUNY Press.

Umbreit, M.S. (1981). "Community Service Sentencing: Jail Alternative or Added Sanction?" *Federal Probation* 45(3):3-14.

U.S. Division of Probation (1974). "The Selective Presentence Investigation Report." *Federal Probation* 38(4):52-53.

Van Dine, S., J.P. Conrad & S. Dinitz (1979). "The Incapacitation of the Chronic Thug." *Journal of Criminal Law and Criminology* 65:535.

Van Voorhis, P. (1987). "Correctional Effectiveness: The High Cost of Ignoring Success." *Federal Probation* 51(1):56-62.

Vining, A.R. (1983). "Developing Aggregate Measures of Disparity." *Criminology* 21(2):233-252.

Visher, C. (1987). "Incapacitation and Crime Control: Does a 'Lock 'Em Up' Strategy Reduce Crime?" *Justice Quarterly* 4(4):513-543.

Vito, G. & T. Keil (1998). "Elements of Support for Capital Punishment: An Examination of Changing Attitudes." *Journal of Crime and Justice* 21(2):17-36.

Vito, G.F. & D.G. Wilson (1988). "Back from the Dead: Tracking the Progress of Kentucky's Furman Commuted Death Row Population." *Justice Quarterly* 5(1):101-111.

von Hirsch, A. (1976). *Doing Justice.* New York: Hill & Wang.

von Hirsch, A. & K.J. Hanrahan (1979). *The Question of Parole.* Cambridge, MA: Ballinger.

Weinrath, M. (1999). "Are New Directions Warranted for the Presentence Report? An Empirical Assessment of Its Predictive Utility in the Adult Court System." *Journal of Crime and Justice* 22(1):113-129.

Wenk, E.A., J.O. Robison & G.W. Smith (1972). "Can Violence be Predicted?" *Crime & Delinquency* 18(3):393-402.

Wilkins, L.T., J.M. Kress, D. Gottfredson, J.C. Calpin & A. Gelman (1976). *Sentencing Guidelines: Structuring Judicial Discretion.* Albany, NY: Criminal Justice Research Center.

Wright, R. & S. Decker (1994). *Burglars on the Job: Streetlife and Residential Break-Ins.* Boston: Northeastern University Press.

Wonders, N. (1996). "Determinate Sentencing: A Feminist and Postmodern Story." *Justice Quarterly* 13(4):611-648.

Zalman, M. (1987). "Sentencing in a Free Society: The Failure of the President's Crime Commission to Influence Sentencing Policy." *Justice Quarterly* 4(4):545-569.

Zatz, M. (2000). "The Convergence of Race, Ethnicity, Gender, and Class on Court Decisionmaking: Looking Toward the 21st Century." In J. Horney (ed.), *Policies, Processes, and Decisions of the Criminal Justice System.* Washington, DC: National Institute of Justice, Criminal Justice 2000, Volume 3:503-552.

Important Cases

Blakely v. Washington, 542 U.S.296 (2004).

Furman v. Georgia, 408 U.S. 238 (1972).

Gardner v. Florida, 430 U.S. 349 (1977).

Gregg v. Georgia, 428 U.S. 153 (1976).

Mempa v. Rhay, 389 U.S. 128 (1967).

United States v. Booker, 543 U.S. 220 (2005).

Williams v. New York, 377 U.S. 241 (1949).

Chapter 10

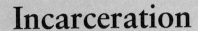

Incarceration

Important Terms

clear and present danger

compelling state interest

congregate system

"hands off" doctrine

institutionalization

"jailhouse lawyers"

jails

least restrictive
    alternative

multijurisdictional jails

"pains of
    imprisonment"

penitentiary

Prison Litigation
    Reform Act

"prisonization"

prisons

reformatory

segregate system

"smug hack"

"total institution"

On any given day there are more than 2.25 million people incarcerated in thousands of jails and hundreds of prisons across the United States (Sabol, Minton & Harrison, 2007). The overwhelming majority of those incarcerated are male, and the U.S. Department of Justice estimated that nearly 5 percent of black males and 2 percent of Hispanic males were in custody at midyear 2006. Less than 1 percent of white males were in custody. Persons born in the United States in 2001 have a 6.6 percent chance of serving a prison term over the course of their lifetime (Bonczar, 2003:1). By midyear 2006, one in every 133 residents of the United States was either in prison or jail (Sabol, Minton & Harrison, 2007). In 2001, expenditures for state prisons were nearly $30 billion (Stephan, 2004) and have increased since then. About 80 percent of state expenditures for correctional services are devoted to prisons. For a variety of reasons, the prison is traditionally seen as our response to crime.

Nonincarcerative sanctions are often viewed by the public as leniency (Newman, 1983; Rhine, 1992). The use of prisons as punishment for serious criminal behavior is an American invention. Most of us view incarceration as the most appropriate penalty to impose on those who violate the criminal laws (Durham, 1989; Tewksbury & DeMichele, 2003). While most offenders are not sentenced to terms of imprisonment, it seems to be our belief that prisons are the core of corrections in the United States.

There is good reason to believe that prisons are central to American corrections. By virtue of their size, history, and cost, prisons receive the lion's share of attention from correctional administrators (and, until recently, from persons studying corrections as well). Further, the threat of imprisonment is considered necessary in order to make less severe sanctions workable (Connolly, 1975). The argument is that without the threat of imprisonment, such sanctions as fines or probation would not be taken seriously by offenders.

Incarceration of criminals (and those accused of criminal behavior) takes place in prisons and jails. These are two distinct types of institutions (see comparison in Box 10.1). **Prisons** generally are state or federal facilities, segregated according to the sex of inmates, which house persons convicted of felonies who are serving sen-

Box 10.1   Characteristics of Prisons and Jails

What are the Characteristics of Confinement Facilities?

Prisons		Jails	
Number of Prisons	1,208	Number of Jails	3,365
Maximum Security	332	Population	
Medium Security	606	< 50	1,573
Minimum Security	370	50-99	544
		100-149	265
Men-only	1,017	150-249	256
Women-only	98	250-499	241
Both Sexes	93	500-999	188
		1,000-1,499	98
Average Population		1,500-1,999	44
		2,000+	156
<250	226		
250-749	327		
750-1,499	417		
1,500-2,499	174		
2,500+	64		
Age of Prison			
< 10 yrs.	378		
10-19	301		
20-49	265		
50-99	207		
100 +	56		
Unreported	1		

Sources: J. Stephan (2001), *Census of Jails*, 1999 (Washington, DC: Bureau of Justice Statistics); J. Stephan & J. Karberg (2003), *Census of State and Federal Correctional Facilities, 2000* (Washington, DC: Bureau of Justice Statistics).

tences of one year or more. **Jails** are usually operated by municipal governments and house a variety of people who are convicted of misdemeanors or are at various stages of criminal case processing. As might be expected, there are far more jails in the country than prisons, but most of the jails are small in size and experience a greater turnover in population (Sabol, Minton & Harrison, 2007).

This chapter examines incarceration in the American criminal justice system. It describes the history, organization, and practice of incarceration in both prisons and jails. Several contemporary issues in the operation of prisons and jails will be addressed in the following chapter.

The Origins of American Incarceration

The jail was established in England during the reign of Alfred the Great. Its purpose was to serve as a detention facility for those accused of seriously breaching the peace. In addition to tax collecting and other duties, the shire reeve (sheriff) was responsible for maintaining the jail. Then, as now, the jail operated on a local level in holding prisoners for a centralized authority.

The American colonists brought the jail with them to the New World, but generally did not need to use it within their small, close-knit communities. As had happened earlier in England, however, towns in the colonies grew larger and jails began to receive more use. Those incarcerated in jails were arrested persons who were not yet convicted, or were debtors or people who failed to pay fines. Incarceration was not yet used as a punishment for crime (Moynahan & Steward, 1980).

Incarceration as a response to criminal behavior developed as part of a larger "discovery" of the asylum in American society in the early 1800s (Rothman, 1971). After the American Revolution, the nature of American society was altered. No longer was it common for people to know all of their neighbors and to maintain a sense of small community in their dealings with others. Mobility (caused by the war), the beginnings of industrialism and immigration, and the growth of commerce and cities led to a more impersonal, less intimate social climate. Problems of poverty, dependency, and crime increasingly came to be seen as requiring a more centralized solution than had been characteristic of the colonial response. The solution to the social problems of poverty, insanity, and crime was found in the "asylum" or institution. Poorhouses, insane asylums, and jails became more common around the nation in the latter part of the 1700s. The first prison in the United States was opened in Newgate, Connecticut, before the Revolution in 1773. The general use of imprisonment did not spread until afterward (Durham, 1990).

The **penitentiary**, a place of punishment and repentance, as a response to crime was particularly attractive. The harsh criminal code of England had been transported to the colonies with the result that most offenses were punished with what Langbein (1976) termed "blood punishments." It was common practice to torture, mutilate, or execute offenders. These "barbaric" penalties violated the assumptions of the Enlightenment, which underlay the New Republic. When Patrick Henry addressed the Virginia House of Burgesses and declared, "Give me liberty or give me death!," he unwittingly identified the perfect penalty. Incarceration gives the convicted offender neither liberty nor death.

Pragmatically, incarceration solved a pressing problem of administration for penal codes that provided for severe punishments. When the penalties for crimes were perceived as being too harsh (e.g., lashes or branding for petty theft, death for repeat offenses), juries dealt with the dilemma by failing to convict the offenders. Some observers saw this as a major obstacle to meeting the deterrent functions of the law. Further, in a rational penalty system, it was difficult to grade penalties to crimes when physical pain was the standard. Incarceration seemed more humane and likely to result in higher conviction rates. It also made an easier task of matching lengths of term to seriousness of offense.

The problem of harsh penalties was very troublesome. If the penalty for stealing a pig was death, what should be the penalty for stealing a cow? What would deter a burglar who faced hanging from killing the homeowner? Jurors faced tough decisions as well. Voting to convict a hungry offender who stole a loaf of bread could ensure that the offender suffered branding, mutilation, or death. By establishing time as a punishment, and describing the prison as a harsh but humane environment, it was possible to better match penalties to offenses, such as one year for stealing a pig or three years for stealing a cow. The availability of incarceration as a sentencing option also led to a higher rate of conviction, as juries were more willing to see a hungry thief spend a few months in prison (where food and clothing would be available).

The centrality of the prison as an appropriate sanction for deterrent purposes was established by Jeremy Bentham, although later historians have overlooked Bentham's focus on deterrence. Robert Sullivan (1996) reviewed Bentham's original work, concluding that, to Bentham, the prison provided a technology of punishment that allowed precise alteration of the intensity and duration of punishment. According to Bentham, this precision would allow punishers to achieve, via scientific application, optimal deterrent value from criminal punishment.

Ideologically, incarceration appeared well-suited to the needs of offender reform. Without the opportunity to transport prisoners to penal colonies, penitentiaries provided internal penal colonies to which offenders could be sentenced. The penitentiary removed the offender from the evil environment of the city, allowed the person to reflect on the error of his or her ways, and taught good work habits. Indeed, in the early days of incarceration, some viewed the penitentiary as a "utopia." Most proponents of the penitentiary felt that crime was caused by an evil environment, and believed that the penitentiary would insulate the offender from further criminal influences. The French philosopher, Michel Foucault (1979) is perhaps the best known proponent of the view that the prison emerged as a means of disciplining or controlling people. The prison emerged as a primary means of criminal punishment for a variety of reasons (Garland, 1990).

The Congregate/Segregate System Debate

During the 1820s, two systems of penitentiary discipline developed. They are compared in Box 10.2. The first, in Pennsylvania, was known as the **segregate system** or the "Pennsylvania system." Here, inmates were housed separately in individual cells, took their meals in their cells, exercised in separate yards, and never interacted with other offenders. Any industry that was conducted was "cottage" industry, in which inmates completed the entire product in their cells.

This system had the advantage of ensuring that offenders were protected from the corrupting influence of other offenders. The major disadvantages were that offenders suffered psychologically from isolation, and the prison was expensive to operate and was not always able to produce a profit from its industry. Nonetheless, the Pennsylvania system had its supporters because it was true to an ideal of penance and isolation.

In contrast, the second penitentiary in the United States was developed in Auburn, New York. This system came to be known as the **congregate system** or the "Auburn system" of prison discipline. Here, inmates were housed in separate cells, but the inmates ate, worked, and exercised in groups. "Isolation" was maintained by a strict rule of silence that prohibited inmates from conversing with each other. This organization reduced costs as a result of mass movement and feeding of prisoners. Further, the ability to work offenders in groups allowed assembly-line methods of production and a wider variety of prison-made products.

The strengths of this system were the more humane mingling of prisoners (even if they were silent, inmates at least were able to see each other) and the cost-effectiveness of the system. The disadvantages were that the congregate system required closer surveillance of inmates to enforce silence, and that prison administrators were unable to keep inmates isolated. In addition, in the congregate system, there was greater potential for riots and fights among inmates.

For several decades, a debate raged about which of these systems was the better method for handling inmates. In the end, the cost-effectiveness of the congregate system emerged the victor of the debate, at least in the United States. Later generations of American penitentiaries most often operated under the Auburn system of congregate feeding, work, and exercise.

The experience of the Virginia Penitentiary illustrates this point. In an attempt to benefit from both the congregate and segregate systems, Virginia law required that inmates, who were initially housed in larger dormitories under a "silent system," spend their last three months in solitary confinement. Keve (1986:41) cited the 1832 report of a legislative study committee, which found the solitary confinement requirement of Virginia prison terms counterproductive:

> Upon the subject of the three month's solitary confinement required by law to be inflicted upon convicts immediately preceding their discharge, the committee have had much reflection; and they have come to the conclusion that this portion of the close confinement ought to

Box 10.2 Segregate versus Congregate Systems

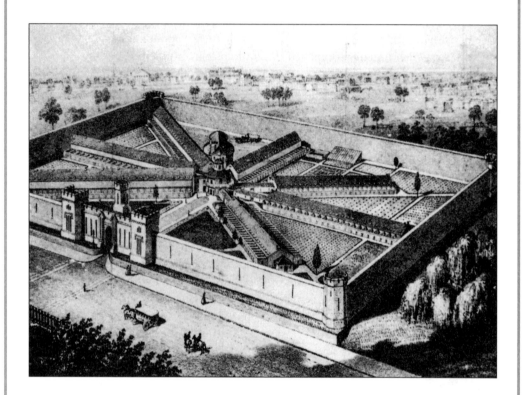

The Eastern State Penitentiary, designed by John Haviland and completed in 1829, became the model and primary exponent of the Pennsylvania "separate" system. The prison had seven original cell blocks radiating from the hub-like center, a rotunda with an observatory tower, and an alarm bell.

A corridor ran down the center of each block, with the cells at right angles to the corridor. Each cell had a back door to a small, uncovered exercise yard and double front doors, the outer one made of wood, and the other of grated iron with a trap so that meals could be passed to prisoners.

Box 10.2 *(continued)*

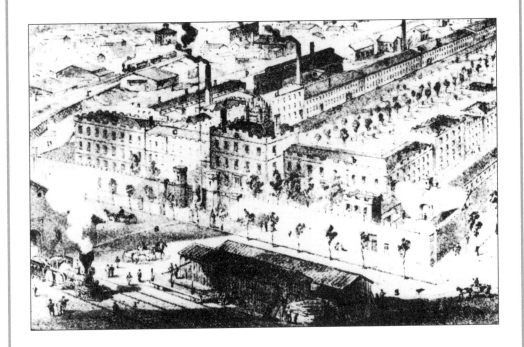

In 1816, New York began the construction of a new prison at Auburn. It was patterned after other early American prisons with a few solitary cells to conform to the law of solitary confinement to be used for punishment, and with sizeable night rooms to accommodate most prisoners.

To test the efficiency of the Pennsylvania system, an experiment was tried in 1821 with a group of inmates who were confined to their cells without labor. Many of these inmates became insane and sick. The experiment was abandoned as a failure in 1823, and most of the inmates studied were pardoned.

A new plan was adopted whereby all inmates were locked in separate cells at night, but worked and ate together in congregate settings in silence under penalty of punishment.

Source: American Correctional Association (1983), *The American Prison: From the Beginning . . . A Pictorial History* (College Park, MD: American Correctional Association):39, 48.

be abolished. They believe that it is productive of no substantial benefit, but is on the contrary, decidedly injurious. It obliterates the habits of industry previously acquired. Upon the score of more interest to the state it is inexpedient because it abstracts from the institution the most valuable portion of the time and labor of the convicts. It exceeds the requisitions of stern justice . . . But above all it ruins the health of the victim and indirectly takes away human life . . . In any aspect which it may be viewed experience proves its inexpediency, if not its absolute inhumanity and injustice.

The Changing Purposes of Prisons

Initially, it was believed that the experience of incarceration alone would lead to improved behavior on the part of offenders. The learning of good work habits, the removal from contaminating influences, and other benefits of incarceration were supposed to result in better citizens. However, over time, it became clear that the reform (prison) was itself in need of reform. By the middle of the nineteenth century, penitentiaries were replaced with reformatories in which offenders were trained to be law-abiding citizens and released from incarceration as soon as it was clear that they had been reformed.

Created as a humanitarian and practical alternative to the corporal and capital punishments of the eighteenth century and earlier, the penitentiary soon came to be recognized as flawed. The early developers of the penitentiary supported isolation of prisoners because they sincerely believed that criminality was caused when people were tempted by their environment. The term "penitentiary" was applied because it was designed to be a place where the offender could do penance. It was thought that lack of adequate discipline and training from the family, combined with the lure of taverns and "bawdy houses," led otherwise law-abiding citizens into a life of crime. Isolation, solitary contemplation on right and wrong, and the discipline of hard work in a "sanitized" environment free from criminal temptations would work to improve offenders and prepare them for lawful living.

By the Civil War period, observers came to believe that simple incarceration was not enough. The penitentiary lacked an incentive to offenders to make them want to change. Further, the imposition of a definite term of confinement seemed counterproductive. If a prisoner with a five-year term had reformed in one year, these observers saw no reason to continue his or her confinement for an additional four years. It was important that prisons take active steps to reform criminals. These steps would include instilling discipline and industry as habits in the inmates, and offering the possibility of early release from incarceration as an incentive to reform.

In the reformatory, inmates were raw materials that were to be shaped into law-abiding citizens (that is, reformed). Upon entering the reformatory, the prisoner lost his or her civilian identity, contact with the outside world, and nearly all rights. The reformatory was a factory producing useful citizens. The process through which this production was to be accomplished was training. Prisoners were conditioned to industry and discipline in the belief that once the habits were established in the prison, they would not be broken after release. As an ex-convict, author Malcolm Braly (1976:202) noted that the habits acquired in the penitentiary did endure, at least for a while. Describing his first few days of freedom after release from San Quentin, Braly wrote, "That first morning and every morning for several weeks I woke exactly at six-thirty when the big bell had begun to pound in the blocks. Rise and shine. It's daylight in the swamps."

Within 50 years of the creation of reformatories, a new correctional ideology developed (O'Leary & Duffee, 1971). The mere training of offenders was not sufficient. Rather, offenders were "ill" and in need of treatment to cure them of their proclivities toward crime. The rehabilitative correctional institution had arrived, with a treatment staff in addition to the custody and industry staffs.

Several problems had plagued the reformatory ideal. First, the habits established in prison did not last long for many prisoners after they were released. Second, over time, early release was used increasingly as a prison management tool rather than recognition of inmate reformation. If the prison became crowded, inmates would be released. If a particular inmate was needed (for example, if he or she was the only barber in the institution), he or she might not be released, no matter how reformed he or she became. Finally, the view of the cause of criminality also changed.

The growth of the social and behavioral sciences, and the development of service professions related to these disciplines, fostered a reexamination of institutional corrections. In 1897, Warren Spalding, Secretary of the Massachusetts Prison Association, remarked (1897:47), "The State is not an avenger, with a mission to right the wrong which the criminal has done, but is to try to right the criminal, that he may cease to do wrong." The emphasis on the individual offender, and on the motives and causes of the individual's criminality, grew in the early twentieth century (Fogel, 1979:50-61). This was the Progressive Era, when there was a general trust in the ability of the state to do good for individuals, and when reformers wanted prisons that met the needs of individual criminals rather than the general needs of society (Rothman, 1980).

In the middle 1960s, yet another shift occurred in correctional ideology. Prisons themselves were now viewed as part of the problem of crime. The best solution to reforming criminal offenders was thought to rest in keeping the criminal in the community where he or she could learn how to live a law-abiding life. Prison populations fell, and those kept in prison increasingly were able to take advantage of furlough programs and to enjoy increased contact with the outside world. Observers of the nation's prisons came to believe that attempts at individualizing treatment, and the focus on the cause of crime as being inside the offender, were ineffective. Rather, to succeed in changing offenders into law-abiding citizens, it would be necessary to deal with the criminal in society. A survey of prison inmates in Norway revealed that the inmates themselves believed that imprisonment alone will neither deter nor rehabilitate inmates (Kolstad, 1996).

Another prison writer, Lou Torok (1974:91), succinctly summarized the arguments in favor of the reintegration philosophy of corrections, which flourished for a decade from the middle 1960s:

It costs the taxpayer up to six thousand dollars each year to keep one convict locked up uselessly in prison. On the other hand, it would only cost about three hundred dollars a year to keep the same man in the community, under close supervision, on parole or probation, where he will pay his own way, earn a salary, keep his family off welfare and live a law-abiding life. Both society and the offender would benefit from this approach but so many people are unwilling to examine the facts and figures objectively. They continue to pour millions of dollars of tax money into an archaic prison system which does not correct, does not reform, simply does not, in any sense work.

In the middle 1970s, correctional ideology again shifted. The purpose of imprisonment came to be defined principally as punishment. Inmates served time as punishment for criminal offenses. Whatever programs and industries were available to inmates were there for voluntary usage. Release from incarceration was based on service of sentence, not on evidence of reform or rehabilitation. Further, more offenders were expected to serve prison sentences as punishment, although the lengths of terms were reduced for most offenders (Twentieth Century Fund, 1976).

One argument in favor of this newest purpose of prisons was that, in the end, punishment had been the only purpose that the tradition of the prison had shown incarceration could serve. Torok (1974:88) wrote, "In actual practice, prisons do little more than punish." Similarly, Braly (1976:362) wrote of the new prisons, "The old timers scorned these new prisons and dismissed them as Holiday Motels. We couldn't be conned by departmental [Department of Corrections] window dressing. We were still under the Man, and the Man still had a gun locked away somewhere nearby . . . Essentially, it was only Folsom with Muzak." A number of commentators support the notion of the prison as a place of punishment. Logan and Gaes (1993) suggest that prisons follow a "confinement model" in which the purpose is the secure, safe, humane custody of inmates. This notion of the purpose of the prison fits well with a resurgence of retributive punishment. If the purpose of punishment is to return harm for harm, then the prison should impose pain safely and humanely (Clear, 1994; Cullen, 1995). When combined with tremendous crowding in prisons, the retributive ideal led to what some called a "new penology" (Feeley & Simon, 1992). In this new penology, the primary purpose of the prison was the efficient management of a large population (Holcomb & Williams, 2003; Rutherford, 1993).

At the turn of the century, the purpose of prisons was again the subject of intense debate (Clear, 1997). Several observers noted that the move to more punitive policies concerning the use of prisons and jails is at least partly responsible for the tremendous growth in America's inmate population over the past quarter century (Lynch & Sabol, 2000). Increasingly punitive conditions in prisons and jails were criticized for failing to prepare inmates for life after incarceration, and for making the management of correctional institutions more difficult (Rhine, 1992; Seiter, 1997; Wright, 2000). In response, an increasing number of commentators called for the reinstitution of rehabilitative programming in correctional institutions (Cullen & Gendreau, 2000; Schriro, 2000). Most Americans believe rehabilitation should be a primary objective of prison programming (Applegate, Cullen & Fisher, 2002; Flanagan, 1996).

The American prison was developed as a humane alternative to the harsh punishments of colonial justice. In a history of slightly less than 200 years, the purpose of prisons has been redefined several times in accord with changing public and social attitudes regarding crime and human behavior. Through it all, the prison has survived. It is instructive to recognize that one of the first prisons ever erected, Auburn Penitentiary, is still in operation today. It has undergone several renovations and name changes, yet it still houses inmates.

The history of prisons in the United States reveals that these institutions are enduring (Schwartz & Travis, 1996). The prison represents the core of our views on how to respond to criminal behavior. It is likely to do so for at least the foreseeable future.

The Organization of American Incarceration

Given the distinct (although related) natures and functions of jails and prisons, it is necessary to give separate treatment to the organizations of the two types of institutions. While both types of institutions hold convicted offenders, their widely divergent structures cannot be combined easily.

Jail Organization

Local control, multiple functions, and a transient, heterogeneous population have shaped the major organizational characteristics of jails. Box 10.3 provides a partial answer to the question "Who is in jail?" Typically jails are under the jurisdiction of county government. In most instances, the local area has neither the necessary tax base from which to finance a jail adequately nor sufficient size to justify even the most rudimentary correctional programs. In addition, local control has inevitably meant involvement with local politics. Jails are left in a paradoxical situation: while clung to tenaciously by localities, they often have been unwilling or unable to meet even minimal standards (National Advisory Commission, 1973:274).

Most jails in the United States are operated by county sheriffs' offices. Of 3,365 jails in the nation, more than 80 percent are operated at the county level, and more than 16 percent are city jails. Less than 1.5 percent of jails are classified as **multijurisdictional jails**, or serving more than one municipality or jurisdiction. All but six states (Alaska, Connecticut, Delaware, Hawaii, Rhode Island, and Vermont) have local jails. In Alaska, five of the state's jails are administered by cities (Perkins, Stephan & Beck, 1995).

As local institutions, jails must compete (often within a larger sheriff's or police department, and with other municipal services such as public works, sani-

Box 10.3 Who's in Jail?

- Persons pending court proceedings like arraignment, trial, or sentencing, including both those unable to secure pretrial release and those denied release.

- Probation, parole, and bail violators and absconders.

- Juveniles pending transfer to juvenile authorities.

- Mentally ill persons pending movement to mental health facilities.

- Military personnel for protective custody, contempt, or as witnesses.

- Persons awaiting transfer to state or federal correctional facilities.

- Federal and state prisoners held because of prison crowding.

- Convicted offenders sentenced to short terms (generally under one year).

- Material witnesses.

- Prison inmates on furlough or other temporary release status.

Source: D. James (2004), *Profile of Jail Inmates, 2004* (Washington, DC: Bureau of Justice Statistics).

tation, health, education, and the like) for resources. Moreover, almost one-half of American jails are designed to house fewer than 50 inmates. About one-fifth of jails are capable of housing more than 250 inmates. Yet, in the early part of this century, one-half of all jail inmates were held in the largest 6 percent of jails (Sabol, Minton & Harrison, 2007). Moreover, almost 90 percent of jail inmates were held in the 37 percent of jails that house more than 100 inmates, which means that the majority of jail inmates are held in large institutions.

On any given day, almost 750,000 inmates are being held in our nation's jails (Sabol, Minton & Harrison, 2007). Annually, millions of prisoners are processed through the jails. The Bureau of Justice Statistics (Stephan, 2001) reported that approximately 219,000 persons entered jails in a one-week period. The median time spent in jail for convicted inmates in 2002 was expected to be less than six months (James, 2004). Over half of those incarcerated in jails have not yet been convicted of a criminal offense and are awaiting trial. Including those who will obtain pretrial release or be sentenced to a penalty other than incarceration, the average length of stay for persons entering jails was estimated at three days (Snell, 1993). Those serving sentences in jail generally face short terms, and the jail population experiences a rapid turnover.

Most jail inmates are male, under the age of 35, unmarried, and minority-group members, with just under 40 percent having completed high school (James, 2004). Only about 13 percent of jail inmates are female, and 92 percent were U.S. citizens (James, 2004:2). Nearly half of all jail inmates have not graduated high school (Harlow, 2003). As a result of short terms and small total population sizes, programs for jail inmates generally either do not exist or are inadequate. Most jails report having programs for education and health care. Box 10.4 describes programs available to jail inmates. Much of a jail inmate's incarceration time is spent in idleness, viewing television, or otherwise attempting to pass the hours. Jail inmates have high levels of medical needs and substance dependence and

Box 10.4 Jail Jurisdictions Reporting Programs Available to Jail Inmates

Program or policy	Jail jurisdictions with a program	
	Number	Percent
Education		
Secondary	1,545	55%
Basic adult	696	25
Special	303	11
Study release	260	9
Vocational	182	6
College	94	3
Counseling		
Religious/spiritual	1,960	70%
Alcohol	1,724	61
Drug	1,528	54
Psychological	1,306	47
Life skills	601	21
Domestic violence	488	17
Pretrial services	468	17
Job seeking	411	15
Health care delivery system		
Fee-for-service	1,101	39%
On-site staff	882	31
Managed care	500	18
Local government physicians	338	12
Mental health services		
Screening at intake	2,152	78%
Psychotropic medication	1,832	66
24-hour care	1,309	47
Routine therapy/counseling	1,283	46
Psychiatric evaluation	1,044	38

Note: The following numbers of jail jurisdictions reported data on policies and programs: education, 2,821 jurisdictions; counseling, 2,804; health care delivery systems, 2,802; and mental health services, 2,769.

Source: J. Stephan (2001), *Census of Jails, 1999* (Washington, DC: Bureau of Justice Statistics):10.

abuse, posing problems for jail treatment programs (Maruschak, 2006; Karberg & James, 2005). It is an understatement to say that the jail population is comprised of offenders with high service needs.

The majority of jail staff are custodial officers, and as a result of the administration of jails by sheriffs and police, many custodial officers are sworn police officers who would rather not be serving in jails. Fewer than 10 percent of jail personnel are service staff members, such as doctors, social workers, and teachers (Stephan, 2001). Most jail personnel are white, non-Hispanic (66%), and male (66%). In 1999 the ratio of inmates to correctional officers in jails was 4.3 to one. Twenty-six percent of correctional officers were black, non-Hispanic, and 28 percent were female. The characteristics of all jail staff, including correctional officers, are shown in Box 10.5.

Box 10.5 Characteristics of Jail Staff

Sex:	N = 207,600
Male	66%
Female	34%
Ethnicity:	
White	65%
Black	26%
Hispanic	8%
Other	1%
Job Classification:	
Administrators	9.0%
Correctional Officers	68.9%
Clerical & Maintenance	13.0%
Educational/Professional	8.4%
Other	.3%

Source: J. Stephan (2001), *Census of Jails, 1999* (Washington, DC: Bureau of Justice Statistics).

The organization and administration of jails has remained relatively unchanged over the years, and there is little chance that speedy change in jail organization will occur (Skoler, 1978:11). Jails historically have been criticized for their lack of programs for inmates, poor physical condition, and inadequate staffing (Fishman, 1923; Goldfarb, 1975; McGee, 1971). Ruddell and Mays (2007:258) studied rural jails and concluded, "Perhaps the most significant finding of this study was that the problems identified in Cronk's (1982) study of rural crime and justice were still major challenges over two decades later."

Although there has been some improvement in jails in recent years, much remains to be done (Katsampes & Neil, 1981). Newer jails often incorporate a redesign of jail facilities. An increasing number of new jails have been built using alternatives to the traditional row of cells. Often called "podular" designs, these jails contain housing units with cells arranged along the exterior walls with a common living/dining area in the center. This design is coupled with the delivery of most services to inmates within the housing unit. Researchers have reported that this design seems to reduce tension and inmate misbehavior (Zupan, 1991; Zupan & Menke, 1988). Jeffrey Senese (1997) evaluated the effect of jail design on inmate behavior and concluded that the new design is associated with lower rates of inmate misbehavior of some types (violence, escape, destruction), but that general disorder infractions are higher. Unfortunately, in many places the construction of these new facilities has not meant that older, traditional jails can be closed (Bikle, 2000). Instead, because of growing populations, many jurisdictions now operate both types of jails. In addition, nearly 10 percent of persons under jail supervision nationally are supervised outside the jail facility, as shown in Box 10.6.

Prison Organization

Prisons are organized on either a state or federal level. Unlike jails, prisons suffer from problems associated with their large size. The National Advisory

---

Box 10.6 Persons Under Jail Supervision by Confinement Status

Percent of Jail Inmates Confined:

Inside Jails	92.7%
Outside Jail	7.3

Status of Jail Inmates Not Confined in Jail:

Community Service	24.4%
Weekend Program	19.0
Electronic Monitoring	18.3
Work Program	13.8
Pretrial Supervision	10.6
Day Reporting	8.0
Treatment Program	2.5
Home Detention	.3
Other	2.1
Total: (60,222 inmates)	100%

Source: W. Sabol, T. Minton & P. Harrison (2007), *Prison and Jail Inmates at Midyear 2006* (Washington, DC: Bureau of Justice Statistics):21.

Commission on Criminal Justice Standards and Goals observed the detrimental consequences of overly large institutions (1973:355):

> The usual response to bigness has been regimentation and uniformity. Individuals become subjugated to the needs generated by the institution. Uniformity is translated into depersonalization. A human being ceases to be identified by the usual points of reference, such as his name, his job, or family role. He becomes a number, identified by the cellblock where he sleeps. Such practices reflect maladaptation resulting from size.

The majority of prisons in the United States are operated by or for state governments. The Bureau of Justice Statistics (Stephan & Karberg, 2003) identified 1,320 state, 264 private, and 84 federal correctional facilities in operation in 2000. The majority of these (1,208) were confinement facilities (prisons), while 460 were community-based. Community-based facilities include prerelease and furlough centers where inmates are allowed to leave the facility for part of the day. Of the more than 1,200 prisons in America, 84 are federal prisons (Stephan & Karberg, 2003). Every state has a prison, or state confinement facility, and about one-third of states operate more than 20. About one-half of state and federal facilities house fewer than 750 inmates but, as with the jail population, most prison inmates are housed in large prisons. The Bureau of Justice Statistics reported that three jurisdictions, California, Texas, and the Federal Prison System, housed more than one-third of all inmates in 2006, while the 21 smallest state systems housed only 8 percent of inmates (Sabol, Minton & Harrison, 2007).

At the end of 1984, the Bureau of Justice Statistics (1985) reported that more than 480,000 offenders were being held in American prisons. That population increased more than 17 percent by the end of 1986, when there were 546,659 prison inmates in the United States (Bureau of Justice Statistics, 1987:1). At the end of 1996, there were 1,182,169 inmates in state and federal prisons, an increase of almost 250 percent (Mumola & Beck, 1997). By the middle of 2006, there were more than 1.5 million people in prison. Most of these offenders are housed in single-sex facilities. Fewer than 8 percent of prisons were co-educational in 2000 (Stephan & Karberg, 2003:6). Because prisons have a much lower turnover rate than jails, fewer than 1.5 million inmates are processed through prisons each year. The median time served prior to first release from state prison in 1991 was 14 months (Perkins, 1994:30); by 1995, median time served had increased to 24 months, and by 1997 it rose to 27 months (Beck & Mumola, 1999; Mumola & Beck, 1997). Between 1986 and 1997, time served by inmates of the federal prison system more than doubled (Sabol & McGready, 1999). Box 10.7 displays the growth in prison populations in the United States.

Most prison inmates, like their counterparts in jails, are male, minority-group members, and young (Harrison & Beck, 2003). Recent data reveal that nearly one-third are age 40 or older and most have graduated from high school and have a history of some drug use. Only about 7 percent of inmates are female, 35 percent are white, 40 percent are black, and nearly 20 percent are of Hispanic origin

Box 10.7 Growth in Prison Population in the United States, 1985-2006

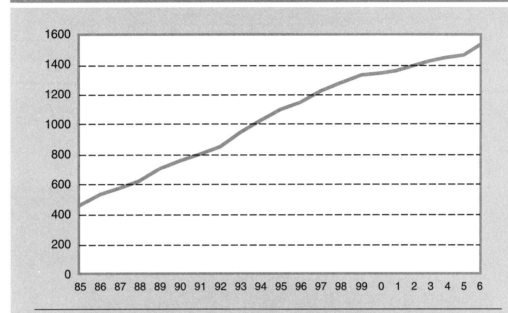

Source: A. Pastore & K. Maguire (2007), *Sourcebook of Criminal Justice Statistics* [online]. Found at: http://www.albany.edu/sourcebook (accessed August 17, 2007); W. Sabol, T. Minton & P. Harrison (2007), *Prison and Jail Inmates at Midyear 2006* (Washington, DC: Bureau of Justice Statistics).

(Sabol, Minton & Harrison, 2007). Greenfeld (1992:16) reported that 93 percent of prisoners in 1991 had been convicted of a violent crime or were recidivists. This is a tricky statistic, however, because it combines violence and recidivism. In 1996, only 29.5 percent of new admissions to prison were convicted of a violent offense. Most persons sentenced to prison have a prior record of criminal behavior and on any day about half of state prisoners were being held for a violent offense.

Because of the longer terms of confinement and generally larger populations, prisons are able to provide a wide range of programs to inmates, including educational, vocational, recreational, social, and psychological counseling programs. Stephan and Karberg (2003:11-13) reported that 94 percent of confinement facilities offered educational programs, 96 percent offered counseling programs, and most facilities provided work assignments to inmates. Relatively few inmates were involved in prison industries. Most work programs involved inmates with assignments dealing with maintenance and service of the facility. Nearly 25 percent of inmates were idle at the start of 1996, having neither an academic nor a work assignment (Camp & Camp, 1996:74).

Similar to jails, the majority of prison staff hold custodial positions (65.2%). The Bureau of Justice Statistics (1997) reported that almost 29 percent of prison personnel in 1995 were female, with almost 19 percent of custody/security staff being women. Camp and Camp (1996) reported that a total of 190,802 persons worked as correctional officers in state and federal prisons in 1996. Nearly 20 percent were female, and two-thirds were white. Since then, the number of persons working as correctional officers in state and federal prisons has grown to more than 250,000. The ratio of inmates to correctional officers in American state prisons in 2000 was reported to be 4.5 to 1 (Stephan & Karberg, 2003).

There are, however, higher percentages of prison staff who hold administrative (2.5%), professional (14.4%), and maintenance and food service/clerical (12.8%) job titles (Stephan & Karberg, 2003:13). Box 10.8 describes the distribution of prison personnel across job titles. Unlike those working in jails, correctional personnel in prisons are hired solely as correctional personnel. The organization and administration of prisons has changed little over the years and does not seem likely to change much in the future.

Box 10.8   Distribution of Prison Employees by Job Category, 2000

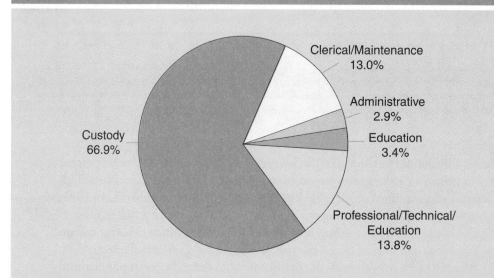

Source: J. Stephan & J. Karberg (2003), *Census of State and Federal Correctional Facilities, 2000* (Washington, DC: Bureau of Justice Statistics).

Doing Time

Incarceration is the foundation of American corrections. With the exception of capital punishment, it is the most severe sanction available to the state. As such, it is the "stick" that supports community corrections programs, such as halfway houses, probation, and parole (Reasons & Kaplan, 1975). Prisons are an American invention, and Americans rely upon the use of incarceration as a response to criminal behavior.

The experience of incarceration differs depending upon where an inmate is incarcerated, yet in large measure, it is the same wherever and whenever it occurs. The inmate in either prison or jail is typically under control and is not a contributing member of any policy-making body. This fact leads to a similarity of experience for all inmates. The experience of "doing time" is painful. The **"pains of imprisonment"** were identified by Gresham Sykes (1969) as: (1) deprivation of liberty, (2) deprivation of goods and services, (3) deprivation of heterosexual relations, (4) deprivation of autonomy, and (5) deprivation of security. Victor Hassine (1996:18), an inmate in the Pennsylvania prison system, described these pains as follows: "At first, I missed the obvious, sex, love, family, and friends. But it wasn't long before I stopped missing these things and started focusing on the next wave of things I no longer have: privacy, quiet, and peace of mind, intangibles that I have never stopped missing to this day."

Many observers have identified what has been called **"prisonization."** This refers to the apparent fact that prison inmates become socialized into a specific prison subculture. Some contend that the experience of deprivation creates a prison "subculture" that provides inmates with norms and rules for living in prison. In contrast, others suggest that the prison subculture is imported by offenders. That is, the type of people sent to prison already have a set of values, norms, and beliefs that is different from and counter to conventional society (Zaitzow, 1999). The research evidence on whether the "prison subculture" is a product of the characteristics of inmates coming to prison (importation model) or emerges from the experience of imprisonment (deprivation model) is unclear. Brent Paterline and David Peterson (1999) surveyed more than 400 federal prisoners and concluded, "The findings of this investigation coincide with some previous research, which concludes that the merger of the importation and deprivation models explains more of the variation in prisonization than either analyzed separately." John McDonald (1999) studied drug use and violence while incarcerated among youths released from California facilities. He also suggests that his research supports a merger of the importation and deprivation models. Hochstetler and DeLisi (2005) expanded on this by observing that different types of inmates are more likely to place themselves in circumstances in which they are exposed to opportunities for good or bad behavior in prison. They suggest that the reality of living in prison is quite complex and that it is a combination of inmate and institution characteristics that explains inmate behavior in prison. Whatever the source, the subculture provides inmates with a means of making sense of the prison and enduring the hardships of incarceration.

Deprivation of Liberty

By definition, those confined in correctional institutions do not have any liberty of movement. Yet, even within the institution, the inmate is not at liberty to move around. As Sykes observed (1969:65), "In short, the prisoner's loss of liberty is a double one: first, by confinement to the institution and second, by confinement within the institution."

Prisoners are moved en masse from cell block to activity, to dining facility, to activity, and back to cell block. Few inmates are allowed the privilege of moving about the institution without an escort. Inmates also are not free to choose to whom they may write or with whom they may otherwise interact. The net effect of this deprivation is isolation from the outside community. This loss of liberty is symbolic of a loss of status as a trusted member of society. As one inmate put it:

> Freedom is the only meaningful thing to a human. Without freedom things lose meaning. The whole system in prison is designed to degenerate a human being, to break him as a man. They take away all of his freedom, his freedom to express himself and his feelings. How can you be human if you can't express yourself? (Wright, 1973:146).

Deprivation of Goods and Services

While options have been increased since Sykes made his observations, inmates today are still deprived of access to, and ownership of, a wide variety of goods and services. Most prisons do not allow inmates to possess money, and most require standardization of clothing and other possessions.

Upon admission to a prison or jail, the "civilian" possessions of inmates

A Hamilton County, Ohio, offender washes windows in his inmate uniform outside the Hamilton County Justice Center. The black-and-white striped jail uniform clearly identifies the inmate and indicates the deprivation of an inmate's personal control over appearance. *Photo credit: AP Photo/David Kohl.*

(e.g., jewelry, money, clothing, etc.) are confiscated and either stored until release or shipped to a destination chosen by the inmate (usually "home"). All of the amenities of free society by which we make a statement about who we are, such as the clothes we wear, the way we wear our hair, the car we drive, and the like, are removed from the inmate. Instead, the inmate is issued a uniform, given a prison haircut, and generally not allowed to exercise personal taste in the selection and purchase of goods and services. Hassine (1996:19-21) describes his first disciplinary infraction as the result of a desire to have a hamburger "his way." He wrote, "My first misconduct at Graterford resulted from missing one of life's simplest pleasures: a fresh-cooked burger." He bought contraband hamburger, buns, butter, onions, and a heating element. While preparing his hamburger, he was discovered and "written-up." He concludes this tale, writing, "For many years afterward, my prison handle became 'Burger King,' even though I had never gotten a chance to taste the object of my crime."

Most penal facilities now have commissaries, where inmates are allowed to purchase toiletries, candy bars, and other small items. Some prisons allow inmates to wear certain articles of civilian clothing, such as hats or tee shirts, but the range of options available to the inmate is very restricted. The effect of this deprivation is that the inmate feels impoverished. His or her self-worth is lessened by reason of the reduced "net worth."

> In prison the slightest distinction is cherished and enlarged . . . Bob, since he had bad feet, had been allowed to keep his own shoes rather than wear the Santa Rosa hightops which were standard issue. He had polished these shoes until they glittered, and, as we spoke, he continued to rub one shoe and then the other against his pants leg. He also wore the watch Big John had given him, and he glanced at it frequently as if he had an important appointment and wasn't just standing around, as I was, killing time until lunch (Braly, 1976:156).

Deprivation of Heterosexual Relations

As noted earlier, most penal facilities in the United States are segregated by sex. The inmate is not only denied liberty and impoverished by reason of incarceration, but is also forced to endure involuntary celibacy. The lack of members of the opposite sex in the prison society leads to anxieties about sexual identity among inmates. Some observers have characterized the prison "culture" as being "ultramasculine" (Lutze & Murphy, 1999).

The effect of sex segregation is not only physical, but also psychological in that the inmate has lost one-half of the audience and comparison group from whom he or she receives a validation of sexual identity. That is, it is more difficult to be masculine or feminine in an all-male or all-female society (respectively) than in mixed company. One of the principal ways in which we know who we are sexually is by comparison with members of the opposite sex. In prison, these comparisons are largely absent (Nacci & Kane, 1984).

> Some men look feminine and looks are enough alone for a man behind these walls to try and get him. It is a hell of a thing to say, but here you are another man and you are behind these walls and before long another man begins to look like a woman to you (Lockwood, 1982:54).

Deprivation of Autonomy

The prison is a "total institution," as described by Goffman (1961). The total institution provides all the necessities for the individual, and makes all the decisions for its residents. This fact leads to what has been called institutionalization, which is the formation of individuals who are almost wholly dependent upon the institution and incapable of caring for themselves in the free society.

The prison inmate is not allowed to decide when to eat, what to eat, when or how often to take a shower, when to go to sleep, when to awaken, what job to do, and how to make other seemingly trivial decisions. Rather, the inmate is subjected to a life in which all major, and most minor, decisions are made by others. The refusal of inmate requests is generally not accompanied by any explanation, thereby adding insult to injury.

The net effect of the loss of autonomy is a reduction in feelings of self-worth, as inmates come to recognize that they are no longer in control of their own destinies. The inmate is reduced to a state of childlike dependency upon the parent (the state). As Sykes (1969:76) explained, "But for the adult who has escaped such helplessness with the passage of years, to be thrust back into childhood's helplessness is even more painful . . ."

In the words of an inmate at San Quentin:

> The worst thing here is the way your life is regulated, always regulated, day in and day out. They tell you what to do almost every moment of the day. You become a robot just following instructions. They do this, they say, so that you can learn to be free on the outside (Wright, 1973:146).

Deprivation of Security

The final pain of imprisonment mentioned by Sykes is paradoxical: the loss of security. In a prison, even one classified as "maximum-security," the prisoner experiences a real loss of personal security. Prisons are not safe places in which to reside. Consider living in a neighborhood where all of those around you are accused criminals, convicted felons, and other criminal offenders. How many people would voluntarily move into such a neighborhood?

At any time, the prisoner must be prepared to fight to protect his or her belongings and personal safety. Living with the constant threat of victimization is stressful, and this constant stress adds to the pain of imprisonment. Cell doors may serve not only to lock in the inmate, but also to lock out others who may harm the prisoner. It is not uncommon for prison inmates to request placement in segregation (solitary confinement) for reasons of personal safety. Existing in the general prison population is generally a frightening experience.

> It used to be a pastime of mine to watch the change in men, to observe the blackening of their hearts. It takes place before your eyes. They enter prison more bewildered than afraid. Every step after that, the fear creeps into them . . . No one is prepared for it.
>
> Everyone is afraid. It is not an emotional, psychological fear. It is a practical matter. If you do not threaten someone, at the very least, someone will threaten you (Abbott, 1981:144).

Correctional Officers: The Other Inmates

If imprisonment is frustrating and painful to inmates, it is not much less so for those whose job it is to work within the walls of penal facilities each day. In recent years, there has been increasing attention paid to the stressful role of custodial officers in prisons and jails (Dowden & Tellier, 2004; Lambert, 2003; Moracco, 1985; Philliber, 1987; Wright, 1993; Wright & Sweeney, 1990; Zupan, 1992). This stress has been linked to physical illness, job dissatisfaction, and job turnover among correctional officers. What happens on the job, stress, and level of job satisfaction also "spill over" to influence general satisfaction with life. Research indicates that correctional officers who report being less satisfied at work are also likely to report lower levels of satisfaction with their lives in general (Lambert et al., 2005). While they may be able to leave the institution at the end of their shifts, most correctional officers, over the span of their careers, will spend more time in prison or jail than will the inmates. They too suffer several pains of imprisonment. Triplett, Mullings, and Scarborough (1996) reported that concerns about safety and career development were important sources of stress for correctional officers. Officers responding to their survey also indicated that conflicting expectations and ambiguity about the job were problems faced by most officers. A meta-analysis of research on correctional officer stress reviewed 20 different studies and concluded that role definition problems contribute to officer stress, but that work attitudes and perceived danger were the most important predictors of stress (Dowden & Tellier, 2004).

The correctional officer serves a dual role: (1) manager of inmates, and (2) line-level worker within the prison. As a line worker, the officer is subjected to frequent "shake-downs" (to control the possibility of officers smuggling contraband into the prison), supervision, and disciplinary action by superior officers, and other controls, which make the occupation of correctional officer similar to the role of prison inmate (Clear & Cole, 1986:306). In a study of supervisory and administrative staff in higher-custody facilities, Reisig and Lovrich (1998) found that those working in facilities in which there was a controlling model of management (strict rules and supervision) were most dissatisfied and reported the highest levels of role strain. Dowden and Tellier (2004) noted that lack of a voice in organizational decisionmaking (similar to "deprivation of autonomy") was an important source of stress for correctional officers.

Starting pay for correctional officers is generally low, and there is little hope for advancement to managerial positions (Fogel, 1979:95-96). Requirements for officers are also minimal, and turnover in the custodial ranks is high. By virtue of the low entrance criteria, relatively low pay, and low status associated with their job, custodial officers suffer many of the same kinds of deprivations as do inmates.

While more than 60 percent of the prison staff hold correctional officer positions, the role of correctional officer had often been ignored (Hawkins, 1976). Investigations of the correctional officer's role have identified the importance of the officer to the operation of the prison (Jacobs & Crotty, 1978; Lombardo, 1989). Guards have the greatest contact with prison inmates, and are most directly responsible for the smooth operation of the prison. Box 10.9 compares correctional officers to inmates.

Box 10.9 Characteristics of Prison Personnel/Inmates

Race:	Prison Staff	Inmates
White	63.9%	34.2%
Black	19.0%	45.1%
Hispanic	7.3%	18.1%
Other	1.8%	2.6%
Sex:		
Male	67.3%	93.8%
Female	32.7%	6.2%

Source: Derived from P. Harris & A. Beck (2003), *Prisoners in 2002* (Washington, DC: Bureau of Justice Statistics); J. Stephan & J. Karber (2003), *Census of State and Federal Correctional Facilities, 2000* (Washington, DC: Bureau of Justice Statistics).

A survey of correctional officers in New Jersey (Cheek & Miller, 1983) identified 21 items that the officers felt were the most stressful aspects of the job. The most important of these can be classified into the categories of organizational or administrative problems. The officers reported being most troubled by a lack of clear job description, absence of support from superiors, and not being able to exercise personal judgment. Cheek and Miller (1983:19) concluded:

> The officer gets no respect from anyone. Not from the outside community, which sees him as the brute portrayed in the old James Cagney movies, not from the inmates who use him as a dumping ground for their hostility, not from prison administrators who expect him to play the tin soldier. . . . A stressful job indeed!

As with any occupational group, it is difficult to generalize about guards, for they differ widely among themselves in terms of how they perceive and perform their jobs. Auerbach, Quick, and Pegg (2003) report that correctional officers perceive higher levels of job stress than do most other types of workers. Mitchell and his colleagues (2000) found that stress was a major factor in correctional officers deciding to leave their jobs. Jackson and Ammen (1996) investigated changes in the composition of the correctional officer force resulting from affirmative action in Texas. They concluded that the recruitment of females and individuals from minority groups resulted in a wider range of officer perceptions of inmates and prison treatment. Camp and his colleagues (2001) found that diversity in the prison workforce was associated with lower job commitment among white, male officers, but did not seem to affect teamwork and job performance. However, Triplett, Mullings, and Scarborough (1999) reported that female officers are more likely to experience stress related to conflicts between the job and their home lives, and Hemmens and his colleagues (2002) reported that the presence of even a few "traditional males" in the prison workforce can support a culture that is antagonistic toward female correctional officers.

Toch and Klofas (1982) reported that perhaps one-fourth of all custodial officers fit the Hollywood image of the brutal, uncaring guard. They called this type of officer the "smug hack." However, this estimate means that 75 percent of the custodial force does not fit the stereotype. Johnson (1987:184) suggested that most guards are not "hacks," but play an important role in providing services to inmates. The guards do this, Johnson argued, at least partly in response to their need to make the job more challenging and important than either the public or the prison administration believes it to be.

Toch and Klofas reported that perhaps one-fourth of all custodial corrections officers fit the Hollywood image of the brutal, uncaring guard, which they term the "smug hack." This estimate means, of course, that about 75 percent of the custodial force does not fit that stereotype. *Photo credit: Mark C. Ide.*

Many officers, however, try to solve the problem of alienation by expanding their roles and making them more substantial and rewarding. These officers discover that in the process of helping inmates, and thereby giving them more autonomy, security, and emotional support, the officers gain the same benefits: more control over their environment, more security in their daily interactions with prisoners, and a sense of community—however inchoate or ill-defined—with at least some of the people under their care. In other words, in solving inmate adjustment problems, staff solve their own problems as well. Hassine (1996:117-118) commented on the symbiotic relationship between guards and inmates:

> . . . an unwritten agreement has been established between inmates and guards: inmates get what they want by being friendly and nonaggressive, while guards ensure their own safety by not strictly enforcing the rules. For the most part, inmates manipulate the guards' desire for safety, and guards exploit the inmates' need for autonomy.

Prison custodial officers then, like inmates and like police in the community, are affected by the nature of their positions within the justice system. In a classic experiment on the effects of incarceration, Philip Zimbardo (1972) concluded that incarceration profoundly affected both the inmates and the guards. He concluded that the social situation (role definitions of guard or prisoner, presence or absence of power, etc.) determines how people will act. John Riley (2000) explored the influence of social setting on guard behavior. He found that correctional officers developed "sensemaking" tactics whereby they could define inmates as different, and less than human, justifying their exercise of control. Hemmens and Marquart (2000) reported a study of prisoners that indicated that inmates tended to report lower levels of satisfaction with correctional officers. Marquart (2005) suggests that relationships between inmates and officers are generally "cooperative" as both groups attempted to maintain order in the institution. Whether because of administrative rules, a lack of training, or some other reason, prison officers have a limited range of actions open to them. As part-time prison inmates, correctional officers too are deprived of liberty, autonomy, and security. What these officers seem to want is not just more respect or support from the public and superiors, but more options. That is, officers seem to believe that they will achieve greater security in the prison if they are granted the liberty to perform their jobs in a more autonomous fashion (Hepburn, 1987).

Incarceration in the Criminal Justice System

For years, the operations of penal facilities were not open to public or court scrutiny. Rather, the prisons and jails were assumed to require no supervision by outsiders, and indeed, it was believed that outside interference would be more harmful than beneficial. In the past several decades, however, this condition has changed with the emergence of prisoners' rights.

David Fogel (1979) suggested that our perceptions of prison inmates have traveled along a continuum, from the earliest days when the offender was seen as a pariah, through periods of viewing the offender as penitent, prisoner, and patient, to the current view of the prisoner as a peer. This shift to seeing prisoners as peers has been status-costly to correctional authorities, for they must now deal with inmates as individuals who retain certain rights. The unreviewed, nearly total power over inmates that traditionally rested with correctional authorities is now subject to judicial review upon the filing of suits by the inmates themselves. In the 1941 case of *Ex parte Hull*, the U.S. Supreme Court ruled that inmates had the right to access of the courts. Initially, this right of access was more theoretical than practical. For years, appellate courts adopted a **"hands off" doctrine** in deciding cases concerning the rights of inmates (Vito & Kaci, 1982). In a series of appellate court decisions, though, rights of inmates have been identified, and due process controls have been placed on the exercise of discretion by prison authorities.

In 1964, the U.S. Supreme Court decided the case of *Cooper v. Pate*, ruling that prisoners in state and federal institutions were protected from arbitrary and capricious violations of their civil rights. Prison inmates were entitled to the protections of the Civil Rights Act of 1871. In deciding the case, the Court provided a vehicle by which inmates could challenge conditions of confinement in the nation's courts. A later decision, *Johnson v. Avery*, further strengthened the position of inmates. In this case, the Court ruled that prison authorities must either allow inmates the use of "jailhouse lawyers" (inmates who assist others in the preparation of court documents) or provide an adequate alternative. In combination, these two rulings meant that inmates were not only entitled to certain rights, but that they were also to be provided with the necessary resources to secure those rights in court. As Cohen (1972:862) noted, "To hold, for example, that a prisoner must be guaranteed reasonable access to the courts, that he must suffer no reprisals for his efforts, and that there is a right to some form of assistance, recognizes the prisoner as a jural entity."

Donald Wallace (1992) observed that commentators often rely upon the decision of the Virginia Supreme Court in *Ruffin v. Virginia* (1871) as support for the hands-off approach of the courts to prisoner's rights. In that decision the court wrote that the prisoner was a "slave of the state," and thus had no protected rights. Wallace observed that indeed there has been a tradition of judicial oversight of prisons and concern with prisoner's issues. The problem for prisoners, however, was that courts were reluctant to intervene directly, except in the most extreme cases, and inmates were often unable to get the attention of either the courts or the public. Abandonment of a general hands-off attitude made court oversight of prisons more likely.

With access to the courts thus ensured, the next stage in the development of prisoners' rights was entered. It was now time for prisoners to seek protections from the more onerous conditions of confinement. In a flurry of litigation, this is precisely what happened. The more important developments in prisoners' rights occurred in three areas, relating to the protections of the First, Eighth, and Fourteenth Amendments.

In deciding questions of prisoners' rights, the courts generally have applied three tests to the reasonableness of prison conditions and regulations: (1) compelling state interest, (2) least restrictive alternative, and (3) clear and present danger. A **compelling state interest** is any concern of the state (prison administration) that is so important that it overrides the protections afforded in the Constitution. Such an interest, for example, would be evident if an inmate were to request the right to go on a pilgrimage for religious reasons; the state "interest" in custody is compelling and justifies the denial of the right to go on a pilgrimage. The **least restrictive alternative** refers to the desire to be no more oppressive than is necessary to meet the needs of the state. For example, a rule punishing an inmate for possession of lewd photographs would probably be too restrictive, given that a rule prohibiting display of the material would meet the state's interests in not arousing other inmates. Finally, **clear and present danger** refers to conditions or behavior that pose an immediate threat to safety or order and relates to controls on the activities of inmates that pose a direct threat to the smooth operation of the facility. For example, rules prohibiting inmates from assembling and making inflammatory speeches will be upheld, as such activities pose a clear and present danger of instigating riots.

Prisoners' Rights

First Amendment Protections

The First Amendment to the U.S. Constitution provides for the freedoms of religion, speech, the press, and assembly, as well as the right to petition the government for redress of grievances. Some of the more noteworthy prisoners' cases focused on the question of freedom of religion, although other First Amendment issues were also litigated. The examples above illustrate some of the kinds of issues that have been decided in the courts.

The major decisions regarding freedom of religion dealt with the emergence and spread of Islam in the prisons. Black Muslims in prisons were initially (and perhaps are to this day) viewed with suspicion by prison administrators. The Muslims were seen more as a political group than a religious sect. Requests for special diets, spiritual mentors (chaplains), access to the Koran, and the like, tended to be seen as challenges to prison authority rather than attempts to practice a religion. The Muslims were required to litigate almost every issue involved in the practice of their religion in prison.

Similar litigation was required to clarify other First Amendment issues, such as access to the media, censorship of mail, visitation rights, formation of prisoners' unions, and other activities. Employing the three reasonableness tests described above, the courts have decided hundreds of cases dealing with First Amendment rights of prisoners.

Eighth Amendment Protections

The Eighth Amendment to the U.S. Constitution provides that cruel and unusual punishments will not be inflicted upon offenders. Prisoners have brought suits under this amendment to protest perceived deficiencies in nearly every aspect of prison life, from food to medical treatment. With the recent surge in prison populations, these suits have become more controversial as inmates seek relief from overcrowded prisons and overburdened prison resources. In *Rhodes v. Chapman* (1982), the U.S. Supreme Court ruled that crowding (housing two inmates in cells designed for one) by itself does not constitute cruel and unusual punishment.

Eighth Amendment suits have been responsible for the cessation of corporal punishment and a general improvement in prison conditions. There is evidence, however, that the courts are reluctant to interfere in the operation of prisons. A leading case in prison conditions was *Holt v. Sarver* (1970), on which the movie *Brubaker* was based. In this case, inmates in Arkansas protested a wide range of prison conditions, from poor sanitary facilities to the use of inmate trustees (including allegations of inadequate medical care, food, sleeping quarters, and almost everything else). The Court found that many of the specific allegations did not constitute cruel and unusual punishment, but when it considered the claims together (the totality of the circumstances), the court decided that conditions at the prison combined to make life there cruel and unusual. Later cases similar to this have led to the appointment of "masters," who are charged by the court with the responsibility of bringing a prison, or even an entire prison system, into compliance with the Constitution.

Fourteenth Amendment Protections

The third major area of development in prisoners' rights lies within the purview of the Fourteenth Amendment, which provides that no state may deprive any citizen of life, liberty, or property without due process of law. This amendment also ensures that the federal courts can apply the requirements of the U.S. Constitution to the states.

Perhaps the most important due process case in the area of prisoners' rights was decided by the U.S. Supreme Court in 1974. In *Wolff v. McDonnell,* the Court determined what due process rights applied to prison disciplinary hearings. Prior to this decision, it was not uncommon for prisoners to face a presumption of guilt and be granted no constitutional protections in disciplinary hearings. The *Wolff* decision required that correctional authorities provide to any prisoner charged with a rules violation: (1) written notice of the charges, (2) a hearing within 72 hours of notice, (3) warnings of possible criminal proceedings that could result from the hearing, (4) a written statement of the findings and evidence, and (5) the right to appeal within five days.

The impact of these rights on the daily lives of prisoners is unclear. While prisons are still not "country clubs" by any stretch of the imagination, one effect of the prisoners' rights movement has been to make prisons less oppressive than they had been. While the pains of imprisonment still do exist, inmates today have somewhat more freedom and autonomy within the institution than did inmates at the time Sykes identified the five "deprivations" associated with prison life. Yet, correctional officials have ways to circumvent the requirements of court rulings such as the procedural protections afforded in *Wolff* (Thomas et al., 1991). Further, a number of court decisions have limited the ability of inmates to bring suit alleging violations of their rights. Rudolf Alexander (1993:115) contends that the courts have "slammed the door" on inmates: "Whether in personal liability, habeas corpus, or rights emanating from the amendments to the U.S. Constitution, the Supreme Court of the 1980s and early 1990s has made it much more difficult for inmates to prevail."

Legal Issues in Incarceration

While most of the major issues around prisoners' rights have been decided in general, there remain a number of questions that continue to bring prisoners' rights cases to the courts. Stephan and Karberg (2003:9) reported that in June 2000, 20 percent of institutions were operating under court orders or consent decrees. Most involved suits regarding conditions of confinement, and about 40 percent specifically required limits on the size of the prison population. About 16 percent involved the totality of conditions, and the remainder involved specific conditions ranging from accommodations for the disabled to fire safety. Recent efforts to make imprisonment more painful have focused on restricting recreational opportunities for inmates. These efforts include calls for the removal of weight-lifting equipment, television, and similar "frills." The right of inmates to recreational time and pursuits has been established, but the definition of what kinds of activities are protected has not been resolved (Lee, 1996). Increasingly, issues associated with the concept of prisoners' rights are being litigated as civil liability cases. Perhaps the prisoners' rights movement has overcome restrictions on the use of criminal law appeals by entering the civil courts (Vaughn, 1996).

Box 10.10 provides a table on selected court cases on prisoners' rights.

Box 10.10 Selected Court Cases on Prisoners' Rights

Ruffin v. Virginia 62 Va. 790 (1871)	Declared prison inmates to be "slaves of the state" while imprisoned.
Cooper v. Pate 378 U.S. 546 (1941)	Granted inmates protection from arbitrary and capricious violations of civil rights.
Ex parte Hull 312 U.S. 546 (1964)	Granted prison inmates the right of access to the courts.
Johnson v. Avery 393 U.S. 483 (1969)	Required prison administrators to provide legal assistance to inmates.
Holt v. Sarver 309 F. Supp. 362 (1970)	Used "totality of circumstances" test to determine that conditions which shocked the conscience of the court violated the Eighth Amendment.
Wolff v. McDonnell 418 U.S. 539 (1974)	Specified due process protections for inmates facing disciplinary charges.
Chapman v. Rhodes 452 U.S. 337 (1982)	Declared that prison crowding, by itself does not violate the ban on cruel and unusual punishments.
Porter v. Nussle 534 U.S. 516 (2002)	Held that the exhaustion requirement of the Prison Litigation Reform Act (PLRA) of 1995 applies to all inmate suits about prison life, regardless of whether they involve systemic conditions or isolated acts of wrongdoing.

Due Process, Crime Control, and Incarceration

The issue of prisoners' rights demonstrates the conflict between due process and crime control in the incarceration process. Even when convicted of a felony offense and sentenced to prison, individuals retain rights and interests that are protected by our laws. Before the government can restrict the liberty of individuals (even incarcerated individuals), it must justify its decisions. Requirements for tests of state interest and the least drastic alternative represent limits on the authority of prison and jail staff. Viewing these concerns within a framework of the totality of circumstances, however, allows courts to consider the operational and crime control effects.

After conviction, and certainly after incarceration, the balance between due process and crime control concerns shifts to some degree. The observations of Alexander (1993) that the federal courts are slamming the door on inmates is partly a reaction to this shift in balance. The courts are attempting to limit the disruption of crime control and operational efforts of correctional administrators by defining causes of action more narrowly. The U.S. Congress passed the **Prison Litigation Reform Act** of 1995 (PLRA), a law requiring inmates to exhaust all administrative remedies (appeals through the prison administration and department of corrections) before they could file a suit in federal court. In 2002, the U.S. Supreme Court decided *Porter v. Nussle*, ruling that the requirement of exhausting all administrative remedies was mandatory, no matter what the basis of the inmate's appeal, including allegations of excessive force.

This narrowing of definition, compared to the heyday of prisoner's rights, seems to be victory for crime control supporters over those concerned with due process. In all likelihood, it is a natural attempt by the justice system to achieve equilibrium between these conflicting concerns. One thing that has not changed is the right of inmates to be protected from unreasonable or malicious interventions by correctional staff. The creation of a prisoner's rights movement settled the question of the existence of due process protections for inmates. What remains is to determine how those protections will be balanced against the crime control concerns of society.

Review Questions

1. Why can incarceration be considered the cornerstone of American corrections?

2. Briefly relate the history of American prisons and jails. Distinguish between the Auburn and Pennsylvania systems of incarceration.

3. With reference to organizational and legal differences, distinguish between prisons and jails.

Review Questions (continued)

4. Identify the "pains of imprisonment."

5. Who are the "other inmates"?

6. Explain what is meant by the "hands off" doctrine.

7. Identify three areas in which prisoners' rights have been granted or expanded.

References

Abbott, J.H. (1981). *In the Belly of the Beast: Letters from Prison.* New York: Vintage.

Alexander, R. (1993). "Slamming the Federal Courthouse Door on Inmates." *Journal of Criminal Justice* 21(2):103-116.

Applegate, B., F. Cullen & B. Fisher (2002). "Public Views Toward Crime and Correctional Policies: Is There a Gender Gap?" *Journal of Criminal Justice* 30(2):89-100.

Auerbach, S., B. Quick & P. Pegg (2003). "General Job Stress and Job-Specific Stress in Juvenile Correctional Officers." *Journal of Criminal Justice* 31(1):25-36.

Beck, A. & C. Mumola (1999). *Prisoners in 1998.* Washington, DC: Bureau of Justice Statistics.

Bikle, B. (2000). "Direct Supervision Jails: What Have We Learned?" Paper presented at the annual meeting of Midwestern Criminal Justice Association, October 2000.

Bonczar, T. (2003). *Prevalence of Imprisonment in the U.S. Population, 1974-2001.* Washington, DC: Bureau of Justice Statistics.

Braly, M. (1976). *False Starts: A Memoir of San Quentin and Other Prisons.* New York: Penguin Books.

Bureau of Justice Statistics (1985). *Jail Inmates, 1983.* Washington, DC: U.S. Department of Justice.

Bureau of Justice Statistics (1987). *Prisoners in 1986.* Washington, DC: U.S. Department of Justice.

Bureau of Justice Statistics (1997). *Correctional Populations in the United States, 1995.* Washington, DC: Bureau of Justice Statistics.

Camp, S., W. Saylor & K. Wright (2001). "Racial Diversity of Correctional Workers and Inmates: Organizational Commitment, Teamwork, and Worker's Efficacy in Prisons." *Justice Quarterly* 18(2):411-427.

Camp, C. & G. Camp (1996). *The Corrections Yearbook 1996.* South Salem, NY: Criminal Justice Institute.

Cheek, F.E. & M.D. Miller (1983). "The Experience of Stress for Correction Officers: A Double-Bind Theory of Correctional Stress." *Journal of Criminal Justice* 11(2):105-120.

Clear, T.R. (1997). "Ten Unintended Consequences of the Growth in Imprisonment." *Corrections Management Quarterly* 1(2):25-31.

Clear, T.R. (1994). *Harm in American Penology: Offenders, Victims, and Their Communities.* Albany, NY: SUNY Press.

Clear, T.R. & G.F. Cole (1986). *American Corrections.* Monterey, CA: Brooks/Cole.

Cohen, F. (1972). "The Discovery of Prison Reform." *Buffalo Law Review* 21(3):855-887.

Connolly, P.K. (1975). "The Possibility of a Prison Sentence is a Necessity." *Crime & Delinquency* 21(4):356-359.

Cullen, F. (1995). "Assessing the Penal Harm Movement." *Journal of Research in Crime and Delinquency* 32(2):338-358.

Cullen, F. & P. Gendreau (2000). "Assessing Correctional Rehabilitation: Policy, Practice, and Prospects." In J. Horney (ed.), *Policies, Processes, and Decisions of the Criminal Justice System.* Washington, DC: National Institute of Justice, 2000:109-176.

Dowden, C. & C. Tellier (2004). "Predicting Work-Related Stress in Correctional Officers: A Meta-Analysis." *Journal of Criminal Justice* 32(1):49-62.

Durham, A. (1989). "Judgments of Appropriate Punishment: The Effects of Question Type." *Journal of Criminal Justice* 17(2):75-86.

Durham, A. (1990). "Social Control and Imprisonment During the American Revolution: Newgate of Connecticut." *Justice Quarterly* 7(2):293-323.

Feeley, M. & J. Simon (1992). "The New Penology: Notes on the Emerging Strategy of Corrections and Its Implications." *Criminology* 30(3):449-474.

Fishman, J.F. (1923). *Crucibles of Crime: The Shocking Story of the American Jail.* Montclair, NJ: Patterson Smith, 1969.

Flanagan, T. (1996). "Reform or Punish? Americans' Views of the Correctional System." In T. Flanagan and D. Longmire (eds.), *Americans View Crime and Justice: A National Public Opinion Survey.* Thousand Oaks, CA: Sage, 1996.

Fogel, D.F. (1979). *We Are the Living Proof…The Justice Model for Corrections.* Cincinnati: Anderson.

Foucault, M. (1979). *Discipline and Punish: The Birth of the Prison.* New York: Vintage Books.

Garland, D. (1990). *Punishment and Modern Society.* Chicago: University of Chicago Press.

Goffman, E. (1961). *Asylums: Essays on the Social Situations of Mental Patients and Other Inmates.* Chicago: Aldine.

Goldfarb, R. (1975). *Jails: The Ultimate Ghetto.* New York: Anchor-Doubleday.

Greenfeld, L. (1992). *Prisons and Prisoners in the United States.* Washington, DC: U.S. Department of Justice.

Harlow, C. (2003). *Education and Correctional Populations.* Washington, DC: Bureau of Justice Statistics.

Harrison, P. & A. Beck (2003). *Prisoners in 2002.* Washington, DC: Bureau of Justice Statistics.

Hassine, V. (1996). *Life Without Parole: Living in Prison Today.* Los Angeles: Roxbury.

Hawkins, G. (1976). *The Prison: Policy and Practice.* Chicago: University of Chicago Press.

Hemmens, C. & J. Marquart (2000). "Friend or Foe? Race, Age, and Inmate Perceptions of Inmate-Staff Relations." *Journal of Criminal Justice* 28(4):297-312.

Hemmens, C., M. Stohr, M. Schoeler & B. Miller (2002). "One Step Up, Two Steps Back: The Progression of Perceptions of Women's Work in Prisons and Jails." *Journal of Criminal Justice* 30(6):473-489.

Hepburn, J. (1987). "The Prison Control Structure and Its Effects on Work Attitudes: The Percep-tions and Attitudes of Prison Guards." *Journal of Criminal Justice* 15(1):49-64.

Hochstetler, A. & M. DeLisi (2005). "Importation, Deprivation, and Varieties of Serving Time: An Integrated-lifestyle-exposure Model of Prison Offending." *Journal of Criminal Justice* 33(3):257-266.

Holcomb, J. & M. Williams (2003). "From the Field: 'Bad Time': The Rise and Fall of Penal Policy in Ohio." *Journal of Crime and Justice* 26(2):153-175.

Jacobs, J. & N. Crotty (1978). *Guard Unions and the Future of Prisons.* Ithaca, NY: New York State School of Industrial and Labor Relations.

Jackson, J. & S. Ammen (1996). "Race and Correctional Officers' Punitive Attitudes Toward Treatment Programs for Inmates." *Journal of Criminal Justice* 24(2):153-166.

James, D. (2004). *Profile of Jail Inmates 2002.* Washington, DC: Bureau of Justice Statistics.

Johnson, R. (1987). *Hard Time: Understanding and Reforming the Prison.* Monterey, CA: Brooks/Cole.

Karberg, J. & D. James (2005). *Substance Dependence, Abuse, and Treatment of Jail Inmates, 2002.* Washington, DC: Bureau of Justice Statistics.

Katsampes, P. & T.C. Neil (1981). "A Decade of Improvement for Our Sick Jails." *Federal Probation* 45(3):45-48.

Keve, P.W. (1986). *The History of Corrections in Virginia.* Charlottesville: University Press of Virginia.

Kolstad, A. (1996). "Imprisonment as Rehabilitation: Offenders' Assessment of Why It Doesn't Work." *Journal of Criminal Justice* 24(4):323-335.

Lambert, E. (2003). "The Impact of Organizational Justice on Correctional Staff." *Journal of Criminal Justice* 31(2):155-168.

Lambert, E., N. Hogan, E. Paoline & D. Baker (2005). "The Good Life: The Impact of Job Sat-isfaction and Occupational Stressors on Correctional Staff Life Satisfaction—An Exploratory Study." *Journal of Crime and Justice* 28(2):1-26.

Langbein, J.H. (1976). "The Historical Origins of the Sanction of Imprisonment for Serious Crime." *Journal of Legal Studies* 5.

Lee, R. (1996). "Prisoners' Rights to Recreation: Quantity, Quality, and Other Aspects." *Journal of Criminal Justice* 24(2):167-178.

Lockwood, D. (1982). "The Contribution of Sexual Harassment to Stress and Coping in Confine-ment." In N. Parisi (ed.), *Coping with Imprisonment.* Beverly Hills, CA: Sage, 45-64.

Logan, C. & G. Gaes (1993). "Meta-Analysis and the Rehabilitation of Punishment." *Justice Quarterly* 10(2):245-262.

Lombardo, L.X. (1989). *Guards Imprisoned,* 2nd ed. Cincinnati: Anderson.

Lutze, F. & D. Murphy (1999). "Ultramasculine Prison Environments and Inmates' Adjustment: It's Time to Move Beyond the 'Boys Will Be Boys' Paradigm." *Justice Quarterly* 16(4):709-733.

Lynch, J. & W. Sabol (2000). "Prison Use and Social Control." In J. Horney (ed.), *Policies, Processes, and Decisions of the Criminal Justice System.* Washington, DC: National Institute of Justice, 2000:7-44.

Marquart, J. (2005). "Understanding the Power of Social Contexts on Criminal Justice Institutions." *Journal of Criminal Justice Education* 16(2):213-225.

Maruschak, L. (2006). *Medical Problems of Jail Inmates.* Washington, DC: Bureau of Justice Statistics.

McDonald, J. (1999). "Violence and Drug Use in Juvenile Institutions." *Journal of Criminal Justice* 27(1):33-44.

McGee, R. (1971). "Our Sick Jails." *Federal Probation* 35(1):3-8.

Mitchell, O., D. Mackenzie, G. Styve & A. Gover (2000). "The Impact of Individual, Organizational, and Environmental Attributes on Voluntary Turnover among Juvenile Correctional Staff Members." *Justice Quarterly* 17(2):333-357.

Moracco, J.C. (1985). "Stress: How Corrections Personnel Can Anticipate, Manage, and Reduce Stress on the Job." *Corrections Today* 47(7):22-26.

Moynahan, J.M. & E. Steward (1980). *The American Jail.* Chicago: Nelson-Hall.

Mumola, C. & A. Beck (1997). *Prisoners in 1996.* Washington, DC: Bureau of Justice Statistics.

Nacci, P.L. & T.R. Kane (1984). "Sex and Sexual Aggression in Federal Prisons: Inmate Involvement and Employee Impact." *Federal Probation* 48(1):46-53.

National Advisory Commission on Criminal Justice Standards and Goals (1973). *Corrections.* Washington, DC: U.S. Government Printing Office.

Newman, G.R. (1983). *Just and Painful.* New York: Macmillan.

O'Leary, V. & D. Duffee (1971). "Correctional Policy: A Classification of Goals Designed for Change." *Crime & Delinquency* 17(4):373-386.

Paterline, B. & D. Petersen (1999). "Structural and Social Psychological Determinants of Prisonization." *Journal of Criminal Justice* 27(5):427-441.

Perkins, C. (1994). *Prison Inmates 1992.* Washington, DC: Bureau of Justice Statistics.

Perkins, C., J. Stephan & A. Beck (1995). *Jails and Jail Inmates 1993-94.* Washington, DC: Bureau of Justice Statistics.

Philliber, S. (1987). "Thy Brother's Keeper: A Review of the Literature on Correctional Officers." *Justice Quarterly* 4(1):9-37.

Reasons, C.E. & R.L. Kaplan (1975). "Tear Down the Walls? Some Functions of Prisons." *Crime & Delinquency* 21(4):360-372.

Reisig, M. and N. Lovrich (1998). "Job Attitudes among Higher-Custody State Prison Management Personnel: A Cross-Sectional Comparative Assessment." *Journal of Criminal Justice* 26(3):213-226.

Rhine, E. (1992). "Sentencing Reform and Correctional Policy: Some Unanswered Questions." In C. Hartjen and E. Rhine (eds.), *Correctional Theory and Practice.* Chicago: Nelson-Hall, 1992:271-287.

Riley, J. (2000). "Sensemaking in Prison: Inmate Identity as a Working Understanding." *Justice Quarterly* 17(2):359-376.

Rothman, D. (1971). *The Discovery of the Asylum.* Boston: Little, Brown.

Rothman, D. (1980). *Conscience and Convenience: The Asylum and Its Alternatives in Progressive America.* Boston: Little, Brown.

Ruddell, R. & G. Mays (2007). "Rural Jails: Problematic Inmates, Overcrowded Cells, and Cash-strapped Counties." *Journal of Criminal Justice* 35(3):251-260.

Rutherford, A. (1993). *Criminal Justice and the Pursuit of Decency.* Oxford, UK: Oxford University Press.

Sabol, W. & J. McGready (1999). *Time Served in Prison by Federal Offenders, 1986-97.* Washington, DC: Bureau of Justice Statistics.

Sabol, W., T. Minton & P. Harrison (2007). *Prison and Jail Inmates at Midyear 2006.* Washington, DC: Bureau of Justice Statistics.

Schwartz, M. & L. Travis (1996). *Corrections: An Issues Approach,* 4th ed. Cincinnati: Anderson.

Schriro, D. (2000). *Correcting Corrections: Missouri's Parallel Universe.* Washington, DC: National Institute of Justice.

Seiter, R. (1997). "A View From The Inside: Setting Correctional Policies." *Corrections Management Quarterly* 1(2):81-83.

Senese, J. (1997). "Evaluating Jail Reform: A Comparative Analysis of Podular/Direct and Linear Jail Inmate Infractions." *Journal of Criminal Justice* 25(1):61-73.

Skoler, D.L. (1978). *Governmental Structuring of Criminal Justice Services: Organizing the Non-system.* Washington, DC: U.S. Government Printing Office.

Snell, T. (1993). *Correctional Populations in the United States, 1991.* Washington, DC: Bureau of Justice Statistics.

Spalding, W.F. (1897). "Indeterminate Sentences." In *Proceedings of the National Conference of Charities and Correction at the 24th Annual Session,* Toronto, Canada, July 7-14, 46-51.

Stephan, J. (2004). *State Prison Expenditures, 2001.* Washington, DC: Bureau of Justice Statistics.

Stephan, J. (2001). *Census of Jails, 1999.* Washington, DC: Bureau of Justice Statistics.

Stephan, J. & J. Karberg (2003). *Census of State and Federal Correctional Facilities, 2000.* Washington, DC: Bureau of Justice Statistics.

Sullivan, R. (1996). "The Birth of the Prison: Discipline or Punish?" *Journal of Criminal Justice* 24(5):449-458.

Sykes, G.M. (1969). *The Society of Captives.* Princeton, NJ: Princeton University Press.

Tewksbury, R. & M. DeMichele (2003). "The Good, the Bad, and the (Sometimes) Ugly Truths: American Penal Goals and Perspectives." *American Journal of Criminal Justice* 28(1):1-14.

Thomas, J., H. Mika, J. Blakemore & A. Aylward (1991). "Exacting Control Through Disciplinary Hearings: 'Making Do' with Prison Rules." *Justice Quarterly* 8(1):37-57.

Toch, H. & J. Klofas (1982). "Alienation and Desire for Job Enrichment Among Correctional Officers." *Federal Probation* 36:35-47.

Torok, L. (1974). *Straight Talk from Prison: A Convict Reflects on Youth, Crime and Society.* New York: Human Sciences Press.

Triplett, R., J. Mullings, & K. Scarborough (1999). "Examining the Effect of Work-Home Conflict on Work-Related Stress among Correctional Officers." *Journal of Criminal Justice* 27(4):371-385.

Triplett, R., J. Mullings & K. Scarborough (1996). "Work-Related Stress and Coping Among Correctional Officers: Implications From Organizational Literature." *Journal of Criminal Justice* 24(4):291-308.

Twentieth Century Fund (1976). *Fair and Certain Punishment.* New York: McGraw-Hill.

Vaughn, M. (1996). "Prison Civil Liability for Inmate-Against-Inmate Assault and Breakdown/ Disorganization Theory." *Journal of Criminal Justice* 24(2):139-152.

Vito, G.F. & J.H. Kaci (1982). "Hands On or Hands Off? The Use of Judicial Intervention to Establish Prisoners' Rights." In N. Parisi (ed.), *Coping with Imprisonment.* Beverly Hills, CA: Sage, 79-100.

Wallace, D. (1992). "Ruffin v. Virginia and Slaves of the State: A Nonexistent Baseline of Prisoner's Rights Jurisprudence." *Journal of Criminal Justice* 20(4):333-342.

Wright, E.O. (ed.) (1973). *The Politics of Punishment: A Critical Analysis of Prisons in America.* New York: Harper Torchbooks.

Wright, K. (2000). "The Evolution of Decisionmaking among Prison Executives, 1975-2000." In J. Horney (ed.), *Policies, Processes, and Decisions of the Criminal Justice System.* Washington, DC: National Institute of Justice, 2000:177-224.

Wright, T. (1993). "Correctional Employee Turnover: A Longitudinal Study." *Journal of Criminal Justice* 21(2):131-142.

Wright, T. & D. Sweeney (1990). "Correctional Institutional Workers' Coping Strategies and Their Effect on Diastolic Blood Pressure." *Journal of Criminal Justice* 18(2):161-170.

Zaitzow, B. (1999). "Doing Time: A Case Study of a North Carolina Youth Institution." *Journal of Crime and Justice* 22(2):91-124.

Zimbardo, P.G. (1972). "The Pathology of Imprisonment." *Society* 9(2).

Zupan, L. (1991). *Jails: Reform and the New Generation Philosophy.* Cincinnati: Anderson.

Zupan, L. (1992). "Men Guarding Women: An Analysis of the Employment of Male Correction Officers in Prisons for Women." *Journal of Criminal Justice* 20(4):297-310.

Zupan, L. & B. Menke (1988). "Implementing Organizational Change: From Traditional to New Generational Jail Operations." *Policy Studies Review* 7:614-625.

Important Cases

Cooper v. Pate, 378 U.S. 546 (1964).

Ex parte Hull, 312 U.S. 546 (1941).

Holt v. Sarver, 309 F. Supp. 362 (1970).

Johnson v. Avery, 393 U.S. 483 (1969).

Porter v. Nussle, 534 U.S. 512 (2002).

Rhodes v. Chapman, 452 U.S. 337 (1982).

Ruffin v. Virginia, 62 Va. 790 (1871).

Wolff v. McDonnell, 418 U.S. 539 (1974).

Chapter 11

Problems and Issues in Incarceration

The development of prisoners' rights is a core issue in the use of incarceration as a sanction for criminal offenders. Like other areas of the justice system, the incarceration of offenders is a practice surrounded by controversy. Indeed, the concept of incarceration—especially as practiced in the United States—is itself controversial. Critics often note that, among all the nations in Western civilization, the United States has the highest rate of imprisonment and imposes the longest prison terms on offenders (Doleschal, 1971). The impact of incarceration on reducing crime and helping criminals has been questioned, and the negative effects of imprisonment described (Crutchfield, 2004; Rogers, 1989). Still, others defend the use of incarceration. Richard Wright (1994, 1997) provides a strong argument for prisons as both a deterrent and incapacitative sanction, and Edwin Zedlewski (1997) notes that there is a value to prisons meeting society's desire to inflict some vengeance on criminal offenders.

It is clear that the United States incarcerates a large number of individuals, but not enough is known about whom we incarcerate and how patterns of incarceration change over time. Those who are incarcerated most often come from the lower classes of society. Jail inmate populations tend to reflect the ethnic composition of our lower and working classes (Stojkovic, Pope & Feyerherm, 1987). In addition, jail use varies by community (Klofas, 1987). Just as with the police and courts, some of the explanation for incarceration can be found in community attitudes and values. This point is illustrated by differences found in the treatment of crack cocaine users versus powder cocaine users. Viewing crack cocaine use as a more serious drug offense than powder cocaine use seems to have added to overrepresentation of minority-group members in the prison population (Barnes & Kingsnorth, 1996). The war on drugs affected all areas of incarceration in the United States by increasing the numbers of offenders incarcerated, and resulted in disproportionate incarceration of minorities (Snyder, 1990). Lynch and Sabol (2000) argue that the long-term consequences of incarcerating large numbers of young, poor, minority males may be an increase in crime. They suggest that current patterns of incarceration serve to disrupt family and social life in poor, minority neighborhoods, creating conditions that are ripe for crime. The research to date indicates that there is a weak link between high rates of incarceration and reduced community cohesion (Lynch & Sabol, 2004). Liedka, Piehl, and Useem (2006) suggest that the effect of imprisonment on crime is curvilinear. They argue that increasing the rate of imprisonment from low levels probably reduces crime, but eventually the increase reaches a point of "diminishing returns" at which continuing to increase the rate of incarceration may actually lead to increases in crime. The trick is to discover the optimum level of imprisonment at which we can obtain the greatest reductions in crime.

Reacting to these observations, several commentators have joined long-standing critics of incarceration by suggesting that the most appropriate strategy for the control of criminal offenders is one that reduces reliance on incarceration (McDonald, 1986; Meares, 2004; Nagel, 1973; National Council on Crime and Delinquency, 1972; Piehl, 2004; Rector, 1975). Norval Morris (1974) took a middle-ground approach in suggesting that prisons are necessary and useful in the control of the small percentage of dangerous offenders, but that the United States currently overuses incarceration.

Logan and DiIulio (1992), however, challenge such assumptions about the rates of incarceration in the United States. They note, for example, that the large number of persons incarcerated in the United States compared to other nations is a function of our higher crime rate. They also observe that while some "petty" criminals may go to prison, such offenders tend to be released early. More serious offenders serve longer terms, thus "stacking up" inside prisons. The net result is that most prisoners have been convicted of serious crimes. They also observe that Americans make widespread use of alternatives to incarceration. They conclude that incarceration, if justly imposed, is a positive feature of our law.

Other observers believe that the problem with American prisons is that they are underused. Some suggest that the solution to the crime problem will be found in the incarceration of offenders for incapacitative purposes (Greenwood, 1982; Wilson, 1975). The approach taken by these observers mirrors that of Morris in that they view prison as a scarce resource. They suggest that prison sentences be reserved for those criminals who commit the most serious offenses.

Some scholars are less discriminating and would impose incarceration on a much wider range of offenders. Edwin Zedlewski (1987) argued that incarceration of the average offender would save money. He calculated that, on average, it cost $25,000 to incarcerate a felon in prison for one year. Basing estimates on a survey of prison inmates, he concluded that the average inmate committed 187 crimes each year, at an average cost of $2,300 each. Thus, according to Zedlewski's model, investing $25,000 to incarcerate an offender would have saved $430,000 in crime costs. The reliability and accuracy of these estimates are questionable, but the model supports a broader use of incarceration.

Fox (1983:299) reported, "The viewpoint taken by the majority of correctional administrators is that prisons are overused and that many people in prison today do not need to be there." Yet, it is also true that abolition of the prison is not likely to occur in the near future. Whether because of its long tradition as a criminal sanction or, as Johnson (1987) suggests, because the urge to incarcerate may be "natural," the continued use of prisons seems assured. Assuming that we will continue to employ incarceration as a sanction for criminal offenses, the issues and controversies surrounding prison and jail operations today are significant. While the processes are unclear, it seems apparent that the experience of imprisonment has effects on prisoners and staff.

It is difficult to choose the issues on which to focus because there are so many problems found in our prisons and jails. Increasing use of imprisonment, along with the lengthening of prison terms imposed, have created a new class of "geriatric" prisoners. Increasing numbers of elderly offenders are serving time in American prisons, and these inmates pose management and medical problems for

prison operation (Maruschak & Beck, 2001; McDonald, Hasol & Carlson, 1999; Neeley, Addison & Craig-Moreland, 1997). In addition, the higher rates of AIDS infection among intravenous drug users has produced a disproportionate number of AIDS-infected inmates, partly as a result of the war on drugs. The health problems posed by these inmates are another contemporary problem in prisons and jails (Maruschak, 2004). A renewed focus on prison treatment of offenders to reduce the risk of future criminality has produced a variety of new programs and rekindled interest in

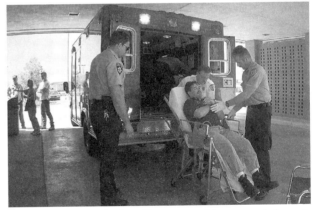

An unidentified Wackenhut officer is moved from an ambulance in Hobbs, New Mexico, after being transported from the Lea County Correctional Facility following a disturbance in April of 1999. At least eight guards were injured in the disturbance at the privately run prison. A "Private Prisons Watch" reported that the facility had been the site of three inmate stabbing deaths and a near-riot in that year. *Photo credit: AP Photo/Hobbs News-Sun, Duane Tinkey.*

traditional programming, such as education (Batiuk, Moke & Rountree, 1997), work (Saylor & Gaes, 1997), and activities by religious groups (Johnson, Larson & Pitts, 1997). Increases in the number of drug-involved persons in prisons and jails, and concern about the mental health problems of inmates, have spurred recent interest in drug and mental health treatment programs in correctional facilities (Mumola & Karberg, 2006). Personnel issues, ranging from changes in correctional officer recruitment and selection (Jackson & Ammen, 1996; Lommel, 2004) through staff training (Stohr, Lovrich & Wood, 1996), as well as officer stress discussed in Chapter 10, have received much attention. Continuing issues, such as the influence of gangs in prisons, the prisoner subculture, civil liability of prison administrators and systems, and facility design and size (Stohr et al., 1994) are still debated.

In this chapter, we will discuss four current issues in American incarceration: (1) privatization, (2) crowding, (3) prison industries, and (4) prison violence. As the history of incarceration has been one of problems, it may be safe to say that there are no new issues in American prisons and jails (Schwartz, Travis & Clear, 1980:212). These problem areas represent continuing issues around incarceration that reveal the structural limitations on the ability of correctional institutions to change—and show the effects of broader social changes on criminal justice system operations.

Privatization

For decades, correctional institutions have contracted for services with private corporations, ranging from facility design and construction to the provision of medical care or food service for the inmate population. There has been increasing privatization, that is, contracting with a private vendor for the entire operation of a prison or jail (Ericson, McMahon & Evans, 1987). Peter Greenwood (1981) suggested that private enterprise could do a better job of running the nation's prisons, at less cost. In 1985, the delegate assembly of the American Correctional Association (ACA) passed a policy statement that was generally supportive of further privatization (*Criminal Justice Newsletter*, 1985:1-2).

Privatizing the operation of correctional facilities began with several detention facilities operated by private businesses (Krajick, 1984). Most of these institutions dealt with special offender populations, such as illegal aliens or juvenile offenders. What followed was the suggestion that private companies be allowed to operate general-purpose prisons and jails (Logan, 1987). The effects of private operation are still debated, but as Box 11.1 illustrates, private firms operate many penal facilities.

By the middle 1990s, contracts for the provision of medical care and food service were common (Camp & Camp 1996:70). The private operation of halfway houses, prerelease centers, or related transitional residential programming was reported in 28 states. Only three states reported that they had contracted for the operations of institutions for adults under state jurisdiction (with a total of 61 beds). Obviously, private operation of penal institutions was limited at that time.

By 1987, however, privatization had spread. Hackett et al. (1987) reported that, by the end of 1986, about 1,200 adults were housed in secure facilities operated by private organizations. For example, the state of Kentucky contracted for the operation of a 200-bed minimum-security facility that opened in January 1986. The authors concluded, "State and local experience in contracting for the

Box 11.1   Correctional Facilities Run by Private Firms

Number of Facilities Under Contract	264
Rated Capacity of All Facilities Under Contract	105,133
Total Inmates in Operating Facilities	93,077
Percent Occupancy of Operating Facilities	89%
Security Level of Facilities:	
Maximum	4
Medium	65
Minimum	195

Source: J. Stephan & J. Karberg (2003), *Census of State and Federal Correctional Facilities, 2000* (Washington, DC: Bureau of Justice Statistics):iv.

entire operation and management of a secure adult institution is still quite limited." The effect of private prisons is still not well understood (Thomas, 2005).

Nonetheless, privatization has emerged as an alternative form of providing incarceration for all jurisdictions. Shover and Einstadter (1988) have suggested that privatization came to the fore in the 1980s because it was congruent with a national social view that the private sector and the "marketplace" are proper forums for the resolution of social problems. This is another example of how corrections reflects changes in social and political ideology.

On June 30, 2006, more than 111,000 inmates were housed in prisons operated by private contractors, comprising more than 7 percent of the total prison population (Sabol, Minton & Harrison, 2007). The Private Corrections Project at the University of Florida reported that the number of privately operated facilities grew by 13.4 percent to 161 institutions between 1997 and mid-1999. These facilities had the capacity to house 121,802 inmates (Maguire & Pastore, 1999:82). In 1999, 47 of the nation's local jails were privately owned or operated, housing 13,814 inmates, or 2.3 percent of the total jail population. By the end of 2005, 33 states and the federal government were using private prisons for about 7 percent of the inmate population. Another 5 percent of that population was held in local jails (Harrison & Beck, 2006). Five states (Alaska, Hawaii, Montana, New Mexico, and Wyoming) had at least a quarter of their prison population housed in private prisons at the end of 2005. More than 14 percent of federal inmates are also housed in private facilities (Harrison & Beck, 2006).

In an assessment of the benefits and drawbacks of private prisons and jails, Travis, Latessa, and Vito (1985) identified three problems with private involvement. First, it is not clear what is the legal authority of private contractors. Second, there is no solid evidence that privatization will prove to be less costly than state operation. Finally, there are unresolved questions about accountability (Mays & Gray, 1996).

Can and should a private company and its agents be authorized to exercise force (including deadly force) to prevent escapes, quell riots, and otherwise control an inmate population? Perhaps more basic is the question of whether a private company can be empowered to deprive citizens of their liberty. Related legal issues surround the question of liability. If an inmate is injured through the negligence of a private company, would the committing state or local government also be liable for damages? These questions need to be answered before any large-scale movement to private prisons can take place. Charles Logan (1987) suggested that the right of the state to imprison people derives ultimately from the citizens, and could be delegated properly to a private company. Further, he suggested that the motives of state agencies cannot be assumed to be any better than the profit motive of a private firm. In contrast, Michael Reisig and Travis Pratt (2000) concluded that private prison management runs counter to our moral and philosophical tradition concerning liberal-democratic constitutional government.

The issue of cost is similarly unsettled. With many services, contracting with private agencies appears to be more cost-efficient than governmental operation. Yet, the question of cost is less clear when discussing the possibility of an entire institution being run by a contractor. Any cost savings realized may be attained by lowering quality control. Might a private company hire custodial officers at minimum wage, thereby limiting the pool from which candidates might be drawn, and enhancing the likelihood of employee turnover? Assessments of private prison and jail operations must attend to both cost concerns and the impact of different types of facilities on future criminality by those who were incarcerated there (Pratt & Maahs, 1999). In one of the few published comparisons of private and public correctional facilities, Lanza-Kaduce, Parker, and Thomas (1999) concluded that privately operated juvenile facilities were more effective than their public counterparts. This study had some limitations, especially the fact that insufficient time had passed to be sure the youths housed in private facilities would continue to refrain from crime. Geis, Mobley, and Shichor (1999) criticized this evaluation because its authors were linked to private prison operations. They suggested that the results of the evaluation might have been influenced by a potential conflict of interest. This type of criticism raises the last major issue with privatization. A later comparison of public and private prisons in Florida revealed no difference in recidivism rates for inmates who were housed in those facilities (Bales et al., 2005).

This third set of concerns deals with accountability for the operation of the institution. If a prison or jail is "contracted," the contracting governmental authority is still accountable for the delivery of incarceration services (Gowdy, 1997:61). The task changes from that of managing the facility to that of overseeing and managing the contract. In addition, other problems of accountability arise because a new layer of administration has been created.

Would the manager of a privately operated prison be allowed to "cap" the population of the facility? Or could the private facility refuse to accept inmates suspected of being "troublemakers"? It is most likely that the governmental agency contracting for the private prison would still be held accountable for its operation, but would be forced to negotiate with the contractor over most aspects of institutional operation (Cooper, 1993). On the other hand, suppose the contracting government cannot supply enough inmates to make the private facility profitable? Clear (1997) reported that when this happened in Connecticut, investors in the private jail lobbied to import offenders from other regions for local incarceration. Until these and other issues are resolved, privatization will pose as many problems as it does solutions (Bowditch & Everett, 1987; Ogle, 1999).

In a review of what was known to date about private operation of correctional facilities, Thomas and Logan (1993:235) concluded:

> . . . the best available evidence reveals that existing privatization efforts have confronted no consequential constitutional barriers, have reduced the legal liability costs contracting units of government previously confronted, expanded the scope of legal remedies made available to prisoners, have decreased correctional costs in the areas of both construction and facility operation, resulted in quality improvements in correctional services provided, and enhanced the ability of government to control and be accountable for its correctional facilities.

In the intervening years, what research has been reported has not indicated any major changes. McDonald and Patten (2003) reported on the management of privatization by government. They studied the operation of private prisons for convicted offenders in 1997, focusing on how government agencies established, monitored, and administered contracts for prisons. They identified two basic models. In the first, the government agency gets bids either for the operation of a state-owned prison or the opening of a new prison in the state. In the second model, the state enters an agreement to house inmates in a contractor's facility that is located out of state. Of the two, McDonald and Patten found that contracts for in-state facilities were better monitored and less costly than those for housing inmates out of state. Whatever else happens, their research indicates that states exercise more control over private facilities when those prisons operate within the state jurisdiction.

Bowditch and Everett (1987) voiced concern over the philosophical implications of the profit motive in the operation of prisons. Ethridge and Marquart (1993), after reviewing the development of privatization in Texas, suggested that private prisons may be limited to particular parts of the incarceration system, notably the operation of minimum-security and prerelease institutions. It would appear that by the start of the twenty-first century, private prisons and jails have become a fixture in American corrections. Voncile Gowdy (1997:62) concluded, "As the industry grows and thereby establishes track records for its usage, the demand on corrections officials to consider using privatization as a means of quickly and economically addressing prison crowding problems is likely to become more prominent." While private prisons house a substantial number of inmates, there has not been a rapid growth in the use of private prisons, and private prisons and jails have emerged as a supplement to public facilities. One of the greatest users of private incarceration is the federal government

Crowding

Perhaps the most pressing concern of correctional administrators today is crowding in the nation's prisons and jails. At midyear 1999, 15 percent of jails responding to a Bureau of Justice Statistics survey reported they were operating under court order (Stephan, 2001). Nearly 80 percent of these (325 jails) stated they were under court order to limit their inmate population. In 1984 the Bureau of Justice Statistics reported that nearly 20 percent of American jails were holding inmates as a result of crowding at other facilities; almost 10,000 jail inmates were being held as a result of crowding in prisons. The situation has not improved, but has worsened over time. At the end of 2005, more than 73,000 prison inmates from 35 state systems and the federal system were housed in local jails, many of them overcrowded (Harrison & Beck, 2006). The Bureau of Justice Statistics (Sabol, Minton & Harrison, 2007) estimated that the total population of prison and jail inmates was nearly 2.25 million persons by the middle of 2006.

Between 1995 and 2006 the jail population grew more than 50 percent from just over one-half million inmates to more than 766,000 inmates. The **incarceration rate** (the number of persons incarcerated per 100,000 population eligible for

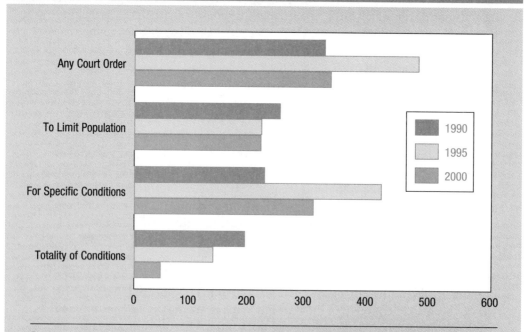

Box 11.2   Changes in Prison Conditions Leading to Court Orders, 1990-2000

Source: J. Stephan (1997), *Census of State and Federal Correctional Facilities, 1995—Executive Summary* (Washington DC: Bureau of Justice Statistics):1; J. Stephan & J. Karberg (2003). *Census of State and Federal Correctional Facilities, 2000* (Washington, DC: Bureau of Justice Statistics):9.

incarceration) reached 497 by midyear 2006. Jail capacity (the number of available beds) grew less than 40 percent and, by June 30, 2006, jail populations were at 94 percent of capacity nationwide, with jails in the largest jurisdictions being the most crowded. Jail costs can be expected to have risen accordingly so that we can estimate that it costs around $20,000 per year to house an inmate in a local jail, and that local governments spend more than $10 billion a year on jails.

A similar picture can be painted for prisons. In the early 1980s, the majority of prison systems in the United States were crowded to the point that court intervention had occurred or was sought. In 1983, eight state prison systems (Alabama, Florida, Michigan, Mississippi, Oklahoma, Rhode Island, Tennessee, and Texas) were either operating under court order to change or had been declared to be unconstitutional. In addition, the District of Columbia and 21 states had one or more institutions operating under court order, while nine others had litigation pending and two states were operating under consent decrees (whereby the court and the state enter into a voluntary agreement about issues raised in court). Box 11.2 describes the types of prison conditions leading to court orders through the end of the twentieth century.

In 1986, the Bureau of Justice Statistics reported that 32 jurisdictions were housing more inmates than their highest capacity. Using a different estimate of capacity, it was reported that as many as 41 jurisdictions could be classified as crowded. At the end of 2005, 23 states and the Federal system were operating at or above their highest capacity. The Bureau reported, "Jurisdictions have employed many methods to alleviate crowding. Construction of permanent and temporary facilities, backups in local jails, double-bunking, intensive community supervision programs, accelerated parole release, and sentence rollbacks have all been used to make room for new inmates." One of the difficulties in assessing prison crowding is the determination of prison population capacity. Box 11.3 presents

Box 11.3 Definitions of Prison Capacity

The extent of prison crowding is difficult to determine because of the absence of uniform measures for defining capacity. The state, federal and District of Columbia jurisdictions apply a wide variety of capacity measures to reflect both the available space to house inmates and the ability to staff and operate an institution. To estimate prison capacity jurisdictions were asked to give three measures for capacity at yearend 2005. These measures were defined as follows:

Rated capacity is the number of beds or inmates assigned by a rating official (such as a fire marshal) to institutions within the jurisdiction

Operational capacity is the number of inmates that can be accommodated, based on a facility's staff, existing programs, and services.

Design capacity is the number of inmates that planners or architects intended for the facility.

Source: P. Harrison & A. Beck (2006), *Prisoners in 2005* (Washington, DC: Bureau of Justice Statistics):7.

three definitions of prison capacity: (1) **rated capacity**, (2) **operational capacity**, and (3) **design capacity**. Nationally, the state prison inmate population equalled 99 percent of the highest capacity of prisons (usually the operational capacity) and 114 percent of the lowest rating (usually the design capacity).

Between 1985 and 2000, state prison capacity grew from under 450,000 beds to more than 1.2 million beds—an increase of more than 267 percent. Expenditures for prisons have also grown dramatically from $6.9 billion to more than $30 billion. States spent more than $1.5 billion each year on prison construction. The crowding problem has not been solved.

In response to the crisis of crowding, states developed ways to reduce their prison populations and continue construction programs to create more prison space. The National Institute of Corrections (NIC) operated a program in several states that involves the use of prison crowding policy teams to assist the states in responding to the crowding problem. Some states have passed legislation enabling correctional administrators to accelerate release dates for certain inmates whenever the prison population reaches the point of crowding. Camp and Camp (1996:49) reported that eight jurisdictions released 3,322 inmates in 1995 through **emergency release programs.** These programs are mechanisms for legally releasing inmates in order to control prison crowding. Fifteen states had laws authorizing such programs in 1995. In addition, there has been an increased interest in probation and parole (to be discussed in the next chapter) as alternatives to incarceration (Latessa, 1985). Over the past several years, while prisons continue to house more inmates than they are designed to hold, the difference between capacity and population has been shrinking.

Crowding in correctional institutions poses several problems for inmates, correctional staff, and correctional administrators. For these reasons, it is simply not acceptable to jam more prisoners into existing space, at least not as a long-term response to crowding. Rather, alternatives must be developed that ensure adequate capacity to house the large numbers of offenders now populating the nation's prisons and jails.

For inmates, crowding places severe demands upon available resources. Simple things that would generally be taken for granted (e.g., hot water for showers) become scarce resources. Privacy, always at a premium in penal facilities, becomes almost totally beyond the reach of most inmates. A crowded facility generally lacks the ability to provide activities or "meaningful" work experiences for inmates. There are more inmates with whom recreational, educational, vocational, and other resources must be shared. It may even become difficult to find a seat from which to view television.

Research indicates that crowding leads to irritability and increased violence among inmates (Jan, 1980). Thus, the crowded institution is a more dangerous place to be. Sechrest (1991) notes that crowding alone contributes to disruptive and assaultive behavior, but that characteristics of staff, programs, classification, and facility design are also important correlates of assault levels. Tartaro (2002) found that population density (crowding) in jails was associated with lower levels of assault, contrary to what might be expected. It is not clear if correctional authorities react to crowding in ways that might reduce the chances of violence (increased programs, reduced inmate freedom in the institution, and other mechanisms to limit the chances of violence). Wooldredge, Griffin, and Pratt (2001) found that prison crowding was related to levels of inmate misconduct of all sorts, indicating that crowding contributes to safety and management problems in prisons. Beyond these pressures, disease and illness spread more rapidly in a crowded institution. The effect of all of these pressures is to make the experience of imprisonment even more painful for inmates, and this increase in pain often breeds resentment toward the prison that may be expressed in the form of riots or assaults on prison staff.

Prison staff also feel the pressures of crowding. In addition to the increased tension in the institution and the perceived increase in the likelihood of attack by inmates, the workload of staff increases. Doubling the inmate population means doubling the caseloads of correctional counselors, increasing the class sizes of educational staff, doubling the demands upon food service staff, and increased activity for the custody staff. There are twice as many inmates to count, escort, search, counsel, and watch. Correctional officers can be overwhelmed by the sheer numbers of inmates. The crowded institution becomes more anonymous and impersonal, making it difficult for officers to recognize and know inmates, or to provide adequate service and protection to them. As a result, correctional officers in crowded institutions are likely to be less attuned to the population and more distant from it. Criminal justice system officials continue to identify prison and jail crowding as one of their most pressing problems (McEwen, 1995).

Correctional managers must provide for the needs of larger numbers of inmates with a constant level of resources (Vanyur, 1997). Managers become more concerned with tranquility and bed space than with the provision of services and opportunities. As Johnson (1987:182) noted, "When prisons become overcrowded, moreover, the temptation to warehouse inmates as a matter of policy, rather than as a failure of policy, is strong." That is, correctional managers facing crowded prisons seek to survive without disruption, rather than to improve either their institutions or the lives of inmates. As McEwen (1995:7) noted, ". . . with the numbers increasing, the emphasis must shift from treatment and programming to containment, diverting resources from programs to security. Mental health programs and recreational programs were among those affected by crowding." For example, several jurisdictions are using what is euphemistically called "bus housing." It has been estimated that large states, like California, may have 1,000 or more inmates "in transit" between prisons at any time. Inmates on a bus do not require cells. Surely, routine transfers for the sake of bed space do not well serve the needs of prisoners (or of the prison system). Yet, faced with severe crowding, it is one strategy that allows correctional managers to retain custody over inmates when there is insufficient space to house them.

Correctional managers face yet another pressure from overcrowding: court intervention. Vanyur (1997) observed:

> A majority of states are under some court order relating to prison crowding or conditions. Judges have intervened in what was previously prison management territory—food service, health care, sanitation, staff practices, and so forth . . . in some cases, judges have served as de facto commissioners.

How to resolve the problem of prison crowding is a question that lacks a ready answer. The solution to crowding depends upon conditions in the jurisdiction. Benton and Silberstein (1983) suggested that the policy adopted by a jurisdiction for dealing with crowding depends upon, among other factors, the size of the prison system, the court rulings, the nature of the increase in population, the prevailing political sentiment, and economic conditions. Thus, the decision whether to build more prisons, to grant early releases, to divert convicted offenders from prison, or to deal with crowding in another manner varies from state to state. The response to prison and jail crowding in any jurisdiction depends upon the nature and characteristics of the justice system and its environment in that jurisdiction. John Klofas (1987) observed that similar factors influence the use of incarceration in a jurisdiction. Thus, the solutions to the crowding problem in a jurisdiction reflect how the jurisdiction views incarceration as a response to crime.

The causes of prison crowding are not clear. Some suggest that the aging of the "baby boom" generation produced a demographic "bulge," a large number of persons in the age group most likely to be imprisoned. Yet, if demography were the cause, crowding should be on the decline. Marvell and Moody (1997) found that demography is related to prison population size, but that other factors must also be contributing to prison population growth. Among these other factors are increased punitiveness (more mandatory prison sentences and longer terms), improvements in detection and prosecution, and a widening of the definition of types of offenses requiring imprisonment. Beck and Mumola (1999) report that increases in the number of parole violators returned to prison, declining rates of parole release, and increasing time served are key contributors to rising prison populations.

Great Britain has opted to alleviate some prison overcrowding with the utilization of "Her Majesty's Prison Weare," the country's first floating prison since the nineteenth century. Britain's Prison Service purchased the prison ship from New York's Department of Correction in 1997. *Photo credit: AP Photo/Dave Caulkin.*

Solutions to the crowding problem are of two basic types (see Schwartz & Travis, 1997:77-80): (1) capacity expansion, and (2) demand reduction. We must either increase the amount of prison space available or reduce our demand for prison space. These two solutions involve three strategies. The capacity expansion strategy relies on construction of more prisons, the conversion of facilities built for other purposes (such as mental hospitals or military bases), and renovations of existing facilities in order to increase the number of prisoners they can accommodate. The demand reduction solution involves two separate strategies. The first is to reduce the number of offenders sent to prison by increasing diversion programs and the use of community-based alternative sentences. The second is to reduce the amount of time inmates are kept in prison, and thereby reduce prison populations. If release dates were accelerated so that offenders served only one-half as much time as they currently do, the present supply of prison space could accommodate twice as many inmates. These strategies have been identified as **"front door" strategies** (diversion from prison), **"back door" strategies** (earlier release of inmates), and capacity expansion (Travis, 1989).

Prison Industries

In the early days of prisons in America, inmates were expected to pay for the costs of incarceration by working in prison industries. Indeed, the early proponents of incarceration hoped that prisons would not only be self-sufficient, but that they might even become profit centers for the state. After decades of prison industry, including contracting prison labor with private companies as well as state-run industries, prison factories were not considered to be profitable.

"Self-sufficiency was a goal pursued by all states where prisons were instituted. Legislators persistently demanded that their penitentiaries pay their way, even though private industries lobbied against prison manufacturing," observed Keve (1986:28). Prison industry was believed to have a number of beneficial effects. First, especially in the early years of the penitentiary, it was hoped that convict labor could be used to defray the expense of constructing and operating prisons and jails, that is, that inmates could be made to pay for their own punishment (Durham, 1989). Second, it was believed that the activity of work would occupy inmates and keep them from breaking prison rules. Finally, it was hoped that a regimen of work for inmates would serve to instill in them good habits. As Johnson (1987:26-27) summarized the approach:

> It was hoped that silent laboring days and solitary contemplative nights would encourage communion with God and effect a transformation of at least some of the wayward prisoners' souls. But simple conformity to the prison routine, a life of pure habits if not pure intentions, was enough to get a prisoner by in the congregate systems.

According to Fox (1983), prison industry has been organized in many ways over time. Six of the more common of these are (1) piece price, (2) contract, (3) lease, (4) public account, (5) state use, and (6) public works. Each has its strengths and weaknesses. The **piece price system** was common in the early years of prisons. The manufacturer supplied the raw materials to the prison, and inmates constructed the finished product, which was purchased by the manufacturer at an established price. The **contract system** involved an entrepreneur contracting with the prison for labor and the use of prison shops for the production of goods. The highest bidder won the right to use prison labor and shops. The **lease system** was common in Southern prisons after the Civil War. The prison simply leased its convicts to a contractor who produced goods with convict labor. All of these methods involved having a private contractor.

The other common methods of organizing prison industry relied upon prison-run operations. In a **public account system**, prisoners in correctional industries produce goods and sell them on the open market. There traditionally have been severe restrictions on what prisons may produce, or to whom the products may be sold. In a **state-use system**, the prison is allowed to produce almost any product, but the sale or distribution of the product is limited to governmental agencies. The state-use method of organization does not allow the prison industry to compete on the open market. The **public works system** uses inmate labor for public service projects, such as road maintenance, construction of parks, and other government services. Sing Sing Prison in the state of New York was an early public works prison project; it was constructed largely through the labors of inmates brought from the penitentiary at Auburn.

Opposition to the use of "slave" convict labor and the unfair advantage given to manufacturers employing convicts led to the passage of several laws limiting the sale of prison-made goods across state lines, and within states to nongovernmental units (Cullen & Travis, 1984). The resulting decline in markets, as well as the lack of capital investment in prison industries, rendered most prison factories noncompetitive with free-world enterprises. More recently, however, there has been a resurgence of prison industry competing in free-world markets (Vito, 1985).

The new prison industries are designed to be more similar to free-world production than were prison industries in the past (Auerbach, 1993). Inmate participation in prison industries is generally voluntary. The inmates receive wages comparable to those paid on the free market, and are required to pay taxes, child support, and other expenses. Local unions are consulted prior to the development of industries to ensure that the new prison jobs do not cause unemployment among law-abiding citizens (Auerbach, 1982). A promising experimental program (called the Free Venture Program) using inmates in state-of-the-art production for private businesses was established in a number of prisons (Fedo, 1981).

The cycle of prison industry, progressing from the production of goods for the open market, through restricted public use, and back again to the free market, shows how difficult it is to resolve the issue of what to do with prison inmates. Some analyses have suggested that introducing free-market practices and pay scales into prison industry programs will benefit both the inmates (Schwarz, 1986) and the general economy of the state (Lonski, 1986:52). Still, there is opposition to the idea of prisoners manufacturing and selling goods. Finally, the old hopes for prison industry have not been changed. Those advocating the expansion of prison industry programs still suggest that the results of these efforts will be, as identified by the Bureau of Justice Assistance (2004:3), the goals of the Prison Industry Enhancement Certification Program, to benefit:

- The corrections administrator, as a cost-effective way to occupy a portion of the ever-growing prison population.

- The crime victim, by providing a means of partial repayment for harm sustained.

- The inmate, through offering a chance to work, meet financial obligations, learn job skills, and increase chances of meaningful employment on release.

- The private sector, by providing a stable and readily available workforce.

- The public, through reducing costs with inmate worker contributions to room and board, family support, victim compensation, and taxes.

As is apparent from these goals, when compared to the history of prison industries, the only change has been that the supporters of industries no longer expect full self-sufficiency or complete rehabilitation to result from convict labor. Box 11.4 presents the distribution of inmate wages under the Prison Industry Enhancement Program at the end of 2005. It shows that while inmates retained much of their earnings, almost one-half of gross wages were applied to inmate financial obligations (Moses & Smith, 2007). In addition, a portion of the "net pay" category (48 percent of total wages) was used by inmates for living expenses, including some healthcare costs, food, and toiletries. These payments by inmates further reduced state expenses.

Industry programs for inmates have expanded to include jail populations in recent years. Miller, Sexton, and Jacobsen (1991) reported on jail industry pro-

Box 11.4	Distribution of Wages Paid Inmates in PIE Program Reported for 2005

Application of Wages	Percent
Inmate	48.1%
Inmate Savings	3.4
Taxes	11.3
Room & Board	24.0
Victim's Fund	8.0
Family Support	5.2
Total	100.0

Source: M. Moses & C. Smith (2007), "Factories Behind Fences: Do Prison 'Real Work' Programs Work?" *NIJ Journal* (June):35.

grams in 15 local and one federal jail/detention center operating inmate work programs. The purposes of jail work programs are similar to those in prisons and include development of inmate work habits and skills, reduction of costs, reduction of inmate idleness, and the meeting of community needs. Most jail programs compensate inmates with "good time" reductions in sentence length, but some pay wages. Some counties allow inmates to continue to work at their own jobs, reporting to the jail after work each day. In cases in which inmates earn wages, it is typical for the jail to bill for room and board or other fees. Still, relatively few inmates participate in prison industries. Almost all prisons operate some sort of work or employment programs, most commonly using inmates to perform tasks required for the operation of the prison. Not surprisingly, inmates rank prison jobs differently. Alarid (2003) found that while male and female inmates preferred somewhat different jobs, the "best" jobs according to inmates were those that provided some useful job skills, allowed a measure of independence, and were highest paid. Physical labor on prison maintenance under close supervision was not considered attractive by either men or women. Alarid also found that inmate job assignments appeared to be based on merit rather than race or other "unfair" criteria. Inmates having served the longest terms and those who were the lowest risks for escape or violence were assigned to the "best" jobs.

Box 11.5   Percentage of Prisons Reporting Types of Work Programs in Prisons, 2000

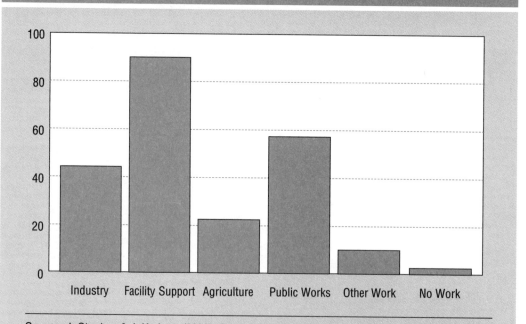

Source: J. Stephan & J. Karberg (2003), *Census of State and Federal Correctional Facilities, 2000* (Washington, DC: Bureau of Justice Statistics):11.

The resurgence of prison industries is a reflection of the current efforts to improve incarceration. Having learned from past problems, correctional administrators are attempting to accentuate the positive aspects of past efforts while controlling the negative effects (Cullen & Travis, 1984). In a sense, the revitalization of prison industries represents a general return to incarceration as a preferred criminal sanction, which is an effect that has occurred since the early 1970s. The appeal of putting prisoners to work, both for their own good and for the good of the state, is strong. Box 11.5 describes the distribution of work assignments in prisons. Inmate wage rates in most cases are substantially lower than wages in the free society. The question is whether it is possible to overcome objections to convict labor and to obtain the expected benefits of prison industries. Flanagan and Maguire (1993) have urged the adoption of a full-employment policy for prisons, believing that such an approach is both necessary and possible. Moses and Smith (2007) report that prisoners who participate in industry programs tend to show a better adjustment to society upon release from prison.

Prison Violence

Violence has long been a part of the incarceration experience (Braswell, Montgomery & Lombardo, 1994). The earliest prison riot in the United States occurred in 1774, when inmates at Newgate Prison of Connecticut revolted (Fox, 1983:114). Newgate was an abandoned copper mine where offenders were sentenced to terms in the old underground mine shafts. Riots and nonviolent strikes by inmates have occurred throughout the history of prisons and jails. In addition, violence on a smaller scale, between inmates and officers, and among inmates, has a long tradition. Prison violence occurs in many forms. We shall briefly examine interpersonal assaults, homicide, sexual assaults, and riots.

Interpersonal Assaults and Homicide

John Conrad (1982) suggested that prison violence results from five factors: (1) violence-prone inmates; (2) the "lower-class value system," which emphasizes masculinity, toughness, and violence; (3) the use of violence by correctional administrators to control inmates; (4) the anonymity of large (especially crowded) prisons; and (5) the utility of violence in furthering inmate objectives. Given that prisons are places where aggressive, often violent, people are locked in close proximity to each other, it is not surprising that so much violence occurs in prisons. Rather, it is surprising that so little violence occurs. Box 11.6 describes the types of offenses for which inmates were imprisoned in 2003. Nearly half had a current conviction for a violent crime. Added to this is the impact of "truth in sentencing" reforms (see Chapter 9), which increase the amount of time inmates convicted of violent crimes will serve in prison. It is likely that the overall inmate population will be comprised of an even greater proportion of violent offenders as these inmates serve longer sentences and begin to "stack up" in prison (Ditton & Wilson, 1999). About one-fifth of jail inmates have been convicted or accused of a violent offense, and about one-third have a prior record of criminal violence (James, 2004).

Box 11.6   State Prison Inmates by Type of Crime Conviction (percents)

Type of Crime	Percent of Responses
Violent	51.7%
Property	20.8
Drug	20.2
Public-Order	6.8
Other	0.5
Total	100.0%

Source: P. Harrison & A. Beck (2006), *Prisoners in 2005* (Washington, DC: Bureau of Justice Statistics):9.

Whether or not a high level of violence exists in any particular institution, the potential for violence is always there, and the threat of harm colors the behavior of inmates and staff alike (Bowker, 1980). Jack Abbott (1981:150), a convict-writer who expressed his prison experiences in his book *In the Belly of the Beast,* wrote, "Everyone in prison has an ideal of violence, murder. Beneath all relationships between prisoners in prison is the ever-present fact of murder. It ultimately defines our relationship among ourselves." Abbott suggested that life in a modern prison is akin to life in the jungle. The rule is "kill or be killed." Correctional officers are not immune to the constant threat of violence inside the institution, as evidenced by the growing interest in and market for "body armor" for correctional officers (Kaplan, 1987).

Most of what we know about violence and misbehavior in prisons is based on research that focused on male offenders (Baskin, Sommers & Steadman, 1991). More recently there has been increasing interest in the violence and misbehavior of female prisoners as well. Kruttschnitt and Krmpotich (1990) reported that about 25 percent of female inmates engaged in aggressive acts against other inmates. Tischler and Marquart (1989) reported no significant difference in disciplinary infractions between minimum-security male inmates and female inmates, but maximum-security female inmates posed the most disciplinary problems. In general, women were more likely to receive disciplinary reports for fighting than were men, but men were more likely to attack guards than were women. It may be that women prisoners are less violent than men because of the lower incidence of gang involvement in women's prisons (Kruttschnitt & Krmpotich, 1990). If women are less violent than men, it may also reflect differences in who goes to prison.

The majority of female violent offenders had attacked a victim known to them, while male violent criminals were more likely to have attacked strangers. Simon (1993) found that male inmates who had attacked strangers were significantly more likely to commit violent acts in prison than those who attacked people they knew. McCorkle (1995) compared male and female prisoners diagnosed with a mental health problem. He found that female inmates were both more likely to receive medication for their illness while incarcerated, and more likely to engage in disruptive behaviors in the institution. He suggested that different experiences with the stress of imprisonment for women as opposed to men may aggravate these behavioral problems. It may be that women inmates who have been convicted of violent crimes are qualitatively different from violent men in that their violent behavior was contextual and not a general pattern of adaptation to stress and conflict. More research needs to be completed before we can assess whether there are differences between men and women in terms of prison violence, and to be able understand any such differences. What is clear from these studies, however, is that violence and disciplinary infractions are not all that rare among female inmates. In a study of women's perceptions and experiences in prison, Pogrebin and Dodge (2001) reported widespread violence and fear of violence among a sample of female prison inmates. This suggests that the experience of violence in prison by women is at least as common as that among men.

Fox (1983:107) wrote, "Homicides in prison appear to be grossly underreported." He further estimated that the official statistics should be doubled to approach a more accurate figure. Eichenthal and Jacobs (1991) noted the underreporting of criminal acts in prisons, and decried the lack of information concerning crimes of all types that occur in prisons. For example, the Bureau of Justice Statistics (Mumola, 2005) reported 48 prison inmate homicides in 2002. Fewer than 2 percent of inmate deaths were reported to be the result of homicide in 2004 (Mumola, 2007). Each year there are thousands of inmate assaults on other inmates. Forty state prison systems responded to a survey asking about assaults and homicides in prisons in 1990 (Maguire, Pastore & Flanagan, 1993:669), reporting more than 8,000 inmate assaults on staff and more than 14,600 inmate assaults on other inmates. Between midyear 1999 and 2000, there were a reported 17,952 inmate assaults on staff, five of which resulted in the death of a prison staff member. Adjusting for the inmate population and number of prison staff for 2000, these yield rates of assault of 4,174 per 100,000 correctional staff and 2,622 per 100,000 inmates. These assault rates alone are five to 10 times higher than similar rates for members of the general public. In 1995, the number of inmate assaults against staff and other inmates in American prisons was 40,113. Box 11.7 compares a "violent crime rate" of prisoners with the similar rate for aggravated assault. The figure shows that rates of violence in prisons greatly exceed those in the free society.

Box 11.7   Comparison of U.S. and Prison Assault Rates

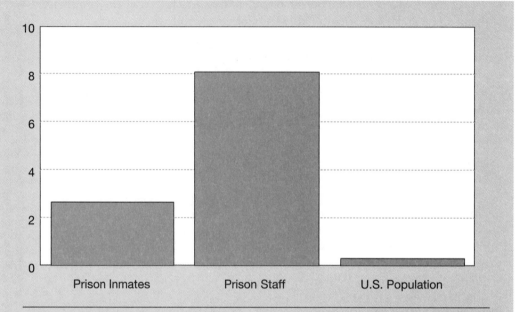

Source: Federal Bureau of Investigation (2001), *Crime in the United States, 2000* (Washington, DC: Bureau of Justice Statistics); J. Stephen & J. Karberg (2003), *Census of State and Federal Correctional Facilities, 2000* (Washington, DC: Bureau of Justice Statistics):10.

Sexual Assaults and Violence

Sexual assaults in prison are a special case of individual violence among inmates. The first reported study of sexual assaults among inmates was made by Alan Davis (1968). Davis studied this type of inmate violence in the Philadelphia prison system and in sheriff's vans transporting prisoners. He included verbal assaults with actual physical attacks in his definition of sexual assault. As a result, Davis concluded that nearly 5 percent of the prison population had been victims of sexual assaults. The problem of sexual violence in prisons has entered "common knowledge" so that the popular media depict and discuss sexual assaults in prisons.

In 2003, the United States Congress enacted the **Prison Rape Elimination Act**. This law provides for the development of better information about the nature and incidence of rape and sexual assault in prisons, and provides funding to correctional authorities to reduce and control sexual violence in prisons. In passing the law, Congress (45 USC 15601, Sec. 2) made several "findings" about sexual violence in prisons. They found that young, first offenders are at greater risk of sexual assault than older offenders; prison rapes generally go unreported and victims untreated; and the high incidence of prison rape "increases the levels of violence, directed at inmates and at staff, within prisons."

The academic literature and popular media have portrayed sexual violence in correctional institutions as widespread (Lockwood, 1994). The image of such violence, however, has been that of the homosexual rape, which helps explain the relatively narrow title of the federal legislation. In fact, other studies (Lockwood, 1980; Nacci, 1988) have revealed that rape is a relatively rare event, with estimates of less than 1 percent of the inmate population being victims of physical sexual assaults. That the actual incidence of homosexual rape is low, however, tells only part of the story. One effect of sexual assault, or the threat of sexual assault, is a general increase in the level of violence in prisons. The fear of sexual assault leads otherwise peaceful inmates to commit acts of violence to deter attackers.

Toch (1965) reported that 25 percent of inmate assaults in six California prisons were attributed to homosexual activity. Nearly 50 percent of these involved cases of rivalry (jealousy, unrequited love), while the remainder were cases of forced sexual contact (rape). Lockwood (1980) argued that the reactions of inmates to sexual harassment probably contributed to the total level of prison violence beyond those cases with a clearly sexual cause.

In response to the Prison Rape Elimination Act, correctional officials are required to report sexual assaults and sexual misconduct in correctional facilities. Beck and Hughes (2006) reported results of a survey of more than 1,800 correctional facilities, covering more than 1.7 million inmates. For this population, there was a total of 6,241 allegations of sexual violence, of which fewer than 1,000 were substantiated by investigations by correctional authorities. Sometimes prison and jail personnel are the offenders. When this happens in jails, the correctional personnel involved are overwhelmingly male and the inmate victims overwhelmingly female. In prisons, nearly two-thirds of correctional staff offenders are female, and most inmate victims are male. Staff misconduct accounts for more than one-third of all reported incidents (Tewksbury, 2007). While it is likely that sexual assaults are grossly underreported in correctional settings, the data indicate that actual sexual assaults are still relatively rare.

In terms of deterring inmate sexual assault, one useful result of fighting in prison is self-defense. Especially given the media portrayal of widespread rape and sexual victimization in prison, inmates may attempt to build a "reputation" in the institution to ensure that they will not become targets of sexual aggressors. Thus, some inmates may assault others in nonsexual circumstances for the purpose of avoiding sexual attack. One inmate interviewed by Lockwood (1980:95-96) explained an assault on another in the dining hall as self-defense. The inmate Lockwood interviewed had been the victim of a sexual assault, and attacking another inmate in the dining hall was designed to prevent future sexual victimization. As the inmate explained his actions:

> They had a code in the prison on the chow line that said no man
> should cut ahead of you in the chow line. And this one man passed me
> a couple of times in the line, and he knew that I was aware of what he

was doing. If I failed to do what I was supposed to do here, then I was lost again [would be a sexual victim again]. So the next day, when they come through the chow line, when this guy cut in front of me, I hit him in the head with a tray as hard as I could. And when he went to the ground, I hit him several more times before the guard could reach me. It is regrettable but it is the only way that you can handle it. And I didn't want to do it, but I did what I had to do to protect myself.

As Lockwood suggested, the importance of sexual violence in prisons may come more from the perception than the reality of sexual assaults. It appears that, in reality, there are relatively few cases of actual sexual assault in prisons. It also appears, however, that inmates believe the threat of sexual assault is both real and great. Many instances of individual violence in prisons, therefore, may result from the fear of sexual assault. In this way, it is possible that most prison violence is a form of sexual violence. A similar explanation for inmate violence can be inferred from Victor Hassine's (1996:23) observations on life in prison. He wrote, "In the life of an inmate, if you catch someone stealing from you, you're compelled to deal with it physically. This is not because you want to or you think it's the right thing to do, but because you absolutely must . . . If you choose to ignore the theft, the man will steal from you again and tell his friends, who in turn will also steal from you. Eventually, you will be challenged for more than just minor belongings."

From the perspective of the inmate, there are few choices available for dealing with other inmates. Reliance on correctional authorities can be viewed as a sign of weakness and is generally seen as ineffective. Not only are correctional officers often unable to protect victimized inmates, those inmates who report incidents to officers come to be labeled "snitches," and are then targets for increased violence. Another alternative is to seek protective custody. **Protective custody** is usually a housing unit kept separate from the general inmate population so that inmates in the unit are separated from attackers. Most protective custody units, however, offer little programming, and inmates are kept locked in their cells for most of the day. In 1995, about 2 percent of the prison population was in protective custody (Camp & Camp, 1996:20). The lack of alternatives to confrontation adds to the sense that the prison is a violent place.

Riots

To the relatively high level of violence among individuals must be added the danger of riot. In the last third of the twentieth century, four large-scale prison riots captured media attention and illustrated the potential violence in prison riots. In 2001, there were more than 600 "major incidents" involving five or more inmates and resulting in serious injury or significant property damage in state prisons (Stephan & Karberg, 2003:10). There were an additional 639 other disruptions that same year.

While similar in some respects, each of the major riots between 1971 and

1993 had different outcomes. The riots at Attica (New York) and the New Mexico State Penitentiary in Santa Fe were among the bloodiest in history. The riots by Cuban detainees at federal institutions (in Atlanta, Georgia, and Oakdale, Louisiana) resulted in only one inmate death. The 1993 riot by inmates at the Southern Ohio Correctional Facility at Lucasville claimed 11 lives, including one correctional officer.

On September 9, 1971, inmates rioted at the New York State Correctional Facility at Attica, and took control of a large part of the prison. On September 13, state police and prison authorities stormed the prison and took command. When the smoke cleared, 43 persons were dead; most of them (30) were inmates killed during the attack. It was the bloodiest prison riot in American history. Nine years later, on February 15 and 16, 1980, inmates rioted for 36 hours at the New Mexico State Penitentiary. When the incident was over, it was learned that the rioting inmates had killed 33 prisoners, and many of these deaths occurred after the victims had been barbarically tortured (Rolland, 1997; Serrill & Katel, 1980). In late 1987, Cuban detainees rioted at the Federal Detention Center in Oakdale, Louisiana; two days later, Cuban inmates also rioted at the Federal Penitentiary in Atlanta (*Newsweek*, 1987). Two weeks after the beginning of the Oakdale disturbance, the Atlanta rioters finally surrendered.

The riots by the Cuban detainees did not involve anything near the level of personal violence that characterized the Attica and Santa Fe uprisings. While only one inmate was killed, the extent of property damage caused by the rioting of Oakdale and Atlanta detainees was massive (Nacci, 1988). The two institutions were almost completely destroyed. In this respect, the federal riots mirrored the Santa Fe experience, in which inmates caused extensive damage to the facility in addition to committing killings. (At Attica, damage to the institution was much less severe.) The Lucasville riot extended over several days and resulted in severe damage to the

An injured inmate is carried on a stretcher from the cell block at the Southern Ohio Correctional Facility in Lucasville, Ohio, in 1993. At the time of the riot, which claimed 11 lives, the inmate population had risen to more than 35,000, and correctional officers were outnumbered nearly nine to one. *Photo credit: AP Photo/Lennox McLendon.*

part of the prison that was under control of the rioting inmates. The death and damage toll at Lucasville was less than New Mexico, but the riot was the most serious in a decade.

Because of their intensity, and the numbers of inmates and staff who are at risk, as well as the possibility of damage to the facility itself, riots are a major concern of correctional administrators. The problem is that not enough is known about the causes of prison riots to allow adequate planning to avoid them (Mahan, 1982). The paradoxical nature of prison violence, including riots, is that the violence may be the result of efforts to reform the prison and improve the quality of life for prison inmates. Camp and colleagues (2003) studied inmate misconduct, especially violence, in federal prisons. They concluded that characteristics of the prison itself account for much of the violence in prisons. In a similar fashion, Huebner (2003) reported that the "style" by which prison staff control inmate behavior is related to levels of violence. As suggested by Conrad (1982), coercive control, or the use/threat of force is related to higher levels of inmate violence than noncoercive controls.

What makes prison violence a contemporary issue, although it has always been a part of the prison experience, is that there is evidence to suggest that violence in prisons today is qualitatively different from such violence in the past. As Johnson (1987:75) stated the issue, "Violence has always been a salient aspect of the convict world. In many of today's prisons, however, the convict culture of violence is unusually pronounced." The question remains: Why is this violent culture so much more pronounced today?

Observers point to many factors that they believe have changed the nature of American prisons and jails (Conrad, 1982). Wright (2000) reported that the correctional administrators he interviewed mentioned the following as contributing to increased violence: the simple increase in the number of prisoners leading to increased chances of conflicts, the impact of crowding on prisoner classification and housing, the increase in gang membership among prisoners, and larger numbers of young predatory offenders. Two additional important contributors have been the emergence of professional prison administrators (Conrad, 1982; Fox, 1983; Johnson, 1987; Mahan, 1982) and the effect of court intervention on prison operations (Jacobs, 1977; Marquart & Crouch, 1984). In effect, the prisoners' rights movement and the prevalence of "professional" prison administrators served to lessen the authority of correctional staff by humanizing the prison.

Recognizing the prisoner as an individual who deserves to be considered and listened to in making decisions about the running of the institution has the effect of lessening the power of correctional personnel. In regard to the prisoners' rights movement, the success of inmates in court was identified by Fogel (1979) as being "status-costly" to correctional staff, as it reduced the staff's position of social and physical superiority over inmates. Perhaps what this means is that a decrease in control over prisons and prisoners by correctional authorities has created a "power vacuum" in our institutions. The perceived increase in prison violence then represents a "power struggle" among inmates to fill that vacuum. As Johnson (1987:81) concluded, "Today's prisons are, as a result, more relaxed in their discipline but more dangerous in their daily operation. The iron hand of the custodian has given way to a 'rule of the cruel,' with the hard-core convicts now setting the tone of prison life."

There is some evidence to suggest that the violence of American prisons that seemed to follow the expansion of prisoner's rights was temporary. Crouch and Marquart (1990:120) state the issue, writing, "If (court) intervention heightens violence and if prisoners thus are exposed not only to the danger of assault and death but also to the stresses created by greater risk, perhaps intervention is not worth the pain to prisoners." Reviewing events in Texas (discussed below), they noted that an immediate effect of court intervention was an increase in violence among inmates. However, they discovered that inmates did not view the prison as any less safe after court intervention.

The Texas prison system was sued in 1972 by inmates who alleged that the crowding, health care, disciplinary policies, and security practices of the prisons were unconstitutional. In particular, Texas employed inmate trustees, called "building tenders," to maintain order in cell blocks. These tenders were supported in their efforts by the correctional staff, and the methods used by them included physical abuse and assault. In signing an agreement to settle the lawsuit, the Texas Department of Corrections agreed to abolish the position of building tender. With the building tenders (and correctional staff's use of force), the Texas prisons were orderly but oppressive. Removal of the building tenders meant that brutality against inmates was reduced, but so was order in the prisons.

In 1985, the Texas Department of Corrections responded to escalating violence by placing all known gang members and inmates who had assaulted guards or other inmates into "administrative segregation." This meant that the most dangerous inmates were locked down in single cells for an indefinite period. Some 3,200 inmates were thus segregated from the general inmate population. As a result, rates of inmate violence decreased, and inmate perceptions of prison safety were improved. Even in the prison, decisions about personal liberty compared with needs for order must be made. The restriction of this 10 percent of inmates made life safer and more orderly for the remaining 90 percent.

The dilemma we face is to solve the problem, if possible, without resorting to the oppressive conditions characteristic of prison life prior to the 1970s. The question is whether it is possible to grant legal rights and protections to prison inmates, as well as giving inmates some level of self-determination, while maintaining control over the operation of the prison. If that question can be answered in the affirmative, there is a chance that we can reduce the current level of prison violence and still retain the progress that has been made in conditions of confinement. The most promising developments are in the area of inmate classification. Classification involves the testing and assessment of inmates to determine inmate treatment needs and prison custody and security needs. Accurate, effective inmate classification can lead to safer, less violent prisons (Berk et al., 2003). John Wooldredge (2003) observes that effective classification can produce benefits beyond reduced violence. He argues that controlling prison violence is a positive goal to protect inmates and staff, but also a requirement for effective correctional treatment.

Continuing Pressures on Incarceration

It does not seem likely that the current problems of incarceration in the criminal justice system will soon be solved. Indeed, current events seem likely to increase the pressure on United States prisons and jails. As noted, efforts to achieve truth in sentencing for violent offenders promise to increase population and concentrate even more violent offenders in the prison and jail populations. Improved police procedures, coupled with the war on drugs, will result in higher numbers of arrests, with corresponding pressures on jails, and higher numbers of convictions leading to increased prison populations.

As states try to deal with crowding, there is likely to be more emphasis on seeking solutions in the private sector and a greater reliance on private provision of incarceration. Thus far we have not been able to build our way out of the prison crowding crisis. Crowding has been linked to privatization, violence, and limited inmate participation in industry programs. Current policy choices, whatever their other consequences, appear likely to aggravate crowding in both prisons and jails.

There are growing pressures to revise and improve prison treatment programs both as something that is owed to inmates and also as a means of reducing crime and future prison populations (Lowenkamp, Latessa & Smith, 2006). In the past 30 years there has been substantial progress in the development of correctional programming. Research indicates that well planned, carefully implemented treatment programs can substantially reduce recidivism among correctional populations. While prisons will also have a punitive and security function, there are increasing calls for the development of more therapeutic efforts in correctional institutions.

Incarceration in the Total System

Prisons and jails are inextricably linked to the larger society in which they exist. As we saw, prison researchers identified what they called a "prisoner subculture," a social system with its own set of values and language set apart from the broader society. The prison subculture placed a positive value on criminality, resistance to correctional officials, and inmate solidarity (Clemmer, 1940; Sykes, 1958). Two explanations for the existence of this subculture emerged: a deprivation model and an importation model (Schwartz & Travis, 1997:127-130). The **deprivation model** suggests that the inmate code or prison subculture develops as a reaction to the losses experienced by prisoners upon arrival in the prison. The loss of freedom, autonomy, goods and services, and the like supports the development of a "new" social order based on the values of the prison inmates born in reaction to their plight as prisoners. The **importation model**, on the other hand, suggests that the prison subculture is actually a product of the selection of inmates. Those persons sent to prison, according to the importation model, already subscribe to an anti-authority code of conduct. Thus, the prison imports its problems from the free society. Cao, Zhao, and Van Dine (1997) argue that the importation model is a better explanation of prisoner behavior than the deprivation model, suggesting that much of the problem of inmate misbehavior in prisons is a reflection of subcultural conflict that exists in the free society.

All of the issues examined in this chapter display links between incarceration and the wider society. Privatization reflects a broader movement to reduce governmental bureaucracy that has "trickled down" to prisons and jails. Prisoners' rights represent, at some level, an expansion of the general due process revolution in American criminal justice that began under the Warren Supreme Court. Violence in institutions reflects the growing violence in American society, including gang- and drug-related violence. The problem of crowding in American prisons and jails, however, is perhaps the best illustration of how the criminal justice system and its subsystems interact with their environment. Crowding in correctional institutions is a product of changes in the justice system as well as broader social changes. Its effects can be felt by all components of the justice process.

One of the explanations for prison and jail crowding is based on demography. The maturing of the baby-boom generation means that the raw material for the justice system—the number of potential criminals—has increased dramatically. Thus, criminal justice agencies must respond to changes in the material environment. Similarly, the war on drugs, mandatory sentencing for drunk drivers, and a general rise in punitiveness among Americans all help to explain both the increasing rate of imprisonment and the longer sentences imposed. Here we can see criminal justice agencies reacting to changes in the philosophical environment.

Wayne Welsh (1993) reported on a study of police arrest practices in jurisdictions in which the courts had ordered jail populations to be reduced. He found no significant statistical support for the view that court intervention changed arrest practices. However, he concluded that part of the change in arrest practices may be attributable to court intervention with the jail. Recognizing the complexity of the justice system and its relationship with its environment, Welsh (1993:112) concluded that increasing the use of citations in lieu of arrest is probably the result of a number of forces. He wrote, "the presence of court orders indeed may contribute to changes in police arrest policy in specific municipalities, but other factors (e.g., local politics, different organizational interests, exchange relationships with other justice agencies) also interact to shape citation policy at the local level." John Klofas (1990) notes that jail crowding and policies aimed at reducing that crowding are intimately linked to the wider community. He suggests that jail crowding can be best understood as a product of changes in community structure and function in general. One response to jail crowding is to change arrest practices by the police, while one effect of jail crowding is to undermine the ability of the police to use arrest powers to enforce the law or maintain order. In this case, the link between the front end and back end of the justice system is clear—as is their relationship to the society in which they exist.

Since the war on drugs and the development of sentencing guidelines for the federal courts, the composition of the inmate population has both increased and changed. The redefinition of drug offenses as more serious crimes, and the attempt to ensure greater retribution in the allocation of criminal punishments, increased the number of drug offenders sentenced to federal prisons. The proportion of the federal prison population comprised of violent offenders decreased as a result. Given the large increase in the total population, however, this change reflects the increased imprisonment of those convicted of drug crimes, not a reduction in the use of prison for violent offenders. At the state level, there has been an increase in the number of violent offenders partly as a result of increasing lengths of terms for those convicted of violent crimes, related to "truth in sentencing." The greatly increased costs of incarceration combined with little perceived reduction in crime has caused some people to question the emphasis we place on prison as a response to crime. This questioning of imprisonment supports an expanded role for community alternatives to incarceration, raising issues in community corrections. Thus, changes in our views of crimes and improvements in our ability to detect and apprehend offenders have ripple effects throughout the justice system that are most keenly felt in the corrections component that is "at the end of the line."

Review Questions

1. Explain what is meant by privatization in institutional corrections, and identify at least three unresolved issues regarding the trend of privatization.

2. Explain how the current crisis of crowding in American prisons has affected our jail populations.

3. Identify three strategies a state may employ to deal with prison crowding, and name some factors that may help explain why a particular state selects a specific option.

4. Identify the effects of prison crowding on inmates, staff, and prison administrators.

5. Identify the six ways in which prison industry has been organized throughout the years.

6. What positive benefits are expected for the state and inmates from successful prison industry programs?

7. Briefly describe three recent prison riots.

8. Some observers believe that recent changes in prison administration that have improved conditions for inmates vis-à-vis prison staff have contributed to increased violence. Briefly explain this argument.

9. Describe how many of the problems faced by prisons and jails are reflections of broader changes and issues in the larger society.

References

Abbott, J.H. (1981). *In the Belly of the Beast: Letters from Prison.* New York: Vintage.

Alarid, L. (2003). "A Gender Comparison of Prisoner Selection for Job Assignments While Incarcerated." *Journal of Crime and Justice* 26(1):95-116.

Auerbach, B. (1982). "New Prison Industries Legislation: The Private Sector Re-enters the Field." *The Prison Journal* 62(2):25-36.

Auerbach, B. (1993). "Federal Government Involvement in Private Sector Partnerships with Prison Industries." In G. Bowman, S. Hakim & P. Seidenstat (eds.), *Privatizing Correctional Institutions.* New Brunswick, NJ: Transaction, 91-104.

Bales, W., L. Bedard, S. Quinn, D. Ensley & G. Holley (2005). "Recidivism of Public and Private State Prison Inmates in Florida." *Criminology & Public Policy* 4(1):57-82.

Barnes, C. & R. Kingsnorth (1996). "Race, Drugs, and Criminal Sentencing: Hidden Effects of the Criminal Law." *Journal of Criminal Justice* 24(1):39-55.

Baskin, D., I. Sommers & H. Steadman (1991). "Assessing the Impact of Psychiatric Impairment on Prison Violence." *Journal of Criminal Justice* 19(3):271-280.

Batiuk, M., P. Moke & P. Rountree (1997). "Research Note: Crime and Rehabilitation: Correctional Education As An Agent of Change." *Justice Quarterly* 14(1):167-180.

Beck, A. & P. Harrison (2006). *Sexual Violence Reported by Correctional Authorities, 2005.* Washington, DC: Bureau of Justice Statistics.

Beck, A. & T. Hughes (2005). *Sexual Violence Reported by Correctional Authorities, 2004.* Washington, DC: Bureau of Justice Statistics.

Beck, A. & C. Mumola (1999). *Prisoners in 1998.* Washington, DC: Bureau of Justice Statistics.

Benton, F.W. & J.A. Silberstein (1983). "State Prison Expansion: An Explanatory Model." *Journal of Criminal Justice* 11(2):121-128.

Berk, R., H. Ladd, H. Graziano & J. Baek (2003). "A Randomized Experiment Testing Inmate Classification Systems." *Criminology & Public Policy* 2(2):215-242.

Bowditch, C. & R. Everett (1987). "Private Prisons: Problems Within the Solution." *Justice Quarterly* 4(3):441-453.

Bowker, L.H. (1980). *Prison Victimization.* New York: Elsevier.

Braswell, M., R. Montgomery & L. Lombardo (eds.) (1994). *Prison Violence in America,* 2nd ed. Cincinnati: Anderson.

Bureau of Justice Assistance (2004). *Prison Industry Enhancement Certification Program.* Washington, DC: Bureau of Justice Assistance.

Bureau of Justice Statistics (1984). *The 1983 Jail Census.* Washington, DC: U.S. Department of Justice.

Bureau of Justice Statistics (1986). *Population Density in State Prisons.* Washington, DC: U.S. Department of Justice.

Camp, C. & G. Camp (1996). *The Corrections Yearbook 1996.* South Salem, NY: Criminal Justice Institute.

Camp, S., G. Gaes, N. Langan & W. Saylor (2003). "The Influence of Prisons on Inmate Misconduct: A Multilevel Investigation." *Justice Quarterly* 20(3):501-533.

Cao, L., J. Zhao & S. Van Dine (1997). "Prison Disciplinary Tickets: A Test of the Deprivation and Importation Models." *Journal of Criminal Justice* 25(2):103-113.

Clear, T. (1997). "Ten Unintended Consequences of the Growth in Imprisonment." *Corrections Management Quarterly* 1(2):25-31.

Clemmer, D. (1940). *The Prison Community.* Boston: Christopher.

Conrad, J. (1982). "What Do the Undeserving Deserve?" In R. Johnson & H. Toch (eds.), *The Pains of Imprisonment.* Beverly Hills, CA: Sage, 313-330.

Cooper, L. (1993). "Minimizing Liability with Private Management of Correctional Facilities." In G. Bowman, S. Hakim & P. Seidenstat (eds.), *Privatizing Correctional Institutions.* New Brunswick, NJ: Transaction, 131-137.

Criminal Justice Newsletter (1985). "Controversial A.C.A. Policy Calls for 'Privatization.'" *Criminal Justice Newsletter* 16(3):1-3.

Crouch, B. & J. Marquart (1990). "Resolving the Paradox of Reform: Litigation, Prisoner Violence, and Perceptions of Risk." *Justice Quarterly* 7(1):103-123.

Crutchfield, R. (2004). "Editorial Introduction—Commentary: Mass Incarceration." *Criminology & Public Policy* 3(2):265-266.

Cullen, F.T. & L.F. Travis, III (1984). "Work as an Avenue of Prison Reform." *New England Journal on Criminal and Civil Confinement* 10(1):45-64.

Davis, A. (1968). "Sexual Assaults in the Philadelphia Prison System and Sheriff's Vans." *Transaction* 6:13.

Ditton, P. (1999). *Mental Health and Treatment of Inmates and Probationers.* Washington, DC: Bureau of Justice Statistics.

Ditton, P. & D. Wilson (1999). *Truth in Sentencing in State Prisons.* Washington, DC: Bureau of Justice Statistics.

Doleschal, E. (1971). "Rate and Length of Imprisonment." *Crime & Delinquency* 23:51.

Durham, A. (1989). "Managing the Costs of Modern Corrections: Implications of Nineteenth-Century Privatized Prison-Labor Programs." *Journal of Criminal Justice* 17(2):441-455.

Eichenthal, D. & J. Jacobs (1991). "Enforcing the Criminal Law in State Prisons." *Justice Quarterly* 8(3):283-303.

Ericson, R., M. McMahon & D. Evans (1987). "Punishment for Profit: Reflections on the Revival of Privatization in Corrections." *Canadian Journal of Criminology* 29(4):355-388.

Ethridge, P. & J. Marquart (1993). "Private Prisons in Texas: The New Penology for Profit." *Justice Quarterly* 10(1):29-48.

Fedo, M. (1981). "Free Enterprise Goes to Prison." *Corrections Magazine* 7(2):5-13.

Flanagan, T. & K. Maguire (1993). "A Full Employment Policy for Prisons in the United States: Some Arguments, Estimates, and Implications." *Journal of Criminal Justice* 21(2):117-130.

Fogel, D.F. (1979). *"We Are the Living Proof . . ." The Justice Model for Corrections,* 2nd ed. Cincinnati: Anderson.

Fox, V. (1983). *Correctional Institutions.* Englewood Cliffs, NJ: Prentice Hall.

Geis, G., A. Mobley & D. Shichor (1999). "Private Prisons, Criminological Research, and Conflict of Interest: A Case Study." *Crime & Delinquency* 45(3):372-388.

Gowdy, V. (1997). "Should We Privatize Our Prisons? The Pros and Cons." *Corrections Management Quarterly* 1(2):56-63.

Greenwood, P. (1981). *Private Enterprise Prisons? Why Not? The Job Would Be Done Better and at Less Cost.* Santa Monica, CA: RAND.

Greenwood, P. (1982). *Selective Incapacitation.* Santa Monica, CA: RAND.

Hackett, J.C., H.P. Hatry, R.B. Levinson, J. Allen, K. Chi & E.D. Feigenbaum (1987). *Contracting for the Operation of Prisons and Jails.* Washington, DC: U.S. Department of Justice.

Harrison, P. & A. Beck (2006). *Prisoners in 2005.* Washington, DC: Bureau of Justice Statistics.

Hassine, V. (1996). *Life Without Parole: Living in Prison Today.* Los Angeles: Roxbury.

Huebner, B. (2003). "Administrative Determinants of Inmate Violence: A Multilevel Analysis." *Journal of Criminal Justice* 31(2):107-117.

Jacobs, J. (1977). *Stateville: The Penitentiary in Mass Society.* Chicago: University of Chicago Press.

Jackson, J. & S. Ammen (1996). "Race and Correctional Officers' Punitive Attitudes Toward Treatment Programs for Inmates." *Journal of Criminal Justice* 24(2):153-166.

James, D. (2004). *Profile of Jail Inmates, 2002.* Washington, DC: Bureau of Justice Statistics.

Jan, L. (1980). "Overcrowding and Inmate Behavior: Some Preliminary Findings." *Criminal Justice and Behavior* 7(3):293-301.

Johnson, B., D. Larson & T. Pitts (1997). "Religious Programs, Institutional Adjustment, and Recidivism Among Former Inmates in Prison Fellowship Programs." *Justice Quarterly* 14(1):145-166.

Johnson, R. (1987). *Hard Time: Understanding and Reforming the Prison.* Monterey, CA: Brooks/Cole.

Kaplan, S. (1987). "Solid Protection—New Advances in Body Armor." *Corrections Today* 49(4):80-82.

Keve, P. (1986). *The History of Corrections in Virginia.* Charlottesville: University of Virginia Press.

Klofas, J. (1987). "Patterns of Jail Use." *Journal of Criminal Justice* 15(5):403-412.

Klofas, J. (1990). "The Jail and the Community." *Justice Quarterly* 7(1):69-102.

Krajick, K. (1984). "Punishment for Profit." *Across the Board* (March):20-27.

Kruttschnitt, C. & S. Krmpotich (1990). "Aggressive Behavior Among Female Inmates: An Exploratory Study." *Justice Quarterly* 7(2):371-389.

Lanza-Kaduce, L., K. Parker & C. Thomas (1999). "A Comparative Recidivism Analysis of Releases from Private and Public Prisons." *Crime & Delinquency* 45(1):28-47.

Latessa, E.J. (1985). "Community Corrections as Diversion." In L.F. Travis III (ed.), *Probation, Parole, and Community Corrections.* Prospect Heights, IL: Waveland, 81-93.

Liedka, R., A. Piehl & B. Useem (2006). "The Crime-Control Effect of Incarceration: Does Scale Matter?" *Criminology & Public Policy* 5(2):245-276.

Lockwood, D. (1980). *Prison Sexual Violence.* New York: Elsevier.

Lockwood, D. (1994). "Issues in Prison Sexual Violence." In M. Braswell, R. Montgomery & L. Lombardo (eds.), *Prison Violence in America,* 2nd ed. Cincinnati: Anderson, 89-97.

Logan, C.H. (1987). "The Propriety of Proprietary Prisons." *Federal Probation* 51(3):35-40.

Logan, C.H. & J. DiIulio (1992). "Ten Deadly Myths about Crime and Punishment in the U.S." *Wisconsin Interest* 1(Winter/Spring):21-35.

Lommel, J. (2004). "Turning Around Turnover." *Corrections Today* (August):54-63.

Lonski, P.D. (1986). "Illinois Shatters Myth—Industries Boost Local Economy." *Corrections Today* 48(7):52-56.

Lowenkamp, C., E. Latessa & P. Smith (2006). "Does Correctional Program Quality Really Matter? The Impact of Adhering to the Principles of Effective Intervention." *Criminology & Public Policy* 5(3):575-594.

Lynch, J. & W. Sabol (2004). "Assessing the Effects of Mass Incarceration on Informal Social Control in Communities." *Criminology and Public Policy* 3(2):267-294.

Lynch, J. & W. Sabol (2000). "Prison Use and Social Control." In J. Horney (ed.), *Policies, Processes, and Decisions of the Criminal Justice System.* Washington, DC: National Institute of Justice, 2000:7-44.

Maguire, K. & A. Pastore (1999). *Sourcebook of Criminal Justice Statistics–1998.* Washington, DC: U.S. Government Printing Office.

Maguire, K., A. Pastore & T. Flanagan (1993). *Sourcebook of Criminal Justice Statistics–1992.* Washington, DC: U.S. Government Printing Office.

Mahan, S. (1982). "An Orgy of Brutality at Attica and the 'Killing Ground' at Santa Fe: A Comparison of Prison Riots." In N. Parisi (ed.), *Coping with Imprisonment.* Beverly Hills, CA: Sage, 65-78.

Marquart, J.W. & B.M. Crouch (1984). "Co-opting the Kept: Using Inmates for Social Control in a Southern Prison." *Justice Quarterly* 1(4):491-509.

Maruschak, L. (2004). *HIV in Prisons, 2001.* Washington, DC: Bureau of Justice Statistics.

Maruschak, L. & A. Beck (2001). *Medical Problems of Inmates, 1997.* Washington, DC: Bureau of Justice Statistics.

Marvell, T. & C. Moody (1997). "Age-Structure Trends and Prison Populations." *Journal of Criminal Justice* 25(2):115-124.

Mays, G. & T. Gray (1996). *Privatization and the Provision of Correctional Services: Context and Consequences.* Cincinnati: Anderson.

McCorkle, R. (1995). "Gender, Psychopathology, and Institutional Behavior: A Comparison of Male and Female Mentally Ill Prison Inmates." *Journal of Criminal Justice* 23(1):53-61.

McDonald, D.C. (1986). *Punishment Without Walls: Community Service Sentences in New York City.* New Brunswick, NJ: Rutgers University Press.

McDonald, D., A. Hassol & K. Carlson (1999). "Can Telemedicine Reduce Spending and Improve Prisoners Health Care?" *National Institute of Justice Journal* (April):20-25.

McDonald, D. & C. Patten (2003). *Government's Management of Private Prisons.* Washington, DC: National institute of Justice.

McEwen, T. (1995). *National Assessment Program: 1994 Survey Results.* Washington, DC: National Institute of Justice.

Meares, T. (2004). "Mass Incarceration: Who Pays the Price for Criminal Offending?" *Criminology and Public Policy* 3(2):295-302.

Miller, R., G. Sexton & V. Jacobsen (1991). "Making Jails Productive." *National Institute of Justice Reports* (January/February) (223):2-5.

Morris, N. (1974). *The Future of Imprisonment.* Chicago: University of Chicago Press.

Moses, M. & C. Smith (2007). "Factories Behind Fences: Do Prison 'Real Work' Programs Work?" *NIJ Journal* (June):32-35.

Mumola, C. (2007). *Medical Causes of Death in State Prisons, 2001-2004.* Washington, DC: Bureau of Justice Statistics.

Mumola, C. (2005). *Suicide and Homicide in State Prisons and Local Jails.* Washington, DC: Bureau of Justice Statistics.

Mumola, C. & J. Karberg (2006). *Drug Use and Dependence, State and Federal Prisoners, 2004.* Washington, DC: Bureau of Justice Statistics.

Nacci, P.L. (1988). "The Oakdale-Atlanta Prison Disturbances: The Events, the Results." *Federal Probation* 52(4):3-12.

Nagel, W.G. (1973). *The New Red Barn: A Critical Look at the Modern American Prison.* New York: Walker & Co.

National Council on Crime and Delinquency (1972). "Institutional Construction." *Crime & Delinquency* 18(3):331.

Neeley, C., L. Addison & D. Craig-Moreland (1997). "Addressing the Needs of Elderly Offenders." *Corrections Today* 59(5):120-123.

Newsweek (1987). "A Cuban Explosion." (December 7, 1987):38-40.

Ogle, R. (1999). "Prison Privatization: An Environmental Catch-22." *Justice Quarterly* 16(3):579-600.

Piehl, A. (2004). "The Challenge of Mass Incarceration." *Criminology and Public Policy* 3(2):303-308.

Pogrebin, M. & M. Dodge (2001). "Women's Accounts of Their Prison Experiences: A Retrospective View of Their Subjective Realities." *Journal of Criminal Justice* 29(6):531-541.

Pratt, T. & J. Maahs (1999). "Are Private Prisons More Cost-Effective Than Public Prisons? A Meta-Analysis of Evaluation Research Studies." *Crime & Delinquency* 45(3):358-371.

Rector, M. (1975). "The Extravagance of Imprisonment." *Crime & Delinquency* 21(3):323-330.

Reisig, M. & T. Pratt (2000). "The Ethics of Correctional Privatization: A Critical Examination of the Delegation of Coercive Authority." *The Prison Journal* 80(2):210-222.

Rogers, J. (1989). "The Greatest Correctional Myth: Winning the War on Crime Through Incarceration." *Federal Probation* 53:21-28.

Rolland, M. (1997). *Descent Into Madness: An Inmate's Experience of the New Mexico State Prison Riot.* Cincinnati: Anderson.

Sabol, W., T. Minton & P. Harrison (2007). *Prison and Jail Inmates at Midyear 2006.* Washington, DC: Bureau of Justice Statistics.

Saylor, W. & G. Gaes (1997). "Training Inmates Through Industrial Work Participation and Vocational and Apprenticeship Instruction." *Corrections Management Quarterly* 1(2):32-43.

Schwartz, M.D. & L.F. Travis III (eds.) (1997). *Corrections: An Issues Approach,* 4th ed. Cincinnati: Anderson.

Schwartz, M., L. Travis & T. Clear (eds.) (1980). *Corrections: An Issues Approach.* Cincinnati: Anderson.

Schwarz, R.J. (1986). "New Mexico: The Anatomy of a Riot." *Corrections Magazine* 6(2):6-24.

Sechrest, D. (1991). "The Effects of Density on Jail Assaults." *Journal of Criminal Justice* 19(3):211-223.

Serrill, M. & P. Katel (1980). "New Mexico: The Anatomy of a Riot." *Corrections Magazine* 6(2):6-24.

Shover, N. & W. Einstadter (1988). *Analyzing American Corrections.* Belmont, CA: Wadsworth.

Simon, L. (1993). "Prison Behavior and the Victim-Offender Relationship Among Violent Offenders." *Justice Quarterly* 10(3):490-506.

Snyder, H. (1990). *Growth in Minority Detentions Attributed to Drug Law Violators.* Washington, DC: Office of Juvenile Justice and Delinquency Prevention.

Stephan, J. (2001). *Census of Jails, 1999.* Washington, DC: Bureau of Justice Statistics.

Stephan, J. & J. Karberg (2003). *Census of State and Federal Correctional Facilities, 2000.* Washington, DC: Bureau of Justice Statistics.

Stohr, M., N. Lovrich, B. Menke & L. Zupan (1994). "Staff Management in Correctional Institutions: Comparing DiIulio's 'Control Model' and 'Employee Investment Model': Outcomes in Five Jails." *Justice Quarterly* 11(3):471-497.

Stohr, M., N. Lovrich & M. Wood (1996). "Service Versus Security Concerns in Contemporary Jails: Testing General Differences in Training Topic Assessments." *Journal of Criminal Justice* 24(5):437-448.

Stojkovic, S., C. Pope & W. Feyerherm (1987). "Confinement Patterns in the Milwaukee County House of Correction: 1907-1965." *Journal of Criminal Justice* 15(4):301-316.

Sykes, G. (1958). *The Society of Captives.* Princeton, NJ: Princeton University Press.

Tartaro, C. (2002). "The Impact of Density on Jail Violence." *Journal of Criminal Justice* 30(6):499-510.

Tewksbury, R. (2007). "Staff Sexual Misconduct." Workforce—Human Resources: American Correctional Association. Found at: http://www.aca.org/committee/home.asp, accessed July 2, 2007.

Thomas, C. (2005). "Recidivism of Public and Private State Prison Inmates in Florida: Issues and Unanswered Questions." *Criminology and Public Policy* 4(1):89-100.

Thomas, C. & C. Logan (1993). "The Development, Present Status, and Future Potential of Correctional Privatization in America." In G. Bowman, S. Hakim & P. Seidenstat (eds.), *Privatizing Correctional Institutions.* New Brunswick, NJ: Transaction, 213-240.

Tischler, C. & J. Marquart (1989). "Analysis of Disciplinary Infraction Rates Among Male and Female Inmates." *Journal of Criminal Justice* 17(6):507-513.

Toch, H. (1965). "Task Force for Institutional Violence, 1965." Unpublished manuscript. Sacramento, CA: California Department of Corrections.

Travis, L. (1989). "Crowding in American Prisons and Jails: Causes, Effects and Possible Solutions." *Justice Professional* 4(2):257-278.

Travis, L.F., E.J. Latessa & G.F. Vito (1985). "Private Enterprise in Institutional Corrections: A Call for Caution." *Federal Probation* 49(4):11-16.

Vanyur, J. (1997). "What It Takes to Be a Warden in the 1990s." *Corrections Management Quarterly* 1(2):65-70.

Vito, G. (1985). "Putting Prisoners to Work: Policies and Problems." *Journal of Offender Counseling, Services, and Rehabilitation* 9(3):21-34.

Welsh, W. (1993). "Changes in Arrest Policies as a Result of Court Orders Against County Jails." *Justice Quarterly* 10(1):89-120.

Wilson, J.Q. (1975). *Thinking About Crime.* New York: Basic Books.

Wooldredge, J. (2003). "Keeping Pace With Evolving Prison Populations for Effective Management." *Criminology & Public Policy* 2(2):253-258.

Wooldredge, J., T. Griffin & T. Pratt (2001). "Considering Hierarchical Models for Research on Inmate Behavior: Predicting Misconduct with Multilevel Data." *Justice Quarterly* 18(1):203-231.

Wright, K. (2000). "The Evolution of Decisionmaking among Prison Executives, 1975-2000." In J. Horney (ed.), *Policies, Processes, and Decisions of the Criminal Justice System.* Washington, DC: National Institute of Justice, 2000:177-224.

Wright, R. (1994). *In Defense of Prisons.* Westport, CT: Greenwood Press.

Wright, R. (1997). "The Evidence in Favor of Prisons." In M. Schwartz & L. Travis (eds.), *Corrections: An Issues Approach,* 4th ed. Cincinnati: Anderson, 95-108.

Zedlewski, E. (1987). *Making Confinement Decisions.* Washington, DC: U.S. Department of Justice.

Zedlewski, E. (1997). "Why Prisons Matter: A Utilitarian Review." *Corrections Management Quarterly* 1(2):15-24.

Chapter 12

Probation, Parole, and Community Corrections

Important Terms

At any given time, there are roughly two and a half times as many people under probation and parole supervision as there are people incarcerated in the United States. As of December 31, 2005, nearly 3 percent of the adult population of the United States could be found either on probation or parole. While incarceration may be the cornerstone of American corrections, the majority of criminal offenders are sentenced to probation.

By the end of 1985, the Bureau of Justice Statistics (1987:1) reported that more than 2.9 million persons were under correctional authority, and 74 percent of all those were under community supervision (probation or parole). By the end of 2005, there were nearly 7.1 million adults under correctional authority, with more than 4.9 million under probation or parole supervision (Glaze & Bonczar, 2006). The majority of persons under community supervision (4.1 million) were on probation. The combined probation and parole populations account for about 70 percent of all those under the custody of correctional agencies. While the percentage of the correctional population that is comprised of inmates (in jails and prisons) has increased over the past 20 years, community supervision is still the most common correctional setting.

Probation and parole supervision as currently operated, like the prison, are American inventions. Both involve the conditional release of convicted offenders into the community under supervision. Probationers and parolees experience similar treatment but, as we shall see, there are important differences between the two.

Box 12.1   Probation and Parole (2005): "The Bookends of Imprisonment"

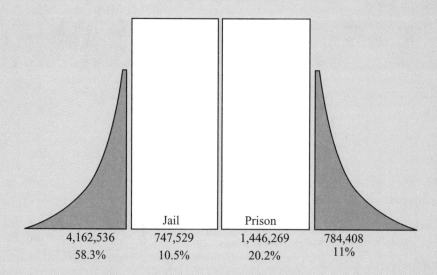

	Jail	Prison	
4,162,536	747,529	1,446,269	784,408
58.3%	10.5%	20.2%	11%

• **Probation** is the sentencing of an offender to community supervision by a probation agency, often as a result of suspending a sentence to confinement. Such supervision normally entails specific rules of conduct while in the community. If the rules are violated a sentence to confinement may be imposed. Probation is the most widely used correctional disposition in the United States.

• **Incarceration** is the confinement of a convicted criminal in a Federal or State prison or a local jail to serve a court-imposed sentence. Confinement is usually in a jail, administered locally, or a prison, operated by the State or Federal Government. In many States offenders sentenced to one year or less are held in a jail; those sentenced to longer terms are committed to a State prison.

Release from prison generally occurs as the result of a decision of a paroling authority, mandatory release, or expiration of sentence.

• **Parole** is the release of a prisoner by the decision of a paroling authority. The offender is placed under the supervision of a parole officer who monitors the offender's compliance with rules of conduct imposed by the paroling authority. Violations of these rules may result in reimprisonment for the balance of the unexpired sentence.

• **Mandatory release** is based on earned "good time" (days earned for good behavior) or other statutory sentence-reduction measures and, though supervision is required after release, does not usually depend on the discretionary decision of a parole board. Supervision rules of conduct, if violated, may result in a return to prison for the time remaining on the sentence.

Source: L. Glaze & T. Bonczar (2006), *Probation and Parole in the United States, 2005* (Washington, DC: Bureau of Justice Statistics):1.

Probation and parole can be considered to be the "bookends" of imprisonment (see Box 12.1). Probation is a sanction generally imposed in lieu of incarceration, and thus, it occurs before imprisonment. Parole involves those who are released early from incarceration sentences, so it occurs after a period of imprisonment. Therefore, probation and parole "flank" imprisonment on either side as criminal sanctions.

This chapter examines community supervision in the criminal justice system of the United States. We will describe probation and parole supervision as well as some other forms of community control of offenders. The history and practice of probation, parole, and other community-based sanctions will be addressed, and the various populations involved in these sanctions will be assessed.

The Origins of Community Supervision

Probation and parole developed in the nineteenth century in the United States, although each had precursors in Western civilization. An examination of the history of community supervision shows how the justice system has changed with the social and intellectual currents in the larger society. Shortly after the creation of the penitentiary, many people came to view incarceration as a less-than-adequate response to all offenders. Probation and parole developed as alternatives to incarceration for select groups of offenders.

Probation evolved from several prior practices in the English courts that allowed judges to grant leniency to offenders who would otherwise be subjected to the harsh corporal and capital punishments provided in the common law. Among these were the benefit of clergy, judicial reprieve, and release on recognizance (Allen et al., 1985:37-40). Each of these practices allowed the sentencing judge to postpone or avoid the execution of sentence.

The benefit of clergy was a practice that developed during the medieval period so that members of the clergy would be held accountable in ecclesiastic (church) courts rather than civil courts. The accused could claim the benefit of clergy to have his or her case moved from the civil courts to the church courts. The test for benefit of clergy came to be one of literacy, in which the accused would be asked to read the text of the 51st Psalm (see Box 12.2) in court. In due time, illiterate common criminals committed the psalm to memory so that they could pretend to read it and thus avoid the punishments of the king's courts (Clear & Cole, 1986:232).

Box 12.2 51st Psalm: The Neck Verse

Have mercy upon me, O God,
according to thy loving kindness,
According to the multitude of thy tender mercies
blot out my transgressions.

The 51st Psalm, because it allowed many offenders to avoid hanging as the penalty for their crimes, came to be known as "the neck verse." After a period of expansion of the benefit of clergy (from the fourteenth through the eighteenth centuries), the practice was disallowed by statute in 1827. No longer was it possible to escape in this way to the less severe sanctions of the church courts.

Judicial reprieve was a common practice in England in the nineteenth century. Under this practice, the offender could apply to the judge for a reprieve, which would require that sentencing of the offender be delayed upon condition of good behavior, for a specific period of time. After the allotted time period, the offender would be allowed to ask for a pardon from the king. Here we see the addition of two components of contemporary probation: (1) a set time period, and (2) the requirement that the offender abide by conditions of good behavior.

Release on recognizance (ROR) was a practice (combined with peace bonds) that was a forerunner to bail. While awaiting the arrival of the circuit magistrate, an accused offender obtained release by posting a surety or by having someone vouch for him or her. It was this practice that most directly led to the development of contemporary probation.

John Augustus, a Boston boot maker, is generally credited as the "father of probation." It was common practice in Massachusetts courts to allow offenders to be released on the recognizance of a third party. Augustus began a nearly 20-year career as a voluntary probation officer by posting bail in the Boston Police Court in 1841 for a man accused of drunkenness. Between 1841 and 1858 he supervised nearly 2,000 people. He was so successful that the state of Massachusetts passed legislation authorizing probation as a disposition and provided for the first paid probation officer. Over time, the Massachusetts practice was emulated by other states. Today, probation is the most common disposition of criminal cases.

Parole also developed in the mid-1800s. By the 1850s, observers of the penitentiary system grew dissatisfied with the effectiveness of incarceration in preventing further criminal behavior by offenders. These critics began to call for a reform of incarceration practices that would serve to "reform" inmates and produce law-abiding citizens. The outcome of this reform movement was parole release and supervision. Parole has two components. First, there can be a discretionary early release from prison. The second component is the period of supervision in the community that follows such a release.

In England and other European countries, several practices were already in place that laid the groundwork for the creation of parole. The term "parole" was taken from the French phrase *parole de honeur,* meaning "word of honor." Prisoners of war were released on their "parole" that they would not again take up arms against their captors. This term was later applied to the procedure for allowing prison inmates to return to society prior to the expiration of their prison terms. Essentially, the prisoners were expected to vow that they would not violate the law, in return for which they were released.

Banishment and transportation also have been considered to be precursors to parole, in that these procedures essentially allowed an offender to avoid a more harsh penalty upon condition that the offender not return to the land of the original crime (Barnes & Teeters, 1959). Closer to modern parole practice, however, were release procedures developed by Walter Crofton and Captain Alexander Maconochie. As superintendents of penal facilities, each of these men created a system of inmate discipline that allowed the prisoners to earn early release.

Crofton devised a ticket of leave for inmates in the Irish prison system. Prisoners were classified into three stages of treatment, ranging from segregated confinement, through work on public projects (which was increasingly free of supervision), until final release "on license." Successful inmates earned their ticket of leave through hard work and good behavior. When Crofton believed an inmate to be ready for release, he would issue a ticket authorizing the inmate to return home and report the offender's return to the local police. There was no supervision of the released inmate.

Alexander Maconochie is often called the "father of parole." His system was very similar to that of Crofton. Maconochie operated the British penal colony on Norfolk Island, in the South Pacific. There he classified offenders into three groups and instituted a **mark system**. All inmates began at the "penal stage," which involved close supervision while engaging in hard labor with a large group of fellow prisoners. Good behavior and industry earned "marks" for an inmate, and upon acquiring enough marks, the prisoner was moved to the next stage. The "social stage" involved working and living in groups of about seven prisoners, with less supervision than the penal stage. Again, marks were earned leading to promotion to the "individual stage," during which the prisoner was allowed a cottage and was given individual work. Prisoners were liable to being moved back to earlier stages for misconduct or laziness. Those in the individual stage who continued to demonstrate good behavior and industry were eventually rewarded with a ticket of leave or conditional pardon. Often they were apprenticed to citizens on mainland Australia (Travis, 1985).

The apparent success of these programs did not go unnoticed in the United States. In 1870, the American Prison Association in Cincinnati provided the forum for reformers to push for the creation of parole and a system of reformatory discipline in the United States (Lindsey, 1925). As a result of the growing support for early release and reformatory discipline, New York enacted legislation creating a reformatory at Elmira, where first offenders would be sentenced to terms that would last "until reformation, not to exceed five years." Parole release had been born in the United States.

Jonathan Simon (1993) has reviewed and assessed the development of parole. He suggests that the practice of third-party recognizance, what he calls "suretyship," was a forerunner to modern parole. **Suretyship** was the practice of a person of good standing in the community taking responsibility for guaranteeing the lawful behavior of another person. When the prison became the dominant form of punishment, Simon suggests, there was a recognition that not all offenders needed to be incarcerated, or at least incarcerated for full terms. Parole release and supervision allowed authorities to select worthy offenders and release them from prison. Parole was used to support discipline, in that well-behaved, industrious inmates who could secure employment (and thus be kept busy at socially acceptable activities) were granted parole. When employment opportunities decreased during the Great Depression, disciplinary parole was replaced with "clinical" parole. In this revised model, the purpose of parole was to support the treatment and rehabilitation of inmates. In both cases, parole enabled authorities to differentiate between those convicted criminals who could be reformed and those who could not.

A similar argument can be applied to the development of probation supervision, as the functions and definitions of probation have mirrored those of parole. The task of probation evolved from diverting selected offenders from prison through control and discipline in the community, to the provision of treatment and rehabilitative services to offenders who did not need the more intensive treatment of prison.

During the first six or seven decades of its existence, a number of legal challenges to parole were raised. The practice of discretionary, early release from incarceration was finally accepted by the 1940s. In addition, during this era (called the Progressive Era), increasing attention was focused on the role of post-release supervision of offenders (as well as probation supervision). This led eventually to the current system of parole involving both early release and supervision in the community (Rothman, 1980).

Since the middle 1990s there has been increased concern about what is called **reentry**, the return of former inmates to life in the community. Throughout the 1990s, as prison populations continued to increase, it became apparent that relatively large numbers of parole violators accounted for a substantial portion of the inmate population (Burke, 2004). In 2005, more than one-third of all inmates admitted to state prisons were parole violators (Sabol, Minton & Harrison, 2005). Box 12.3 shows that the percentage of prison admissions comprised of parole violators has remained relatively stable at about one-third.

The twin concerns of assisting released inmates to adjust to law-abiding life in the community and reducing the risk of new crime posed by released offenders led to the development of **reentry courts**, where services for and supervision of parolees

Box 12.3 State Prison Admissions by Type, Percents

| Year | Type of Admission | | | |
	New Court Number	Commitment Percent	Number	Parole Violator Percent
2000	350,431	65.0%	203,569	35.0%
2001	365,714	63.7	215,450	36.3
2002	392,661	66.1	207,961	33.9
2003	399,843	66.9	209,753	33.1
2004	411,300	66.2	219,033	33.8
2005	421,426	65.7	232,229	34.3

Source: W. Sabol, T. Minton & P. Harrison (2007), *Prison and Jail Inmates at Midyear 2006* (Washington, DC: Bureau of Justice Statistics):4.

are coordinated and monitored in a court environment. These operate much like "drug courts" in which a "judge" meets frequently with the offender to monitor progress and, if needed, to change conditions of supervision and release (Lindquist, Hardison & Lattimore, 2003; Travis, Solomon & Waul, 2001). In many ways, the contemporary focus on prisoner reentry is like the original interest in developing parole. It might be said that we have rediscovered parole in the past decade.

An evaluation of one such program compared offenders enrolled in a specific reentry program with others who either received traditional prerelease services or no reentry programming at all (Wilson, 2007). Of the three groups, those who received no programming had fewer arrests and lower rates of revocation than either the reentry or traditional programming groups. The evaluators and others (Rhine, Mawhorr & Parks, 2006) suggest that the reentry program was not properly designed and implemented. Correctional personnel seek to learn from their mistakes and improve programs for the future. It remains to be seen how well reentry programs will do in improving parole supervision and outcomes.

The Organization of Community Supervision: Probation and Parole

Probation and parole, although very similar, differ in how they are organized. While many states charge supervising officers with the responsibility of serving both parolees and probationers, there are other states in which the two tasks are administratively separate. Probation tends to be organized as a county and municipal function. Parole, on the other hand, usually is a state function, even in states where parolees are supervised by probation officers (U.S. Department of Justice, 1978).

According to the U.S. Department of Justice (1978), parole supervision is exclusively a state function in 44 states. Seven states (the total included the District of Columbia) supplement state-level authority with local systems. Probation supervision is attached to the criminal court, but in most cases, probation officers are employees of the executive branch of the state government. About a quarter of agencies responsible for the supervision of adult and juvenile probationers are state-level, while nearly 70 percent are organized at the county level. The remaining probation agencies are city and municipal organizations. For parole supervision, the numbers are reversed, with more than 99 percent of agencies charged solely with the supervision of parolees organized at the state level. In places where the same agency supervises both probationers and parolees, more than 90 percent of the organizations are administered at the state level (U.S. Department of Justice, 1978). Thus, for the most part, probation is a local function and parole is a state function.

A survey of correctional systems in 1996 (Camp & Camp, 1996) revealed that 31 (two-thirds) of the systems reported combined probation and parole officers, while 15 maintained separate probation and parole supervision staff. In five of the systems, the state corrections agency was responsible only for parole supervision, and in one, only probation officers were on the state staff. Even in states reporting dual roles for officers (probation and parole supervision), often there is a separate local system of probation. In many states, counties can choose to provide probation supervision themselves, or may turn responsibility for the supervision of probationers over to the state.

Probationers are under the jurisdiction of the sentencing court, and are held to a set of conditions imposed by the sentencing judge. Probation officers are responsible for carrying out the wishes of the sentencing judge. Parolees, on the other hand, are under the jurisdiction of the state paroling authority, and are held to a set of conditions imposed by that authority. Parole officers are responsible for carrying out the wishes of the parole authority, although in most cases parole supervision is administered independently of the parole authority (Rhine, Smith & Jackson, 1991). In jurisdictions in which the same officers supervise both parole and probation, the officers wear two hats, and their behavior is contingent upon the legal status (probationer or parolee) of the client.

Fewer than 25 percent of those released from prison in 2004 were granted a discretionary parole. About 40 percent achieved mandatory release. **Mandatory release** occurs at the expiration of a prison term reduced by good behavior, or when a sentencing law requires that inmates completing their prison terms must be supervised in the community for some period of time (Glaze & Bonczar, 2006:8). The status of mandatory releasees is like that of parolees. For the period of their supervision, they are on a conditional release and must obey the rules and conditions of parole or face re-imprisonment. Discretionary release on parole has been steadily decreasing since the 1970s, with a corresponding increase in the

Box 12.4	Changes in Percentage of Prison Releases by Discretionary Parole 1977-2004

Year	Discretionary Parole Releases
1977	69.0%
1980	58.5
1985	42.5
1990	39.4
1992	39.5
1995	32.3
1999	23.7
2004	22.0

Source: Table constructed from, T. Hughes, D. Wilson & A. Beck (2001), *Trends in State Parole, 1990-2000* (Washington, DC: Bureau of Justice Statistics); L. Glaze & T. Bonczar (2006), *Probation and Parole in the United States, 2005* (Washington, DC: Bureau of Justice Statistics).

Box 12.5	Characteristics of the Probation and Parole Population, 2005	

Characteristic	Probation	Parole
Sex:		
Male	77%	88%
Female	23	12
Race:		
White	55%	41%
Black	30	40
Hispanic	13	18
Other	1	1
Supervision Status:		
Active	70%	83%
Inactive	9	4
Absconded	10	7
Out-of-State	2	4
Other	9	1

Source: Glaze, L. & T. Bonczar (2006), *Probation and Parole in the United States*, 2005 (Washington, DC: Bureau of Justice Statistics).

number of inmates receiving a mandatory release. In 1977, 69 percent of inmates released from prison received discretionary parole release. At the same time, the number of persons under parole supervision has more than tripled. Box 12.4 describes changes in discretionary parole release over time.

Few systematic data exist on the characteristics of probationers and parolees. It is generally safe to say that probationers, for the most part, are offenders who have less extensive criminal records than do prisoners. Kathleen Auerhahn (2007), however, has estimated that the probation population in California is increasingly composed of offenders with prior felony records and who were convicted of violent crimes. If this is true, then the traditional differences between probationers and parolees may be disappearing. Parolees, on the other hand, having been prisoners themselves, can be expected to mirror the prison population. In those states where release is discretionary, we might expect parolees to be slightly less dangerous than the general prison population, but this is speculation.

In 2004, 28 percent of persons convicted of a felony in state courts were sentenced directly to probation, and 40 percent were sentenced to prison (Durose & Langan, 2007). Felons sentenced directly to probation represented nearly 300,000 offenders, with an average supervision term of just over three years. In 2005, 480,300 persons entered parole supervision from state prisons (Glaze & Bonczar, 2006:6). Box 12.5 presents a description of the characteristics of the probation and parole populations in 2005. The probation population contains more females, fewer persons convicted of a violent offense, and fewer ethnic minorities than does the parole population. Given that ethnic minorities and males are more likely to be imprisoned, it would follow that the parole population (comprised of those who had been in prison) would have disproportionately fewer women and whites.

Not only do parole populations generally tend to be comprised of offenders with more serious criminal records, but further, largely as a result of incarceration, parolees tend to have greater needs in the areas of housing, employment, and personal relations than do probationers. One major difference is that parole caseloads tend to be significantly smaller than those served by probation officers. Camp and Camp (1996) reported that the average caseload for regular probation in the United States in 1995 was 142 offenders; for parole, the average caseload was 90 offenders. However, even though parole caseloads are smaller, the greater needs of the parole population often make them more difficult to supervise than the probation population. Box 12.6 compares supervision outcomes of probationers and parolees. Of those removed from supervision, nearly 60 percent of probationers successfully completed their terms, while less than one-half of parolees did so.

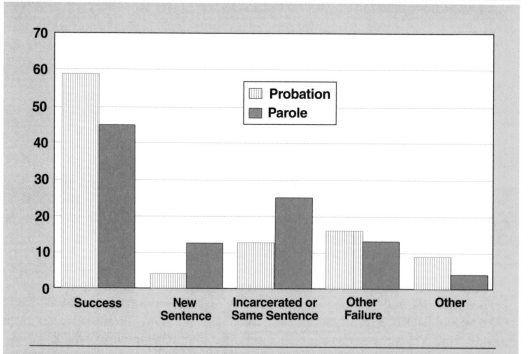

Box 12.6 Supervision Outcomes for Adults Leaving Probation and Parole, 2005

Source: L. Glaze & T. Bonczar (2006), *Probation and Parole in the United States, 2005* (Washington, DC: Bureau of Justice Statistics):6;9.

Other Forms of Community Supervision

While probation and parole are the major components of community supervision of criminal offenders, there are other programs that play a role in the nonincarceration treatment of convicted offenders. These programs include halfway houses, community service, furlough, home incarceration, and various diversion programs. Very frequently, these programs are imposed as conditions of release under probation or parole. Nonetheless, we will briefly discuss each of these separately.

Halfway Houses

Halfway houses are generally small residential programs that are based in the community and serve populations of less than 30 people (Wilson, 1985). Changes in thinking about the role of the community in the development of socially acceptable behavior spurred the development of halfway houses for both criminal offenders and the mentally ill (Beha, 1975). While these houses have a long tradition, their application to criminal corrections has experienced tremendous growth in the past three decades (Allen et al., 1978; Latessa & Travis, 1992).

Halfway houses are so named because they represent an intermediate step that is halfway between incarceration and community supervision. They can be either "halfway-out" houses that deal with parolees and other ex-inmates, or "halfway-in" houses for probationers and others not imprisoned (Keller & Alper, 1970). In either case, treatment is a part of the halfway-house routine.

In addition to providing room and board, halfway houses generally offer counseling services that include group and individual counseling sessions. Some halfway houses restrict their client population to "special needs" offenders, such as abusers of alcohol and other drugs. Other houses accept a

The Talbert House in Cincinnati, Ohio, was one of the first community-based agencies to receive accreditation from the American Correctional Association's Commission on Accreditation for Corrections. It is a privately administered agency that offers residential programs for offenders. *Photo credit: E.S. Boyne.*

wider range of persons, and provide or contract for a wider range of services. While we lack a clear picture of the characteristics and number of such halfway houses, estimates suggest that such facilities house upwards of 30,000 offenders per year in the United States (Latessa & Travis, 1992). At any given time, upwards of 20,000 offenders are housed in nearly 600 halfway houses across the country. Almost 90 percent of these halfway houses were operated by private organizations that contracted with correctional agencies to provide services (Camp & Camp, 1996:90-91).

Community Service Programs

Community service orders are programs in which convicted offenders are sentenced to a number of hours of service to community organizations or governmental agencies (Perrier & Pink, 1985). The work takes place in the community, and the offender is generally at liberty except for the scheduled work hours. The work of the convicted offender is supervised (Umbreit, 1981).

These programs have not been widely used with felons. Langan and Dawson (1993) reported that 4 percent of felons sentenced in state courts in 1990 were ordered to complete some form of community service. By 2002, that number had not changed with only 4 percent of felons ordered to complete community service as part of their sentence (Durose & Langan, 2003:10).

Community service is often seen as symbolically retributive in that the offender is typically sentenced to render some service related to the offense. For example, drunk drivers may be ordered to assist in a hospital emergency room, vandals may be ordered to clean and repair damaged buildings, and similar reflective penalties may be imposed on other offenders. A variant on community service is the chain gang, in which inmates work on public projects such as cleaning litter from roadsides while chained together in groups. Once discredited as too demeaning, chain gangs have recently resurfaced in some places. Those completing community service sentences generally are supervised by probation officers. Frequently, community service is imposed as a condition of probation (Hurd & Miller, 1981).

One of the most ambitious community-service sentencing programs reported to date was operated by the Vera Institute of Justice in New York City (McDonald, 1986). In this program, minor offenders were sentenced to perform 70 hours of community service work, such as cleaning and maintaining parks and senior citizen centers, or restoring buildings for low-income housing. The community-service sanction was imposed on those offenders likely to receive jail terms of 90 days or less, and on those likely to receive no sanction because of the pettiness of their offenses. In a five-year span, nearly 3,500 offenders served community-service sentences in three boroughs of New York.

Community service is often a core component of restorative justice programs. The term **restorative justice** refers to efforts to repair the harm to victims and/or communities caused by crime through interventions with the offender. David Karp and Kevin Drakulich (2004) reported on a statewide program of restorative justice in Vermont that involved those convicted of less serious offenses being placed on probation with a condition that they participate in the restorative justice program. Nearly two-thirds of restorative justice cases included community service orders. If restorative justice efforts increase, we can expect an increased reliance on community service in the future.

Furlough Programs

Furlough programs also are relatively recent alternatives to the traditional sanction of incarceration. At base, a furlough program allows an inmate to leave the penal facility for a specified period to perform an identified function. Several prisons and jails operate work and educational furlough programs. Inmates are released, without escort, to participate in educational programs or to report to work. After work or school, they return to the institution where they are incarcerated.

These programs are designed to eliminate some of the more debilitating effects of incarceration, such as the loss of a job or the severance of community ties. Furloughs also are employed to help inmates prepare for re-entry to the community by gradual exposure to release (Doleschal, 1971). Inmates on these types of furloughs are expected to seek work and housing, which they will need upon release from the institution.

Furloughs have a relatively long history in American corrections, but their use has changed and grown in recent years. Traditionally, furloughs were available to prison inmates in cases of family emergencies (e.g., to visit seriously ill relatives or to attend funerals). In these traditional furloughs, the inmate and the inmate's family were required to pay all expenses, including the cost of an escorting officer (Fox, 1983:147). In the 1960s, several states began granting furloughs to qualifying inmates for social visits, issuing weekend passes to certain inmates. Today, many states use furlough programs to allow inmates that are near the time of their release on parole to seek employment or arrange for residences. Each year thousands of prison inmates receive furloughs from prison in more than 40 jurisdictions.

LeClair and Guarino-Ghezzi (1991) studied furlough programs in Massachusetts. They found that prisoners who received furloughs were significantly less likely to commit new offenses after release than were those not receiving furloughs. They suggest that furlough programs serve as a positive reward for good behavior by inmates, and that by going on furlough, inmates may become more committed to adopting a lawful lifestyle. This is, indeed, the theory behind furlough programs. As LeClair and Guarino-Ghezzi (1991) suggest, we need to learn more about how furlough programs may work to reduce recidivism.

Work and Educational Release Programs

In a move related to furloughs, which tend to be brief releases for a specified period of time, correctional agencies are making use of work or study/educational release. Work or study release refers to the practice of allowing inmates of correctional facilities to leave the institution during the day to attend classes or work at a job. More than 9,000 jail inmates in 1995 were involved in work release programs (Gillard & Beck, 1996), and more than 55,000 prison inmates participated in work or study release programs in that year (Camp & Camp, 1996).

Work release programs are designed to allow inmates to secure and/or maintain employment while serving terms of incarceration. The benefits of work release programs are considered to be the opportunity for inmates released to work to maintain ties to conventional lifestyles and to their communities. Such inmates also can help support their families and often must contribute to the cost of their incarceration. This reduces overall correctional costs to the community. While relatively few inmates participate in such release programs, those who do participate benefit from being allowed to leave the correctional facility and by being able to keep jobs or secure an education (Wright & Travis, 1996).

Turner and Petersilia (1996) reported an evaluation of work release programming in the state of Washington. They found that almost 40 percent of inmates were placed in work release programs at some point during their term. Most work release participants successfully completed the program, with only 5 percent committing new crimes. However, the work release program was not found to reduce later recidivism or correctional costs when compared to what happened with inmates who did not receive a work release placement. In recent years, the use of work release programs has decreased compared to the early 1970s. Turner and Petersilia suggest that the decreased use of work release is a product of increased concerns about public safety and reduced program funding available from the federal government.

Home Incarceration

As a response to crowded prisons and jails, there has been a resurgence of interest in the practice of "house arrest" or home incarceration (Petersilia, 1986). Offenders sentenced to home incarceration are essentially "grounded." They are ordered to remain at home except for approved absences, such as attending school, going to work, or keeping medical appointments. While thus incarcerated, the offender is kept out of society yet is not confined in a jail. Ties to family and the community are retained, costs to the state are reduced, and the conditions of confinement for the offender are generally better than would exist in a penal facility.

Proponents of home incarceration argue that this practice is more humane and less costly than incarceration (Corbett & Fersch, 1985). Box 12.7 reports a comparison of the costs of home incarceration (house arrest) with other possible sanctions. These proponents suggest that, for many offenders, home incarceration represents a more satisfactory alternative to incarceration than do the traditional practices of fines or probation. With home incarceration, someone (usually a probation officer) must be responsible for monitoring the offender to ensure that he or she stays home. At midyear 2006, more than 800 jail "inmates" were placed on home detention with no other monitoring, and an unknown portion of the nearly 11,000 inmates being electronically monitored were also on home detention (Sabol, Minton & Harrison, 2006).

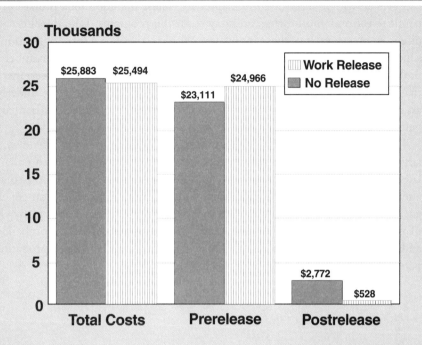

Box 12.7 House Arrest Costs: Comparison of Released and Nonreleased Offenders

Source: S. Turner & J. Petersilia (1996), *Work Release: Recidivism and Corrections Costs in Washington State* (Washington, DC: National Institute of Justice):11.

Diversion

The general rubric of **diversion** incorporates a wide variety of programs that occur at all stages of the justice system. Diversion is included in the discussion of community supervision because its most common formal application is at some point in the court process prior to conviction or sentencing. In most places, supervision of both diverted and sentenced offenders is conducted by the same office: the probation department (McSparron, 1980).

Diversion programs are designed to prevent some offenders from being processed through the justice system, or to minimize the extent of their processing. It is hoped that diverting offenders from the system will enable them to avoid the stigma of a criminal label and other negative effects of justice-system processing. While used for adults in many jurisdictions, diversion programs are most commonly used with juvenile offenders (Latessa, Travis & Wilson, 1984).

Being "On Paper"

Additional types of community sanctions or forms of probation and parole supervision will be discussed in Chapter 13. These include shock probation and parole, electronic monitoring, and day reporting programs. Like the alternatives discussed above, each of these innovations either represents a form of community supervision, or is imposed as a condition of probation or parole. Remember that probation and parole are the core components of community corrections, and that each of these is a form of conditional release from prison. The underlying assumption is that the offender would be incarcerated if not for his or her participation in community programming.

Community supervision is the punishment of choice for most offenders. The large role community supervision plays in the justice system has been enhanced lately as a result of prison crowding. Community supervision is often used as an alternative to imprisonment. Offenders under community supervision generally are held to a higher moral standard than are members of the free society, by virtue of the conditions of release. "On paper" is a term often used by probationers and parolees to refer to their status. This is a reference to the written probation or parole agreements that set out the conditions of release.

Supervision Conditions

In the final analysis, probation and parole represent an agreement between the offender and the state. In return for the decision not to incarcerate (or for the decision to release from incarceration), the offender agrees to abide by several conditions while at liberty in the community. Violation of any of these conditions can be used as the basis for revocation of liberty and subsequent incarceration of the offender.

Probation and parole conditions cover a wide variety of behavior and serve a number of purposes (Travis & Latessa, 1984:599). The primary goal of supervision conditions is to prevent future criminality on the part of probationers and parolees. Conditions can be classified into two general types: standard conditions that are imposed on everyone under supervision in a jurisdiction, and special conditions imposed on individual offenders that relate directly to the offender's status and characteristics (Hartman, Travis & Latessa, 1996).

Standard conditions of parole and probation vary across jurisdictions. They usually include restrictions on travel and on the freedom to change addresses or jobs, and involve instructions on reporting to the supervising officer. These conditions ensure that the probation or parole officer will be able to monitor the offender. Box 12.8 presents standard conditions of parole in the United States. Special conditions vary greatly (Jaffe, 1979). They include such things as restrictions on association with particular people, requirements of attending treatment programs, restrictions on the consumption of alcoholic beverages, and restitution orders.

The conditions of probation and parole are designed to achieve a number of purposes. Some conditions are necessary to ensure that supervision can occur. Thus, offenders may not be allowed to change their jobs or addresses without notifying the supervising officer. They may be required to report to a probation or parole officer on a regular schedule. Offenders who fail to submit to supervision (do not report as directed, change jobs or addresses without notifying their supervising officer, etc.) are called absconders. They are said to have absconded (escaped) from supervision. A study of probation absconders (Mayzer, Gray & Maxwell, 2004) found that these offenders often seem to abscond in the face of probable revocation and that they do not appear to differ from probationers who ultimately have their conditional liberty revoked. It seems likely that those who abscond from supervision have violated the conditions of release in other ways as well.

Other supervision conditions are aimed at imposing punishment, such as a requirement that an offender pay restitution, write a punishment lesson, or do community service work. A judge in Painesville, Ohio, was reported to sentence men convicted of soliciting a prostitute to wear a chicken suit and carry a sign that read, "No Chicken Ranch in Painesville." The sign is a reference to a famous "Chicken Ranch" prostitution house in Nevada (*Cincinnati Enquirer*, 2007). Still other conditions seek to ensure that offenders receive treatment for their problems by requiring participation in educational, psychological, or substance abuse programs. Conditions are also imposed to reduce the risk of new criminality. For instance, the U.S. Parole Commission has imposed conditions on some parolees that prohibit them from using computers. The "no computers" condition is a result of evidence that some offenders (sex offenders, confidence artists, etc.) use the Internet to gather information or contact others for criminal purposes (Schiesel, 1997). Finally, some conditions are imposed not as restrictions on behavior, but to give the offender notice. This may be the case, for example, when a condition of supervision is that the offender remain on probation or parole until discharged. What this condition does, of course, is tell the offender that supervision does not end until he or she is notified by the supervising authority.

Client Perspectives

The experience of being "on paper" reflects the number and content of conditions as well as the characteristics of the probation or parole officer. A probationer facing conditions that include a curfew, requirements of restitution, restriction on associating with friends, and some period of incarceration will have a qualitatively different experience than will a probationer under less restrictive conditions. Similarly, a parolee whose supervising officer is rule-oriented and unsympathetic will experience a different sanction than one whose officer is flexible and empathetic.

The ability to impose special conditions of probation has led to the use of probation to accomplish many correctional goals that are not necessarily authorized by statute. For example, in a jurisdiction in which there is no law authorizing "split sentences," a judge wishing to impose such a sentence can place the offender

Box 12.8   Parole Conditions in Effect in the United States, 1995

STATE	AL	AK	AR	ARK	CA	CO	CT	DE	FL	GA	HA	ID	IL	IA	IN	KS	KY	LA	TOTAL
1. Out of state travel	Xj	Xj	Xj	Xj	Xa	Xa	Xa	Xa	Xa	Xa	Xa	Xa	Xj	Xa	Xj	X	Xj	X	17
2. Comply with law	X	X	X	X	X	X		X	X		X	X	X	X	X	X	X	X	16
3. Regularly report/scheduled meeting		Xg					X												5
4. Weapons possession prohibited	X	X	X	X	X	X	X	X	X	X	X	X	X	X	X	X	X	X	18
5. Change residence	X	Xd	Xj	X	Xf	Xf	Xe	Xf	Xa	Xa	Xj	Xj	X	X	X	X	X	X	16
6. Special request from PO			X																1
7. First arrival report	Xh	X	Xd	Xe	Xd	X	X	Xf	Xa	Xa	Xj	Xh	Xj	X	X	X	X	Xe	12
8. Employment (change/maintain)		X	X	X	Xf	X	X	Xf	Xa	X	Xj	Xj		X	X	X	X		16
9. Narcotics usage/paraphanelia	Xb	Xb	Xb	Xb		Xb		Xb	Xb		Xb	Xb			Xb	Xb	Xb	Xb	13
10. Undesirable assoc./correspondence		Xb	Xb			Xb		Xb			Xb				Xb	Xc		Xb	6
11. Report, if arrested					Xh	Xh	Xe	Xg	X	Xh	Xh		X	Xd		X	Xf		11
12. Waive extradition	X		X	X														X	4
13. Support dependants						X			X								X		4
14. Liquor establishment/usage			Xb	Xi		Xb			Xb		Xb	Xb			Xb	Xb	Xb	Xb	10
15. Searches (house/work)			X	Xa		X	X	X	X			X			X		X	X	11
16. Auto registration				Xa										Xa	Xj				3
17. Change in marital status							Xe										Xa		2
18. May not be an informant		X	X														X		3
19. Program (drug/alcohol/vocational)				X				X				X		X					4
20. Curfew								X			X								2
21. Urinalysis	X		X	X		X		X				X		X		X	X		9
22. Restitution/fees	X		X	X				X	X	X				X		X		X	9
23. Give written/oral information	Xh					X		X	X	Xh	X	Xg			X		X	X	10
24. Indebtedness/no credit cards																			0
25. Intermediate sanction (EM/ISP/CS)								Xf										X	2
26. Away from victim																X			1
27. Refrain from assaultive behavior		X									X	X					X		4
28. Away from correctional facility											X	X					X		3
29. Other																			1
TOTALS	10	11	17	13	7	13	10	14	12	7	14	14	6	12	11	12	16	14	

Box 12.8   *(continued)*

STATE	ME	MD	MA	MI	MN	MO	MT	MS	NE	NV	NH	NJ	NM	NY	NC	ND	OH	OK	TOTAL
1. Out of state travel	Xa	Xa	Xa	Xj		Xj	Xj	X	Xj	Xj	Xa	X	Xa	Xa	Xa	Xj	Xj	Xa	17
2. Comply with law	X	X	X	X		X	X	X	X	X	X	X	X	X	X	X	X	X	17
3. Regularly report/scheduled meeting	X	X			X	X	X	X			X	X							8
4. Weapons possession prohibited	X		Xd	Xb	Xi	X	X	X	X	X	X	X		Xb	Xj	Xb	X	Xb	16
5. Change residence	X	Xa	X	X		Xj	Xa	X	Xa	Xa	Xa	X	Xa	Xd	Xh	Xd	Xa	X	17
6. Special request from PO				Xd				X	Xd	Xh					Xh			Xh	6
7. First arrival report				Xd	Xd					X		X	X	Xd	X	Xd			9
8. Employment (change/maintain)			X	X		X	X	X	Xj	Xa	Xa		Xa			X	Xb	X	15
9. Narcotics usage/paraphanelia		Xa	Xb	Xb	Xb	Xb		Xb	Xb	Xb	Xb	Xb	Xb	Xb	Xb	Xb	Xb	Xb	14
10. Undesirable assoc./correspondence				Xb		Xb	Xe	Xb	Xb	Xb	Xb		Xf	Xb		Xb	Xj		10
11. Report, if arrested	Xd			Xd		Xe		Xe			X	Xh	X	X	Xd		Xd	Xh	13
12. Waive extradition		X		X				X			X			X	X		X		6
13. Support dependants										X	X				X				3
14. Liquor establishment/usage								X	Xb	Xb	Xi		Xb		Xb	Xb	X	X	7
15. Searches (house/work)							X		X	X	X		X	X	X	X			10
16. Auto registration																			0
17. Change in marital status			Xd					X		Xa			X		X			Xa	4
18. May not be an informant			X						X							Xb			5
19. Program (drug/alcohol/vocational)																X			2
20. Curfew								X	X					X	Xj				1
21. Urinalysis				X				X	X	X	X				X	X	X	X	6
22. Restitution/fees								X	X	Xh	X			X		X	X	Xh	6
23. Give written/oral information						X		X		X		X				Xf		X	9
24. Indebtedness/no credit cards						X	X						Xg						3
25. Intermediate sanction (EM/ISP/CS)																			0
26. Away from victim																			0
27. Refrain from assaultive behavior							X	X											2
28. Away from correctional facility								X											1
29. Other										X									1
TOTALS	6	6	8	12	4	10	9	18	14	17	15	9	12	12	15	15	12	13	

Box 12.8 (continued)

STATE	OR	PA	RI	SC	SD	TN	TX	UT	VA	VT	WI	WA	WV	WY	US	TOTAL
1. Out of state travel	Xj		X		Xa	X	Xj	Xj	Xa	Xa	Xa	Xa	Xj	X	Xj	12
2. Comply with law	X	X	X	X	X	X	X	X	X	X	X	X	X	X	X	14
3. Regularly report/scheduled meeting		X				X	X				X					4
4. Weapons possession prohibited	Xb	X	Xd		X	X	X	Xb	X	X	X	X	X		X	13
5. Change residence	Xa	Xj				X	Xa	Xb	Xf				Xf	X	Xe	8
6. Special request from PO						X	X			X					X	5
7. First arrival report		Xe					Xh	Xh	Xf	X		X	Xd		Xd	9
8. Employment (change/maintain)	X	Xf	Xd		Xa	X		X	Xf	X		Xd	Xf	X	Xd	11
9. Narcotics usage/paraphernalia	Xb	X	Xb		Xb	Xb		Xb	Xb	Xd			Xb	Xb	Xb	9
10. Undesirable assoc./correspondence			Xb		Xb		Xb	Xb	Xb				Xb		Xb	7
11. Report, if arrested		Xf	Xh			X		Xe	Xf	X	Xf		Xf		Xb	9
12. Waive extradition		X	X						X	X					Xe	3
13. Support dependants			X		X								X			4
14. Liquor establishment/usage	Xb	Xb	X			X							X		X	5
15. Searches (house/work)	X	X	X		X		Xa		X	X	X	X		X	X	11
16. Auto registration			Xa		Xa		Xa			Xa						4
17. Change in marital status																0
18. May not be an informant			X	X			Xa		X	X	X					5
19. Program (drug/alcohol/vocational)	X	X	X	X					X	X				X	X	6
20. Curfew			X		X					X	X		X		X	3
21. Urinalysis	Xh		X	X		X		X	X	X		X	X		X	6
22. Restitution/fees	X	X	X	X	X	X	X	X	Xh	X			X		X	9
23. Give written/oral information	X			X			X	X		X			Xg		X	10
24. Indebtedness/no credit cards			Xa	Xa	Xa											3
25. Intermediate sanction (EM/ISP/CS)				X		X		X								3
26. Away from victim															X	1
27. Refrain from assaultive behavior		X								X						2
28. Away from correctional facility																0
29. Other	X	X	X												X	3
TOTALS	12	14	16	8	12	11	11	12	14	17	9	5	10	8	20	

a=permission; b=prohibited; c=must report; d=within 24 hours; e=within 48 hours; f=within 72 hours; g=monthly; h=immediately; i=allowed, but not to excess; j=written permission.

Other: Kentucky: lost the right to vote and hold public office. Pennsylvania & Nevada: if recommit, no good time. Oregon: not allowed to have dangerous animals. Rhode Island: revocation.

Source: J. Hartman, L. Travis & E. Latessa (1996), "Thirty-nine Years of Parole Rules." Paper presented at annual meeting of the Academy of Criminal Justice Sciences, Las Vegas, NV, March 1996.

on probation on condition that he or she serves some time in jail (Talarico & Myers, 1987). In a like fashion, absent a statutory authority to impose restitution, a judge can simply make restitution a condition of probation. Probation and (to a lesser extent) parole are the most flexible of sanctions. This may account, in part, for their popularity among justice system officials.

Recently, criminal justice scholars have begun to ask probationers and parolees for their views on community supervision (Allen, 1985; Gibbs, 1985; McCleary, 1978; Spelman, 1995; Wood & May, 2003). In large part, these offenders prefer probation or parole to any form of incarceration. Many feel fortunate to have been granted an opportunity to prove themselves in the community, but most also identify problems associated with being under supervision. In some cases, however, offenders see community supervision as a less desirable sanction than incarceration (Crouch, 1993; Petersilia, 1990; Wood & May, 2003). If the prison or jail term is relatively short and followed by unsupervised release, while probation or parole supervision will entail close supervision and restrictive conditions, many offenders would rather just "get it over with." They would prefer a short term of incarceration followed by freedom instead of what they expect will be a period of close supervision followed by prison when they are found in violation of conditions. This suggests that, at some level, it is possible to design a community supervision sanction that is as unpleasant as incarceration.

Probationers and parolees most often complain about what they perceive as the pettiness and unfairness of some conditions of release. They also dislike the requirement that they seek approval of their supervising officers for many minor decisions. Wood and May (2003) suggest that blacks or other minority group members may perceive greater discrimination and unfairness in community supervision than in prison, leading them to conclude that prison is often a less severe sanction than community alternatives. Finally, many are dissatisfied with their officers. Many probationers and parolees feel that their officers do not act as advocates for them, and many believe their officers are too intrusive.

As probation and parole have become more intrusive and controlling in recent years, the perceived difference between being "on paper" and "doing time" may have decreased. Chapter 13 describes these changes in supervision in more detail, but in general the increase in punitiveness has made com-

Tonya Harding, famous for her involvement in the 1994 Olympic scandal in which competitor Nancy Kerrigan was clubbed on the knee, attends a court appearance for a probation violation at the municipal court in Washougal, Washington. At a hearing held to determine whether she violated her probation conditions by consuming alcohol, Harding was sentenced to 30 days detention, with 20 days suspended. *Photo credit: AP Photo/John Gress, Pool.*

munity supervision more troublesome to offenders. At the same time, because of crowding, incarceration terms have been reduced in many jurisdictions. As a result, when offered release on parole for a given period or incarceration for a short period, many offenders choose incarceration. In a sample of Texas prisoners, Crouch (1993:79) found that almost half would choose one year in prison instead of five years of probation. A study compared probationer and probation officer perceptions of the burden of certain community sanctions relative to imprisonment and found that officers routinely overestimated the severity of sanctions. In general, probationers were much less likely to agree to additional sanctions, such as fines, restitution, and the like in order to avoid incarceration. Similarly, offenders reported that community service was much less onerous than probation officers thought it to be. The implications of this research are that probation and parole officers may be very limited in their ability to control offender behavior through the threat of sanctions (Flory et al., 2006). If offenders would prefer jail time to intensive supervision, the threat of jail is unlikely to convince them to abide by the conditions of supervision.

Officer Perspectives

Camp and Camp (1996) reported that in the United States correctional systems the total probation and parole staff (including support staff and others) exceeded 57,000. In about 40 percent of the jurisdictions responding to the survey, probation and parole officers were considered "peace officers" (like police) in their respective jurisdictions. Most agencies required both pre-service and in-service training of officers, with the average required training totaling about four weeks. It is common for parole and probation agencies to require officers to have a college education or even a graduate degree. Starting salaries for probation and parole officers differ by type of organization (probation only, parole only, or probation and parole), but average about $37,000 per year. Maximum salaries also vary, with an average high salary of less than $50,000.

Probation and parole officers lead a "schizophrenic" existence in relation to their jobs. For years, research into the role of the community supervision officer has identified conflicting dimensions of the responsibilities to help and to control (Clear & Cole, 1986). The officer is expected both to befriend and assist his or her clients, as well as to monitor and control them. With reference to parole officers, Studt (1973) identified officer "style" as critical to an understanding of the supervision process. She observed two basic styles: service (emphasis on helping the offender) and surveillance (emphasis on controlling criminal conduct).

Crean (1985:118) reported, "Within a typical work week, a line officer is usually called upon to be an investigator, a biographer, a watchdog, counselor, friend, confidant, reporter, expert witness and broker of outside services." The line officer is a public employee and responsible to the authority that placed the offender under the officer's supervision. Further, the officer must interact on a regular basis with the offender, the offender's family, law enforcement officials, and representatives of community agencies (Sigler, 1988).

As with most criminal justice jobs, community supervision involves a rather large degree of discretion and responsibility. It also entails a tremendous amount of paperwork. While there are psychological, monetary, and social rewards in being a probation or parole officer, there are the concomitant costs of dealing with offenders, danger, and bureaucracy. Nevertheless, probation and parole officers exhibit the characteristics of professionals, and they frequently do not work steady hours. Those who remain at their positions learn to separate work from the other aspects of their lives.

In a study of role conflict among probation officers working in intensive supervision programs, Clear and Latessa (1993) failed to find evidence of effects of different role definitions on individual officers. They compared officers working in one program that was clearly control-oriented with those working in another that was clearly treatment-oriented. They found that individual officers displayed differences in role definition (seeing themselves as more control- or treatment/support-oriented), but not in how they approached the jobs. The organizational philosophy of the probation agency appeared to be more important in explaining differences in case treatment than did individual attitudes. Regardless of whether the officer personally prefers control or support as an orientation to the job, the officer is able to perform only in compliance with organizational expectations. As Clear and Latessa (1993) note, a key question that remains is to discover how agencies select officers whose role definitions meet agency philosophy, or how agency philosophy is transmitted to officers and how it influences officer behavior. Fulton and colleagues (1997) reported that officer role orientation can be changed through training, again suggesting that it is the organizational policy more than individual officer attitudes that affects a probation or parole officer's "style" of work.

Probation and (to a lesser extent) parole are correctional interventions that often employ citizen volunteers. As probation was originated by a volunteer, this volunteer involvement is not surprising. Because the primary task of community supervision is to see that offenders can reside safely in the community, there are good reasons for using volunteers. Volunteers can perform many functions for probation and parole officers. The use of volunteers also helps clients by connecting them with law-abiding citizens (Lucas, 1987).

The dual roles of service and surveillance, coupled with heavy caseloads and frequently inadequate community services, often frustrate probation and parole officers and managers. Some areas of inquiry have included burnout and job satisfaction among the ranks of probation and parole officers (Whitehead, 1986). While there are many demoralizing facets of the job of community supervision agent, most officers report that the benefits outweigh the drawbacks of the job.

Offender Rights in Community Supervision

Probation and parole normally are considered privileges and not rights (del Carmen, 1985). Once placed on probation or parole, however, the offender does have a constitutionally protected interest in retaining that status, as opposed to being incarcerated. To date, there have been relatively few U.S. Supreme Court decisions dealing with the acceptability of various conditions of release and supervision practices. Most of the existing cases in this area were decided by state or federal appellate courts.

Essentially, courts have supported all types of probation and parole conditions, as long as those conditions were constitutional, reasonably related to criminality, clearly written, and/or contributed to the rehabilitation of the offender. The decisions of courts vary across jurisdictions, and are indeed case-specific. For example, a prohibition against the consumption of alcoholic beverages is likely to be upheld in a case in which the offender's criminality stemmed from drunkenness, and is likely to be voided in a case in which the offender has no history of alcohol abuse.

Probation and parole conditions often serve as an arsenal of leverage for correctional authorities. Because violation of any of the conditions of parole or probation constitutes grounds for revocation and incarceration, the conditions provide the officer with tools for controlling the offender. With regard to revocation, however, the U.S. Supreme Court has set forth due process protections for probationers and parolees.

In 1972, the Court decided the case of *Morrissey v. Brewer*, in which a parolee sought relief after his parole had been revoked. The Court ruled that parolees facing revocation must be granted the following protections: (1) written notice of the claimed violations, (2) disclosure of evidence against the parolee, (3) the opportunity to be heard and to present evidence, (4) a limited right to confront and cross-examine witnesses, (5) a hearing before a neutral body, and (6) a written statement of the decision and evidence upon which it was based.

The following year, the Court decided the case of *Gagnon v. Scarpelli* (1973), which dealt with probation revocation. In this case, the Court stated that, at least in regard to revocation procedures, there was no substantial difference between probationers and parolees. They granted probationers the same protections as those given to parolees.

Persons under community supervision generally are less restricted and suffer fewer pains than those incarcerated. Nonetheless, community supervision is still a punishment for crime, and the status of conviction and being under sentence sets probationers and parolees apart from free citizens. Even with the protections afforded by the *Morrissey* and *Gagnon* decisions, probationers and parolees may have their liberty revoked and may be incarcerated for "offenses" that would not carry similar penalties for free citizens. In addition, incarceration may follow hearings for which the burden of proof is not as high as the trial standard of proof beyond a reasonable doubt.

Hoffman and Beck (2005) described a pilot program of the U.S. Parole Commission that involved expedited revocation hearings. In many cases the alleged misbehavior involves violations of the technical conditions of parole and the parolee admits the violation. In these cases, the function of the revocation hearing is to determine the sanction. If the parolee consents, the probable cause hearing is waived and the parolee is returned to the institution for a dispositional hearing. The researchers concluded that the expedited process was cost-effective and supported by all parties, including defense counsel.

Community supervision serves crime control functions by allowing the state to limit the risk of new crimes through relaxed requirements for revocation (as compared to conviction). Yet, probationers and parolees have protected interests in conditional liberty, and the actions and decisions of probation and parole authorities are constrained by some due process requirements. It is instructive to observe that while a number of states and the federal government have taken steps to eliminate discretionary parole release, most have retained a period of post-release supervision. Community supervision itself represents a balance between individual interests in avoiding incarceration and community interests in controlling potential criminality. See Box 12.9 for a table of selected court cases on probation and parole.

Box 12.9   Selected Court Cases on Probation and Parole

Morrissey v. Brewer 408 U.S. 471 (1972)	Parolees facing revocation must be granted: written notice of the claimed violations; disclosure of evidence against the parolee; the opportunity to be heard and to present evidence; a limited right to confront and cross-examine witnesses; a hearing before a neutral body; and a written statement of the decision and the evidence upon which it was based.
Gagnon v. Scarpelli 411 U.S. 778 (1973)	At least in regard to revocation procedures, there is no substantial difference between probationers and parolees; therefore, probationers are granted the same protections as parolees. (For specific protections granted, see *Morrissey v. Brewer*.)

Supervision conditions also represent part of the "arsenal of the prosecutor." As we discussed earlier, it is fairly common for prosecutors to dismiss new criminal charges when they can proceed to a probation or parole revocation. Kingsnorth, MacIntosh, and Sutherland (2002) studied probation violation processing in eight California counties. They report that prosecutors frequently seek probation violations rather than file new criminal charges. This is especially true when the new offense is less serious than the one for which the offender was placed on probation.

Community Supervision
in the Whole System

In previous chapters, we have discussed several areas of overlap between community supervision and other components of the justice system. Pretrial release, diversion from court, prosecutorial charging, incarceration, and the size of the prison population all involve decisions that depend (more or less) directly on the operation of community supervision. For example, if probation and parole were not available as alternatives to incarceration, absent the development of other practices, the prison and jail population would increase threefold. The growth of intermediate sanctions and other changes in community supervision practices show how the criminal justice process is an "open system."

The development of intermediate sanctions and their effects on community supervision agencies and practices illustrate the open nature of the criminal justice system. The primary motivation for these new alternatives has been the need to control correctional costs in general, and the prison population specifically. As the prison population grew, so did community supervision populations. The same forces that produced the increase in prisoners have worked to swell community supervision populations. The war on drugs, for example, brought a large number of offenders into the justice system. Low-level drug offenders are now often seen as prime candidates for intermediate sanctions while under community supervision. A common adjustment to "truth in sentencing," which requires longer prison terms for violent offenders, has been to divert property and public order offenders from prison to probation or parole.

The prison population crisis has changed the nature of the community supervision population so that there are increased numbers of felons and more serious offenders under probation and parole supervision than historically was the case. The increase in the numbers of offenders has, in turn, been the impetus for changes in community supervision management, financing, and programs. Some of these programs, because they involve closer supervision and more restrictive conditions of release, have experienced relatively large rates of supervision failure. Those revoked from intermediate sanction programs often are imprisoned, but now come to prison as community supervision failures.

In these ways we can see the links between the components of the justice system, and between the justice system and the larger society. A redefinition of the seriousness of drug offenses led to enhanced drug crime enforcement. Increased enforcement changed the size and composition of the correctional population, both those incarcerated and those under community supervision. Seeking ways of managing the larger populations, we have developed intermediate sanctions that have altered traditional community supervision programs. Changes in community supervision, in turn, seem to have put increased pressure on prison populations through increased numbers of supervision failures. The next chapter explores changes in community supervision in more detail.

Review Questions

1. Distinguish between probation and parole.

2. Briefly trace the origins of community supervision in corrections.

3. Describe the organization of community supervision.

4. Tell what is meant by the term "re-entry."

5. Identify five forms of community supervision, excluding traditional probation and parole.

6. Distinguish between "standard" and "special" conditions of probation or parole.

7. Describe the role and importance of community supervision in the criminal justice system.

8. Identify the due process rights of probationers and parolees at revocation.

References

Allen, G.F. (1985). "The Probationers Speak: Analysis of Probationer's Experiences and Attitudes." *Federal Probation* 49(3):67-75.

Allen, H.E., E.W. Carlson, E.C. Parks & R.P. Seiter (1978). *Halfway Houses*. Washington, DC: U.S. Government Printing Office.

Allen, H.E., C.W. Eskridge, E.J. Latessa & G.F. Vito (1985). *Probation and Parole in America*. Monterey, CA: Brooks/Cole.

Auerhahn, K. (2007). "Do You Know Who Your Probationers Are? Using Simulation to Estimate the Composition of California's Felony Probation Population, 1980-2000." *Justice Quarterly* 24(1):28-47.

Barnes, H.E. & N.D. Teeters (1959). *New Horizons in Criminology*. Englewood Cliffs, NJ: Prentice Hall.

Beha, J.A. (1975). "Halfway Houses in Adult Corrections: The Law, Practice, and Results." *Criminal Law Bulletin* 11(4).

Bureau of Justice Statistics (1987). *Probation and Parole, 1985*. Washington, DC: U.S. Department of Justice.

Burke, P. (2004). "Parole Violations: An Important Window on Offender Reentry." *Perspectives* 28(1):24-31.

Camp, C. & G. Camp (1996). *The Corrections Yearbook 1996.* South Salem, NY: Criminal Justice Institute.

Cincinnati Enquirer (2007). "Sex Offenders Must Wear Chicken Suit." Found at: http://news.enquirer.com, accessed July 27, 2007.

Clear, T.R. & G.F. Cole (1986). *American Corrections. Monterey,* CA: Brooks/Cole.

Clear, T.R. & E.J. Latessa (1993). "Probation Officers' Roles in Intensive Supervision: Surveillance Versus Treatment." *Justice Quarterly* 10(3):441-459.

Corbett, R.P. & E.A.I. Fersch (1985). "Home as Prison: The Use of House Arrest." *Federal Probation* 49(1):13-17.

Crean, D.M. (1985). "Community Corrections: On the Line." In L.F. Travis III (ed.), *Probation, Parole and Community Corrections.* Prospect Heights, IL: Waveland, 109-124.

Crouch, B. (1993). "Is Incarceration Really Worse? Analysis of Offenders' Preferences for Prison Over Probation." *Parole and Community Corrections.* Prospect Heights, IL: Waveland, 47-70.

del Carmen, R.V. (1985). "Legal Issues and Liabilities in Community Corrections." In L.F. Travis III (ed.), *Probation, Parole, and Community Corrections.* Prospect Heights, IL:Waveland, 47-70.

Doleschal, E. (1971). *Graduated Release.* Rockville, MD: NIMH.

Durose, M. & P. Langan (2007). *Felony Sentences in State Courts, 2004.* Washington, DC: Bureau of Justice Statistics.

Durose, M. & P. Langan (2003). *Felony Sentences in State Courts, 2000.* Washington, DC: Bureau of Justice Statistics.

Flory, C., D. May, K. Minor & P. Wood (2006). "A Comparison of Punishment Exchange Rates Between Offenders Under Supervision and Their Supervising Officers." *Journal of Criminal Justice* 34(1):39-50.

Fox, V. (1983). *Correctional Institutions.* Englewood Cliffs, NJ: Prentice Hall.

Fulton, B., A. Stichman, L. Travis & E. Latessa (1997). "Moderating Probation and Parole Officer Attitudes to Achieve Desired Outcomes." *The Prison Journal* 77(3):295-312.

Gibbs, J.J. (1985). "Client's Views of Community Corrections." In L.F. Travis III (ed.), *Probation, Parole and Community Corrections.* Prospect Heights, IL: Waveland, 97-108.

Gillard, D. & A. Beck (1996). *Prison and Jail Inmates, 1995.* Washington, DC: Bureau of Justice Statistics.

Glaze, L. & T. Bonczar (2006). *Probation and Parole in the United States, 2005.* Washington, DC: Bureau of Justice Statistics.

Hartman, J., L. Travis & E. Latessa (1996). "Thirty-nine Years of Parole Rules." Paper presented at the annual meeting of the Academy of Criminal Justice Sciences, Las Vegas, NV, March 1996.

Hoffman, P. & A. Beck (2005). "Revocation by Consent: The United States Parole Commission's Expedited Revocation Procedure." *Journal of Criminal Justice* 33(5):451-462.

Hurd, J.L. & K.D. Miller (1981). "Community Service: What, Why, and How." *Federal Probation* 45(4):39-41.

Jaffe, H.J. (1979). "Probation with a Flair: A Look at Some Out-of-the-Ordinary Conditions." *Federal Probation* 43(1)25-36.

Karp, D. & K. Drakulich (2004). "Minor Crime in a Quaint Setting: Practices, Outcomes, and Limits of Vermont Reparative Probation Boards." *Criminology & Public Policy* 3(4):655-686.

Keller, O. & B. Alper (1970). *Halfway Houses: Community Centered Corrections and Treatment.* Lexington, MA: D.C. Heath.

Kingsnorth, R., R. MacIntosh & S. Sutherland (2002). "Criminal Charge of Probation Violation? Prosecutorial Discretion and Implications for Research in Criminal Court Processing." *Criminology* 40(3):553-578.

Langan, P. & J. Dawson (1993). *Felony Sentences in State Courts, 1990.* Washington, DC: Bureau of Justice Statistics.

Latessa, E.J. & L.F. Travis III (1992). "Residential Community Correctional Programs." In J. Byrne, A. Lurigio & J. Petersilia (eds.), *Smart Sentencing: The Emergence of Intermediate Sanctions.* Beverly Hills, CA: Sage, 166-181.

Latessa, E.J., L.F. Travis III & G.P. Wilson (1984). "Juvenile Diversion: Factors Related to Decision Making and Outcome." In S.H. Decker (ed.), *Juvenile Justice Policy.* Beverly Hills, CA: Sage, 145-165.

LeClair, D. & S. Guarino-Ghezzi (1991). "Does Incapacitation Guarantee Public Safety? Lessons from the Massachusetts Furlough and Prerelease Programs." *Justice Quarterly* 8(1):9-36.

Lindquist, C., J. Hardison & P. Lattimore (2003). *Reentry Courts Process Evaluation (Phase 1).* Washington, DC: National Institute of Justice.

Lindsey, E. (1925). "Historical Sketch of the Indeterminate Sentence and Parole System." *Journal of Criminal Law & Criminology* 16(1925):9-126.

Lucas, W. (1987). "Perceptions of the Volunteer Role." *Journal of Offender Counseling, Services & Rehabilitation* 12(1):141-146.

Maguire, K. & A. Pastore (1998). *Sourcebook of Criminal Justice Statistics—1997.* Washington, DC: U.S. Government Printing Office.

Mayzer, R., M. Gray & S. Maxwell (2004). "Probation Absconders: A Unique Risk Group?" *Journal of Criminal Justice* 32(2):137-150.

McCleary, R. (1978). *Dangerous Men.* Beverly Hills, CA: Sage.

McDonald, D. (1986). *Punishment Without Walls: Community Service Sentences in New York City.* New Brunswick, NJ: Rutgers University Press.

McSparron, J. (1980). "Community Corrections and Diversion: Cost and Benefit, Subsidy Models, and Start-up Recommendations." *Crime & Delinquency* 26(2):226-247.

Perrier, D.C. & F.S. Pink (1985). "Community Service: All Things to All People." *Federal Probation* 49(2):32-38.

Petersilia, J. (1986). "Exploring the Option of House Arrest." *Federal Probation* 50(2):52-55.

Petersilia, J. (1990). "When Probation Becomes More Dreaded Than Prison." *Federal Probation* 54(1):23-27.

Rhine, E., W. Smith & R. Jackson (1991). *Paroling Authorities: Recent History and Current Practice.* Gaithersburg, MD: American Correctional Association.

Rhine, E. T. Mawhorr & E. Parks (2006). "Implementation: The Bane of Effective Correctional Programs." *Criminology and Public Policy* 5(2):347-358.

Rothman, D.J. (1980). *Conscience and Convenience.* Boston: Little, Brown.

Sabol, W., T. Minton & P. Harrison (2007). *Prison and Jail Inmates at Midyear 2006.* Washington, DC: Bureau of Justice Statistics.

Schiesel, S. (1997). "On Parole and Out of Cyberspace." *The New York Times* (January 5, 1997:E-5).

Sigler, R. (1988). "Role Conflict for Adult Probation and Parole Officers: Fact or Myth?" *Journal of Criminal Justice* 16(2):121-130.

Simon, J. (1993). *Poor Discipline.* Chicago: University of Chicago Press.

Spelman, W. (1995). "The Severity of Intermediate Sanctions." *Journal of Research in Crime and Delinquency* 32(1):107135.

Studt, E. (1973). *Surveillance and Service in Parole.* Washington, DC: U.S. Government Printing Office.

Talarico, S. & M. Myers (1987). "Split Sentencing in Georgia: A Test of Two Empirical Assumptions." *Justice Quarterly* 4(4):611-629.

Travis, J., A. Solomon & M. Waul (2001). *The Dimensions and Consequences of Prisoner Reentry.* Washington, DC: Urban Institute.

Travis, L.F., III (1985). "The Development of American Parole." In H.E. Allen, C. Eskridge, E.J. Latessa & G.F. Vito, *Probation and Parole in America.* New York: Free Press, 19-35.

Travis, L.F., III & E.J. Latessa (1984). "'A Summary of Parole Rules—Thirteen Years Later': Revisited Thirteen Years Later." *Journal of Criminal Justice* 12(6):591-600.

Turner, S. & J. Petersilia (1996). *Work Release: Recidivism and Corrections Costs in Washington State.* Washington, DC: National Institute of Justice.

Umbreit, M.S. (1981). "Community Service Sentencing: Jail Alternative or Added Sanction?" *Federal Probation* 45(3):3-14.

U.S. Department of Justice (1978). *State and Local Probation and Parole Systems.* Washington, DC: U.S. Government Printing Office.

Whitehead, J. (1986). "Job Burnout and Job Satisfaction Among Probation Managers." *Journal of Criminal Justice* 14(1):25-36.

Wilson, G.P. (1985). "Halfway House Programs for Offenders." In L.F. Travis III (ed.), *Probation, Parole and Community Corrections.* Prospect Heights, IL: Waveland, 151-164.

Wilson, J. (2007). "Habilitation or Harm: Project Greenlight." *NIJ Journal* (June):2-7.

Wood, P. & D. May (2003). "Racial Differences in Perceptions of the Severity of Sanctions: A Comparison of Prison with Alternatives." *Justice Quarterly* 20(3):605-631.

Wright, J. & L. Travis (1996). "Work Release." In M. McShane & F. Williams (eds.), *The Encyclopedia of American Prisons.* New York: Garland:510-512.

Important Cases

Gagnon v. Scarpelli, 411 U.S. 778 (1973).

Morrissey v. Brewer, 408 U.S. 471 (1972).

Chapter 13

Issues in Community Supervision

Important Terms

boot camp

casework model

community corrections
  legislation

day reporting

drug testing

electronic monitoring

intensive supervision

model case management
  system

net-widening

Probation Subsidy Act

restitution

"shock incarceration"

shock parole

shock probation

split sentence

supervision fees

team supervision

technical violations

Many important issues in community supervision center around developments in the financing, management, and technology involved in probation and parole. Largely in response to crowded institutions, there is renewed interest in community supervision as an alternative to incarceration. Many recent developments are attempts to improve and enhance the effectiveness and economy of probation and parole. In the past 20 years, however, the central practices of community supervision (probation and parole supervision) have themselves come under attack. This chapter examines the current controversy over community supervision, and discusses specific attempts to improve the efficiency of community corrections.

Does Community Supervision Work?

In 1978, Andrew von Hirsch and Kathleen Hanrahan published a report to the U.S. Department of Justice titled "Abolish Parole?" In this brief document, they suggested that parole supervision might be useless. On both rational (practical) and philosophical grounds, the authors concluded that there was little reason to continue the practice of parole supervision. They held that a period of supervision under conditions constituted an added penalty. That is, assuming the offender served a prison sentence as punishment, there was no reason to impose conditional release in addition to incarceration. From a practical standpoint, they argued that the research to date did not support parole supervision as a crime-control strategy. The authors also argued that parole officers were not very effective in providing needed services to parolees.

Von Hirsch and Hanrahan were not the first to question parole supervision, but they may have been the most eloquent critics. Later reports (e.g., Gottfredson, Mitchell-Herzfeld & Flanagan, 1982) showed that success of supervision in preventing crimes by parolees often depends on how "new crimes" are defined. If a parolee returned to prison for violating the conditions of release without committing a new crime is counted as a "failure," parole supervision may be less effective in preventing recidivism than no supervision at all. Because parolees must obey the conditions of release, they may be returned to prison for "technical violations." Technical violations are infractions of the rules of supervision that do not involve any new criminality. Examples would include violating curfew, failing to report to a parole officer, and other noncriminal behavior. If returns to prison based on technical violations are counted as "failures," parolees have more chances to "fail" than do nonparolees, who must be convicted of new crimes to be incarcerated. The research shows mixed findings. It is difficult, if not impossible, to decide whether parole supervision is an effective crime prevention method (Flanagan, 1985). See Box 13.1 for a description of outcomes of probation supervision.

Box 13.1 Outcome of Probation Supervision, 1986-89

100 felons tracked through their first 3 years of probation

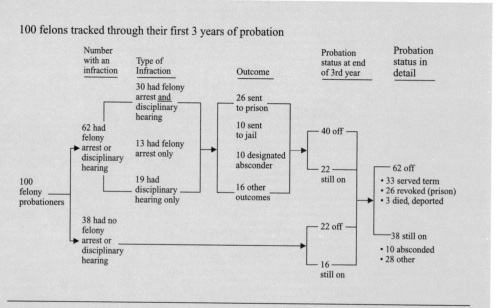

Source: P. Langan (1992), *Recidivism of Felons on Probation, 1986-89* (Washington, DC: U.S. Department of Justice):5.

Other critics have raised similar concerns about probation supervision. With the increased use of both probation and parole in response to prison crowding, these concerns have grown. Observers believe that not only are more offenders being placed under community supervision, but that probation and parole now include more dangerous offenders (Auerhahn, 2007; Guynes, 1988). Critics are beginning to re-examine the degree to which community supervision protects public safety.

Joan Petersilia (1985) studied probationers convicted of felonies in two large California counties. Her conclusions raised serious questions about the ability of community supervision to control crime. Petersilia and her colleagues concluded that a 65 percent rate of new criminality among their sample showed that granting probation to those convicted of felonies was not in the best interests of public safety. She later summarized the results of this study (1986:2):

> These results would seem to support the contention that routine probation is not an appropriate or effective sanction for convicted felons. It evidently could not provide the kind of supervision that might have prevented the majority of our sample of felony offenders from returning to crime.

The importance of Petersilia's study was exaggerated by news media attention (Goldstein, Burrell & Talty, 1985). In the weeks following the release of her report by the RAND Corporation, newspapers across the country reported the story. They summarized the research, often with forbidding headlines telling of the dangers posed by felony probation. Reactions to the report were quick, but failed to achieve the same level of media coverage.

Vito (1986) replicated the RAND study on a sample of Kentucky probationers. He reported that felons on probation in Kentucky were much less likely to commit new crimes than were those studied by Petersilia. Similarly, McGaha, Fichter, and Hirschburg (1987) replicated the study with probationers in Missouri, finding results similar to those found by Vito. In addition, Goldstein, Burrell, and Talty (1985) concluded that probationers in New Jersey did not pose as great a threat to public safety as those examined in Petersilia's study in California. It is possible that the results of Petersilia's study were unique to California, as they are different from findings in other states. In support of this conclusion, the Bureau of Justice Statistics (Hughes, Wilson & Beck, 2001) notes that national averages of successful completion of parole supervision increase when California's cases are removed from the sample.

In attempting to answer the question of whether community supervision works, we must first determine what we mean by the word "work." In the evaluations of felony probation reported by Petersilia, Vito, and Goldstein, the criterion was new crime by probationers. That is, probation was considered to "work" if people under supervision did not commit too many new crimes. In general three criteria can be applied to community supervision in order to determine "what works." Alan Harland (1996:2-3) noted that the definition of what works depends on the perspective of the individual asking the question. Elected officials and the public often define "working" as "reducing rates of recidivism." Policy makers may define "working" as "reducing rates of commitment or lengths of stay for prison and jail inmates." Budget officials may define what works by "managing offenders at a lower cost." For retributivists, what works is a system of sanctions that matches the pain of punishment with the harm of the crime and blameworthiness of the offender. In short, probation, parole, and other community supervision practices work to the degree that they (1) can control risk of new crime, (2) reduce incarceration and correctional costs, and/or (3) match punishments with offenders.

Edward Rhine (1997) observed that the entire criminal justice system is facing a crisis of legitimacy resulting from increasing concern about crime, and the perceived inability of the criminal justice system to control crime. This crisis has produced a movement toward more punitive and incapacitative sanctions, with a greater reliance on incarceration. Nonetheless, as Rhine notes, more than two-thirds of convicted offenders are supervised in the community. In response to the call for punitive treatment of offenders and greater emphasis on crime control, community supervision administrators "have adopted a set of practices and a discourse that represent a discernible shift toward risk management and surveillance" (Rhine, 1997:72). The practice of probation and parole supervision, in Rhine's view, is driven more by a desire to increase risk control and surveillance than by an attempt to reform or reintegrate criminal offenders.

Controlling Risk

Peter Jones (1991) discussed the development of community corrections in Kansas. One of the primary goals of the movement to community correctional alternatives to imprisonment in that state was to protect public safety. As Jones (1991:51) observed, however, "while a public-safety interest was frequently cited, it was usually in the sense of representing an obvious and necessary constraint on how the other goals (reducing prison crowding and developing more appropriate responses for offenders) would be pursued." Thus, protecting public safety was a baseline concern. In the extreme, we could reduce crowding by not sending anyone to prison. If doing so led to a significant increase in crime, however, this policy would be unacceptable.

It seems that much has been made lately of the ability or inability of community correctional programs to control risk. As Bennett (1991:95) noted, "The public is upset, and perhaps rightly so, that people placed on regular probation often do not receive either help or supervision because of large caseloads and inadequate supervision." The critical question is how safe is safe enough? As Jones (1991) describes it, risk control can range from a definition of no new criminality through acceptance of levels of crime no greater than those among persons incarcerated. Harland and Rosen (1987) suggest that minimizing public risk is the primary goal of most intermediate sanctions. Thus, while no new crime would be preferred, achieving similar levels of new crime among a population that is diverted from prison that is less than (or no more than) the level among incarcerated offenders may be "safe enough." There is also the question of what kind of "crime" is being committed.

In an assessment of recidivism among parolees in Tennessee, James Wilson (2005) observed that wide fluctuations in the rate of discretionary parole release were not correlated with changes in revocation rates. This indicates that more offenders could be placed on parole with little or no change in the rate of parole failures. In addition, he observed that a major explanation for the levels of failure had to do with increasingly harsh responses (revocation) for technical violations of parole. This too would indicate that public safety (at least in terms of the threat of new crime) was not endangered by those parolees.

Evaluations of the effectiveness of community supervision use different measures of outcome. The inclusion of violations of technical conditions of supervision, including absconding, with new criminality produces relatively high rates of failure, but may not represent high rates of crime. John Worrall and his associates (2004) studied the link between the size of the probation caseload and the crime rate in California counties. They concluded that the size of the probation caseload is positively associated with the rate of property crime. It is not possible to tell if the crime rate causes probation or the number of probationers causes the crime rate, but there is no evidence that large probation caseloads are associated with any reduction in crime rates. Worrall and colleagues observe that large caseloads are also associated with reduced levels of treatment and reintegration services for probationers. This research suggests that it may be the administration of supervision (large numbers of offenders assigned to too few officers) that explains failure. In contrast, some observers contend that smaller caseloads provide close supervision, which translates into higher rates of technical violations and, thus, higher rates of failure. In a study of "community probation" in Maryland, Nicole Piquero (2003) suggests that the probationers receiving closest supervision were more likely to fail early than those not subjected to such intensive supervision.

Over the past two decades there has been some substantial progress in the development and use of risk assessment devices in both probation and parole. Many classification and prediction instruments have been developed, and several appear to offer valid predictions of the risk of recidivism among correctional populations (Holsinger, Lowenkamp & Latessa, 2006). One problem with these instruments is the incredible diversity of correctional populations. Most risk-assessment devices are not designed for specific subpopulations such as females or racial and ethnic minorities. As a result, the accuracy of risk predictions can vary across different groups. As important is that these general risk-screening instruments are not especially well-suited to the prediction of specific risks, such as the risk that a particular offender will commit a violent offense (Davies & Dedel, 2006). Surely the safest course of action in terms of protecting the community from convicted offenders is to incarcerate the offenders. To do so, however, does not really manage risk, but rather seeks to avoid it. At some point most of these offenders will return to the community, regardless of their level of risk. Attempts to identify and manage risk through probation and parole supervision are necessary, if difficult.

Reducing Incarceration and Costs

As Jones observed in Kansas, a primary factor motivating the development and spread of community supervision sanctions is a desire to reduce prison crowding and correctional costs. Clear and Byrne (1992:321) flatly say, "The frank bottom line for the intermediate sanction movement must be whether it is able to reduce overcrowding in corrections." The impetus behind the movement to expand community supervision sanctions is our inability to deal with the large numbers of persons whom we believe need or deserve more severe sentences than traditional probation. Our inability emerges, in large part, from the cost of incarceration. Thus, if we had excess prison space, we would simply incarcerate offenders who required tougher punishment than probation. We do not have that excess, and we cannot afford to build enough prisons to house all of these offenders.

The creation of alternative sanctions in the community can have the effect of reducing demand for prison space (Gowdy, 1993). Conversely, the development of more severe community-based sanctions may simply result in **net-widening**. Morris and Tonry (1990) argue that in many cases, the result of alternative sanctions has been to make sentences more severe for those who would not have gone to prison anyway. In this way, the "net" of punishment has been cast wider to catch more people. If they are correct, alternative sanctions as presently developed will not meet the goal of reducing correctional costs and prison crowding. Beck and Mumola (1999), reported that one of the primary reasons for prison population growth in 1998 was the large number of parole violators returned to prison. As Rhine (1997:73) pointed out, the new, risk-centered community supervision strives to identify and arrest probationers and parolees who violate conditions of release. To the extent that this strategy is successful, the "failure" rates for probation and parole increase, and more community supervision violators are sent to prison.

Community supervision can work as an alternative to incarceration and many of the intermediate punishments developed in the past few decades are designed to accomplish just that purpose. The problem arises when, as a result of these more restrictive community punishments, failure rates increase, leading to increased levels of imprisonment. To the extent that offenders originally destined for prison can be placed into community settings, community supervision programs can reduce incarceration costs and prison population sizes.

Matching Punishments with Offenders

A third goal of the development of intermediate sanctions in the community is to create a range of penalties that can be appropriately applied to the range of offenses and offenders who come before the courts. The traditional choice between probation and incarceration is seen by many as inadequate for responding to the wide array of crimes and criminals that exist. Morris and Tonry (1990:38) argue that, "A variety of intermediate punishments, along with appropriate treatment conditions, should be part of a comprehensive, integrated system of sentencing and punishment."

Community supervision programs and practices have undergone tremendous change in recent times as we struggle to develop this range of punishments. The matching of punishments to offenders includes two dimensions as anticipated by Morris and Tonry. First, the severity of the penalty should be matched more closely to the seriousness of the crime. In this way, there needs to be a range of punishments. Second, the needs of specific offenders should be addressed by the correctional system while the offenders are under sentence. This necessitates a range of appropriate treatment conditions.

Even if Petersilia's findings of risk of future criminality among probationers may not be accurate for the nation, the question that she raised about the ability of probation supervision to provide for community safety remains critical. At a minimum, the perception exists that probation populations are more dangerous today than ever before. There is growing concern about the risk posed by offenders placed under community supervision. One result of this perception can be seen in that probation and parole officers, in order to better ensure public safety, are changing the way that they do their jobs. Other changes involve making both probation and parole more punitive, such as the increasing use of "shock incarceration" and "intensive supervision," electronic monitoring, day reporting, and other sanctions that are more severe than traditional probation or parole supervision. Box 13.2 shows the imposition of selected supervision conditions on adult probationers.

Box 13.2 Felons Having Additional Penalties, 2002

Additional Penalty	Percent of Felons Receiving
Fine	25%
Restitution	12
Community Service	4
Treatment	3
Other	7

Source: M. Durose & P. Langan (2004), *Felony Sentences in State Courts, 2002* (Washington, DC: Bureau of Justice Statistics):10.

Harris and her colleagues (2001) investigated the use of intermediate sanctions in one county to assess the way in which a range of intermediate sanctions was used. The focus of the research was to determine whether a true "continuum" of sanctions was in place so that the severity of the punishment was linked to the seriousness of the crime. They found that there was a significant relationship between severity of sanction and seriousness of offense, but that the link was relatively weak. They interpreted this to mean that the availability of a range of intermediate sanctions supports efforts to match penalties to crimes. However, other factors still influence the application of penalties in specific cases. They concluded that without the range of intermediate penalties, it would be much more difficult, if even possible, to link crimes and punishments in any meaningful fashion

Shock Incarceration

Programs of shock incarceration and intensive supervision have affected the operation of traditional probation and parole. They illustrate most clearly how community supervision serves as an alternative to incarceration. In both programs, the attempt is made to use community supervision to meet sentencing goals normally associated with incarceration. Specifically, the desired result is the enhancement of both the deterrent and incapacitation effects of community supervision.

Shock probation and shock parole attempt to deter offenders from continued criminality by imposing a prison sentence that is later "commuted" to a period of supervision. The initial incarceration is expected to "shock" the offender by the severity of the punishment. It also informs offenders what to expect if they continue to break the law (Vito, 1985). Thus, with shock probation, the judge might sentence the offender to a long prison term but, within six months, alter the sentence to a probation period. In some states, such as Ohio, the inmate could petition the court for shock probation. In other states, such as Texas, shock probation is solely at the discretion of the judge.

Shock parole is similar to shock probation in that it involves an early release from a relatively long prison term. The difference here is that it is the parole authority rather than the judge that grants an early release from incarceration to parole supervision. For example, a convicted forger who receives a 10-year prison sentence could receive shock probation from the judge after four or five months. If shock probation is not granted, in several states the parole authority is empowered to grant early or shock parole to the offender at his or her first hearing before the board. Like shock probation, states differ as to whether inmates must petition the parole board in order to be considered for shock parole.

In practice, the effectiveness of shock programs is unclear. Many of the programs provide no shock value because offenders expect to be released. Ideally, the incarcerated offender is "shocked" when released. In practice, however, the only shock may come if the offender is not granted an early release. Through a combination of a short prison term followed by community supervision, shock programs attempt to gain the benefits of both incarceration and supervision as sanctions. The offender is expected to be deterred. In theory, shock probation and parole provide a stern warning to the inmate. Without the kindness of the judge or parole authority, the offender would be serving a long prison term. In effect, the released inmate is expected to realize that he or she is living "on borrowed time" and will face a long term of incarceration if supervision is unsuccessful. Camp and Camp (1996:163) reported that probation agencies in half of the state and federal jurisdictions operate shock probation programs.

An innovation on the practice of shock probation and parole has been the development of the prison **boot camp** (Anderson, Dyson & Burns, 1999). These programs are sometimes referred to as **"shock incarceration"** because the conditions of incarceration are much more severe but limited in duration. Boot camp programs in prisons subject inmates to austere conditions, including physical conditioning and strict discipline combined with hard labor, akin to the boot camp experience of new recruits in the military. Boot camps were discussed in Chapter 9 as evidence of attempts to make punishment more physically painful for offenders. These camps are also linked to community supervision because they serve to reduce the length of term served by participants. On June 30, 2000, a total of 12,751 inmates were enrolled in boot camp programs operating in 95 correctional facilities across the nation. Many of these programs release their graduates to community supervision as probationers or parolees. Box 13.3 provides a description of these programs.

Box 13.3 Prison Boot Camp Programs, June 30, 2000

Number of Inmate Participants	12,751
Number of Prisons with Programs	95
Security Level of Facility	
Maximum	13
Medium	31
Minimum	51
Gender of Inmates	
Males Only	67
Females Only	11
Both Sexes	17
Type of Facility	
Federal	3
State	87
Private	5

Source: J. Stephan & J. Karberg (2003), *Census of State and Federal Correctional Facilities, 2000* (Washington, DC: Bureau of Justice Statistics):12.

Mackenzie and Parent (1991) studied the impact of boot camps on prison crowding in Louisiana. They observed that if careful selection criteria are developed, such camps can reduce the number of inmates admitted to regular prison terms. Further, Mackenzie and Shaw (1990) reported that graduates of boot camps appear to have more socially positive attitudes than other prisoners. They suggest that boot camps may meet offender needs in ways that will improve their chances of avoiding crime in the future. Faith Lutze (1998) surveyed prisoners and found that while boot camp programs provide stricter controls on inmate behavior in prison, they are no more likely to support personal growth and development among inmates than traditional minimum-security incarceration. That is, boot camp participants do not differ from regular prisoners in terms of their learning ways to avoid future problems with the law. In a later study, Lutze (2001) reported that the increased severity of boot camp was associated with negative attitudes and adaptations to prison, when not linked to supporting future improvement for inmates. Being "tough" for the sake of being tough was perhaps seen by the inmates as unnecessary and unfair. As Mackenzie and Parent noted, legislators may support boot camp programs because the conditions in these programs are more punitive than in the typical prison, and thus shorter terms are seen as equally tough on crime. However, the available evidence suggests that boot camps do not reduce rates of new crime (recidivism) by program graduates, and may actually hinder inmates in making a positive adjustment (Mackenzie, 1997). Benda, Toombs, and Peacock (2006) found that boot camp programs appear to have different effects for different kinds of offenders. Like the problem of general risk assessments being applied to diverse populations, boot camp programs seem to help some offenders but be harmful with others. Improvement in boot camps (and other correctional efforts) may depend on our ability to match the right program to the right type of offender.

Another practice that is somewhat akin to shock probation is the imposition of split sentences. A split sentence is a penalty that is divided (split) between a period of incarceration and a period of probationary supervision. Because of the great flexibility that judges are allowed in determining the conditions of probation, split sentences are relatively widely used. This is true even in jurisdictions where there is no law that specifically allows the judge to use split sentencing.

Parisi (1980) described four historical methods of imposing split sentences, including shock probation as it is practiced in several states.

1. If a defendant is convicted of several offenses or counts, the judge may order incarceration for some offenses and probation for others. Thus, a defendant convicted of two counts of theft may be sentenced to 90 days on the first count and two years of probation on the second.

2. In shock probation, the same offender may receive an initial five-year prison term, and be "shocked" to probation in 90 days.

3. Another way to impose split sentences can be seen in legislation that allows the judge to combine incarceration and probation in one sentence, such as a sentence of 90 days of incarceration followed by two years of probation.

4. Finally, most states have legislation allowing the judge to use incarceration as a condition of probation. In this case, the offender might receive two years probation with the condition that the first 90 days be spent in jail.

Regardless of the method used to impose split sentences, the outcomes are the same. Probation is often seen by judges, offenders, and the general public as a lenient sanction. The use of split or combination sentences allows judges to increase the harshness of the penalty. A judge may not wish to send a minor offender to prison for a long period, but may want the offender to spend some time in jail. Split sentences allow judges to adjust the severity of sanctions. In 2005, 8 percent of persons placed on probation had received a split sentence while more than half were sentenced directly to probation. Of all those on probation in 2003, 22 percent had a sentence combining probation and incarceration, and 6 percent had been placed on probation in some other fashion, before all court proceedings were completed, as is shown in Box 13.4.

Box 13.4   Types of Sentences to Probation, 2003

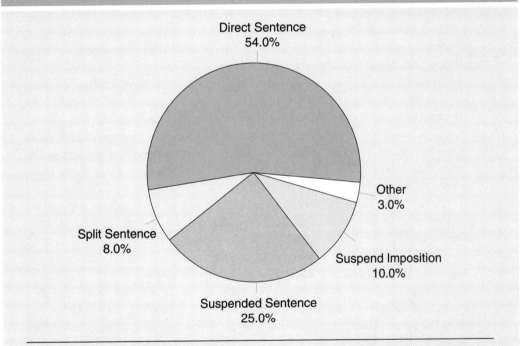

Source: L. Glaze & S. Palla (2004), *Probation and Parole in the United States, 2003* (Washington, DC: Bureau of Justice Statistics):4.

Intensive Supervision

Intensive supervision programs seek to provide more control and service to offenders who otherwise would be incarcerated (Travis, 1984). In practice, these programs rely upon lower client-to-officer ratios, and thus, they assume a higher level of supervision and service delivery (Cullen, Wright & Applegate, 1996; Latessa, 1980). Evaluations of intensive supervision programs show some promise of their effectiveness. However, they do not show that intensive supervision yields better results for the intensive populations than does regular supervision for the regular caseload (Mackenzie, 1997; Fulton et al., 1997).

In the intensive supervision programs in which the level of service delivery actually increased, intensive supervision programs do appear to be modestly effective. Intensive supervision appears to effect the release of many offenders who otherwise would be incarcerated. What is perhaps more important is that the mental picture caused by the label "intensive supervision" may make it politically possible to retain a number of relatively serious or persistent offenders under community supervision, as opposed to incarcerating them (Clear & Shapiro, 1986). This is consistent with the traditional role of community supervision as the "overflow valve" for incarceration.

Several states have implemented intensive supervision programs (ISPs). The state of Georgia, perhaps the leader in ISPs, began a program in 1982 (Erwin, 1986). Evaluations of programs in several states (Petersilia, Turner & Peterson, 1986:41) show that these programs may be successful in preventing criminality among probationers, at least during periods of supervision.

Typically, an intensive supervision program requires the probationer to have more contacts with his or her probation officer. By reducing the size of caseloads, we expect officers to be more vigilant in intensive supervision programs (Byrne, 1986). The net effect of these differences is to make the penalty more painful. The probationer experiences more intrusions by the officer. The penalty is also more incapacitative. The offender is more closely watched, and thus he or she is prevented from relapsing into crime.

Byrne and Pattavina (1992) reviewed evaluations of intensive supervision programs in probation and parole. They reported that by the middle of 1989 there were 40 states operating intensive supervision programs. These programs, they found, were generally effective in meeting the goals of alternative sentencing. Noting limitations of the research, they reported that evaluations of intensive supervision programs report them to be both more cost-effective than imprisonment, and to have achieved true diversion of cases from incarceration. They also found that, in general, intensive programs did not seem to reduce recidivism. Jones (1991) reported similar results in an evaluation of intensive supervision in Kansas. He noted that, while offenders under intensive supervision did not show a decrease in new crime compared to those who were incarcerated, they also did no worse. In an assessment of intensive supervision with juveniles, Sontheimer and Goodstein (1993) suggested that while rates of new offenses may not have decreased, the intensive supervision program was effective in identifying recidivists early and removing them from the community. Thus, while the proportion of offenders under supervision who commit new crimes may not differ, in this program, the number of new crimes committed was fewer for the intensive group than for the nonintensive group. This is probably because offenders under intensive supervision were more likely to be detected and removed from supervision.

Intensive supervision programs that provide increased treatment along with closer supervision may have effects on reducing future crime (Latessa, 1993; Petersilia & Turner, 1993). Fulton and her colleagues (1997:74) concluded a review of intensive supervision programs, writing, "ISP has held its ground as a key element of community corrections programming since its reemergence in 1982. Although the research suggests that ISP has not fulfilled its promise of alleviating prison crowding, it does appear to be serving the important function of providing an intermediate sanction…More importantly, it appears that ISPs that emphasize treatment and services are producing better results than strict surveillance-based ISPs in terms of addressing offender needs and reducing recidivism."

Electronic Monitoring

In electronic monitoring programs, offenders are fitted with transmitting devices that allow correctional staff to monitor their whereabouts. Annesley Schmidt (1989) reported a survey of electronic monitoring usage that showed programs existing in 33 states. Later, Renzema (1992) reported that electronic monitoring programs existed in 47 states by 1990. Estimates of the number of offenders under such monitoring have risen to nearly 100,000 in approximately 1,500 programs (National Institute of Justice, 1999:1). According to Ford and Schmidt (1985), the first operational use of electronic surveillance for monitoring convicted offenders occurred in early 1983.

While the use of surveillance technology to monitor criminal offenders is relatively new, the potential of such technology for crime control has long been recognized. As early as 1966, Ralph Schwitzgebel described a potential telemetric monitoring system for probationers and parolees. In 1968, a prototype of the system was developed and tested. An assessment of the legal ramifications of electronic monitoring was published in the Harvard Law Review in 1966. Later, Robert Schwitzgebel, Ralph's brother, experimented with telemetric monitoring with volunteers in California (Schwitzgebel, 1969). For years, a debate about the acceptability of electronic monitoring continued, and the debate periodically found expression in commentary (Ingraham & Smith, 1972; Szasz, 1975). The debate con-

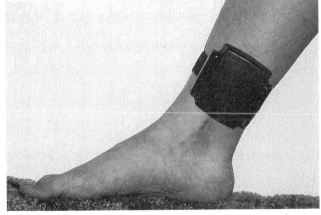

An offender wears an electronic monitoring transmitter. In electronically monitored home detention programs, devices worn by offenders may transmit a signal to inform authorities of the offender's whereabouts. *Photo credit: E.S. Boyne.*

tinues today (Corbett & Marx, 1991; del Carmen & Vaughn, 1986), but the sheer practicality of the technology has meant that, while many important issues remain to be solved, electronic monitoring of criminal offenders is an ongoing practice.

Currently, there are two basic types of radio frequency electronic surveillance systems in use (Ford & Schmidt, 1985; Huskey, 1987; National Institute of Justice, 1999; Schmidt, 1987). These systems can be described as either active or passive surveillance. In an active system, the supervising agency takes positive steps to monitor the offender. Generally, this system involves fitting the offender with a transmitting device. The transmitter sends a tone over the telephone. A computer program randomly calls offenders at times when they are supposed to be at home. The offender must answer the phone, and place the transmitter in a special telephone connection, so that the transmitter sends a message to the computer. In the passive system, a transmitter attached to the offender emits a continuous signal. The transmitter must be kept within range of an amplifier/transmitter or the signal will not reach a monitoring computer. This continuously signaling system requires the offender to remain within 150-200 feet of the fixed amplifier, which is usually installed in the offender's home (Huskey, 1987:19-20). See Box 13.5. A more recent innovation is the use of the global positioning system (GPS) to maintain constant surveillance of the whereabouts of a person being electronically monitored (Padgett, Bales & Blomberg, 2006).

Electronic monitoring systems have tamper alarms that signal a warning to monitors if the devices are removed or altered. The random calling system allows for both voice identification and the transmission of a monitoring signal. As it operates over telephone lines, this system is unaffected by interruptions in transmission caused by walls, structural steel, or other radio transmissions. The active surveillance random calling system appears to have a lower false-alarm rate than the passive surveillance system. The passive surveillance continuous transmission system, while more prone to false alarms, provides a continuous monitoring of the offender's whereabouts.

Most jurisdictions have adopted one or the other form of monitoring technology, and a few have used both. The random calling system allows somewhat greater freedom. For example, the offender could be next door at a neighbor's house and still be called to the telephone. The use of both systems could provide a gradation in the severity of monitoring. Thus, a probationer who is given the random calling monitor and then misses a call could be "punished" by being issued a continuous transmission monitor. The possibility of varying the level of restriction within a category of penalty called "monitoring" adds to the attractiveness of this sanction.

Baumer, Maxfield, and Mendelsohn (1993) evaluated three electronically monitored home detention programs. They found that these programs differed in their effectiveness based upon the agency under which they were operated and the characteristics of the people placed on monitoring. Pretrial detainees were more likely to violate program conditions, but these offenders were more clearly diverted from jail. Further, there was some evidence to suggest that one effect of electronically monitored home confinement was to encourage offenders to seek em-

Box 13.5   Systems for Electronic Monitoring of Offenders

Purpose: to monitor an offender's presence in a given environment where the offender is required to remain.

Devices that use a telephone at the monitored location

Continuously signaling	Programmed contact
A miniaturized **transmitter** is strapped to the offender and it broadcasts an encoded signal at regular intervals over a range.	A **computer** is programmed to call the offender during the hours being monitored either randomly or at specifically selected times. It prepares reports on the results of the calls.
A **receiver-dialer,** located in the offender's home, detects signals from the transmitter and reports to a central computer when it stops receiving the signal from the transmitter and when it starts receiving the signal again; it also provides periodic checks.	Strapped on the offender's arm is a **wristlet,** a black plastic module.
A central **computer** or **receiver** accepts reports from the receiver-dialer over the telephone lines, compares them with the offender's curfew schedule, and alerts correctional officials to unauthorized absences.	When the computer calls, the wristlet is inserted into a **verifier box** connected to the telephone to verify that the call is being answered by the offender being monitored.
	The computer functions similarly to that described above, calling the offender and preparing reports on the results of the call.
	However, **voice verification** technology assures that the telephone is answered by the offender being monitored.

Devices that do not use a telephone

Continuously signaling	Radio signaling
A **transmitter** is strapped to the offender which sends out a constant signal.	The **link** is a small transmitter worn by the offender.
A **portable receiver,** in the car of the officer who is monitoring the offender, is tuned to receive the signal from the specific transmitter when the officer drives within one block of the offender's home.	The **locator unit,** placed in the offender's home or other approved location, receives the signal from the link, records it and relays the information by radio signals to the local area monitor.
	The **local area monitor** is a microcomputer and information management system. This equipment is placed with the network manager (the leader of a small group of people who supervise the offender and encourage him to succeed). It receives information from the offender and coordinates communications among the network members. Each local network can handle 15 to 25 people.
	If required, a **central base station** can be added to provide increased security and back-up functions.

Source: A. Schmidt (1986), "Electronic Monitors," *Federal Probation* 50(2):59.

ployment. Finally, the assessment indicated that offenders on home confinement were not as securely incapacitated as are those incarcerated. Renzema and Mayo-Wilson (2005) reviewed scores of studies of electronic monitoring and concluded that the best evidence available suggests that the effect of electronic monitoring on reducing recidivism is limited. Padgett, Bales, and Blomberg (2006) compared GPS systems to radio frequency systems and found no differences between either of the electronic monitoring systems and offenders not being monitored in terms of recidivism.

In 1949, George Orwell's book *1984* was published. In that book, Orwell assessed the future of the human race under the conditions of the arms race. He suggested that society would become increasingly bureaucratized, and governments would become more totalitarian. The leader of one government, "Big Brother," would retain power through torture and brainwashing. The dominant aspect of life in this society would be that everyone was under surveillance by the government. It was in *1984* that Orwell coined the slogan, "Big Brother is watching." Because of the time period in which he wrote the book, much of what he described appeared to be science fiction. However, as evidenced by our current level of sophistication, it appears that George Orwell only missed by a few years when he titled his book *1984*. Lilly's (1992) assessment of the electronic monitoring movement on an international scale is reminiscent of Orwell.

The issues involved in electronic surveillance recall the questions raised about the development of probation and parole supervision. On the one hand are critics who suggest that monitoring is an insufficient penalty for many offenders. They contend that this leniency reduces the deterrent effect of the law. Other critics argue that the use of monitoring technology to allow the release from incarceration of "dangerous" offenders poses too great a risk to the community. On the other hand are those who criticize this technology as too oppressive, that is, it violates current standards of privacy and infringes on constitutional rights to protection against unreasonable searches and seizures. Finally, some critics fear that electronic monitoring, in practice, will be used to increase the severity of community supervision for those who would otherwise have been released to traditional probation or parole.

Proponents of surveillance argue that the technology enhances public safety by ensuring supervision of offenders in the community. Further, surveillance itself deters offenders from committing crimes. Similarly, the proponents suggest that the ability to monitor offenders results in a lessening of penalty severity. They argue that some offenders are sent to prison who do not actually need to be incarcerated. Continual supervision will allow judges and parole boards to leave these offenders in the community. While the current focus may be on the electronics of contemporary surveillance, at base, the questions and criticisms are the same ones that have always surrounded community supervision.

Despite the ongoing debate, electronic monitoring as a sanction, either alone or in combination with other forms of community supervision, appears to be here to stay. Harry Boone (1996) surveyed judges and policymakers about their perceptions of electronic monitoring. More than 90 percent of both groups said they felt electronic monitoring was here to stay, with almost two-thirds noting that they believed the use of electronic monitoring would grow in the future. Most observers believe that electronic monitoring is a cost-effective alternative to incarceration for many offenders (Evans, 1996). Camp and Camp (1996:160) reported that more than 90 percent of probation agencies responding to their survey indicated that they used electronic monitoring with a capacity of monitoring more than 12,000 offenders. The typical offender was monitored for a period of about three months.

Learning how well electronic monitoring can meet the other goals of community supervision (e.g., fairness; a reduction in future crime; etc.) must await further study (Cohn, Biondi & Flaim, 1996). Thus far, evaluations of electronic monitoring have not shown these programs to have an impact on future crime (Austin & Hardyman, 1991; Mackenzie, 1997).

Day Reporting and Other Sanctions

Unlike many other intermediate sanction alternatives, **day reporting** is of relatively recent origin. While there was earlier use of day reporting in England, the first day reporting program in the United States was started in Massachusetts in 1986 (McDevitt, 1988). This program was designed as an early release alternative for prison and jail inmates near the date of their parole. Participants in the program were required to report to the center each day, prepare an itinerary for their next day's activities, and report by telephone to the center throughout the day (Larivee, 1990).

At midyear 2003, jails reported supervising almost 8,000 offenders in day reporting programs. Parent (1990) reported that day reporting programs were operational in six states by the late 1980s, and many more states were considering the option. These programs (and the clients they served) varied. McDevitt and Miliano (1992:153) observed that programs tend to have similar components, including frequent contact, formalized scheduling, and drug testing. In general, day reporting represents a significant increase in surveillance and contact over even intensive probation or parole supervision programs. By 1992, there were six day reporting centers in operation in Massachusetts, with a total average daily population of several hundred offenders. By 1994, there were 114 day reporting centers operating in the United States (Parent et al., 1995). Box 13.6 offers a description of day reporting centers in the United States in 1994.

At midyear 2003, more than 12,500 jail inmates were supervised outside the jail facility through electronic monitoring (Harrison & Karberg, 2004). Day reporting clients typically make at least one in-person and several telephone contacts with center staff daily, yet they are allowed to remain in the community throughout much of the day. Most programs are limited to between two and four months in duration, followed by a period of probation or parole supervision. Often, day reporting clients work with program staff to develop and obtain substance abuse, psychological and employment treatment and services. These programs are still too new to have been adequately evaluated, but they promise to reduce prison crowding and costs, protect community safety, and provide needed services to offenders.

Box 13.6   Services Provided by Day-Reporting Centers

Total Number of Centers: 114

Services:	At Center	Elsewhere	Both	Centers Providing
Job seeking skills	79%	13%	8%	98%
Drug abuse education	69%	17%	14%	96%
Group counseling	80%	12%	8%	96%
Job placement	62%	34%	4%	93%
Education	55%	31%	14%	93%
Drug treatment	31%	54%	15%	92%
Life skills training	92%	6%	2%	91%
Individual counseling	72%	17%	11%	89%
Transitional housing	13%	81%	6%	63%
Recreation & leisure	74%	16%	10%	60%

Source: D. Parent, J. Byrne, V. Tsarfaty, L. Valade & J. Esselman (1995), Day *Reporting Centers, Volume 1* (Washington, DC: National Institute of Justice):13.

In Chapter 12 we discussed furlough programs. Work and study furloughs, as well as prerelease programs, have been developed to help inmates make the adjustment from incarceration to living in the community. Placements in residential community corrections facilities are also used to provide custodial supervision of offenders who are not seen as needing or deserving jail or prison incarceration (Holsinger et al., 1997). Other changes in probation and parole have similarly bridged the gap between traditional supervision and incarceration. There has been an increasing use of community service sentencing and the imposition of monetary penalties (such as fines and restitution to crime victims). All of these changes in traditional community supervision have worked to make probation and parole more severe as penalties, and to provide greater restrictions and controls over offenders in the community.

Shock probation and parole, split sentencing, and intensive supervision programs blur the distinction between incarceration and community supervision. The experience of being "on paper" becomes much more like that of being incarcerated. In these programs, the probationer or parolee faces additional deprivations of autonomy, liberty, and the like. It is difficult to determine whether the development of these programs has led to the increasing use of community supervision for felons and dangerous offenders. It is possible that these developments are in response to a changing population. Alternatively, these changes may have been successful in creating community-based sanctions that are seen as appropriate for prison and jail-bound offenders. In that case, the changing population of community corrections programs may be a response to changes in programs available.

Issues in Community Supervision

As prison populations have increased since the 1970s, so have the numbers of people under community supervision. The change in types of offenders being placed on probation and parole supervision is an important factor in understanding changes in community supervision. The simple growth in the size of the population, regardless of its characteristics, also has led to changes. Three areas in which such changes can be seen are the financing, management, and technology of probation and parole. These changes merit attention, regardless of whether they involve special programs such as shock or intensive supervision.

Financing

Several states implemented community corrections legislation that includes various funding formulas to support community supervision activities. These laws provide financial incentives to counties to reduce their prison commitments and to retain offenders in the community. The typical law either authorizes a subsidy for counties that reduce their commitment rates, or provides financial support for improved and increased community corrections programs. The state reduces the subsidy if the commitment rate is increased (Clear & Cole, 1986:399-400; National Advisory Commission, 1973:315). The Kansas Community Corrections Act, for example, "penalizes" counties for not reducing their commitments to state prisons (Jones, 1991).

California was the first state to employ an incentive program in order to encourage communities to keep offenders out of the prison system. In 1965, the California legislature passed the Probation Subsidy Act, which paid counties for each offender who was not sentenced to prison in each county. The state developed a formula that estimated the number of offenders expected to be sentenced to prison, and then paid $4,000 to the county for each offender less than that number who was not sentenced to prison. If a county was expected to commit 1,000 offenders to prison, but actually committed only 900, the county received a subsidy of $400,000 ($4,000 x 100). Subsidy funds were earmarked for the improvement of local correctional services. Other states subsequently developed similar models.

The California subsidy program faced several obstacles (Clear & Cole, 1986). There was no subsidy assistance to law enforcement, although the effect of the program was to keep offenders in the community. There was no inflation factor included, so that within 10 years, the purchasing power of the subsidy declined by more than one-third. There also was no adjustment for counties that historically had kept offenders in local correctional custody. For example, a county traditionally may have kept nonviolent offenders in the community on probation. Under the subsidy formula, that county had a lower estimate of commitments. Another county may have traditionally incarcerated nearly every felony offender. Under the subsidy program, the first county could only receive aid by keeping violent or more serious offenders in the community. The second county could begin to use probation for minor, nonviolent offenders, and could reap a large subsidy.

Later funding formulas for community corrections attempted to overcome some of the original difficulties in the California subsidy program. Minnesota, Oregon, and Colorado passed community corrections legislation that included more options for counties. These states also tried to adjust for crime and incarceration rates, and included inflation factors. Other states, such as Ohio, began subsidy programs for specific practices that counties could adopt to reduce prison commitments. In each of these cases, funding is tied to the development and expansion of community programs. The effects are to support probation and other community services and to assist the counties in handling their increasing caseloads.

Another more recent development is in the charging of supervision fees. Several state parole authorities and probation offices now require that the client make a monthly payment to the agency to offset the costs of supervision (Wheeler et al., 1989). This requirement further increases the cost advantage of probation and parole over incarceration. Similarly, it is common for a condition of supervision to be the payment of court costs. This requires that probation and parole officers serve (at least part time) as bill collectors for the courts.

A related financial alteration in the operation of probation and parole is the growing use of restitution. Offenders on probation and parole are increasingly being ordered to make restitution to the victims of their crimes. One-quarter of felony convicts in 2002 were assessed fines, and 12 percent were ordered to pay restitution (Durose & Langan, 2004). Probation and parole officers are then required to manage the payment process for restitution (Clear & Cole, 1986:110-111).

Box 13.7 Percent of Probationers with Selected Financial Conditions Imposed, 1995

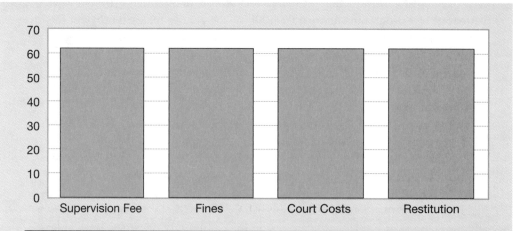

Source: T. Bonczar (1997), *Characteristics of Adults on Probation, 1995* (Washington, DC: Bureau of Justice Statistics):7.

On the one hand, these developments assist community supervision by providing enhanced resources and by reducing costs of operation. On the other hand, these programs also add to the burden of probation and parole officers, who generally dislike working in the role of "bill collector." These practices reflect the tradition of experimentation with correctional practices in probation and parole. Box 13.7 shows financial conditions imposed on probationers in 1995, the most recent year for which data are available.

Management

The traditional approach to probation and parole supervision consisted of the casework model. In casework, each officer was responsible for a caseload of offenders. The officer was a generalist expected to supervise a variety of persons having a variety of needs. The casework model expected the single officer to be capable of providing needed services to all of the offenders.

Beyond this, several other models of organization and caseload management have been proposed and adopted. Several jurisdictions now use teams of officers responsible for large groups of offenders. In team supervision, officers can take advantage of their varied strengths and skills. Thus, an officer who is particularly effective with offenders that require employment services can concentrate on that type of case for the entire team (Dell'Apa et al., 1976).

Another development involves the classification of offenders by objectives of supervision, rather than the general assignment of offenders to officers. This process clarifies the goals of supervision for the officer, and it allows officers to set priorities in responding to the needs of offenders (Clear & O'Leary, 1983). A related adaptation involves identifying the offenders who are least in need of supervision and service, and assigning them to a very low level of monitoring. This practice reduces the caseloads of officers who are providing service, and it maximizes (at least in theory) utilization of supervision resources (Vito & Marshall, 1983). As with objectives-based supervision classification, recent practice involves the identification of supervision levels on the basis of assessments of both the needs and risk of offenders.

The National Institute of Corrections has developed a model case management system (NIC, 1981). The system relies upon two case-assessment instruments: a risk assessment and a needs assessment. Each supervising officer completes these two questionnaires and then reviews them with the offender. Through discussion of the instruments, the officer and the offender develop a plan for dealing with needs. They develop case objectives from that plan. This system helps identify concrete actions that the officer should take, and it provides an ability to assess case progress.

As a management system, the model system involves three components: (1) classification, (2) case planning, and (3) the assignment of workload units. Classification is accomplished through the assessments mentioned above. Depending upon the levels of need or risk, or upon combinations of the two, the offender is placed in a supervision category that is somewhere between "high" (frequent officer attention) and "low" (little or no direct contact by officer). The second component, case planning, creates case objectives based upon a structured interview with the client. The officers' supervisors review the objectives and approve or modify them. Finally, cases are assigned varying "degrees of difficulty" or workload units. These units describe how much of an officer's time will be consumed by the case. In this manner, the officer and his or her supervisor know how much effort to expend on that case, and know how much effort is being spent on the total caseload.

From the information derived through individual case planning, it is possible for the agency or office to assess its needs, objectives, and progress. If 35 percent of the agency's caseload has high employment needs, administrators can see the utility in providing officers with employment development training. The agency might assign some officers as employment specialists. If a large enough percentage of the caseload has high-risk scores, administrators may want to create special surveillance units that would serve risk-control goals distinct from service delivery (Clear & O'Leary, 1983).

The National Institute of Corrections devoted considerable resources to the development and dissemination of this case management program. Training, technical assistance, and the provision of written documentation have spread the model program to probation and parole agencies across the country. With some adaptation for local considerations, the model program may have revolutionized the organization and administration of community supervision. Since then, other models of case classification and management have emerged and been adopted in a variety of institutional and community settings (Dowdy et al., 2002; Holsinger et al., 2003). These models sort offenders into distinct categories based on the expected risk of supervision or program failure, and identify treatment needs of offenders allowing correctional personnel to target treatments to the most important needs of offenders.

Not only has the spread of case assessment and classification technology changed the organization of service delivery and the assignment of cases to types of supervision, it has been linked to what some have called a "flight from discretion." Schneider, Ervin, and Snyder-Joy (1996) observed that even when case assessment and classification do not result in better case processing, community supervision staff support these practices. They suggest that the existence of classification and assignment procedures make case decisions more routine, and reduce the responsibility of supervising officers for what may turn out to be "wrong" case decisions. The increasing numbers of more serious offenders in community programs have raised the stakes and produced increased public scrutiny of supervision practices.

Management innovations in community supervision include the development and adoption of automated information systems to improve case supervision and monitoring. Edwin Zedlewski (1996) observed that existing software programs designed for salespeople are also well suited to probation and parole use. This software manages scheduling, keeps tracks of contacts, and otherwise performs the information storage and retrieval functions most useful to probation and parole officers. In recent years there has been increased emphasis in two important management areas. First, community supervision agencies are moving toward "evidence-based practice" (Latessa et al., 2002). Coupled with automated information systems, administrators seek to assess the effects of different practices on specific types of offenders or specific problems. Boone and Fulton (1996) reported the development of performance-based measures of community supervision effects. Increasingly, community supervision managers seek information about how to affect the behaviors of offenders. In 2001, the American Probation and Parole Association began revising accreditation standards for probation and parole agencies to include performance-based standards. As described by Taylor (2004:21), the new standards not only include compliance with policies and procedures but also include "measurement not only of what an agency does, but how well it does it."

Technology

A final area of recent innovations in community supervision involves the application of communications and other technologies to supervision. These applications have taken a number of forms, such as the information technologies mentioned above. Developments in areas including word processing, telecommunications, and video recording have had some effects and can be expected to play a larger role in the future. We have already addressed some of the effects of improved information systems and classification and assessment procedures as a form of information technology.

Drug testing is currently a hot topic throughout all of our society. Repeated or continuing wars on drugs, increasingly tough drunk-driving laws, deaths of celebrities from drug-related causes, and notorious transportation accidents attributed to drug use all have focused attention on substance abuse. There are today a number of relatively simple technologies for the detection of alcohol and other drug consumption. They range from the Breathalyzer test to determine if a person has been driving under the influence of alcohol, to blood tests to determine alcohol or other drug content. Urine testing is becoming an increasingly common component of community supervision conditions.

Judges and parole boards seek to reduce the incidence of substance abuse among convicted offenders in the hopes of reducing future criminality. They traditionally have prohibited probationers and parolees from the consumption of excessive amounts of alcohol or the use of other recreational drugs. When this author worked for the Oregon Board of Parole, a standard condition of parole limited drinking for all parolees. Parolees were either not allowed to drink alcohol to excess, were not allowed to drink alcohol at all, or were required to take Antabuse. Antabuse is a drug that reacts with alcohol to produce very unpleasant symptoms in the drinker. These symptoms include nausea, shortness of breath, dizziness, and other sensations that are generally unpleasant enough to deter the drinker.

Regardless of the attempts to control substance abuse, probationers and parolees continue to acquire and use alcohol and other drugs. The development of easily administered detection tests has strengthened the ability of probation and parole officers to identify and control substance abuse among their clients. Many believe that merely testing for use will deter offenders. As Atmore and Bauchiero (1987) reported:

> We have noted significant behavioral improvements when we test regularly, because it serves as a deterrent. Therefore, we are returning less people to higher security for positive urines because they know they are taking a huge risk by substance use. In other words, test regularly! You need to have a consistent policy for testing and sanctions for positive results, or else word will get around quickly that one should not take this seriously.
>
> There are some easy to use and very reliable machines for urine testing now available . . . Any probation or parole officer could be trained to use basic urinalysis equipment in a short period of time . . .

In addition to the urine test described by Atmore and Bauchiero, probation and parole officers have a wide array of other testing technologies available to them. These include the Breathalyzer and blood tests, as well as some newer developments, such as a saliva test for alcohol use. With the saliva test, the subject's saliva is placed on a "blotter" that is actually a form of litmus paper. If the subject has recently used alcohol, the paper will change colors. Efforts are currently underway to develop similar saliva tests for other drug use.

Camp and Camp (1996:158-159) reported that all community supervision agencies responding to their survey used drug testing in 1995. These agencies reported a total of nearly 3.7 million drug tests. Most of these tests (98.7%) did not result in revocation of supervision for offenders. Often, even positive drug tests do not result in revocation. The development of drug courts, with their emphasis on drug treatment, for example, use tests as measures of case progress. A positive test result (showing the use of drugs) is likely to result in some change in status (assignment to a new treatment, increased contact, etc.), but is unlikely to result in revocation. Nonetheless, offenders seek ways to avoid detection, and officers must continually guard against altered urine samples (Elbert, 1997).

Substance abuse testing technologies enhance the ability of officers to control the risks of crime posed by their clients. These procedures also may change the nature of the job. The officers must now test their clients, serve as medical technicians, and otherwise assume the role of "cop" instead of "helper." Some believe that testing alters the nature of the officer's job and his or her relationship with offenders. In the Georgia Intensive Supervision program, special officers were designated as "surveillance officers" and charged with conducting urine tests and investigations. Using special officers protected the helping relationship between the probation or parole officer and the offender (Erwin & Clear, 1987).

Developments in geographic information systems have been applied to community supervision. Harries (2003) described a program in which the Maryland Division of Probation and Parole used geographic information to improve supervision. As described by Piquero (2003), Maryland used geographic analysis of crime to develop programs involving police, probation, community members, and other agencies to develop coordinated efforts to reduce and prevent crime. Geographic analysis can improve community supervision in a variety of ways ranging from describing "good" and "bad" environments in which to place offenders through minimizing supervision officer travel time by assigning caseloads based on geography. Related to this, as mentioned earlier, it is now possible to use the global positioning system (GPS) to track offenders. A popular service available on new motor vehicles (known as OnStar or by other titles) is now available for the tracking of offenders. With GPS monitors, it is possible to monitor the location of probationers and parolees at all times.

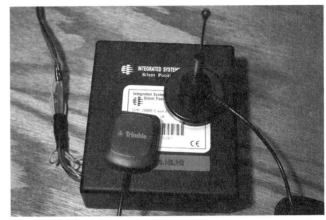

The Global Positioning System (GPS) tracking device that was used to track a murder suspect in 1999 is seen at the Spokane County Sheriff's office in Spokane, Washington. The GPS tracker led investigators to the shallow grave of nine-year-old Valiree Jackson in 1999 and helped put her father, William Bradley Jackson, in prison for murder. *Photo credit: AP Photo/Jeff T. Green.*

Due Process, Crime Control, and Community Supervision

Many of the changes in community supervision were grafted onto existing practices of probation and parole supervision. Thus, restitution orders and supervision fees have been added as conditions of probation. Periods of confinement have been added to supervision conditions to enable courts to achieve split sentencing, or to create programs like shock incarceration. Supervision has been changed to create intensive monitoring programs for the more serious offenders now placed in probation and parole caseloads.

Some of the changes in community supervision represent the development of new programs that complement traditional probation and parole supervision. Day reporting centers, for example, are often operated as adjuncts of the jail or as institutional components of local community corrections agencies. The growth of residential community correctional facilities similarly has been outside of probation and parole agencies. Such facilities serve as a resource to those agencies.

Indeed, one of the problems inherent in estimating the numbers of persons participating in these various programs is that the participants may be reported as members of the probation and parole population. Thus, probation and parole supervision now includes thousands of cases in which offenders are under electronic monitoring, residing in halfway houses, attending day reporting centers, or receiving other forms of intermediate sanctions. As perceptions about the adequacy of sentences have changed, and as the number of offenders eligible for correctional supervision has increased, a large proportion of the burden of adapting to these changes has fallen on the community supervision agencies of the criminal justice system.

Traditionally, community supervision has taken the role of assistance to convicted offenders through the provision of services and a reduction in the severity of criminal sanctions. In this regard, throughout most of the twentieth century, probation and parole could be viewed as supporting the interests and needs of the individual, and thus having a due process orientation. In more recent years, however, the role of community supervision in crime control has come to dominate. Sluder, Sapp, and Langston (1994) have suggested that offender reform for the purposes of crime control is becoming the guiding philosophy of community supervision. In response, Jennifer Hartman (1997) has argued that current changes in community supervision represent extensions of state power and control over individuals. Garland (1990) and Simon (1993) take similar positions. Hartman (1997:193) concluded, "The definition, technology and expectations of community supervision today are such that control is the operating principle and dominates practice."

Joan Petersilia (1996) presented the argument that criminal justice policymakers must invest in community corrections if they hope to reduce crime in the future. Consistent with the position taken by Sluder, Sapp, and Langston, she contends that community supervision and alternative sanctions can support crime control efforts efficiently. The choice is not whether to mitigate the severity of criminal punishments, or whether it is better for offenders to be kept in the community. Rather, her position is that community supervision, including intermediate sanctions, is best designed to achieve reductions in future crime.

While crime control advocates might argue that sanctions short of incarceration inadequately protect the public and fail to deter offenders, due process advocates fear increasing the numbers of offenders who are subjected to criminal justice processing (i.e., net widening) or increasing the restrictiveness of interventions on the lives of offenders. In addition, due process proponents fear that the proliferation of intermediate sanctions has simply meant that offenders who would otherwise have received regular probation now are being subjected to such programs as electronic monitoring, intensive supervision, and day reporting (Harland, 1996). They believe that instead of providing true alternatives to incarceration, intermediate sanctions have brought more offenders under tighter control by the correctional system.

The growth of the community corrections population, especially if coupled with that of the prison and jail populations, suggests the due process proponents may be correct. By the end of 2003, more than 3 percent of the adult population of the United States was under correctional control. What remains unsettled is whether the offenders or society as a whole have benefited as a result of this increased correctional intervention. On one hand, more offenders than ever before are in the custody of corrections officials. On the other hand, intermediate sanctions may have saved tens of thousands of offenders from serving prison and jail terms, and may result in improved conditions for them in the future.

Community supervision represents a compromise between due process and crime control proponents. Offenders under community supervision are subjected to supervision, restrictions, and control. Still, these offenders are under less onerous control than those who are incarcerated. Community supervision often seeks to provide the "right" level of state control over the lives and behavior of convicted offenders. We will return to this issue in the final chapter, but growing interest in restorative justice seeks to balance the interests of the community, victim, and offender. In most restorative justice programs, community supervision plays a key role precisely because it is well suited to serve both due process and crime control ends.

Review Questions

1. How have probation and parole populations changed in recent years?

2. Name and describe two innovations in probation and parole that allow community supervision to approximate the severity of incarceration more closely.

3. What are "split sentences," and how may they be imposed by a judge?

4. Take a position on the question of whether community supervision is "effective." Include public risk, cost, and other relevant factors in arguments for your position.

5. Describe funding approaches that serve to encourage communities to keep offenders out of state prisons, and argue either in favor of or in opposition to them.

6. How can classification of probationers and parolees aid in the use of community supervision resources?

7. Describe two ways in which emerging technologies have affected the ability of probation and parole agencies to supervise offenders in the community.

8. Are current changes in community supervision evidence of a growing dominance of the crime control perspective in American criminal justice?

References

Anderson, J., L. Dyson & J. Burns (1999). *Boot Camp: An Intermediate Sanction.* Lanham, MD: University Press of America.

Atmore, T. & E. Bauchiero (1987). "Substance Abusers: Identification and Treatment." *Corrections Today* 49(7):22-24, et seq.

Auerhahn, K. (2007). "Do You Know Who Your Probationers Are: Using Simulation Modeling to Estimate the Composition of California's Felony Probation Population, 1980-2000." *Justice Quarterly* 24(1):28-47.

Austin, J. & P. Hardyman (1991). *The Use of Early Parole with Electronic Monitoring to Control Prison Crowding.* Washington, DC: National Institute of Justice.

Baumer, T., M. Maxfield & R. Mendelsohn (1993). "A Comparative Analysis of Three Electronically Monitored Home Detention Programs." *Justice Quarterly* 10(1):121-142.

Beck, A. & C. Mumola (1999). *Prisoners in 1998.* Washington, DC: Bureau of Justice Statistics.

Benda, B., N. Toombs & M. Peacock (2006). "Distinguishing Graduates From Dropouts and Dismissals: Who Fails Boot Camp?" *Journal of Criminal Justice* 34(1):27-38.

Bennett, L. (1991). "The Public Wants Accountability." *Corrections Today* 53(4):92-95.

Boone, H. (1996). "Electronic Home Confinement: Judicial and Legislative Perspectives." *APPA Perspectives* (Fall):18-25.

Boone, H. & B. Fulton (1996). *Implementing Performance-Based Measures in Community Corrections.* Washington, DC: National Institute of Corrections.

Byrne, J. (1986). "The Control Controversy: A Preliminary Examination of Intensive Probation Supervision Programs in the United States." *Federal Probation* 50(2):4-16.

Byrne, J. & A. Pattavina (1992). "The Effectiveness Issue: Assessing What Works in the Adult Community Corrections System." In J. Byrne, A. Lurigio & J. Petersilia (eds.), *Smart Sentencing: The Emergence of Intermediate Sanctions.* Beverly Hills, CA: Sage, 281-303.

Camp, C. & G. Camp (1996). *The Corrections Yearbook 1996.* South Salem, NY: Criminal Justice Institute.

Clear, T.R. & J. Byrne (1992). "The Future of Intermediate Sanctions: Questions to Consider." In J. Byrne, A. Lurigio & J. Petersilia (eds.), *Smart Sentencing: The Emergence of Intermediate Sanctions.* Beverly Hills, CA: Sage, 319-331.

Clear, T.R. & G.F. Cole (1986). *American Corrections.* Monterey, CA: Brooks/Cole.

Clear, T.R. & V. O'Leary (1983). *Controlling the Offender in the Community.* Lexington, MA: Lexington Books.

Clear, T.R. & C. Shapiro (1986). "Identifying High Risk Probationers for Supervision in the Community: The Oregon Model." *Federal Probation* 50(2):42-49.

Cohn, A., L. Biondi & L. Flaim (1996). "The Evaluation of Electronic Monitoring Programs." *APPA Perspectives* (Fall):28-37.

Corbett, R. & G. Marx (1991). "Critique: No Soul in the New Machine: Technofallacies in the Electronic Monitoring Movement." *Justice Quarterly* 8(3):399-414.

Cullen, F., J. Wright & B. Applegate (1996). "Control in the Community: The Limits of Reform." In A. Harland (ed.), *Choosing Correctional Options That Work.* Thousand Oaks, CA: Sage, 69-116.

Davies, G. & K. Dedel (2006). "Violence Risk Screening in Community Corrections." *Criminology & Public Policy* 5(4):743-770.

del Carmen, R. & J. Vaughn (1986). "Legal Issues in the Use of Electronic Surveillance in Probation." *Federal Probation* 50(2):60-69.

Dell'Apa, F., W.T. Adams, J.D. Jorgensen & H.R. Sigurdson (1976). "Advocacy, Brokerage, Community: The ABC's of Probation and Parole." *Federal Probation* 40(4):3-8.

Dowdy, E., M. Lacy & N. Unnithan (2002). "Correctional Prediction and the Level of Service Inventory." *Journal of Criminal Justice* 31(1):29-39.

Durose, M. & P. Langan (2004). *Felony Sentences in State Courts, 2002.* Washington, DC: Bureau of Justice Statistics.

Elbert, M. (1997). "The Use of Creatinine and Specific Gravity Measurement to Combat Drug Test Dilution." *Federal Probation* 61(4):10.

Erwin, B. (1986). "Turning Up the Heat on Probationers in Georgia." *Federal Probation* 50(2):17-24.

Erwin, B. & T.R. Clear (1987). "Rethinking Role Conflict in Community Supervision." *Perspectives* 11(2):21-24.

Evans, D. (1996). "Electronic Monitoring: Testimony to Ontario's Standing Committee on Administration of Justice." *APPA Perspectives* (Fall):8-10.

Flanagan, T. (1985). "Questioning the Other Parole: The Effectiveness of Community Supervision of Offenders." In L.F. Travis III (ed.), *Probation, Parole, and Community Corrections: A Reader.* Prospect Heights, IL: Waveland, 167-183.

Ford, D. & A. Schmidt (1985). "Electronically Monitored Home Confinement." *NCJRS Update* (November).

Fulton, B., E. Latessa, A. Stichman & L. Travis (1997). "Up to Speed: The State of ISP: Research and Policy Implications." *Federal Probation* 61(4):65-75.

Garland, D. (1990). *Punishment and Modern Society.* Chicago: University of Chicago Press.

Goldstein, H., W. Burrell & R. Talty (1985). "Probation: The RAND Report and Beyond." *Perspectives* 9(2):11-12, et seq.

Gottfredson, M., S. Mitchell-Herzfeld & T. Flanagan (1982). "Another Look at the Effectiveness of Parole Supervision." *Journal of Research in Crime & Delinquency* 18(2):277-298.

Gowdy, V. (1993). *Intermediate Sanctions.* Washington, DC: National Institute of Justice.

Guynes, R. (1988). *Difficult Clients, Large Caseloads Plague Probation, Parole Agencies.* Washington, DC: U.S. Department of Justice.

Harland, A. (ed.) (1996). *Choosing Correctional Options That Work.* Thousand Oaks, CA: Sage.

Harland, A. & C. Rosen (1987). "Sentencing Theory and Intensive Supervision Probation." *Federal Probation* 51(4):33-42.

Harries, K. (2003). "Using Geographic Analysis in Probation and Parole." *NIJ Journal* (July):32-33.

Harris, P., R. Petersen & S. Rapoza (2001). "Between Probation and Revocation: A Study of Intermediate Sanctions Decision-Making." *Journal of Criminal Justice* 29(4):307-318.

Harrison, P. & J. Karberg (2004). *Prison and Jail Inmates at Midyear 2003.* Washington, DC: Bureau of Justice Statistics.

Hartman, J. (1997). "Operating Principles in Community Supervision." In M. Schwartz & L. Travis (eds.), *Corrections: An Issues Approach*, 4th ed. Cincinnati: Anderson, 187-195.

Holsinger, A., C. Lowenkamp & E. Latessa (2006). "Exploring the Validity of the Level of Service Inventory-Revised with Native American Offenders." *Journal of Criminal Justice* 334(3):331-337.

Holsinger, A.., C. Lowenkamp & E. Latessa (2003). "Ethnicity, Gender, and the Level of Service Inventory-Revised." *Journal of Criminal Justice* 31(4):309-320.

Holsinger, A., E. Latessa, M. Turner & L. Travis (1997). "High Level Alternatives to Incarceration: Examining Community Based Correctional Facilities." Paper presented at the annual meeting of the Academy of Criminal Justice Science, Louisville, KY, March 1997.

Hughes, T., D. Wilson & A. Beck (2001). *Trends in State Parole, 1990-2000.* Washington, DC: Bureau of Justice Statistics.

Huskey, B. (1987). "Electronic Monitoring: An Evolving Alternative." *Perspectives* 11(3):19-23.

Ingraham, B. & G. Smith (1972). "Electronic Surveillance and Control of Behavior and its Possible Use in Rehabilitation and Parole." In *Issues in Criminology*, Vol. 7. Beverly Hills, CA, Sage, 35-52.

Jones, P. (1991). "The Risk of Recidivism: Evaluating the Public-Safety Implications of a Community Corrections Program." *Journal of Criminal Justice* 19(1):49-66.

Larivee, J. (1990). "Day Reporting Centers: Making Their Way from the U.K. to the U.S." *Corrections Today* 52(6):84.

Latessa, E.J., F.T. Cullen & P. Gendreau (2002). "Beyond Correctional Quackery: Professionalism and the Possibility of Effective Treatment." *Federal Probation* 66(2):43-49.

Latessa, E.J. (1980). "Intensive Diversion Unit: An Evaluation." In B. Price & P.J. Baunach (eds.), *Criminal Justice Research.* Beverly Hills, CA: Sage, 101-124.

Latessa, E. (1993). *An Evaluation of the Lucas County Adult Probation Department's IDU and High Risk Groups.* Cincinnati: University of Cincinnati.

Lilly, R. (1992). "Selling Justice: Electronic Monitoring and the Security Industry." *Justice Quarterly* 9(3):493-503.

Lutze, F. (2001). "The Influence of a Shock Incarceration Program on Inmate Adjustment and Attitudinal Change." *Justice Quarterly* 29(3):255-267.

Lutze, F. (1998). "Are Shock Incarceration Programs More Rehabilitative than Traditional Prisons? A Survey of Inmates." *Justice Quarterly* 15(3):547-563.

Mackenzie, D. (1997). "Criminal Justice and Crime Control." In L. Sherman, D. Gottfredson, D. MacKenzie, J. Eck, P. Reuter & S. Bushway (eds.), *Preventing Crime: What Works, What Doesn't, What's Promising?* Washington, DC: National Institute of Justice, 9.1-9.76.

Mackenzie, D. & D. Parent (1991). "Shock Incarceration and Prison Crowding in Louisiana." *Journal of Criminal Justice* 19(3):225-237.

Mackenzie, D. & J. Shaw (1990). "Inmate Adjustment and Change During Shock Incarceration: The Impact of Correctional Boot Camp Programs." *Justice Quarterly* 7(1):125-150.

McDevitt, J. (1988). *Evaluation of the Hampton County Day Reporting Center.* Boston: Crime and Justice Foundation.

McDevitt, J. & R. Miliano (1992). "Day Reporting Centers: An Innovative Concept in Intermediate Sanctions." In J. Byrne, A. Lurigio & J. Petersilia (eds.), *Smart Sentencing: The Emergence of Intermediate Sanctions.* Beverly Hills, CA: Sage, 152-165.

McGaha, J., M. Fichter & P. Hirschburg (1987). "Felony Probation: A Re-examination of Public Risk." *American Journal of Criminal Justice* 12(1):1-9.

Morris, N. & M. Tonry (1990). *Between Prison and Probation: Intermediate Punishments in a Rational Sentencing System.* Oxford: Oxford University Press.

National Advisory Commission on Criminal Justice Standards and Goals (1973). *Corrections.* Washington, DC: U.S. Government Printing Office.

National Institute of Corrections (1981). *Model Probation and Parole Management Project.* Washington, DC: National Institute of Corrections.

National Institute of Justice (1999). *Keeping Track of Electronic Monitoring.* Washington, DC: National Law Enforcement and Corrections Technology Center Bulletin, October.

Note (1966). "Anthropotelemetry: Dr. Schwitzgebel's Machine." *Harvard Law Review* 80:403.

Padgett, K., W. Bales & T. Blomberg (2006). "Under Surveillance: An Empirical Test of the Effectiveness and Consequences of Electronic Monitoring." *Criminology & Public Policy* 5(1):61-92.

Parent, D. (1990). *Day Reporting Centers for Criminal Offenders: A Descriptive Analysis of Existing Programs.* Washington, DC: U.S. Department of Justice.

Parent, D., J. Byrne, V. Tsarfaty, L. Valade & J. Esselman (1995). *Day Reporting Centers, Volume 1: Issues and Practices.* Washington, DC: National Institute of Justice.

Parisi, N. (1980). "Combining Incarceration and Probation." *Federal Probation* 44(2):3-11.

Petersilia, J. (1985). *Probation and Felony Offenders.* Washington, DC: U.S. Department of Justice.

Petersilia, J. (1996). "A Crime Control Rationale for Reinvesting in Community Corrections." *APPA Perspectives* (Spring):21-29.

Petersilia, J. & S. Turner (1993). *Evaluating Intensive Supervision Probation/Parole: Results of a Nationwide Experiment.* Washington, DC: National Institute of Justice.

Petersilia, J., S. Turner & J. Peterson (1986). *Prison Versus Probation in California: Implications for Crime and Offender Recidivism.* Santa Monica, CA: RAND.

Piquero, N. (2003). "A Recidivism Analysis of Maryland's Community Probation Program." *Journal of Criminal Justice* 31(4):295-307.

Renzema, M. & E. Mayo-Wilson (2005). "Can Electronic Monitoring Reduce Crime for Moderate to High-Risk Offenders?" *Journal of Experimental Criminology* 1(2):215-237.

Renzema, M. (1992). "Home Confinement Programs: Development, Implementation, and Impact." In J. Byrne, A. Lurigio & J. Petersilia (eds.), *Smart Sentencing: The Emergence of Intermediate Sanctions.* Beverly Hills, CA: Sage, 41-53.

Rhine, E. (1997). "Probation and Parole Supervision: In Need of a New Narrative." *Corrections Management Quarterly* 1(2):71-75.

Schmidt, A. (1987). "Electronic Monitoring: Who Uses It? How Much Does it Cost? Does it Work?" *Corrections Today* 49(7):28-34.

Schmidt, A. (1989). "Electronic Monitoring of Offenders Increases." *NIJ Reports* (January/February:2-5).

Schneider, A., L. Ervin & Z. Snyder-Joy (1996). "Further Exploration of the Flight From Discretion: The Role of Risk/Need Instruments in Probation Supervision Decisions." *Journal of Criminal Justice* 24(2):109-121.

Schwitzgebel, R. (1969). "A Belt from Big Brother." *Psychology Today* 2(11):45-47, 65.

Simon, J. (1993). *Poor Discipline.* Chicago: University of Chicago Press.

Sluder, R., A. Sapp & D. Langston (1994). "Guiding Philosophies for Probation in the 21st Century." *Federal Probation* 58(2):3-10.

Sontheimer, H. & L. Goodstein (1993). "An Evaluation of Juvenile Intensive Aftercare Probation: Aftercare Versus System Response Effects." *Justice Quarterly* 10(2):197-227.

Szasz, T. (1975). "The Control of Conduct: Authority vs. Autonomy?" *Criminal Law Bulletin* 11.

Taylor, D. (2004). "Agency Accreditation: The Performance-Based Standards Experience." *Perspectives* 28(2):21-23.

Travis, L.F., III (1984). "Intensive Supervision in Probation and Parole." *Corrections Today* 46(4):34.

Vito, G.F. (1985). "Probation as Punishment: New Directions." In L.F. Travis III (ed.), *Probation, Parole and Community Corrections.* Prospect Heights, IL: Waveland, 73-80.

Vito, G.F. (1986). "Felony Probation and Recidivism: Replication and Response." *Federal Probation* 50(4):17-25.

Vito, G.F. & F.H. Marshall (1983). "The Administrative Caseload Project." *Federal Probation* 46(3):33-41.

von Hirsch, A. & K. Hanrahan (1978). *Abolish Parole?* Washington, DC: U.S. Department of Justice.

Wilson, J. (2005). "Bad Behavior or Bad Policy? An Examination of Tennessee Release Cohorts, 1993-2001." *Criminology & Public Policy* 4(3):485-518.

Wheeler, G.R., T.M. Macam, R.V. Hissong & M.P. Slusher (1989). "The Effects of Probation Service Fees on Case Management Strategy and Sanctions." *Journal of Criminal Justice* 17(1):15-24.

Worrall, J., P. Schram, E. Hays & M. Newman (2004). "An Analysis of the Relationship Between Probation Caseloads and Property Crime Rates in California Counties." *Journal of Criminal Justice* 32(3):231-241.

Zedlewski, E. (1996). "NIJ News: Gotta Get IT." *APPA Perspectives* (Fall):16-17.

Chapter 14

The Juvenile Justice System
by Steven P. Lab and John T. Whitehead

Important Terms

abandonment

apprenticeship

blended sentencing

cottage reformatories

detached workers

divestiture

forays

Houses of Refuge

infanticide

involuntary servitude

parens patriae

rumble

status offenses

Misbehavior by juveniles poses special problems for agents of social control. Foremost among the concerns is the general societal belief that juveniles should be handled differently from adults. Indeed, an entire system of social control has been developed for dealing with problem youths. The "juvenile justice system" operates under a different set of assumptions about deviant behavior than does the adult "criminal justice system," and it works somewhat independently of the adult system. This does not mean that there is no overlap between the adult and juvenile systems. In actuality, there is a great deal of similarity in the operations of the two systems. Some individuals claim that the differences are little more than semantic exercises. The aim of this chapter is to briefly familiarize the reader with the problem of juvenile delinquency, the operations of the juvenile justice system, and the major issues currently facing that system.

Defining Delinquency

Perhaps the first point of departure between the adult and juvenile systems appears in the behavior each is charged with handling. Delinquency has been defined in a number of different ways. Many definitions reflect the same behavior outlined as criminal in the adult system. Such criminal law definitions often define a delinquent as a juvenile who violates the criminal laws of the jurisdiction. The Ohio Revised Code (see Box 14.1) is one such statute. The emphasis is on the same behavior prohibited for adults.

Box 14.1   A Criminal Law Definition of Delinquency

(F) "Delinquent child" includes any of the following:

(1) Any child, except a juvenile traffic offender, who violates any law of this state or the United States, or any ordinance of a political subdivision of the state, that would be an offense if committed by an adult;

(2) Any child who violates any lawful order of the court ...

(3) Any child who violates [prohibitions against purchasing or owning a firearm or handgun (Section 2321.211)];

(4) Any child who is a habitual truant and who previously has been adjudicated an unruly child for being a habitual truant;

(5) Any child who is a chronic truant.

Source: Ohio Revised Code (2005) Section 2152.02. Anderson Online Docs. Found at: http://onlinedocs.andersonpublishing.com.

Besides adult criminal acts, the juvenile justice system intervenes in a variety of specific juvenile offenses. Such actions are usually referred to as **status offenses** because they are applicable only to persons of a certain "status." Acts typically considered to be status offenses include smoking, drinking, fighting, swearing, running away, being disrespectful to parents, truancy, and various other actions that are allowable for adults. While "status offense" is the most common term for these actions, various jurisdictions refer to "unruliness," "incorrigibility," "dependency," and other similar terms. Regardless of the term used, such statutes are generally very vague, leaving the interpretation of what is not acceptable behavior to the reader's discretion, and ensuring that all youths could be subjected to intervention. An example of one such statute appears in Box 14.2.

Implicit in the various definitions of delinquency is a definition of "juvenile." While some delinquency statutes provide a specific age, others simply refer to the age of majority of another statute. Clearly, juveniles are young persons who are not yet considered adults. The legal definition, however, varies from place to place (see Box 14.3). For example, 37 states and the District of Columbia set age 18 as the age at which youths move to adult court. Ten states move those age 17 or older to adult court jurisdiction, and three states do so with those age 16 and over (King & Szymanski, 2006). At the same time that an upper age limit is set, some states also set a lower age limit for system intervention (see Box 14.4). These lower ages typically range from age six to age 10. A further age consideration deals with the "waiver or transfer" of youths to adult jurisdiction. While this issue will be dealt with later in the chapter, it is important to note that in 22 states and the District of Columbia there is no minimum age at which juveniles

Box 14.2 A Status Offense Definition of Delinquency

Ohio Chapter 2151.022 defines an "unruly child" as:

(A) Any child who does not submit to the reasonable control of the child's parents, teachers, guardian, or custodian, by reason of being wayward or habitually disobedient;

(B) Any child who is an habitual truant from school and who previously has not been adjudicated an unruly child for being an habitual truant;

(C) Any child who behaves in a manner as to injure or endanger the child's own health or morals or the health or morals of others;

(D) Any child who violates a law ... that is applicable only to a child.

Source: Ohio Revised Code (2005) Section 2151.022. Anderson's Online Docs. Found at: http://onlinedocs.andersonpublishing.com

Box 14.3 Ages at Which Criminal Courts Gain Jurisdiction over Young Offenders

Age 16 (3 states)	Age 18 (38 states)	
Connecticut	Alabama	Montana
New York	Alaska	Nebraska
North Carolina	Arizona	Nevada
	Arkansas	New Jersey
	California	New Mexico
	Colorado	North Dakota
Age 17 (10 states)	Delaware	Ohio
	District of Columbia	Oklahoma
Georgia	Florida	Oregon
Illinois	Hawaii	Pennsylvania
Louisiana	Idaho	Rhode Island
Massachusetts	Indiana	South Dakota
Michigan	Iowa	Tennessee
Missouri	Kansas	Utah
New Hamphsire	Kentucky	Vermont
South Carolina	Maine	Virginia
Texas	Maryland	Washington
Wisconsin	Minnesota	West Virginia
	Mississippi	Wyoming

Source: M. King & L. Szymanski (2006), "National Overviews." *State Juvenile Justice Profiles* (Pittsburgh: National Center for Juvenile Justice). Found at: http//www.ncjj.org/stateprofiles/

can be considered as adults and handled by the adult criminal justice system (see Box 14.5). Varying maximum age, minimum age, and waiver provisions mean that youths subject to the juvenile statutes in one location may be handled as adults in another jurisdiction.

Measuring the Scope of the Problem

How large is the delinquency problem? What characterizes the typical delinquent? Answers to both of these questions can present different images. The varied responses are attributable to the range of possible considerations in defining delinquents and the various methods used for measuring delinquency. Despite the potential variability, some common features about delinquency emerge.

Official Records

The most common source of information on delinquency is the official records of the criminal and juvenile justice system. The Uniform Crime Reports (UCR), court records, and correctional figures are among the varied official crime measures that present information concerning the level of juvenile misbehavior.

Box 14.4 Lower Age Limits for Juvenile Court Jurisdiction

Age 6	Age 7	Age 8	Age 10	
North Carolina	Maryland	Arizona	Arkansas	Pennsylvania
	Massachusetts		Colorado	South Dakota
	New York		Kansas	Texas
			Louisiana	Vermont
			Minnesota	Wisconsin
			Mississippi	

No Specified Lowest Age in Statute or Court Rule

Alabama	Hawaii	Michigan	New Mexico	Tennessee
Alaska	Idaho	Missouri	North Dakota	Utah
California	Illinois	Montana	Ohio	Virginia
Connecticut	Indiana	Nebraska	Oklahoma	Washington DC
Delaware	Iowa	Nevada	Oregon	West Virginia
Florida	Kentucky	New Hampshire	Rhode Island	Wyoming
Georgia	Maine	New Jersey	South Carolina	

Source: M. King & L. Szymanski (2006), "National Overviews." *State Juvenile Justice Profiles* (Pittsburgh: National Center for Juvenile Justice). Found at: http//www.ncjj.org/stateprofiles/

Box 14.5   Minimum Ages for Transfer to Criminal Court

Age 10		Age 15	
Kansas		New Mexico	
Vermont			

Age 12		**No Minimum Age**	
Colorado		Alaska	Nebraska
Missouri		Arizona	Nevada
Montana		Delaware	Oklahoma
		District	Oregon
Age 13		of Columbia	Pennsylvania
Illinois		Florida	Rhode Island
Mississippi		Georgia	South Carolina
New Hampshire		Hawaii	South Dakota
New York		Idaho	Tennessee
North Carolina		Indiana	Washington
Wyoming		Maine	West Virginia
		Maryland	Wisconsin

Age 14	
Alabama	Michigan
Arkansas	Minnesota
California	New Jersey
Connecticut	North Dakota
Iowa	Ohio
Kentucky	Texas
Louisiana	Utah
Massachusetts	Virginia

Source: P. Griffin (2006), "National Overviews," *State Juvenile Justice Profiles* (Pittsburgh: National Center for Juvenile Justice).

Box 14.6 presents data from the 2005 UCR. Youths under the age of 18 accounted for 15 percent of all arrests (approximately 1.6 million), 16 percent of the violent Index crimes (70,482), and 26 percent of the property Index crimes (310,887) (Federal Bureau of Investigation, 2006). The size of the juvenile problem appears even larger when you consider that youths between the ages of 10 and 17 (inclusive) make up roughly 11 percent of the total United States population (U.S. Bureau of the Census, 1992). Juveniles, therefore, are contributing more than their share to the arrest statistics.

Official figures also serve to provide a profile of delinquents. In terms of type of offense, youths confine most of their deviance to property offenses (82% of Index arrests). The sex distribution of juvenile offenders is heavily skewed; males

Box 14.6   Juvenile Index Arrests, 2005

		Percent Under 18	Percent Juvenile Arrestees				American Indian or Alaskan Native	Asian or Pacific Islander
	Under 18		Males	Females	White	Black		
TOTAL	**10,369,819**	**1,582,068**	**15.3**	**70.1**	**29.9**	**67.5**	**29.9**	**1.3**	**1.3**
Murder and nonnegligent manslaughter	10,335	929	9.0	89.8	10.2	43.0	54.0	1.9	1.1
Forcible rape	18,733	2,888	15.4	97.5	2.5	64.3	34.0	1.1	0.6
Robbery	85,309	21,515	25.2	90.0	10.0	30.7	67.5	0.4	1.3
Aggravated assault	331,469	45,150	13.6	76.6	23.4	55.6	42.2	1.1	1.0
Burglary	220,391	57,506	26.1	87.9	12.1	67.1	31.0	1.0	0.9
Larceny-theft	854,856	219,881	25.7	57.7	42.3	68.6	28.1	1.5	1.9
Motor vehicle theft	108,301	27,666	25.5	81.9	18.1	53.8	43.4	1.3	1.5
Arson	12,012	5,834	48.6	86.1	13.9	79.1	18.6	1.1	1.3
Violent crime[1]	445,846	70,482	15.8	81.6	18.4	48.2	49.8	0.9	1.1
Property crime[1]	1,195,560	310,887	26.0	65.7	34.3	67.2	29.8	1.3	1.6

Source: Constructed by authors from UCR.

represent 70 percent of all arrestees. Both males and females, however, commit roughly one-quarter of their offenses in the Part I Index categories. The racial breakdown in official figures shows an overrepresentation of minorities. Although blacks make up approximately 30 percent of youthful offenders, their population representation is only about 15 percent.

The trend in youthful crime reveals declines over recent years. UCR data shows significant decreases since 1989 for every Index category. Unfortunately, juveniles still account for 381,000 Index offense arrests and roughly 1.6 million arrests for all offenses.

In summary, official statistics show that the delinquency problem mainly involves property offenses, is dominated by males, and is overrepresented by minority youths. The data, however, show signs of decreasing arrests in recent years. While the official measures uncover a large amount of delinquency, these numbers probably underrepresent the actual level of juvenile misbehavior in society. First, not everyone reports all the crimes they know about to the police; thus, any unreported deviant act is not included. Second, official records do not adequately reflect status offenses. The police may ignore or simply not record youthful misbehavior that is not also an adult criminal act. The possibility that official records underreport delinquency has led to the use of other measures of deviance. The greatest advantage of the official records lies in the fact that they are collected on an ongoing basis and in a reasonably consistent fashion.

Self-Reports of Delinquency

Delinquency also can be measured through self-report surveys. Self-reports ask the respondent what crimes he or she has committed. These measures have the potential of uncovering deviant acts that are not reported to the police. Indeed, self-report surveys were developed in part as a means of finding out about deviance about which the police were unaware.

Self-report surveys have a fairly long history in juvenile justice. In fact, the earliest such surveys were constructed specifically for the study of juvenile misbehavior. One of the most well-known self-report scales is the Short-Nye Self-report Delinquency Scale (see Box 14.7). It is apparent that the items in the scale are dominated by status and minor offenses. Seven of the items (see the asterisks in Box 14.7) are more commonly used as a set in place of the entire scale. These self-report scales typically uncover a great deal of delinquency. Various studies using these types of scales show that virtually every person is a delinquent. This can be directly attributed to the minor nature of the acts probed in the questions.

Criticisms that the scales were dominated by trivial actions have prompted some researchers to construct scales that include more serious property and personal offenses. The National Youth Survey (NYS) included acts that qualify as felony assault, grand theft, sale of stolen items, and robbery. Unfortunately, the NYS is no longer being conducted. An ongoing self-report survey, the Monitoring the Future (MTF) project, questions high school students and young adults every

Box 14.7 Short-Nye Self-Report Delinquency Items

Driven a car without a driver's license or permit*
Skipped school*
Had a fist fight with one person
"Run away" from home
School probation or expulsion
Defied parents' authority*
Driven too fast or recklessly
Take little things (worth less than $2) that did not belong to you*
Taken things of medium value ($2-$50)
Taken things of large value (over $50)
Used force (strong-arm methods) to get money from another person
Taken part in "gang fights"
Taken a car for a ride without the owner's knowledge
Bought or drank beer, wine or liquor (including drinking at home)*
Bought or drank beer, wine or liquor (outside your home)
Drank beer, wine or liquor in your own home
Deliberate property damage*
Used or sold narcotic drugs
Had sex relations with another person of the same sex (not masturbation)*
Had sex relations with a person of the opposite sex
Gone hunting or fishing without a license (or violated other game laws)
Taken things you didn't want
"Beat up" on kids who hadn't done anything to you
Hurt someone to see them squirm

* Commonly used items in subsequent self-report studies.

Source: J.F. Short & I. Nye (1958), "Extent of Unrecorded Delinquency: Tentative Conclusions." *Journal of Criminal Law, Criminology, and Police Science* 49:296-302.

year. As with the NYS, the MTF includes more serious offenses, such as hitting a teacher, using a weapon to steal something from someone, stealing a car, and fighting in a group. The result of including these more serious items is a reduction in the number of persons claiming to have participated in deviance. In fact, the level of offending for the serious crimes is often close to that uncovered in official records. The level of minor offending, however, remains high.

The demographic profile of offenders presented by self-report studies is somewhat different from the picture evident in official records. First, the peak age of offending appears around age 13 to 15. This earlier peak may be partly due to the use of minor and status offenses in the surveys. Second, differences in the racial and social class distribution are minimal in self-report surveys. Where racial and social class differences appear, they are generally small (Elliott et al., 1983; Hindelang, Hirschi & Weis, 1981). The greatest similarity to official records appears in the sex distribution of offenses. Males again exceed females in the level of offending. An interesting point to note is that, despite the numerical differences, males and females tend to commit similar types of behaviors. That is, there do not appear to be any acts that are primarily restricted to one or the other sex (Elliott et al., 1983).

Comparing the Delinquency Measures

The different sources of delinquency data show both similarities and differences. In general, both show that delinquency is a widespread problem. It is not restricted to any one group or type of offense. The level of offending increased throughout the 1960s and early 1970s, leveled off and showed some decreases in the late 1970s and 1980s, increased in the late 1980s and early 1990s (particularly in serious personal offenses), and has been decreasing in recent years. There is a clear diversity in offending. Youths are involved in all types of behavior— from

While status offenses, such as underage cigarette smoking, are frequently ignored or not recorded by police, they are often included as delinquency measures in self-report surveys. A status offense is a form of juvenile misbehavior that would not constitute a criminal act for an adult. *Photo credit: E.S. Boyne.*

status offenses to serious personal crimes. Property crimes dominate in all measures, and personal offenses are the least common. Males dominate in all but a couple of delinquency categories, such as prostitution and running away.

Most differences in the measures appear in the relative magnitude of offending and by offending subgroups in the population. Self-report measures uncover more offending than do official measures. In terms of demographics, official figures show a much larger number of black offenders than self-report measures. Self-report statistics find little racial difference in offending. Social class differences also tend to disappear when most self-report data are considered. Similar discrepancies emerge when considering the sex of the offenders. While males dominate in magnitude of offending, official figures show the sexes committing different types of offenses. Self-report data, however, tend to portray the sexes as participating in the same types of behavior.

The differences between the measures are a result of the measurement techniques. Official records provide an ongoing look at the level and change in delinquency from year to year according to the formal justice system. These records reflect offenses that are brought to the attention of the authorities. Actions that are not reported but are withheld from public officials are lost to these records. Self-reports typically portray a larger delinquency problem than official figures. The cause of this is the type of activities that are probed in the survey. Surveys that inquire about minor status offenses will always find high delinquency levels.

When more serious offenses form the core of the questionnaire, however, the number of delinquents falls to lower levels.

No single method of measuring delinquency should be considered better than the others. The usefulness of the measures depends entirely on the question that is being answered. Each method provides a different set of information about delinquency. Official records are useful for noting change in official processing and handling of youths over time. They also provide a long-term set of data that allows the inspection of changes over time. Official data are also rich in information about various demographic and offense factors not found in other measures. Self-reports provide a measure of delinquency based on the offender's viewpoint. They are capable of addressing behaviors that may not result in arrests and lead to official records. These measures are rich in data on minor crimes, the number of offenses an individual commits, demographics on offenders, and why an individual acts in a certain way.

Gang Delinquency

The study of juvenile misbehavior consistently portrays delinquency as a group phenomenon (Erickson, 1971; Erickson & Jensen, 1977; Hindelang, 1971). Much of the interest in group delinquency revolves around the existence of juvenile gangs. One source of the public's concern about gangs may be the portrayal of gang behavior in the mass media. Movies and plays such as *The Blackboard Jungle* and *West Side Story* in the 1950s, and *Colors* and *Boyz N the Hood* in more recent years, dramatize the lure of gangs for youths and the aggressive nature of these groups. Social and scholarly interest in gangs was particularly high in the early 1900s until the early 1960s. For a variety of reasons, including overall increases in social unrest and changes in theoretical approaches to deviance, gangs received little specific attention in the late 1960s, 1970s, and early 1980s. It is only within the past 15 years, as gang-related violence increased, that academic and social interest in gangs reemerged.

Defining Gangs

While there has been a great deal of interest and research in gang activity, no single, universally accepted definition of a gang has developed. Curry and Decker (1998) identify a number of factors that are common to most definitions (see Box 14.8). These elements are a group, symbols, communication, permanence, turf, and criminal behavior. Gangs also are more common in poor, disorganized areas of the community.

Rather than attempt to arrive at a single definition for gangs, some authors opt to identify different types of gangs. Knox (1991) offers a typology that presents gangs as developing through identifiable stages from a loose group of youths only marginally involved in criminal activity to a formal gang organized around

Box 14.8   Typical Elements of a "Gang" Definition

GROUP	usually a specified minimum number of members, certainly more than two
SYMBOLS	clothes, hand signs, colors, etc., which serve to indicate membership
COMMUNICATION	verbal and nonverbal forms, such as made-up words, graffiti, hand signals, etc.
PERMANENCE	gangs must persist over time, generally at least one year or more
TURF	territory claimed and/or controlled by the gang (not as common in many definitions)
CRIME	involvement in criminal behavior

Source: Compiled from G.D. Curry & S.H. Decker (1998), *Confronting Gangs: Crime and Community* (Los Angeles: Roxbury).

criminal behavior for profit. Not all gangs will successfully move to the most formalized end of the development continuum. Taylor (1990) offers a typology of gangs based on the motivational factors underlying the gang behavior. While some gangs center on protecting territory, others may exist to make money for its members. Using typologies of gangs negates the need for a single definition. By suggesting that there are different degrees or types of gangs, such typologies suggest that different problems and solutions are needed for the different types.

The Extent of Gang Deviance

The extent of gang deviance is very difficult to gauge, particularly given the varied definitions one can use to identify a gang. What was perhaps the earliest study of gangs identified 1,313 gangs with roughly 25,000 members in Chicago (Thrasher, 1936). These gangs were comprised mostly of adolescent males and usually ranged in size from six to 20 members, although some were as small as two to three members and others numbered more than 100. The great number of gangs in part reflected the fact that Thrasher considered almost any consistent grouping of youths (what he referred to as "play groups") to be a gang. Based on data from six United States cities in the 1970s, Miller (1975, 1980) identified high and low estimates of the number of gangs and the number of gang members (see Box 14.9). His top estimate for these cities was 2,700 gangs with roughly 81,500 members. Research since the 1970s, relying primarily on the National Youth Gang Survey (NYGS) of police and sheriff's departments, suggests that the gang problem is very large and appears in every state and in cities of every size. While we do not know the exact extent of gang participation, we do know that gangs are not uncommon, and they exist in all 50 U.S. states (Office of Juvenile Justice and Delinquency Prevention, 1999).

Box 14.9 Estimates of the Number of Gangs and Gang Members

	# of Gangs	# of Members
Miller (1975)- 6 cities		
low estimates	700	28,450
high estimates	2,700	81,500
Spergel et al. (1999)- 45 cities	1,400	121,000
Curry et al. (1993)- 79 cities	4,881	≈250,000
OJJDP (1997)- 3,440 jurisdictions	23,388	≈665,000
Egley and Arjunan (2002)- 2,542 jurisdictions	24,500	>772,000
Egley and Major (2004)- 2,182 jurisdictions	21,500	731,500

Why Do Youths Join Gangs?

Gang members come together and associate with one another for a wide array of reasons. The early work of Thrasher (1936) suggests that the gang provides inner-city youths with a sense of belonging and acceptance. Several early writers (Bloch & Neiderhoffer, 1958; Cohen, 1955; Miller, 1958) argue that the relative disadvantages of being a lower-class youth faced with middle-class goals leads youths to join gangs as a response to their inability to succeed through normal channels. The lower-class youths find support and unity with others facing similar problems, and gang activity can offer status and a sense of success not available elsewhere. The extent to which the gang is entrepreneurial may provide the members with an income (possibly significant) that is otherwise not available.

More recent research on gangs, particularly that dealing with different racial and ethnic gangs (Horowitz, 1983; Moore, 1991, 1993; Sanders, 1994; Vigil, 1993, 1997; Zatz, 1985) and Asian (Chin, 1990; Chin, Fagan & Kelly, 1992; Huff, 1993; Joe & Robinson, 1980; Sanders, 1994; Toy, 1992), also portray gang membership and activity as a result of life in lower-class communities. Many gang members are recent immigrants or are first-generation Americans. The youths often face problems with success in the schools and other social situations. The gang provides marginal ethnic youths with many of the same things desired by other youths. The gang offers its members a sense of belonging, self-esteem, and status, which may not be forthcoming at home (Moore, 1991; Vigil, 1993, 1997). Brown (1978) portrays the gangs as a form of extended family. This view of gangs is not unlike the explanations for gang behavior set forth in earlier analyses. Clearly, juveniles who find themselves faced with poverty, poor opportunities for advancement, poor school performance, lack of familial support, or other factors may find support and acceptance in the gang.

Gang Activity

The typical view of gang activity, especially as it has been portrayed in the media, has not changed much over the years. Gangs are portrayed as in constant violent confrontation with one another and with the general public. Contrary to this media portrayal, gangs participate in a variety of different behaviors. This does not mean that the gang fights and drive-by shootings are fictional. Such confrontations have taken place in the past and continue to occur today. The image, however, is distorted. Past and present research suggests that such violent confrontations are rare relative to other gang behavior. Jankowski (1990) points out that gangs provide a forum for recreation, partying, and companionship.

When gang aggression does occur, it is not necessarily physical in nature. Miller, Gertz, and Cutter (1961) note that less than 7 percent of one gang's aggressive acts involved physical attacks, and none of those actions involved a weapon. Almost 94 percent of the aggression was verbal, and most did not contain anger (Miller et al., 1961). Miller (1966) reported that gang sentiments in favor of violence are rarely manifested in actual physical expression.

While gang violence is not as common as many believe, gang violence does occur and has changed greatly over the years. The gang fight, or **rumble**, has been the traditional image associated with gang confrontations. The common scenario of the past was of two groups of youths bedecked in leather jackets and wielding chains, knives, or broken bottles in a prearranged fight. Such rumbles, however, were relatively rare, and few members were killed in these exchanges. Violence in recent years does not conform to the image of a rumble. Instead, rumbles have given way to **forays**, in which one or two gang members attack a single rival gang member. The attack usually involves a firearm fired from a moving vehicle. The victim's gang then reciprocates against the transgressor's gang in a like fashion. There emerges an ongoing series of small, isolated attacks between gangs. Counter to public perception, the forays are typically aimed at rival gang members and not the general public. Violence against the public mainly appears in accidental injuries to bystanders. Two factors often pointed to as causes of modern gang violence are the heavy use of firearms and the role of violence in the drug trade.

The role of firearms in increased levels of violence, whether by gang members or individual youths, is very clear. Sheppard et al. (2000) note that the great increases in juvenile homicides in the mid- to late-1980s and early-1990s was due to the increased availability and use of firearms by youths. From 1984 to 1993, there was a 158 percent increase in the age 15-24 homicide rate involving handguns (Sheppard et al., 2000). According to UCR data, almost nine out of 10 murder victims are age 18 or younger, and 65 percent of the murder victims are killed with a firearm (Snyder, 2000).

Firearm use by gang members is a major problem. According to the 1998 NYGS, more than half the law enforcement respondents claim that gang members use firearms often (21%) or sometimes (32%) in assault crimes (National Youth Gang Center, 2000). Gang members are the most likely to own guns (Decker et al., 1997) and recruit youths who already own guns, and are more likely to carry guns than are non-gang youths (Bjerregaard & Lizotte, 1995). Access to firearms has altered the confrontational approach of gangs from more face-to-face personal interaction to more impersonal drive-by shootings. The result of this use of lethal weapons by gangs is a much higher mortality rate among gang members when compared to the general population (Decker & Van Winkle, 1996; Morales, 1992).

The involvement of drugs in gang activity has changed in recent years. There is no doubt that many gang members use and sell drugs, and that the sale of drugs is an integral part to some organized gangs. The degree to which gangs are involved in drugs, however, is highly variable. For example, drug sales in one gang may involve simple sale among its own members, really amounting to little more than a pattern of use, while another gang may be integrally involved in the drug trade throughout the community. Fagan (1990), in a survey of gang members in Los Angeles, San Diego, and Chicago, found that roughly 28 percent were rarely involved in drug use, while 35 percent were seriously involved in drug use and sales. In addition, he found little support for the claim that drug sales were integrally related to the formal organization of the gang. Similarly, Klein et al. (1991) noted that drug sales were not dominated by gangs in Los Angeles County. While these findings argue that gangs are not the most important component of the drug trade, they do show that some gangs and gang members are involved. Whether drug involvement is a driving force behind gang violence is not clear. Klein, Maxson, and Cunningham (1991) report little evidence that drugs are more prevalent in gang homicides than non-gang homicides, and that violence is rare in both gang and non-gang drug arrests. Despite these findings, there is no doubt that conflicts over drugs and sales territories do escalate to violence. It is the extent to which such instances occur that needs further exploration.

A member of the Providence Street Boys gang is tackled by two unidentified members of the Oriental Rascals street gang during their football contest at Classical High School in Providence, Rhode Island. The match was part of an ongoing effort with the Providence Police Department to help gangs battle it out on the football field rather than the streets. *Photo credit: AP Photo/Tim Martin.*

Responding to Gangs

Responding to gangs and gang problems is an area in which much work needs to be done. Unfortunately, the first response by many cities to an emerging gang problem is one of denial (Hagedorn, 1988). Cities often do not want to admit that they have gangs. The outcome of such denial is the emergence of a full-blown problem before the authorities are prepared to deal with it.

The most common approach for dealing with gangs in the past involved the use of **detached workers**. This approach was designed to place gang workers into the environment of the gang. The workers were expected to spend considerable time in the neighborhoods, maintain contact with the gangs, and provide input geared toward more acceptable activities. One key problem of these programs, however, was the inadvertent strengthening of gangs by the worker's presence and the provision of activities (Klein, 1971). Consequently, the impact of these programs on the level of deviance was negligible.

A wide variety of alternative responses has emerged over the years. Box 14.10 lists five general gang intervention strategies identified in a survey of personnel in 245 cities (Spergel & Curry, 1990). These strategies are listed in order of prevalence with 44 percent of the cities reporting the use of suppression of gangs through arrest, incarceration, and supervision. This is closely followed by social interventions (31.5%). The least used response is opportunities provision, although most survey respondents claimed that this is the most effective approach.

Box 14.10   Gang Intervention Strategies

Suppression	Any form of social control in which the criminal justice system (police, courts, or corrections) or society attempt to impose formal or informal limits on behavior.
Social Intervention	Basically a social work approach to working with gangs in the neighborhoods (such as detached worker programs).
Organizational Change and Development	An approach designed to alter the organization(s) that respond to gang problems, such as through the establishment of gang units or specialized training of personnel.
Community Organization	Efforts aimed at mobilizing the comunity toward self-improvement and change, including both physical and social alterations.
Opportunities Provision	An approach recognizing the lack of meaningful jobs and the training needed to succeed, and taking steps to change the problems. Education, vocational training, and job placement are elements.

Source: Adapted from I.A. Spergel & G.D. Curry (1990), "Strategies and Perceived Agency Effectiveness in Dealing with Youth Gang Problems," in C.R. Huff (ed.) Gangs in America (Newbury Park, CA: Sage).

One of the interventions growing in popularity is the Gang Resistance Education and Training (GREAT) program. GREAT began in 1991 under a grant from the Bureau of Alcohol, Tobacco, and Firearms (known as the ATF, and now named the Bureau of Alcohol, Tobacco, Firearms, and Explosives) to the Phoenix, Arizona, Police Department. GREAT mimics the Drug Abuse Resistance Education (DARE) program in that it is taught by police officers to middle-school youths. Lessons deal with individual rights, cultural sensitivity, conflict resolution, drugs, neighborhoods, personal responsibility, and goal setting. The program also targets self-esteem. Esbensen and Osgood (1997) and Esbensen et al. (2001) report that the program seems to have some impact on youths' attitudes toward gangs and drugs. Program participants also display "more prosocial behaviors and attitudes" toward police, the school, family, and peers. Unfortunately, the longitudinal analyses fail to find any significant impact on the level of self-reported gang participation. The promising results found in the evaluations, however, have led to the revised curriculum displayed in Box 14.11.

Box 14.11   GREAT Middle School Curriculum

1. **Welcome to GREAT**
   - Program Introduction
   - Relationship Between Gangs, Violence, Drugs, and Crime

2. **What's the Real Deal?**
   - Message Analysis
   - Facts and Fiction About Gangs and Violence

3. **It's About Us**
   - Community
   - Roles and Responsibilities
   - What You Can Do About Gangs

4. **Where Do We Go From Here?**
   - Setting Realistic and Achievable Goals

5. **Decisions, Decisions, Decisions**
   - GREAT Decision-Making Model
   - Impact of Decisions on Goals
   - Decision-Making Practice

6. **Do You Hear What I Am Saying?**
   - Effective Communication
   - Verbal vs. Nonverbal

7. **Walk In Someone Else's Shoes**
   - Active Listening
   - Identification of Different Emotions
   - Empathy for Others

Box 14.11 *(continued)*

8. Say It Like You Mean It
- Body Language
- Tone of Voice
- Refusal-Skills Practice

9. Getting Along Without Going Along
- Influences and Peer Pressure
- Refusal-Skills Practice

10. Keeping Your Cool
- GREAT Anger Management Tips
- Practice Cooling Off

11. Keeping It Together
- Recognizing Anger in Others
- Tips for Calming Others

12. Working It Out
- Consequences for Fighting
- GREAT Tips for Conflict Resolution
- Conflict Resolution Practice
- Where to Go for Help

13. Looking Back
- Program Review
- "Making My School a GREAT Place" Project Review

Source: Bureau of Justice Assistance (2005), *Gang Resistance Education and Training*. Found at: http://great-online.org

Miller (1990) offers four reasons for our failure to deal with gangs. First, we have no comprehensive national strategy to deal with the problem. Instead, most programs are locally based and are implemented on a piecemeal basis. Second, the resources provided to deal with the problem are inadequate. Third, there is no central focus for the implementation and evaluation of gang programs. Finally, we have failed to identify the problems of the social context within which gang activity flourishes. He argues that until we seriously commit ourselves to dealing with gangs, we will not have any appreciable impact on gangs.

The History of Juvenile Justice

The history of juvenile delinquency and juvenile justice is a relatively short one. While deviance on the part of young persons has always been a fact of life, societal intervention and participation in the handling of juvenile transgressors has gained most of its momentum in the last 100 to 150 years. The reasons for this are easy to see. Throughout most of history, youthful members of society did not enjoy a distinct status as "child." The young were either property or people. The very young, from birth to age five or six, held much the same status as any other property. They were subject to being bought, sold, and disposed of at the wishes of the owner (the parents). Once the individual reached the age of five or six, he or she became a full-fledged adult member of society, subject to the same rules of conduct governing all "adults."

Box 14.12   Milestones in the History of Juvenile Justice

Pre-1800s	Children viewed as property or little adults Deviant youths handled in adult criminal system
1825	Establishment of Houses of Refuge —view that youths can be saved through education, moral training, hard work
1838	*Ex parte Crouse* —establishment of *parens patriae* as basis of intervention with youths
1869	Juvenile probation established in Massachusetts
late 1880s	Move to cottage reformatories —same rationale as Houses of Refuge provided in surrogate family set-up
1899	Juvenile court established in Chicago —totally separate from adult court, heavy reliance on *parens patriae* doctrine
1905	*Commonwealth v. Fisher* —court rules that *parens patriae* and good intentions are sufficient for intervention without concern for due process
1920-1960s	Various new approaches to treatment
1966	*Kent v. United States* —Justice Abe Fortas questions whether the juvenile system is providing the benevolent treatment promised by *parens patriae*, beginning of move toward due process in juvenile court

This state of indifference toward youths can be seen as a result of the health and economic conditions in society. The infant mortality rate typically exceeded 50 percent. The failure to develop a personal, caring attitude toward infants, therefore, was an emotional defense mechanism for reducing or eliminating any pain or sorrow attached to the death of a child. The economic conditions also meant that the birth of an infant was a financial burden on the family. Families lived from day to day on what they could produce. The very young were incapable of caring for themselves or contributing to the family. A child represented a drain on the family's resources.

A variety of practices were used over the centuries for dealing with unwanted or burdensome children. One practice was infanticide, or the deliberate killing of an infant, usually by the mother. Infanticide was a common practice prior to the fourth century and appeared as late as the fourteenth century. A similar practice, which gained prominence after the fourth century, was abandonment. The abandoning of children was seen as less offensive than outright infanticide despite the fact that the end result was the same. Children who survived the first few years of life were often subjected to new actions such as apprenticeship and involuntary servitude. These actions were basically the sale of youths by families. This again alleviated the need to care for the youth and brought an economic return to the family. In addition, these youths provided labor during the rise of industrialization.

Once children entered the labor force they were viewed as adults and subjected to the same rules and regulations as adults. A separate system for dealing with youthful offenders did not exist. At best, the father was responsible for controlling the child and his choices for punishment had no bounds. At the societal level, youths could be (and were) sentenced to the same penalties (including death) as were adults. While harsh punishments were permitted, there is little evidence that the youths received them (Faust & Brantingham, 1979; Platt, 1977).

Changes in the societal view of children did not occur until the seventeenth and eighteenth centuries (the Progressive Era). During this time, medical advances were beginning to have a major impact on infant mortality and life expectancy. Additionally, scholars and religious leaders began to pay attention to the young as a means of attacking the ills of society. Education and protection of the young was seen as a means of creating a moral society. Accompanying these views were alterations in how youthful offenders should be disciplined.

Methods for dealing with problem youths grew out of the establishment of ways to handle the poor. A key method of dealing with the poor was the removal of children from the bad influences and substandard training of poor parents. The establishment of Houses of Refuge in the early 1800s conformed to this idea. The first such institution was established in New York in 1825. Key features of these institutions were the use of education, skills training, hard work, and apprenticeships— all geared toward producing productive members of society. Despite the goals of the Houses of Refuge, various problems emerged. Among the concerns were the mixing of adults and juveniles, the mixing of criminals and noncriminals, overcrowding, the failure to supply intended education and training, the use of harsh physical punishment, and the exploitive use of the clients for monetary gain.

The failure of the early houses of refuge gave rise to the establishment of cottage reformatories in the second half of the 1800s. These new institutions attempted to closely parallel a family; surrogate parents provided the education and moral training for a small number of youths. Probation and the use of foster homes also emerged at the same time as the reformatories. Unfortunately, like the earlier houses of refuge, these new alternatives suffered from many of the same problems.

In response to the failures of institutions to deal with problem youths and the call for new interventions, the juvenile court was established in Chicago in 1899.

The late 1800s continued to experience great levels of immigration by lower-class Europeans, delinquency was on the rise, and there was an emergent body of sociological and psychological study attempting to explain the reasons for social ills. The new juvenile court reflected the general belief in the ability to alter youthful behavior through application of informal intervention and a desire to educate and train the child. Benevolent assistance, caring, training, and guidance were the watchwords of the new juvenile court. The mandate to help youths did not restrict the court to dealing with youths who committed criminal acts. Rather, the court could intervene in any situation in which a youth was in need of assistance. It was during this time that status offenses were included under the purview of the court. The growth of the court was phenomenal, and almost every state had at least one juvenile court by 1920.

The Philosophy of the Juvenile Justice System

The underlying philosophy of the new juvenile court was the doctrine of *parens patriae.* Parens patriae, or the state as parent, was based on the actions of the English Chancery Court, which dealt with overseeing the financial affairs of orphaned juveniles. The court was to act as guardian until the child was mature enough to assume responsibility. Early interventions with juveniles also relied on the *parens patriae* doctrine. For example, in the case *Ex parte Crouse*, the Pennsylvania Supreme Court ruled that the state had a right to intervene into a juvenile's life, against the wishes of the juvenile or the juvenile's parents, if the state felt that the parents were not capable of properly caring for the youth (*Ex parte Crouse*, 1838).

The new juvenile court borrowed this idea of guardianship for the cornerstone of its operations. Debate over the *parens patriae* doctrine was largely settled in 1905 when the Pennsylvania Supreme Court ruled in *Commonwealth v. Fisher* that intervention based on protecting, caring for, and training a youth was a duty of the state and did not violate the constitution, regardless of the youth's actions (*Commonwealth v. Fisher*, 1905). The *parens patriae* philosophy stood largely unchallenged until the 1966 case of *Kent v. United States*. In this case, Justice Abe Fortas questioned the denial of due process for juveniles when he noted:

> There is evidence . . . that there may be grounds for concern that the child receives the worst of both worlds: that he gets neither the protections accorded to adults nor the solicitous care and regenerative treatment postulated for children (*Kent v. United States*, 1966).

Parens patriae remained the dominant force behind interventions with juveniles through the 1970s. Several critics, however, have proposed radical changes in juvenile justice that threaten the traditional *parens patriae* philosophy.

The Juvenile Court Process

Once a police officer takes a youth into custody, it is fairly likely that the police will then refer that youngster to juvenile court. In 2003, 71 percent of the youths taken into custody were referred to juvenile court. The remaining cases were either handled by the police or referred to another agency (Federal Bureau of Investigation, 2004). When police refer a youth to juvenile court, the court per-sonnel must then make one or more critical decisions: whether or not to detain (jail) the youth, whether or not to actually file a peti-tion (charges) against the youth, whether to find (adjudicate) the youth a delinquent, and how to dispose of the petition. These deci-sions correspond to the adult court decisions of bail or jail, the filing of a formal charge versus dismissal, determination of guilt by plea or by trial, and sentencing. Several ju-venile court actors—probation officers, de-fense attorneys, prosecutors, and judges—are involved in these important decisions. While the judge is the primary decisionmaker, oth-er court personnel play important roles in deciding the fate of juvenile suspects.

The Allegheny County Department of Human Ser-vices, Office of Children, Youth, and Families (formerly Children and Youth Services) is a public agency mandated by law to protect children from abuse and neglect. The agency was created in 1963 to comply with federal and state laws requir-ing that child abuse be investigated. *Photo credit: E.S. Boyne.*

This section will examine the critical de-cision points in the juvenile court process: detention, intake, waiver (transfer), adjudi-cation, and disposition. We will look at the roles the various court personnel play (and should play) in the court process. We will de-scribe what happens when a juvenile suspect goes through the juvenile court process, and the ideal will be compared with the reality. Finally, we will examine some of the controversial issues facing juvenile court today, such as the question of how adversarial the attorneys in juvenile court should be and whether juveniles should have the right to a jury trial. It should be noted that we do not focus on the critical question of the police and juveniles. However, many of the law enforcement issues raised earlier in the book apply to juveniles as well as to adults.

The Detention Decision

The first decision that juvenile court personnel must make is the detention decision. They must decide whether to keep a juvenile in custody or allow the youth to go home with his or her parents to await further court action. The **de-tention decision** is the juvenile court counterpart of the bail decision in adult court. It is very important because it concerns the freedom of the child and, therefore, resembles the disposition (sentencing) decision. In fact, children sent to detention may stay there for an extensive period of time, for perhaps even a longer time than children sent to state training schools (youth prisons for juveniles determined to be delinquent). Sickmund and Baunach (1986) reported that youths sentenced to detention spent an average of 12 days in detention even though they had not been adjudicated delinquent.

Detention workers or probation officers usually make the initial detention decision and have several options. Releasing a child to his or her parents is the most frequently used option and the preferred decision in most states. Secure detention— placing a child in the juvenile equivalent of a local jail— is another alternative. It involves placement in a locked facility that houses 10, 20, or more youths who are awaiting further court action or are awaiting transfer to a state correctional facility. **Nonsecure detention** is another option in some places— for youths involved in less serious crimes, youths who do not pose much threat to the community, and youths who are not a threat to themselves. Such youngsters may be placed in small group homes that are either not locked at all or at least not locked as comprehensively as a secure detention facility (hence the term "nonsecure"). Youngsters in nonsecure detention centers may even go to regular public school classes during the day. Alternatives to detention, such as home detention, have developed in recent years. These alternatives are important in light of extensive overuse of detention in the past (McCarthy, 1987b).

The Intake Decision

The second major decision point in juvenile court is the **intake decision,** analogous to the filing or charging decision in adult court. At intake, a court official (either a probation officer, a prosecutor, or both) decides whether to file a court petition of delinquency, status offense, neglect, abuse, or dependency in a particular case. Traditionally, a probation officer makes the intake decision. The *parens patriae* philosophy of the court dictated this approach because its treatment orientation indicated that the probation officer, ideally a trained social worker, should consider the best interests of the child as well as the legal aspects of the case (as an adult court prosecutor might). That is, an intake probation officer is supposed to consider the welfare of the child and the legal demands of the police and victim, and then attempt to resolve every case in light of those considerations.

A frequent decision of the intake officer is to refrain from filing a petition alleging delinquency or a status offense, instead resolving the matter without resorting to a formal petition against the child. This action is usually called "adjustment at intake" or "informal adjustment." It is important to note that such informal adjustment practices occur as frequently as 25 percent of the time (Stahl, 2000) and have been part of juvenile court since its inception.

The Prosecutor's Role

If an intake probation officer decides to file a petition against a child, often that decision requires the approval of an attorney, normally the prosecutor. The prosecutor's approval of the probation officer's decision to file a petition ensures that a legally trained official has reviewed the legal criteria for a properly authorized petition. The prosecutor checks the legal wording of the petition, determines that enough evidence is available for establishing the petition (finding the delinquent or status offender "guilty"), and ensures that the offense occurred in the court's jurisdiction and that the child was of proper age at the time of the offense.

Because of the importance of such legal criteria, and because of the growing emphasis on more punitive juvenile models, some jurisdictions have turned away from the traditional probation officer model of intake to models in which the prosecutor is either the first or the only intake decisionmaker. Such models are more consistent with legalistic views of juvenile court in which the state has abandoned the traditional *parens patriae* philosophy. For example, the state of Washington has switched responsibility for the intake decision to the prosecutor for all felony charges and most misdemeanors. This action represents a radical break with traditional juvenile court thinking and practice. It constitutes a close approximation of adult processing with its retributive emphasis.

The Waiver Decision

For some youths petitioned to juvenile court, the most critical decision point is the **waiver decision** (also called the transfer decision). Many states allow the court to waive or transfer certain offenders (generally older offenders who commit serious crimes) to adult court. This is a crucial decision because the transfer to adult court makes the transferred youth subject to adult penalties (such as lengthy incarceration in an adult prison or even the death penalty) as opposed to a relatively short period of incarceration in a juvenile training school. Such a decision also results in the creation of an adult criminal record, which is public and may hinder future opportunities for employment in certain occupations. A juvenile court record, on the other hand, is confidential, and therefore should not harm the child in any way.

The waiver decision can be invoked through a variety of methods (see Box 14.13). The most common is in a hearing that is analogous to the preliminary hearing in adult court. At a waiver hearing, the prosecutor only must show probable cause that an offense occurred and that the juvenile committed the offense. The prosecutor does not have to prove guilt beyond a reasonable doubt. Proof of guilt is reserved for the trial in adult court if waiver is successful, or for the adjudication stage in juvenile court if the waiver motion fails. The juvenile transfer hearing differs from an adult court preliminary hearing in that the prosecutor

Box 14.13 Forms of Waiver*

Judicial Wavier (46 states)

Discretionary—judge makes decision to waive youths after hearing

> *Mandatory*—state mandates the juvenile court judge to waive jurisdiction under certain circumstances; requires a hearing

> *Presumptive*—statute sets presumption that certain cases are to be waived; not mandatory

Direct File (14 states)—prosecutor has right to choose whether to file in adult or juvenile court

Statutory Exclusion (29 states)—state excludes certain categories of cases from juvenile court jurisdiction

Reverse Waiver (23 states)—permits waiving a juvenile being prosecuted in adult court to be transferred back to juvenile court

Once an Adult/Always an Adult (31 states)—juvenile court jurisdiction is permanently terminated once prosecuted as an adult

Blended Sentencing (15 states juvenile; 17 states criminal)—either the juvenile court or the adult court imposes a sentence that involves either the juvenile or adult correctional systems, or both

*number of states exceeds 50 due to multiple methods in some states

Source: Based on D.M. Bishop (2000), "Juvenile Offenders in the Adult Criminal Justice System," in M. Tonry (ed.), *Crime and Justice: A Review of Research* (Chicago: University of Chicago Press): Volume 27:81-167; P. Griffin, P. Torbet & L. Syzmanski (1998), *Trying Juveniles as Adults in Criminal Court: An Analysis of State Transfer Provisions* (Washington, DC: U.S. Department of Justice); and Office of Juvenile Justice and Delinquency Prevention (2002), *OJJDP Statistical Briefing Book*, online at http://ojjdp.ncjrs.org/ojstatbb/html/qa088.html

must establish that the juvenile is not amenable to juvenile court intervention or that the juvenile is a threat to public safety. An example of nonamenability would be the case of a youth who is already on parole from a state training school for an earlier delinquent act who then commits another serious offense (e.g., armed robbery). If probable cause were established that the youth committed the robbery, then the judge would have to find that the juvenile court had a history of contacts with the youth dating back several years and that one more juvenile court effort to deal with the youth's problems, either through probation or a training school placement, would be futile. An example of a case involving a threat to public safety would be a murder case or an offender with a history of violent offenses.

A number of other forms of waiver have emerged in recent years, including direct file, presumptive waiver, and statutory exclusion. Many of these are due to the more punitive attitudes toward juvenile delinquents. Box 14.14 shows the use of the varying forms of waiver found throughout the United States. Because these measures are relatively new, there are no national data available on the exact number of youths being sent to adult criminal court in such ways.

In 2004, approximately 9,300 juveniles were waived to adult court (Stahl et al., 2007). This was considerably below the peak of 12,100 cases waived in 1994, but higher than the 5,600 cases waived in 2000. Forty-three percent of waived cases in 2004 involved personal crimes, and 33 percent involved property offenses (Stahl et al., 2007). One reason that the number of waiver cases is lower than in 1994 is that states use other methods (such as direct file or statutory exclusion) to prosecute juveniles in adult criminal courts. For example, a survey of 40 of the nation's largest urban counties showed that of 7,100 juveniles charged with felonies in adult criminal court in 1998, three-quarters of them got to criminal court by direct file or statutory exclusion. Approximately one-quarter (24%) were waived to adult court, about 35 percent resulted from prosecutor adult file, and 42 percent were the result of statutory exclusion (Rainville & Smith, 2003). If these proportions are accurate for the entire nation, then the 2004 juvenile court number of 9,300 juveniles waived would suggest a significantly higher total number of youths overall being tried in adult court.

Research on transfer and other methods of placing youths into adult court has produced mixed results. Donna Bishop and her colleagues have done extensive research on transfer in the state of Florida. Comparing a sample of 2,738 youths transferred in 1987 and nontransfer matches, they report that the transferred youths were more likely to receive longer sentences in the adult system than their juvenile-system matches. They were also more likely actually to be incarcerated for longer periods (they actually served longer sentences) than nontransferred youths. The two groups had similar recidivism rates, but the transferred youth were arrested more frequently and more quickly than nontransferred youths (Winner et al., 1997).

Examining robbery and burglary cases handled in criminal and juvenile court, Fagan (1995) found that rearrest rates were higher for the robbery offenders processed in criminal court and that there were no differences in recidivism for the burglary offenders. Robbery offenders processed in criminal court offended more often and more quickly than their juvenile court counterparts. Fagan (1995) concluded that "public safety was, in fact, compromised by adjudication in the criminal court."

A study of 1,042 juveniles prosecuted and sentenced in Pennsylvania adult criminal court between 1997 and 1999 showed that juveniles received harsher sentences in adult court than did young adults, even controlling for legal factors such as offense seriousness and prior record. Specifically, the juveniles were 10 percent more likely to be incarcerated and received a 29-percent increase in sentence length (average sentence length of 2.18 months per juvenile, compared to 1.69 months per adult). These findings "suggest that judges may assign greater levels of culpability and dangerousness to transferred juveniles than to young adult offenders" (Kurlychek & Johnson, 2004).

In general, the research suggests that transfer and other means of putting juveniles into adult court are not magic solutions to some of the perceived problems in the juvenile court. There is conflicting evidence regarding whether youths placed into adult court are more likely to be sentenced to incarceration or are more likely to serve longer time in incarceration. Recidivism statistics do not

Box 14.14 States Use of Waiver and Blended Sentencing

State	Judicial Waiver			Direct File	Statutory Exclusion	Reverse Waiver	Once/ Always	Juvenile Blended	Criminal Blended
	Discretionary	Presumptive	Mandatory						
Total States	**45**	**15**	**15**	**15**	**29**	**25**	**34**	**15**	**17**
Alabama	x						x		
Alaska	x	x			x		x	x	
Arizona	x			x	x	x	x	x	
Arkansas	x			x	x	x		x	x
California	x	x		x	x	x	x	x	x
Colorado	x	x		x		x	x	x	x
Connecticut			x			x		x	
Delaware	x		x		x	x	x	x	
DC	x			x			x		
Florida	x	x		x	x		x		x
Georgia	x		x	x	x	x			x
Hawaii	x						x		
Idaho	x				x		x		x
Illinois	x	x	x		x	x	x	x	x
Indiana	x		x		x		x		x
Iowa	x				x	x	x		x
Kansas	x	x					x		
Kentucky	x		x			x			x
Louisiana	x		x	x		x	x	x	x
Maine	x	x		x			x		
Maryland	x			x	x	x	x		
Massachusetts					x			x	x
Michigan	x	x		x	x		x	x	
Minnesota	x				x		x	x	x
Mississippi	x				x	x	x	x	
Missouri	x						x		
Montana			x	x	x	x		x	x

Box 14.14   (continued)

	Judicial Waiver			Direct File	Statutory Exclusion	Reverse Waiver	Once/Always	Juvenile Blended	Criminal Blended
	Discretionary	Presumptive	Mandatory						
Nebraska				x		x			x
Nevada	x	x				x	x		
New Hampshire	x	x			x		x		
New Jersey	x	x	x						
New Mexico					x			x	x
New York					x	x			
North Carolina	x		x				x		
North Dakota	x	x	x				x	x	
Ohio	x		x				x	x	
Oklahoma	x			x	x	x	x		x
Oregon	x				x	x	x		
Pennsylvania	x	x			x	x	x		
Rhode Island	x	x	x			x	x	x	
South Carolina	x		x		x				
South Dakota	x		x		x	x	x		
Tennessee	x					x			
Texas	x						x	x	
Utah	x	x		x	x		x		
Vermont	x			x	x	x		x	
Virginia	x		x	x		x	x		x
Washington	x				x		x		
West Virginia	x		x						x
Wisconsin	x				x	x	x		x
Wyoming	x			x		x			

Source: Griffin, P. (2006), "National Overviews." State Juvenile Justice Profiles (Pittsburgh: National Center for Juvenile Justice). Found at: http://www.ncjj.org/stateprofiles/

indicate any advantage for transferred youths. In several instances the transferred youths do worse than nontransferred youths. Nevertheless, the current climate favoring punishment suggests that transfer and other mechanisms to get juveniles into adult court will continue. This probably will occur even though some research evidence questions whether this trend is actually protecting the public more than juvenile court processing could.

Adjudication and Disposition

For children not waived to adult criminal court, the next steps after the filing of a petition are adjudication and disposition. In the adjudication and disposition decisions, a judge determines whether there is enough evidence to establish the petition and then decides what to do if there is enough evidence. The **adjudication decision** is comparable to the conviction (plea or trial), and the **disposition decision** is like the sentencing decision in adult court.

Since the United States Supreme Court ordered that certain procedural rights do apply to juveniles as well as to adults (see Box 14.15 for a summary of key court decisions), the ideal is that the determination of the truth of the petition occurs in a rational fashion, with the prosecutor, defense attorney, and judge using their abilities and training to seek justice. Realistically, juvenile court sessions often are hectic and hurried, and they may reflect the self-interests of the parties involved rather than justice or the best interests of the child (Baker, 1991; Prescott, 1981).

Attorneys in the Juvenile Courtroom

There are several problems concerning attorneys in juvenile court. First, many juveniles do not have attorneys. Many juveniles waive their right to an attorney, often because they do not fully understand their rights, especially the importance of the right to an attorney (see, e.g., Brooks & Kamine, 2003). A second critical problem is the burden of high caseloads for public defenders in juvenile court. Depending on the state, the caseload for the average public defender can range from 360 to 1,000 cases per defender (Jones, 2004). With attorneys being so overworked, many juvenile defendants have gotten the clear impression that "their attorneys do not care about them" (Puritz et al., 1995:47).

Many attorneys in juvenile court, both public defenders and private attorneys, are reluctant to utilize the zealous advocate approach that is, at least theoretically, the norm in adult criminal court. Attorneys in adult criminal courts justify such zealous advocacy (in which the attorney fights as hard as possible for all defendants, even defendants who have admitted that they are factually guilty) on the grounds that the system is adversarial and that the adversarial process is best for bringing out the truth. In juvenile court, some attorneys, parents, and judges feel that the adult criminal court norm of zealous advocacy is inappropriate. They may worry that strong advocacy can result in an outcome in which a child who "needs help" will not get it because failure to establish the petition leaves the court with no juris-

Box 14.15   Selected Court Decisions on Juveniles

Kent v. United States 383 U.S. 541 (1966)	Certain minimum safeguards apply to transfer (waiver) cases. The juvenile being considered for transfer to adult criminal court has the right to the assistance of counsel (an attorney), the right to a hearing, and a statement of the reasons for transfer if the judge decides to transfer the case to adult court.
In re Gault 387 U.S. 1 (1967)	The Fifth Amendment privilege against self-incrimination (the right to remain silent) and Sixth Amendment rights to adequate notice of charges against oneself, the right to confront and cross-examine accusers, and the right to the assistance of counsel do apply in delinquency proceedings with the possibility of confinement.
In re Winship 397 U.S. 358 (1970)	The standard proof of guilt beyond a reasonable doubt applies to juvenile delinquency proceedings as well as to adult criminal trials.
McKeiver v. Pennsylvania 493 U.S. 528 (1971)	Juveniles do *not* have a constitutional right to a jury trial.
Breed v. Jones 421 U.S. 519 (1975)	Juveniles cannot be adjudicated delinquent in juvenile court and then waived to adult court for trial without violating double jeopardy.
Fare v. Michael C. 442 U.S. 707 (1979)	Trial court judges must evaluate the voluntariness of any confession obtained from a juvenile based on all the circumstances of the confession. There is no rule that mandates the police consult the child's parent or an attorney before they can question a juvenile suspect. The child can waive his or her privilege against self-incrimination and the right to consult an attorney prior to interrogation.
Eddings v. Oklahoma 455 U.S. 104 (1982)	The age of the defendant should be considered as a mitigating factor in death penalty deliberations.
Schall v. Martin 467 U.S. 361(1984)	A juvenile who is awaiting court proceedings can be held in preventive detention if there is adequate concern that the juvenile would commit additional crimes while the primary case is pending further court action.
Stanford v. Kentucky 492 U.S. 361 (1989)	The constitutionality of the death penalty was upheld for youths who were either 16 or 17 at the time they committed a murder
Roper v. Simmons 543 U.S. 551 (2005)	Ruled that the death penalty for juveniles is unconstitutional..

diction over the child. As a result, at least some attorneys act more like a concerned adult than a zealous advocate, encouraging youths to admit to petitions in cases in which an adversarial approach may have resulted in a dismissal of the petition.

The situation in America's juvenile courts appears to be that some attorneys are adversarial, some are still traditional and act as concerned adults, and some are in between the two extremes. The chief advantage of the zealous advocate model is that it is probably the best insurance that only truly guilty youths will come under court jurisdiction. Because the attorney does not pressure the child to admit to the petition (plead guilty), there is less danger that the court will attempt some type of intervention program with youths who are not really guilty. An added advantage is that this approach may well generate the most respect from juveniles for the court system. Fewer youths will feel that they have been betrayed or tricked into something that some adult thought was best for them, despite their own wishes.

The biggest danger of the zealous advocate approach is that it may contribute to what Fabricant (1983) calls the contemporary version of benign neglect. Because many youths appearing in juvenile court come from families racked with problems, such as low income, public assistance, and/or broken homes, they indeed do need assistance. An adversarial approach may prevent these children from being railroaded into juvenile prisons or other types of intervention due to insufficient legal defense.

The advantage of the concerned adult model is that it seeks to address the problems of the child that presumably led the child into delinquency. The problem is that this helping philosophy has been the rationale of the juvenile court since 1899, and, as Rothman (1980) has so aptly phrased it, the rhetoric of individualized attention has always far outstripped the reality of ineffective if not abusive programs.

Jury Trials for Juveniles

Because the United States Supreme Court has not mandated the right to a jury trial for all juveniles, only 10 states specify that juveniles have a right to a jury trial, and another 11 allow juries in special circumstances (Szymanski, 2002). Some feel that it is critical for juveniles to have the right to a jury trial. For example, Barry Feld (1987b, 1993) has argued that judges require less proof than juries and, therefore, it is easier to convict a youth in front of a judge than in front of a jury. The American Bar Association agrees that judges may be biased and thus it calls for jury trials in juvenile court (Institute of Judicial Administration–American Bar Association, 1980).

Having the right to a jury trial, however, may not make very much difference in juvenile court. In her study of a suburban juvenile court, Mahoney (1985) found that only seven cases out of the 650 she studied actually went to trial. For those seven youths, and for 87 other youths who initially requested a jury trial but later settled without a jury trial, there appeared to be no impact of setting (scheduling) a case for trial on outcomes. Recent research in Ohio showed that most attorneys reported that 10 percent or fewer cases went to trial, and trials were almost nonexistent in some counties (Brooks & Kamine, 2003).

The Recent Emphasis on Punitiveness

Traditionally, the disposition stage of juvenile court has been the epitome of the *parens patriae* philosophy. With the advice of probation officers, social workers, psychologists, and psychiatrists, it was presumed that the judge would do his or her best to act in the best interests of the child. Recently, however, disposition (sentencing) in juvenile justice has taken on an increasingly punitive character.

One indicator of this increasingly explicit focus on punishment is the revision of the purpose clauses of state juvenile codes. Forty-two states have more punitive purpose clauses, and virtually all have some mention of what amounts to a focus on the best interests of the child. However, the last decade has seen 11 states amend their juvenile code purpose clauses to include such goals as punishment, the protection of society, or accountability (Feld, 1987a, 1993). Furthermore, from 1992 to 1997, most states changed their laws expanding criminal court jurisdiction over juveniles or reducing confidentiality provisions for juveniles.

Parallel to the amendment of the purpose clauses, the states have taken more concrete measures to emphasize punishment. Three states (Washington, New Jersey, and Texas) have adopted determinate sentencing statutes with an emphasis on proportionality. The law in such states limits the discretion of judges at disposition and attempts to set penalties that are proportionate to the seriousness of the offense. Some states have enacted mandatory minimum provisions. This means that if the judge commits a child to the state youth authority, the law dictates that the youth must serve a certain minimum amount of time. Some states have adopted dispositional guidelines or suggested sentences for most adjudicated delinquents. Unless a case has some unusual factors, judges are supposed to sentence within the ranges stipulated in the guidelines. Finally, there is the concern that the conditions of confinement have become more negative. For example, in 1991 almost two-thirds of all juveniles in long-term public institutions were in a facility in which the population exceeded design capacity (Office of Juvenile Justice and Delinquency Prevention, 1995).

One other development is blended sentencing. **Blended sentencing** allows either the juvenile court or the adult court to impose a sentence that can involve either the juvenile or the adult correctional system or both. The adult sentence may be suspended pending either a violation or the commission of a new crime. The rationale is to give the judge greater flexibility in sentencing. The judge has greater discretion to adjust the sentence to the offender and the offense. At the end of 1997, 20 states had laws authorizing some type of blended sentencing. It is still too early, however, to gauge the impact of these reforms. Preliminary lessons are that resources have not kept up with legislative changes, the laws seem to encourage plea bargaining, and minorities are overrepresented in the affected populations (Torbet et al., 2000).

Issues in Juvenile Justice

Modern juvenile justice is faced with a variety of concerns and issues. Many of these topics are interrelated and reflect different approaches and concerns. Among the issues are the future of juvenile court, capital punishment for youths, and jurisdiction over status offenders.

The Future of Juvenile Court

There is widespread dissatisfaction with the juvenile court system. Everyone seems to agree that it had noble ideals, but no one seems to feel that it has put those ideals into everyday practice. There are numerous suggestions for the reform of juvenile court. We will examine several reform proposals.

Rehabilitating the Rehabilitative *Parens Patriae Court*

One approach to the problems of the juvenile court is try to return to the rehabilitative and *parens patriae* roots of the court. Reformers who support this option think that the failures of juvenile court are failures of implementation: the juvenile court has not delivered the rehabilitation that it initially promised. A major factor behind this failure of implementation is lack of funding. Legislators have not provided the money needed to help youths obtain education, counseling, family counseling, and vocational training.

If juvenile courts received adequate funding and if they followed the advice of the research on effective rehabilitation programs, the juvenile court could be the ideal youth court envisioned by the Progressives at the beginning of the twentieth century. Juvenile court judges could act like concerned parents trying to help children.

Feld (1999) points out flaws with the argument that juvenile court failure is simply a failure of implementation and that all that is needed is a rededication to the original rehabilitative ideals of juvenile court. He agrees that adequate funds have not been devoted to juvenile court, but argues that funds will always be inadequate. One reason is that there is "pervasive public antipathy" to helping the poor, disadvantaged, disproportionately minority youths who are the clients of juvenile court. Another reason is that because committing a crime is the condition for receiving "help" from juvenile court, there is a built-in punishment focus. Feld argues that providing for children is a societal responsibility, not just a responsibility of juvenile court. In fact, the mere existence of juvenile court is an excuse or alibi for not providing for poor, minority youths.

Feld (1999) also argues that the juvenile court does not provide procedural fairness to children. Traditionally, some of the procedural protections of adult court, such as the right to jury trial, have been denied children on the justification that the juvenile court was not a punitive court like adult court. Even worse than denying procedural protections, juvenile courts have treated children in similar circumstances who commit similar offenses in unequal and disparate fashion. This individualized handling was originally justified on the supposed rehabilitative foundation of juvenile court. But because juvenile court is punitive and does not provide rehabilitation, this denial of due process safeguards makes juvenile court unfair and unjust (Feld, 1999). In summary, Feld thinks that efforts to return the juvenile court to its rehabilitative ideal are doomed to failure: "The current juvenile court provides neither therapy nor justice and cannot be rehabilitated" (Feld, 1999: 297).

Calls for the Elimination of Juvenile Court

Feld (1999) thinks that the problems of juvenile court are too extensive and too fundamental to fix and that now is the time to abandon the sinking ship of juvenile court. The juvenile court provides neither help nor stops crime. In its place, Feld proposes adult criminal court for all—both juveniles and adults.

Adult court would mean that juveniles would receive adult procedural protections. Juveniles would have the right to a jury trial, and defense attorneys would act as zealous adversaries. At the same time, Feld argues that juveniles should still get shorter sentences because shorter sentences have been a saving feature of juvenile court and they "enable most young offenders to survive the mistakes of adolescence with a semblance of their life chances intact" (Feld, 1999:304). Adult courts could "discount" sentences for youths. Specifically, 14-year-olds would receive 25 to 33 percent of the adult penalty; 16-year-olds, 50 to 66 percent; and 18-year-old youths, the full adult penalty.

Feld (1999) fails to note that adult court sentencing for juveniles would also require some type of protection of the youth's record. New York State, for example, has a "youthful offender" provision that makes convictions and sentences under its provisions like juvenile court adjudications and dispositions that do not count against the individual. In other words, one benefit of juvenile court is that a youth can legally say that he or she has not been "arrested" or "convicted," but instead has been "taken into custody" and "adjudicated." Such legal protections against arrest and conviction records can be extremely important if one is applying for a job, graduate school, or the military.

Vandervort and Ladd (2001) raise a serious objection to Feld's proposal. They argue that Michigan has changed its juvenile code to the point that many juveniles are now handled in adult court and the results have been harmful for juveniles. They contend that procedural rights are eroding in adult court. A juvenile transferred to adult court actually receives fewer due process protections in adult court than he would have in juvenile court. Juveniles are simply getting punishment in adult court, not treatment.

Another problem with Feld's suggestion of discounted sentencing for youths in adult court is that even discounted sentences might not be much of a bargain. Recall that Feld (1999) suggests that 16-year-olds should receive a youth discount of 50 to 66 percent. If a life sentence is equivalent to a sentence of 50 years, a 16-year-old processed in adult court would actually stay in prison until age 41 (half of 50 is 25 plus 16 equals age 41) or age 49 (66 percent of 50 plus 16). Thus, even with a youth "discount," youths processed in adult court would pay a heavy price compared to juvenile court, in which the maximum jurisdiction is until age 21.

Kerbs (1999) notes two other problems with Feld's suggestion to switch juveniles to adult criminal court. First, politicians are not saying "discount"; they are crying out "adult crime, adult time." Politicians are mouthing a simplistic formula that suggests that they regard youthful offenders as simply younger but fully responsible offenders. Second, Kerbs fears that African-American juveniles transferred to adult court will continue to receive unfair treatment compared to whites: "unequal justice under law" (Kerbs, 1999:120). Thus, there is reason to believe that abolishing juvenile court would not have the positive effects Feld envisions and might well produce very negative effects.

A Restorative Justice Juvenile Court

Gordon Bazemore (1999) suggests that now is the time to take the "fork in the road," to try a new path for juvenile court. He argues that now is the time to adopt a restorative justice model.

In Pittsburgh, Pennsylvania, young offenders are involved in service projects such as home repair for the elderly and voter registration drives. In Utah, offenders are paying victim restitution out of wages from public service jobs. In Oregon, offender work crews cut firewood and deliver it to the elderly. More than 150 cities are utilizing victim-offender mediation. In Colorado and Florida, offenders work with Habitat for Humanity building homes for lower-income families. In Florida, probation officers are walking neighborhood beats to help promote local guardianship of communities. In Boston and Florida, probation officers are helping police monitor probationers at night.

What all of these efforts have in common is a restorative justice focus that emphasizes the victim and the community. The approach is "focused less on achieving public safety by incarcerating individual offenders and more on reducing fear, building youth-adult relationships, and increasing the capacity of community groups and institutions to prevent crime and safely monitor offenders in the community" (Bazemore, 1999:98).

This represents a radical rethinking of the role of juvenile court. Instead of sanctioning and supervising offenders, the role of the court would be to build community so that neighborhoods can better respond to, but also prevent, delinquency. Communities would be more involved in sentencing through community panels or conferences or dispute resolution programs. Communities would return to their role of being responsible for youths. Bazemore argues that the community must address socialization needs with "caring adults who spend time with young people not because they are paid to do so but because they share a commitment to the idea that youth development is a community responsibility" (Bazemore, 1999:101).

A positive feature of Bazemore's proposal is that many restorative justice programs are already in place. This is not a hypothetical proposal. As noted, numerous communities already are working at restorative justice. A major question, however, is how far restorative justice can go. How willing are citizens to assume the responsibilities that restorative justice would give them in deciding cases and monitoring sanctions such as community service? If people are not available to staff the restorative justice programs, they will not work.

Creating a New Juvenile Court

Still another suggestion is to make a new juvenile court. Noriega (2000) suggests that we create a new juvenile court that has two branches: one for children and one for adolescents. The children's court would be rehabilitative and would presume that children are inculpable, that is, they do not have criminal responsibility. The adolescent court would presume partial culpability and would be more punitive than the children's court. The adult court would continue to presume that adults are culpable and would be the most punitive of the three courts.

Waiver would be by judicial hearing only. There would be no prosecutorial or legislative waiver. Waiver also would be only to the next step. Thus, children could only be waived to adolescent court, and only adolescents could be waived to adult court.

Juveniles (children and adolescents) would not be allowed to waive their right to counsel. Noriega's (2000) reasoning for this is that children and adolescents are generally presumed not competent; they are not allowed to enter into contracts, cannot drink alcohol, and cannot vote or drive (until late adolescence).

This is an interesting proposal. Noriega (2000) disagrees with Feld that abolishing juvenile court is the best course of action. Noriega argues that abolishing juvenile court will not guarantee that adult courts treat children/adolescents properly. He argues that it will be hard to treat a juvenile as a juvenile after he has been designated an "adult" and that it will be difficult to actually give discounts, à la Feld, to juveniles in adult court "as if they were getting their sentence on sale from Kmart" (Noriega, 2000:692-693).

An attractive feature of this proposal is that it offers a more complex and more realistic view of development. Instead of assuming that one day a juvenile is a child and the next day he or she is an adult, it recognizes the intermediate stage of adolescence. Noriega is also probably more realistic than Feld about the actual results of abolishing juvenile court and letting adult court handle juvenile matters. Adult courts are probably not going to be as caring and protective or concerned about youth discounts as Feld hopes.

Unfortunately, Noriega (2000) just gives a sketchy outline. He says states should have a children's court and an adolescent's court. He does not, however, give us specific age limits for each; nor does he specify punishment limits (e.g., incarceration terms) for each. Still another problem is that his strategy could result in yet another bureaucracy—adolescent court and adolescent corrections—when the current juvenile and adult bureaucracies already both have myriad problems. To note just one issue, will states be willing to create a new adolescent court and corrections system (assuming the current juvenile court becomes children's court)? Will they be willing to hire more personnel? Build more courtrooms? Build more prisons? As Garland (2000–and see below) so aptly points out, the recent trend has been to cut back the welfare state in general. Noriega's proposal goes against that trend; governmental bodies are looking to cut expenditures, not embrace new spending initiatives.

A "Youth Justice System" within Adult Criminal Court

Finally, Butts (2000) offers still another variation: a youth justice system within adult court. Butts notes that the juvenile justice system is disappearing before our very eyes. Presumptive waiver provisions, mandatory waiver, blended sentencing, mandatory minimums and sentencing guidelines, open hearings, and the use of juvenile records in adult court (e.g., to count as first or second strikes in three-strikes cases) are all nails in the coffin of the traditional juvenile court. Thus, he states, "[i]t is too late to save the traditional [juvenile justice] system because the traditional system is already gone" (Butts: 2000:52). He also notes that widespread opposition to the idea of delinquency dictates the end of delinquency cases in juvenile court. When the public hears "delinquent," he says, it thinks "weak and lenient" (Butts: 2000:55).

His suggestion is to transfer all delinquency matters to adult court but to create a separate arm of adult court to deal with criminal acts allegedly committed by juveniles. He argues that adults courts are creating new specialized courts such as drug courts and mental health courts that do specialized intake and treatment. He thinks that specialized youth justice courts could do the same for juveniles. The benefit would be to stop fighting over which court—juvenile or adult—gets which offender and to start focusing "on ensuring the quality of the process used for all youth" (Butts, 2000:56). Butts is proposing a specialized court like drug and mental health courts.

Butts is accurate that many of the changes in juvenile court in the last 10 years have taken away many of the clientele (via some type of waiver/transfer). He is also accurate that some of the new drug courts and mental health courts (therapeutic jurisprudence) have made significant strides in dealing with their particular clients. A major question, however, is whether most jurisdictions would in fact start such courts and would devote the resources needed to allow them to carry out their mission. Creating new youth services courts in the adult system without adequate funding and resources would be a sham.

Zimring's Caution

Zimring (2000) adds a cautionary note to the various proposals about keeping, abolishing, or modifying juvenile court. He reminds us that even juvenile court is in the business of imposing punishment. As rehabilitative as the intentions of the founders may have been, the truth, as noted in *In re Gault*, is that juvenile court "dispositions" often deprive youths of their freedom. For Zimring this truth of punishment means that a crucial element, even if we abolish juvenile court, is reduced punishment. In other words, even if all juveniles went to adult court, there still would be a legitimate issue of deciding on lesser punishments for such offenders. Second, Zimring points out that the United States is inconsistent about juveniles. We prohibit them from voting until age 18 and from drinking until age 21 because we consider them immature, but we want to submit them to adult court and punishment at lower and lower ages. Zimring agrees that youths are immature and argues that states need to address this inconsistency and not just ignore it.

Capital Punishment for Juveniles

In 2003, an estimated 1,130 juveniles (youths under 18 years of age) were arrested for murder. This was a decrease of 10 percent from 2002 and a decrease of 18 percent from 1999. It is also dramatically lower than the approximately 3,800 juveniles who were arrested for murder in 1993, the peak year for murders by juveniles (Snyder, 2005). Despite this decrease, we will probably see continued media attention on juveniles who kill.

Considerable discussion has taken place about the appropriateness of the death penalty for juveniles. The increase in juvenile homicide in the late 1980s and early 1990s makes this debate more critical than ever. In 1996 approximately 2,900 juveniles were arrested for murder, an increase of 50 percent over 1987 (Snyder, 1997). In 2000 an estimated 1,200 juveniles were arrested for homicide, down 55 percent from 1996 and 65 percent from 1991 (Snyder, 2002). Although the 2000 statistics represent a continuing decline since 1993, involvement in murder is still alarming and prevalent enough that we will see increasing numbers of juveniles on the nation's death rows. In addition, highly publicized juvenile homicides, especially shootings at schools, generate calls for either criminal court processing or capital punishment or both for youthful murderers.

At year end 2000 there were 78 death row inmates (out of a total of 3,312 death row inmates) who were younger than 18 at the time of their arrest for a capital offense (Snell, 2001). Another 353 death row inmates were either 18 or 19 at the time of their arrest for a capital offense. Thirteen states that have death penalty statutes set 16 or less as the minimum age for eligibility for execution, and four states set a minimum age of 17 years (Snell, 2001).

The Supreme Court recently ruled that the death penalty is unconstitutional for juveniles. In *Roper v. Simmons* (2005), writing for the majority, Justice Kennedy wrote that "[t]he Eighth and Fourteenth Amendments forbid imposition of the death penalty on offenders who were under the age of 18 when their crimes were committed." The ruling came in a case in which Christopher Simmons, age 17, with two accomplices, broke into and entered a home at 2:00 A.M., took a woman captive, drove away, and threw the woman from a railroad trestle into a river. The majority opinion reasoned that the juvenile death penalty is rejected by a majority of the states and is used infrequently in states that authorize it. The majority went on to cite scientific evidence that juveniles under 18 are less mature and responsible than adults, more susceptible to peer pressure, and have character that is less well formed than that of an adult.

Horowitz (2000) argues that there should be no death penalty for juveniles for several reasons. First, she claims that reasoning ability, maturity, and experience levels are lower for juveniles than for adults. Second, subjecting juveniles to the death penalty is arbitrary in that it is contrary to other laws that assume that children under 18 need protection and are not ready for certain responsibilities or privileges such as the right to vote, sit on juries, consent to treatment, and marry. Horowitz also thinks that juveniles have greater potential for rehabilitation than adults. Another part of her argument is that many juveniles have not had a chance to get away from the abuse or other problems they have suffered. Finally, Horowitz (2000) contends that considerations of deterrence and retribution often do not apply to juveniles. In general, youth impulsiveness, poor judgment, and feelings of invincibility prevent them from regarding even the death penalty with the rational calculation necessary for an adequate deterrent impact.

Jurisdiction Over Status Offenses

Also related to the fundamental issue of the future of juvenile court is the issue of divestiture: the elimination of juvenile court jurisdiction over status offenders. Assuming that a state chooses not to completely eliminate juvenile court, should it continue to exercise control over disobedient, runaway, and truant adolescents? The state of Washington has opted to continue juvenile court but to eliminate jurisdiction over status offenses. Maine is the only other state that has written full divestiture into law. Most states have retained jurisdiction but have implemented policies of deinstitutionalization (i.e., they have stopped confining status offenders in state institutions). Additionally, they have established diversion programs to handle status offenders instead of relying on the juvenile justice system (Schneider, 1985).

Despite such efforts, status offenses and status offenders continue to take up a considerable portion of the juvenile court's time and effort. In 1997, juvenile courts handled 158,500 petitioned status offense cases, an increase of more than 90 percent over 1986. Runaway, truancy, and liquor law violation cases increased more than 50 percent, while ungovernable cases increased only 14 percent. Despite more than a decade of discussion about ending juvenile court jurisdiction over status offenses, approximately 11,600 youths were adjudicated status offenders and placed in out-of-home placements in 1997 (Puzzanchero et al., 2000). The 2001 census of juveniles in custody showed more than 5,000 youths in custody for a status offense (Sickmund et al., 2004).

Arguments for Ending Jurisdiction

There are several arguments in favor of complete divestiture. First, it allows the juvenile court more time and resources to deal with juvenile delinquents, especially violent and chronic delinquents. Second, the elimination of status offense jurisdiction would prevent any possible violations of the due process rights of status offenders, such as being prosecuted for very vague charges. Status offense statutes typically are unclear or vague on when youthful disobedience or adolescent rebellion turns into a status offense. Third, elimination of this jurisdiction recognizes the reality that juvenile courts are not adequately staffed and equipped to deal with status offenders. Elimination of jurisdiction over status offenses would be an admission that private agencies with trained social workers and counselors are better equipped to handle the complex personal and interpersonal problems of status offenders, by means of individual, group, and family counseling as well as other professional techniques. Furthermore, elimination of juvenile court jurisdiction would force any intervention to be voluntary, which some writers argue is the proper way to deal with status offenders.

Arguments for Continuing Jurisdiction

Some still feel, however, that juvenile court jurisdiction over status offenses is both desirable and necessary. Proponents of continued jurisdiction contend that parents and schools need the clout or authority of juvenile court to impress adolescents with the need to obey their parents, attend school, and not run away from home. In addition, proponents of court jurisdiction argue that private agencies in the community will not handle (or will not be able to handle) all of the status offense cases if the juvenile court cannot intervene. Private agencies intervene only with willing clients, and many status offenders taken to such agencies will simply refuse assistance.

Proponents also contend that status offenders are properly under juvenile court jurisdiction because their behavior often escalates into delinquent activity. Hence, they feel that early intervention can prevent much delinquency. This escalation hypothesis, however, is controversial. Some proportion of status offenders do indeed escalate or progress but most do not (Lab, 1984; Rojek & Erickson, 1982; Shannon, 1982). Therefore, it is questionable whether all status offenders should be subject to juvenile court jurisdiction. Proponents of court jurisdiction over status offenses feel that court jurisdiction might prevent some children from becoming involved in associated dangerous behaviors. Another argument in favor of continued jurisdiction is that it prevents status offenders from being processed as delinquents. Where system processing of status offenders has been ended, there is some evidence of treating status offenders as minor delinquents and thereby "relabeling" them (Schneider, 1985).

Summary

At the beginning of the twenty-first century, the future is very much in question for the juvenile justice system. Juvenile crime continues to evoke concern and fear among citizens. Such concern sparks calls for harsher measures for juveniles who commit serious, violent offenses. Legislators have been changing state laws to deal with such juveniles in a manner that holds them accountable and protects the public. On the other hand, research suggests that many interventions can be effective in reducing the recidivism of juveniles (Lipsey, Wilson & Cothern, 2000). Hopefully, whatever changes continue to be implemented for court processing and correctional intervention with juveniles will retain some of the hope that the founders of juvenile court had for troubled youths.

Review Questions

1. What is "delinquency"?

2. Identify three types of gangs.

3. How did the juvenile court come to be?

4. What is meant by *parens patriae?*

5. Briefly describe the juvenile justice system.

6. How does the juvenile justice system differ from the adult criminal system?

7. Identify at least three current controversies in juvenile justice.

References

Baker, F. (1991). *Saving Our Kids from Delinquency, Drugs, and Despair.* New York: Harper Collins.

Bazemore, G. (1999). "The Fork in the Road to Juvenile Court Reform." *Annals of the American Academy of Political and Social Science* 564:81-108.

Beger, R.R. (1994). "Illinois Juvenile Justice: An Emerging Dual System." *Crime & Delinquency* 40:54-68.

Bishop, D.M. (2000). "Juvenile Offenders in the Adult Criminal Justice System." In M. Tonry (ed.), *Crime and Justice: A Review of Research*, vol. 27, pp. 81-167. Chicago: University of Chicago Press.

Bloch, H.A. & A. Neiderhoffer (1958). *The Gang: A Study in Adolescent Behavior.* New York: Philosophical Library.

Bjerregaard, B. & A.J. Lizotte (1995). "Gun Ownership and Gang Membership." *Journal of Criminal Law and Criminology* 86:37-58.

Brooks, K. & D. Kamine (2003). *Justice Cut Short: An Assessment of Access to Counsel and Quality of Representation in Delinquency Proceedings in Ohio.* Columbus: Ohio State Bar Association.

Brown, W.K. (1978). "Black Gangs as Family Extension." *International Journal of Offender Therapy and Comparative Criminology* 22:39-45.

Bureau of Justice Assistance (2005). *Gang Resistance Education and Training.* Found at: http:// great-online.org

Butts, J.A. (1996). *Offenders in Juvenile Court, 1994.* Washington, DC: U.S. Department of Justice.

Chin, K. (1990). *Chinese Subculture and Criminality: Non-traditional Crime Groups in America.* Westport, CT: Greenwood.

Chin, K., J. Fagan & R.J. Kelly (1992). "Patterns of Chinese Gang Extortion." *Justice Quarterly* 9:625-646.

Cohen, A.L. (1955). *Delinquent Boys: The Culture of the Gang.* Glencoe, IL: Free Press.

Costanzo, M. (1997). *Just Revenge: Costs and Consequences of the Death Penalty.* New York: St. Martins Press.

Curry, G.D., R.J. Fox, R.A. Ball & D. Stone (1993). *National Assessment of Law Enforcement Anti-Gang Information Resources: Final Report.* Washington, DC: National Institute of Justice.

Curry, G.D. & S.H. Decker (1998). *Confronting Gangs: Crime and Community.* Los Angeles: Roxbury.

Decker, S.H., S. Pennel & A. Caldwell (1997). *Illegal Firearms: Access and Use by Arrestees.* Washington, DC: National Institute of Justice.

Decker, S.H. & B. Van Winkle (1996). *Life in the Gang: Family, Friends, and Violence.* New York: Cambridge University Press.

del Carmen, R.V., M. Parker & F.P. Reddington (1998). *Briefs of Leading Cases in Juvenile Justice.* Cincinnati: Anderson.

Egley, A. & M. Arjunan (2002). *Highlights of the 2000 National Youth Gang Survey.* OJJDP Fact Sheet (February #4). Washington, DC: Office of Juvenile Justice and Delinquency Prevention.

Egley, A. & A.K. Major (2004). *Highlights of the 2002 National Youth Gang Survey.* OJJDP Fact Sheet. Washington, DC: Office of Juvenile Justice and Delinquency Prevention.

Elliott, D.S., S.S. Ageton, D. Huizinga, B.A. Knowles & R.J. Canter (1983). *The Prevalence and Incidence of Delinquent Behavior: 1976-1980.* Boulder, CO: Behavioral Research Institute.

Erickson, M.L. (1971). "The Group Context of Delinquent Behavior." *Social Problems* 19:114-129.

Erickson, M.L. & G. Jensen (1977). "Delinquency is Still Group Behavior: Toward Revitalizing the Group Premise in the Sociology of Deviance." *Journal of Criminal Law and Criminology* 68:262-273.

Esbensen, F. & D.W. Osgood (1997). *National Evaluation of GREAT.* NIJ Research in Brief. Washington, DC: National Institute of Justice.

Esbensen, F., D.W. Osgood, T.J. Taylor, D. Peterson & A. Freng (2001) "How Great is G.R.E.A.T.? Results from a Longitudinal Quasi-experimental Design." *Criminology & Public Policy* 1:87-118.

Fabricant, M. (1983). *Juveniles in the Family Courts.* Lexington, MA: Lexington Books.

Fagan, J. (1990). "Social Processes of Delinquency and Drug Use Among Urban Gangs." In Huff, C.R. (ed.), *Gangs in America.* Newbury Park, CA: Sage.

Fagan, J. (1995). "Separating Men from the Boys: The Comparative Advantage of Juvenile versus Criminal Court Sanctions on Recidivism Among Adolescent Felony Offenders." In J.C. Howell, B. Krisberg, J.D. Hawkins & J.J. Wilson (eds.), *A Sourcebook: Serious, Violent and Chronic Juvenile Offenders* (pp. 238-260). Thousand Oaks, CA: Sage.

Faust, F.L. & P.J. Brantingham (1979). *Juvenile Justice Philosophy: Readings, Cases and Comments.* St. Paul, MN: West.

Federal Bureau of Investigation (2001). *Crime in the United States 2000: Uniform Crime Reports.* Washington, DC: U.S. Department of Justice.

Federal Bureau of Investigation (2003). *Crime in the United States 2002: Uniform Crime Reports.* Washington, DC: U.S. Department of Justice.

Federal Bureau of Investigation (2004). *Crime in the United States 2003: Uniform Crime Reports.* Washington, DC: U.S. Department of Justice.

Federal Bureau of Investigation (2006). *Crime in the United States 2005: Uniform Crime Reports.* Washington, DC: U.S. Department of Justice.

Feld, B. (1987a). "The Juvenile Court Meets the Principle of the Offense: Changing Juvenile Justice Sentencing Practices." Paper presented at the 1987 Annual Meeting of the American Society of Criminology.

Feld, B. (1987b). "The Juvenile Court Meets the Principle of the Offense: Legislative Changes in Juvenile Waiver Statutes." *Journal of Criminal Law and Criminology* 78:471-533.

Feld, B. (1993). "Juvenile (In)justice and the Criminal Court Alternative." *Crime & Delinquency* 39:403-424.

Feld, B. (1999). *Bad Kids: Race and the Transformation of the Juvenile Court.* New York: Oxford University Press.

Griffin, P. (2000). "National Overviews." *State Juvenile Justice Profiles.* Pittsburgh: National Center for Juvenile Justice.

Griffin, P. (2006). "National Overviews." *State Juvenile Justice Profiles.* Pittsburg: National Center for Juvenile Justice.

Griffin, P., P. Torbet & L. Szymanski (1998). *Trying Juveniles as Adults in Criminal Court: An Analysis of State Transfer Provisions.* Washington, DC: U.S. Department of Justice.

Hagedorn, J.M. (1988). *People and Folks: Gangs, Crime, and the Underclass in a Rustbelt City.* Chicago: Lake View Pres).

Hindelang, M.J. (1971). "The Social versus Solitary Nature of Delinquent Involvement." *British Journal of Criminology* 11:167-175.

Hindelang, M.J., T. Hirschi & J.G. Weis (1981). *Measuring Delinquency.* Beverly Hills, CA: Sage.

Horowitz, R. (1983). *Honor and the American Dream.* New Brunswick, NJ: Rutgers University Press.

Horowitz, R. (2000). "Kids Who Kill: A Critique of How the American Legal System Deals with Juveniles who Commit Homicide." *Law and Contemporary Problems* 63:133-177.

Huff, C.R. (1993). "Gangs in the United States." In A.P. Goldstein and C.R. Huff (eds.), *The Gang Intervention Handbook* (pp. 3-20). Champaign, IL: Research Press.

Institute of Judicial Administration–American Bar Association (1980). *Juvenile Justice Standards: Standards Relating to Adjudication.* Cambridge, MA: Ballinger.

Jankowski, M.S. (1991). *Islands in the Street: Gangs and American Urban Society.* Berkeley, CA: University of California Press.

Joe, D. & N. Robinson (1980). "Chinatown's Immigrant Gangs: The New Young Warrior Class." *Criminology* 18:337-345.

Jones, J.B. (2004). *Access to Counsel.* Washington, DC: U.S. Department of Justice.

Kerbs, J.J. (1999). "(Un)equal Justice: Juvenile Court Abolition and African Americans." *Annals of the American Academy of Political and Social Sciences* 564:109-125.

King, M. & L. Szymanski (2006). "National Overviews." State Juvenile Justice Profiles. Pittsburgh: National Center for Juvenile Justice. Found at: http://www.ncjj.org/stateprofiles/

Klein, M.W. (1971). *Street Gangs and Street Workers.* Englewood Cliffs, NJ: Prentice Hall.

Klein, M.W., C.L. Maxson & L.C. Cunningham (1991). "'Crack,' Street Gangs, and Violence." *Criminology* 29:623-649.

Knox, G.W. (1991). *An Introduction to Gangs.* Berrien Springs, MI: Vande Vere.

Kurlychek, M.C. & B.D. Johnson (2004). "The Juvenile Penalty: A Comparison and Young Adult Sentencing Outcomes in Criminal Court." *Criminology* 42:485-515.

Lab, S.P. (1984). "Patterns in Juvenile Misbehavior." *Crime & Delinquency* 30:293-308.

Lipsey, M.W., D.B. Wilson & L. Cothern (2000). *Effective Intervention for Serious Juvenile Offenders.* Washington, DC: U.S. Department of Justice.

Mahoney, A.R. (1985). "Jury Trial for Juveniles: Right or Ritual?" *Justice Quarterly* 2:553-565.

Mahoney, A.R. (1987). *Juvenile Justice in Context.* Boston: Northeastern University Press.

McCarthy, B.R. (1987). "Preventive Detention and Pretrial Custody in the Juvenile Court." *Journal of Criminal Justice* 15:185-200.

Miller, W.B. (1958). "Lower Class Culture as a Generating Milieu of Gang Delinquency." *Journal of Social Issues* 15:5-19.

Miller, W.B. (1966). "Violent Crime in City Gangs." *Annals* 343:97-112.

Miller, W.B. (1975). *Violence by Youth Gangs and Youth Groups as a Crime Problem in Major American Cities.* Washington, DC: National Institute for Juvenile Justice and Delinquency Prevention.

Miller, W.B. (1980). "Gangs, Groups and Serious Youth Crime." In D. Shichor & D.H. Kelly (eds.), *Critical Issues in Juvenile Delinquency* (pp. 115-138). Lexington, MA: Lexington Books.

Miller, W.B. (1990). "Why the United States has Failed to Solve Its Youth Gang Problem." In C.R. Huff (ed.), *Gangs in America.* Newbury Park, CA: Sage.

Miller, W.B., H. Gertz & H.S.G. Cutter (1961). "Aggression in a Boys' Street-corner Group." *Psychiatry* 24:283-298.

Moore, J. (1991). *Going Down to the Barrio: Homeboys and Homegirls in Change.* Philadelphia: Temple University Press.

Morales, A. (1992). "A Clinical Model for the Prevention of Gang Violence and Homicide." In R.C. Cervantes (ed.), *Substance Abuse and Gang Violence* (pp. 105-118). Newbury Park, CA: Sage.

National Youth Gang Center (2000). *1998 National Youth Gang Survey: Summary.* Washington, DC: Office of Juvenile Justice and Delinquency Prevention.

Noriega, C. (2000). "Stick a Fork in It: Is Juvenile Justice Done?" *New York Law School Journal of Human Rights* 16:669-698.

Office of Juvenile Justice and Delinquency Prevention (1995). *Juvenile Offenders and Victims: A National Report.* Washington, DC: U.S. Department of Justice.

Office of Juvenile Justice and Delinquency Prevention (1999). *Promising Strategies to Reduce Gun Violence.* Washington, DC: Office of Juvenile Justice and Delinquency Prevention.

Office of Juvenile Justice and Delinquency Prevention (2002). *OJJDP Statistical Briefing Book* [Online]. Found at: http://ojjdp.ncjrs.org/ojstatbb/html/qa088.html, accessed April 25, 2002.

Ohio Revised Code Annotated (2005). Anderson Online Docs. (Cincinnati: Anderson). Found at: http://onlinedocs.andersonpublishing.com

Platt, A.M. (1977). *The Child Savers: The Invention of Delinquency.* Chicago: University of Chicago Press.

Prescott, P.S. (1981). *The Child Savers: Juvenile Justice Observed.* New York: Alfred A. Knopf.

Puritz, P., S. Burrell, R. Schwartz, M. Soler & L. Warboys (1995). *A Call for Justice: An Assessment of Access to Counsel and Quality of Representation in Delinquency Proceedings.* Washington, DC: American Bar Association Juvenile Justice Center.

Puzzanchera, C., A.L. Stahl, T.A. Finnegan, N. Tierney & H.N. Snyder (2004). *Juvenile Court Statistics 2000.* Pittsburgh: National Center for Juvenile Justice.

Rainville, G.A. & S.K. Smith (2003). *Juvenile Felony Defendants in Criminal Courts: Survey of 40 Counties, 1998.* Washington, DC: U.S. Department of Justice.

Rojek, D.G. & M.L. Erickson (1982). "Delinquent Careers: A Test of the Career Escalation Model." *Criminology* 20:5-28.

Rossum, R.A., B.J. Koller & C.P. Manfredi (1987). *Juvenile Justice Reform: A Model for the States.* Claremont, CA: Rose Institute of State and Local Government and the American Legislative Exchange Council.

Rothman, D. (1980). *Conscience and Convenience.* Boston: Little, Brown.

Sanders, W.B. (1994). *Gangbangs and Drive-bys: Grounded Culture and Juvenile Gang Violence.* New York: Aldine de Gruyter.

Schneider, A.L. (1985). *The Impact of Deinstitutionalization on Recidivism and Secure Confinement of Status Offenders.* Washington, DC: U.S. Department of Justice.

Seis, M.C. & K.L. Elbe (1991). "The Death Penalty for Juveniles: Bridging the Gap between an Evolving Standard of Decency and Legislative Policy." *Justice Quarterly* 8:465-487.

Shannon, L.W. (1982). *Assessing the Relationship of Adult Criminal Careers to Juvenile Careers.* Iowa City: Iowa Urban Community Research Center, University of Iowa.

Sheppard, D., H. Grant, W. Rowe & N. Jacobs (2000). *Fighting Juvenile Gun Violence.* OJJDP Juvenile Justice Bulletin. Washington, DC: Office of Juvenile Justice and Delinquency Prevention.

Short, J.F. & I. Nye (1958). "Extent of Unrecorded Delinquency: Tentative Conclusions." *Journal of Criminal Law, Criminology and Police Science* 49:296-302.

Sickmund, M. & P.J. Baunach (1986). *Children in Custody: Public Juvenile Facilities, 1985.* Bureau of Justice Statistics Bulletin. Washington, DC: U.S. Department of Justice.

Sickmund, M., T.J. Sladky & W. Kang (2004) "Census of Juveniles in Residential Placement Databook." Found at: http://www.ojjdp.ncjrs.org/ojstatbb/cjrp

Snell, T.L. (2000). *Capital Punishment 2000.* Washington, DC: U.S. Department of Justice.

Snyder, H.N. (1997). *Juvenile Arrests 1996.* OJJDP Juvenile Justice Bulletin. Washington, DC: U.S. Department of Justice.

Snyder, H.N. (2000) *Juvenile Arrests 1999.* OJJDP Juvenile Justice Bulletin. Washington, DC: Office of Juvenile Justice and Delinquency Prevention.

Snyder, H.N. (2002). *Juvenile Arrests 2000.* OJJDP Juvenile Justice Bulletin. Washington, DC: U.S. Department of Justice.

Snyder, H.N. (2005). *Juvenile Arrests 2004.* OJJDP Juvenile Justice Bulletin. Washington, DC: U.S. Department of Justice.

Synder, H.N. & M. Sickmund (1999). *Juvenile Offenders and Victims: 1999 National Report.* Washington, DC: Office of Juvenile Justice and Delinquency Prevention.

Spergel, I.A. & G.D. Curry (1993). "Strategies and Perceived Agency Effectiveness in Dealing with Youth Gang Problems." In C.R. Huff (ed.), *Gangs in America.* Newbury Park, CA: Sage.

Stahl, A.L. (2000). *Delinquency Cases in Juvenile Courts, 1997.* Washington, DC: U.S. Department of Justice..

Stahl, A.L. (2001). *Drug Offense Cases in Juvenile Courts, 1989-1998.* OJJDP Fact Sheet (September #36). Washington, DC: U.S. Department of Justice.

Stahl, A., T. Finnegan & W. Kang (2007). *Easy Access to Juvenile Court Statistics: 1985-2004* [data analysis and presentation package]. Pittsburgh: National Center for Juvenile Justice [producer]. Washington, DC: Office of Juvenile Justice and Delinquency Prevention [distributor], 2007. Found at: ojjdp.ncjrs.gov/ojstatbb/ezajcs/

Szymanski, L.A. (2002). *Juvenile Delinquents' Right to a Jury Trial.* NCJJ Snapshot 7(9). Pittsburgh: National Center for Juvenile Justice.

Taylor, C.S. (1990). "Gang Imperialism." In C.R. Huff (ed.), *Gangs in America.* Newbury Park, CA: Sage.

Thrasher, F.M. (1936). *The Gang.* Chicago: University of Chicago Press.

Torbet, P., P. Griffin, H. Hurst Jr. & L.R. MacKenzie (2000). *Juveniles Facing Criminal Sanctions: Three States That Changed the Rules.* Washington, DC: Office of Juvenile Justice and Delinquency Prevention.

Toy, C. (1992). "A Short History of Asian Gangs in San Francisco." *Justice Quarterly* 9:647-666.

U.S. Bureau of Census (1992). *1990 Census of Population: General Population Characteristics: United States.* Washington, DC: U.S. Department of Commerce.

van den Haag, E. & P. Conrad (1983). *The Death Penalty: A Debate.* New York: Plenum.

Vandervort, F.E. & W.E. Ladd (2001). "The Worst of All Possible Worlds: Michigan's Juvenile Justice System and International Standards for the Treatment of Children." *University of Detroit Mercy Law Review* 78:202-258.

Vigil, J.D. (1993). "The Established Gang." In S. Cummings & D.J. Monti (eds.), *Gangs: The Origins and Impact of Contemporary Youth Gangs in the United States* (pp. 95-112). Albany, NY: SUNY Press.

Vigil, J.D. (1997). "Learning from Gangs: The Mexican American Experience." *ERIC Digest* (Feb.)

Winner, L., L. Lanza-Kaduce, D.M. Bishop & C.E. Frazier (1997). "The Transfer of Juveniles to Criminal Court: Re-examining Recidivism over the Long Term." *Crime & Delinquency* 43:548-563.

Zatz, M.S. (1985). "Los Cholos: Legal Processing of Chicano Gang Members." *Social Problems* 33:13-30.

Zimring, F.E. (2000). "Penal Proportionality for the Young Offender: Notes on Immaturity, Capacity, and Diminished Responsibility." In T. Grisso & R.G. Schwartz (eds.), *Youth on Trial: A Developmental Perspective on Juvenile Justice* (pp. 271-289). Chicago: University of Chicago Press.

Important Cases

Breed v. Jones, 421 U.S. 519 (1975).

Commonwealth v. Fisher, 213 Pa. 48 (1905).

Ex parte Crouse, 4 Wheaton (Pa.) 9 (1838).

Fare v. Michael C., 442 U.S. 707 (1979).

In re Gault, 387 U.S. 1 (1967).

In re Winship, 397 U.S. 358 (1970).

Kent v. United States, 383 U.S. 541 (1966).

McKeiver v. Pennsylvania, 403 U.S. 528 (1971).

Roper v. Simmons, 543 U.S. 551 (2005).

Schall v. Martin, 467 U.S. 253 (1984).

Stanford v. Kentucky, 492 U.S. 361 (1989).

Chapter 15

Discharge and Developments

In 2005, approximately 2.8 million persons were released from some form of prison, probation, or parole supervision (Glaze & Bonczar, 2006; Sabol, Minton & Harrison, 2007). The great bulk of these people were released or discharged from probation supervision. More than 100,000 prison inmates were discharged from incarceration at the end of their terms, and more than 500,000 parolees were released or discharged from supervision. Fewer than 1 percent of the correctional population died while under sentence, and life sentences are imposed on less than 1 percent of those convicted of felonies (Durose & Langan, 2007). In 1987, Burton, Cullen, and Travis estimated that more than 14 million convicted felons lived in the population at large. In the 20 years since then, it is almost certain that the number of felons in the population has increased. More than 5 percent of all Americans are expected to serve a prison sentence some time in their lives, and only about one-half of all felons go to prison, so as much as 10 percent of the adult population may become ex-offenders.

This chapter examines what happens to those people who progress through the justice system to the point of discharge from custody, or to where the justice system stops. In doing so, we see that, for many released offenders, the effects of justice system processing do not stop, but start anew. We will also examine changes in the criminal justice system that can be anticipated, or that seem to be beginning now.

Discharge

The last major point in the criminal justice process is the discharge of offenders. In many cases, discharge is not actually a decision point, but rather an event that occurs at a point in time. For example, if you were convicted of theft and sentenced to five years in prison on January 1, 2008, the sentence would expire at midnight on December 31, 2013. You would have to be discharged from custody at that point, as there would no longer be a legal justification for custody. In many states, however, discharge itself is a decision.

Traditionally, a convicted offender was considered to be under the custody of the justice system until his or her sentence had expired. With the imposition of relatively long sentences, this meant that a person sentenced to a life term could be in custody for his or her entire lifetime. Most states developed mechanisms for limiting the period of custody, and empowered the parole authority to grant a discharge from sentence after a period of successful parole supervision. As a

| Box 15.1 | Estimated Time to be Served in Prison by Most Serious Conviction Offense, 2002 |

Most Serious Conviction offense	Time to be served in prison, estimated		
	Mean Prison sentence	Percent of sentence	Time
All offenses	53 mo.	51%	27 mo.
Violent offenses	82 mo.	62%	52 mo.
Murder	225	63	142
Sexual Assault	100	64	64
Rape	132	68	90
Other Sex Assault	84	62	52
Robbery	91	58	53
Aggravated Assault	54	66	36
Other violent	51	61	31
Property offenses	41 mo.	49%	20 mo.
Burglary	50	49	24
Larceny	34	52	18
Motor Vehicle Theft	30	49	15
Fraud	38	44	17
Drug offenses	48 mo.	43%	20 mo.
Possession	35	40	14
Trafficking	55	45	24
Weapon offenses	38 mo.	63%	24 mo.
Other offenses	38 mo.	50%	19 mo.

Source: M. Durose & P. Langan (2004), *Felony Sentences in State Courts, 2002* (Washington, DC: Bureau of Justice Statistics):5.

Box 15.2 — Time Served in Prison Prior to First Release by Type of Offense and Type of Release

Type of release and offense	1990 Mean sentence length[a]	1990 Mean total time served[b]	1990 Percent of sentence served[c]	1999 Mean sentence length[a]	1999 Mean total time served[b]	1999 Percent of sentence served[c]
Discretionary release	82 mo.	29 mo.	34%	89 mo.	35 mo.	37%
Violent	118	49	40	126	59	44
Property	77	25	31	83	31	34
Drug	70	20	29	80	28	33
Public-order	44	18	37	49	21	39
Mandatory release	42 mo.	27 mo.	55%	48 mo.	33 mo.	61%
Violent	54	41	59	66	47	63
Property	38	23	52	43	30	59
Drug	33	20	50	40	27	59
Public-order	27	19	61	38	25	61
Expiration of sentence	56 mo.	31 mo.	53%	49 mo.	36 mo.	67%
Violent	81	44	53	69	52	68
Property	50	27	52	41	30	65
Drug	35	21	57	41	29	65
Public-order	43	28	62	35	25	66

Note: Based on prisoners with a sentence of more than 1 year. Excludes persons released from prison by escape, death, transfer, appeal, or detainer.

[a]Excludes sentences of life without parole, life plus additional years, life and death.

[b]Includes time served in prison and jail.

[c]Based on total sentence length (not shown) for all consecutive sentences.

Source: T. Hughes, D. Wilson & J. Beck (2001), *Trends in State Parole, 1990-2000.* (Washington, DC: Bureau of Justice Statistics).

pragmatic alternative, many parole authorities created a custody class of unsupervised parole, in which the offender was no longer required to report to a parole officer and was no longer subjected to supervision. Unsupervised parole allowed an offender to "serve" a sentence until discharge without actually being restricted. Further, many states have specifically empowered correctional officials to grant final releases or discharges from sentence. Box 15.1 describes the distribution of expected time served in prison for felons sentenced in the year 2002. Time served in prison prior to release on parole has increased, and the rate of parole release from prison has decreased. Felons sentenced to state prisons in 2002 were expected to serve an average of 27 months before gaining release from prison. As we entered the twenty-first century, prisoners were serving a greater percentage of their total sentence in prison than had previously been the case. It is likely that today's prisoners will have spent more time in prison and less time under parole supervision before being discharged. Box 15.2 compares time served prior to release by offenders sentenced for different types of crimes and type of release.

Some states allow offenders to apply for **executive clemency**, or mercy. That is, a convict could ask the governor for a commutation or pardon. If the request was granted, the prisoner would receive a discharge from sentence. Someone serving a 20-year term, for example, might be imprisoned for two years, serve an additional two years under parole supervision, and still "owe" 16 years on the sentence. That offender could ask the governor to commute the sentence to four years and receive a discharge, or the offender could be pardoned for the offense.

Regardless of the method, the fact remains that, at some point, most offenders will be discharged from sentence. At the point of discharge, whether by a discretionary decision made by a justice system official, or at the expiration of sentence, the offender is free from direct intervention by the criminal justice system. The effects of conviction, however, will linger.

Collateral Consequences of Conviction

Once convicted of a criminal offense, an individual experiences several negative effects. The sentence imposed for crime is a direct consequence of conviction, and is intentionally painful. Other effects that result from conviction are called **collateral consequences**. In many ways, these effects can be more disturbing and painful than the imposed sentence. Box 15.3 identifies some of the collateral consequences of a felony conviction.

There is a stigma that attaches to a person who has been convicted of a crime. The label of "ex-con" is difficult to overcome. If you were hiring people to work for a company, and had two equally qualified candidates, one of whom was an ex-con, which applicant would you hire? At a party, how would you react when meeting someone who was an ex-con? The fact that we can discuss a set of people simply by using the label "ex-con" illustrates the point of stigma. The fact of a prior conviction is meaningful to us in our dealings with ex-cons. Robert Homant and Daniel Kennedy (1982) assessed the stigma of ex-cons relative to that of ex-mental patients, obese people, and neutral or nonstigmatized people. They found that there was little difference in how the four groups were treated by their subjects. Earlier research, however, has shown that ex-offenders do suffer the stigma associated with their convictions (Reed, 1979; Schwartz & Skolnick, 1962).

In addition to the stigma of having a criminal record, other collateral consequences attend criminal conviction. Some avenues of employment are closed to offenders (Finn & Fontaine, 1985). Many jobs in our society require that the employee be bonded (insured), and ex-offenders normally are not considered good risks by bonding companies. Thus, an ex-offender may even have difficulty obtaining employment as a cashier in a convenience store. Other occupational groups, such as barbers, beauticians, teachers, physicians, nurses, and attorneys, require licensure. In many cases, a felony conviction is a bar to licensure (Davidenas, 1983).

Assuming the offender served a prison term, he or she may have a particularly difficult time in securing credit or employment because of the incarceration. How

Box 15.3   Collateral Consequences of Felony Convictions in American Jurisdictions

RESTRICTIONS OF FELONY OFFENDERS' CIVIL RIGHTS
Restrictive vs. Less Restrictive, by Right & Jurisdiction

Jurisdiction	Voting *Permanently Lost vs. Restorable*	Parental *Yes vs. No*	Divorce *Yes vs. No*	Public Employment *Permanently Lost vs. Restorable*	Juror *Permanently Lost vs. Restorable*	Holding Office *Permanently Lost vs. Restorable*	Firearm *"Violent" Felony vs. "Any" Felony*	Criminal Registration *Yes vs. No*	Civil Death *Yes vs. No*
Alabama	X	X	X	X	X	X		X	
Alaska		X			X		X		
Arizona		X					X	X	
Arkansas	X		X		X	X	X		
California		X			X	X¹	X	X	
Colorado		X							
Connecticut			X				X		
Delaware				X	X	X	X		
D.C.			X		X	X¹	X		
Florida	X				X	X	X	X	
Georgia			X		X	X	X		
Hawaii					X		X		
Idaho			X		X				X
Illinois			X				X		
Indiana		X	X		X		X		
Iowa	X			X	X	X	X		
Kansas		X					X		
Kentucky	X				X	X	X		
Louisiana			X						
Maine						X¹			
Maryland			X		X				
Massachusetts		X				X¹	X		
Michigan		X					X		
Minnesota			X						
Mississippi	X	X	X	X		X	X	X	X
Missouri					X				
Montana					X		X		
Nebraska					X		X		
Nevada	X	X			X	X	X	X	
New Hampshire			X				X		
New Jersey			X		X	X			
New Mexico	X				X	X	X		
New York			X		X	X	X		X
North Carolina									
North Dakota			X						
Ohio			X		X	X			
Oklahoma			X		X		X		
Oregon		X					X		
Pennsylvania			X		X		X		
Rhode Island	X	X	X	X	X	X			X
South Carolina				X	X	X			
South Dakota		X	X						
Tennessee	X	X	X		X	X		X	
Texas			X		X	X	X		
Utah			X		X			X	
Vermont			X						
Virginia	X		X		X	X			
Washington									
West Virginia			X				X		
Wisconsin		X				X	X		
Wyoming		X			X				

X = right is restricted or jeopardized   1 = right is restricted for specific offenses

---

Source: V.S. Burton, F.T. Cullen & L.F. Travis III (1987), "The Collateral Consequences of a Felony Conviction: A National Survey of State Statutes," *Federal Probation* 51(3):55.

does an ex-inmate answer questions about where he or she was employed for the past two years, or about where he or she resided? (One of the author's students, an ex-convict, routinely answered such questions by saying that he had "worked for the state" for the past seven years.) Kurlychek, Brame, and Bushway (2006) report that employers are more frequently conducting criminal history checks of employees and applicants. In some cases, state laws require employers to check the criminal history of workers. They found that in most cases there was little difference between employees with and without prior arrest records, and that in some cases "good" employees were dismissed when a previous arrest was found. The impact of a prior conviction on employment prospects continues to be negative.

As if the natural consequences of conviction were not severe enough, most states impose specific limitations on the rights of those convicted of felonies. These limitations are added to whatever sentence may be ordered (Buckler & Travis, 2003; Burton, Cullen & Travis, 1987; Vile, 1981). Only two states, North Carolina and Washington, do not routinely restrict a convicted offender's rights. Two states, Idaho and New York, have provisions allowing certain offenders (generally, those receiving life sentences) to be declared civilly dead (Rottman & Strickland, 2006). **Civil death** means that as far as civil rights (contracting, marriage, voting, etc.) are concerned, the offender is "dead." Most states restrict some civil rights for at least as long as the offender is serving his or her sentence. In many jurisdictions, conviction of a felony carries the permanent loss of some civil rights. All states now require the registration of at least some sex offenders and more than half the states restrict parental rights for those convicted of specified crimes. Given the collateral consequences of conviction, for many offenders, criminal justice processing never ends.

Restoration of Rights

Most states today have provisions for the restoration of all, or most, of the civil rights that are lost upon conviction of a felony. For example, Rottman and Strickland (2006:260-262) reported that all 50 states and the District of Columbia impose some restrictions on public employment, but the right is restorable in two-thirds of those jurisdictions. In many states, such as Ohio, the parole authority is empowered to grant a full restoration of rights upon discharge from parole supervision and sentence. In other places, such as California, the ex-convict may apply for a restoration of rights after certain conditions are met (Allen & Simonsen, 1986). The California provisions require that the offender petition the court for a pardon. To qualify for the pardon, the ex-offender must have led a crime-free life for 10 years after final release from parole. The court then conducts a formal hearing, at which it receives opinions from the district attorney and law enforcement officials. The probation department investigates the petitioner and reports to the court. If all of the evidence is favorable, the court approves the application and forwards it to the governor. The governor instructs the parole authority to investigate and then to recommend a pardon decision. In the end, based on this recommendation from the parole authority, the governor decides whether to grant the pardon.

Other states have less-involved restoration processes, but most processes generally include a petition by the ex-offender and a subsequent investigation. These states also require some period of good behavior after discharge from sentence (usually five or 10 years). While the ex-convict may eventually be restored to full citizenship, the effect of the conviction will last through the sentence and for many years afterward. Many states provide for the automatic restoration of rights, at least for first offenders (Burton, Travis & Cullen, 1988).

Burton, Cullen, and Travis (1987) suggested that there is a movement afoot for states to become less restrictive of the rights of convicted offenders. With the exception of parental rights and the right to possess firearms, most of the restrictions on civil rights that traditionally were imposed by states have been relaxed. The commentators contended that this reduction in restrictiveness represents an extension of the "due process movement," in which courts are more likely to require the state to provide reasons for restrictions. They also summarized the arguments in favor of, and in opposition to, the restriction of civil rights. In contrast, Buckler and Travis (2003) identified a shift in the application of collateral consequences that they identified as being the product of increased concerns for public safety. The development and spread of offender registration requirements, limits on access to children, and other such restrictions are consistent with an emphasis on crime prevention and public safety.

Those opposed to the imposition of collateral consequences of felony conviction argue that restrictions may be counterproductive. Adding to penalties by limiting rights may cause ex-offenders to become bitter toward society in general and the justice system in particular. Especially in regard to employment rights, restrictions may be harmful. They limit an ex-offender's ability to lead a law-abiding life by closing opportunities for socially accepted means of earning a living. In addition, many restrictions on civil rights, such as restrictions on the voting rights of someone with a prior conviction for theft, are unrelated to the offender's

Former University of Kentucky basketball player Tanya Fogle goes over an application for the restoration of her civil rights with Kentucky Governor Ernie Fletcher's general counsel in July 2006. Fogle, who served prison time after a felony drug conviction, supports a bill that would allow citizens to vote on whether to change the state Constitution to allow felons of nonviolent crimes to vote as soon as they complete their sentence. *Photo credit: AP Photo/Ed Reinke.*

crime. Finally, there are those who argue that the imposition of additional restrictions after the sentence has been served means that the offender can never pay his or her debt to society.

Those favoring the restriction of civil rights for people convicted of criminal offenses argue that such restrictions serve several purposes. First, rights are balanced by duties and, by failing to meet the duty of obeying the law, offenders have lost the privilege of exercising their rights (Vile, 1981). Others suggest that a "principle of least eligibility" applies, in that ex-offenders are least eligible of all citizens to be protected in their rights to vote, work, and so on (Simon, 1993:265-266). Others suggest that the fact of conviction evidences unacceptable character flaws, so that restricting offenders from holding public office, serving on juries, and voting actually protects law-abiding citizens from possible election fraud and malfeasance in office by ex-offenders. Other restrictions on rights are justified by proponents as pragmatic concessions. In many states, incarceration is grounds for divorce; it is justified by the argument that it is not fair to require the spouse to stand by an absent mate. Loss of parental rights has been justified because a felony conviction is said to represent proof of being an unfit parent. Finally, civil death has been justified to enable family members to dispose of the convicted offender's debts and property.

Recidivism

Ex-convict Malcolm Braly (1977) wrote an autobiography, aptly titled *False Starts*, in which he recalled 20 years of criminal justice experience, during which he spent time in and out of reform school and prison. His first incarceration was in a reform school before he had turned 18. Describing his years as an offender, Braly remembered his "false starts" at living a conventional, law-abiding life. Through four releases from custody, three of which became failed paroles, Braly learned how to live in the free world, and finally was successfully settled after his fifth release, at age 40.

As a "business," the criminal justice system is not supposed to encourage repeat "customers." If the system operated at peak effectiveness, anyone that committed a crime most assuredly would not commit a second offense. Unfortunately, the data indicate that the justice system produces many "customers" who return again and again. These repeat offenders are called recidivists.

Defining Recidivism

Perhaps no other concept in criminal justice has been as fully studied and debated as has recidivism. Recidivism is hard to define, but generally means a return to crime or other trouble with the criminal justice system. In fact, the notion of recidivism is so controversial that contemporary writers tend to use other labels for it, such as "failure" or "return." At base, recidivism means repetition of crime. The term is confusing because it is not exactly clear what "repetition" should include. For example, if a convicted robber is released from custody and commits a theft, has the offender repeated? If the offender is arrested, but not convicted, is it recidivism? If the offender's parole is revoked for failing to report to the supervising officer, is the offender a recidivist? On the surface, these seem to be technical distinctions, but they can be very important.

Whatever definition one adopts for "recidivism," the concept is crucial to evaluations of the effectiveness of criminal justice processing. Gottfredson, Mitchell-Herzfeld, and Flanagan (1982) suggested that the definition employed has an effect on the level of recidivism that will be detected. For example, if technical violations of probation or parole rules are counted as recidivism, the rate of return to crime will be higher. Counting arrests yields higher recidivism rates than counting only convictions. Counting only returns to prison as repeat offenses leads to still lower rates of recidivism, and counting only repeated convictions for the same crime yields the lowest rates of all.

Flanagan (1985) argued that time is yet another important component of the definition of recidivism. The longer the period over which offenders are tracked, the higher the total level of recidivism. Hoffman and Stone-Meierhoefer (1979) indicated that, for federal parolees at least, rates of return remain relatively stable for up to three years after release. This finding means that, if recidivism is measured for only one year, the rate of return might be 20 percent. Extending the time frame to three years might yield a total return rate of 48 percent. As Box 15.4 indicates, it is important to measure not only the total number of returns to prison but the percentage of failure of the "at-risk" population for each year. While most offenders who return may fail in the first year or two, the rate of return of those at risk may not change for three or more years.

Box 15.4	Rate of Return to Prison as Percentages of the "At-Risk" Population

At-Risk Population	Returns	% of Those at Risk	Cumulative % Returned
1,000	200	20%	20.0%
800	160	20%	36.0%
640	128	20%	48.8%
512	51	10%	53.9%

From this example, the rate of return to prison for those at risk remains stable at 20 percent for three years and then decreases. While most of those who return to prison do so within two years (360 of the 480 total returned), the rate of return for the population at risk remains the same (20%) for the third year as well.

Recidivism and Criminal Justice Policy

One problem with recidivism is that it is very difficult to measure. Knowledge of the effectiveness of correctional programs and judicial sentencing decisions based on the rate of return to crime can help us to design crime control policies. The fact that recidivism depends so heavily on what is counted, and for how long, means that we must be especially careful in interpreting and using recidivism statistics as the basis for policy decisions (Hoffman & Stone-Meierhoffer, 1980).

The RAND study of probation supervision effectiveness (discussed in Chapter 13) illustrates this point. Without sufficient care in interpreting the results of that study, a wise policy decision might be to ban felons from receiving probation. After all, Petersilia, Turner, and Peterson (1986) reported that nearly two-thirds (65%) of their sample were arrested for new offenses. However, only about one-third (34%) were sentenced to jail or prison terms, and less than one-fifth (19%) of the probation sample were sentenced to new prison terms. As a policymaker, what does this information tell you about the use of probation for felons?

Unfortunately, it tells us little. Paradoxically, it also tells us much. Ultimately, the decision about using probation supervision with convicted felons will depend upon this and other information, and upon the attitudes of the policymakers themselves. If they count new prison terms as recidivism, 80 percent of felony probationers will be successes, and probation will be considered a useful disposition for felons. If the policymakers count arrests as failures, 65 percent of felony probationers will fail, and probation may not be considered an appropriate disposition for felons. What is important is that in order to make an informed judgment, the decisionmakers need to know not only the statistics (65% or 19% "failures"), but also what the statistics mean.

In a study of correctional boot camp graduates, Benda, Toombs, and Peacock (2003) reported that within five years, more than 60 percent had recidivated. They identified three distinct categories of recidivism: felony, technical violation, and drug offense. If only new felons are counted, then nearly 60 percent of graduates "succeed." Just as importantly, they found that different factors were associated with different types of recidivism. This suggests that criminal justice officials might need to target different aspects of the lives of offenders to reduce different types of recidivism. Lumping all the ways in which offenders may "fail" into a single category of recidivism may actually make it more difficult to intervene successfully in the lives of offenders.

William Sabol and his colleagues (2000) studied returns to federal prison by inmates released between 1986 and 1994. They had no information on how many inmates might have been incarcerated in state prisons, but fewer than 20 percent of those released returned to federal prison within three years. Not surprisingly, the bulk of those returned to prison came back in the first year after release. Sabol and associates also found that the rate of return was higher for those who had served longer terms in prison. It may be that long-term incarceration makes reentry more difficult, but it may also be that those who pose the greatest risk or who are the "worst" offenders serve the longest terms.

A study of parolee recidivism (Beck & Shipley, 1987) reported that nearly 70 percent of a group of young parolees released in 1978 had been rearrested for a serious crime within six years. Based on this finding and a similar recidivism rate for the probationers in the RAND study in California, it appears likely that most offenders will again be subjected to criminal justice processing. Yet, other research indicates that the criminal justice system can have a positive effect on the lives of offenders

(Sechrest, White & Brown, 1979). There is some evidence to suggest, as may have been the case with Malcolm Braly, that some offenders simply mature and grow out of crime as they get older (Hoffman & Beck, 1984). For many (between one-third and one-half of all convicted offenders), discharge means the start of a law-abiding life. Still, for many others, the end of the justice system represents a continuation in their lives of crime, which eventually leads them back into the justice system.

A study of prison inmates released in 1994 revealed that more than two-thirds were rearrested within three years of release, almost one-half were convicted of a new crime, and more than one-quarter were returned to prison with a new sentence (Langan & Levin, 2002). Nearly one-half of all those rearrested within three years were arrested within six months of release, and about two-thirds of those rearrested in the three-year period had already been arrested by the end of the first year. Most of those who "failed" did so in the first year, but the "failure rates" for the at-risk population (offenders who had not yet been rearrested) remained relatively high (more than 20%) for the next two years.

Developments in Criminal Justice

Bennett (1987) coined the phrase "crime-warps" to describe what she saw as changes in the future of criminal justice in the United States. Crime-warps referred to the alterations that she expected to occur in our definitions of—and our responses to—crime. She anticipated that the form, if not the substance, of crime will take on new shapes in the future. Consequently, the justice system will need to adapt to these new developments as well. Bennett identified several crime-warps, ranging from new types of criminals to changes in the balance between the protection of individual liberties and the requirements of social defense. She predicted there would be increasing emphasis on white-collar and computer crimes. According to Bennett, many "victimless" crimes, such as prostitution, homosexuality, gambling, and drug use, would be legalized, while other offenses, such as manufacturing and distributing pornography, will be subjected to greater restrictions. She anticipated greater technological development in criminal justice, an enhanced role for private enterprise, and a reduction in privacy. According to her predictions, civil liberties will be increasingly threatened as citizens are subjected to increasing surveillance by both their neighbors and justice officials.

It is always risky to predict the future. As we have seen, criminal justice practices and policies are the products of a complex set of forces. Ideological shifts, economic changes, demographic variations, organizational goals, and the attitudes of individual agents and offenders all affect criminal justice decisionmaking. Attempting to predict how these factors will change and develop, and how they will interact to produce different decisions and patterns of criminal justice practice, is hazardous and error-prone. Consider, for example, Bennett's prediction that drug use would be legalized in light of recent and continuing "wars on drugs." Nonetheless, it is incumbent upon us to attempt to foresee the future so that we can try to shape it.

In an effort to discern the future of criminal justice in the United States, we shall examine three trends and project possible futures. In doing so, our attention must be drawn to the forces that gave rise to the trends, as well as to the powerful forces opposing any real change in the operation of the criminal justice system. Hedging our bets, we shall call these trends "possibilities." It should be remembered, of course, that it is likely that nothing much will change in the foreseeable future. The possibilities that we shall examine are increased federalism, private justice, and technological justice.

Increased Federalism

We have described the American criminal justice system as fragmented, with multiple sets of crime control apparatus operating in thousands of counties and/ or cities across the country. Traditionally, criminal justice and crime control policy have been local issues. America has not had a single national criminal justice system comprised of federal laws, police, courts, and corrections. Rather, each state has its own criminal code, and most municipalities have their own police and courts. Over the past 50 years, however, the federal role in criminal justice has expanded greatly. In the late 1960s, the United States Congress passed the Omnibus Crime Control and Safe Streets Act, creating a federal bureaucracy that influenced local justice policy and practice through the provision of federal aid. As Charles Friel (2000:2) put it, "Beginning with this Act and the Federal funds that then flowed to State and local criminal justice agencies, the Federal Government would become a major player in local crime control and justice policy . . . On top of the long litany of decisions by the Federal courts that have tempered almost every area of the justice system in the past 40 years, we now question whether there is too much federal involvement. Some argue for more, while others demand less."

During the last 45 years or so, the federal government has provided funding, training, and technical support to local criminal justice agencies on a variety of topics. The debate over the role of the federal government in local justice policy hinges on a disagreement about the motive for, and impact of, this assistance. Those who believe the federal government is exerting too much influence over local policy contend that this aid acts as an inducement, or bribe, to states and local criminal justice agencies. Accepting federal support requires accepting any "strings" attached to the support. In essence, the federal government is paying local criminal justice agencies to change their policies and practices.

For example, in 1998, the Office of Juvenile Justice and Delinquency Prevention began funding what was called the Juvenile Accountability Incentive Block Grants (JAIBG) Program. The program provides funding and other support to local juvenile justice systems that agree to implement "accountability" efforts. "Holding a juvenile offender 'accountable' in the juvenile justice system means that once the juvenile is determined to have committed law-violating behavior, by admission or adjudication, he or she is held responsible for the act through consequences of sanctions, imposed pursuant to law, that are proportionate to the offense. Consequences or sanctions that are applied swiftly, surely, and consistently, and are graduated to provide appropriate and effective responses to varying levels of offense seriousness and offender chronicity, work best in preventing, controlling, and reducing further law violations" (Hurst, 1999). To receive JAIBG funding, a state or local juvenile justice agency must demonstrate a plan to hold juveniles accountable in accordance with the JAIBG program's definitions and purposes.

Similarly, types of federal assistance have been made available for programs involving "truth in sentencing," where federal support is available to states that propose to ensure that offenders convicted of violent crimes will serve at least 85 percent of their sentence in prison. Traditionally, these offenders would serve one-half or less of their sentence incarcerated. States could receive support for the construction of new prisons, or to develop alternatives to prison for nonviolent offenders. They had to ensure, however, that violent offenders would serve 85 percent of their sentences in prison. There was also the federal initiative supporting community-oriented policing, in which the Office of Community Oriented Policing Services (COPS) was created to disburse funds to law enforcement agencies to support efforts to place an additional 100,000 police officers on the streets of the nation. Funding was available, over the life of the program, for hiring new officers, paying overtime to existing officers, and for other efforts (hiring civilians, implementing new technologies, etc.) aimed at making more time available for police officers to serve on the streets. Thousands of police agencies took advantage of these programs. Of course, it was not enough to simply increase the number of police officers on patrol. The increased personnel were required to be dedicated to "community policing."

Critics view these funding and support programs as efforts by the federal government to standardize and direct local criminal justice practices. On the other side of the issue, however, are those who support and applaud this increased federal role. They argue that no one forces local officials to participate in the programs. Indeed, many jurisdictions did not apply to participate in each of these programs. Local justice officials are free to ignore offers of federal assistance that do not meet local needs, and to apply only for those that fit local priorities.

The impact of federal incentives on local operations is still unclear. Helms and Gutierrez (2007) report that COPS funding is associated with important innovation and organizational change in large police agencies. Worrall and Kovandzic (2007), however, found that the influx of community policing dollars had little impact on rates of serious crime. It is also unclear how permanent any changes may be, with the expiration of federal funding for community policing. Some cynics suggest that local agencies "follow the money" and accept federal funding without planning any long term reforms. For example, in 2003, fewer than half of local police departments had a written plan concerning terrorist attacks (Hickman & Reaves, 2006). With the advent of the Department of Homeland Security and the availability of some federal support for counter-terrorism efforts, it is likely that local justice agencies will take on an increased role in combating terrorism, at least as long as federal support is available.

Beginning in fiscal year 1996, the federal Bureau of Justice Assistance began offering Local Law Enforcement Block Grants (LLEBGs), awarding more than $1.3 billion to local communities in the first three years of the program. The distribution of LLEBG funds is described in Box 15.5. The Bureau of Justice Assistance (2000:1) describes the program as one that, "encourages communities to craft their own responses to local crime and drug problems." Still, the LLEBG funds are constrained by legislation to "authorized spending areas" (Bureau of Justice Assistance, 2000:3). In addition, applicant jurisdictions must create advisory boards comprised of identified representatives (law enforcement, prosecutor, court, school system, and community organizations active in crime prevention or substance abuse treatment) to review and develop plans for spending any money received through the LLEBG program. Despite the fact that the purpose of the LLEBG program is to assist local communities to define and solve their own problems, the requirements of federal funding place restrictions on applicants and require specific processes for making decisions about how to allocate the funds. Funding available to local agencies through the LLEBG program has decreased from almost .5 billion dollars in 1996 to $115 million in 2004 (Bauer, 2004). At the same time, federal support for a variety of homeland security initiatives increased dramatically.

Box 15.5   Allocation of Law Enforcement Block Grant Funds: Fiscal Year 1998

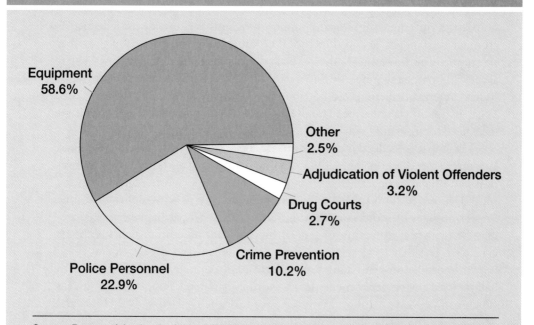

Source: Bureau of Justice Assistance (2000), *A History of the Local Law Enforcement Block Grants Program: Supporting Local Solutions to Crime* (Washington, DC: Bureau of Justice Assistance):2.

Beyond the provision of additional funds, the federal role in local justice policy and practice has also increased in two additional areas. First, the federal government has taken the lead in publiciz-ing successful criminal justice practices by supporting a range of conferences, training, and information dissemination activities. One result of this has been to make the same information available to criminal justice offi-cials all over the nation, creating a "common knowledge" of criminal justice. Second, the past two decades have seen greatly increased collaboration between federal and local agencies. Malcolm Einhorn (2003) has de-scribed the increasing collaboration between federal and local justice officials, especially police and prosecutors. He notes that federal criminal procedures are often less stringent than state rules, making investigation, pros-ecution, and conviction easier. Perhaps the most important criminal justice initiative of President George W. Bush's administra-tion is "Project Safe Neighborhoods," which joins local and state police and prosecutors to crack down on gun crimes (Healy, 2002). And, of course, after the terrorist attacks of September 11, 2001, the provisions of the USA PATRIOT Act and the effort to pre-vent future acts of terrorism have combined to support increased centralization of terror prevention activities and broader information sharing between local, state, and federal law enforcement agencies (International Association of Chiefs of Police, 2004).

Neighborhood Watch programs, which have gained popularity across the United States, are often publicized by signs, such as this one in a Northern Kentucky city. Such programs rely upon citizen vol-unteers to act as the "eyes and ears" of the police. *Photo credit: E.S. Boyne.*

The past several decades have seen an increased role for the federal govern-ment in local criminal justice policy and practice. The provision of direct support for specific criminal justice policies has increased in recent years, and the federal courts have been involved in all aspects of the justice process. It remains to be seen what the ultimate impact of increased federal involvement may be, but at present it seems certain that the federal role in local criminal justice is not likely to dimin-ish in the near future.

Private Justice

In earlier chapters, we discussed developments that tend toward the priva-tization of criminal justice. These include, but are not limited to, contracted services for the operation of correctional programs and institutions, citizen crime prevention, private security, and alternative dispute resolution. Additionally, continuing developments in **victims' rights**, that is, efforts to protect the interests of crime victims, can be considered to be indicative of a trend toward a privatization of justice.

Historically, the criminal justice system evolved from a tradition of private retaliation for wrongdoing. In the past, if a member of one family should injure a member of another family, the families would settle the dispute. Either you and your kin would seek revenge, or my kin and I would pay reparations. With the emergence of stronger leaders and central governments, offenses came to be defined as crimes against the state, rather than as wrongs against individuals. With the growing division of labor within society, the duty to prevent and control crime came to be the province of a set of defined agents and organizations. This relieved the average citizen of the necessity to intercede in criminal matters. Over time, both the definition of crimes and the response to them became matters of public domain.

Today we can see the beginnings of a reversal of that trend. Increasingly, crime and crime control are becoming defined as private concerns. This new definition goes beyond acceptance of private industry provision of criminal justice services, such as the contract prisons discussed earlier. There is a recognition that private individuals are harmed by crimes, and that private individuals must be involved in solving the problem of crime (Finn & Lee, 1988).

Rosenbaum, Lurigio, and Lavrakas (1986) reported that, between 1978 and 1986, the number of **"crime stoppers" programs** in the United States grew from just five to more than 600. Today, one function of community-oriented policing is to develop and support Neighborhood Watch and similar citizen crime-prevention programs. There is an increased awareness of the need for citizens to take steps on their own to prevent crime.

By granting anonymity and cash rewards for tips that lead to arrests and convictions in criminal cases, these programs encourage citizens to provide information to the police. Programs rely upon private citizens to provide leads and evidence to public law enforcement agencies. Further, the majority of funding for these programs comes from private (usually business and industry) donations. The past decade has seen a tremendous growth in this form of private crime control, which essentially uses the police to process cases that are detected and solved privately (Kelling, Edwards & Moore, 1986).

Pfuhl (1992) characterizes crime-stopper programs as legitimized snitching. He notes the long-held social disapproval of "tattletales" in the United States, and assesses how it has happened that this form of snitching has become acceptable. He suggests that public fear of crime, media portrayals of the value of crime stoppers, and police support for crime-stopper programs combine to define this form of tattling as a positive public service. Nor does Pfuhl discount the effect of rewards paid to informers. He suggests that crime-stopper programs are congruent with general social attitudes that the citizenry must take an active role in the "war on crime." In attempting to assess the implications of socially approved snitching, he is concerned about the promise of anonymity given to those who report to crime-stopper programs. While unsure of the final effects of such programs on American society, Pfuhl (1992:525) notes that legitimizing anonymous informing might "pose an even greater threat than the criminality it was intended to combat."

Neighborhood Watch programs have experienced similar growth (Latessa & Travis, 1987). Beginning in 1967, criminal justice observers noted the importance of citizen involvement in assisting the police in controlling crime. Projects designed to increase citizen cooperation with the police began across the country. Variously named, the most common of these projects are Neighborhood Watch or crime-watch programs. They rely upon citizen volunteers to act as "the eyes and ears" of the police. Again, the effect of these programs is that private citizens are taking responsibility for crime control. One interesting product of a crime-watch program studied by Latessa and Travis (1987:48) was that fewer citizens believed the police were successful in controlling crime. It may be that crime-watch programs led citizens to appreciate their role in crime control, and therefore, to devalue the role of the police. These programs may develop a "they-couldn't-do-it-without-us" attitude toward the police. Still, over the past 20 years, there has been a sustained national effort to increase citizen participation in crime prevention (Bureau of Justice Assistance, 1997).

Steven Lab (1990) studied participation in crime prevention activities among a sample of American citizens. He found five distinct crime prevention activities: (1) personal access control (multiple locks, peepholes on doors), (2) target-hardening (installing alarms, marking property), (3) personal security (buying a gun or dog for self-defense), (4) surveillance (joining a crime-watch program), and (5) avoidance (changing behavior to reduce risk, e.g., staying at home at night). Moreover, different personal characteristics were associated with participation in different types of crime prevention. Thus, citizen participation in crime prevention actions is partly a product of the characteristics of the citizens themselves. For instance, Lab (1990:481) found that crime-watch participants were likely to be older, better-educated females who did not own their homes and who had previously been victims of property crimes. Zhao and his colleagues (2002) found that citizens who volunteer to participate in crime prevention programs tend to report higher levels of fear of crime than those who do not. In that regard, participation in crime prevention programs may represent self-interest, as those most afraid of being crime victims are most likely to join programs.

Another area receiving increased attention is known as "crime prevention through environmental design" or CPTED. CPTED (pronounced "sep-ted") programs change environmental conditions to reduce the likelihood of crime. Strategies such as the increased use of lighting, alarms, surveillance cameras, locks, bars, chains, and other security devices; the marking of property; and the changing of traffic flow patterns all seek to make crime less attractive to potential offenders. Ralph Taylor and Adele Harrell (1996) identified four basic approaches to CPTED (see Box 15.6). Allen Wagner (1997) reported that blocking the through traffic in a neighborhood may reduce the amount of crime that occurs there. Hakim, Rengert, and Shachmurove (1996) calculated the costs and benefits of increased use of alarm systems by citizens. They concluded that such systems

> ## Box 15.6   Approaches to Crime Prevention Through Environmental Design (CPTED)
>
> **Housing design/block layout:** Making it more difficult to commit crimes by reducing the availability of crime targets, removing barriers that prevent easy detection of potential offenders or crimes in progress; increasing physical obstacles to crime.
>
> **Land use and circulation patterns:** Creating safer use of neighborhood space by reducing exposure of areas to potential criminals. Can be accomplished by changing traffic patterns, location, and hours of operation of public spaces and facilities. Can include street closings.
>
> **Territorial features:** Encouraging the use of territorial markings or fostering conditions that lead to more extensive markings to indicate vigilant residents, such as Neighborhood Watch signs. Neighborhood cleanup and beautification to indicate that residents are observant and concerned about neighborhood conditions.
>
> **Physical deterioration:** Controlling deterioration to change offender perceptions that areas are vulnerable to crime. Includes closing vacant buildings, removal of trash and abandoned cars, razing condemned buildings, repaving sidewalks.
>
> ---
>
> Source: R. Taylor & A. Harrell (1996), *Physical Environment and Crime* (Washington, DC: National Institute of Justice):3-4.

do save money by reducing the likelihood of crimes at protected places, but that the costs of police investigating false alarms are higher than generally thought and usually not charged directly to the alarm owner. Fleissner and Heinzelmann (1996) reported a link between CPTED efforts and community policing, and urged increased consideration of environmental solutions to crime problems by both police and citizens. Ward (1997) found that even if such programs do not affect actual levels of crime, they appear to reduce the level of fear of crime among neighborhood residents.

Dispute resolution is yet another area where there is a movement away from the criminal justice system as the solution to crime. Dispute resolution programs generally attempt to take less serious offenses and citizen disputes out of the criminal justice arena, and put them into a private negotiation format. Rather than neighbors pressing criminal charges or landlords bringing charges against tenants, under these programs, a forum is provided in which the conflicting parties can resolve their differences without recourse to the criminal law. Dispute resolution centers appear to provide alternatives to criminal justice processing, and participants generally seem satisfied with the programs.

McGillis (1986) reported the results of a survey of 29 dispute resolution centers, including information on the widespread use of these programs. Though the programs were intended to increase access to justice and to reduce the number of cases filed in criminal and civil courts, they faced a major difficulty in the lack of citizen participation. The solution, according to McGillis, lies in encouraging greater participation, that is, increasing the private (or at least semi-public) resolu-tion of disputes. Television shows based on dispute resolution (such as "The People's Court") illustrate this trend. Another example of the trend is evident in the increas-ing number of "trouble shooters" who investigate consumer complaints or govern-ment malfeasance as part of local news programs (Pfuhl & Altheide, 1987).

A related development involves what are known as **victim/offender media-tion** programs in which criminal offenders are brought to meet with their vic-tims to negotiate a resolution to the criminal event (Umbreit, 1986). In a survey of programs, Umbreit identified more operating mediation projects, the first of which was begun in 1974. The majority of these programs were developed by private-sector organizations. The major goals of such projects are to provide sen-tencing alternatives, to allow the victim a voice in the justice process, to reduce the harm done to the victim (generally through restitution), and to increase the offender's accountability to the victim.

Outlaw and Ruback (1999) examined restitution orders imposed as a condi-tion of probation on offenders. They found that more than 40 percent of pro-bationers failed to pay restitution, but that most offenders met their restitution orders. More troubling was their finding that perhaps the most important factor in explaining the imposition of restitution was the ease with which judges could put a price on the harm done to the victim. Property loss and medical expenses are easily quantified and more likely to result in restitution, while emotional and psychological suffering are difficult to quantify and less likely to result in restitution orders. The U.S. Department of Justice's Office for Victims of Crime (2002a) reports that judges have authority to impose **restitution** an order to repay the victim for the costs and loss resulting from the crime. In two-thirds of states, constitutional amendments give victims a right to restitution. Still, the same office (2002b) notes that many victims do not receive payment—or, at least, not full payment.

In criminal justice system mediation programs, the offender and the victim meet face-to-face in the presence of a trained mediator. In addition to providing for restitution, the programs seek to allow the victim and offender to reconcile their conflict arising from the criminal event (Umbreit, 1986:54). Two-thirds of the programs hold these meetings prior to sentencing, although three-fourths of the programs also schedule reconciliation meetings after sentencing.

In a later work, Umbreit (1989) examined the goals of victims who partici-pate in these programs. His conclusion was that victims obtain a better sense of fair treatment through mediation programs than they do in traditional criminal justice processing. The majority of crime victims he studied were not seeking revenge, but rather hoped that mediation would either help the offender, or solve their own problems that resulted from the crime. Malsch and Carriere (1999) reported that mediation programs met the needs of victims for involvement in the process and being kept informed about case status and progress better than traditional justice system procedures. Umbreit suggested that most victims seek a resolution to the crime that they feel is fair in terms of both the offender and themselves. Box 15.7 presents Umbreit's typology of crime victims' perspectives.

Box 15.7   Typology of Victim Perspectives of Fairness

	Type A "The Healer" N=24	Type B "The Fixer" N=14	(N=50) Type C "The Avenger" N=12
Focus:	Offender	Victim	Society
Primary Concerns:	(1) Kids need help, counseling, and guidance. (2) Rehabilitation can reduce future criminal behavior. (3) Punishment is important but not as important as taking responsibility for their lives.	(1) Need to face consequences by repairing damages. (2) Full compensation to victim is required. (3) Direct accountability to victim is important.	(1) [Criminal justice system] too lenient, most often just a slap on the hand. (2) Firm punishment is needed, jail or institution. (3) Rehabilitation: restitution often important, but secondary concern.
Examples:	(1) "I'm not so worried about the money, as the kids." (2) "If the choice was for restitution or help for the kid, I would go for the betterment of the kid." (3) "Fairness is consequences. Those who make mistakes should get the help they need so that they stop doing it."	(1) "I didn't want any vindictiveness, all I wanted was restitution." (2) "It's only fair that I should get what was wrongfully taken from me returned." (3) "Restitution is the major thing, they need to personally make restitution—strong connection between their actions/consequences."	(1) "The punishment isn't harsh enough—it was too lenient." (2) "It's been a slap on the wrist, he should serve time in a prison." (3) "A good-sized deterrent is the only thing that is going to make these people take notice."

Note: Each category in this typology is not mutually exclusive. Rather, each group represents the dominant or primary characteristics expressed by victims of burglary in this study. For example, while the primary concern of most victims fits Type A, these same individuals may also be concerned about some of the characteristics in Type B or Type C, but at a more secondary and less intense level.

Source: M.S. Umbreit (1989), "Crime Victims Seeking Fairness, Not Revenge: Toward Restorative Justice," *Federal Probation* 53(3):54.

Current interest in community courts and community prosecution (Boland, 1996; Brienza, 1998) and community justice (Barajas, 1996) indicates that there has been an expansion of these earlier programs into a more comprehensive approach to the problem of crime in communities. Community justice programs, sometimes considered under the title "restorative justice," seek to achieve a balance between offenders and victims. This balance is expected to reflect community values and restore order, not just determine who is guilty and impose punishment. Such programs involve mediation, restitution, and similar practices. Box 15.8 compares community justice with restorative justice. One difficulty with such programs, of course, is that not all offenders (or victims) are well-suited to participate. Lois Presser and Christopher Lowenkamp (1999) urge the development of a mechanism for screening offenders to ensure that they will be able to participate effectively in restorative justice programs, including victim-offender mediation. Community justice programs seek to empower communities to solve disputes and problems without recourse to the formal system of criminal justice (Robinson, 1996; Stone, 1996). Karp and Clear (2000:324) define community justice, writing, "Community justice broadly refers to all variants of crime prevention and justice activities that explicitly include the community in their processes and set the enhancement of community quality of life as a goal."

Box 15.8   Community and Restorative Justice Continuums

Community Justice	No community involvement	Information sharing	Formal and informal links	Collaboration with joint goals and shared measures of success
Restorative Justice	No victim or community involvement	Victim referred to services, and notified of case status	Staff trained in victimology, restitution in all cases, informal links to the community	Victim participates and remains involved in policy committees, sanction geared to repairing the harm done to the victim

Source: Adapted from "Restorative Justice: An Interview with Visiting Fellow Thomas Quinn," *NIJ Journal* (March 1998):11.

The growth and development in restitution also reflects the increasing emphasis on the private wrongs that accompany crime. In restitution programs, the offender is directed to repay the victim for losses incurred as a result of the crime (Galaway & Hudson, 1978). While restitution had always been a traditional practice (Schwartz, Clear & Travis, 1980:268-270), in the middle 1970s, several jurisdictions began experimenting with restitution as an official part of a criminal sanction (Galaway, 1977). The age-old practice of the offender paying restitution or reparation to erase or minimize the crime before sentencing became a part of the official sentence itself.

In addition to ordering that the offender make restitution to the crime victim, most states operate victim compensation programs for those who suffer a violent crime (McCormack, 1991). **Victim compensation** programs are designed so that the state can pay crime victims for the loss they experienced. However, relatively few victims of violent crime receive any compensation for the harm they have suffered. Only about 6 percent of violent crime victims sought compensation. Nearly two-thirds of those who apply for compensation receive some payments, but ratios of payments to claims vary widely between the states. McCormack (1991) concluded that, among other factors, the lack of resources and failure to inform crime victims of their eligibility for compensation explain the low rates of claims and the low levels of compensation.

Perhaps the clearest indication of a movement toward private justice today can be found in the development of programs for crime victims. Until very recently, the victim of crime was generally ignored by the criminal justice system. At best, the victim was treated as an important witness; at worst, the victim was treated almost as if he or she were the offender. In the 1980s, the separate threads of restitution, dispute resolution, and victim/offender mediation programs came together in comprehensive crime victim legislation (Walker, 1994).

Davis (1987) wrote that future historians may declare the 1980s as the period when crime victims were finally recognized by the justice system. He reported that more than 30 states had passed victims' rights legislation. This legislation recognizes the plight of the victim and tries to attend to victim concerns through providing compensation and requiring that victims be notified of the progress of their case. Programs for crime victims run the gamut from counseling to compensation. Once again, the victims of crime have come to be defined as the injured parties in criminal acts. Technically, the offense may still be against the state, but today, the state is beginning to accept a responsibility to protect the individual interests of the victim. Finn and Lee (1988) reported that more than 4,000 programs existed to assist crime victims. In late 1998, the U.S. Office for Victims of Crime reported that more than 10,000 such programs existed and, "Today, there are more than 27,000 crime victim-related state statutes, 29 state victims' rights constitutional amendments, and basic rights and services for victims of federal crimes" (Office for Victims of Crime, 1998:3). By the end of 2001, 39 states gave crime victims the right to attend criminal justice proceedings, including trials (Office for Victims of Crime, 2002c).

In many jurisdictions, legislation has been passed that allows the victim to address the court at sentencing, or the parole authority at release determinations (Erez & Tontodonato, 1992). It is increasingly common for presentence investigation reports to include a **victim impact statement**, which explains the loss incurred by the victim as a result of the crime. One of the most far-reaching of laws providing for victim input is California's Victim's Bill of Rights, which was passed in 1982. This law allows the victim to appear before the court and parole authorities. Other states have adopted similar procedures that allow victims to speak at critical decision points in the justice process. As Walker (1985:183) observed, "The great danger is that the presence of the victim would add a note of vengeance to the criminal process, or at least a greater one than presently exists."

Villmoare and Neto (1987) reported that the California legislation appeared to have little impact on criminal justice processing. Fewer than 3 percent of victims actually exercised their right to speak at sentencing. Of those who spoke at sentencing, fewer than one-half felt their comments had any effect on the disposition of the case. Villmoare and Neto concluded that such victim rights could

not be successful if simply added on to the existing justice system. They concluded that one reason for the lack of impact of victim statements was the fact that so many cases had already been decided through plea bargaining. To give the victim of crime a real voice in case processing, they suggest it would be necessary to make profound changes throughout the justice system. In short, decision-making authority in the criminal justice system, from bail

Larry Meyers, far right, brother of sniper victim Dean Meyers, delivers victim impact testimony prior to the sentencing of John Allen Muhammad in the death of Dean Meyers at the Prince William County Circuit Court in Manassas, Virginia, in March of 2004. Prince William County Circuit Court Judge Leroy Millette upheld the jury's two death sentences for Muhammad. *Photo credit: AP Photo/Steve Helber.*

through sentencing, would need to be shared between the official agents and the victims of crime. Davis and Smith (1994a, 1994b) reported that victim impact statements appeared to have no effect on criminal justice agent considerations of harm caused to victims, and no impact on the severity of sentences imposed.

Due Process, Crime Control, and Private Justice

As is true whenever we attempt to predict the future, it is unclear where we are headed with our current privatization of justice. In many ways, current trends can be easily dismissed as a natural reaction to the due process revolution of the 1960s, which, according to many observers, "handcuffed the police." It is quite possible that what we see today is an effort to return the justice process to a point of equilibrium. Perhaps one result of the Supreme Court's decisions on criminal matters in the 1960s was to tip the scales too far in favor of offenders, and the contemporary focus on the victim is an effort to restore the previous balance. From the perspective of criminal justice agents, introduction of the crime victim creates an identified individual whose interests compete with those of the offender. The role of the crime victim may be most influential as a check on concerns for the liberty and rights of offenders.

It also may be that those who proclaimed the 1980s to be the "me generation" were correct. A fundamental shift in our perceptions of government and its duty to the citizenry may be reflected in criminal justice processes. Paradoxically, government today is expected to leave us alone as much as possible, yet it is supposed to protect our interests to the maximum. Insured loans to businesses are expected as a function of government, yet government is also expected not to tax too greatly or regulate too strictly. Perhaps, then, we feel that the justice system should not control our behavior too closely, yet should serve our individual needs if we become victims.

The implications of increased citizen participation in crime control, especially through such practices as Neighborhood Watch and crime-stoppers programs, may extend the scope of government control (Pfuhl, 1992). With our neighbors watching and willing to call the police anonymously, we may lose our privacy—and thus our liberty to do things in our private lives. With so many extra eyes and ears, the surveillance capability of the government will be greatly enhanced, at a cost to individual liberty. On the other hand, to the degree that fear of crime keeps people from doing the things they like (such as going out in the evenings), increased citizen surveillance may enhance our personal freedom by increasing our level of perceived safety. Fears of terrorist attack have led to unprecedented government power to monitor communications and citizens and have added to travel delays as airline passengers undergo security checks.

One can predict that the next several years will be a period of adjustment. Evidence thus far indicates that most victims of crime do not seem to want a direct voice in criminal justice processing (Davis, 1987; Forer, 1980); as mentioned earlier, less than 3 percent of all victims actually exercise their rights to speak at sentencing and parole hearings. More recent reviews of the exercise of rights by victims of crime indicate that most victims make (or file) a victim impact statement at sentencing, but few still exercise the right to make recommendations at bail or parole hearings (Kilpatrick, Beatty & Howley, 1998). In the end, it appears that the results of the privatization of criminal justice will be mixed. Victims may be treated more humanely, and services and compensation to reduce the traumatic effects of victimization may be maintained, but decisions about the handling of offenders will likely revert to the detached, professional judgments of criminal justice agents and officers. Citizens may engage in surveillance and reporting of criminality, but will probably focus their attention on more serious, traditional crimes by strangers. Agencies of the justice system encourage victim participation that helps "balance" concern for offender rights by introducing the competing concern for victim's interests. Still, these same agencies are not well suited to the provision of direct services to victims (Bryant & Brown, 2002). In short, over a span of years, it is likely that we will learn the limits to privatization, both practical and philosophical, and the system will be adjusted accordingly.

Technological Justice

Earlier we devoted considerable attention to the development and impact of surveillance technologies on community supervision. In all aspects of life, technological changes have caused adjustments in behavior. We take for granted such advances as household electricity, indoor plumbing, telephones, automobiles, and other commonplace technological conveniences, yet, as recently as 50 years ago, these technologies were unavailable to large segments of our population. The computer age is now upon us, but 50 years ago we still used vacuum tubes in large, complicated computing devices. One hundred years ago, we did not even have aircraft (other than hot air balloons).

The effects of technological advances on criminal justice have been staggering, as they have been on other areas of life. The telephone and the automobile changed the nature of policing. No longer did the neighborhood cop walk a beat and know everyone. Now a simple telephone call to an impersonal dispatcher results in the arrival, by automobile, of an equally impersonal police officer. In the past, offenders could simply give the police an alias or cross a state line to avoid prosecution. Today, computerized criminal records and fingerprint checks can lead to quick identifications (Johnson, 1998). A simple traffic stop may lead to a felony arrest when a computer check yields outstanding warrants.

Warehouses full of paper documents have been reduced to a few boxes of microfiche. Some observers anticipate "paperless" criminal justice (Duffie & Graham, 1986), with records and documents stored on computer files. The availability of electronic databases and powerful search engines has made the police, courts, and correctional agencies more effective in identifying and tracking known and/or wanted offenders. Television, videotapes, and computer simulations can be used to great effect in investigations and at trial to present and test evidence and to reduce delays and costs. "Teleconferencing" can be used to replace on-site hearings for parole or probation revocation, or even for parole release hearings; this advance reduces costs and increases efficiency.

Scientific advances (including genetic testing) have been adapted to criminal justice uses. Currently, DNA "fingerprinting" is being used to help identify offenders conclusively, as well as to help identify innocent suspects (Rau, 1991). DNA evidence has been used in trials in most states. While there are still some problems with this technology (Herrera & Tracey, 1992), including improper laboratory procedures, it would appear that the technique is firmly established. Other investigatory aids include computer-generated offender profiles to assist police in identifying likely suspects, and a variety of drug detection tests to both locate contraband and establish drug use among criminal suspects.

Modern prisons and jails are making use of a variety of technological innovations to improve custody and services. Electronic perimeter security (microwave, electric eye, and vibration sensors, which are increasingly replacing towers and stone walls) has reduced construction costs and accelerated construction schedules for new prisons (Camp & Camp, 1987; Donohoe & Greloch, 1997; Latessa et al., 1988). Closed-circuit television, automatic locking devices, and careful planning have reduced the need for custodial staff in prisons and jails. Gabrielle deGroot (1997) described cutting-edge correctional technologies including satellite monitoring, heartbeat monitoring, and "smart cards" that allow corrections officials to track each inmate with little paperwork. Some states are experimenting with "smart cards" that contain inmate information on microchips to expedite processing of inmates in need of medication. Additional uses of these cards include identification, access control, and monitoring of inmate locations (Pilant, 1998). Automated video surveillance has enhanced the ability of correctional personnel to monitor inmate behavior and prison safety (Turner, 2007).

With technological development, the justice system now is able to detect, apprehend, and process offenders more quickly and economically. The technologies have allowed us to conduct business as usual, but in a more efficient manner. Advances in medical science have also affected crime. Giacopassi, Sparger, and Stein (1992) note that improved emergency medical care may have suppressed the homicide rate. That is, many of today's felonious assaults would have been homicides but for the fact that medical care has been improved. Saving the life of the crime victim reduces the seriousness of the crime. Indeed, Penelope Hanke and James Gundlach (1995) suggested that differences in access to quality emergency medical care may explain the observed differences in seriousness of crime between white and black offenders. They provide evidence that lack of access to quality emergency medical care in minority, inner-city neighborhoods may help account for higher rates of homicide and more serious injuries to victims of violent crime. Other technologies have arisen that may alter the conduct of criminal justice business in more significant ways.

New technologies have affected the types of crimes that will be the focus of criminal justice efforts. Box 15.9 describes "cybercrimes" reported by a sample of businesses. New technologies also have affected the delicate balance between the rights of individuals and those of the community. The future of crime seems more easily predictable than does the outcome of the balance of state and individual interests. For example, there has been an increased interest in the use of pretrial drug testing of criminal defendants (Visher, 1992). Those who test positive may be subjected to stricter conditions of pretrial release. In essence, on the basis of the results of a drug test, unconvicted defendants receive more punitive conditions of pretrial release. As Visher (1992:6) observed, the constitutionality of these tests and resulting differences in treatment have not yet been resolved. Rhodes, Hyatt, and Scheiman (1996) reported the results of a study of pretrial drug test results as predictors of rearrest or failure to appear. They suggest that judges can use the results of such pretrial tests to deny release or set special conditions of pretrial release. Tony Fabelo (2000) urges us to consider the ethical and legal questions involved in applying technological solutions to crime problems. He observed (2000:1), "The techno-correctional apparatus may provide the infrastructure for increased intrusiveness by the state and its abusive control of both offenders and law-abiding citizens."

Johnson (1981) explained that changes in police organization and operation were partly due to the changes in the nature and extent of crime. Similarly, Lundman (1980) explained the development of police, in part, as a result of changes in the rates and images of crime. That is, the police (and, by extension, the entire criminal justice system) must be responsive to those acts that we view as seriously threatening public order and safety. Technological change also changes crime.

Willie Sutton, a famous bank robber, is credited with a witty response to a question about his actions. When asked why he committed bank robberies,

Sutton is said to have replied, "Because that's where the money is." If we look at crimes throughout American history, we see that, very often, they take place "where the money is." Criminals such as Jesse James robbed stagecoaches because these coaches carried large sums of money (corporate payments, payrolls, etc.). These men became train robbers when cash began to be transported by rail. Bank robberies became more common when cash transactions were replaced by checks and fund transfers. Today's offender might well be described as a "lineman," that is, he or she often steals by computer. Fraud with computerized banking, already a problem, is likely to become more important in the future.

Not only is money itself at risk in an increasingly computerized commercial system, but information is also more often the target of theft. Trade secrets, customer lists, business records, and all sorts of other information (including national defense secrets) are stored in computer databases. Theft of such information often is more damaging (and more profitable for the thief) than fraudulent fund transfers. As quoted by Bennett (1987:109), Wolfgang predicted, "By the turn of the century, the main concern of criminal justice will be information crime."

Detection of computer crime (and enforcement of laws against it) will require a different type of law enforcement response than that required by traditional street crime. The officer in the patrol car may be replaced by the systems analyst at the terminal. This does not mean that street crime will disappear; it means that computer-related offenses will increase in frequency and importance, which will lead to justice system adaptations to combat them. Harris (1995) reported that there is growing recognition of the need for law enforcement officers with computer skills. She quoted one respondent who noted, "We need to begin recruiting people with technological skills, or at least basic computer system operation skills." The knowledge and skills required for effective search and seizure of computers are lacking in most law enforcement agencies (Harris, 1995). A survey of law enforcement officials by Burns and his colleagues (2004) revealed that while most felt Internet fraud was being investigated by police at all levels, it would best be pursued by federal agencies. A lack of resources and inadequate organizational structure hamper local law enforcement efforts to respond to Internet fraud and similar computer crimes. A pilot study of almost 200 businesses in 2001 revealed that almost three-quarters had suffered a computer crime victimization. Most of these were attacks by computer viruses, and the offender is rarely an employee of the company (Rantala, 2004). We can only expect that all sorts of computer crime will increase in the future. Box 15.9 describes the types of computer crimes prosecuted by state court prosecutors in 2000. Hugh Nugent (1991) reviewed existing state computer crime statutes and found that since 1978, 40 states and the federal government have passed laws defining some types of computer crimes. Box 15.10 describes the most common forms of computer offenses identified in state statutes.

During the 1970s, especially during the Carter administration, a shift toward increased efforts against corporate and white-collar crime could be detected in changes in federal law enforcement. In that time period, the FBI sought agents with the skills required to track white-collar crime, and recruits were trained in accounting, computers, or law. These backgrounds were to prepare the agents

Box 15.9 Types of "Cybercrime" Reported by Businesses

Type of Incident	Companies that detected incidents:		
	One Event	More than one	Missing
Theft			
Embezzlement	75.0	--	--
Fraud	41.2	52.9	5.9
Of Proprietary Info	50.0	41.7	8.3
Computer Attack			
Denial of Service	34.0%	64.0	2.0
Vandalism or sabotage	51.4	48.6	0
Computer virus	7.9	86.6	5.5
Other	34.6%	57.7%	7.7%
Total	8.2%	89.1%	2.7%

Source: R. Rantala (2004), *Cybercrime Against Businesses* (Washington, DC: Bureau of Justice Statistics):3.

Box 15.10 Categories of Behavior Addressed by State Computer Crime Statutes

- **Intellectual Property**—expanded the idea that computer programs, computer data, and computer services are property or intellectual property.

- **Computer tampering**—made illegal "knowingly or recklessly" degrading or disrupting computer services to the extent that such actions impair the ability of authorized users to obtain full use of their computer systems.

- **Computer trespass**—made illegal the unauthorized access of a computer and its contents, including using the contents of a computer to aid and abet the commission of a crime.

- **Unlawful duplication/disclosure**—made illegal copying and distributing the contents of a computer without authorization.

- **Defenses**—allowed some defenses to restrict anauthorized access.

- **Venues/Sites of offense**—specified the jurisdiction for purposes of prosecuting the theft of computer information.

Source: M. Brown (2000), "Criminal Justice Discovers Information Technology," in G. LaFree (ed.), *The Nature of Crime: Continuity and Change* (Washington, DC: National Institute of Justice, Criminal Justice 2000) Volume 1:219-259.

for the shifting emphasis of federal law enforcement to corporate and white-collar crimes. Since then, however, a re-emergence of drug-related crimes and an increased concern about terrorism resulted, at least partially, in a return of federal law enforcement to more traditional practices during the Reagan administration. This focus on more traditional crimes has continued through the Clinton years and into the administration of President George W. Bush. Michael Lynch and his colleagues (2004) note a "disappearing act" in terms of attention paid to corporate crime in the criminological literature. That scholarly disappearance mirrors a similar one in practice. Of course, scandals such as the Enron fraud case and the obstruction-of-justice conviction of Martha Stewart have served to heighten again the interest in corporate and white-collar crime.

A change in social attitudes about the responsibilities and duties of businesses and corporations led to increasing concern over corporate and white-collar crime (Clinard & Yeager, 1980; Cullen, Maakestad & Cavender, 1987). As recently as 50 years ago, white-collar crime was virtually unknown. Businesses and business-persons committed wrongs against the public, but these acts were not necessarily considered crimes. The consumer protection movement, which developed in the 1960s, was responsible for the identification of white-collar crime as a serious criminal justice problem. A specific form of corporate or business crime receiving increased attention today is the violation of environmental protection laws. The National Institute of Justice (1994) reported that criminal prosecutions for environmental crimes increased 132 percent between 1990 and 1992. Factors affecting the decision to prosecute environmental crimes include the amount of harm caused, the offender's degree of criminal intent and prior record, and the availability of civil remedies, among other things. In 1997, about 17 percent of all defendants charged with environmental violations by federal prosecutors were organizations (Scalia, 1999).

Technology affects the types of crimes that can be (and are) committed. In response, the qualifications of justice system officials, the nature of cases in the criminal justice process, and responses to offenders will be altered. There is little doubt that, similar to the shift from stagecoach robbery to bank robbery, the practices of criminal justice will be required to adapt to high-technology crimes of computer fraud. These changes, however, do not appear likely to change the criminal justice system in any fundamental way.

Computer crimes may pit justice-system investigators skilled in systems analysis against offenders skilled in programming. Evidence at trials may come to be comprised of documents and disks more often than of hairs and weapons, but the process itself can continue in its present form. In this case, the type of crime and criminal may be different, but the basic response to crime can be maintained. Other effects of technology, however, pose a greater likelihood of altering the way in which criminal justice is accomplished.

In addition to the opportunities for crime that computers offer, computerized record keeping can aid the efforts of criminal justice officials. Tremendous amounts of information about almost every citizen are kept somewhere on computer records. If a suspected offender has ever applied for credit, or if he or she operates a motor vehicle, police can garner much information, quickly and easily, by requesting computer records. Credit applications generate data about employment, earnings, savings, debts, addresses, dependents, references, demographic characteristics (such as age, sex, race, education, and marital status), and even height and weight. Access to a person's credit report can provide a tremendous amount of personal information about him or her. Operation of a motor vehicle provides similar background data, important identifying numbers (e.g., social security numbers), as well as information about possible criminal record. It is possible to conduct a relatively thorough background check on the average citizen without ever leaving a computer terminal.

Credit card purchase records allow investigators to track travel patterns of individuals. Credit card purchasing and payment information exist on computer records that do not require a check on access (other than perhaps knowledge of a correct password). This means that personal data are potentially available to anyone. Consider what information about your private life could be learned by someone with access to computer records. If someone had unlimited access, could that person discover your name, address, telephone number, income, age, sex, race, general whereabouts over the past month, courses you are taking, and your grade-point average? How difficult would it be for such a person to identify your friends, family, or taste in clothes or music? Of course, the more you use credit cards and electronic tellers, the more can be discovered about you. However, we are all known to some computer somewhere, and we would consider much of the available information to be personal. Our right to be protected from unreasonable "searches and seizures" is increasingly at risk, and we are frequently unaware of the risk. The sheer availability of information about suspects, witnesses, and offenders could lead to increased surveillance by the justice system. There is no doubt that much of this information would prove useful not only in criminal investigations, but also for what is called "intelligence gathering."

Intelligence gathering relates to the compilation of information that may be helpful in solving crimes, but with no specific probable cause to believe the information will lead to solving a particular crime. As the emphasis on proactive, preventive efforts of criminal justice agencies increases, with a complementary focus on problem-solving, we can expect justice agencies to compile and use larger and more diverse sets of information. Crime mapping and geographic analysis have become important planning tools for law enforcement agencies (Rich, 1995), and their use has spread to courts and to correctional agencies (Harries, 2003). In most applications, the criminal justice analyst ties a variety of data sources to a known location and then seeks relationships that help explain the presence or absence of crime so that policy can be directed at reducing the likelihood of crime or other problems.

Yet another computer-generated technological change promises to alter the way in which criminal justice decisions are made. It is increasingly common for justice agencies to employ statistical models to assist in the determination of resource allocation and case processing decisions. Spelman and Eck (1987) reported on "smart policing," in which police reactions to crime problems (in the form of changing patterns of patrol, enlisting community assistance, and selecting police problems for enforcement attention) are "incident-driven." That is, crime reports are analyzed, and computer-generated patterns of police problems are then created to guide the deployment of police resources. In the latter part of the 1990s, police agencies began using computerized crime mapping and geographic analysis of crime to inform decisions about where and how to allocate police resources (Harries, 1999; Mamalian & LaVigne, 1997).

Some commentators call for increasing use of such models for making police decisions. They suggest that criminal complaints should be ranked according to solvability, and that detective and patrol officers should be assigned to respond to cases on the basis of the likelihood that the case can be solved (Cordner, Greene & Bynum, 1983; Greenberg & Wasserman, 1979). Therefore, the lower the probability that the case will be solved, the less should be the urgency for police response to the complaint.

Many prosecutors' offices differentiate cases on the basis of factors associated with successful prosecution, or on other models of case importance. Cases are selected for special attention when an analysis of factors present in the case (witnesses, physical evidence, etc.) indicates a high probability of conviction. That is, prosecutorial resources are to be focused on those cases for which there is the greatest probability of successful prosecution.

The courts and parole authorities rely upon various analyses to assist in the determination of criminal sanctions. The tradition of research-generated guidelines for criminal justice decisionmaking is longest in parole and sentencing (Travis & O"Leary, 1979). Block and Rhodes (1987) assessed the federal sentencing guidelines, noting that the Federal Sentencing Commission (which authored the guidelines) did not expect federal judges to deviate from guideline sentences very often. William Wilkins, Chairman of the Commission, predicted that "if this effort at the Federal level is generally found to be successful, these guidelines will foster the development of guidelines by many States that do not already have them" (Wilkins, 1987:8). As we saw, many states have implemented guidelines and/or sentencing commissions.

As discussed earlier, probation and parole supervision levels in many states are determined with reference to risk and needs assessment measures. Gettinger (1981) described the California system for assigning levels of supervision, referring to the system as "doing parole by the numbers." In that system, each case was assessed for risk and determined to be either a "control case" or a "service case." Control cases received close supervision and an emphasis on crime prevention; service cases received counseling and assistance in receiving community services. Like the parolees, the parole officers were broken into classes of: minimum-supervision agents, who administered large caseloads of parolees requiring little attention; control officers, who served as "personal police" for dangerous parolees; and service agents, who arranged social services for parolees needing them.

Partially an outgrowth of research over the past three decades that identified inefficiencies in criminal justice processing, the use of these classification technologies is expected to ensure that criminal justice resources are wisely expended on those cases for which they are most needed. The use of "problem-oriented policing," setting prosecution priorities, sentencing guidelines, and correctional classification also reflects the contemporary emphasis on career criminals (see Chapter 3).

The problem posed by this new decision-making technology for criminal justice revolves around the question of who makes the decisions. To the extent that all of these classification and prediction technologies provide information and guidance to decisionmakers, they do not significantly alter justice-system processing. These devices simply become another factor in the equation that produces criminal justice outcomes. The problem is that these technologies may actually alter the decisions themselves.

In regard to community supervision case classification, there is evidence that many jurisdictions simply adopted the National Institute of Corrections case management models, and that they did so without adjusting the models for local characteristics. Indeed, an evaluation of the application of the model system to several local departments indicated that the risk assessment instruments did not work very well at predicting risk in some places (Wright, Clear & Dickson, 1984). Nonetheless, classification decisions were made on the basis of an existing (albeit inappropriate) model; one could say that the model made the decisions.

In regard to prosecutorial guidelines, David Weimer (1980) found that a more effective use of prosecution resources would be obtained by focusing resources on cases with lower probabilities of conviction. After all, cases with high probabilities of conviction do not need as much special attention. Further, lacking an effort to deal strongly with lower-probability cases, and lacking continual evaluation of case decisionmaking and outcomes, the model becomes self-perpetuating. Nothing will change, because there will be no new information generated that will lead to change.

For sentencing decisions, guidelines are often stifling. Convicted offenders receive predetermined sentences because of factors that often are beyond their control. For example, to the extent that prior criminal record affects the severity of sentence, there is nothing the offender can do to alter his or her sentence. The prior record never gets better. When one considers that parole and sentencing guidelines are often based on past experience (what kinds of sentences were imposed in the past), the problem is more apparent. Arguably, one reason for the development of these models is to improve decisionmaking, but the models are based on the very decisions they are expected to improve (Gottfredson et al., 1978).

For the foreseeable future, the tendency to adopt and use decision-making aids will probably continue and spread throughout the justice system. The effects of these models are presently unknown. By relieving decisionmakers of responsibility for decisions, the guidelines allow them to claim that they were forced to make a certain decision. As a result, there will probably be a tendency toward uniformity in decisions. This uniformity would have the effect of masking differences between individual cases, which could result in less humane treatment of offenders. Further, it can be expected that such guidelines will further strengthen the justice system's ability to resist change. One long-range result may well be a call for greater individualization in criminal justice case processing, which would return us, full cycle, to where these guidelines began.

Technology and Criminal Justice in the Total System

Technological advances in all areas of society continue at an accelerated pace. The effects of these changes for society are both positive and negative. Increased communication capability, for example, applies to both good news and bad. Having voicemail means the phone will be answered, but the chance of speaking with a living person is greatly decreased. Changes in technology affect the environment of the criminal justice system, and thus must be expected to produce changes in criminal justice processing.

As illustrated in the previous discussion, most of the effects of technological change have occurred in the material environment. Types of crimes and methods of detection and investigation have changed. The relative frequency of homicide as compared to assault, or white-collar crimes as compared with street crimes, may have been altered. Similarly, the characteristics of criminal justice personnel, and the equipment they need to do their jobs, may change in response to technological innovation.

The impact of technology on the operations of criminal justice indicates the open-system nature of the justice process. These changes occur in the means of criminal justice operations but probably have little impact on the ends of processing. Other technological advances, such as decision-making aids, are more subtle, but may have more far-reaching effects because they alter the ends of criminal justice operations. To the extent that information technology assists criminal justice actors to achieve effective and fair decisions, the impact of technological change in the environment will be positive. To the degree that these alterations produce unintended consequences, such as institutionalizing discrimination, their effects may be negative. Whatever the effect on the means and ends of criminal justice, one factor to be considered in assessing the future of criminal justice remains the future environment of the system.

Technological advances affect jurisprudence in many ways. The courtroom of State Supreme Court Justice Lewis Friedman was the test site for technology providing nearly instant video display of testimony transcribed by the stenographer. The system is meant to streamline trials by allowing videotaped testimony, documents, and other exhibits to be viewed on the screens. *Photo credit: AP Photo/Mark Lennihan.*

Criminal Justice in the Early Twenty-First Century

What will the structure and practice of criminal justice in the United States be like as the twenty-first century progresses? If current developments continue on their present course, we can expect some changes. Three related developments promise to alter the fundamental nature of American criminal justice from its most recent tradition. There is a growing emphasis on crime prevention (Sherman et al., 1997) that has resulted in an expansion of the role of criminal justice in our society. The justice system is increasingly being held accountable for a broader quality of life than simply crime control. In part, this expansion of the role of criminal justice is a function of information suggesting that if we wish to reduce crime, we must attack problems of social order. Focusing on problems of social order has meant that the community has become an identified client and partner in criminal justice policymaking. Concern about the costs of justice-system operation has risen at the same time that the criminal justice system is experiencing role expansion. This has meant that cost considerations have gained new prominence in criminal justice policy. Thus, concern about social order beyond crime has produced an expanded role for agents of the criminal justice system. This expanded role has increased costs, but also opened new avenues of funding for criminal justice operations. Finally, current assessments of criminal justice practices place greater emphasis on effectiveness than on democracy. In terms of our themes, contemporary criminal justice practices stress crime control over due process more than in the recent past.

In 1964, Francis Allen voiced concern about the role of the criminal justice system in dealing with social problems like alcoholism. Allen suggested that many problems of social order lie on the borderland of the criminal justice system. His solution was that we limit the kinds of behaviors that should be the focus of criminal justice operations. Failing to limit the criminal justice system to the control of crime, Allen feared, would have negative consequences for both the system and society. As we enter the twenty-first century, the border of criminal justice has become less distinct.

Throughout the book we have explored community policing, community prosecution, community courts, community corrections, and community justice. All of these developments assume the existence of an identifiable community. What happens when there are no (or few) agreed-upon community values? Suppose some members of the community are concerned about loitering, but others are not? To whom do justice system officials listen?

The tradition in American criminal justice has been to let the community decide what issues were important and communicate this by their complaints to the police. Increasingly, justice-system agents are becoming involved in community-organizing activities in which they bring neighborhood residents together and help them to define problems and select solutions. To the extent that it is criminal justice agents who "create" these communities, the justice system is being "proactive." A proactive justice system, you will recall, is associated with a less democratic society.

People, in general, may be more willing to use the law—and the criminal law in particular—to resolve disputes and conflicts (Miethe, 1995). Therefore, the range of issues that reach the attention of police, court, and correctional authorities has expanded. So, too, have the range of solutions. Justice system officials increasingly employ noncriminal justice solutions to problems of crime and disorder. Prosecutors use civil court processes such as eviction and license revocation to remove offenders from communities, and to close problem businesses (Finn, 1995). "Zero-tolerance" policing, which seeks to minimize disorderly behavior, can produce negative police/community relations, as some parts of the community experience repressive policing (National Institute of Justice, 2000). Asset forfeiture, in which justice agents seize the property of criminal offenders, provides a "profit motive" for criminal justice and may alter the selection of enforcement targets and the establishment of enforcement priorities in justice agencies (Holden, 1993; Miller & Selva, 1994). Rather than working for us, justice agents may be working for themselves.

The emphasis on crime prevention that is characteristic of recent changes in criminal justice operations is qualitatively different from an emphasis on crime control. In crime control, the justice system can be reactive and respond to instances of crime or potential crime. The system is effective to the extent that criminals are arrested and processed. A potential benefit may be that crime control efforts have preventive effects, such as deterrence and education. The emphasis on crime prevention, however, means that the justice system works to stop crimes that might happen, or that are predicted to happen. The difference is that these crimes have not yet occurred, and the offenders who might commit these crimes have, as yet, done nothing wrong. What is the basis on which justice system authorities intervene in the lives of citizens who have not yet committed a crime?

At present, the balance between due process and crime control seems to have shifted in the direction of a greater emphasis on crime control. This can occur only at a cost to due process. In the foreseeable future, at least, we can expect increased criminal justice system efforts at crime prevention, accompanied by less concern about individual liberty and due process. We can expect that at some time in the future the balance will shift again to give primacy to individual liberty, due process, and the control of government power.

Criminal Justice: A Final Thought

The term "criminal justice" is paradoxical. Does it mean that justice is criminal, or that crime is just? We now know that it refers to how we define, detect, and react to behaviors that we deem criminal. We should also have an appreciation for how complex a topic it really is.

We have seen how present practices reflect various mixes of historical, political, economic, social, philosophical, and individual traits and factors. We can appreciate how the justice system, in balancing these many demands, is highly resistant to reform. There are so many places where reforms can be made, and so many levels at which reform can be stymied, that the justice process seems immune to change. Still, we have seen that changes have indeed occurred in criminal justice over the years. Some changes have been more fundamental than others. Some appear to have been more long-lasting. Others are not yet complete.

Through our examination of criminal justice, we have come to see that no single purpose does (or can) predominate the system. The central dilemma is that of controlling behavior in a free society. The tension is between individual liberty and the need for an orderly and predictable society. The pendulum shifts over the decades from an emphasis on one to an emphasis on the other. The result is the appearance that no change has occurred. Criminal justice seems to proceed in a circular fashion, continually returning to earlier points. The effect is enough to make us despair in our hopes to achieve progress, but that is not the intent of the study of criminal justice.

An understanding of criminal justice promotes an understanding of our society and culture. Similarly, it is not possible to grasp the intricacies of the justice system without understanding its larger context. The failure of past reforms often can be traced to either or both of two mistakes. First, we must be reasonable in our expectations for change. It is probably not possible to eliminate injustice or inefficiency, and it may not even be desirable to do so. Second, change in the justice process is accomplished only by thorough planning and careful execution. As a system (or collection of separate systems), criminal justice is elastic and resists alteration. The would-be reformer must anticipate and prepare for reactions to change.

One thing that we can predict with confidence is that there will be a criminal justice process in the future. It is incumbent on us to try to understand it, and to work to improve it.

Review Questions

1. Identify two ways in which an offender can receive a discharge from criminal justice custody.

2. What are collateral consequences of conviction? Identify five such consequences.

3. Describe a process by which an ex-offender may have his or her constitutional rights restored.

4. What are some of the problems in arriving at a definition of recidivism?

5. What are the implications of the concept of recidivism for criminal justice policy?

Review Questions *(continued)*

6. It is argued that there is a trend toward privatizing criminal justice. Summarize this argument, and discuss whether you agree with it.

7. One recent trend in criminal justice has been the development and use of decision-making guidelines. Give three examples of such guidelines, and discuss their possible effects.

8. Has the justice system moved more toward an emphasis on crime control than due process?

References

Allen, F. (1964). *The Borderland of Criminal Justice.* Chicago: University of Chicago Press.

Allen, H. & C. Simonsen (1986). *Corrections in America: An Introduction,* 4th ed. New York: Macmillan.

Barajas, E. (1996). "Moving Toward Community Justice." *APPA Perspectives* (Spring):32-35.

Bauer, L. (2004). *Local Law Enforcement Block Grant Program, 1996-2004.* Washington, DC: Bureau of Justice Statistics.

Beck, A. & B. Shipley (1987). *Recidivism of Young Parolees.* Washington, DC: U.S. Department of Justice.

Benda, B., N. Toombs & M. Peacock (2003). "Discriminators of Types of Recidivism Among Boot Camp Graduates in a Five-Year Follow-up Study." *Journal of Criminal Justice* 31(6):539-551.

Bennett, G. (1987). *Crime-Warps: The Future of Crime in America.* New York: Doubleday.

Block, M. & W. Rhodes (1987). "The Impact of Federal Sentencing Guidelines." *NIJ Reports* (September/October):2-7.

Boland, B. (1996). "What is Community Prosecution?" *NIJ Journal* (August):35-40.

Brienza, L. (1998). "New York Community Court Honored for Innovation." *Justice Technology Monitor* 1(1):1-2, 18.

Buckler, K. & L. Travis (2003). "Reanalyzing the Prevalence and Social Context of Collateral Consequence Statutes." *Journal of Criminal Justice* 31(5):435-453.

Bureau of Justice Assistance (1997). *National Citizen's Crime Prevention Campaign.* Washington, DC: Bureau of Justice Assistance.

Bureau of Justice Assistance (2000). *A History of the Local Law Enforcement Block Grants Program: Supporting Local Solutions to Crime.* Washington, DC: Bureau of Justice Assistance.

Braly, M. (1977). *False Starts: A Memoir of San Quentin and Other Prisons.* New York: Penguin Books.

Bryant, K. & N. Brown (2002). "Victim Service Delivery at the Federal Level: A Case Study." *Journal of Crime and Justice* 25(2):121-128.

Burns, R., K. Whitworth & C. Thompson (2004). "Assessing Law Enforcement Preparedness to Address Internet Fraud." *Journal of Criminal Justice* 32(6):477-493.

Burton, V., F. Cullen & L.F. Travis III (1987). "The Collateral Consequences of a Felony Conviction: A National Study of State Statutes." *Federal Probation* 51(3):52-60.

Burton, V., L.F. Travis III & F.T. Cullen (1988). "Reducing the Legal Consequences of a Felony Conviction: A National Survey of State Statutes." *International Journal of Comparative and Applied Criminal Justice* 12(1):101-109.

Camp, G.M. & C.C. Camp (1987). *Stopping Escapes: Perimeter Security.* Washington, DC: U.S. Department of Justice.

Clinard, M.B. & P. Yeager (1980). *Corporate Crime.* New York: Free Press.

Cordner, G., J. Greene & T. Bynum (1983). "The Sooner the Better: Some Effects of Police Response Time." In R. Bennett (ed.), *Police at Work: Policy Issues and Analysis.* Beverly Hills, CA: Sage, 145-164.

Cullen, F.T., W.J. Maakestad & G. Cavender (1987). *Corporate Crime Under Attack: The Ford Pinto Case and Beyond.* Cincinnati: Anderson.

Cullen, F.T., W.J. Maakestad, G. Cavender & M.L. Benson (2006). *Corporate Crime Under Attack: The Fight to Criminalize Business Violence.* Newark, NJ: LexisNexis Matthew Bender.

Davidenas, J. (1983). "The Professional License: An Ex-Offender's Illusion." *Criminal Justice Journal* 7(1):61-96.

Davis, R. (1987). "Crime Victims: Learning How to Help Them." *NIJ Reports* (May/June):2-7.

Davis, R. & B. Smith (1994a). "Victim Impact Statements and Victim Satisfaction: An Unfulfilled Promise?" *Journal of Criminal Justice* 22(1):1-12.

Davis, R. & B. Smith (1994b). "The Effects of Victim Impact Statements on Sentencing Decisions: A Test in an Urban Setting." *Justice Quarterly* 11(3):453-469.

deGroot, G. (1997). "Hot New Technologies." *Corrections Today* (July):60-62.

Donohoe, S. & A. Greloch (1997). "Keeping it Simple: Design Techniques Can Enhance Security." *Corrections Today* (July):90-92.

Duffie, H. & G. Graham (1986). "A Paperless Probation Department?—Solutions to the Endless Paper Chase." *Corrections Today* 48(1):46;50.

Durose, M. & P. Langan (2007). *Felony Sentences in State Courts, 2004.* Washington, DC: Bureau of Justice Statistics.

Einhorn, M. (2003). *Fighting Urban Crime: The Evolution of Federal-Local Collaboration.* Washington, DC: National Institute of Justice.

Erez, E. & P. Tontodonato (1992). "Victim Participation in Sentencing and Satisfaction with Justice." *Justice Quarterly* 9(3):393-417.

Fabelo, T. (2000). "'Technocorrections': The Promises, the Uncertain Threats." In *Sentencing & Corrections: Issues for the 21st Century* (May) No.5. Washington, DC: National Institute of Justice.

Finn, P. (1995). *The Manhattan District Attorney's Narcotics Eviction Program.* Washington, DC: National Institute of Justice.

Finn, P. & B. Lee (1988). *Establishing and Expanding Victim-Witness Assistance Programs.* Washington, DC: U.S. Department of Justice.

Finn, R. & P. Fontaine (1985). "The Association Between Selected Characteristics and Perceived Employability of Offenders." *Criminal Justice & Behavior* 12(3):353-365.

Flanagan, T. (1985). "Questioning the 'Other' Parole: The Effectiveness of Community Supervision of Offenders." In L.F. Travis III (ed.), *Probation, Parole, and Community Corrections: A Reader.* Prospect Heights, IL: Waveland, 167-183.

Fleissner, D. & F. Heinzelmann (1996). *Crime Prevention Through Environment Design and Community Policing.* Washington, DC: National Institute of Justice.

Forer, L. (1980). *Criminals and Victims: A Trial Judge Reflects on Crime and Punishment.* New York: W.W. Norton.

Friel, C. (2000). "A Century of Boundary Changes." In C. Friel (ed.), *Boundary Changes in Criminal Justice Organizations.* Washington, DC: National Institute of Justice, Criminal Justice 2000, Vol. 2.

Galaway, B. (1977). "The Use of Restitution." *Crime & Delinquency* 23(1):57-67.

Galaway, B. & J. Hudson (eds.) (1978). *Offender Restitution in Theory and Action.* Lexington, MA: Lexington Books.

Gettinger, S. (1981). "Separating the Cop from the Counselor." *Corrections Magazine* 7(2):34-38.

Giacopassi, D., J. Sparger & P. Stein (1992). "The Effects of Emergency Medical Care on the Homicide Rate: Some Additional Evidence." *Journal of Criminal Justice* 20(3):249-259.

Glaze, L. & T. Bonczar (2006). *Probation and Parole in the United States, 2005.* Washington, DC: Bureau of Justice Statistics.

Gottfredson, D., C. Cosgrove, L. Wilkins, J. Wallerstein & C. Rauh (1978). *Classification for Parole Decision Policy.* Washington, DC: U.S. Government Printing Office.

Gottfredson, M., S. Mitchell-Herzfeld & T. Flanagan (1982). "Another Look at the Effectiveness of Parole Supervision." *Journal of Research in Crime and Delinquency* 18(2):277-298.

Greenberg, I. & R. Wasserman (1979). *Managing Criminal Investigations.* Washington, DC: National Institute of Justice.

Hakim, S., G. Rengert & Y. Shachmurove (1996). "Estimation of Net Social Benefits of Electronic Security." *Justice Quarterly* 13(1):153-170.

Hanke, P. & J. Gundlach (1995). "Damned on Arrival: A Preliminary Study of the Relationship Between Homicide, Emergency Medical Care, and Race." *Journal of Criminal Justice* 23(4):313-323.

Harries, K. (1999). *Mapping Crime: Principle and Practice.* Washington, DC: National Institute of Justice.

Harries, K. (2003). "Using Geographic Analysis in Probation and Parole." *NIJ Journal* (July):32-33,

Harris, K. (1995). *Computer Crime: An Overview.* Sacramento: SEARCH, 5.

Healy, G. (2002). *Policy Analysis: "There Goes the Neighborhood: The Bush-Ashcroft Plan to 'Help" Localities Fight Gun Crime."* Washington, DC: CATO Institute.

Helms, R. & R. Gutierrez (2007). "Federal Subsidies and Evidence of Progressive Change: A Quantitative Assessment of the Effects of Targeted Grants on Manpower and Innovation in Large U.S. Police Agencies." *Police Quarterly* 10(1):87-107.

Herrera, R. & M. Tracey (1992). "DNA Fingerprinting: Basic Techniques, Problems, and Solutions." *Journal of Criminal Justice* 20(3):237-248.

Hickman, M. & B. Reaves (2006). *Local Police Departments, 2003.* Washington, DC: Bureau of Justice Statistics.

Hoffman, P. & J. Beck (1984). "Burnout—Age at Release from Prison and Recidivism." *Journal of Criminal Justice* 12(6):617-624.

Hoffman, P. & B. Stone-Meierhoefer (1979). "Post Release Arrest Experiences of Federal Prisoners: A Six-Year Follow-Up." *Journal of Criminal Justice* 7(3):193-216.

Hoffman, P. & B. Stone-Meierhoefer (1980). "Reporting Recidivism Rates: The Criterion and Follow-Up Issues." *Journal of Criminal Justice* 8(1):53-60.

Holden, R. (1993). "Police and the Profit Motive: A New Look at Asset Forfeiture." *ACJS Today* 12:2.

Homant, R. & D. Kennedy (1982). "Attitudes Towards Ex-Offenders: A Comparison of Social Stigmas." *Journal of Criminal Justice* 10(5):383-392.

Hurst, H. (1999). *Workload Measurement for Juvenile Justice System Personnel: Practices and Needs.* Washington, DC: Office of Juvenile Justice and Delinquency Prevention.

International Association of Chiefs of Police (2004). *Executive Summary: National Criminal Intelligence Sharing Plan.* Gaithersburg, MD: International Association of Chiefs of Police.

Johnson, D. (1981). *American Law Enforcement: A History.* St. Louis: Forum Press.

Johnson, E. (1998). *From the Inkpad to the Mousepad: IAFIS and Fingerprint Technology at the Dawn of the 21st Century.* Washington, DC: Bureau of Justice Assistance.

Karp, D. & T. Clear (2000). "Community Justice: A Conceptual Framework." In C. Friel (ed.), *Boundary Changes in Criminal Justice Organizations.* Washington, DC: National Institute of Justice, Criminal Justice 2000, Volume 2:323-369.

Kelling, G., S. Edwards & M. Moore (1986). "Federally Funded Community Crime Control: Urban Initiatives Anti-Crime Program." *Criminal Justice Policy Review* 1(1):58-75.

Kilpatrick, D., D. Beatty & S. Howley (1998). *The Rights of Crime Victims—Does Legal Protection Make a Difference?* Washington, DC: National Institute of Justice.

Kurlychek, M., R. Brame & S. Bushway (2006). "Scarlet Letters and Recidivism: Does an Old Criminal Record Predict Future Offending?" *Criminology & Public Policy* 5(3):483-504.

Lab, S. (1990). "Citizen Crime Prevention: Domains and Participation." *Justice Quarterly,* 7(3):467-491.

Langan, P. & D. Levin (2002). *Recidivism of Prisoners Released in 1994.* Washington, DC: Bureau of Justice Statistics.

Latessa, E. & L.F. Travis III (1987). "Citizen Crime Prevention: Problems and Prospectives in Reducing Crime." *Journal of Security Management* 10(1):38-51.

Latessa, E., L.F. Travis, III, R. Oldendick, B. McDermott & S. Noonan (1988). *The Impact of Technology in Prisons: Final Report.* Washington, DC: National Institute of Corrections.

Lundman, R. (1980). *Police and Policing: An Introduction.* New York: Holt, Rinehart & Winston.

Lynch, M., D. McGurrin & M. Fenwick (2004). "Disappearing Act: The Representation of Corporate Crime Research in Criminological Literature." *Journal of Criminal Justice* 32(5):389-398.

Malsch, M. & R. Carriere (1999). "Victim's Wishes for Compensation: The Immaterial Aspect." *Journal of Criminal Justice* 27(3):239-247.

Mamalian, C. & N. LaVigne (1997). *The Use of Computerized Crime Mapping by Law Enforcement: Survey Results.* Washington, DC: National Institute of Justice.

McCormack, R. (1991). "Compensating Victims of Violent Crime." *Justice Quarterly* 8(3):329-346.

McGillis, D. (1986). *Community Dispute Resolution Programs and Public Policy.* Washington, DC: National Institute of Justice.

Miethe, T. (1995). "Predicting Future Litigiousness." *Justice Quarterly* 12(3):563-581.

Miller, J. & L. Selva (1994). "Drug Enforcement's Double-Edged Sword: An Assessment of Asset Forfeiture Programs." *Justice Quarterly* 11(2):313-335.

National Institute of Justice (1994). *Environmental Crime Prosecution: Results of a National Survey.* Washington, DC: National Institute of Justice.

National Institute of Justice (2000). "At-A-Glance: Recent Research Findings—Effective Police Management Affects Citizen Perceptions." *NIJ Journal* (July):24-25.

Nugent, H. (1991). *State Computer Crime Statutes.* Washington, DC: National Institute of Justice.

Office for Victims of Crime (1998). *New Directions from the Field: Victims' Rights and Services for the 21st Century.* Washington, DC: Office for Victims of Crime.

Office for Victims of Crime (2002a). *Ordering Restitution to the Crime Victim.* Washington, DC: Office for Victims of Crime, Legal Series Bulletin #6.

Office for Victims of Crime (2002b). *Restitution: Making It Work.* Washington, DC: Office for Victims of Crime, Legal Series Bulletin #5.

Office for Victims of Crime (2002c). *The Crime Victim's Right to be Present.* Washington, DC: Office for Victims of Crime, Legal Series Bulletin #3.

Outlaw, M. & R. Ruback (1999). "Predictors and Outcomes of Victim Restitution Orders." *Justice Quarterly* 16(4):847-869.

Petersilia, J., S. Turner & J. Peterson (1986). *Prison Versus Probation in California: Implications for Crime and Offender Recidivism.* Santa Monica, CA: RAND.

Pfuhl, E. (1992). "Crime Stoppers: The Legitimation of Snitching." *Justice Quarterly* 9(3):505-528.

Pfuhl, E. & D. Altheide (1987). "TV Mediation of Disputes and Injustice." *Justice Quarterly* 4(1):99-116.

Pilant, L. (1998). "Smart Cards: An Information Tool for the Future." *NIJ Journal* (July):21-23.

Presser, L. & C. Lowenkamp (1999). "Restorative Justice and Offender Screening." *Journal of Criminal Justice* 27(4):333-343.

Rantala, R. (2004). *Cybercrime against Businesses.* Washington, DC: Bureau of Justice Statistics.

Rau, R. (1991). "Forensic Science and Criminal Justice Technology: High-Tech Tools for the 90's." *National Institute of Justice Reports,* June (224):6-10.

Reed, J. (1979). "Civil Disabilities, Attitudes, and Reentry: Or How Can the Offender Reacquire a Conventional Status?" *Journal of Offender Rehabilitation* 3:219-228.

Rhodes, W., R. Hyatt & P. Scheiman (1996). *Predicting Pretrial Misconduct with Drug Tests of Arrestees.* Washington, DC: National Institute of Justice.

Rich, T. (1995). *The Use of Computerized Mapping in Crime Control and Prevention Programs.* Washington, DC: National Institute of Justice.

Robinson, L. (1996). "Linking Community-Based Initiatives and Community Justice: The Office of Justice Programs." *NIJ Journal* (August):4-7.

Rosenbaum, D., A. Lurigio & P. Lavrakas (1986). *Crime Stoppers—A National Evaluation.* Washington, DC: U.S. Department of Justice.

Rottman, D. & S. Strickland (2006). *State Court Organization, 2005.* Washington, DC: Bureau of Justice Statistics.

Sabol, W., W. Adams, B. Parthasarathy & Y. Yuan (2000). *Offenders Returning to Federal Prison, 1986-97.* Washington, DC: Bureau of Justice Statistics.

Sabol, W., T. Minton & P. Harrison (2007). *Prison and Jail Inmates at Midyear 2006.* Washington, DC: Bureau of Justice Statistics.

Scalia, J. (1999). *Federal Enforcement of Environmental Laws, 1997.* Washington, DC: Bureau of Justice Statistics.

Schwartz, M., T. Clear & L.F. Travis III (1980). *Corrections: An Issues Approach.* Cincinnati: Anderson.

Schwartz, R. & J. Skolnick (1962). "Two Studies of Legal Stigma." *Social Problems* 10:133-142.

Sechrest, L., S. White & E. Brown (1979). *The Rehabilitation of Criminal Offenders: Problems and Prospects.* Washington, DC: National Academy of Sciences.

Sherman, L., D. Gottfredson, D. Mackenzie, J. Eck, P. Reuter & S. Bushway (1997). *Preventing Crime: What Works, What Doesn't, What's Promising?* Washington, DC: National Institute of Justice.

Simon, J. (1993). *Poor Discipline.* Chicago: University of Chicago Press.

Spelman, W. & J. Eck (1987). "Newport News Tests Problem-Oriented Policing." *NIJ Reports* (January/February):2-8.

Stone, C. (1996). "Community Defense and the Challenge of Community Justice." *NIJ Journal* (August):41-45.

Taylor, R. & A. Harrell (1996). *Physical Environment and Crime.* Washington, DC: National Institute of Justice.

Travis, L.F., III & V. O'Leary (1979). *Changes in Sentencing and Parole Decision Making: 1976-78.* Hackensack, NJ: National Council on Crime and Delinquency.

Turner, A. (2007). "Automated Video Surveillance: Improving CCTV to Detect and Prevent Incidents." *Corrections Today* (June):44-45.

Umbreit, M. (1986). "Victim/Offender Mediation: A National Survey." *Federal Probation* 50(4):53-56.

Umbreit, M. (1989). "Crime Victims Seeking Fairness, Not Revenge: Toward Restorative Justice." *Federal Probation* 53(3):52-57.

Vile, J. (1981). "The Right to Vote as Applied to Ex-Felons." *Federal Probation* 45(1):12-16.

Villmoare, E. & V. Neto (1987). *Victim Appearances at Sentencing Under California's Victims' Bill of Rights.* Washington, DC: U.S. Department of Justice.

Visher, C. (1992). *Pretrial Drug Testing.* Washington, DC: U.S. Department of Justice.

Wagner, A. (1997). "A Study of Traffic Pattern Modifications in an Urban Crime Prevention Program." *Journal of Criminal Justice* 25(1):19-30.

Walker, S. (1985). *Sense and Nonsense about Crime: A Policy Guide.* Monterey, CA: Brooks/Cole.

Walker, S. (1994). *Sense and Nonsense about Crime and Drugs: A Policy Guide,* 3rd ed. Belmont, CA: Wadsworth.

Ward, C. (1997). "Community Crime Prevention: Addressing Background and Foreground Causes of Criminal Behavior." *Journal of Criminal Justice* 25(1):1-18.

Weimer, D. (1980). "Vertical Prosecution and Career Criminal Bureaus: How Many and Who?" *Journal of Criminal Justice* 8(6):369-378.

Wilkins, W. (1987). "Sentencing Commission Chairman Wilkins Answers Questions on the Guidelines." *NIJ Reports* (September/October):7-9.

Worrall, J. & T. Kovandzic (2007). "COPS Grants and Crime Revisited." *Criminology* 45(1):159-190.

Wright, K., T.R. Clear & P. Dickson (1984). "Universal Applicability of Probation Risk-Assessment Instruments: A Critique." *Criminology* 22(1):113-134.

Zhao, S., C. Gibson, N. Lovrich & M. Gaffney (2002). "Participation in Community Crime Prevention: Are Volunteers More or Less Fearful of Crime Than Other Citizens?" *Journal of Crime and Justice* 25(1):41-61.

Glossary

A

abandonment: a way of disposing unwanted or burdensome children, which gained prominence after the fourth century; the desertion of an infant or child by her or his parents.

absconders: offenders who fail to submit to supervision (do not report as directed, change jobs or addresses without notifying their supervising officer, etc.).

actuarial prediction: a method of forecasting that focuses on the characteristics of the group to which the individual belongs. Like insurance company life-expectancy tables, it presents the "odds" of a future event.

actus reus: the behavioral or action element of a criminal offense.

adjudication: the determination of the facts in a case by a judicial body. Specifically in the juvenile justice system, it refers to the fact-finding process that is similar to the trial in the adult system.

appellate courts: tribunals authorized to hear and settle questions of law that arise from lower courts. In most cases, appellate courts do not hear factual matters, and most often the appellate court is comprised of panels of judges or justices.

apprenticeship: a system of education or training in which a youth learned a trade by working as an assistant to a craftsperson. An apprenticeship typically had a set term of training.

arraignment: a formal stage of the criminal justice process at which the accused is informed of the criminal charges against her or him, and asked to plead to those charges.

arrest: taking a person into custody; one of the decision points of the criminal justice system.

assigned counsel: a system for providing criminal defense services for the indigent in which attorneys are assigned or appointed to the case of a defendant from a list of candidates maintained by the court.

B

"back door" strategies: a demand reduction solution aiming to reduce the amount of time inmates remain in prison (e.g., earlier release of inmates).

bail: a monetary surety required of a defendant prior to release from custody to assure the defendant's appearance at later court hearings.

bench trial: a criminal trial held before a judge alone, without a jury. The judge in a bench trial both presides over the trial and serves as the finder of fact.

benefit of clergy: a forerunner to contemporary practices such as probation; the practice of excusing members of the clergy from state criminal responsibility in English courts, the benefit was later extended to all literate citizens.

blended sentencing: a practice that allows either the juvenile court or the adult court to impose a sentence on a juvenile offender that can involve either the juvenile or the adult correctional system, or both.

booking: the point in the criminal justice process at which the arrest of a criminal suspect is officially recorded (written in the police log book).

boot camp: a specialized prison program in which offenders (typically young) are subjected to a regimen of physical training and strict discipline, but are granted release earlier than more traditional incarceration.

C

career criminal: a label given to repeat offenders, generally those who have a lengthy and involved history of criminality.

casework model: a model of organizing service delivery in probation, parole, and other settings in which the criminal justice official is assigned subjects (cases) and is responsible for generally serving all of their needs.

charging: the process by which the prosecutor (or state's attorney or district attorney) applies the criminal law to the facts of the case and identifies which provisions of the criminal code have been violated.

circuits: districts or territories assigned to courts in the federal system; 11 circuits cover the United States; the District of Columbia comprises an additional circuit.

civil death: loss or restriction of civil rights so that for legal purposes, the individual is "dead." Often a consequence of conviction in felony cases.

classification: the testing and assessment of inmates to determine inmate treatment needs and prison custody and security needs.

clear and present danger: conditions or behavior that pose an immediate threat to safety or order and relates to controls on the activities of inmates that pose a direct threat to the smooth operation of the facility.

clinical prediction: a method of forecasting that focuses on the characteristics of an individual and estimates the likelihood of that specific person engaging in certain behavior in the future.

closed system: a system or collection of interrelated parts that are relatively isolated or insulated from their environment.

cohort studies: research based on the longitudinal study of an indentifiable group of individuals. The indentified group is the "cohort" about which the study seeks information.

"cold case squads": teams of detectives dedicated to pursuing cases (usually homicide cases) that have not been solved and lack significant leads.

collateral consequences: effects or "products" of a criminal conviction that are in addition to any criminal penalty, for example, the loss of civil rights.

community corrections legislation: statutes that create, and often encourage, the development of sentencing alternatives to imprisonment that involve dealing with the offender in her or his community.

community courts: courts that attempt to resolve problems and disputes by addressing all concerned, including the community at large. Such courts are usually linked to community resources.

community justice: the empowerment of communities for solving problems and disputes without recourse to the formal system of criminal justice.

community prosecution: a type of prosecution in which the prosecutor is assigned to the case from initial appearance through disposition and works with the police, community, and other agencies not just to secure conviction, but to solve the problems that led to the criminal behavior.

community-oriented policing: an approach to policing that relies on community definitions of police functions and a partnership between the police and the community in the production of public safety.

community service orders: a command by the court that a convicted offender work, without compensation, at some task or job of benefit to the community.

compelling state interest: a legal criterion used to judge the reasonableness of a practice or condition. In general, the state must justify its use of intrusive practices or conditions by showing that the practice accomplishes an objective that the state must achieve.

concurrent term: a sentence for a criminal conviction that is executed ("runs") at the same time as another sentence.

conditional release: permission for an offender to remain in the community if he or she abides by certain conditions, such as reporting regularly to a supervising officer, refraining from consuming alcohol, etc.

congregate system: the "silent" or Auburn model of prison discipline in which inmates ate, worked, recreated, and worshipped together, but were housed in separate cells at night and prohibited from talking with each other.

consecutive term: a sentence for a criminal conviction that is delayed in execution until after the sentence for another conviction has expired.

consent decrees: decrees whereby the court and the state enter into a voluntary agreement about issues raised in court.

constable: a court office in Norman England that had many administrative and public safety duties; a forerunner to the police.

contract systems: the practice of leasing to the highest bidder inmate labor and the use of prison work areas and shops.

corporate gang: a group of individuals that has a well-organized formal structure and whose purpose is to make money.

cottage reformatories: institutions for juvenile offenders established in the mid- to late 1800s that attempted to parallel a family setting.

count: a specific criminal charge in an indictment so that "three counts of robbery" means three separate charges of robbery.

courtroom work group: the people who comprise the major actors in the court process and who generally develop common understandings and norms for how the business of the court will be conducted.

CPTED: Crime Prevention Through Environmental Design (pronounced "sep-ted"); programs that change environmental conditions to reduce the likelihood of crime; for instance, by increased lighting and other security devices.

crackdown: usually short-term, an intensive police response to a perceived problem. For example, strict enforcement of traffic or parking laws, saturation patrol, and other intensive police efforts focused at specific problem areas.

crime: an act or omission in violation of a law, which is punishable by the state.

crime control model: an analytic device developed by Herbert Packer that describes how the criminal justice process would operate if the control of crime were the only (or the predominant) goal served by the system.

Crime Index: the total number of eight specific types of offenses that are known to the police in any given year, as reported by the Federal Bureau of Investigation.

crime rate: a standardized measure of the amount of crime per unit of population. Typically, the number of crimes known to the police per 100,000 members of the population.

"crime stoppers" programs: programs that offer citizens anonymity and rewards for providing information about crimes and criminals to the police.

crime-warps: a term coined by Georgette Bennett to describe changes in the nature and definition of crime and criminal justice in America in the future.

criminal justice: the formal social institution designed to respond to deviance defined as crime.

crystallized gang: a group that has achieved recognition as a gang, has a leadership hierarchy, specialized roles and statuses, and is active in criminal activity.

cynicism: in terms of police, the perception or belief that citizens, department leaders, politicians, and other criminal justice officials are not truthful and honest in their dealings with police officers.

D

"dark figure" of crime: the amount of criminal activity that is unreported and undetected; specifically, the amount of crime that is not included in official statistics such as the Uniform Crime Report.

day reporting: a community corrections program in which convicted offenders are required to check in with (or at) a supervising center each day, but are allowed to remain in their homes at night and to engage in approved activities (i.e., work or school) during the day.

decoy operation: an investigative technique in which police officers act as potential crime victims in order to attract the attention of criminals. The officers serve as "decoys" to lure offenders into a trap.

defounding: the practice of reducing the seriousness of a crime alleged by a victim or complainant, such as recording a reported felony as if it were a misdemeanor.

deinstitutionalization: the practice of refraining from confining juvenile status offenders in state institutions.

delinquent: a juvenile who violates the criminal laws of the jurisdiction.

deprivation model: a model that explains the development of prisoner subculture as a reaction to the loss of freedom, goods, services, and ties to life outside the prison.

design capacity: the number of inmates that a prison was designed to house or hold.

detached workers: workers placed in the environment of a gang to provide input geared toward more acceptable activities for the gang.

detection: the decision point in the criminal justice process at which police officers come to believe that a crime has occurred.

detention decision: the decision whether to keep a juvenile in custody or to allow the youth to go home with parents or guardians to await further court action.

determinate sentencing: a sentencing to incarceration in which the exact length and nature of punishment is known at the time it is imposed.

deterrence: a reason for criminal punishment based on the idea that punishment of the individual offender produces benefits for the future by making the idea of criminal behavior less attractive.

deviance: behavior that violates socially accepted standards of proper conduct.

discharge: release from sentence and custody or control by the criminal justice system.

disparity: inequality; especially in sentencing when two similarly situated offenders receive different penalties.

disposition: outcome; in the juvenile justice system and with probation and parole revocation, a specific hearing stage during which penalty/sentence is decided.

dispute resolution: less formal mechanisms for reducing conflicts and resolving criminal complaints between individuals, including mediation, arbitration, and other alternatives to criminal justice processing.

diversion: preventing cases from entering the criminal justice system or reducing how far cases progress into the system; avoiding criminal justice processing.

divestiture: the elimination of juvenile court jurisdiction over status offenders.

drug courts: special courts dedicated to the processing and supervision of drug cases.

drug testing: chemical testing for the presence of drugs in the urine, blood, hair, etc. of the test subject. A relatively common practice for suspected drug users in criminal justice populations, and often a requirement of employment in criminal justice agencies.

dual system: a term used to describe the existence of two sets of courts in the United States, one federal and the other state.

due process model: an analytic device created by Herbert Packer to describe a criminal justice system in which the most important goal is the protection of individual liberty.

E

electronic monitoring: any of several systems in which criminal offenders are tracked and supervised, at least in part, by radio and or telephone contact.

emergency release programs: mechanisms for legally releasing inmates in order to control prison crowding.

emergent gang: a group of individuals that has some degree of structure and that engages in some minor offenses but lacks much formalized structure and a commitment to group criminality.

entrapment: a defense to criminal charges that applies when the idea for the crime and the motivation to commit the crime are produced by the police and did not arise with the offender.

exclusionary rule: created by the appellate courts as protection of constitutional rights and a sanction against police misbehavior, this rule prohibits the use of illegally obtained evidence in criminal prosecutions.

exculpatory evidence: evidence that tends to establish the innocence of the accused or defendant.

executive clemency: the authority of the executive officer of a jurisdiction to grant mercy or forgiveness to those accused or convicted of a crime. Clemency includes pardon, commutation, and reprieve.

F

false negative: in criminal justice prediction, someone who is predicted to be safe, not to pose a threat of future criminality, but who is, in fact, dangerous and commits additional crimes.

false positive: in criminal justice prediction, someone who is predicted to be dangerous, to pose a threat of future criminality, but who is, in fact, safe and would not commit additional crimes.

family model: an analytic device developed by John Griffiths (in opposition to Packer's due process and crime control models) that contends that the criminal justice system should operate under the assumption that the interests of society and the interests of the offender are the same.

federalism: the structure of government in the United States that distinguishes between federal, state, and local governmental interests, duties, responsibilities, and powers.

felony: serious criminal offense defined by statute; usually punishable by a term of one year or longer in a state or federal prison.

forays: attacks in which one or two gang members attack a single rival gang member, usually using a firearm from a moving vehicle, resulting in an ongoing series of small, isolated attacks between gangs.

forgetting: in regard to victim surveys, the possibility that a respondent will forget a crime that occurred during a specific time period.

formal charges: the official accusation of criminal conduct that the prosecutor must prove beyond a reasonable doubt if the case goes to trial; established by indictment or the filing of an information in court.

formal social control: sanctions that are applied by some authorized body after a public finding of fault.

formalized gang: a group of individuals that has a formal structure and organization, owns a meeting place, is committed to criminality as a group, and claims a wide territory.

frisk: a limited search (pat down) of the outer clothing of a suspect for the purpose of self-protection through the discovery of any weapons.

"front door" strategies: a demand reduction solution aiming to reduce the number of offenders sent to prison by increasing diversion programs and the use of community-based alternative sentences.

functions: the purposes or goals served by social institutions or practices. They can be both manifest (stated, expressed) purposes and latent (hidden) purposes.

"funnel effect": the effect by which the criminal justice system operates like a giant sieve, continuously filtering the huge volume of crimes and criminals to the relatively small number of offenders who are incarcerated in the nation's prisons.

furlough: temporary release from custody; programs of short-term release of prison inmates for specific purposes such as seeking employment and housing prior to release, attending to a personal or family emergency, and the like.

G

general deterrence: a subtype of deterrence based on the notion that punishing a specific offender will frighten or warn the general population to avoid criminal behavior.

general jurisdiction: a term used to describe the authority of some trial courts that indicates that the court is empowered to settle questions of fact in almost all civil and criminal matters arising within its geographical area.

good faith exception: the tenet that if the police conduct a search believing in good faith that the search is permissible, then the evidence can be used at trial.

good time: reductions in the length of sentence granted to inmates as a reward for "good behavior" in the institution.

grand jury: a panel of citizens (usually 23, with a quorum of 16) that reviews evidence in criminal cases to determine whether sufficient evidence exists to justify trial of an individual.

H

habitual offender statutes: legislative statutes that allow for increased penalties for repeat offenders.

halfway houses: a generic term describing residential programs operating in the community in which criminal offenders are housed and provided various treatments. The term indicates that this option is "halfway" between incarceration in prison or jail and release to the community under supervision.

"hands off" doctrine: phrase describing the reluctance of appellate courts to intervene in the operation of prisons, jails, and other correctional facilities. The term implies that courts grant wide latitude to correctional administrators by keeping their (the court's) hands off of questions of facility administration.

home incarceration: a sanction of "incarceration" that is served in the offender's home, essentially a restriction on liberty that requires the offender to remain in his or her residence during specified hours for a set term, and typically enforced by the use of electronic monitoring.

"hot pursuit": a circumstance in which the police are closely chasing a crime suspect. Officers engaged in a "hot pursuit" are not required to seek a warrant to search the area in which the suspect is caught or trapped.

"hot spots" of crime: a term coined by Sherman, Gartin, and Buerger to refer to locations where much more crime can be found than at other places.

Houses of Refuge: institutions established in the early 1800s for youthful offenders; they were designed to use education, skills training, hard work, and apprenticeships to produce productive members of society.

hung jury: a jury that cannot reach consensus about the verdict.

I

importation model: a model that explains the existence of a prisoner sub-culture as the result of inmates bringing criminal and anti-authority values with them from their lives in the community.

incapacitation: a reason for criminal punishment based on the notion that the penalty will prevent the offender from having the chance to com-mit a crime in the future.

incarceration rate: the number of persons incarcerated per 100,000 pop-ulation eligible for incarceration.

indeterminate sentencing: a sentencing to incarceration that is stated as a range of time between some minimum and some maximum term and in which, at the point of sentencing, the exact length of confinement is unknown.

indictment: a true bill issued by a grand jury that establishes that the jury found probable cause to have a defendant respond to criminal charges in court. A mechanism of filing formal criminal charges against a defendant.

indigent: poor; a criminal defendant or convict who is unable to afford the cost of defense counsel and for whom counsel will be provided at state expense.

infanticide: literally, the killing of an infant; the practice in history of killing unwanted or burdensome children shortly after birth.

informal social control: mechanisms that influence behavior without the need for a public finding of fault or the use of group-authorized sanctions.

information process: a process occurring in open court in which the defendant and his or her attorney are present and are allowed to examine witnesses.

initial appearance: the criminal suspect's first appearance in a court hearing, at which the question of pretrial release is decided.

innocence projects: coordinated efforts to investigate claims of innocence maintained by persons convicted of criminal offenses.

institutionalization: the tendency for residents of "total institutions" (e.g., prison inmates) to become habituated to and dependent upon the institutional routine so that they lose the ability to make independent decisions.

intake decision: a screening point in the juvenile justice system at which a court official, often a probation officer, decides whether a juvenile's case will be processed through the court or handled outside the formal court process.

intelligence gathering: the compilation of information that may be helpful in solving crimes, but with no specific probable cause to believe the information will lead to solving a particular crime.

intensive supervision: a form of probation and parole supervision in which offenders receive an increased level of attention from supervision officers that usually includes more in-person contact and closer monitoring by the officer.

intermediate sanctions: the term given to describe a range of criminal penalties developed as alternatives to traditional probation or incarceration. These include intensive supervision, house arrest, community service, and other penalties.

interrogation: questioning; specifically, the in-custody questioning of crime suspects by the police.

inventory search: the routine check of seized property to establish what has been taken by the police. The term specifically applies to inventorying the contents of seized automobiles.

investigation: the search for and accumulation of evidence that links a particular crime to a particular person or persons.

involuntary servitude: slavery, the requirement that someone work for another; a practice once common for moving children from the family home through placing them in indentureships or apprenticeships.

J

jails: relatively short-term custodial facilities, typically operated at the municipal (county) level, used to house a variety of offenders and criminal suspects.

"jailhouse lawyers": inmates who assist others in the preparation of court documents.

judicial reprieve: a practice in early English courts that served as a forerunner to probation, it was essentially a suspended sentence ordered by the judge.

jurisdiction: the limits of authority or interest placed on a criminal justice agent or agency and comprised generally of geographic boundaries and the identification of case or offender characteristics.

jury: a panel of citizens selected to hear evidence and render a decision in a criminal matter. Grand juries make charging decisions; petit juries render conviction decisions.

jury nullification: the power and practice of a petit jury rendering a not guilty verdict despite overwhelming evidence of wrong; this is a statement that the law involved is inappropriate, thus the jury nullifies the law by nonenforcement.

jury trial: the determination of guilt by adjudication before a jury at which the state must prove, in open court, all elements of the offense beyond a reasonable doubt, and the jury members make the final determination concerning guilt.

just deserts: a justification for criminal penalties based on the notion that criminals, by virtue of breaking the law, have earned their punishment, and noncriminals have earned the right to have criminals punished; therefore, crime deserves punishment.

juvenile: a person who by virtue of their age as defined in applicable statute, has not yet reached majority and thus is subject to different treatment than adults. The age limits for juvenile status vary among the states.

L

latent functions: the unstated or hidden goals of an institution.

lease system: a model of prison labor in which the state rented the labor of convicts and the use of prison shops to the highest bidder.

least restrictive alternative: the principle that requires that the state use the least intrusive or least controlling practice or regulation to achieve its legitimate aims.

legalistic style: coined by James Q. Wilson, this label is attached to those police organizations in which the normal practice is to intervene frequently and formally with citizens and in which the police role and activities are more narrowly defined by law and law enforcement obligations.

level of abstraction: with reference to the systems approach or systems theory, the degree of complexity of the topic under study. For example, the social control system is at a higher level of abstraction than the criminal justice system.

lifecourse criminality: the involvement in crime of a person over his or her entire lifetime, including both childhood and adulthood.

limited jurisdiction: used to describe courts or other judicial offices, this phrase generally refers to circumstances in which the court is authorized to hear only the early stages of serious cases, or only to hear less serious or specific types of cases.

lineups: an investigatory practice in which the crime suspect, in the company of a group of similar persons, is brought before the witness for identification.

local autonomy: a component of federalism, the freedom of local governmental units to define and respond to problems in their own way.

low visibility: lacking review; as used by Joseph Goldstein, discretionary decisions by police not to invoke the criminal law. These decisions would not be reviewed by courts or others in the police administration and thus would have "low visibility."

M

mala in se: "bad in itself," a term used to describe certain traditional crimes about which there is general agreement that the behavior is wrong.

mala prohibita: "bad because prohibited," a term used to describe those crimes about which there is more general disagreement among people concerning whether the behavior is wrong. Often applied to vice and regulatory offenses.

mandatory minimum sentences: sentences that reflect a required period of incarceration defined by statute that must be imposed as a sanction if the offender is convicted of a particular crime.

mandatory release: release based on earned good time or other statutory sentence-reduction measures; usually does not depend on the discretionary decision of a parole board.

manifest functions: the stated purposes of an institution.

mark system: the "token economy" of Alexander Maconochie at Norfolk Island by which inmates could earn marks by good behavior and labor. These marks then allowed inmates to progress to increasingly less strict conditions of confinement.

mens rea: "mental things," the mental element of a crime such as intention, voluntariness, and other cognitive conditions required by the law.

Miranda warnings: notification of rights (to remain silent and to have an attorney present) that are required to be given to suspects prior to interrogation; named for the 1966 Supreme Court case, *Miranda v. Arizona*, which established these rights.

misdemeanor: a crime that is generally considered to be less serious than a felony and that is usually punishable by a term of no more than one year in a local jail.

Missouri Plan: a method of judicial selection by which judges are appointed from a slate of qualified candidates and are periodically reviewed by means of a retention election in which citizens decide if the judge, running unopposed, should continue to serve.

model case management system: a process for classifying offenders on probation and parole based on both risk of further crime as well as the service needs of the offender, using this information to structure and direct the activities of officers and entire field supervision agencies. The model system was developed and disseminated by the National Institute of Corrections beginning in the early 1980s.

multijurisdictional jails: jails that serve more than one municipality or jurisdiction.

N

National Crime Victimization Survey (NCVS): an annual survey of a representative sample of Americans asking their experiences as crime victims. The NCVS is the primary source of victimization data concerning crime in America.

Neighborhood Watch: citizen crime prevention programs involving the mobilization of residents to serve as the "eyes and ears" of the police and to watch for and report any crimes or suspicious activities.

net-widening: the term used to describe the phenomenon of increasing the number of persons touched by some aspect of the justice system. In particular, it is applied to cases where a new program or service results in more people being subjected to criminal justice intervention because the new program is seen as appropriate to them.

nolle prosequie: Latin term meaning "I do not prosecute"; a prosecutor may choose to refuse to prosecute, or "nol pros," a case.

nolo contendere: Latin term meaning "no contest," or "I do not contest the charges"; a plea available to criminal defendants, with the consent of the court, in most jurisdictions. The effect of the *nolo contendere* plea is similar to that of a plea of guilty, except the defendant is not "proven" to have broken the law and thus is better able to defend against a civil suit.

O

observations: as used here, a type of research that relies upon the on-site, in-person observations of criminal justice practice or the behavior of criminals by the research staff; more generally, "field research."

official statistics: any data routinely collected and reported by official agencies of criminal justice. The best known example is the Uniform Crime Reports.

"on paper": serving a term of probation or parole supervision. The phrase refers to the supervision agreement or conditions of supervision that govern the behavior of the offender as the "paper" the offender is "on."

open system: a system that is relatively sensitive to its environment and thus adapts and reacts to changes in the environment.

operational capacity: a method of rating the size of a population appropriate for a given correctional institution, based on the facility's staff, existing programs, and services.

order maintenance: functions of the police that serve to maintain order, including settling disputes, dispersing crowds, keeping traffic flowing smoothly, etc.

organized/corporate gang: a well-organized group that exists and functions for the purpose of making money through criminal activities.

P

"pains of imprisonment": a term originated by Gresham Sykes to refer to the social psychological deprivations experienced by prison inmates that combine to make the experience of incarceration personally painful to inmates.

panel attorneys: assigned counsel in the federal system, named as such because defense counsel are assigned from a list or panel of approved lawyers.

paramilitary structure: military-like structure; having the characteristics of a military organization such as formal ranks, a chain of command, pyramidal organizational structure, etc.

parens patriae: "the state as parent," a doctrine that suggests that the state or government has a parental interest in the welfare of children and can act as a parent when needed. The doctrine underlies the concept of the juvenile court as a nonadversarial, nonpunitive solution of juvenile offending.

parole: from the French term meaning "word of honor," it refers to the release of prison inmates, prior to expiration of term, on the condition that they agree to abide by certain restrictions. It also describes the process of conditional liberty, which includes supervision by a state official. Parole can mean either the decision to release, or supervised release in the community.

parole eligibility: established by the legislature, this defines which types of inmates can be paroled at what points in their sentence.

partial disclosure: when the judge summarizes the facts and the reasons for sentence, allowing the defense to contest any errors.

penitentiary: prison; while no longer commonly used in the names of correctional institutions, early prisons were considered to be places in which convicted offenders could "pay" for their crimes and "do penance." Thus, they were call penitentiaries.

peremptory challenges: authorization to exclude someone from a particular trial jury without the requirement that a cause for exclusion be shown.

piece price system: a method of organizing prison labor that was common in the earliest years of prison, in which the private contractor supplied raw materials and agreed to buy finished products made by inmates at fixed price for each piece of finished product.

plain view doctrine: a doctrine that states that police do not need to obtain a warrant to seize contraband or criminal evidence that is plainly visible and requires no search.

plea bargaining: the practice of exchange between the prosecution and defense in which the defendant agrees to plead guilty to criminal charges in return for some concession from the prosecution.

pre-gang: a loose-knit group of individuals who regularly congregate but rarely engage in criminal activity.

preliminary hearing: a hearing in open court at which the prosecution introduces evidence to establish probable cause to have a defendant bound over for trial on criminal charges.

presentence investigation (PSI): a background report on a convicted criminal offender designed to provide the judge with information about the offender's social and criminal history and current status, for use in making a sentencing decision.

presumptive sentencing: suggested sanction for conviction of a particular offense, the expected or "presumed" sentence can be modified by the judge for cause.

preventive detention: a practice by which defendants suspected to be dangerous are denied bail until their cases are tried.

priority prosecution: a prosecutorial style in which offenders are selected to receive increased attention to ensure conviction. Rather than treating each case as unique, cases are classified into types that typically receive different treatments.

prisons: typically larger institutions used to house convicted adult felons for terms of one year or longer.

Prison Litigation Reform Act: a 1995 law requiring inmates to exhaust all administrative remedies (appeals through the prison administration and department of corrections) before they can file a suit in federal court.

Prison Rape Elimination Act: a 2003 law providing for the development of better information about the nature and incidence of rape and sexual assault in prisons, and providing funding to correctional authorities to reduce and control sexual violence in prisons.

"prisonization": the term given to describe the process by which prison inmates come to learn and accept the values and norms of the inmate subculture.

private court: offices or commissions for dispute resolution that divert cases away from the formal courts, usually staffed by volunteers or paid staff whose salaries are lower than that of a judge.

privately retained counsel: counsel or attorney for the defense in a criminal matter, who is hired and paid privately by the defendant.

privatization: the movement to turn government functions over to operation by private sector (profit or not-for-profit) organizations.

pro se defense: "defense for self," the provision of defense services in court proceedings by the defendant acting on his or her own behalf rather than by relying upon a representative.

proactive: self-motivated or self-initiated; specifically as related to policing, efforts to detect or respond to crimes that are motivated by the police themselves without reliance upon a formal complaint.

probable cause: evidence that leads a reasonable person to conclude that a crime has occurred and evidence of the crime may be found to support the search.

probation: a sentence of conditional and revocable release into the community, generally under supervision, usually imposed in lieu of incarceration. The process of supervising and enforcing conditions of release in lieu of incarceration.

Probation Subsidy Act: an early form of community corrections legislation in California that provided financial incentives to counties to retain convicted offenders at the local level under probation supervision as an alternative to incarceration in state prisons.

prosecutorial case management: a system for assigning, managing, and conducting the work of a prosecutor's office, generally involving case classification and the establishment of priorities for the expenditure of prosecutorial resources.

protective custody: a method for protecting inmates from attacks by other inmates, usually a housing unit kept separate from the general inmate population.

public account system: a model of prison industry in which prison labor is used in the production of goods for sale on the open market, and the prison industry, as a public agency, operates like a private business.

public defender: common in larger and busier criminal jurisdictions, a model for the provision of defense counsel to the indigent that relies upon a public office organized similarly to that of the prosecutor.

public works system: a model of prison industry in which inmate labor is used in the completion of public works such as road construction and maintenance, the building or repair of public buildings, and similar public projects.

Q

quality-of-life policing: a style in which the police focus on minor crimes as a means of preventing serious crime. Improving the "quality of life" in the neighborhood is seen to lead to effective informal social control and, ultimately, less serious crime.

R

rated capacity: a method for determining the size of a population that is appropriate for a specific correctional institution, based on a judgment or rating of some official such as a health inspector or fire marshal.

reactive: responsive; specifically as it relates to policing, efforts of the police to detect or prevent crime, which are initiated by or in reaction to a formal complaint.

recidivism: the commission of criminal behavior by a person after release or discharge from the criminal justice process.

reentry: the return of former inmates to life in the community.

reentry courts: courts in which services for and supervision of parolees are coordinated and monitored in a court environment.

reformatory: a prison typically reserved for youthful adult felony offenders.

rehabilitation: a justification for the imposition of a criminal sentence based on the idea that crime is symptomatic of problems an offender has with regard to living within society. The punishment is imposed "for the offender's own good," and is intended to change the offender's need or proclivity to engage in crime.

release on recognizance (ROR): generally used at the pretrial stage of the process, the order allowing a defendant to remain at liberty in the community pending further court actions without posting any bond or surety.

restitution: repayment for the harm caused by criminal behavior; an increasingly common part of criminal sanctions that requires convicted offenders to repay their victims.

restorative justice: efforts to repair the harm to victims and/or communities caused by crime through interventions with the offender.

retribution: a justification for criminal penalties that is based on the principle that wrong deserves to be punished, regardless of whether the punishment produces any benefit.

revocation: recall; the cancellation of conditional liberty (usually probation or parole) upon a finding that the offender has violated the conditions of release.

"routine activities" theory: a theory suggesting that crime occurs when a motivated offender and a suitable target (victim or property) come together in time and space in the absence of an effective guardian.

rumble: the traditional image of the gang fight involving two groups of youths in a prearranged fight.

S

scavenger gang: a group that exists without particular goals or organizational structure but serves to give members a sense of belonging.

search: an investigatory technique in which police or other officials seek physical evidence of criminality or contraband.

segregate system: an early form of prison discipline, practiced in the Pennsylvania penitentiaries, in which inmates were kept isolated from each other for the duration of their confinement.

self-report studies: surveys that attempt to measure the amount of crime committed and describe the characteristics of offenders by asking people if they have committed offenses.

sentencing: the imposition of a sanction upon conviction of a crime; the decision and process of deciding upon an appropriate penalty for a specific criminal act or acts.

sentencing commissions: formal bodies assigned to assess and oversee criminal sentencing and recommend reforms.

separation of powers: the reservation of specific functions and authority to particular branches of government that enables the system of "checks and balances" to operate.

service style: coined by James Q. Wilson, the term refers to a method of policing in which officers intervene frequently, but informally, in the lives of citizens.

shire reeve: an early Saxon political office representing the head of a large group of families (shire); forerunner to the contemporary office of sheriff.

"shock incarceration": short-term prison programs in which the conditions of incarceration are much more severe but limited in duration (e.g., boot camps).

shock parole: early release to parole supervision after a comparatively brief period of incarceration. The purpose is to "shock" the offender with a small period of incarceration followed by an unexpected early release to supervision.

shock probation: see shock parole; a grant of probation to an offender previously sentenced to prison after serving a relatively small portion of the prison term.

situational crime prevention: an approach to controlling crime through efforts to change the context in which crime happens, including changing the physical, organizational, and social environment.

"smug hack": a brutal, calloused, authoritarian correctional officer; a prison guard who behaves as a petty tyrant.

social control: the process of directing and limiting the behavior of individual members of a social group or society.

special conditions: requirements for release and/or supervision written into the supervision agreement for probation or parole. These are not generally imposed on all probationers or parolees.

special jurisdiction: a nontraditional authorization; for example, in policing, special jurisdiction agencies may have full police powers within a park, on transportation routes or on waterways but lack general police powers throughout the municipality.

special prosecutor: an attorney appointed by a governmental authority for the purpose of conducting investigations and pursuing criminal cases arising from particularly complex or politically sensitive circumstances.

specific deterrence: a subtype of deterrence in which the purpose of the penalty is to frighten the individual offender into conformity, regardless of the effect of the sanction on the broader, general public.

split sentences: sentences combining a period of incarceration with a period of community supervision as part of the sentence order; splitting the total sentence between incarceration and community supervision.

standard conditions: requirements for release and/or supervision that are imposed on everyone under supervision in a given jurisdiction.

state-use system: a model of prison industry in which prison labor and prison factories are operated to produce goods solely for the use of governmental entities and not for sale on the open market; for example, using prison factories to produce state-issued automobile license plates.

status offenses: regarding juvenile offenders, acts prohibited by law or justifying juvenile justice system intervention that apply to youth solely by virtue of their status as juveniles (e.g., truancy, running away, etc.).

sting operation: a police decoy operation in which officers pretend to be involved in a criminal operation such as a stolen automobile "chop shop" or a "fencing" operation and in which criminal offenders who sell the proceeds of their crimes are "stung" or caught by these decoy officers.

street sense: intuition based on experience that enables police officers to detect criminality; a phrase describing how police officers develop hunches and suspicions in circumstances that would not attract a second thought from civilians.

strict liability: an offense in which the mental state or mens rea is presumed to be present so that mere behavior constitutes the elements of the crime regardless of intention.

supervision fees: costs charged to offenders on probation and parole supervision that are used to offset the expenses of operating the supervision process. These fees are typically billed in monthly installments for the length of the supervision period.

suretyship: the practice of a person of good standing in the community taking responsibility for guaranteeing the lawful behavior of another person; the forerunner to modern parole.

system: a collection of interrelated parts working together toward a common goal.

T

team supervision: a model of organizing probation or parole offices in which a group or "team" of personnel are assigned to provide service and surveillance to offenders. In theory, this model allows officers to specialize, thus improving the efficiency of the supervision process.

technical violations: infractions of the rules of supervision that do not involve any new criminality (e.g., violating curfew).

telescoping: in regard to victim surveys, the possibility that a respondent will erroneously include an earlier event in reporting on criminal victimizations during a specific time period.

territorial gang: a group having a clear identity and leadership that is organized around specific, identifiable geographic areas.

theory: a logical explanation for reality; a statement of how things work.

third-party policing: a policing style in which the police work with outside parties to exert control over offenders or criminal contexts. For example, the police might pressure a landlord to evict a tenant who is selling drugs from his apartment.

three-strikes laws: laws that increase prison terms for offenders having been convicted of a serious criminal offense on three or more separate occasions.

throw-downs: a process of criminal suspect identification in which a set of photographs, including a picture of the suspect, is presented (thrown down) before a witness who is asked to pick out the photograph of the person who committed the crime.

ticket of leave: a practice of early release developed by Sir Walter Crofton by which prisoners could be released early by issuance of a "ticket of leave" from the prison. A forerunner to modern parole.

tort: a civil action; an offense against an individual settled in a civil court.

"total institution": a concept developed by Irving Goffman to refer to settings, like prisons and mental hospitals, in which residents are completely dependent upon facility staff and where virtually all decisions are made by staff rather than by the individuals.

transportation: a practice of England in the eighteenth and nineteenth centuries in which offenders convicted of several types of crimes were banished to English colonies. Convicted offenders were "transported" to these distant locations as a punishment for crime. This practice was a forerunner to modern parole.

treatment: see rehabilitation; a justification for sentencing based on the belief that criminal offenders can be helped to prevent them from committing future crimes; the delivery of services—and the services themselves—provided to criminal offenders as a means to reduce future criminality.

trial: the fact-finding point in the criminal justice process; the court stage at which the state must present evidence sufficient to convince the judge or jury beyond a reasonable doubt that the defendant committed the crimes charged, or else the defendant is released from further processing.

trial courts: those courts in which criminal (and often civil) cases are heard to determine the facts of the case.

"truth in sentencing": the concept that offenders should actually serve at least 85 percent of the term they receive; legislation requiring truth in sentencing has been passed in many states.

U

undetected crime: crime that is not known to the criminal justice system or the victim; crimes that are not recognized as crimes.

unfounding: the process that takes place when police decide that a citizen's complaint of a crime is not supported by available evidence. The unfounding of a complaint essentially "erases" the event as a crime known to the police.

unified court system: a system that combines general-jurisdiction and limited-jurisdiction courts into one.

Uniform Crime Reports (UCR): published annually by the Federal Bureau of Investigation, the most well-known source of official statistics on crime. Among other things, the report includes a count of all crimes "known to police" participating in the UCR program, as well as a description of the characteristics of persons arrested for crimes.

unofficial statistics: in regard to crime and criminal justice, statistics and data concerning the amount and distribution of crime and the activities of criminal justice agents and agencies that are collected and reported by persons who are not themselves involved in the official criminal justice processing of cases.

unreported crime: crime that victims recognize as law-breaking behavior, but is not brought to the attention of authorities.

unsolved: an adjective used to describe criminal cases in which the police have been unable to identify an individual or group as the offender.

unsupervised parole: a practice used in some jurisdictions in which active supervision of a parolee is terminated before the expiration of sentence and the discharge of the parolee from criminal justice custody.

V

venire: the panel of citizens from which a jury can be chosen.

vertical prosecution: the practice of assigning the responsibility of a case to a single prosecutor who then follows that same case throughout the entire court process.

victim compensation: the payment of damages to victims of crime to compensate them for the losses experienced by virtue of being a crime victim. The program by which states establish funds and procedures for the payment of claims by crime victims.

victim impact statement: an official statement by a victim that explains the loss incurred by the victim as a result of the crime.

victim/offender mediation: an alternative to criminal justice processing in which the crime victim and criminal offender are brought together to negotiate a "settlement" of the criminal complaint without full criminal justice processing.

victimization data: estimates of the rate and distribution of crime derived from survey respondents' reports of experiences of being the victims of crime.

victims' rights: a term referring to the status of crime victims in the criminal justice system and to summarize a movement designed to increase concern for crime victims and change criminal justice processing to be more sympathetic to the needs and concerns of crime victims.

violation: a minor criminal offense typically punishable by a fine or restriction of privileges such as speeding, overtime parking, etc. The breaking of a condition of supervision by a probationer or parolee.

voir dire: "speak the truth"; the jury selection process in which members of a venire are interrogated by both sides (prosecution and defense, in criminal trials) to determine their suitability for service on the jury.

W

waiver decision: the decision to transfer a juvenile offender to the adult court; a determination that, though a juvenile in terms of age, an offender should be tried and punished as an adult by virtue of the seriousness of the crime or the characteristics of the offender.

watchman style: coined by James Q. Wilson, the term refers to police agencies in which officers only infrequently intervene in the lives of citizens.

wrongful conviction: the result when innocent persons are convicted of criminal acts.

Subject Index

Author Index

Table of Important Cases

About the Author

Lawrence F. Travis III is Professor of Criminal Justice at the University of Cincinnati. He received his Ph.D. in criminal justice from the State University of New York at Albany. He has previously served as research director for the Oregon State Board of Parole and as a research analyst for the National Parole Institutes.

His published works include *Corrections: An Issues Approach* as well as *Changes in Sentencing and Parole Decision Making: 1976-1978; Policing in America: A Balance of Forces;* and *Probation, Parole, and Community Corrections: A Reader.* He is editor of *Policing: An International Journal of Police Strategies and Management* and has contributed frequently to criminal justice journals.

Travis's research interests lie in policing, criminal justice policy reform, sentencing, and corrections. He is an active member of several professional organizations, including the Academy of Criminal Justice Sciences, the American Society of Criminology, and the American Correctional Association.